Shane Denson
Postnaturalism

Film

Für Karin und Ari

Shane Denson (PhD) is a postdoctoral research associate at the Leibniz University of Hanover, Germany and a DAAD postdoctoral fellow at Duke University. His research interests include film and media theory, seriality, and the philosophy of technology.

Shane Denson

Postnaturalism
Frankenstein, Film, and the Anthropotechnical Interface
(With a Foreword by Mark B. N. Hansen)

[transcript]

Bibliographic information published by the Deutsche Nationalbibliothek
The Deutsche Nationalbibliothek lists this publication in the Deutsche Nationalbibliografie; detailed bibliographic data are available in the Internet at http://dnb.d-nb.de

© 2014 transcript Verlag, Bielefeld

All rights reserved. No part of this book may be reprinted or reproduced or utilized in any form or by any electronic, mechanical, or other means, now known or hereafter invented, including photocopying and recording, or in any information storage or retrieval system, without permission in writing from the publisher.

Cover layout: Kordula Röckenhaus, Bielefeld,
 according to an idea of the author
Cover illustration: Promotional photo of Boris Karloff as Frankenstein's monster from Universal Studios' »Bride of Frankenstein« (1935). Public domain. Source: Wikimedia Commons – http://commons.m.wikimedia.org/wiki/File:Frankenstein%27s_monster_(Boris_Karloff).jpg
Printed by Majuskel Medienproduktion GmbH, Wetzlar
Print-ISBN 978-3-8376-2817-3
PDF-ISBN 978-3-8394-2817-7

Contents

Acknowledgements | 7

Foreword: Logics of Transition
Mark B. N. Hansen | 11

1. **Introduction: Monster Movies and Metaphysics** | 23
   Monster Movies: Adaptation, Myth, Genre, and Beyond | 27
   Metaphysics: Film and the Anthropotechnical Interface | 40

PART ONE

2. **Frankenstein's Filmic Progenies:
   A Techno-Phenomenological Approach** | 51
   Film as Frankensteinian Technology? | 52
   Techno-Phenomenology and the Structure of Cinematic Revolutions | 61
   Frankenstein Films and the Noetic Arrow, Or:
   Watch Where You Point That Thing! | 76

3. **Monsters in Transit: Edison's *Frankenstein*** | 101
   An Interstitial Space | 103
   Seeing Double: Material and Discursive Monsters
   in the Transition and Beyond | 126

PART TWO

4. **To the Heart of (the) Matter:
   Frankenstein, Embodiment, Materiality** | 149
   Frankenstein as a Tale of Two Monsters:
   Feminist Interventions and Beyond | 154
   Parabolic Mutations: From Textual Allegory to Machinic Parable | 175

5. **Of Steam Engines, Revolutions, and the (Un)natural History
   of Matter: A Techno-Scientific Interlude** | 205
   Scientific Revolution: A Matter of Discourse
   or the Discourse of Matter? | 208
   Postnaturalism and the Thermodynamic Revolution | 230
   Coda: Fiction Meets Friction | 268

6. **Re-Focusing Cinematic Double Vision: Seriality, Mediality, and Mediation in Postnatural Perspective** | 279
Prelude: Maurice and Henri at the Cosmic Picture Show | 282
Media in the Middle | 298
Segue: Seriality and the Mediation of Medial Change | 332

PART THREE

7. **Universal Monsters and Monstrous Particulars** | 353
Incorporations: Melodrama and Monstrosity | 357
About-Face: Anthro-, Techno-, Xeno-Phenomenology | 379

8. **Lines of Flight:
Transitional Thoughts by Way of Conclusion** | 403
The Continuing Adventures of the Uncanny Body | 406

Works Cited | 417

Acknowledgements

Many people (and not a few nonhumans) have helped me to realize this project, and, as Bruno Latour once said of one of his books, many people have tried to make it less unreasonable. Sometimes, perhaps, it even worked (though probably not very often). In any case, it definitely helped that people cared enough to try. (I suspect that the nonhumans, for their part, either couldn't care less or were quite happy to see a little more rather than less unreason creep into the pages that follow. All the more important, then—and especially for a book that tries to balance the demands and contributions of human and nonhuman agencies—that friends, colleagues, and other humans were there to help me out.)

This book has its origins in a doctoral dissertation that I completed at the Gottfried Wilhelm Leibniz Universität Hannover. During that phase, I received material and intellectual support for the project from the Studienstiftung des deutschen Volkes, who provided me with a stipend for several years. During the final months of writing the manuscript, the Gleichstellungsbüro at the Leibniz Universität Hannover also provided crucial support. And Ruth Mayer helped me pay my bills by finding short-term jobs at the university that filled the gaps between, while also laying the groundwork for more long-term employment thereafter.

I would like to thank Ruth Mayer also—and more importantly—for her invaluable support in her role as advisor for the project during those early stages. She went above and beyond what was required of her in her engagement and belief in my project. (Not that she didn't try to make it less unreasonable.) Since then, it has been a pleasure and an honor to continue working with her in Hannover, where I have learned invaluable lessons from our collaborative teaching and research projects. I would also like to thank Mark B. N. Hansen, who served as second reader for the dissertation, and who in more ways than one got me where I am today: it was he who first piqued my interest in literary theory and later in media theory, and my first trip from Texas to Germany was made with him (in the context of a student exchange). More recently, he has been instrumental in helping me return to the US with the aid of a postdoctoral fellowship, funded by the German Academic Exchange Service (DAAD), at the Program in Literature at Duke University.

Other teachers and mentors who have helped me along the way include Frank Schulze-Engler, with whom I first started thinking about *Frankenstein*, and whose humane manner impressed me deeply. In Texas, Peter Hutcheson also believed in me, and his philosophical rigor continues to goad me to make a better argument. (Though I'm sure he would wish that some of the ones I make here turned out a bit less unreasonable). Jeffrey Gordon also made an essential contribution to my philosophical formation, instilling in me a deep appreciation of contingency, indeterminacy, and the non-absoluteness of (disciplinary) boundaries.

During the writing of this project, I profited from discussions with Don Ihde and N. Katherine Hayles, and I thank them for taking the time. Matthias Bauer provided me with fascinating *Frankenstein*-related materials. A number of online contacts also helped me, among them people at the Classic Horror Film Board, Luke McKernan of the Bioscope, and inhabitants of the speculative realism corner of the blogosphere. My arguments benefited from discussions at Studienstiftung-supported research colloquia on the topics of "Funktionen von Kunst" and "Mediales Erzählen." Both in person and online, I profited immensely from exchanges and conversations with Steven Shaviro, Julia Leyda, Therese Grisham, Adrian Ivakhiv, James Stanescu, Jussi Parikka, Bernard Dionysius Geoghegan, Michael Chaney, Catherine Grant, and many, many others.

Over the past few years, I have had the honor to be a part of an incredible research group on "Popular Seriality—Aesthetics and Practice," expertly chaired by Frank Kelleter and funded by the Deutsche Forschungsgemeinschaft. The seriality group has taught me a great deal, and I thank everyone involved for creating such a supportive environment and for making the journey so far such an edifying experience. I would especially like to thank Frank Kelleter for his efforts in putting things together and keeping them from falling apart, Ruth Mayer (again) for getting me involved and for being an awesome collaborator, Andreas Jahn-Sudmann for his great ideas and his contagious excitement about media theory, Daniel Stein for involving me in new projects, and Jason Mittell for bringing in new perspectives.

In Hannover, I have profited from my involvement in the doctoral colloquium in American studies, the Film & TV Reading Group, and the Initiative for Interdisciplinary Media Research. I am particularly grateful to Florian Groß, Felix Brinker, Ilka Brasch, Vanessa Künnemann, Kirsten Twelbeck, Christina Meyer, Regina Schober, Bettina Soller, and Jana Wachsmuth for their helpful discussions. And I especially thank Jatin Wagle, Stefan Hautke, and Christoph Bestian, who have been true friends. Other friends who have helped me in one way or another include Ulf Kossatz, Rüdiger Zilm, and Steffen Wallat.

Finally, I would like to thank my family for all of their support over the years: my late grandfather for encouraging and nurturing my inquisitiveness at a very young age; my mother for always supporting my pursuits, no matter how crazy they must have seemed to her; my father for supplying me with media at a formative age (cable TV and an Atari 2600 may not have made me a better person, but they made me who I am); my brothers for bringing me down to earth. Above all, I thank Karin and Ari, who are always there for me, and who make everything worth it. (Sorry I couldn't be just a little bit less unreasonable.)

Foreword: Logics of Transition

MARK B. N. HANSEN

At one point in the complex and astute engagement with theories of media and technology that makes up the core of *Postnaturalism,* Shane Denson advances what appears on first glance to be an absolutely astounding claim concerning Niklas Luhmann's systems-theoretical account of media. "In contrast to the usual worries that systems theory's treatment of media is too abstract," Denson cool-headedly explains, "my concern is that it paradoxically *may not be abstract enough*"; Luhmann's theory may not be abstract enough, Denson clarifies, "to capture the dynamic processes concretely embodied by media" (311). In a sense, Denson's entire meditation in *Postnaturalism* is a massively concentrated effort to substantiate just this claim by way of a central thesis concerning the nature and operationality of media. In its contemporary operations but also in its historical formations, media functions to empower the environment itself in ways that give rise to phenomena of the living but that also produce inanimate becomings of the material domain both for itself and as it interpenetrates with higher-order, living operations. Media in Denson's understanding, and here we discover the deep motivation for his appeal to Luhmann (and his insistence on the limitations of Luhmannian systems theory), operate less as agents *within* any given system, than as environmental forces conditioning the development of an autonomous material domain and informing the disparate becomings that compose such development.

Anthropotechnical Interface

At the heart of Denson's argument is the figure of the "anthropotechnical interface." Denson introduces this concept to describe materiality as it operates before and beneath the human-nonhuman couplings that comprise the history of representations. To formulate this concept, Denson brings together two philosophical traditions that are normally held at a distance from one another. From naturalism,

Denson derives the crucial theme of matter's absolute resistance to linguistic or representational capture; and from phenomenology, the fundamental perspectival anchoring of any sensorimotor apprehension of materiality. By confronting each tradition with the other, Denson calls for their respective transformations: naturalism becomes postnaturalism; phenomenology, techno-phenomenology.

Naturalism, as Denson develops it, sheds any lingering connection to what we might call "negative" semiotic demonstrations, as well as to forms of constructivism that undergird such demonstrations. The result, however, is not a simple repudiation of linguistic-constructivist foundations, but their subsumption into a more encompassing, materialist ontology. This is precisely the subtle point of Denson's explication of the continuity from naturalism to postnaturalism when, for example, he writes: "the virtue of postnaturalism lies in its naturalist point of departure. Taking the material evolution of organic bodies for granted, methodologically speaking, means that we *begin* by assuming that our linguistically elusive interface with the unrepresentable material real is already, literally, *fleshed out*" (226). Far from taking place in some purified void, the linguistic-representational interface is itself part of the larger materiality at issue in any given moment of techno-material history, meaning that *both* its transparencies or "correlations," *and more importantly*, its opacities or "non-correlations," are deeply relevant to material process and to human (and extra-human) efforts to think that process.

In a similar way, Denson broadens the mandate of phenomenology to encompass not just human-centered intentional relations, but relations involving embodied agents of all sorts, nonhuman organisms to be sure, but technological entities as well. "Techno-phenomenology," Denson clarifies, "assumes that there is a plethora of embodied perspectives or standpoints that are no less real for the fact that phenomenology cannot countenance or occupy them, and between which standpoints occur inter-agential transactions and evolutionary transformations, defining a sub-phenomenological space of liminal matter and a sub-phenomenological time of transitionality" (283). What is involved here, once again, is not a simple repudiation of orthodox phenomenology, but rather, its far more complex embedding within a larger context where its endemic opacities—what phenomenological consciousness cannot intend—count as much, indeed much more, than the "contents" it secures through reduction.

Together, the postnatural operationality of matter and the post-phenomenological operationality of technics open up a "non-empirical stratum of materiality." Denson introduces this stratum as something like the "real condition" for experience as such, where the latter is not limited to the schematization of a manifold by the understanding, as it is on the Kantian account, but rather captures and names the impact of the sub-phenomenological force of matter on whatever entity or composition of entities, whether human mind or technical assemblage, serves to provide focal perspective on material process.

Again, Denson cuts to the heart of the stakes of his argument when he characterizes this non-empirical stratum as the very space of anthropotechnical embodiment: "from whichever direction we approach the impasse [between prioritizations of the human and the nonhuman], that of phenomenology or of naturalism, we arrive through this confrontation of perspectives at a non-empirical stratum of materiality that, in the evolutionary conjunction of organic and inorganic variation, constitutes the postnatural space of anthropotechnical embodiment. This material realm must be pre-empirical, as it concerns the very means of our access to the world: embodiment and technology, conceived not as organic or technical objects but as the bidirectional pathways through which experience and agency must pass" (257). From this clarification, we grasp how embodiment and technology are co-implicated at a level more fundamental or primitive than that of any integrated organic or inorganic "body," the human included: as the twin operations of the anthropotechnical interface, embodiment and technology work together in a cosmic dance that continuously generates nature itself. "The hybrid materiality of the anthropotechnical interface conditions all access to objective reality and, in a postnatural sense, *actually undergirds nature itself*" (257).

Non-Correlational Access

Denson's elucidation of the logic of the anthropotechnical interface is a particularly welcome development when contextualized against the backdrop of recent developments in cultural theory that have sought to escape from various logics of the human. In marked contrast to the critique of "correlationism" at the heart of today's various speculative realisms as well as to the over hasty enfranchisement of material processes and events at issue in the so-called "new materialisms," Denson's perspective forcefully asserts the necessity to proceed through and with the human in order to get to a position where the human need no longer function as a bottleneck on what can be presented to thought. To this end, Denson installs media in the role played by the "ancestral" (Quentin Meillassoux) or the "object" (Graham Harman). Proffering the materialist concept of "metabolism" as an alternative to the "realtime representational fluxes" central to Bernard Stiegler's media philosophy, Denson invests media themselves—media understood as "distributed materiality" or "distributed embodiment"—as "originary correlators" that operate before and as the very basis of the dual evolutionary lineages of the human and the technical. "[B]esides further counteracting Stiegler's all-too-cognitive view of technics," the payoff of Denson's approach "is that we reach a more robustly anti-correlationist account of media *as the originary correlators*. By taking a wholly ahuman realm of non-organic metabolic materiality into account, we counteract the impression of anthropocentrism that adheres to the asymmetrical privileging of the human bodily synthesis of time and space as the primary determinant of empirical reality" (328).

Like Whitehead (and unlike the speculative realists), Denson views the problem of correlationism less as an epistemological issue than a material-ontological one: the problem with Kant is not that he correlates what is with what can be thought, but rather, as Helmholtz already pointed out more than 100 years ago in his indictment of Kant's commitment to Euclidean geometry, that he gives an account of nature far too fully tailored to human experience. To break this correlationist circle does not require us to hypostatize and then reject the role Kant accords thought. What is needed, rather, is a non-anthropocentric account of the production of space and time, as well as an expanded view of how humans, understood as elements within a larger "postnatural" process, are both encompassed within and permeated by the very forces that generate the spatiotemporal continuum. For Denson, this means theorizing how media operate as forces of "distributed embodiment": "We then conceive the production of the empirical, the constitution and maintenance of its spatio-temporal foundations, as a matter of distributed embodiment—of the transduction of materially intersecting entities, each with their own form of embodiment, their own manner of marking the boundary, embodying the membrane, between material flux and the emergent realm of discrete objects" (328).

We might say that Denson's effort to locate media beneath the evolutionary split between the human and the technical yields an account of "non-correlational access" in the place of a simple critique of correlationism. If Denson is right that the metabolic operationality of media displaces the anthropocentrism of the human bodily synthesis of space and time, then what he proffers as the anthropotechnical interface holds forth the promise to access this metabolic materiality, this domain of distributed embodiment, without imposing on it the specific form of *human* embodiment. The result is an account of the power of distributed embodiment that does not need to sacrifice human participation but that can celebrate the more fundamental sensory and preperceptual "worldliness" of humans *as a crucial component in metabolic materiality.*

Transitionality

The form of this argument concerning correlation and the question of the human exemplifies a critical maneuver that is characteristic of Denson's various deployments of the vast theoretical archive he mobilizes in *Postnaturalism*. His procedure, here and at numerous points along the continuum he postulates from cinematic "double materiality" to the anthropotechnical interface itself, is to think with, through, and beyond a given concept in order to resituate or reapply that concept in a larger field or context, where whatever limitations it had appeared to possess are resolved (in the sense of *aufgehoben*) and where the concept in question takes on renewed scope and urgency. The result is a mind-dazzling exfoliation of the technicity informing the living that proceeds through stages of theoretical expansion, punctuating the story of the anthropotechnical interface like spikes rising up from the noise of an fMRI readout.

While this "Hegelian style of thought" reflects Denson's ruminative mode of dwelling with theory, and while it facilitates the impressively wide-ranging synthetic scope of his theoretical vision, it also directly implicates what I take to be the fundamental theoretical argument animating *Postnaturalism* as a whole, namely, the argument for the *generativity of the transitional*. Whether the focus in question be the historical transition between the so-called "primitive" mode of cinema and its later "classical" mode, or the material transition (flux) between environmental energy and embodied life, or the onto-epistemological transition between pre-perceptual, impersonal sensation and representational, conscious experience, Denson takes up residence in the space of process or relationality, and refuses to fall prey to any temptation to privilege one or another of the states, terms, or levels in correlation. By so doing, Denson puts himself in a position to discern and to track the "energies" driving the processes or relationalities that he puts into correlation prior to their solidification into terms: thus, in each of the cases mentioned above and in a series of other relationalities engaged in *Postnaturalism*, the movement is less that of a *from* ... *to* than a bidirectional and recursive *between*. Material transitionality replaces critical correlationalism as the mode of thinking connection.

The Singularity of Frankenstein

Denson's critical engagement with debates in early cinema perfectly exemplifies the power of transitionality. In a manner that typifies *Postnaturalism*'s theoretical excavations, Denson begins his account of early cinema with a pointed and helpfully explanatory reconstruction of arguments concerning the initial formation of a "primitive" mode of cinematic expression, characterized by the operation of "attraction" and the absence of narrative motivation, and its subsequent transformation into a "classical" mode that has—following the majority of extant film histories—remained relatively stable from the early 1930s until today. Drawing on arguments from film scholars like Tom Gunning and Miriam Hansen, Denson puts into question the notion of a straight-forward, linear and progressive transition from the primitive to the classical mode, and seeks to revalue the so-called "transitional period" as something far less "transitional" than it in fact has historically been treated. Rather than a "mere transition" on the way to cinema's maturity, the transitional period is here treated as a period of openness and heterogeneity, a period in which divergent potentialities of the cinematic medium came together, led in various directions, and seeded often incompossible future potentialities for cinema.

What is striking about Denson's critical engagement is his success in bringing new significance to a historical claim about early cinema's "transitional" phase. He does this *precisely* by treating cinema as an element *within a larger technomaterial transitionality*: accordingly, the so-called period of transition of early cinema describes a power of transitionality possessing a scope greater than any particular trajectory in cinema's history, and indeed, greater than that of the institution of cinema itself. In Denson's reconstruction then, the so-called transitional period names nothing less than a historical-material configuration that arose when a host of divergent material energies—both intra- and extra-cinematic—came together to create unprecedented potentialities for emergence.

At a moment when scholars have been challenged to reinvent the scope and singularity of the cinematic institution itself, Denson's broad and theoretically-driven approach might well inaugurate a new mode of expansion: as an alternative to arguments that further specify the materiality of cinema (e.g., arguments concerning the historical specificity of film as a celluloid support for cinema), Denson's exfoliating approach reembeds the institution of cinema in a much larger, technomaterial history, in relation to which questions concerning the ontology of cinema and its role within the history of the anthropotechnical interface can become orienting points for analysis.

Mangling as History

Denson engages in a formally similar analysis—and always one sensitive to the substantive matters at hand—in relation to a host of quite different moments of historical transition, including the reversal of the hierarchy between science and technology following the industrial revolution, and the complex material shifts ensuing from the proliferation of computational technologies that mark our contemporary historical moment. Denson also extends his account of the force of transitionality beyond the historical proper and into the domain of cultural theory and criticism: thus, a similar logic of what we might (following Denson following Pickering) call "mangling" informs Denson's nuanced theoretical characterizations of the material flows between environment and embodiment and of the difficult correlation of material life and representation.

The point, in all of these divergent cases, is the same, though the means taken to make it are always different, i.e., technically and historically specific: an adequate account of the anthropotechnical condition that characterizes the human, or better, the cosmos in which humans are implicated, requires a mode of analysis that does not discover "answers" within itself and its own history, but "generates" knowledge on the basis of the complex relationalities of divergent forces and the emergences they yield. In relation to questions of historical methodology, the payoff of Denson's focus on transitionality is the hard-to-come-by recognition that mangling precedes history: mangling describes the complex interpenetration and cross-fertilization of technomaterial energies that generate the very changes forming the raw material of the discipline of history.

Postnaturalism

Nowhere is the synthetic power of this logic of transitionality more clearly exemplified than in the striking correlation Denson forges between Frankenstein films and what he calls "postnaturalism." This correlation begins from the outset of the book and is woven into its various structural levels as Denson moves from close-readings of scenes from particular films outward to synoptic characterizations of critical positions (e.g., feminist interpretations of Shelley's *Frankenstein*), engagements with sociology of science/technology and science studies (the generalization of Pickering's "mangle of practice"), and ultimately to the broad ontological arguments that inform his characterization of the postnatural condition of humanity (or again, of the cosmos implicating human life and phenomenality). Not only can we say that this correlation structures the argumentation here in general, but we can say that it institutes a certain critical-theoretical imperative: the imperative to think nonhuman, cosmological becoming together with human, phenomenal experience. As I see it, this is the fundamental function of the focus on the *Frankenstein* myth and its various cultural expressions: in addition to furnishing exemplary historical moments at which the thematic concern with technological exteriorization of human experience becomes most salient, most formally complicated, and also most pressing, the *Frankenstein* complex constitutes something like an *interface* that, on the one hand, facilitates and structures our (human) experiential contact with cosmological techno-material becoming, while on the other, insists on the importance of representation—or better, of self-reference—as an irreducible aspect of our cultural negotiation of what I might be tempted to call our human technogenesis (and what Denson might want to generalize into something like cosmological technogenesis).

Cinematic Double Articulation

The significance of Denson's isolation of and focus on the cinematic legacy of the Frankenstein myth can be pinpointed in this context: with its own constitutive double articulation, cinema materializes, and thus perfectly exemplifies, the kernel of the Frankenstein narrative. As we have seen, cinema on Denson's account has from its origin functioned in a transitional space, or better, as an agent of transitionality between materiality and representation. Part of the story of cinema's maturation (even for a critic as critical of any progressive narrative as Tom Gunning) concerns the way that subjective focus gets introjected into the space of a filmic image that presents a wealth of worldly detail in excess of any subjective synthetic capacity. From the very beginning and by way of its technical "automatism" (Cavell), cinema presents a world that cannot be fully captured as representation, which means that it functions on a double register: it operates simultaneously at the level of embodiment and at the level of representation.

It is entirely to Denson's credit that he sees this double vision of cinema not simply as constitutive of cinema as a technomaterial institution but, crucially, as resistant to any kind of correlationism, meaning that what cinema does capture representationally *cannot be equated with* a representation of what it presents to embodied experience, but is a qualitatively different material experience altogether. Indeed, it is central to Denson's argument concerning cinema's "internal Frankenstein complex" that the two levels of "experience" differentiated here *not* correlate: their tension is itself implicated in the larger logic of (human and cosmological) technogenesis, and it is thus requisite upon us, as critics, to avoid the reciprocal temptations either to totalize representation, following the trajectory of Derridean deconstruction, or simply to abandon it as mere ideology, whether that be conceptualized as de Man's "phenomenality" or Kittler's "eyewash."

Perhaps more than the very impressive feats of synthesis and the daunting scope that mark the highpoints of *Postnaturalism*, for me it may well be this sensitivity to the irreducible double operation of the anthropotechnical interface that best demonstrates the maturity of Denson's meditation: this well-nigh ethical refusal to give up the category of phenomenality, and with it the "non-optionality" of the human, is, in my opinion, responsible for the degree of complexity and nuance that Denson is able to bring to his consideration of postnaturalism. Not only is it what takes him, in the impressive series of broadenings (as well as correlative contractions) I have already mentioned, *directly* and *obligatorily* from individual Frankenstein films to the overarching onto-logic of contemporary postnaturalism, but it is also—perhaps paradoxically—what allows Denson to indict the lingering anthropocentrism of many of his sourcepoints (my own work included) and to rethink the human not as the ontological, epistemological, or ethical center point of the analysis, but as a contingently or "in-certain-circumstances" privileged component of a greater cosmological onto-logic. Put in more simple terms: in the wake of Denson's account, the phenomenal is not irreducible because it furnishes the necessary perspective for the human to be implicated in techno-material cosmogenesis; the phenomenal is, rather, a *necessary element* of such cosmogenesis and one that, at least in our cosmos, implicates the human as its "agent." Denson puts this difference into operation at several points in the analysis, most notably (for me) when he engages the event of "digital convergence" and takes a critical distance from arguments that see something entirely unprecedented in the microtemporal, subrepresentational operationality of digital computation. On Denson's account, this is simply the latest in a long history of phases in technogenesis that are differentially structured by the double articulation of—and constitutive tension between—embodiment and representation.

Whither the Postnatural?

In a development that resonates with Walter Benjamin's brilliant account of cinema as a psycho-physiological training ground for life in modern times, Denson effectively presents cinematic double vision as a training ground for life in postnatural times. "Would it be possible," he asks, "on the basis of a cinematic double vision, to imaginatively feel our way into profoundly different, non-anthropomorphic filmic bodies and to describe their difference from our own being, that is, their specific positions between objective framings and subjective framers of material experience? If something like this is possible—and this of course remains to be seen—then the task of cinematic double vision could be understood as a sort of anthropotechnical ethnography, one that would offer, by means of its break with correlationism, a hope not unlike that promised (though certainly not always fulfilled) by traditional ethnography: that we may become more tolerant, open, and just with respect to difference and variation—in both the human *and the nonhuman* realm of agency" (298).

Denson's profound insight here—which carries forward Benjamin's conviction that cinema both impacts us tactilely and mediates the tactile energies of the technomaterial domain—is that humans are connected to the material domain through a host of avenues, most of which do not find their way into any cognitive channels of correlation. But what Denson proposes, by way of his conception of an anthropotechnical ethnography, is a form of practice that could exploit the "double articulation" of cinema, and beyond it of technical objects and processes generally, as the very vehicle for a broadened appreciation of the complex interpermeation of human life and material world. If cinema is exemplary in such an ethnography, that is because cinema does not simply represent the operationality of material forces that evade capture by Kantian *Vorstellungen*, but itself operates, as an expressive form but also as a technomaterial agent, at a host of levels, many of which evade representational capture.

Cinema, in other words, performs what it shows: indeed, it *cannot but perform what it shows*. This, I think, is the very kernel of Denson's argument (discussed above) for media as "originary correlators": to the extent that technical media are imbricated deep within the material fluxes at the heart of cosmological process, they are agents of a very general and multi-faceted correlation that, in marked contrast to the correlation criticized by Meillassoux and company, does not link the human and the world in a one-to-one correspondence, but describes the complexity and multi-dimensionality of the human's implication within the technomaterial world. Fortunately for us, and this is the crux of Denson's specification of the cinema as functionally privileged form of mediation, the technogenetic history of media has created anthropotechnical interfaces—like cinema itself—that give us noncorrelational, yet in some sense representational access to the extra-representational domain of material forces and operations subtending not just our existence in and as part of the world, but the cosmological genesis of the world itself. Beyond the narratives and images it presents, what cinema mediates is, ultimately, nothing other than our belonging to such a broader technomaterial, cosmological process.

Shane Denson's *Postnaturalism* develops this ambitious, wide-ranging, and deeply compelling argument concerning the originary operation of media in a way that sketches out a much-needed alternative to destructive developments which, expanding the darker strains of poststructuralist anti-humanism, have pitted the human against the material in some kind of cosmological endgame. *Postnaturalism* will provide a very powerful and timely addition to the literature on posthuman, cosmological technogenesis. Perhaps more clearly than any other account, it reconciles the irreducibility of phenomenality and the imperative to move beyond anthropocentrism as we seek to fathom the *postnatural* techno-material "revolutions" that have repeatedly remade—and that will no doubt continue to remake—the environments from which we emerge and to which "we" belong before we become and as a condition of becoming human subjects.

Denson's thought is permeated by a generosity that effectively places him in a similar relation to his sources as the human is to its cosmological envelope. By living the complexity and multi-dimensionality of his own anthropotechnical inheritance, Denson is able—and here his thinking stands in marked contrast to much of contemporary theoretical discourse—to synthesize where others can only divide. He is thus able to achieve a singular feat: to engage constructively, indeed, compositionally, with an impressively vast archive of ideational and worldly materials. His accomplishment in *Postnaturalism* shows convincingly that such wide-ranging synthesis is the key to derailing overly formalistic conceptions of correlation in favor of the broad correlation linking humans to postnatural materiality through a relational texture of mutual implication that confounds any and all efforts at purification.

1. Introduction:
Monster Movies and Metaphysics

> Unnatural participations or nuptials are the true
> Nature spanning the kingdoms of nature.
> GILLES DELEUZE AND FÉLIX GUATTARI[1]

What is postnaturalism? One might say, as a first approach, that it is post-postmodernism in a very basic, literal form: not so much the "return of the real" after having worked through all the intricate deconstructive constructivisms and paradoxically ornate aesthetic levelings that dominated an era of not-quite-late-enough capital. No, though it might have a touch of that too, postnaturalism is "after postmodernism" in a much more basic sense, in the same way that Aristotle's metaphysics was after physics, that is, arranged canonically after his *Physics*: likewise, postnaturalism comes after postmodernism in the banal sense of situating itself on alphabetically ordered bookshelves (and in corresponding databanks) right after all those books with "postmodernism" in their titles. But apart from playfully justifying a strategically useful position on the bookshelf, the comparison with Aristotle's *Metaphysics* is not entirely spurious. For just as the posthumous arrangement of his treatises gave rise to the mistaken notion that Aristotle was concerned to delineate a field of study that is categorically *beyond* physics, my notion of postnaturalism runs the risk that it will be understood as an attempt to move categorically *beyond* nature and/or naturalism. The relations amongst these terms is, however, more complex, and I will not be able fully to specify them until much later in this work. For the time being—I might as well come right out with it—let it be known that postnaturalism is in fact an emphatically *metaphysical* position: metaphysical in the sense of the philosophical discipline to which Aristotle's librarians so innocently but so momentously gave rise, i.e. the speculative study of the fundamental nature of being, whose very enterprise has been so demonized in large segments of recent thought.

---

1 *A Thousand Plateaus: Capitalism and Schizophrenia* 241.

By returning to metaphysics—and admitting it, no less—postnaturalism is therefore "after postmodernism" in another, more substantial sense than mere alphabetical order. But just as postmodernism maintained relations to modernism in its various senses, postnaturalism remains indebted to postmodernism's achievements, most centrally its deconstructive critique of essentialism. And this is where postnaturalism defines its basic opposition to naturalism: that is, it is a refusal of nature as essence (human nature, the natural order of things, benevolent nature as opposed to malignant culture or the evil of technical artificiality), as well as a refusal of naturalism *qua* reductivism (the dogma that empirical science is the sole yardstick of being, the surreptitious metaphysics that establishes the successors of "natural philosophy" as first philosophy). Thus, postnaturalism is largely continuous with that aspect of postmodern thought that taught us the significance of supplements and that gave us cyborg manifestoes. At the same time, though, postnaturalism is also in a sense continuous with scientific naturalism—sharing with it a belief in the primacy of the material world over the constructions of human thought—and this emphasis on materiality marks a break with the focus on discourse that dominates broadly postmodern thinking. Finally, like postmodernism, postnaturalism encompasses a historical dimension—defined by its attention to the historicity of technological changes, conceived as qualitative transitions of a genuinely ontological order—but the "post" in postnaturalism is not meant to indicate that we are living *after* or *beyond* nature, whatever that might mean. For the basic idea behind postnaturalism might be summed up, to adapt a phrase from Bruno Latour, thus: *We have never been natural.*[2] (And neither has nature, for that matter.)

If that is the philosophical import of postnaturalism, it is important to note that this will not be a conventional work of philosophy. Instead, I begin and I end with filmic adaptations and variations on Mary Shelley's *Frankenstein*, which for a full century now (since Thomas Edison's one-reeler *Frankenstein* appeared in 1910) have been reflecting, commenting upon, and treating in the most diverse of fashions the uneasy relations that obtain between modern humans and their technologies. So-called Frankenstein films also engage social and cultural constructions of human normalcy and deviance, along with their consequences for bodies and identities marked as unnatural, anomalous, freakish, or queer. These films thus offer a particularly rich index of the historical transformations to which normative conceptions and images of humanity have been subject in the twentieth century: they document anxieties about the technological alienation of human beings, and they combine these with (often propagandizing) representations of social processes of exclusion

---

2   The inspiration, of course, is Bruno Latour's *We Have Never Been Modern*, the influence of which on my line of thinking will become clear later, in the theory-dominated Part Two of this book.

through which privileged forms of subjectivity negatively derive their shape—and power—from abnormal or monstrous Others. On a narrative or thematic level, that is, cinematic adaptations of the Frankenstein story depict "human nature" as threatened by both the technical/artificial and the non-normative. Upon this basis, Frankenstein films can be investigated in terms of semiotic correlations between processes of oppression and their historically specific sociocultural contexts; one may ask how these correlations inform the filmic texts and, more generally, our thinking about ourselves and our technologies as filtered through those texts.[3]

Beyond this rather traditional, representationalist focus, however, I aim to situate my analyses in a robustly material realm of human-technological interaction, a realm of lived relations underlying and largely unperceived in human thinking about, and cultural images of, technology.[4] Not just an arena for the production, reproduction, and circulation of images and ideas, it is important to conceive the cinema also as a site of material interchange between human bodies and technologies. Frankenstein films' thematic contents are presented by means of constantly

---

3   Esther Schor, in her chapter "Frankenstein and Film" in *The Cambridge Companion to Mary Shelley*, characterizes this type of approach thus: "In the history of Frankenstein films, we can trace a Rohrschach—a psychologist's inkblot—of our collective fears. Critics have explored the implication of racism and lynching in the 1931 *Frankenstein*; of eugenics and the threat of a 'master race' in Whale's 1935 *Bride of Frankenstein*; of nuclear danger in the 1957 *Curse of Frankenstein* (dir. Terence Fisher) and the Hammer Studios sequels of the 1950s and 1960s; of organ transplants in various films of the 1960s and 70s; of sexual perversity in *Andy Warhol's Frankenstein* (dir. Antonio Margheriti and Paul Morrissey, 1974); and of replicants, cyborgs, and artificial intelligence in such films as Ridley Scott's *Blade Runner* (1982) and Steven Spielberg's *Artificial Intelligence: AI* (2001 [...])" (64). Schor sets this type of perspective aside in her text, but she remains in a representationalist framework by asking what filmic depictions of animation have to say about, or how they might influence our readings of, the monster as depicted in Shelley's novel. That is, the focus is framed by an intertextual relation between films and the novel, and both relata are queried as to what animation *means* or *signifies*. In what follows, I break with both of these framing choices by dissociating the films from Shelley's novel (though a reading of the novel, in Chapter 4, will be essential to my argument about what the films materially do) and by subordinating the question of discursive meaning to questions of embodiment, materiality, and interfacing.

4   Here I follow Mark Hansen, who defines representationalism thus: "By representationalist approach I mean any approach that legitimizes representation as its frame of reference, whether for ends either affirmative or critical, positivist or deconstructive" (*Embodying Technesis* 265). The expression "robust *materiality* of technology," to which he opposes representationalist approaches, also stems from Hansen (4).

changing cinematic technologies; indeed, the films often highlight their own technical foundations as much as—and often by means of—their displays of the technological creation of the diegetic monster. Discursive analyses, though indispensable, cannot therefore be sufficient for understanding the reflexive feedback loops that exist here between spectator, technological milieu, and the thematic representations on the screen. The material conditions of the cinema and the embodied constitution of historically situated spectators must also be accounted for if we are to grasp Frankenstein films' assertions of a doubly articulated anthropotechnical interface: as these movies intimate—though they often work to repress their own recognition—not only the filmic monster but also *we* as spectators are "bio-technical" hybrids, and our imbrication in technical networks (cinematic and otherwise) presents an additional complication in the cultural-political negotiation of "the human."

Hybridity, though, has a history. *Frankenstein* is not a timeless tale, nor do its filmic progenies act in a historical vacuum. Indeed, Frankenstein films confront us with precisely the *historicity of human-technological interfaces*—at least, that is, if we confront the films in a vigorously historicizing manner. Seen in the context of the historical connections that obtain amongst their narrative contents, their social settings, and contemporaneous cultural conflicts; set in relation to media-technical infrastructures, innovations, and transitions; and located squarely in the material and experiential parameters of historically situated spectatorship, Frankenstein films reveal specific, changing configurations of human-technological interaction: patterns, tendencies, and deviations that mark moments in a richly variable history that is at once a history of cinema, of media, of technology, and of the affective channels of our own embodiment. Clearly, there is nothing obvious about this claim, which would seem to aggrandize a rather trivial cinematic phenomenon and invest Frankenstein films with a function that they cannot possibly fulfill. It shall take some work, then, to demonstrate the reverse, and I undertake this task by situating the films within a history of phenomenological patterns of cinematic reception, of changing relations amongst spectatorial subjects, filmic objects, and mediating technologies. Seen in this light, as I hope to demonstrate, we find Frankenstein films making certain demands on their human users, at times altogether *unreasonable* demands that challenge the very coherence and stability of viewing subjects and pressure them to submit to a disorienting affective experience. As the material locus of this experience, human embodiment is opened to the direct, non-cognitive and pre-personal, impact of cinematic technology. In this way, viewers are brought into contact with a realm of diffuse materiality—that of the anthropotechnical interface itself, the relational substrate which underlies the socially, psychically, and otherwise subjectively or discursively organized relations that humans maintain with technologies. Though typically only a momentary, fleeting experience, viewers are exposed to a domain of radically alterior agencies in flux, into which subjectivities are plunged and out of which emerge new configurations of human-nonhuman relationality. This is the realm of postnatural transitionality, in which occur historical movements that outstrip the scope of any empirical or discursive historiography. In this realm is grounded a history of material agency itself, as it is shaped and bent, expanded and attenuated, formed and deformed in concert with our technological environments.

The link, then, that my project forges between monster movies and metaphysics is one that attempts to answer the call issued by Frankenstein films themselves, to live up to the demands that they make upon viewers by developing a framework capable of countenancing those demands and the affective experiences to which they give rise. Postnaturalism, as a metaphysics of anthropotechnical change, thus acknowledges these films' provocations, to which it offers in response a theory that promises a sort of rapprochement between over-challenged humans and misunderstood technical agencies. My project, in accordance with these relations and goals, is organized into three main parts: Part One locates the experiential challenges posed by Frankenstein films; Part Two theorizes embodiment, transitionality, and mediality in an attempt to articulate a framework—postnaturalism—that will meet those challenges; and Part Three returns to Frankenstein films, now with postnatural theory in hand, to demonstrate the films' special relations to the historicity of the anthropotechnical interface. But before I go any further, I need to address two topics, which will occupy the remainder of this introduction—namely: What do I mean by Frankenstein film? And what is an anthropotechnical interface?

Monster Movies:
Adaptation, Myth, Genre, and Beyond

What is a Frankenstein film? The answer to this question may seem obvious at first glance. Surely we know one when we see one. And yet, when pressed to give a definition capable of drawing clear lines of inclusion and exclusion, we may find ourselves unable to respond. We can name a few clear-cut cases, for example James Whale's *Frankenstein* (1931) and *Bride of Frankenstein* (1935)—the very paradigms of the Frankenstein film, with Boris Karloff as the iconic embodiment of the monster—along with the rest of the Universal cycle and the Hammer series that began with *The Curse of Frankenstein* (1957).[5] Surely we would include Kenneth

---

5   Production histories for all of the Universal Frankenstein films are contained in Gregory William Mank's *It's Alive! The Classic Cinema Saga of Frankenstein.* Each of the individual films is covered, and the original scripts reproduced, in the books of the Magi-

Branagh's *Mary Shelley's Frankenstein* (1994, starring Robert de Niro as the creature[6]), as well as *Flesh for Frankenstein* (1973, better known as *Andy Warhol's Frankenstein*). And then there's a slew of other films with "Frankenstein" in their titles: *I Was a Teenage Frankenstein* (1957), *Frankenstein's Daughter* (1958), *Frankenstein 1970* (1958), *Dracula Vs. Frankenstein* (1971), *Lady Frankenstein* (1971), *The Erotic Adventures of Frankenstein* (1971), *Frankenstein's Castle of Freaks* (1974).[7] But a titular mention of "Frankenstein" might not be a reliable indicator: *Frankenstein Meets the Spaceman* (1965) is iffy—Martians land on Earth, damage a NASA-built android, which then goes haywire and terrorizes bikini-clad girls—while *Frankenstein Conquers the World* (also 1965, from the Toho Company of Godzilla fame) is perhaps even more questionable, with its story of a heart, stolen from the Nazis during WWII and exposed to radiation during the bombing of Hiroshima, which then sprouts into a giant boy who eventually faces a showdown with a giant reptile. What about spoofs such as *Abbott and Costello Meet Frankenstein* (1948) and Mel Brooks's *Young Frankenstein* (1974)? Or how about films with a clearly *Frankenstein*-inspired story of creation, such as *Rocky Horror Picture Show* (1975) or *Edward Scissorhands* (1990)? But if we take these on board, should we also include such films as *Hulk* (2003), *Robocop* (1987), or even *Blade Runner* (1982)? Do we still know a Frankenstein film when we see one?

Now I do not have any definitive answers to these questions, and I am inclined to concede that such precision here may not, ultimately, be all that important; however, we do need a general idea of what kind of objects we're after here, and taking the question of definition seriously provides an opportunity for me both to outline these objects and to explore what it is that makes Frankenstein films so attractive for my larger project. First of all, it seems unreasonable to maintain that the category of Frankenstein films is limited in any strict sense to *adaptations* of Mary Shelley's novel, for this would rule out almost all of the films that we commonly accept under the rubric, including such paradigmatic examples as *Bride of Frankenstein*, which imagines the consummation of a project never completed in the novel: the

---

cimage Filmbooks Universal Filmscripts Series, all edited by Philip J. Riley. The Hammer series is covered in Marcus Hearn and Alan Barnes, *The Hammer Story*; David Pirie, *A New Heritage of Horror*; and Wayne Kinsey, *Hammer Films: The Bray Studios Years* and *Hammer Films: The Elstree Studios Years*.

6 Background and screenplay are included in Diana Landau, ed., *Mary Shelley's Frankenstein: The Classic Tale of Terror Reborn on Film*.

7 Compendia of film facts, primary materials, and secondary sources for Frankenstein films include Donald Glut's *The Frankenstein Catalog* and Caroline Picart's more recent *The Frankenstein Film Sourcebook*.

creation of a female monster.[8] As this example demonstrates, any definition in terms of "adaptation" will have to take that concept in a very loose sense, one which allows both for lines of derivation but also major deviations from Shelley's narrative. It is questionable, though, whether a notion of adaptation stretched far enough to include even the core films of the Universal and Hammer series would still be a useful concept.[9] It would have to accommodate the monster's resurrection

---

8   Of course, the traditional reply would be to say that the film is faithful to the "spirit" rather than the details of Shelley's plot. But this form of reply, itself questionable enough in its vagueness, will not be able to accommodate all of the various filmic deviations from Shelley's narrative. A number of more recent theoretical approaches to adaptation might be better suited to deal with such cases. Critics such as Brian McFarlane, Robert Stam, Thomas Leitch, Julie Sanders, and Linda Hutcheon have criticized the so-called "fidelity discourse" that is operative in my counterexample. (See, for example, McFarlane's *Novel to Film*, Stam's "Beyond Fidelity," Hutcheon's *A Theory of Adaptation*, Leitch's *Film Adaptation and its Discontents*, and Sanders's *Adaptation and Appropriation*.) It is the notion of fidelity to an original (in this case Mary Shelley's novel) that defines the "strict sense" of adaptation that I refer to above. I turn to "looser senses" of adaptation in a moment. For clarity's sake, though, at issue in my denial of the reasonableness of a strict sense is not so much whether we can conceive the films as "*adaptations* of Shelley's novel" as whether we can or should conceive them as "adaptations *of Shelley's novel*," with emphasis on the narrow relation between adaptation and "original," whether that relation be evaluated in terms of the spirit or the letter of the alleged source.

9   To be more precise about this, it is less a question of *whether* such a loose conception would be useful as it is a question of *what it would be useful for*. Thus, Linda Hutcheon's evolutionary theory, which puts aside the hierarchical relation of an adaptation to the "original" and the related focus on fidelity and instead envisions a network of dialogical adaptation relations amongst a whole ecosphere of texts, is better suited to a macroscopic view of cultural practices, but less well suited, in my opinion, to a detailed study of a particular line of development. (An explicit "homology between biological and cultural adaptation" has been proposed in a jointly authored article by Gary R. Bortolotti and Linda Hutcheon: "On the Origin of Adaptations.") To be sure, this type of theory is a major advance over the older binarizing fidelity model, in that it allows us to understand our own and past "remix cultures" better, giving us a means to trace broad cultural mutations, but the light it sheds on the particular formation of Frankenstein films, for example, is one that tends not so much to explain their unity as to *dissolve* it into a number of subpopulations constituted by the relations of adaptations to other adaptations. And indeed, this can be a useful perspective if we are primarily interested in *what culture does to Frankenstein films* (as the diversifying action of an environment on groups of organisms)

first by one son of Frankenstein (in *Son of Frankenstein*, 1939) and then another (*Ghost of Frankenstein*, 1942); it would have to suffer the creature's encounters with the Wolf Man (*Frankenstein Meets the Wolf Man*, 1943), and again with the Wolf Man *and* Dracula (in both *House of Frankenstein*, 1944, and *House of Dracula*, 1945). The situation is similar when we turn to Hammer, where Baron Frankenstein takes the spotlight: he first constructs a creature (*The Curse of Frankenstein*, 1957), then builds a new body for his hunchback assistant (*The Revenge of Frankenstein*, 1958), employs the services of a mesmerist for the act of animation (*The Evil of Frankenstein*, 1964), installs the soul of a man in the corpse of a woman (*Frankenstein Created Woman*, 1967), performs the first ever brain transplantation (*Frankenstein Must Be Destroyed*, 1969), repeats his first act of creation (*The Horror of Frankenstein*, 1970), and finally, himself completely mad, pairs up with a lunatic to stitch together a homicidal hairy ape-like monster (*Frankenstein and the Monster from Hell*, 1974). What do all of these films have in common with Mary Shelley's Gothic novel? At the end of the day, not much—certainly not a particular set of narrative events; at most, there is a shared focus on acts of creation and the consequences of such acts, along with a very general thematic exploration of human-technology relations and attendant socio-cultural conflicts.[10]

Starting from this thematic basis, there is a temptation to cast the net wide, to include any film that shares the focus on the technological animation of artificial creatures. Thus, for example, in his introduction to the collection *We Belong Dead:*

---

rather than a focus on *how Frankenstein films act as a group* (where it should be understood that there is no immutable essence common to them all, but that their constitution as a group is possible by means of an observational selection, which does not involve any backsliding into the fidelity model). The "myth" approach that I consider in a moment can be seen as one such observational selection, but one that is too vague and ahistorical to be of much use. The notion that Frankenstein films constitute a genre or quasi-genre, which I consider thereafter, is another, more promising but ultimately limited, observational selection. In Chapter 6, I return briefly to this question and propose that Frankenstein films constitute, in fact, a type of *series*.

10 Thomas Leitch discusses Frankenstein films as examples of "*secondary, tertiary, or quaternary imitations*" which give fidelity models trouble, but which can be conceived as "adaptations not of an earlier story but of an earlier character, setting, or concept" (120). My problem with this suggestion, however, is that it gives the impression of describing a more or less well-defined class of objects while it in fact trades on a vacillation between, on the one hand, an endless subdivision amongst "secondary, tertiary, or quaternary" formations without an overarching unity and, on the other hand, an open unity based on vague notions such as the "adaptation of a concept" that make it difficult to exclude anything. The latter tendency opens onto the "myth" approach that I discuss presently.

Frankenstein on Film, which itself treats more or less non-controversial candidates for inclusion in the Frankenstein film category, editor Gary Svehla describes how a tendency to generalize once took shape in himself: "Growing up in the 1950s and 1960s, we saw the recreation of the Frankenstein myth rewritten first by England's Hammer Film Productions and later recast in science fiction terms, where even *The Thing* and *It! The Terror from Beyond Space* became variations on a theme: Frankenstein Monsters from outer space" (9). Similarly seeing the Frankenstein story as a "myth," the theme of which is taken to be "*parthenogenesis* or male self-birthing" (3), Caroline Picart restricts herself, for the most part, in *The Cinematic Rebirths of Frankenstein: Universal, Hammer, and Beyond* to the canonical films of the Universal and Hammer series, and plays it safe with the "beyond," treating only *Frankenstein 1970* and *Mary Shelley's Frankenstein*; but she suggests that this is a more or less arbitrary limitation, and that not only "comedic or parodic versions" such as *Abbott and Costello Meet Frankenstein*, *Young Frankenstein*, and *The Rocky Horror Picture Show*, but also science fiction films such as *Blade Runner* and *Alien* (1979) "effectively rewrite the Frankenstein narrative" and could therefore be treated as Frankenstein films proper (200). And this she does in her follow-up book, *Remaking the Frankenstein Myth on Film*, where Picart looks at the theme of "parthenogenetic births" and the "tensions regarding gender, power, and technology" (2) that it encodes in a broader range of films, including both the complete *Alien* quadrilogy and the *Terminator* series, which for her are an integral part of the "Frankensteinian cinemyth" (1). But while I can certainly understand Svehla's youthful experience, and while I grant that there may be good reasons for *comparing* the films that Picart treats to Frankenstein films, I question the usefulness of *identifying* them as Frankenstein films. This inflationary approach, based on a very broad thematic foundation, stretches the category beyond recognition. Moreover, the (widespread) generalization of the Frankenstein story into a "myth" is itself a sort of mythical approach, one that tends to reduce the tale's historicity to a general relation it has to modern technology while neutralizing any significant changes in that relation or in technology itself.[11]

---

11 A recent incarnation of the myth approach is Susan Tyler Hitchcock's *Frankenstein: A Cultural History*. Identifying the tale as "a myth of claiming long-forbidden knowledge and facing the consequences," and relating it to Joseph Campbell's Jungian take on an archetypal "myth of the search for meaning in human life" that pervades geographically and historically disparate cultures (4), Hitchcock sees the Frankenstein story's "crucial, haunting, modern twist" as consisting in the secularization of the myth, raising the "dark possibility of a godless world" (6). The pop-Nietzschean-existentialism-cum-Jungian-essentialism notwithstanding, Hitchcock's anecdotal study offers a highly readable overview of the pervasion of Shelley's tale across popular culture. Other examples of the

Thus, Picart in particular stretches the category of Frankenstein films too far for my taste, and my uneasiness with this move is based ultimately in my belief that one of the salient characteristics of Frankenstein films is their ability to invoke an experience of the postnatural historicity of anthropotechnical relations. It would, of course, be question-begging for me to *define* the films in this way, and that is not what I wish to suggest; indeed, not all Frankenstein films manage to call forth this experience, and that's far from being all that they do. But, as we shall see later, when Frankenstein films do in fact pull it off, they do so only as a function of their own historicity and their relation to a historically contingent juncture of spectating subjects, mediating technologies, and material settings—and it is precisely this rich historicity of the films that a "mythical" approach underemphasizes. On the other hand, though, what Svehla and Picart demonstrate by stretching the category as they do is that the category is itself inherently flexible, and that a set of family resemblances unites the films as a group more than any common lineage that might be traced back to Shelley's novel. This I take to be an important insight, but one that does not compel us to expand the category of Frankenstein films to the status of "cinemyth." (*Alien* and *Terminator*, for me, are perhaps distant relatives, hardly next of kin.) *Typically*—and typicality all that we can hope for when considering "family resemblance"-type groupings—Frankenstein films have the thematic focus that we have been considering (artificial creation, human-technological conflict, etc.), but beyond that they are staged according to one of a limited repertoire of

---

"Frankenstein myth" approach include Chris Baldick's *In Frankenstein's Shadow: Myth, Monstrosity, and Nineteenth-Century Writing*, Christopher Small's *Mary Shelley's Frankenstein: Tracing the Myth*, and Martin Tropp's *Images of Fear*. Finally, an interesting variation is Pedro Javier Pardo García's article "Beyond Adaptation: Frankenstein's Postmodern Progeny," which reasons: "it is not just the literary source that has been ceaselessly reproduced: most film versions do not take Mary Shelley's text as a point of departure, but previous film versions. In fact, what different versions have in common is not so much the book as the myth created by its dramatic and cinematic reproduction, to the extent that the book has become one more version of that myth—the founding, but not necessarily the most influential one. The mediation of myth in the transference from page to screen must be taken into account in any study of the film adaptations of *Frankenstein*" (224). For García, this translates into the following: "The story of Shelley's *Frankenstein* on film is therefore one of distortion, of omissions, and additions, simplification and elaboration, or simply, one in which the myth has supplanted the novel" (226). What we see here is how the overly narrow view of adaptation on the "fidelity" model gives way to the overly broad view of the "myth" model. In my opinion, we need to steer a course between the two if we are to have a useful but non-reductive view of Frankenstein films as a group formation.

narrative patterns, visualized according to a conventional iconography, enacted according to standard patterns of characterization, and generally connected to other Frankenstein films by means of allusion, quotation, and other intertextual means of signaling a nodding awareness of one another.

Repetition of a basic thematic conflict and variation on the theme, narrowed according to factors of conventional resemblance and interconnection—this suggests that we are dealing with something like a genre. I would like to pursue this suggestion a bit further, but let me state up front that I do not ultimately believe that the requisite generic coherence obtains to warrant the strong label of genre or even the weaker one of sub-genre (of what?); for though all but a handful of Frankenstein films are uncontroversially "genre films," they are dispersed across a range of film genres. Most of them share the broader characteristics of horror and/or science fiction, but it is not at all obvious why we should rule out comedy versions like *Young Frankenstein*, exploitation pictures such as *Blackenstein* (1973), or action-adventure movies like *Van Helsing* (2004). Do we not, however, miss this cross-generic nature of the category when we seek to identify the films as a generic unit? Besides, and more importantly, if we take the genre designation over-seriously we run the risk again of over-generalizing and thereby de-historicizing the films, and thus of overlooking the significant intra- and inter-generic transformations marked by Frankenstein films. James Whale's *Frankenstein*, for instance, was instrumental in defining the emerging genre of horror, which in turn effectively died before Hammer revived it with *The Curse of Frankenstein*; but theirs was a new type of horror, which in some ways anticipated splatter films but was hardly comparable to the graphic displays of disembowelment that we find (presented in 3D, no less) in *Andy Warhol's Frankenstein* or the recent over-the-top body-gore-fest *Vampire Girl Vs. Frankenstein Girl* (2009). Moreover, if it is now common to classify even the classic Frankenstein films of the 1930s as horror/sci-fi hybrids, the science fiction genre was not solidified as such until after World War II; other films—such as *Frankenstein 1970*, starring an aged Boris Karloff as Dr. Frankenstein's descendant seeking to clone himself with an atomic reactor, or the much later time-travel tale *Frankenstein Unbound* (1990)—can more plausibly be treated as hybrids, where this hybridity marks a historically determinate act of probing genre boundaries. Nor is horror/sci-fi the only type of hybridity—fittingly enough for films centered around a hybrid monster—that we find among Frankenstein films. There is horror/comedy (such as *The Monster Squad*, 1987), horror/porn or horror/sexploitation (*Lust for Frankenstein*, 1998; *Mistress Frankenstein*, 2000; *Bikini Frankenstein*, 2010), and even a horror/sci-fi-Western mix-up (*Jesse James Meets Frankenstein's Daughter*, 1966). In short, there are just too many trans-generic hybridities, cross-overs, and spin-offs, and too much heterogeneous trash and treasure to be reduced to a genre.

However, if we bear in mind the caveat that it is merely a heuristic fiction, it will nevertheless be instructive as a preliminary exercise to tentatively treat the films as a quasi-generic formation. In this way, we can begin to approach those aspects that I find most interesting about them, and which effectively take us beyond genre. We have seen that Frankenstein films share a thematic focus on human-technological interactions and attendant conflicts of various sorts. Consider now this statement from Thomas Schatz's classic book *Hollywood Genres*: "In addressing basic cultural conflicts and celebrating the values and attitudes whereby these conflicts might be resolved, all film genres represent the filmmakers' and audience's cooperative efforts to 'tame' those beasts, both actual and imaginary, which threaten the stability of our everyday lives" (29). Now there might or might not be better ones, but there are certainly a lot worse starting points for thinking the unity of Frankenstein films (as opposed to the disparity that I have largely emphasized up to now). The interesting thing about Schatz's statement, in this connection, is that Frankenstein films typically represent a very *literal* interpretation of the "cooperative efforts" he describes: these films embody the threats to stability of which Schatz speaks in an actual monster, a material "beast" that must be physically "tamed" or, more commonly, destroyed to restore order. Now for Schatz, who has in mind a more figurative enactment of this scenario, the repeated staging of more or less the same conflicts in highly conventionalized manners indicates that genres are a matter of *"cultural ritual"* (12)—ritualized means of confronting, which is not to say solving, a society's contradictions. Whatever we might think about the *function* of such ritual (whether we think it serves psychological, sociological, or even metaphysical purposes), the ritualistic aspect is clearly present in Frankenstein films, where a basic pattern can be identified that, though not universal, is repeatedly rehearsed not only in the paradigmatic horror and horror/sci-fi versions but also in the comedy and other, more marginal hybrid productions.

Thus, Frankenstein films largely conform to the basic "plot structure of a genre film" that Schatz describes as involving the following four stages (30):

establishment (via various narrative and iconographic cues) of the generic community with its inherent dramatic conflicts;

animation of those conflicts through the actions and attitudes of the genre's constellation of characters;

instensification of the conflict by means of conventional situations and dramatic confrontations until the conflict reaches crisis proportions;

resolution of the crisis in a fashion which eliminates the physical and/or ideological threat and thereby celebrates the (temporarily) well-ordered community. (30)

In your typical Frankenstein film, just about everything leading up to the act of creation is *establishment* in Schatz's sense; narrative cues (such as Frankenstein's increasing neglect of his fiancée, his undertaking of illegitimate studies, cruelties to humans or animals, desecrations of hallowed ground, etc.) and iconographic cues (Gothic architecture, tower labs or their modern-day equivalents, weird machinery, graveyards by night, etc.) establish the community's inherent conflict between renegade science and traditional community, between the seductions of forbidden knowledge and the sanctioned appeals of romantic love, family, *Heimat*, and nature. The next step, *animation*, is particularly literal in the Frankenstein film's typically central event: the act of creation, the animation of the monster, which brings the latent conflict (i.e. the monster) to life. The conflict then *intensifies* when the monster fails to submit, when it kills innocent victims, when it escapes, resulting in the community's alarm and panic. The *resolution* of the crisis is just as literal as its animation: the community "eliminates the physical and/or ideological threat" by banding together, hunting down the creature, torches in hand, and (apparently) killing it; but the community, as Schatz indicates, is only "(temporarily) well-ordered" as a result, for the restoration of order is unmasked as illusory when the next film reveals that the creature is not in fact dead, or that Dr. Frankenstein or some relative or former student is about to resurrect it.

As Schatz points out, a genre's success over time depends on both the continued "thematic appeal and significance" accorded its central conflicts and a certain "flexibility" in its treatment of them (31). In the case of Frankenstein films, motivation for the basic plot structure's ceaseless repetition is surely sustained, at least in part, by the apparently unresolvable conflicts generated by technological innovation, which is the source both of hopes and of fears, intimately tied and yet irreconcilably opposed to one another. And Frankenstein films are sufficiently flexible in their trips to this inexhaustible well, ever adapting the tale to the most ambivalently promising and threatening technologies of the day: filmic Frankensteins utilize atomic energy, perform organ transplants, pursue bioethically dubious eugenic or genetic research, become experts in AI and robotics; and so can the monster be made to stand for just about any potential technological menace we can think of. Frankenstein films' human-technology conflicts (meaning, typically, conflicts of the type technology-out-of-control and/or technology-in-the-wrong-hands) are, in Schatz's terms, the "static nucleus" of the (quasi-)genre, while the various forms this conflict takes are its "dynamic surface structure" (31). However, if generic variation were restricted to the choice of technologies employed to frame the basic conflict, the genre view would again not yield much in the way of a historicizing perspective. Or, conversely, no plausible theory of genre can maintain that the basic patterns are static and unchanging over the course of a genre's history. Variation—and not just surface variation but historical transformation of the generic core—is essential to the utility of the notion of "genre" itself, which in the actual practice of generic formations is always susceptible to decline, always has some "golden age" or high point (either in qualitative or quantitative terms), can always subdivide into new formations, or be transformed through contact with other genres. A genre, in short, always has a history; without it, we would not have a generic category but instead an immutable essence, the same film over and over again rather than a collection of films of more or less the same type.[12]

In his own take on historical variation, which draws on suggestions made by Christian Metz and Henri Focillon, Schatz develops a model of the "evolution" of genres (36-41). He argues that,

at the earliest stages of its life span, a genre tends to exploit the cinematic medium *as a medium*. If a genre is a society collectively speaking to itself, then any stylistic flourishes or formal self-consciousness will only impede the transmission of the message. At this stage, genre films transmit a certain idealized cultural self-image with as little "formal interference" as possible. Once a genre has passed through its experimental stage where its conventions have been established, it enters into its classical stage. We might consider this stage as one of *formal transparency*. Both the narrative formula and the film medium work together to transmit and reinforce that genre's social message—its ideology or problem-solving strategy—as directly as possible to the audience. (38)

This message, of course, must be renegotiated in each new incarnation, varied to the extent—but no further—that it succeeds in communicating the central message in a compelling, yet conventional, but nevertheless non-redundant way. There is a subtle give and take in the so-called classical stage, but at some point something's got to give:

Thus, the end of a genre's classic stage can be viewed as that point at which the genre's straightforward message has "saturated" the audience. With its growing awareness of the formal and thematic structures, the genre evolves into what Focillon termed the age of re-

---

12 Indeed, without this qualification, the genre designation would collapse back into the myth view: the co-presence of hope and fear occasioned by technological innovation is the basis for the archetypal view taken, for example, by Susan Tyler Hitchcock (see previous footnote above), while the "dynamic surface structure" of adaptation to currently controversial technologies accords with the various manifestations of the alleged archetypal myth as they occur in various cultures.

finement. As a genre's classic conventions are refined and eventually parodied and subverted, its transparency gradually gives way to *opacity*: we no longer look *through* the form (or perhaps "into the mirror") to glimpse an idealized self-image, rather we look *at the form itself* to examine and appropriate its structure and its cultural appeal. (38)

In terms that come quite close to the substance and tone of a systems-theoretical approach, Schatz sums up his view thus: "A genre's progression from transparency to opacity—from straightforward storytelling to self-conscious formalism—involves its concerted effort to explain itself, to address and evaluate its very status as a popular form" (38).

We can imagine how this might apply to Frankenstein films. Universal's "classic" cycle perfected the Frankenstein film genre in the mode of horror. Hammer "refined" the basic formula, which means not so much that they improved upon it as that they embellished it and adapted it on the basis of an "awareness of the formal and thematic structures" established by Universal. This awareness is demonstrated, for example, in the dramatic shift from the creature to the creator as the central character of the Hammer series. Through such deviations, Hammer significantly transformed the formula, but they did not yet go beyond the "age of refinement" into what Focillon termed "the baroque age." This occurred later, when Mel Brooks parodied (but also paid tribute to) the formula, when Warhol's Frankenstein subverted it (or "fucked it in the gall bladder," in the words of the film's Baron Frankenstein), when other productions of the 1970s and beyond—such as *Rocky Horror*, Tim Burton's *Frankenweenie* (1984, 2012), and even an episode of *The X-Files* ("The Post-Modern Prometheus," 1997)—subjected it to further scrutiny, pastiche, deconstruction, made it "opaque" in order to examine its cultural function and appeal, and to display the hidden politics of that appeal.

There is, however, a problem with this view of Frankenstein films' development—namely: James Whale's "golden age" horrors, *Frankenstein* and *Bride of Frankenstein*, which together form the very epitome of the classical Frankenstein film, are themselves already extremely self-reflexive, full of camp and irony. On the other hand, some of the most "serious" or "straightforward" retellings of the Frankenstein tale (adaptations such as *Terror of Frankenstein*, 1977, or that better-known attempt at "faithfulness," *Mary Shelley's Frankenstein*) appear very late in the day. Frankenstein films, or so it would seem, simply do not follow the evolutionary pattern described by Schatz. Perhaps this deviation can be attributed in part to the long cultural prehistory of the (hypothetical) film genre, which includes Shelley's novel, satirical political cartoons, and a rich theatrical tradition of stage plays of all sorts.[13] On the other hand, though, it might simply be that genres do not develop in the manner of an "evolution from transparent social reaffirmation to opaque self-reflexivity" (40-41). Steve Neale, for one, opts for the latter alternative and argues that Schatz's model is far too hermetic, too closed off from the types of extrinsic influences that I have identified as forming the Frankenstein film's prehistory—which never in fact ended but instead developed in parallel with cinematic incarnations across a wide range of media (comics, radio, TV, video games, etc.).[14] Indeed, though Schatz allows that there can be exceptions to the evolutionary model, the latter remains a more or less self-enclosed system; interestingly, the exceptional cases he acknowledges involve factors that are not so different in kind from the genre-extrinsic influences highlighted by Neale: Schatz maintains that "external pressures" such as "the threat of government censorship and religious boycott" can disturb the "internal evolution" of genres (40) rather than, as Neale would have it, militating against the notion of internal evolution itself.

Now my point is not to invalidate Schatz's model or even to engage in this debate, which is far-ranging and goes beyond Schatz and Neale. To put it bluntly, genre theory is not my primary interest here at all, but only ancillary to another purpose. I raise the question of genre historicity, that is, not in order to learn about the history of genres but because the question focuses attention on a peculiar and significant feature of Frankenstein films—one that is touched upon in Schatz's use of the terms "transparency" and "opacity" and that presents a much greater obstacle to the subsumption of Frankenstein films under Schatz's model than the factors raised by Neale. Quite apart from those largely external factors (which would either invalidate the model *or* prove the rule by exception), there are in fact formal characteristics of Frankenstein films, factors *internal* to the films themselves, that militate against a purely formal or intertextual approach to their "internal evolution" as a genre. These characteristics, which are typical of Frankenstein films *as* a quasigeneric formation, are anchored in the films' previously discussed realization *à la*

---

13 As Steven Forry details in his *Hideous Progenies*, "the years between 1823 [when Richard Brinsley Peake's theatrical adaptation *Presumption* appeared] and 1832 were years of proliferation during which the Frankenstein myth was transformed for popular consumption. From the passage of the first Reform Bill to the turn of the century, however, the myth spread among the populace, taking on new media, the most important of which was the political cartoon" (43). See Forry for an overview of pre- and non-filmic incarnations, especially the many theatrical productions, for which Forry reprints selected scripts.

14 See, for example, Neale's article "Questions of Genre," where he links historical change within a genre to a variety of factors, from changes in filmic technologies and social patterns of moviegoing to the relations between film and non-filmic entertainments and media such as vaudeville, comics, and popular literature and music.

lettre of the generic plot structure—in which the conflict, once established, is literally *animated* before the crisis intensifies and eventually finds resolution in the communal purging of the monster. In connection with this literalness, Frankenstein films' central thematic questionings of human-technological relations are consistently related, as we shall see in more detail later, to a formal or *medial* questioning of film-viewer relations—a self-reflexive questioning enacted by way of a competition staged between two filmic modes: between film as a transparent medium for the representation of characters, events, and dramatic conflicts on the one hand, and film as an opaque spectacle in its own right, a matter of special effects and the presentation of images *as* images on the other. Playing, that is, on the self-reflexive relation between the diegetic monster's animation through technical means and a view of film as itself a technology of animation, films such as Whale's foreground the mediality of film and set it in conflict with the mediated narrative.[15] This establishes a conflict for the spectator between the appeals of narrative integration and an alternative appeal, a pleasure in the spectacle and the technology of film as itself something wondrous, hearkening back to the "operational aesthetic" of so-called primitive film.[16] Caught between these poles, the viewer is implicated in the probing of a dynamic, phenomenally unstable realm not unlike that which characterized the historical transition, in the 1910s, from early to classical film.[17] Far from charting an evolutionary course from transparency to opacity, then, Frankenstein films possess a motivation, at once thematic and medial, for "baroque" formal opacity and self-reflexivity right from the start.

---

15 The self-reflexive relation between film-as-animating-technology and Frankenstein films as films-about-technological-animation provides the jumping off point, in Chapter 2, for a historicizing approach to the phenomenological structure of cinematic spectatorship in general and in the specific case of Frankenstein films.

16 The term "operational aesthetic" was coined by Neil Harris and taken up by Tom Gunning to explain the non-narrative, techno-centric appeals characteristic of early film. See, for example, Gunning's "Crazy Machines in the Garden of Forking Paths: Mischief Gags and the Origins of American Film Comedy." I return to early cinema and its phenomenological relevance for Frankenstein films in Chapter 2.

17 I set up the argument for this claim in Chapter 2. A full exploration of the thesis follows in Chapter 3.

Metaphysics:
Film and the Anthropotechnical Interface

Frankenstein films thus involve a probing of the filmic medium itself. But in what does the medium consist? While I am not concerned to formulate a definition per se, we can identify, as a start, the following least common technical denominator: film consists in a series of photographic images shown in rapid succession. Film's realization therefore requires an apparatus for capturing these images (the camera), a material base for storing them (film stock), and a means of reproducing them (a projector and a screen), not to mention a venue for viewing films and the humans who operate the machinery and view the films.[18] Frankenstein films, I contend, challenge us to probe our own relations to this technical infrastructure of film. And when we accept the challenge, as I intend to demonstrate in this book, what we discover is a historically variable material interface that challenges the primacy of human thought over technology: an embodied interface that subsists below the threshold of subjectivity. But if it eludes the advances of conceptual thought, then the task of grasping the anthropotechnical interface for the conceptual purposes of definition is difficult to say the least. Our initial approach, it would seem, has to be a negative one. Part One of this project can largely be understood as mounting such a negative approach, one which locates the anthropotechnical interface symptomatically, by means of the experiential gaps and lacunae that Frankenstein films confront us with. In Part Two, these gaps will serve as the basis for a more positive characterization in terms of my theory of the postnatural historicity of the interface.

Before that, however, I would like to offer a preliminary and orientational exploration of the anthropotechnical interface, by means of which my overall argu-

---

18 Clearly, I am focusing on a certain historical configuration of technical apparatuses here; I am ignoring alternatives such as the camera-less (or camera-virtualizing) digital production of images, the storage of images on video or in digital formats, and the reproduction of images by means of DVD player/TV or computer/monitor combos, for example, or the pre-cinematic kinetoscopes and similar peep-hole apparatuses that allowed only a single person at time to view recorded images. Besides these major variations, there are also many more significant shifts within the basic apparatus I describe, for example the shift from nitrate stock to acetate and then polyester film, or even more apparent changes such as the advent of sound, color, widescreen, 3D, and so on. My point here is not to downplay historical variation by excluding these alternatives and changes, but merely to highlight the existence of a material infrastructure. Historical changes in the constitution of this infrastructure will indeed be central to my argument, which will correlate such changes with (but not equate them with) the postnatural history of the anthropotechnical interface.

ment can be better understood. I shall begin this exploration in what might at first seem an unlikely and perhaps even unnecessarily indirect manner, by addressing the question: "Can film be art?" While it may seem gratuitous at present, this oblique strategy is necessitated by the resistance to conceptual capture of the anthropotechnical interface, to which the historical question of film's artistic status is related by the series of attempts, on the part of film theory, to navigate a course between cheap entertainment and high culture, ostentatious technological show and refined aesthetic expression. This negotiational process of redefinition, which was most pronounced in the transitional era of the 1910s and involved such pioneers of film aesthetics as Vachel Lindsay and Hugo Münsterberg, necessarily implicated the medium in efforts to isolate and elevate it by containing film in aesthetic and cultural categories of discursive thought, making it a medium *qua* channel for the communication of artists' inspired ideas, and thus capable of addressing essentially human, transhistorically stable faculties and subjectivities. Endowed with this timeless, transcendent communicative ability, film would thus be purified of the material taint of its lowly origins as a spectacle in the mode of technological exhibitions. At issue here, as I have elsewhere endeavored to show, was not only the social status of the cinema but also the corporeal impact of film's technical materiality, which transformatively displaced human thought by revising the embodied basis of sensorimotor contact with the world.[19] In Lindsay's struggles to tame what he calls "the non-humanness of the undisciplined photograph" (*Art of the Moving Picture* 193) and "the uncanny scientific quality of the camera's work" (194), and in Münsterberg's attempts to configure film as a vehicle of genius, which is freed from all causal constraint and "overcomes reality" (*The Photoplay* 144) in order to achieve "a new form of true beauty in the turmoil of a technical age" (233), we recognize transitional-era film aesthetics as motivated by the goal of buffering or warding off the impact of technology by subsuming film under a model of art as timeless, disinterested, and amenable to faculties of a static human essence.

As I have already intimated, the transitional-era context in which Lindsay and Münsterberg undertook their film-aesthetic projects is of central importance to my attempt to locate Frankenstein films' experiential challenges; and as shall become increasingly clear in the course of my arguments in the coming chapters, the transitional-era conflicts these early theorists record are central not only to my film-historical outlook but to a broader metaphysical theory of transitionality per se, which stands at the heart of the anthropotechnical interface's postnatural historicity. Perhaps the clearest view, however, of what Lindsay and Münsterberg were up against can be provided from a different vantage, far removed from the transitional

---

19 See my article "Between Technology and Art: Functions of Film in Transitional-Era Cinema" for a fuller treatment of what follows.

era of the 1910s. In his 1981 article "Photography and Representation," philosopher Roger Scruton takes up the question, by then no longer fashionable, of whether film can be art; his argument, which poses a fundamental challenge to film aesthetics, can be summarized as follows. Film is essentially dependent on photography as the source of its images. And while photography appears to share the property of *representation* that characterizes (non-abstract) painting's relation to its objects, there is a significant difference between the two that distinguishes painting, and *not* photography, as a representational art. Representation in art, according to Scruton, is a matter of the communication of an artist's thoughts about a subject by means of a mediated depiction of that subject. Accordingly, representational painting embodies in visual form an intentional relation between the painter and the depicted subject-matter. To appreciate the painting, the spectator must be able, on the basis of visible traces alone, to decipher the meaning of the artist's intention—which is equivalent to understanding what the picture represents and at the same time comprehending the artist's expressed thought about it—whereby the communicative act is consummated. An aesthetic interest in the painting is an interest in the representation as such and for its own sake—not an interest in the object represented but in the thoughts that the representation communicates and essentially *is*.

By contrast, the photographic image stands in a purely *causal* rather than intentional relation to the object it depicts. Based on the causal mechanism of the camera, the image is transparent to the world in such a way that bypasses the intention of the photographer, who is unable to completely control the details of the image and embody in it the expression of a representational thought. The photographer can attempt to assert his or her control over details by carefully staging the scene before taking the picture; but, Scruton reasons, if the scene is representational in the relevant sense, the photograph itself will be irrelevant to the representation—merely existing as a reminder of a dramatic scene. Or one might intervene in the developing or printing process, but the resulting image, if representational and not abstract, will then embody the artist's thoughts more in the mode of painting than as a photograph. According to Scruton, then, the interest we take in a photograph can be either non-aesthetic (as when we view press photos in search of information), aesthetic but abstract (and thus not representational), or representational but not essentially photographic (because the representation involved is logically—and usually temporally—prior or subsequent to the mechanically causal process of photography). As a concatenation of photographs, film will similarly fall into one of these categories. If a film manages to be art, and if this art is representational, the film itself will be inessential to the representation involved. *Q.E.D.*: films will either not be artworks, or their artistic status will be dependent on another art form, most likely a pro-filmic drama for which the film itself serves as a mere conduit.

The argument goes straight to the heart of the Lindsay-Münsterberg project of establishing film as an independent art not reducible, in the parlance of their day, to "canned drama." Both Lindsay and Münsterberg conceive the narrative film or "photoplay" as an author-centered, expressive medium, and each of them accepts Scruton's premise that pictorial representation requires perfect coextension with the artist's intention for communication to take place. That is, the representational artwork must embody completely, and without remainder, the thought it expresses. For example, due to his notion of "harmony, in which every part is the complete fulfillment of that which the other parts demand, when nothing is suggested which is not fulfilled in the midst of the same experience" (153), Münsterberg is committed to precisely this isomorphism of intention, expressive embodiment, and spectatorial experience—and thus also to an ideal of complete artistic control. Furthermore, Münsterberg explicitly extends this ideal from the film as a whole to its atomic parts as well: "Every single picture of the sixteen thousand which are shown to us in one reel ought to be treated with this respect of the pictorial artist for the unity of the forms" (190). Each frame, in short, should be a work of representational art.

But according to Scruton, "[t]he causal process of which the photographer is a victim puts almost every detail outside of his control" (593). Thus:

The history of the art of photography is the history of successive attempts to break the causal chain by which the photographer is imprisoned, to impose a human intention between subject and appearance so that the subject can be both defined by that intention and seen in terms of it. It is the history of an attempt to turn a mere simulacrum into the expression of a representational thought [...]. (594)

Here we have Lindsay's "struggle against the non-humanness of the undisciplined photograph." And Münsterberg is engaged in a similar battle, emphasizing that "[t]o imitate the world is a mechanical process" (144) that has little to do with art. Artistic representation, for Münsterberg, takes reality as its starting point, "[b]ut it becomes art just in so far as it overcomes reality, stops imitating and leaves the imitated reality behind it" (144). What could be a more "mechanical process," though, than photographic "imitation"? The photographic image cannot simply and definitively "leave the imitated reality behind it" because, as the result of sheer causality, the photograph captures "the real things which are enchained by the causes and effects of nature," freedom from which Münsterberg stipulates as a necessary condition of artistic beauty (151).

It would seem, then, that transitional-era film aesthetics was doomed from the start to failure. Today, however, this conclusion is likely to be greeted with complacency, and the entire discussion itself is likely to strike us as quaint and outdated. It seems we are simply not worried any longer about whether film can be art, a question that we tend to affirm but without attaching much importance to the answer. The reason, of course, is that substantive notions of art like the one held by Scruton, Lindsay, and Münsterberg have largely fallen out of fashion. For one thing, the requirement of total artistic control seems hopelessly unrealistic, damning not only of photography but also of representational painting: does not the painter's embodiment as an organism, subject to physiological and chemical processes not completely within his or her control, imply that it will never be possible for a flesh-and-blood human to achieve the painterly mastery that Scruton demands of true, unadulterated expressions of artistic vision and thought? Besides, from our vantage point today, after postmodernism and in the wake of cultural studies, Scruton's ideas are likely to strike us not only as unrealistic abstractions but also as politically dubious notions that encode an elitist resistance to popular culture. Scruton writes: "Art is essentially serious; it cannot rest content with the gratification of mere fantasy, nor can it dwell on what fascinates us while avoiding altogether the question of its meaning" (602). But a commercialized entertainment industry, against which Lindsay defines his ideal filmic art, is ignorant of these deeper significances, is content in its pursuit of profit to cater to the superficial desires of the masses. The latter are desperately in need of reform, and art, in the form of the artistic photoplay, will save them from their fallen state. Münsterberg writes in this vein: "The people still has to learn the great difference between true enjoyment and fleeting pleasure, between real beauty and the mere tickling of the senses" (230). Thus, very much in accordance with Scruton's open conservatism, the film-aesthetic theories of Lindsay and Münsterberg were complicit in the transitional era's larger efforts to police the cinema as a public sphere, to gentrify it and free it from its unseemly history as a fairground attraction.[20]

So why not simply reject the stipulated notion of representational art and move on? Why dwell on these discussions of film as art? And why on earth should we bring them to bear on Frankenstein films, of all things, which themselves are largely indifferent, or so it would seem, to the question of film's artistic status? The answer, in short, is that what is ultimately at stake in these arguments over the artistic potential of film is precisely the impact of filmic technology that is also at stake in Frankenstein films. That is, by demonstrating that film cannot live up to the definition of representational art that he shares with Lindsay and Münsterberg, Scruton is in fact pointing out something crucial about the nature of the filmic apparatus's contact with human beings. The photographic causality that causes the

---

20 Miriam Hansen's *Babel and Babylon*, which will be central to my arguments in Part One, is especially illuminating with regard to the competition of interests at work in transitional-era cinema.

filmic image to elude the artist's control suggests that film is *opaque to thought* precisely because it is *transparent to the material world*.[21] And apart from the problem of authorial control, this indicates that film at least in part bypasses representational thought, thereby establishing a channel for non-cognitive impacts on its spectators. In other words, cinema, like other technologies, has a direct impact on human *bodies* and the *material lifeworlds* that ground psychic subjectivities and social formations. The impact is *direct* in the sense that it bypasses conscious, discursive perception and affects human beings at the level of pre-reflective experience; technology, that is, makes up a part of the phenomenally unthematized "flesh" of the world. Herein lies the anthropotechnical interface, which is basic to the constitution of the people we take ourselves to be.

In the case of cinema, on my view, film's technical materiality therefore haunts the soul itself, unmasks its alleged timelessness and sets it in historical relation to the shocks, velocities, and technologies of modernization. This is not just a matter of film's content, of the prevalence of technologies in the subject-matter of popular films. Instead, it is a question of an entirely new type of vision, one that is only possible with cinema's enabling technical infrastructure. The camera does not just extend the vision of filmmakers and spectators; it significantly reduces *and* augments direct experience. Like painting, it channels experience into a framed visual form, but it also enables new visions that are impossible to the unaided eye. Substitution techniques, slow and reverse motion, for example, are not seen directly by the cinematographer but made possible only when the camera's photographic record is processed and projected properly. In this way, the projector offers the specta-

---

21 To say that the camera captures the objects of reality so that we really see *them* in mediated form—and not (just) *representations* of them—is emphatically not equivalent to the claim that the image is identical with its object. However, in discussions of photographic and cinematic realism there has been considerable slippage between the two positions. André Bazin, for example, claims in "The Ontology of the Photographic Image" that "[t]he photographic image is the object itself" (14), a claim of identity that he relates to the causal claim that "an image of the world is formed automatically, without the creative intervention of man" (13), so that the relation between it and the object is similar to "a fingerprint" (15). Arguably, Christian Metz also equivocates between the two views: "The cinema is the 'phenomenological' art *par excellence*, the signifier is coextensive with the whole of the significate, the spectacle its own signification, thus short-circuiting the sign itself" (*Film Language* 43). Kendall L. Walton, in "Transparent Pictures," makes a strong case for the transparency of photographs—"the viewer of a photograph sees, literally, the scene that was photographed" (252)—while clearly distinguishing his position from the identity thesis. Furthermore, he argues that this transparency is not equivalent to, and is irreducible to, an alleged "illusion" of seeing reality.

tor a visible spectacle that is radically incommensurate with the structure of a pre-technical or pre-modern mind. The introduction of film therefore marks a radical change in humans' relations to the world, but the scope of this change eclipses thought and points to the presence of a sub-personal, material interface; accordingly, the anthropotechnical interface subtends human agency as the site of its historical transformation. More than the social status of the cinema, I suggest, it was this transformation that transitional-era film aesthetics took aim at: with their theories of a timeless, universal art of the photoplay, Lindsay and Münsterberg tried to shore up the deterritorializing force of anthropotechnical transitionality itself.

As I have pointed out, Frankenstein films tend to foreground their own mediality, making it formally "opaque" in the manner that Schatz associates with the so-called baroque stage of generic evolution, and in this way they challenge us to reassess our relations with technology and its material opacity with regard to thought. Scruton's argument about photographic causality, while ostensibly designed to show why cinema can never be art, ironically helps us to rethink the means by which Frankenstein films pose their challenges. Near the end of his article, Scruton writes: "the cinema [...] provides us with a ready means of realizing situations which fascinate us. It can address itself to our fantasy directly without depending upon any intermediate process of thought" (602-03). Probably this is meant to suggest that, in contrast to "serious" art, popular productions like Frankenstein films are just superficial fluff; but, as we have seen, it can also be taken to highlight film's direct address of the body. This immediacy or directness, Scruton continues,

is surely what distinguishes the scenes of violence which are so popular in the cinema from the conventionalized death throes of the theatre. And surely it is this too which makes photography incapable of being an erotic art, in that it presents us with the object of lust rather than a symbol of it: it therefore gratifies the fantasy of desire long before it has succeeded in understanding or expressing the fact of it. The medium of photography, one might say, is inherently pornographic. (603)

Now rather than trying to refute this claim, my suggestion is that we take Scruton's hyperbole seriously, that we accord to film a basically pornographic ontology which is grounded in its ability to move our bodies directly, "long before it has succeeded in understanding or expressing the fact of it." At their most effective moments, Frankenstein films manage to turn this ability of film—and therefore the anthropotechnical interface that materially connects us with filmic technology—into the very object of our longing. In a sense more fundamental than arousing sexual desire, Frankenstein films are pornographic by virtue of gratifying us directly, "present[ing] us with the object of lust rather than a symbol of it," and thus submitting our bodies to material transformation without the mediation of representational thought. Linda Williams, discussing pornography in the narrower sense, calls it, along with horror and melodrama, a "body genre."[22] Though perhaps lacking the coherence of a determinate genre, Frankenstein films must be seen as a preeminent formation of the body-genre type. Whether they arouse us, terrify us, or move us to tears, the power of Frankenstein films derives from a sort of archepornographic interest in the filmic medium's power to transform us; at their best, the films cultivate this interest and focus it on the anthropotechnical interface itself, allowing us to savor our own vulnerability to chance and our lack of conscious control over the postnatural course of our becoming.

A Preview of Coming Attractions

As I indicated earlier, the body of this work is divided into three main parts, the task of Part One being to *locate* the experiential challenges posed by Frankenstein films. Towards this end, Chapter 2 develops a historically indexed "techno-phenomenology" of the dominant film-viewer relations under the paradigms of early and classical film; I then apply this perspective to the analysis of two Frankenstein films from the respective film-historical periods, each of which is shown to instantiate a vacillating destabilization of spectatorial relations, pointing to a volatile intermediate realm between the phenomenological regimes of early and classical cinema. In Chapter 3, I follow this cue to the transitional era of the 1910s, and specifically to the first known Frankenstein film proper: the Edison Studios' 1910 production *Frankenstein*. As I argue in that chapter, the dualities of address exemplified in this film point to a broader experience of *transitionality* which, on the move between more determinately stabilized situations, presents itself negatively to phenomenological subjectivity—as an indeterminate gap.

It is in these gaps of transitionality that I locate Frankenstein films' characteristic challenge, and in Part Two I take up that challenge by formulating a theoretical framework, that of postnaturalism, that would be able to *answer* the films' provocations. Chapter 4 first circles around the gaps that feminist readers have located in the text of Mary Shelley's Gothic novel before diving into them to discover a theory of a pre-personal and therefore non-discursive contact between human embodiment and technological materiality. On the basis of this contact, as I argue, technological revolutions (such as the industrial revolution in the wake of which Shelley

---

22 See Williams's "Film Bodies: Gender, Genre, and Excess." The epilogue to the second edition of Williams's *Hard Core* (280-315) is also highly relevant to the present discussion.

composed her novel) are capable of radically destabilizing human agency, causing us to draw experiential blanks and to produce textual gaps—which, however, are quickly filled in and forgotten in the process of novel technologies' habituation and naturalization. In the techno-scientific interlude of Chapter 5, I trace these processes in the context of the industrial steam engine's recuperation by thermodynamic science in order to uncover the postnatural historicity of natural science's nature itself—i.e. the fact, not reducible to an epistemic phenomenon of discursive construction and projection on the part of human subjects, that material nature itself is constantly in motion, in transition, and that—due to the role of technologies in this history—nature has thus never been "natural." Chapter 6 translates these findings into a specifically postnatural media theory, which pertains not only to empirically determinate apparatuses but to the very historicity of the phenomenological realm as it is co-articulated between human and nonhuman agencies; as a film-theoretical correlate of this theory, I put forward what I call a "cinematic double vision," which alternates between a Merleau-Ponty inspired phenomenological perspective and a Bergsonian metaphysics to reveal film experience as animated by the interchange between human situations and technological displacements.

Part Three then returns to Frankenstein films to demonstrate the films' special relations to the postnatural historicity of the anthropotechnical interface and, in effect, to execute a *rapprochement* between the conflicting human and nonhuman agencies inhabiting these films. In order to do so, Chapter 7 turns to the paradigmatic filmic progenies, James Whale's *Frankenstein* and *Bride of Frankenstein*, and, on the theoretical basis of postnaturalism, alternately illuminates the human and nonhuman perspectives that come together to animate the films' central creature. In this confrontation—the staging of which is inextricable from the films' historical moment and specifically from their relations to the then-recent transition to sound cinema—I seek a non-reductive means of apprehending the alterior agency that occupies the gaps in subjective experience provoked by Frankenstein films. Chapter 8, by way of conclusion, briefly pursues this line beyond the paradigm case, taking a more synoptic view of the continuing proliferation of the Frankenstein film; here I seek to illuminate the active role played by cinematic technologies in eliciting a fleeting experience of transitionality, which lies submerged beneath the weight of our habituated or "natural" relations to those technologies. The rapprochement of which I spoke consists, then, of a recognition of the mutual articulation of experience by human and nonhuman technical agencies, whereby the affective and embodied experience of anthropotechnical transitionality is not arrested and subjugated to human dominance, but approached experimentally as a joint production of our postnatural future. This is the ultimate challenge posed for us by Frankenstein films.

Part One

2. Frankenstein's Filmic Progenies: A Techno-Phenomenological Approach

> I am kino-eye, I create a man more perfect than Adam. I create thousands of different people in accordance with preliminary blueprints and diagrams of different kinds.
> I am kino-eye.
> From one person I take the hands, the strongest and most dexterous; from another I take the legs, the swiftest and most shapely; from a third, the most beautiful and expressive head—and through montage I create a new, perfect man.
> DZIGA VERTOV

When Mary Shelley "bid [her] hideous progeny go forth and prosper" (10) in the 1831 Introduction to the revised edition of *Frankenstein*, she suggested certain parallels between herself and the eponymous protagonist of her story. Just as Frankenstein had given life to a creature that refused to bow to his purposes, Shelley's authorial control was challenged as her text began taking on a life of its own.[1] And yet, at that early date, she could scarcely have imagined how successful her

---

1 It is thus not insignificant that the 1831 Introduction, in which Shelley spells out a moral message that was far less apparent in the novel's original version, follows a series of theatrical adaptations that transformed Shelley's tale into a sensational and melodramatic story. The first adaptation, which wears its moral in its title and which Shelley herself saw performed, was Richard Brinsley Peake's 1823 production, *Presumption; or the Fate of Frankenstein*. An electronic edition of the play, edited by Stephen C. Behrendt, is now available online. It is also included in Steven Earl Forry's *Hideous Progenies*, which provides a detailed study of the theatrical history of *Frankenstein*. See also Elizabeth Nitchie, "The Stage History of *Frankenstein*" and Albert J. Lavalley, "The Stage and Film Children of *Frankenstein*: A Survey."

"monster" (that is, both her tale and its monster) would be in gaining autonomy and reproducing itself. From cereal boxes to bioethics, Frankensteinian images and references positively permeate Western (popular) culture today, and, as we have seen, its reproductive success in the cinema has been astounding in both breadth and diversity. It has been estimated that over 200 film versions of *Frankenstein* have been produced, spanning from Thomas Edison's 1910 silent film to 2014's digitally enhanced *I, Frankenstein* and beyond.[2] Fulfilling Shelley's (perhaps half fearful) wish for her "hideous progeny," Frankenstein films continually rewrite Shelley's narrative and tirelessly reanimate its creature. Beyond this, however, film "adaptations" of *Frankenstein* strain and expand the already double reference of her dictum. Frankenstein's *filmic* progenies, that is, are not limited to the multiplications of story and creature that Frankenstein films obviously are; for in the process of recreating and transferring the tale to a new medium, the content does not remain untouched. On the contrary, the medium of film and the monstrosities of Shelley's text inform and transform one another in quite unpredictable ways. Not only are narrative events, settings, and even ideologies changed by the many directors and others involved in the filmic appropriation of *Frankenstein*; also the medium of film itself and the notion of the spectator, as I shall endeavor here to show, are explored and challenged on a number of levels in the process. Thus, the question of *Frankenstein*'s filmic descendants becomes a great deal messier than could be accommodated by a simple enumeration of the many film versions or a comparative ideological analysis of them. Concomitantly, though, a comparative analysis of Frankenstein films can be quite revealing with regard to the historically variable status of film as a mediating technology and the types of subjectivities that interact with it.

FILM AS FRANKENSTEINIAN TECHNOLOGY?

We can begin to approach the issues I am raising by noting that film itself, on a very formal and abstract level, bears a certain comparison with Frankensteinian technology. V.I. Pudovkin quite poignantly suggests the basis for the comparison: "Editing is the basic creative force, by power of which the soulless photographs (the separate shots) are engineered into living, cinematographic form" (xv). Like Frankenstein selecting parts from corpses and infusing life into a composite body,

---

2   See Forry 127. The estimate, however, is problematic, for it begs a question of definition. What is included? What gets excluded? The same problem plagues compendia such as Donald Glut's *Frankenstein Catalog* or the more recent *Frankenstein Film Sourcebook* edited by Picart, Smoot, and Blodgett.

directors and editors utilize the technical means of film to (re)animate the "dead" (photographically preserved) traces of living organisms (actors) into new narrative components and wholes (e.g. characters and the film-as-narrative in which they live).[3] However, this invitingly simple analogy is far too abstract to be of much use in a historically sensitive analysis of the filmic medium. It works toward establishing a timeless ontology for film and thereby overlooks historically specific transformations in terms of style, technologies, and the contexts of film's presentation and consumption. Ultimately, the comparison may be best suited to the classical Hollywood style, wherein editing techniques became central to situating the spectator with regard to the narrative world of diegesis. Early film, with its "primitive" narratives, less sophisticated editing, and eclectic pleasures and modes of address, is less well accounted for. Recognizing the analogy's shortcomings suggests the need to situate an analysis of film as a mediating technology within a phenomenology of film experience that is sensitive to the historical paradigm shift from early or "primitive" to classical modes of film production and reception.

The analogy, limp as it may, is not however completely irrelevant to my purpose. The point is not that *all* (or even most) films, due to their technical means of "animation," are somehow "Frankenstein films." On the contrary, the analogy suggests the potential for a motion picture to be a "Frankenstein film" in two distinct but interrelated senses: that is, the narrative adaptation of Shelley's tale, which grounds the notion of the Frankenstein film in its common acceptation, lends itself simultaneously to formal and thematic reflection on the filmic technologies that allow for the trans-medial appropriation in the first place. This is not to accord a privileged position to these films, but merely to point out, initially, that such adap-

---

3 Indeed, I am not the first to note this formal analogy. For example, James A.W. Heffernan writes that "film versions of *Frankenstein* implicitly remind us that filmmaking itself is a Frankensteinian exercise in artificial reproduction" (139). And in his discussion of film adaptations of *Frankenstein*, William Nestrick writes: "The film is the animation of the machine, a continuous life created by the persistence of vision in combination with a machine casting light through individual photographs flashed separately upon the screen. Since 'life' in film is movement, the word that bridges the worlds of film and man is 'animation'—the basic principle by which motion is imparted to the picture" (294-95). Identifying this "point where film art and scientific creation are able to mutually comment on each other," Bouriana Zakharieva adds "montage as the cinematic principle proper of creating a screen character," a principle that also "accounts for the originality of Mary Shelley's monster" (417-18). The focus on montage brings Zakharieva's comments into close connection with the epigraph of this chapter, provided by Dziga Vertov, a contemporary and compatriot of Pudovkin's. The epigraph is taken from Vertov's "Kinoks: A Revolution" (102).

tations—even in a narrow sense of adaptation—may be "about" more than just the stories they tell.

Of course, Mary Shelley's novel is also about more than just the creation of a monster by technical means, but exactly what it is about is a matter of ongoing controversy. To name just a few of the many approaches that have been taken, the novel has been read as everything from an "introduction" to Romantic themes,[4] to a critique of the male model of Romantic literary creation, to an allegorical tale of the marginalization of women by science.[5] This is not the place to decide on the strengths and weaknesses of the various readings. But at least two strains of interpretation seem particularly relevant here. First, the novel may be seen as crucially concerned with the rise of industrial technologies and their "monstrous" potential to elude human control.[6] It thus articulates and probes large questions concerning the hopes and fears we have with regard to technological innovation, and this fact helps explain our continued cultural preoccupations with *Frankenstein* well into the postindustrial age—witness, for example, the central position accorded the tale and its monster in popular discussions of biotechnology. Second, Shelley's text has also been seen to engage in a self-reflexive interrogation of its own medium.[7] Acts of writing (and reading) structure the unfolding of the novel's plot from start to finish: from the frame story recorded in Walton's letters to his sister to the creature's self-education through a small canon of books and his discovery of Frankenstein's journal. By burying the monster's own (spoken) tale of how he came to self-awareness (and the priority of written texts in this process) at the center of a thoroughly textual structure, Shelley effectively undermines the traditional phonocentric subordination of writing to spoken language as a deviant, because mediated, aberration from nature and self-presence. Concomitantly, the novel problematizes the Rousseauian notion of the natural, organic self by highlighting the inherent mediation of subjectivity.

The distinctive potential of filmic appropriations of *Frankenstein* lies, I suggest, in their ability to combine these two lines of reflection—concerning human-technological relations and concerning media and mediation—and to update Shelley's self-reflexivity into a critical treatment of the filmic medium. Shelley's narra-

---

4   This is the gist of Harold Bloom's afterword to the Signet edition of the novel.

5   I return to the feminist reception of the novel in Chapter 4.

6   This theme has of course been discussed by numerous critics and to various ends. When I return to the novel in Chapter 4, I will concern myself most directly with Mark Hansen's reading, as put forth in his article "'Not thus, after all, would life be given': *Technesis*, Technology, and the Parody of Romantic Poetics in *Frankenstein*."

7   This is a common theme in poststructuralist feminist readings, which I consider in detail in Chapter 4.

tive, therefore, provides filmmakers with a ready means to channel the questions it raises about the fascinations and dangers of technology, originally formulated against the background of the industrial revolution, into a self-reflexive probing of filmic mediality and the phenomenal experience of cinematic spectatorship. It is worth emphasizing, though, that the fact that a film appropriates Shelley's narrative is neither a sufficient nor a necessary condition for its providing valuable insights into the medium. The narrative content contains no guarantee of success, and thus the view of Frankenstein films I am here developing has no problems countenancing the existence of poorly made monster movies without any deeper significance. On the other hand, the establishment of a self-reflexive connection between medial form and narrative content is far from being the exclusive dominion of Frankenstein films. But for those films that pursue this line of (self)reflection, that appropriate Shelley's narrative and set it to work on the medial basis of that appropriation, Marshall McLuhan's famous dictum—"the medium is the message"—is capable of assuming a meaning more specific and perhaps even more enlightening than that implied by McLuhan himself, and it is well worth investigating the cultural and historical circumstances that make this possible.

The type of investigation I propose undertaking is what might be called a "techno-phenomenological" one. Its starting points, in the present context, are the resonances between a preeminent tale of technological fascination, seduction, and danger on the one hand, and the technological medium by and through which the tale is told on the other. But not content with abstract analogies or formalistic self-reflexivity for its own sake, this analysis is interested above all in the phenomenal conditions of a particular form of human-technological interaction (that of film spectatorship) and what the aforementioned resonances can do to illuminate or transform them. Human-technological relations come in various stripes, and film spectatorship is no exception: different genres, for example, make different demands on viewers and establish implicit rules or models of spectatorship which they deem appropriate. Moreover, spectatorship is a normative construct and a set of practices with a history tied to variations in predominant entertainment forms and settings and to inflections provided by their broader cultural contexts. A techno-phenomenological analysis cannot, therefore, assume a timeless model of filmic reception or posit a transcendental (viewing) subject. It thus needs a set of conceptual tools that highlight variation and allow for the appropriate contextualization.

Tools of the Trade

For this purpose I turn to philosopher of technology Don Ihde's phenomenological analysis of human-technology relations, of which he identifies several major types:

embodiment relations, hermeneutic relations, and background relations.[8] Instances of human-technology interaction are classed into one of these categories according to where the technological artifact in question enters into the basic noetic relation between subject and object (symbolized thus: I → world). Embodiment relations obtain in situations where a technological artifact or system functions as an extension of the human body and the senses grounded therein, as prosthetic extensions of human activity or perception. Here the subject and the mediating technology are grouped together on the left-hand side of the noetic arrow, with the object of the relation on the right: I – tech → world. The technological mediator is relatively transparent with relation to human intentionality. Examples of such relations include Heidegger's famous hammer—where the tool withdraws from the field of objects and goes more or less unnoticed in the execution of the human aim towards which it is employed[9]—or Merleau-Ponty's blind-man's cane—by and indeed *through* which the user probes the ground and makes his or her way through the world, thus extending tactile perception and enabling unhindered ambulation.[10] As prostheses, such technologies are incorporated *into* human embodiment; they do not stand out phenomenally as something distinct from the body and its subjective intentionality—not, that is, so long as they are actively being employed and they are functioning properly.

The second type of human-technological relation, which Ihde calls a "hermeneutic" relation, obtains in cases where there is a relative opacity of the mediating technology with regard to the world of noetic intentionality. The technology, that is, itself becomes phenomenally visible as an object of perception, though it remains a mediating conduit for the further perception of, or action upon, an intended world beyond it. The mediating technology is thus relegated to the right-hand side of the noetic arrow: I → tech – world. Whereas a conventional telescope is embodied by the user, prosthetically and more or less invisibly extending his or her perception of the phenomenal object, a radio telescope itself becomes an object of perception, though not the final one of intentional concern. The user is engaged in a more active and more apparent act of "interpretation"; the audial or visual output of the telescope must be interrogated for its meaning, and thus phenomenally isolated

---

8   See Ihde's *Technics and Praxis* and especially his *Technology and the Lifeworld* for a thorough exploration of these concepts. In addition to the relations discussed here, Ihde describes a fourth category: "alterity relations," which, though I do not consider them here, will make an appearance in Chapter 5.
9   See the famous tool analysis in Division One, Chapter III, "The Worldhood of the World," in Heidegger's *Being and Time*.
10 See Merleau-Ponty's *Phenomenology of Perception* (165-166).

from the interrogating subject, if it is to reveal something about the unseen heavens—the real object of concern.

Finally, in background relations the technological artifact or system more or less recedes from view in the phenomenal relation of subject to object by contributing to the establishment of the very framework for perception or action. Electric lighting and heating systems, for example, are not typically perceived as objects of our concern (unless, of course, they malfunction or our profession requires that we so perceive them); however, they invisibly help to structure the active and perceptual relations we have with the world. Falling on neither side of the noetic arrow, such technologies may be seen to enable the arrow of intentionality itself, for example by providing light for the perception of objects at night and the necessary warmth in the winter for a variety of active dealings with these objects. Such technologies thus tend to produce "cocoons" within which our relations to the phenomenal world take place; this may take the form of a small-scale niche, or background technologies may link up in an encompassing techno-sphere or techno-ecology underlying and enabling human action and perception.

All of these relations are relevant to an analysis of film as a mediating technology,[11] but a few words of caution are in order before they can be properly applied. First, the distinctions between embodied, hermeneutic, and background relations are neither static nor discrete. There is a range of possibilities with regard to where exactly in the phenomenal subject-object relation a mediating technology may announce or fail to announce itself. Embodiment relations involve a *relative* invisibility or transparency of the technology, hermeneutic relations a *relative* opacity—and some technologies, in some phenomenal situations, may be more transparent or opaque than others at other times. Moreover, the various relations are not instantiated solely by the technologies themselves but result from their placement in the intentional interrelations of subject and phenomenal world. Thus, there can be no technology-specific determination beforehand with regard to what relation a given technology will engender. A telescope can be embodied as an extension of our

---

11 Vivian Sobchack, in her important book *The Address of the Eye*, has applied Ihde's concepts in an intricate analysis of filmic human-technology relations. My own application of Ihde's concepts may seem simplistic in comparison, but there is an important reason for my departure from Sobchack's analysis, consideration of which I defer until Chapter 6: namely, as I argue there, Sobchack's application leads to a relatively ahistorical, formalistic view of human-film interactions that privileges classical Hollywood as the telos of cinematic and cinema-technological development. By way of contrast, my application of Ihde's concepts highlights historical change—paradigm shifts that correspond to a change in dominant human-film relations—leading to a non-teleological view of film-technological development and messier formal relations as well.

perceptual abilities, or it can become an object of perception itself—either due to breakage, when we marvel at the craftsmanship that produced it, or when we put it in a museum as a historical artifact. This does not mean, however, that technologies are neutral with regard to our relations with them and the world they mediate and condition for us. Indeed, as Ihde argues, they may harbor within themselves tendencies of their own towards the production of a given type of human-technology relation.[12] Certainly, a conventional telescope *typically* lends itself to an embodiment relation—at least, that is, when it is *in use* and functional. And yet, a given technology—and film technologies are indeed among them—may be open to a range of uses, thus implying a variety of possibilities with regard to human-technological relations.[13] In the case of film, typical uses are defined in terms of historically variable normative paradigms of film style and viewership, for example, so that we should expect to discover important changes over time in the phenomenal constitution of film and its situation in the noetic relations between (viewing) subjects and their worlds.

Of the three human-technology relations outlined above, background relations are perhaps those that can be applied to an analysis of film most straightforwardly and least controversially. Focusing on them will, however, point us towards some of the more difficult aspects of a techno-phenomenological analysis of film. In any film-viewing situation, there is a rich technological infrastructure at work in enabling our perception of and involvement with the images we see on the screen. The machinery at work may be of quite diverse types: we typically think of projectors as being located behind and above our heads in the back of a movie theater, but early projectors were often located on the other side of the screen, and home cinema systems may be centered around television sets of different types and sizes or digital projectors connected to an optical disk player; if the film has a soundtrack, any number of speakers may be responsible for transforming analogue or digital impulses into a perceptible sound pattern—whether it be a mono-aural track transmitted by one or more loudspeakers, a stereo track with audial left-right differentiation,

---

12 Ihde speaks of "telic inclinations." See Ihde's *Technics and Praxis*, 42-44.

13 The dynamic nature of human-technological relations is well illustrated by the example of the automobile. When we are just learning to drive, the car, itself a means to an end (transportation), typically occupies a quasi-objective position in our phenomenal dealings with it. We have not yet learned to "embody" it; it poses interpretive problems for us: when should I release the clutch? How hard should I apply the brakes? Later, such questions typically disappear from consciousness as the car becomes a transparent extension of our bodies. Our bodies enter into a symbiotic relationship with the machinery and act without the need for thought. (We continue, however, to relate to certain instruments in the auto in a hermeneutic manner.)

or a state-of-the-art surround sound system. These material differences are by no means neutral with regard to our perception of the films we view: certain films are more likely to impress when shown on a big screen but tend to disappoint when viewed on a small-screen television; we may even miss important visual and audial information when a film is transferred to video and adjusted for differences in screen formats and audio systems. Moreover, since these differences in material infrastructure are the products of historical developments in film and video technologies, we can expect to find alongside them significant historical changes in the phenomenal reception of films. However, so long as we are engaged in watching the images on the screen and delving into the narrative worlds they depict, all such infrastructural technologies tend, *typically*, to recede into the background. Only when we focus on a historical comparison of them, or when we view a film under (by our own historically situated standards) poor projection conditions, for example, do these mechanisms tend to stand out phenomenally. Significant exceptions notwithstanding, as film spectators we tend not to notice the technologies involved in producing the sights and sounds of film, for they occupy a background relation to the objects of our intentionality—they enable our perception of these objects in the first place. In such cases, the material technologies themselves become mysteriously immaterial.

Focusing, as I have done, on the material setting and technological backdrop of film viewership highlights the physical setting of spectators seated in this or that type of auditorium, surrounded by this or that type of machinery within a structure of such and such architectural design. It thus brings to the fore our own physical embodiment as film spectators. But emphasizing the fact that the technological infrastructure tends to recede from view as we become engrossed in the film itself indicates that the physical environment, and our awareness of ourselves as concretely embodied subjects within it, can also take a phenomenal backseat in inverse relation to the "hermeneutic" activity of engagement with (especially narrative) films. This dialectic between embodiment and hermeneutics is crucial to an assessment of the phenomenological experience of film, but there are a number of pitfalls that we must be wary of here if we are to do justice to the historicity of the filmic medium on the one hand and to the integrity of Ihde's phenomenological analysis of human-technology relations on the other.

For one thing, there is a risk of terminological confusion that must be borne in mind here. "Embodiment" has become something of a buzz-word in recent years; in a variety of discourses and in a variety fields, the term has come to indicate an opposition to a wide range of rationalistic abstractions. For example, embodiment has played a central role in feminist scholarship interested in deconstructing the patriarchal construct "man."[14] In film studies, embodiment has also been a focal point for reversing trends in psychoanalytic and semiotic film theory. Here it is set against essentializing constructions of the spectator to emphasize bodily difference and the non-discursive, and often non-normative, affective involvements that concrete individuals have with films.[15] The embodiment at issue here is a flesh-and-blood, i.e. "real-world" or non-diegetic, aspect of viewers' being; an awareness or consciousness of one's own embodiment stands therefore in an *inverse relation* to the instantiation of *embodiment relations*, whereby filmic technologies are subjectively incorporated and spectators are engrossed or absorbed into the diegesis. Conversely, focusing on technologies as phenomenal objects in their own right, which is characteristic of *hermeneutic relations*, can *stand in the way* of narrative interpretation and the "normal" hermeneutic activities conducted by moviegoers. However, these correlations, which admit of exceptions but which characterize mainstream cinema as dominated by a hermeneutic mode that privileges phenomenological embodiment relations at the expense of spectators' own embodiment, is a historically contingent product of a specific normative construction of the spectator. In particular, as I shall argue shortly, the view of spectatorship that idealizes absorption into the diegetic world and thereby enables an analysis along the lines of Ihde's embodiment relation is a part of the paradigm known as classical Hollywood. Early film, on the other hand, engaged its viewers in different ways, often undercutting the spectatorial "identification" encouraged by classical film. The fascination of moving pictures for early audiences lay elsewhere than in the prospect of engrossment in a captivating story, and Ihde's hermeneutic relations were an important part of, rather than a distraction from, this cinema's particular attraction.

Ihde's concepts will help us to characterize a major shift in the history of film-viewer relations, which will in turn bring a historical dimension to bear on the phenomenology of filmic technologies or the techno-phenomenology of film. As we shall see, though, there is no clear break between early or "primitive" and classical modes of reception, and there is no bright line, phenomenally speaking, between the diegetic and non-diegetic worlds at stake. The Frankenstein films that I will analyze later in this chapter pay tribute to these facts by thematizing human-technology relations on a narrative level while simultaneously (and thereby) problematizing these relations in the real world. As we delve into these problematizations, we will find ourselves increasingly pushed towards a liminal realm, a realm of transition. The transitionalities in question, moreover, are at once the phenomenological experiences of individual viewers, but they are simultaneously indexed to

---

14 In Chapter 4, I look at several notions of embodiment as they are used, towards this end, in feminist interpretations of Shelley's *Frankenstein*.
15 One of the first and best examples is Steven Shaviro's *The Cinematic Body*.

broader historical processes of technological change. Before turning to those films, it therefore behooves us to apply the tools of techno-phenomenological analysis to the historical question of cinematic paradigms and their specific configurations of film-viewer relations.

TECHNO-PHENOMENOLOGY AND THE STRUCTURE OF CINEMATIC REVOLUTIONS

Recent work in film studies, following in the wake of Tom Gunning's pioneering work, has contributed to a reconceptualization of early film that no longer views the products of cinema's formative era as merely "primitive"—in a vaguely deprecating sense invoking a teleological development towards the classical style—but as embodying a categorically different paradigm than that articulated after, say, 1917.[16] On this revisionist view, the classical system did not merely gather together the false starts and loose ends of primitive film and synthesize out of them a coherent aesthetic form; instead, as Miriam Hansen has persuasively argued in *Babel and Babylon*, the shift from one paradigm to another was nothing less than a revolution in the modes of cinematic address, involving the creation of a normative model of cinematic subjectivity: that of the "spectator," who stands in sharp contrast to the diverse viewing audiences of the earlier "cinema of attractions." The difference here is not just one of demographics but of the phenomenological constitution and experiential position of the viewer with regard to the spectacle of film. Accordingly, the shift from early to classical cinema involved a radical transformation of "the conception of the relations between film and spectator" (Hansen 24), which is to say that a phenomenal reorientation of human-technology relations lies at the heart of the primitive/classical periodization scheme.

Moreover, the reconfiguration of film-viewer relations was tied to concrete changes in viewing situations: the shift was accompanied and expedited by a move from the fairgrounds and World Expositions where film was one attraction among others, to the vaudeville theaters where it competed with more traditional forms of popular entertainment, via the rise and fall of the nickelodeons with their own local and ethnic colorings, and eventually into the film palaces of the 1920s—by when exhibition practices had been effectively standardized. As Hansen argues, "early film-spectator relations were determined—and overdetermined—by the contexts in which films were first exhibited: vaudeville and variety shows, dime museums and penny arcades, summer parks, fair grounds, and traveling shows. These institutions

---

16 The now classic text in this revision is Gunning's "The Cinema of Attraction: Early Cinema, Its Spectator and the Avant-Garde."

provided not only the locations and occasions for film exhibition, but also a particular format of programming, the *variety format*" (Hansen 29). Thus, early cinema implied a mode of address "predicated on diversity, on distracting the viewer with a variety of spectacles (rather than absorbing him or her into a coherent narrative by way of a unified spectatorial vantage point)" (Hansen 34). Implicit in Hansen's account of the shift from one paradigm to the other is the idea that the format of film exhibition, the mode of filmic address, and thus ultimately the very phenomenological constitution of the viewer being addressed were influenced by the human-technological "background relations" instantiated in the various settings for cinematic consumption. By tying the shift in spectatorial constitution to material-technical changes in cinema, Hansen therefore lays the groundwork for a techno-phenomenological view of the historical process by which the classical system came to replace the primitive paradigm.

In this section I would like to expand upon this approach and to deepen its purview by focusing on the roles of human-technological embodiment and hermeneutic relations as dominant structural components of the respective cinematic paradigms. My immediate purpose is to demonstrate the relevance of the techno-phenomenological approach to the historical periodization and analysis of film. In this way, I hope to show that such an analysis can live up to the demands I have imposed for it: that it be sensitive to and illuminating with regard to the historical nuances of cinematic realities and the role of technological change. The results of this analysis are also to serve, in the next section, as a background for the more detailed analysis of three "Frankenstein films." That investigation, in turn, will serve to complicate the picture I draw here of the techno-phenomenological constitution of the two paradigms. I begin therefore with a rather sweeping claim, which is to be progressively relativized and problematized, though not rejected—viz.: *paradigmatically*, early film viewership is characterized by hermeneutic relations, classical cinema by embodiment relations. But as with any paradigm shift, whether scientific, technological, or otherwise, the break between the models is not clear-cut, nor was it effected in a once-and-for-all manner. Precursors existed, pressures mounted, the old paradigm was eventually overwhelmed, but traces remained. Paradigms are never pure, only paradigmatic.

Early Film

From cinema's quasi-mythical origins in the Lumière brothers' first public screening on December 28, 1895 in the Grand Café in Paris, the technology of film exhibition itself was the center of attraction; the "content" of the projected images was of secondary importance in relation to the astonishing fact that these could be captured and exhibited to an assembled public. As an industry arose around the production, distribution, and exhibition of film, many facets of the cinema underwent significant change, but this much remained the same: early cinema, at least in its first decade, was not primarily concerned with the production and staging of narrative events.[17] Far more important was the thrill of sitting in the machine—a wonderful machine capable of bringing images to life. Hyperbolically romantic and naïve as this description of early viewers may seem, the claim is borne out both by the social-cultural positionings of early cinema and by its phenomenological structures. On the first count, cinema itself overshadowed "the film" as an attraction; films (and narrative productions were initially by far in the minority) were transitory diversions amidst other entertainments—magic lantern shows, vaudeville, singing acts, etc.—in the variety format. Film-viewing thus shared a common space with these other attractions, both physically and phenomenologically. This meant that the fascinating occurrence of images projected onto a screen stood out in the context of "live" entertainments as a specifically technological object of attention, but one situated spatially within a material venue shared with living entertainers. Furthermore, "the image on the screen [was mediated] by exhibitors or by personnel present in the theater—lecturers, musicians, or sound-effect specialists" (Hansen 42), with the effect that the very distinction between "live" and non-live attractions was blurred. Cinema as an attraction was thus not focused upon the screen but instead diffused throughout an inclusive expanse. There was, as Hansen puts it, "a perceptual continuity between the space on the screen and the social space of the theater, including projection and other elements of exhibition" (36).

This atmosphere encouraged a predominance of hermeneutic relations: filmic technologies and film *as* technology were phenomenally opaque in this context as objects of intentional perception. And yet the images on the screen were of course seen as images *of* something; the perception of them was not that of pure sense-data, flickering mindlessly and without significance, but as related to and intimating a reality beyond. Film thus insinuated itself into the phenomenal field towards its objective pole, but retained thereby a distance of mediation to the physical objects captured by the camera. Just as the technologies of exhibition obtruded perceptually in contrast to the non-technological attractions while simultaneously receding from absolute objectivity *as* technology in the common arena, so too did the image at once announce itself in a dominating claim to attention and partially withdraw to make way for its referential function.

Instantiating a hermeneutic relation between subjective viewer and objective world, early film is thus characterized phenomenologically by an objective ambigu-

---

17 A detailed history of the cinema in this period is provided by Charles Musser's *The Emergence of Cinema: The American Screen to 1907.*

ity or an ambiguity in its objectivity. And the integration of narrative representation, though initially secondary to cinematic presentation, was in part made possible by this ambiguity. But even when engaged in the telling of stories, early film highlighted itself in enacting a mode of address quite different from that of the classical system. Thus, an actor's direct address of the camera, and by extension of the viewer, was not uncommon—one of the most shocking examples is provided by the opening scene (or closing, depending on the editorial prerogative of the early exhibitor) of *The Great Train Robbery*, in which an outlaw points his gun at the viewer. Such occurrences prevent the viewer from being absorbed into the illusion of a diegetic world, and they thus became taboo in the classical mode (Hansen 37). The direct address highlights, by way of shock, the presence of the screen within the space of the venue, and it is thus only possible within a paradigm that fails to articulate a clear segregation of the two spaces. In this regard, the direct address must be seen alongside a number of early techniques designed to emphasize the specifically cinematic nature of the spectacle. The Méliésian tradition of illusion and the so-called "trick film" highlighted the magic of the movies and thereby drew attention to the unique capabilities of film itself. And as Hansen argues, even the "documentary" types of early film were often engaged in "provid[ing] an occasion for demonstrating specifically cinematic techniques and possibilities" (33). The early illusionist tradition, like the early story film with its shocking interruptions to narrative flow, was thus part of a paradigm that placed film, its technologies, and its images in a quasi-objective position with regard to noetic subjectivity.

However, both the possibility of illusion and the ability to shock inherent in the camera's direct address are ambiguously predicated on the *referential* potential of the image: in order for such phenomena to be appreciated, the image must be seen not only as vaguely indicative of a transcendent reality but as providing a clear view of events that are amazing or threatening *because* they are real. This referential potential, in turn, derives from the camera's ability, in principle, to instantiate a techno-phenomenological embodiment relation at odds with the early paradigmatic hermeneutic relation. As an optical technology, the film camera follows in the wake of telescopes, microscopes, and other optical devices that themselves disappear phenomenally in the process of tunneling the perspective of the subject in his or her perception of an object. Moreover, in being embodied in this way, these technologies are seen to provide an unadulterated view of the objects as they are in reality, aiding the observer in overcoming the limitations of human perception and bridging the gap to a micro- or macro-level otherwise unseen. Another optical technology, that of photography—upon which the cinema depends for its technical conditions of possibility—provides the paradigm example of an allegedly undistorted, verisimilar view of the world, superior even to human vision by virtue of the camera's disinterestedly faithful reproduction of reality. Only against this technological background of reference and the reliability of optical devices could the cinematic depiction of a magic trick amaze or the outlaw's gun frighten early audiences.

This is to say that the positioning of film as an opaque but mediating object in the hermeneutic relation typical of early film could only take place despite—and, supplementarily, *contingent upon*—the factual possibility for film to be embodied as a transparent medium. Actuality films and panorama views of distant locales encouraged momentary instantiations of embodiment relations in this sense: they offered themselves as vehicles for perception at a distance, both spatially and temporally. But even here the cinematic apparatus itself continued to loom phenomenally large, as a "vehicle" for traveling great distances at an unparalleled speed and even capable of traversing the fourth dimension. In this regard, these films resemble the so-called "kinesthetic films," for which a camera was attached to the front of a car or train, for example, in order to record, and later reproduce, the dizzying velocity of technological transportation; and of all early-film types, the kinesthetic film is that which relies most heavily on the possibility of human-technological embodiment relations. Here the exhibition venue itself was transformed into a vehicle— and quite literally so in the genre's culmination in Hale's Tours, which employed a theater designed like a realistic railroad car. The appeal of the kinesthetic film, much like that of today's IMAX 3D spectacles or the still futuristic VR fantasies, depends crucially on the ability of the spectator to project him- or herself into the world of the screen, to see and feel as if that were the world of unmediated or "real" experience. This requires that the viewer unconsciously merge his or her own perspective with that of the camera or the vehicle to which it is attached in order to move beyond the visual recognition of winding railway tracks and the like—and towards a haptic experience of speed, the inertial pull of the curves, and the anxiety induced by running along a seaside cliff.

The goal of such fantasies, that is, is a thoroughly embodied relation to the filmic medium. Ideally, the images on the screen become so transparent to the viewer that they are taken for the real thing; film and filmic technologies disappear completely from the phenomenal field and only the referential objects of the images are left over—as the objects of apparently direct perception. But in the early period of the cinema, the ideal remained a fleeting ideal. The shock of racing towards a cliff, like the shock of a gun aimed at the viewer, could draw attention back to the cinematic conditions of its occurrence, as could the "unsettling effect," as Hansen puts it with regard to a subway-perspective kinesthetic film, of "the viewer's inescapable consignment to the place of the invisible camera, experienced in terms of an overpowering orality" (32). The merging of perspectives, seemingly at odds with the hermeneutic paradigm, in fact reinforced that paradigm by highlighting particularly cinematic possibilities and thus offering an attraction, *as* attraction, vying to top all others. With reference to Hale's Tours, Hansen argues: "While the realistic environment motivates the kinesthetic experience (and thus to some extent contains its destabilizing effect), it still betrays a distinctly primitive attitude toward the cinematic illusion, one that includes the spectator in the space and process of make-believe" (32). Thus, cinema itself remained the attraction, and the phenomenology of cinematic space retained its continuity with the physical space of exhibition. These facts, coupled with the sheer novelty of the cinematic spectacle, helped to insure, even in this apparently extreme case, that hermeneutic relations remained dominant.

Classical Film

By about 1917 this hierarchy had been inverted. The classical paradigm had reached ascendancy, its system of representational and aesthetic principles codified, and sweeping changes in exhibition practices effected.[18] Phenomenologically, embodiment relations became the norm. And though we can point to the occurrence—and even *necessity* (as supplement)—of embodiment relations in the primitive paradigm, the stubborn resistance by which such phenomenological modes were subordinated there to hermeneutic relations entails the erroneousness of viewing the classical paradigm as the latent entelechy of primitive cinema. The type of embodiment relation exploited in the direct address of the camera or in kinesthetic films was much too excessive and disruptive to be of use to the classical system. An actor's acknowledgement of the camera thwarted the possibility of immersion in the illusion of the screen and encouraged a heightened awareness on the part of the viewer of being located physically in a material environment that included the screen and its images; and the virtual train ride was too extreme in demanding the viewer's identification with a machine, the kinesthetic fascination thus too alienating to serve as anything but an advertisement for the technological wonder of the cinematic machine. Though linked by the referential function of the camera, there is thus a gulf of separation rather than a relation of continuity between embodiment relations as they functioned in early cinema and in the classical system.

Very schematically, embodiment relations in the classical paradigm function to integrate the spectator into the world depicted on the screen so that the screen as such phenomenally disappears from view. The achievement of this phenomenal reorientation, as Hansen argues, "involved representational strategies aimed at suppressing awareness of the theater space and absorbing the spectator into the illusionist space on screen: closer framing, centered composition, and directional light-

---

18 The classic study is *The Classical Hollywood Cinema* by David Bordwell, Janet Staiger, and Kristin Thompson.

ing; continuity editing which created a coherent diegetic space unfolding itself to an ubiquitous invisible observer; and the gradual increase of film length, culminating in the introduction of the feature film" (44). It was necessary to reduce the influence of situational contingencies, including local variations in exhibition practices and improvisational elements, and to isolate cinema from its early milieu as one attraction among many. The development of the feature-length narrative, moreover, was instrumental in positioning "the film" itself, as opposed to the cinematic machinery, as what one went to see. As Tom Gunning reminds us, "Early audiences went to exhibitions to see machines demonstrated (the newest technological wonder, following in the wake of such widely exhibited machines and marvels as X-rays or, earlier, the phonograph) rather than to view films. It was the Cinématographe, the Biograph or the Vitascope that were advertised on the variety bills in which they premiered, not *The Baby's Breakfast* or *The Black Diamond Express*" ("Cinema of Attraction" 66). But with the feature film, and thanks to the refinement and expansion of distribution processes, one could now see the same film in New York or Chicago or Los Angeles in (almost) exactly the same form. A new metaphysics of film resulted from these material changes, for they effected not only a factual abstraction of the film-as-packaged-product from the location of its exhibition but, more importantly, a phenomenal segregation of diegetic and theater spaces. This separation was essential to the transformation of the screen into a transparent window, and it required that classical embodiment relations were of a more modest sort than their shocking precursors in early film—lest the window suddenly shatter and reveal itself *as* a window.

How, though, could the *segregation* of theater space from narrative space paradoxically effect an *integration* of spectator and film? Should it not, on the contrary, *separate* the spectacle from the spectator—who, after all, or at least apparently, is an embodied being occupying a very real seat in the physical space of the venue? The answer to the conundrum lies in a radical reconceptualization of the film-viewing subject—the creation, that is, of the spectator *per se*, as distinct from the viewers addressed by early film. The latter, as we have seen, were addressed as embodied subjects occupying a material arena they shared not only with fellow viewers but also with film and its technological infrastructure of projector, screen, and so forth. The spectator implied by the classical paradigm, on the other hand, was not primarily a concrete individual but an abstract subject devoid of the bodily, physiological differences and social markers that together distinguish us from one another according to race, gender, or class, for example. As Hansen has pointed out, it is not coincidental that film, in the formative years of the classical system, was figured as a "universal language" that—because of its photographically direct and thus visually unambiguous mode of communication—was addressed to and understandable by all of humanity, regardless of background or current standing in society (76-86). The film-viewing subject was thus implicitly asked to identify with this inclusive humanity and to forget temporarily the identifications and identities that individualized him or her as potentially marginal to that normative construct. This implied that the particularities of embodiment defining the empirical audience member in relation to the physical surroundings of the theater also had to be suppressed.

In terms of technology's contribution to this feat, camera and editing techniques such as the 180-degree rule, shot-reverse shot, and eyeline match, among others, helped to produce a closed and internally coherent diegesis, a logically ordered space within which causally coherent narratives could unfold. More importantly, these and other devices offered the spectator a privileged perspective from which to view narrative events: a perspective at once *inside* the diegetic world, orientated perspectively within that imaginary space through the devices that revealed its layout, and yet mysteriously *invisible* to the characters populating it. The spectator was thus guided and "situated" with regard to the filmic spectacle, "assumed [...] as an implicit reference point, functionally comparable to the vanishing point in Renaissance perspective" (Hansen 81). In this way, the spectator became a veritable part of the film product, anticipated by it and yoked by its technical apparatus—which itself had to become invisible—to induce a deeper sense of phenomenal and emotional involvement with the film world. The wedge of separation introduced by the segregation of filmic and theater spaces was thus lodged not between spectator and film but instead insinuated itself between an abstract spectator and the embodied viewer—between a normative viewing subject on the one hand and the physicality of theater, body, and film technology on the other.

In short, classical film-viewer relations were decidedly embodiment relations, but of a type demanding a relative *disembodiment* of the viewer-as-spectator. Techno-phenomenologically, the integration of spectator and spectacle into the film-as-packaged-product was made possible by the fact that the filmic medium, when "embodied" according to the classical paradigm, implies an abstract relational equivalence between the phenomenal results of either bringing the spectator closer to the objects observed (i.e. the referential objects of the images on the screen and their spatial situations) or, alternatively, of these objects actively approaching the stationary viewer. That is, in the phenomenal erasure of the mediating technology required for and definitive of its being subjectively "incorporated," the apparent spatial relations between the seer and the seen are transformed, the two brought closer to one another; but passing judgment on which of the pair now occupies a different position is a matter of (external) perspective. In this sense, cinema as an embodied technology is quite similar to optical technologies of magnification. As Ihde points out:

Lensing, in the telescope and microscope, transformed the phenomenological sense of space-time. Apparent distance, in technical language today, is a description of the changed relative distance between observer/observed. It is relativistically equivalent to say that the telescope brought the mountains of the Moon "closer" to Galileo or Galileo "closer" to the mountains. It was in the difference of direct and telescopically mediated distances that the sense of space was transformed. Similarly, the microscope repeats for the miniscule the same feat of transformed sense of distance, and phenomenologically speaking, it may be said to be equivalent regarding telescope and microscope. (Moon mountains and paramecia both take up focal places within the now instrument-mediated apparent space and are "same-sized" objects within central vision.) (*Bodies in Technology* 46)

However, the cinematic apparatus is not merely a technology of magnification; the alterations of "the phenomenological sense of space-time" effected in the embodiment relations of classical cinema are indeed more radical than those of the telescope, for they do not just transform apparent distance but more globally affect the spectator's sense of location and spatial orientation. The phenomenal integration of filmic observer/observed depends on classical film's ability to approximate the phenomenal properties of "natural" spatial orientation—hence the need to codify a set of editing techniques that reveal a "coherent" space, i.e. one approximately analogous to our experience of real-world coordination and the visual estimation of distance. When effective, these techniques induce in the viewer a "bracketing" of real-world space, which implies the aforementioned phenomenal equivalence between two views of the situation: either the spectator has been transported into the space of diegesis, or that space has come forward to surround the spectator.

Objectively, we tend to think (in psychological terms) of the diegetic space experienced by the spectator as being constructed "in his or her head"; what the viewer, looked at from this third-person perspective, "really" sees are only flickering images. The spatial relations among them, from this perspective, are not inherent to the images themselves but "read into" them by the viewing subject. But subjectively, at least when wrapped up in the narrative and its space, we (and the shift to first-person is here intentional) experience ourselves as if we were a part of the film world, inhabiting it and navigating its spaces. In science, the third-person perspective has been dominant; skeptical voices notwithstanding, an "instrumental realism" established itself such that "[w]hat could be seen through the lensing systems was taken as real, in part because it retained its analog qualities to unmediated vision" (Ihde, *Bodies* 46). As moviegoers, however, we are more often than not willing participants in a fantasy world; we *know* that the spectacle of film is fiction, but we not unwillingly suppress this knowledge, suspend disbelief, and dive in. The "analog qualities to unmediated vision" and spatial coordination that the fictional film-world retains encourage not unqualified belief but a counterfactual "as-if" attitude, allowing us to be immersed in the illusion and thus enlisting us in an attenuation—but not total elimination—of our sense of the materially concrete embodiment that we are.

The Question of the Transition and the Scope of Techno-Phenomenology

The techno-phenomenological approach I have taken here emphasizes a lack of continuity between so-called primitive film and classical cinema, but how, it might be asked, can it explain the shift from the early hermeneutic paradigm to the classical paradigm of embodiment relations? Certainly changes in venue, exhibition practices, and background relations involving projection technologies, for example, are pertinent from a techno-phenomenological perspective. But while an analysis along these lines will help to *assess* the paradigmatic differences, it will remain incomplete as an *explanation* of them. It seems, indeed, that the descriptive methodology of a techno-phenomenological approach is simply not suited to the task of revealing the historical causalities generative of the break—and that it would be best, lest we fall into a form of technological determinism, to admit this up front. However, technological "neutralism," or the view that autonomous human agents employ technologies as passive tools without risk of themselves being transformed, is not the only alternative to determinism.[19] A techno-phenomenology may reveal that the aesthetic program of classical cinema was actively shaped in significant respects by transformations of cinematic technologies, even if the reasons for the latter changes have to be sought elsewhere than in the technologies themselves.[20] "Machines," after all, "do not invent themselves" (Gomery 110). Yet, appealing to science as a necessary condition of technological innovation will not suffice, for an explanation along these lines tends once again to reassert a teleological progression, suggesting that its classical form is what cinema *would have been* from the start given the opportunity—i.e. provided the tools for its realization, the development of

---

19 This is a recurring theme running through all of Ihde's work.
20 Transitional-era film aesthetics, e.g. in the film-theoretical texts of Vachel Lindsay and Hugo Münsterberg, display an ambivalent to and fro between, on the one hand, an insistence on the active role of cinematic technologies in the aesthetic maturation of film, and on the other, an attempt to shore up technical agency and place humans squarely in control. These texts are highly instructive with regard to assessing the transitional experience from a techno-phenomenological perspective. See my "Between Technology and Art: Functions of Film in Transitional Era Cinema."

which had to wait for a more advanced science.[21] A techno-phenomenological approach reveals precisely the fallaciousness of this scientistic view by highlighting the extent of the difference between human-technological (film-viewer) relations under the two paradigms. Primitive film was simply not striving to be what classical cinema became.

Following in the wake of *The Classical Hollywood Cinema*, by David Bordwell, Kristin Thompson, and Janet Staiger, the most influential approach to the "generative mechanisms" explaining the shift from primitive to classical cinema has been formulated in terms of economic factors motivating the transformation of stylistic norms. Accordingly, the codification of classical aesthetic principles went hand in hand with the standardization of distribution and exhibition practices, the ultimate goal of which was to increase profits by appealing to and reaching as wide an audience as possible. This is an intuitively sensible and admirably argued approach; however, as Miriam Hansen argues, it tends to blot out the losses incurred by emphasizing the perspective of the victors (88), making us forget that the standardization involved in engineering a more inclusive audience also implied a shutting off of "locally and culturally specific acts of reception" and a closing down of the "margin of participation and unpredictability" that early film's quasi-live exhibition practices held open (43). Or, read from another perspective, it tends to overemphasize the power of an oligarchical economic elite, casting the masses of cinematic spectators in the role of a duped herd helplessly at their mercy. Certainly, the perspective of cultural studies has taught us to be skeptical of such implications; cultural products regulated normatively by the powers that be—and which embody a politics aimed at normatively regulating legitimate identities—are open to ironic, non-normative uses and thus leave open a "margin of participation and unpredictability" of their own. Economic and technoscientific forces of normalization cannot, it would seem, totally suppress the power of difference. But whereas cultural studies' celebration, at least in its less poststructuralist moments, of an inherently subversive potential of (popular) media use tends to encourage a naïve humanism in the place of determinism, there is a correlated factor that is more directly germane to the techno-phenomenological perspective: viz., technologies do not determine their own use, nor do their designers.[22] Technologies are always open to "hacking,"

---

21 For discussions of these tendencies in film historiography, see, for example, Douglas Gomery's "Technological Film History," contained in Gomery and Allen's *Film History: Theory and Practice*; also see Andrew Utterson's "General Introduction" to *Technology and Culture: The Film Reader*, edited by Utterson.

22 Ihde provides a useful discussion of what he calls the "designer fallacy," which parallels the "intentional fallacy" in literary criticism, in "The Designer Fallacy and Technological Imagination," which is contained in Ihde's *Ironic Technics* (19-30).

to unintended uses that result not only from attempts at subversion but also from intended or accidental changes in the circumstances of use, including acquisition by new user groups, the discovery of new contexts of use, or the emergence of new goals to be achieved. A techno-phenomenological approach therefore supplements—and is supplemented by—cultural and social considerations of, among others, gender, class, and ethnic differences, along with economic and aesthetic aspects of technological innovation, diffusion, and change; this expanded focus is essential, as we shall see in more detail in Chapter 3, to the assessment of the cinema's transitional era—it helps us to appreciate it as an overdetermined and differentially realized *experiential transition*.

I have raised the question of the transition from one paradigm to another in order to delineate the limits of, and proper scope of, a techno-phenomenology of film. The very existence of a transition complicates both the neat picture of techno-phenomenological paradigms I set out from and, more generally, the conceptual integrity of paradigms themselves. The dominant metaphor for describing paradigmatic change is that of "revolution."[23] On the one hand, the term is quite appropriate, for it emphasizes the radicality of the break or rupture—the incommensurability of pre- and post-revolutionary states. On the other hand, however, the "revolution" metaphor can be quite misleading, for it also suggests that the break is sudden and violent like an armed uprising. In fact, the disjunction between paradigms is seldom if ever so abrupt or decisive. In the case of cinema, we are dealing with a slow revolution—a protracted period of overlap, articulation, and negotiation—the transitional period lasting from approximately 1909 to 1917.[24] And because of the extensive extra-technological factors at play in this slow changing of

---

23 The convention, of course, derives from Thomas Kuhn's *The Structure of Scientific Revolutions*.

24 The dates are not only approximate but also disputed. Miriam Hansen locates the period, as I have, between 1909 and 1917, while others estimate the length and time-frame of the transition variously. For instance, in *The Transformation of Cinema*, Eileen Bowser covers the years 1907-1915. In her chapter "From primitive to classical" in *The Classical Hollywood Cinema*, Kristin Thompson places the "transitionary phase" between primitive cinema (itself broken into two phases, 1895-1902 and 1902-1908) and classical cinema in the years 1909 to 1916 (159). Charlie Keil, in *Early American Cinema in Transition*, claims that "the years 1907 to 1913 constitute the period of transitional cinema" (3), though he respects the general consensus that 1917 marks the firm establishment of classical cinema, thus leaving room for an additional undefined phase between 1913 and 1917. These disagreements over periodization are not, in my opinion, insignificant, for they attest to the overdetermined nature and the differential realization that I have attributed to the transitional era.

the guard, we must respect the limitations of a techno-phenomenological approach not only in terms of its restricted ability to provide an *explanation* of the transition itself but also its limited capacity to deliver definitive *descriptive* results for the transitional period. To state this more positively, a techno-phenomenology of film paradigms reveals its strengths in the analysis of relatively "pure" cases of paradigmatic stability. The question of transitions, however, indicates that the techno-phenomenological view—even when analyzing "pure," i.e. non-transitional, cases—is not self-sufficient but must be responsive to a number of things apparently beyond its own proper purview: these include extra-filmic technologies (in the contexts of entertainment, science, industry, and elsewhere), extra-technological aspects of film (such as genre, narrative representation, and, beginning in the late 1920s, recorded dialogue), and extra-filmic, extra-technological aspects of culture and society.

In fact, the necessary inclusion of such factors does not contradict the essential impulse or focus of a techno-phenomenology. For its objects of analysis are never simply technologies, conceived as cold and hard material realities or "things" standing in opposition to and isolated from human subjects. Instead, at the very heart of this way of looking is a focus upon the active interchange between technologies and humans beings—the various anthropotechnical interfaces that are articulated when humans relate to technological artifacts, systems, and environments. As we have seen, these relations may take a variety of shapes, part of the reason being that the *relata* themselves are multidimensional, multistable—never simply reducible to clearly defined "entities." Human subjectivity, of course, is overdetermined by psychology, physiology, social interaction, language, and a range of public and private identities and identifications. Likewise, technologies are dynamically situated within a wide spectrum of material and discursive contexts, and they interact simultaneously in small-scale systems (the single user with a simple tool and a goal) and large-scale structures (science, economics, and the global environment). Heidegger famously claimed that "the essence of technology is nothing technological" ("The Question Concerning Technology" 35); and though I shy away from the totalizing philosophy of technology in which the statement occurs, Vivian Sobchack's gloss on its meaning is quite revealing in the present context: "Technology never comes to its particular specificity in a neutral context for neutral purpose. Rather, it is always 'lived'—always historically informed by political, economic, and social content, and always an expression of aesthetic value" (*Screening Space* 223). Thus, extra-technological factors are integral, not alien, to a view which takes anthropotechnical interactions as its basic units of analysis; their inclusion therefore in no way represents a compromise to the "proper" focus of a techno-phenomenology.

As I envision it, and as it has been practiced by Don Ihde and, in the context of film, Vivian Sobchack, techno-phenomenology thus avoids many of the charges that are often (rightly or wrongly) leveled against classical phenomenology of the Husserlian sort.[25] Typical worries are that the phenomenological method, aimed at uncovering the "essences" of intentional objects, is a particularly bloodless approach to reality, one that cannot countenance the messier aspects of the social, cultural, and always political world of human beings. Moreover, the bracketing *epoché* of phenomenology insures that the objects in question and their supposed essences are nothing more than the projections of their essentialistic counterpart, the "transcendental subject," and that phenomenology is itself nothing more than a solipsistic idealism at root. However, these popular arguments, presented here in much clichéd form, are hardly decisive. Techno-phenomenology takes its cue from a Merleau-Pontean line of existential phenomenology, which places subjectivity not in a transcendental vacuum but in the immanent materiality of the lived body (*corps vécu*).[26] Simultaneously subjective and objective, this is a concretely situated, physically instantiated, embodied form of being that is nevertheless endowed with an intentional subjectivity that opens it up and exceeds the limits of the skin. The lived body provides a clear antidote to solipsism and, in its openness, helps to explain the potential we have as material beings to "incorporate" and "inhabit" our equally material technologies.

Nevertheless, transitionality poses a real problem for techno-phenomenological analysis. I have argued that the primitive/classical distinction can be elucidated in terms of the dominant modes of anthropotechnical relationality governing spectatorship in the respective paradigms. But we have also seen that embodiment relations, for example, play an entirely different role in early as opposed to classical film; they instantiate *qualitatively different relations* in the two contexts. In other words, "primitive" embodiment relations never mature into classical form, as if there were a linear progression from early naiveté to classical restraint and sophistication. Instead, one form of naiveté—which in phenomenology goes by the special name of the "natural attitude"—somehow gives way to another; the habitual and taken-for-granted background of experience is transformed. This demonstrates, in effect, that there's nothing so very "natural" about the natural attitude, for it is responsive to changes of normative construction and to the habituation of once novel phenomena, including experiences of new material technologies. On this basis, Vivian Sobchack has suggested it would be more appropriate to speak of the

---

25 As I have already indicated in a previous footnote, Sobchack's phenomenology of film experience in *The Address of the Eye* is nevertheless compromised by a teleological essentialism, to which I return in Chapter 6.

26 Again, the central text is Merleau-Ponty's *Phenomenology of Perception*.

"naturalized attitude" (*Carnal Thoughts* 5). Transitionality concerns the "naturalization" of a once "unnatural" form of experience. But when the natural ground of experience shifts in this manner, from what position, or upon what ground, is it possible to describe the experience of transition? Not only is the nature/culture split destabilized, but technology insinuates itself into and transforms nature as well, which means that it not only redefines nature's discursive opposition to technology, but also materially and actively shapes and reshapes it. Nor is the lived body immune to such change. The advent of transitionality suggests that anthropotechnical symbioses, which the techno-phenomenology outlined here takes as the basic units of its analysis, are subject to transformations according to processes and mechanisms of a postnatural history that must remain opaque to phenomenological inquiry.

In fact, the "problem" that transitionality poses for techno-phenomenology is the central *opportunity* for a specifically postnatural theory that a techno-phenomenological investigation of Frankenstein films helps to uncover. We shall return, therefore, to the question of transitionality and the specific challenges and chances it presents, which I take up most directly in Part Two. But first let us turn to a series of Frankenstein films—one each from the early, the classical, and the transitional period of cinema—in order to situate our inquiry and observe the complexities of human-technological engagement involved in these self-reflexive productions. As we shall see, these are not merely narratives about human-technological relations in general; they also reflect in various ways on the specific relations of viewers to the cinematic technology of their time. At the same time, they are variously sensitive to their social contexts, thematizing monstrosity in terms both of human-technological hybridity and the interplay between normative and marginal identities. The conjunction of discursive-semiotic and material-technical forms or aspects of monstrosity lends itself to a contextual analysis that insists on viewing cinema itself as a contested "public sphere" (as Miriam Hansen, drawing on the work of Oskar Negt and Alexander Kluge, puts it[27]), where the social interchanges that take place in and around this sphere are deeply informed by the variable structures of technological mediation instantiated in the cinema as a simultaneously social, material, and technological environment. As we shall see, then, these Frankenstein films do not merely relate narratives about human-technological distinctions and indistinctions; more importantly, they performatively enact profound and unsettling interrogations of the tangled interrelations among cinematic technologies, spectatorial subjectivities, filmic objects, and lived bodies.

---

27 See the Introduction and Chapter 3 of Hansen's *Babel and Babylon*.

Frankenstein Films and the Noetic Arrow, or: Watch Where You Point That Thing!

Establishing Shot

A straight-on and level long shot reveals a bearded man, apparently bored, leaning against a machine about the size of a mobile hot-dog stand, labeled "Patent Dog Transformator," in the center of the frame. We see another man dusting rows of coiled sausages hanging on the back wall, each identified according to a given dog breed or type: "Pointer," "Setter," "Terrier," "Mut," "Bull," "Plain Dog," etc. A sign above reads "Dog Factory" and, in somewhat smaller print: "Dogs Made While You Wait" and "Dogs Mixed to Order."

A man walks into the frame accompanied by three dogs. One after another, the canines are lifted up and placed into an opening in the top of the machine, disappearing into it as one of the partners turns a crank and the other removes the sausage links that appear from a smaller opening on the right side of the apparatus. The operators pay the man and he leaves. Another man comes on the scene, points at the sausages labeled "Spaniel," and the process is now reversed: the sausages are cranked into the top opening of the "transformator" and out comes a living dog on the left. The man, satisfied with the results, pays and goes. Next, a woman in an extravagant hat approaches, surveys the sausages, and orders a dachshund. As she waits, she clasps her hands and expresses her anticipation with broad gestures of her arms. The dog, however, proves to be too unruly for her taste, so it is transformed back into hot dogs. She then orders a terrier and happily leaves with her new companion. After a few seconds, a man in a suit orders a "trained dog." One of the operators demonstrates just how well trained it is, inducing it to perform tricks, including a reverse somersault. The next woman points at the sign reading "Bull Pups," and the sausages yield four small dogs. She chooses one, and the remaining three are converted back to their original form. Finally, a man orders a "Boston Bull," but it is apparently not tough enough for his liking. He then orders a "Fighting Bull." The first dog snaps at the sausages as they are taken from the wall and carried to the machine, one of the operators kicking it out of the way. When the "Fighting Bull" jumps out of the machine, it bites the man's bottom, sends him rolling on the floor, and chomps into his arm. The operators burst into uproarious laughter, gesticulating uncontrollably their pleasure at the man's misfortune as he runs away.

We have arrived in the world of early cinema. The film, aptly entitled *Dog Factory*, was shot by Edwin S. Porter at Thomas Edison's New York studio and bears a copyright in Edison's name dating from April 21, 1904. Cinema, understood as the public screening of motion pictures to a paying audience of more than one person, was not quite a decade old, and the nickelodeon had not yet appeared on the scene and transformed it. *Dog Factory* is thus undeniably situated in the context of the variety format, as a brief attraction among others. It is accordingly unspectacular by today's standards, both in terms of cinematography and narrative development. The long shot with which the film opens remains static over the film's entire course of approximately four minutes (at a projection speed of 14 fps).[28] The plot, if it can be called such, is similarly "primitive": though there is a comic climax of sorts, there is no real development, certainly no depth of characterization. Early film, more concerned to demonstrate its own ability to magically project moving images than to develop captivating stories, was not particularly choosy with regard to its subject matter. Often filmmakers turned for content to the live entertainments with which film coexisted and competed in the variety format, and *Dog Factory* is no exception. The "trained dog's" back-flip allowed for the incorporation of elements from the crowd-pleasing animal acts. And apparently the machine-transforms-dog-into-sausage theme was a popular premise for vaudeville acts of the time.[29] Those acts, in turn, were intertextually connected to a series of popular songs: "Der Deitcher's Dog," composed and published by Septimus Winner in 1864, and sung in a comic mixture of English and German, tells the tale of a man slowly realizing, while indulging in the stereotypical Teutonic pleasures of beer and sausage, that his meal has been provided by his missing dog. (The song, in less gruesome and politically incorrect form, has survived as the children's tune "Oh Where, Oh Where Has My Little Dog Gone?") And the tune "Dunderbeck," also known as "Dunderback's Terrible Machine" or "Johnny Verbeck" (in the Boy Scouts Handbook version), has a man of German or Dutch origin invent a steam-powered sausage machine with

---

28 Of course, the projection speed was variable, depending upon how fast the the film was hand-cranked through the projector. The Library of Congress, in reconstructing the film from its paper print, chose the 14 fps speed, resulting in a total running time of 4:27. A more "objective" measure of the film's length is given by the Edison Catalog, which indicates that film no. 5925 was 240 feet long (roughly one-fourth of a reel).

29 Tom Gunning writes: "The sausage machine had been a joke apparatus for at least a century (one tradition claims its inventor was the famous early nineteenth-century British clown, Joseph Grimaldi) and had appeared in circuses, vaudeville and minstrel shows for decades" ("Crazy Machines" 98). See also Brooks MacNamara, "Scavengers of the Amusement World: Popular Entertainment and the Birth of the Movies." *American Pastimes*. Brockton, Mass.: Brockton Art Center, 1976. 18. According to Gunning, MacNamara also found reference to a sausage machine sketch in the form of a shadow play in a late nineteenth-century "minstrel guide": Frank Dumont, *The Witmark Amateur Minstrel Guide and Burnt Cork Enyclopedia*. New York: M. Witmark and Sons, 1899. 146-49.

which he grinds up dogs, cats, and other animals. But Dunderbeck must pay for his invention and the resulting scarcity of pets: when the machine malfunctions and he crawls inside to repair it, his sleep-walking wife gives "the crank an awful yank, / And Dunderbeck was meat." Finally, the hot dog received its name in this same context of gastronomic suspicion and xenophobia. The first known written occurrence of the term appeared on October 19, 1895 in the *Yale Record*; students at Yale University had begun referring to the wagons peddling sausages in buns on campus as "dog wagons," calling into question the origins of the meat served and perhaps connecting it with the sausage-shaped dachshunds popular among German immigrants.[30] As the example of *Dog Factory* shows, understanding the short attractions of early cinema, which were hardly self-contained entities, depended on relating them to a wide variety of subtextual and intertextual references to other forms of entertainment and larger social discourses.

Furthermore, the scope of early cinema's "remix culture" extended beyond the practice of ransacking culture and society at large for its inspirations; borrowing themes, quoting from other films, reenacting scenes, copying whole productions, and downright plagiarism were also widespread. Though filmmakers often strived in these recyclings for (usually technical) innovation, it served less the purpose of demonstrating the originality of a particular film than of impressing the viewer with the novelty of cinema itself—and, importantly, of *renewing* this impression with ever advancing cinematic techniques and effects. Indeed, *Dog Factory* was not the first film to pick up on the sausage theme: it was preceded by Edwin Porter's own *Fun in A Butcher Shop* (1901), George A. Smith's *Making Sausages* (1897), the American Mutoscope and Biograph Company's *The Sausage Machine* (1897), and, most famously, Louis Lumière's *La Charcuterie Mécanique* (1895).[31] These films must be viewed not only in the context of a popular culture strangely pervaded by sausage stories but also that of an emerging cinematic culture fascinated with its own technology. The "trick film" and, more generally, the fantastic tradition pioneered by the magician Méliès exploit and depend for their fascination on the unique capabilities of film, those aspects that set it apart from theater or live magic shows, for example. Filmic technologies allowed for otherwise impossible specta-

---

30 The National Hot Dog & Sausage Institute reports this and other hot dog origin stories on its website: <http://www.hot-dog.org/ht/d/sp/i/38594/pid/38594>.

31 It is also followed by Biograph's *The Deceived Slumming Party* (1908, directed by D.W. Griffith), which, in the context of a tour of Chinatown, presents the view of a woman falling into a sausage machine that begins turning her into links. The process is reversed, however, by turning the crank backwards, and the woman is restored to her former shape. Even later, the sausage machine trick is repeated in the Kalem Company's *Ham and the Sausage Factory* (1915).

cles to be realized, simultaneously concealing from view the technological underpinnings of film's sleight of hand and thereby drawing attention to the wondrousness of that very infrastructure. The transformation of an animal into processed food provided an opportunity to exercise the cinema's amazing potential in just this manner. *Dog Factory's* director Porter had himself studied and imitated the work of Méliès, distinguishing himself in films such as *The Finish of Bridget McKeen* (1901) and *Jack and the Beanstalk* (1902) as a master of the art of film magic or "special effects." *Dog Factory* itself, however, relies not so much on the specific technologies of film for the transformations it depicts as on less sophisticated theatrical effects. Rather than utilizing special editing techniques or trick photography, *Dog Factory*'s metamorphoses could be realized in a single, uninterrupted shot by means of a much simpler trick: a human helper responsible for the substitution of dogs for sausages and sausages for dogs was presumably concealed by the bulky and stationary contraption at the center of the frame. Even by the standards of live magic shows, this is a very primitive form of *trucage*. Moreover, *Dog Factory*'s central technological wonder is a farce, the mere shell of a machine, quite literally inhabited by an organic rather than a technical force—and it is unlikely to have fooled even the most naïve of primitive audiences.[32]

Yet this technically unsophisticated film accomplishes much the same effect as the trick films that served as showcases for the latest filmic techniques and visual effects: like them, *Dog Factory* is capable of diverting attention from the action on the screen to an awareness of the screen itself as a component in cinema's technological apparatus. And what sets *Dog Factory* apart from previous cinematic incarnations (so to speak) of the sausage theme is the film's emphasis on the reversibility of the transformation process, which it relentlessly demonstrates again and again, and a self-reflexive allegorization of cinematic technology. Visually, the "Patent Dog Transformator" resembles the film camera developed for Thomas Edison by W.K.L. Dickson in the late 1880s, the Kinetograph. Both apparatuses are bulky, square devices, cranked by hand, and hardly mobile—the Kinetograph thus producing scenes as static in their composition as *Dog Factory*'s own. Significantly, Edison referred to the Kinetograph as the "dog house" (presumably because of its size and wooden construction). But the Kinetograph had to be supplemented by the

---

32 Indeed, the theme of cinematic naiveté was playfully taken up by productions of the early period. Porter's *Uncle Josh at the Moving Picture Show* (1902) makes the cinematically uneducated Uncle Josh, a country rube who mistakenly takes the images on the screen as real, the butt of a very significant joke: the comedy of the spectacle depends on the fact that the viewer knows better than to be duped in such a manner. The film stands as testimony of a discourse, initiated quite early in the history of movies, of "progress" and a distancing from "naiveté" in film-viewership. See Miriam Hansen, 25-28.

Kinetoscope, which was capable of displaying its images only to a single viewer, and thus the dog house was superseded by the Lumière camera, the Cinématographe. The latter had the advantage not only of increased portability but also of combining the functions of camera and projector in a single device, thus paving the way for the birth of cinema. Functionally, *Dog Factory*'s machine thus approximates the more versatile Cinématographe, as the repeated reversals of the transformation process reveal. Like a camera, the apparatus captures life itself (the dogs), transforms and preserves it in "suspended animation" (coils of sausage/rolls of film), and finally, like a projector, restores it in all its original vividness to paying customers.[33] Camera/projector systems such as the Vitascope and Biograph bear witness to a discourse, prevalent in cinema's early years, that equated the ability to reproduce captured motion with an infusion of "life" into otherwise "dead," discrete photographs. *Dog Factory* picks up on this discourse, literalizes it, and thus stages its representations of a technological wonder as an analogy for the technological wonder of cinema itself.[34]

We are back to the formal analogy of cinematic and Frankensteinian technologies with which I opened this chapter. On the basis of the film's self-reflexive exploration of its own technologies of realization, we might thus claim *Dog Factory* as an early "Frankenstein film" of sorts—but one obviously lacking a key ingredient: viz. an identifiable relation to the Frankenstein legend itself. Where *Franken-*

---

33 Though he does not explicitly link *Dog Factory*'s apparatus to the camera-projector of early film, Tom Gunning does suggest that the sausage machine films partook in the "operational aesthetic" (a term borrowed from Neil Harris) which linked early film's advertisement of its technologies rather than individual films to a broader "show-biz strategy" at the time, one which "reflected a fascination with the way things worked, particularly innovative or unbelievable technologies" ("Crazy Machines" 88). Similarly, what Gunning calls "mischief gag films" typically employed some sort of apparatus, whether a simple garden hose (as in *L'Arroseur arrosé*) or a more complicated technical device, which "possesses its own fascination, one which brings us back in an unexpected way to the operational aesthetic" ("Crazy Machines" 91). Such films therefore indirectly reinforced the intended fascination with the cinematic apparatus of camera-projector-screen.

34 Ironically, the film-as-sausage trope was to have an incredibly long life span, though in a critical vein rather than in the context of early film's celebration of an "operational aesthetic." Thus, years later D.W. Griffith, tired of making primitive films for Biograph and eager to make more complex features, wrote to cameraman Billy Bitzer and complained: "We are just grinding out sausages, Billy, and will continue to do so as long as we remain here" (qtd. in Brown 39). In the 1920s, King Vidor also picked up on the metaphor, referring to assembly-line techniques enforced under the studios' central-producer system as "the sausage-factory method of making films" (qtd. in Ross 260).

stein explores both the allure and the anxieties with which modern technologies confront humans, *Dog Factory* dwells only on their fascinations. Indeed, like so many early films, it works to heighten viewers' sense of cinema as a benignly enchanting machinery. The film's central spectacle, the reversible transformation of dogs into consumable flesh and vice versa, is perhaps a morbid premise, but it is anything but frightening. The reanimation of dead matter is not presided over by a mad scientist; on the contrary, the "creation" process as depicted in *Dog Factory* is tuned to the creative process as it was configured in early cinema: the conjunction of camera and projector in the "transformator" entails a partnership between filmmakers and exhibitors in shaping the attractions consumed by a paying public. One of the operators, apparently the boss, seems to emulate a director, overseeing operations and supervising his assistant who doubles as cameraman and exhibitor. But this doubling reflects the active contribution made by early exhibitors, who were anything but mere projectionists. The operators are thus magicians perhaps, but certainly not evil or even threatening. If anything, *Dog Factory*'s operators are socially marginalized characters, bearing a mark of "monstrosity" due to their presumed ethnic background. Early viewers were surely aware of the rather malicious jokes, songs, and stories connecting Germans, dachshunds, sausages, and hot dogs. And the film draws upon this background, which it can only imply (but about which the Edison catalog is quite explicit in identifying the men as Germans), to help create its comic atmosphere. Monsters or not, the operators, unlike Victor Frankenstein, do not fall victim to an act of "revenge" on the part of their technology. In keeping with early cinema's figuration of itself as a fascinating but non-threatening technology, the two men retain control over their machine. (Though perhaps the revenge theme is merely lying dormant, latent in the cultural subtext provided by "Dunderback's Terrible Machine," for example, and hinted at in the aggressiveness with which the "Fighting Bull"—the dog itself a "projection" of the allegorical machine—attacks the final customer.)

My interest in *Dog Factory* is thus not based on its thematic connections to *Frankenstein*, tenuous connections that would have to be stretched if not fabricated altogether to be established. Instead, the film provides a book-end of sorts, an early example of a film self-reflexively exploring its own filmic medium and structures of mediation, against which to measure comparable practices in adaptations proper of *Frankenstein*. In order for *Dog Factory* to serve this purpose, though, we need to turn our analysis to a specifically techno-phenomenological assessment of its engagement with film-viewer relations. The question thus concerns the "direction" of the noetic arrow, the place of mediating technologies within the relations of subjects to their objects, and the role of self-reflexivity in the equation. I have argued that the early cinematic paradigm is one conducive to hermeneutic relations: here cinematic technologies inhabit a quasi-objective position with regard to viewing subjects. But, as I have also contended, embodiment relations play a supplementary role in moments of medial transparency—moments, however, that are generally either too weak or indeed too radical to be sustained and therefore give way to an often intensified hermeneutic relation. *Dog Factory* exhibits a similar interplay of tendencies and induces phenomenal relations that see-saw between transparency and opacity of the cinematic apparatus—ultimately resulting, however, in a victorious promotion of the cinema itself by casting a spotlight on its technologies.

In effect, *Dog Factory* exploits the potential embodiment relations inherent in film's referential properties, based in turn on the indexical function of photography, but only to short-circuit them. That is, the viewer is drawn briefly into the primitive "diegesis" of the film (distinguished by the concealment of the "transformator's" technological hollowness, for example, from the "real" scene of the studio where the film was shot), but he or she is directed by way of the allegorical machine back out—to the technological conditions of film itself: most proximally to the camera and the projector for which the contraption stands. The initial (in a non-temporal sense) immersion in the fictional world, meagerly furnished as it is, is essential to grasping the film as a comedy; an exclusive fixation on the surface of the images would yield no punch-line. And yet the comic quality of the film is heightened by the obviousness of the technological farce that the "transformator" is: the concealment of its literal hollowness drives a conceptual wedge between the real world of the film-shoot and the fictional world represented on the screen, but the transparency of the screen that is thereby established is almost simultaneously shattered by the very transparency of the *trucage*: we "see through" the trick almost immediately.[35] We must for a moment believe—or perceive "as if"—a machine is performing

---

[35] I employ the first-person plural here under advisement. It is used to signal my attempt to place myself among the viewers of the film, in their historical context, in order to gain a vantage point for a phenomenological analysis that is sensitive to the paradigmatic otherness of early film-viewer relations. Obviously, this attempt is fraught with methodological difficulties. Phenomenological investigation aims to recover the vicissitudes of its objects from a first-person perspective. I am separated, however, from the original viewers of *Dog Factory* not only by a hundred years but also by my very different sociocultural conditioning, including the influences of classical and post-classical film on my perception of cinematic phenomena. I can never fully merge my own subjectivity with that of a concretely situated viewer of 1904, never see with his or her eyes. I can at best approximate the ideal perspective I am striving for by recovering the social, cultural, technological, and cinematic contexts informing the film and its original viewership. My lengthy preliminary discussion of these contexts is thus not extraneous to the phenomenological analysis proper; it is necessitated by the task of describing the phenomena in question from a historically situated perspective that is not merely my own.

miraculous feats in order to derive comic pleasure from the spectacle, but the conspicuousness of the hoax thwarts us in this belief, intensifying the comic effect. We are expelled by this recognition from the world on the screen, brought back to an awareness of the screen in the world. And here is where the analogy between sausage machine and cinematic machine takes over, pointing us first towards an awareness of the camera as essential to the construction of a world distinct from our own (the onscreen world) and of the projector as instrumental in staging our brief fantasy (here, in the offscreen world). Wider circles are drawn: we begin to notice the screen as framing the spectacle but failing to contain it, become sensitive to the presence of the exhibitor and other personnel in the room, and alive to the venue itself as a material environment in which we, the physically concrete and socially engaged viewers, are seated. Our foray into another world is short-circuited by the self-reflexive object of attention at the heart of that world, the arrow of noetic investment hijacked and set upon a trajectory leading back to the sociocultural and material world of the cinema, and the cinema's technological background relations thus highlighted by way of a spectacle that depends on their very invisibility.

The "process" outlined here is not to be taken as a description of a temporal sequence; the "moments" of immersion, of recognition, of expulsion are not discrete and ordered but coexist in an unsettled tension with one another. The illusion of the film's fiction is both sustained and broken—continually, not chronologically. The film's comic effect depends on both belief and non-belief, and the self-reflexive analogy embodied by the machine is located at once on (or in) and off the screen. Because of the illogical interplay between conflicting phenomenal conditions and relations involved, talk of "belief" and other conscious states should also not be overestimated. To be sure, consciousness is not ruled out altogether, but the dynamic tension of conflicting but coexisting "moments" (a tension which should not be reduced to an intellectual dilemma) is possible, I contend, because it largely takes place on the pre-personal level of non-thematized embodiment. And the overall effect (which need not be the *final* effect) of the film is to focus our attention, or channel our pre-reflective awareness, towards both the materiality of cinematic technology and the concreteness of the lived body. But because these "objects" are hardly thematizable, serving as bodily and environmental conditions or grounds of lived subjectivity, to focus attention upon them is also to blur the perspectival standpoint from which they are "seen," to disperse personal consciousness and the seeing subject itself.[36]

---

36 We should thus not expect that an empirical survey of *Dog Factory*'s original viewers would yield results in any way resembling the phenomenological description I have offered. Not only would linguistic expression distort the viewing experience in the ways I have noted with regard to my own account, imposing temporal orderings and subjective

Thus, *Dog Factory*'s relation to *Frankenstein* lies not merely in the abstract analogy that figures cinematic technologies as capable of infusing life into dead matter. The film's central allegory leads, as we have seen, to a *phenomenal* probing and problematization of human-technological relations—thereby approximating the *thematic* focus of Mary Shelley's *Frankenstein*, a book which, due to this focus, is occasionally claimed as the first science-fiction novel.

This quasi-convergence raises an intriguing question about genre. In film, the genre that has most persistently interrogated human-technology relations has been sci-fi. And though critics generally agree that it was not established as a coherent film genre until the 1950s, it is also intuitively plausible to see Méliès's *Le Voyage dans la Lune* (1902), which draws its narrative content from SF authors Jules Verne and H.G. Wells, as the first exemplar of sci-fi cinema. More radically, Brooks Landon has suggested a "revisionist history" which casts none other than *La Charcuterie mécanique*—the original sausage-film precursor of *Dog Factory*—in this role; indeed, Landon goes so far as to claim "*all* films made before 1906 as science fiction" (31). The rationale for Landon's revision lies, in fact, in the non-narrative engagement by early films of the narrative themes taken to be definitive of sci-fi literature as a genre. As I have argued, *Dog Factory* raises its questions about human-technological relations by according to its own mediating technologies a quasi-objective status, inducing a volatile hermeneutic relation between the viewer and the cinematic apparatus. Sci-fi film, especially through its extravagant displays of technology in special effects, is capable of something similar; as Landon argues: "special effects events in science-fiction film can be profitably considered as self-reflexive celebrations of film technology itself, as a kind of counter-narrative that often conflicts with the ostensible discursive narrative, and even as a kind of liberatory or utopic moment quite independent from the utopian representations of science-fiction narrative" (39). Opposed in this way to diegetic absorption, special effects displays approximate the early hermeneutic paradigm, and sci-fi film thus presents an extension of Gunning's "cinema of attractions."

It remains, I believe, problematic to stretch the historical notion of the "cinema of attractions" in this way, widening the category's penumbra to include such historically disparate phenomena as the sausage film, 1950s sci-fi, IMAX, CGI, and

---

states incompatible with the ambivalences and tensions involved; moreover, the dispersal of subjectivity need never have been (and is indeed quite difficult to be) registered subjectively, i.e. consciously. In any case, the interpersonal interchange between interviewer and respondent demands a recuperation of subjective positionality, and any awareness of the radical diffusion of subjective focus I am claiming would likely sink back to the level of pre-reflective "knowledge"—where the non-thematized knowledge of our lived bodies normally resides and informs our being as "habit."

VR, situated as they are in such different cultural contexts and against such various technological backgrounds.[37] The "utopic moments" of sci-fi film only function against the backdrop of the classical paradigm and its privileging of narrative, of embodiment relations, and of spectatorial immersion in the diegetic world. Obviously, the same cannot be said for pre-classical film. Landon's radical claim that all pre-1906 film is science fiction therefore puts the cart before the horse. Nevertheless, his provocative thesis, when read the other way around, serves the positive purpose of suggesting sci-fi as one of the places where early spectacle-based cinema went underground in the classical period (and beyond), highlighting structural similarities and phenomenological (as opposed to narrative) commonalities between a once dominant mode of film-viewer relations and explosive moments of release from a later mode of immersive, prosthetic embodiment relations. As I have been arguing, these are moments that not only phenomenally accentuate cinematic technologies but that also problematize human relations to them on the level of human embodiment itself.[38] When looking at "genuine" *Frankenstein* films, those that appropriate Shelley's science-fictional narrative engagement with anthropotechnical interaction and its bodily inscription, we shall have to be attentive to both the thematic representations of human-technological interaction and the presence of such non-narrative, self-reflexive moments. It is the latter, I contend, that offer the most fruitful base for a specifically techno-phenomenological analysis of Frankenstein films and that do the most to highlight and problematize the various configurations of film-viewer relations generally.

---

37 Vivian Sobchack also makes this point in her essay "What My Fingers Knew: The Cinesthetic Subject, or Vision in the Flesh" (57), contained in her *Carnal Thoughts*.

38 Tom Gunning suggests that there is also a continuity between the early "mischief gag" and sausage machine films, on the one hand, and classical silent-era comedy à la Buster Keaton on the other ("Crazy Machines" 97-104); he argues that in their engagements with technical devices, later comedians enact spectacles that appeal to the "operational aesthetic" of early film through "show-stopping" gags that interrupt and subvert the narratives in which they are embedded. Citing instances where the comedian "merges with the central device, becoming a projectile in thrall to the laws of mechanics" (99), Gunning argues that the gags not only interrupt narrative flow but also depend on "an interaction between devices, consciousness (and unconsciousness) and grace" (103), a submission of the character's will to the mindless operations of machines. Thus, "the comedy of gags which begins with the tricks of naughty boys [a reference to *L'Arroseur arrosé*] extends to images of an unbelievable grace, as the human blends with the unconscious functioning of the machineries of physical laws" (103-04), thereby enacting, again non-thematically, the human-technological hybridity central to *Frankenstein* and its filmic progeny.

Jump cut—

1931: The classical paradigm has long been established, the nickelodeon has come and gone, lavish film palaces have been erected, and the Depression has set in. Feature-length narrative films (with identifiable genres) have become the dominant attractions of cinema, the techniques of continuity editing (such as the 30-degree rule and cutting on action) have been perfected, the aesthetic principles regulating their use codified, and sound recently added to the repertoire of sensorial stimulations—all intensifying the immersive potential of embodiment relations under the paradigmatic sway of classical Hollywood. In this context, James Whale directs *Frankenstein*, and Boris Karloff's embodiment of the creature fixes our image of the monster, seemingly forever. Certainly, the film exploits continuity techniques to render the process of its own making invisible, subordinating its cuts to the coherency of spatial, temporal, and logical structures of diegesis; the film's masterful editing creates suspense, helping to ensure that the spectator will not be distracted from the narrative world but rather positioned within it, both spatially and psychologically, via a triangulated relation (later theorized as "suture"[39]) to the objects, events, and characters represented on the screen. And yet Whale's *Frankenstein* poses a number of disruptive problems for the embodiment relations it so crucially depends upon. In particular, and far more important in this respect than its stylized expressionistic *mise-en-scène*, the film indulges in the self-reflexive allegorization of cinematic technologies that we have seen at work in *Dog Factory*, a "teasing alignment of monster-making and movie-making" that Marc Redfield identifies as "the film's central pun" (par. 6). More than a mere pun, though, Whale's playful association of the technologies productive of, and those depicted in, the film threatens to upset the balance of classical film-viewer relations. The monster created exceeds the bounds of diegesis—is not localizable strictly as a figure in the film but is distributed within and without it due to the generative alliance of the machinery *in* the film frame and the machinery *producing* the frame. The creature with its scarred face and body, moreover, challenges spectatorial "identification"; the (literal) stitches holding the monster tenuously together problematize the (figurative) suture binding spectator to spectacle, revealing simultaneously the bodily and technological (and thus very real, material) bases of the bond.

Whale's *Frankenstein*, according to Redfield, is "an exemplary act of cinematic appropriation" (par. 1), not only because it adapts Mary Shelley's tale to the medium of film but because it uses the tale to explore and comment upon that medium. Right from the start, argues Redfield, "[s]eeing, and the seeing of seeing, is an-

---

39 A classic treatment of "suture" is to be found in Chapter 5 of Kaja Silverman's *The Subject of Semiotics*.

nounced as the film's main theme by images of eyes that drift behind the opening credits"—eyes that recall the "dull, yellow eye" of Shelley's monster but also signal the film's central concern with the mediated visuality of cinema (par. 4). The film's main visual attraction, the object of our ocular desires (and fears), is, of course, Frankenstein's monster. By means of a number of devices, many of which are themselves optical in nature, Whale focuses these desires in a protracted cultivation of suspenseful anticipation; in addition to narratively motivated setbacks that prolong the wait before we can "feast our eyes" on the monster, the effect is achieved through elements of *mise-en-scène* that would be quite illogical if not for their exclusive *visual* motivation—a cloth draped over the creature prior to the animation scene, for example, or the monster's backward entry into the room the first time his face is revealed. In terms of the story, these things literally fail to make sense; in terms, though, of the film *qua* film, they serve to heighten the spectator's visual sensibility. Moreover, once we do finally see the monster, our preoccupation with its outward appearance is sustained by a move that privileges sight to the exclusion of other sensory means of perceiving the creature: the monster is denied speech, rendering it mute in a (cinematic) world wired for sound. The sympathies we develop for it must therefore be based, in stark contrast to Shelley's novel, purely on our visual perceptions: we see the creature plead, express confusion and desire solely through gesture. Redfield points out that the creature's "voicelessness shores up the silent-film theatricality of his efforts to touch light when Frankenstein first exposes him to it" (par. 4). Indeed, the creature's muteness serves at once to highlight the centrality accorded to vision in the cinema generally (by contrast with the linguistically eloquent creature of the novel) and to question the effects of the introduction of sound (by means of "silent-film theatricality"). Thus, as Redfield argues: "This monster's visibility is a *cinematic* visibility: the hypervisibility of an image in the age of mechanical reproduction" (par. 4).

However, as Redfield notes, "if one claims that the monster embodies 'the cinematic' in Whale's film, one is simply paying homage to the film's own interpretive emphases" (par. 5). The self-reflexive play is explicit, and it is perhaps nowhere more apparent than in the famous creation scene. While preparations are being made for the animation of the lifeless corpse, Elizabeth, Victor Moritz (Henry [sic] Frankenstein's friend), and Dr. Waldman (Frankenstein's former teacher) show up at the lab to prevent Frankenstein from making a fatal mistake. Allowed in, they are instructed to sit down and shut up; instead of stopping the show, they end up as spectators to it. Michael Sevastakis argues that the onlookers function here as "the filmgoer's surrogates and the kinesthetic conductors of emotional responses indicating how the audience is to respond to the action" (69). Frankenstein himself drives the point home: "Quite a good scene, isn't it?" What follows is an extended allegorization of cinematic creation. In Redfield's words:

In Shelley's novel, Victor Frankenstein labors in sick solitude, but in Whale's film monster-making is a collective activity, involving a tyrannical director, an assistant, an audience, and a grand spectacle, the ur-scene of monster-movie tradition: the lab, the slab, the sheet-covered body rising heavenward amidst chains and pulleys, switches and coils, and great bursts of life-giving lightning. Hoisted up, the slab flickers with light exactly as if an old-fashioned projection bulb were being trained on it. And now it moves down; the sheet over the body is a teasing veil, for one of Karloff's long, elegant hands hangs loose and exposed, and, as the camera moves in, begins to curl its fingers. Cinema has animated it, figuratively as well as literally. It is thus hardly an exaggeration to say that Whale self-consciously stages here a primal scene readable as cinema's own. (par. 5)

Indeed, the creation scene is not an isolated example:

Other carefully composed shots elsewhere in the film reinforce the lesson. [For example, in] the monster's first introduction to light, which occurs a little after the animation scene, when Frankenstein, interested in viewing the effects of light on a creature that he has thus far kept (literally) in the dark, hauls on chains to open a skylight, so that a theatrically precise spot-light falls on Karloff. And near the end of the film Whale stages another almost coyly self-reflexive joke: Henry Frankenstein and his monster face each other in an abandoned wind-mill, separated by the mill's large, wooden, slowly turning cogwheel; as the wheel turns, their faces flicker through its square reticulations—a brilliant evocation of the moving celluloid strip that allows cinema to animate bodies, which is to say, to be cinema per se. (par. 5)

Reinforcing the double sense of *Frankenstein*'s "cinematic appropriation," we might add, the mill scene also gives a particularly cinematic twist to the *Doppelgänger* theme already present in Shelley's novel.

Asking "what such self-reflexivity means in such a context" (par.6), Redfield turns to Walter Benjamin's classic essay, "The Work of Art in the Age of Mechanical Reproduction." According to Redfield, Whale's "cunning attention to his medium tends [...] to uncover that dimension of cinema that drew Benjamin's attention: its inherent reproducibility, which is to say its deep, if ambivalent, hostility to the 'aura' of the artwork" (par. 6). "[T]he monster's hypervisibility bears the mark of [...] the 'shock effect' (*Chockwirkung*), as Benjamin famously called it, of modernity as mechanical reproducibility" (par. 6). But, the argument continues, what Whale's film is attempting in its self-reflexive playfulness is nothing less than a *transcendence* of this shock, presenting us with "fantasies of seeing the mechanisms of seeing—of mechanically reproducible seeing—itself. Lab and slab trope the lighting, the cables, the stage set, in short, everything that you do *not* see when you see a film" (par. 7). Here is the relevant passage in Benjamin's text:

The shooting of a film, especially of a sound film, affords a spectacle unimaginable anywhere at any time before this. It presents a process in which it is impossible to assign a spectator a viewpoint which would exclude from the actual scene such extraneous accessories as camera equipment, lighting machinery, staff assistants, etc.—unless his eye were on a line parallel with the lens. This circumstance, more than any other, renders superficial and insignificant any possible similarity between a scene in the studio and one on the stage. In the theater one is well aware of the place from which the play cannot immediately be detected as illusionary. There is no such place for the movie scene that is being shot. Its illusionary nature is that of the second degree, the result of cutting. That is to say, in the studio the mechanical equipment [*Apparatur*] has penetrated so deeply into reality that its pure aspect freed from the foreign body of equipment is the result of a special procedure, namely, the shooting by the specially adjusted camera [*Apparat*] and the mounting of the shot together with other similar ones. The equipment-free [*apparatfreie*] aspect of reality here has become the height of artifice; the sight of immediate reality has become a blue flower in the land of technology. (232-233)[40]

Redfield relates this passage back to Whale's *Frankenstein* thus:

Yet though the "equipment-free" gaze of the camera is the height of artifice, no self-reflexivity is adequate to this artifice. One can film (portions of) one's own equipment as one shoots, but the camera and its supporting apparatus will never entirely be able to film itself filming. Such, however, is the fantasy animating the monster's animation in *Frankenstein*. Even as it records its world as saturated with technology, the film dreams of a monstrous moment in which it could expose itself to itself, capture and possess itself for itself, and thus ward off the shock of its own self-replication, its mechanical self-differentiation and dissemination—in a word, its *mediation*." (par. 7)

Despite his apparent admiration for the ingenuity of Whale's "cinematic appropriation," Redfield finally condemns the film for its unfaithfulness to Shelley's novel—not, of course, on the simplistic basis of Whale's alteration of the original plot, but because the film, according to Redfield, indulges in a fantasy of human autonomy and control over technology-as-tool that the novel systematically deconstructs—notably, but not solely, in the establishment of the *Doppelgänger* relation between Frankenstein and the creature. The novel's Frankenstein insists on his autonomy to the bitter end, even to the point of accepting responsibility for a chain of events that exceeds his controlling agency—and in which he has been merely "instrumental," as much a side-effect as the monster itself in relation to a vastly broader technologi-

---

40 Redfield, in quoting this passage (par. 7), omits four sentences, beginning with "This circumstance, more than any other" and ending with the sentence "Its illusionary nature is that of the second degree, the result of cutting."

zation of the world. According to Redfield, the film's self-reflexivity continues Frankenstein's delusion, promising to obliterate the alienating distance of technological mediation between ourselves and reality (and thereby dispel the shock effect of which Benjamin speaks) by making that mediation itself apparent to us as an object of perception, restoring us to the safe vantage point of sovereign subjectivity. Thus, "the novel, for its part, provides us with a powerful critique of the fantasy of self-seeing that inhabits and in a sense makes possible Whale's film" (par. 7)—a fantasy that Redfield identifies with the "illusions of transparency and self-mastery that technoculture propagates about itself" (par. 1).

I contend, however, that the effect of Whale's self-reflexive association of "monster-making and movie-making" is quite different. Rather than renewing Frankenstein's fantasy, the film *exposes* it as a particularly cinematic fantasy (though not a timeless one), subverts it phenomenologically, and therefore heightens rather than diminishing the shock effect that film has on us as spectators. Let us reconsider the passage quoted above, where we find Benjamin describing, in effect, the conditions for the construction of cinematic embodiment relations. That is, he is concerned here to lay bare the means whereby the cinema of his day achieves the illusion of a prosthetic *enhancement* of vision (of seeing reality as it is, only magnified, so to speak). Paradoxically, the enhancement is achieved, according to Benjamin's analysis, by way of a radical *attenuation* of the field of vision itself. This attenuation is both literal and figural: literally, it depends on the camera's restriction of our perspective to include only a certain aspect of the studio setting (a function of the camera's physical placement); in addition, it requires that the "reality" subsequently perceived is that of the diegetic (rather than physical) world. The two aspects of attenuation are co-dependent; together, they enable the spectator to enter the space marked out by narrative film as the realm in which the true and proper objects of our attention have their existence, so that characters rather than actors are perceived, along with the objects and events that populate and complicate their worlds, not the photographed representations thereof.

Benjamin's meditations pertain foremost to classical cinema, in which embodiment relations are dominant. In this context, Benjamin's reference to the "sound film" as the very "height of artifice" is not spurious. The inclusion of diegetic sound, or so it would seem, greatly facilitates the illusion of transparency and offers new possibilities for the integration of the spectator into the film.[41] And the contrast between the "scene in the studio" and its counterpart "on the stage"—though a

---

41 However, as we shall see in Chapter 7, in conjunction with Robert Spadoni's arguments in his *Uncanny Bodies*, this was not always true. In particular, the sound transition leaves significant marks on Whale's *Frankenstein*.

perennial topic since the beginning of cinema[42]— speaks, in Benjamin's text, not to film in general but to the classical paradigm whose embodiment relations required a radical segregation of spaces that was not possible either in the theater or in the semi-live variety format of early cinema. The decisive factor is the classical era's use of continuity editing and montage as the means for creating a coherent diegesis and distinguishing it, as a self-sufficient or closed realm, from theater space: "[Film's] illusionary nature is [...] the result of cutting."

Benjamin extends the sense of the word "cutting" by developing an analogy between the filmmaker and the surgeon (contrasted with the painter as "magician")— thus also extending the basis for viewing Whale's film as self-reflexive. Whereas "[t]he painter maintains in his work a natural distance from reality" (like a magician who "heals [...] by the laying on of hands"), the cameraman obliterates this distance—like a "surgeon [who] cuts into the patient's body" (233). Because his equipment materially permeates the scene of shooting, "the cameraman penetrates deeply into [reality's] web" (233). Whereas the painter's picture of reality "is a total one, that of the cameraman consists of multiple fragments which are assembled under a new law" (233). That is, "cutting" in the ordinary sense of editing is necessitated by technology's more fundamental "cutting into" or "penetration of" reality in the studio setting. If the surgeon's goal is not to murder but to heal, then the incisions made must be closed back up, the patient's body sewn back together. Likewise, for the illusion of reality to be conveyed, the filmmaker must not only take care to avoid revealing the equipment pervading the scene but also stitch together the resulting images into a seemingly organic whole.

The cameraman/surgeon analogy adds yet another facet to our view of the cinematic nature of Frankenstein's activities, his literal cutting of corpses to obtain the raw materials for his "edited" creature. As Redfield puts it, the monster's "theatrical scars and prostheses and his awkward mechanical movements offer a displaced figure for the utter constructedness of cinematic vision—as though the record of angled shots, cutting, editing, etc. could be inscribed on a visible body" (par. 7). But this simply confirms Redfield in his conclusion that Whale is attempting to objectify the process of mediation, to overcome it by putting it at arm's length. What is being overlooked, however, is a third resonance of the "cutting/sewing"

---

42 Several early films took up this distinction as the basis for demonstrating the unique capabilities of film. Edison's *May Irwin Kiss* (1896), for example, recreates a scene from a popular play, consisting of nothing more than a kiss, but offers to the viewer a position and proximity to the actors unavailable to a theatergoer. His *Kiss* (1900) does much the same, but it also demonstrates the lack of segregation between diegetic screen space and non-diegetic viewing space through the male actor's repeated winking at the camera and, by extension, the viewer.

trope, one that brings the spectator into the picture. At stake centrally in Benjamin's discussion of the cameraman's surgical acts (both the technological penetration of reality and the resulting need to cut the images together) is also what has come to be called "suture," the "stitching-in" of the spectator into the film spectacle to produce a "seamless" whole—not just the edited film as organic narrative but an overarching structure that includes and envelops the spectator as one of its components.

Though suture has traditionally been theorized in terms of "subject-positions" opened up by film—thus as an incorporeal relation between spectator and diegetic content—Benjamin's comparison of the filmmaker with the "surgeon [who] cuts into the patient's body" allows for a radically material reconceptualization of the bond between concrete viewers and the material medium of film in its technological milieu. If we read the "patient's body" not just as a metaphor for the inanimate reality into which film technologies penetrate (a reading supported by the narrow context of the passage), but also take it literally, as a reference to the concretely lived body at the base of every spectator, we are in a better position to understand the physical, "tactile" nature of cinema's "shock effects." Though Benjamin sometimes writes of shock as if it were a matter of cognitive dissonance, a function of incongruities within or among images, and whose primary value is thus ideological in nature, he also refers to the physiological and phenomenological impact of the film medium itself on human experience.[43] That is, the psychic bonds of suture connecting a spectator-subject and his or her intentional image-objects are always also subtended by material relations between lived bodies and cinematic technologies of mediation. The concept of suture emphasizes the spectator's integration, primarily by means of continuity editing, into the diegetic world of film, the assumption of a subject-position in that world most literally realized in the "identification" with absent characters in shot/reverse-shots and point-of-view. Thus, a presumed presence-absence dialectic, which explains the "as-if" nature of (classical) cinema's reality illusion, is established as the heart of cinematic subjectivity. The underlying (and largely suppressed) interface of body and technology, on the other hand, is a matter of pure presence, a "positivist" phenomenon (in a Deleuzo-Guattarian sense). It is at this level of subjectively non-thematized material interaction between bodies and machines that a pre-personal shock effect occurs: it is here

---

43 Cf. Mark Hansen, *Embodying Technesis*, 231-63 for a detailed exploration of these issues. Hansen contrasts the "Work of Art" essay with Benjamin's later "On Some Motifs in Baudelaire," where the corporeal nature of shock is made clearer, but he rightly points out that the distinction is present in the earlier essay as well. There Benjamin writes: "By means of its technical structure, the film has taken the physical shock effect out of the wrappers in which Dadaism has, as it were, kept it inside the moral shock effect" (238).

that cinema's technologies "cut" into the lived body, and only against this background that a sublimating suture can be effected.[44]

Frankenstein's monster (both in Shelley's novel and in Whale's film version) can of course be read as a trope for the direct impact of modern technology on human embodiment. But can a film like Whale's, one which so prominently displays this interface as a visual phenomenon, go beyond such figuration and resist the temptation to reduce the monster to a mere object? Can it, that is, avoid neutralizing the shock effect of its own medium and propagating among its spectators the fantasies of transparency and mastery to which Frankenstein falls prey? The narrative development of Whale's film, with its rehabilitation of the mad scientist, his reunion with Elizabeth, and the restoration of order through the expulsion of the monster, would suggest that it fails to escape this pitfall. On another level, though, the film may in fact succeed. To see how, I return once more to Benjamin's description of the film-shoot, to the point where the spectator *almost* manages to make it onto the scene. Here, again, "it is impossible to assign a spectator a viewpoint which would exclude from the actual scene such extraneous accessories as camera equipment, lighting machinery, staff assistants, etc.—unless his eye were on a line parallel with the lens." As I indicated above, Benjamin is explicating a basic condition for the realization of embodiment relations in classical cinema. The impossible perspective—impossible for an embodied, spatially extended human agent—which is nevertheless made occupiable for the spectator through the mediating lens of the camera (in conjunction with that of the projector), is the basis for the illusion of a direct perception of reality; along with editing techniques, it thus enables the bond of suture. The counterfactual nature of the viewpoint from which a human could "really" view the diegetic world (i.e. from a physical location in the studio) reflects the play of presence and absence in the subjective perception of filmic phenomena. Suture, that is, requires the impossible: that our eyes are always "on a line parallel with the lens"; under the classical paradigm, this is a near constant requirement, allowing us to "embody" all types of shots and experience them as transparent.

Now a particularly powerful means of involving the spectator in the world of the filmic characters is to make his or her "identification" with those characters concrete in a subjective shot. However, it is precisely in such a moment of subjective identification, at the very "height of artifice," so to speak, that Whale's *Frankenstein* manages to expose the illusion of transparency *as* an illusion—not by reducing it to an object of perception and thus insulating the viewing subject from the effects of mediation, as Redfield would have it, but by radically reducing the spec-

---

44 This view resonates with the picture of spectatorship developed by Steven Shaviro in *The Cinematic Body*. In Part Two, I shall approach the pre-personal material contact and shock posited here from several different angles.

tator's distance from the mediated object and foregrounding film's shock effect in a manner reminiscent of primitive film. The scene in question occurs shortly after the monster's face has been revealed for the first time. We see the creature chained in the basement of the tower lab, desperately trying to free itself from its bondage, Frankenstein's assistant Fritz whipping it brutally. Frankenstein enters, takes the whip away from the childish Fritz, and tries to pull him away. In his disillusionment, though, Frankenstein forgets his torch on the ground and leaves. In a brief but significant shot, the only unambiguously subjective shot of the entire film, the camera assumes the perspective of the tormented creature. In a shocking close-up, Fritz waves the burning torch before the monster's face, giving the impression that the flames are just inches from the creature's eyes—*and from our own*, as mediated by the camera lens. Behind the flames, Fritz's hideous, sadistic facial expressions reveal him as truly monstrous—more so, perhaps, than "the monster" itself.

Narratively, the scene marks a significant turning point. It in part enables the rehabilitation of Frankenstein, as his baser instincts are transferred onto the cruel and already unsympathetic Fritz. Furthermore, it provides a base upon which sympathies for the initially horrifying creature can be built. Through our brief identification with the creature, which is terrifying for viewer and creature alike, it is difficult to feel pity for Fritz when he is killed by the creature (offscreen) shortly afterwards. Instead, there is an ambiguous feeling of justice served, though still mixed with fear of the avenger. Beyond the plot, however, the subjective coincidence of viewer and creature *vis-à-vis* a monstrous Fritz functions to pry open the stitches of suture that a subjective shot usually serves to sew. For a brief moment, the spectator who has been systematically pulled into the film, seduced by its appeal of suspense and spliced into its world through skillful continuity editing, is forced into the unstable "subject position" of the film's ultimate "object" (an object of scientific experimentation, of cruel torture, and of spectatorial fear and desire). The effect is a destabilization of classical film-viewer relations and a deconstruction of suture.

The concept of suture, it should be emphasized, is not worthy of deconstruction at any cost; on the contrary, the pleasures of classical cinema depend crucially on the sort of structures articulated under its heading. Moreover, suture's deconstruction depends for its possibility on its initial construction. In the context of Whale's film, the subjective shot would be without significance if not for the active (and quite effective) involvement of the spectator in the diegesis. In this respect, the camera—as part of a much larger technological-material and semiotic-discursive apparatus, including editing, lighting, *mise-en-scène*, narrative development, advertising propaganda, and larger social discourses of technological hopes and fears—has systematically trained us to focus our attention on the monster. The creature has been hidden from view, causing our intentional desire to actively seek it out, despite and even in service of our fear of it. In effect, we have been bound to this object like it, the monster, has been bound in chains. Just prior to the pivotal subjective shot, our desire has finally been consummated in the revelation of the monster's face; that scene has played with our ambiguous yearnings, heightening our fascination through the monster's suspenseful entry—preceded by the sound of footsteps, then backing into the doorway, slowly turning towards the camera to reveal first a profile, and then framing the hideous visage in a series of close-ups, each more extreme than the last.[45] When we now see through the monster's eyes, what we see is not simply Fritz's face, but the face of our own sutured desire: brutal, base, and overwhelmed with its own lust. *We* are thereby indicted as complicit in the creation of a monster. The shock we experience is based not on our "identification" with the subjectivity of the monster as a diegetic character: until this point, the creature remains devoid of psychological texture, contour, or depth. The monster's face is a mere surface, pure object rather than a node of potential intersubjective contact. We have in fact made it that way through our investment in the transparency of the medium, by constructing our own subjectivity as autonomous, empowered, and endowed with mastery over the objects of our intention. What we now see, though, is that our training in classical embodiment relations—the yoking of our subjectivity to the medium so that it seemingly disappears into transparent nothingness—has been responsible for this self-construction. And now, confronted with the face of our desire, our claim to superiority is shattered, the means of its construction made opaque—not in the mode of intentional object but in a dissolution of the presence-absence dialectic, a dissolution experienced as positive abjection.

What we experience is indeed a "seeing of seeing"—but not configured as seeing-subject in relation to seeing-as-object. Instead, we experience a vacillating, unstable non-dualism of pure subjecthood or pure objecthood. The "self-reflexivity" of this single shot is more radical than all the ingenious analogies and allegories between cinematic and monster-making technologies established in Whale's film. Those still allow for a subject to view them as objects, and they do indeed tend towards an objectification of mediation—but only as figure. Indeed, they offer no hope of real transcendence or escape from mediation; if that were their purpose, Redfield would certainly be right to condemn them. But apart from the intentional fallacy involved in Redfield's imputation of such a purpose to Whale as auteur, there is a greater oversight involved in his argumentation. When we look at the film as a whole, it is easy to condemn it for its neutralization of mediation, its erasure of the non-neutral effects of technology on us as living bodies and social subjects. As I mentioned before, the shot in question marks an important turning point in the narrative and can thus be contextualized in terms of two narrative tra-

---

45 I return to this scene in Chapter 7.

jectories: one, leading up to here, emphasizes horror, sin, and hubris, and another, beginning here, works toward rehabilitation, re-humanization, reintegration, and overall a happy end. It is inevitable and necessary that we contextualize thus—otherwise, there is no film, no story, and no subject. However, the shot itself works against these trajectories, is itself transcendent—not in the sense of "holy" or "immune," but simply *outside* the narrative structures surrounding it. It explodes our subject positions of mastery—both the leering desire motivating our viewership up to now, as well as the relatively humbled but largely self-righteous search for justice and order to follow. For a moment, neither of these are possibilities. We are thrown back upon ourselves—which is to say, we are thrown *out* of the discursive structures defining our "identity" in relation to the film, back onto our lived body in communication with the materiality of technological mediation. Such "transcendence" is thus far from empowering. It does not stabilize the subject and offer insulation from mediation's effects. It destroys rather than continues what Redfield calls the "illusions of transparency and self-mastery that technoculture propagates about itself."

In its passive objectivity (the result of the creature's subjugation to spectatorial desire and the implicit denial of psychic subjectivity with which we have been taught by the film to treat it), the monster's face contains eyes that see nothing on their own; because they are incapable of subjective depth, they record but do not interpret. The monster's eyes thus reflect the supposed passivity of the camera itself as a neutral extension of our senses and intentionality. The subjective shot therefore implies a radical conjunction of vision with the camera; my eye is on a line not just parallel but *identical* with the lens. However, the passive, unthinking, and unfeeling camera through which we see (the mechanical eye of the monster) is focused upon a radically non-passive camera, one invested with and indeed productive of the passion with which we perceive its objects. As an "assistant" to Frankenstein, Fritz is to be a mere tool in the realization of a genius-subject's project; however, he is far from neutral. His eyes are thus those of the "embodied" camera—a putatively passive instrument with a secret, impassioned agenda of its own. In the face-off between Fritz and the monster, we do in fact experience something like "film filming itself," the logical impossibility that Redfield claims is the general aim of Whale's *Frankenstein*. The camera is indeed turned back upon itself in a "monstrous moment" of self-identity. The result is not, however, to "ward off the shock of its own self-replication" but to reveal the radical *attenuation* of vision, and of subjectivity itself, centrally involved in vision's apparent enhancement—to expose the compromise of autonomy, of vision as well as of subjective agency, involved in creating the illusion of mastery.

In Fritz's face, we see the supposed neutrality of the camera lens unmasked: far from being a simple extension of our perceiving selves, it is a productive force in a non-neutral feedback loop in which our subjective desire is also at stake. In a word, we experience ourselves as "the monster," as an anthropotechnical hybrid; we "feel" but do not "see" (as intentional object) the chains of suture, the transparent bond between our subjectivity and technological mediation. The world of diegesis collapses as the enabling mechanisms of classical cinema's embodiment relations—the non-innocent symbiosis of subjectivity and technology which allows for a seemingly clear view onto another world—come up against an unassimilable point of resistance, a space of material positivity always underlying the spectator's absorption into cinematic spaces defined by absence as well as presence. The "eye contact" between the monster and Fritz is not an intersubjective dialectic of gazes; it is rather a material, tactile, and literal form of contact—that of our own bodies with the material apparatuses of filmic mediation. As subject melds with object, we live our mediation, we become the apparatus—or discern that we have long been a part of it. We feel the incision as the apparatus "cuts" into "the patient's body," as technology penetrates into reality's web. We feel it, moreover, on the surface and in the depths of our lived bodies as a tactile shock.

But the show must go on. Spectatorial subjectivity and diegetic objecthood must, of course, rise again, phoenix-like, from their own ashes. The experience cannot be sustained if there is to be a film-as-narrative in the classical mode. And the existence of such a film is the precondition for its subversion as such. It is understandable, then, that the rest of the film can offer only self-reflexive *figures*, visual and conceptual approximations of the radical self-reflexivity enacted in our brief moment of monstrous vision. If we pay attention to these figures, though, they seem to be anticipating and pointing back to the "utopic moment" (in Landon's phrase) of a subjective shot that ironically denies itself a subjective point of reference. Later, at the film's narrative zenith, the scene in which Frankenstein and the monster face off in the mill—separated by the cog wheel which causes their faces to flicker in visual reminiscence of the cinema's animation of photographic images—can be seen as a figural re-enactment of the shocking face-off that has preceded it. As I said earlier, the mill scene gives a cinematic twist to the old human-technological *Doppelgänger* theme of Shelley's novel; moreover, it makes the point—albeit on a figural, personal level secondary to the pre-personal deconstruction experienced earlier—that we, the spectators, are in fact the singular embodiment of that *Doppelgänger* relation. It is we who inhabit the camera's mediating perspective—literally situated *in the middle* of the two characters—and it is we who must realize the integration of shots, the healing of the "cut," in the form of "suture."

The relation between the two face-off scenes recalls the double sense of Benjamin's "shock effect." Both scenes are shocking in their own way, but one of them, as I have argued, involves a radical and immediate experience of human-technological interpenetration, while the other, as a figural re-enactment, remains assimilable to a subject-position created for us by the film. The latter, though it is of course charged with emotion, depends for its shock value upon a cognitive operation, a recognition of dissonance and a symbolic association. It may "re-mind" us of the corporeal shock highlighted by the former scene, but this already presupposes that we have in the meantime been forced to forget the experience, which itself defies subjective recuperation. A tropic play of self-reflexivity may invoke in us a certain sense of fear; the bodily registration of cinematic technology's "cut" into the material fabric of the world, on the other hand, evokes a deeper sense of *Angst*—without an object or even a stable subject, our cinematic Being-in-the-world is itself at stake. Can it be a coincidence, then, that censors in 1937 literally "cut," i.e. removed, this excruciating scene? For, as a destabilizing threat to suture, the experience opened up by the subjective shot stands opposed to classical film itself as a paradigm of embodiment relations. More so than the violence portrayed *in* the scene—as contextualized and related back, that is, to diegesis in a subjective reconstruction—the pre- or non-subjective violence enacted *by* the scene on the body of the viewer had to be suppressed.

So where does the noetic arrow point us in Whale's *Frankenstein*? Obviously, the answer must be a complicated one. On the one hand, the film skillfully utilizes the conventions of the classical paradigm, directing the spectator towards the diegetic world through its establishment of technologically transparent embodiment relations. At the same time, it introduces conceptual hindrances to such transparency. The muteness of the creature presents an affront to the sound film's extended methods of spectatorial absorption, and the compensating use of exaggerated, theatrical gesture points back to the pre-transitional era of film—before the development of new cinematographic and editing techniques began taking on the weight of narrative expressivity previously carried by pantomimic acting. Along with its scarred face and body, which conceptually if not phenomenally problematize spectatorial identification and suture, the creature thus attests to the significance of corporeality in the anthropotechnical interface of film. The creature poses a "hermeneutic" problem—not only a problem *of* interpretation but an obstacle *to* interpretation under the classical paradigm and thus serves as a reminder of the hermeneutic relations of early film.[46]

All of this takes place within the diegesis, at a subjective level of interpretation, but the film's self-reflexive allegorization of cinematic and Frankensteinian technologies points insistently *beyond* that level, tending always toward the subjective shot I have been discussing—a "black hole" at the middle of the narrative structure towards which everything else gravitates and which spells the phenomenal undoing

---

46 I return to these ideas in Chapter 7.

of narrative and subjective suture itself. It is there that the film articulates a genuine resistance to the classical paradigm and its standardizing immersion of the spectator into diegesis. Indeed, the shot recalls the phenomenal experience of early kinesthetic films: by mounting the camera onto a machine (car or train), those films exaggerated the potential for embodiment relations inherent in optical technologies to the point of their own breakdown: the "identification" of viewer with technology highlighted the material interaction of body and cinematic technology, thereby shattering the illusion of transparency. Likewise, by mounting the camera on the monster's machine-body, *Frankenstein*'s pivotal subjective shot effects a kinesthetic subversion of classical embodiment relations, phenomenally (rather than merely conceptually) problematizing the human-technological hybridity demanded of the spectator, exploding diegesis and bringing the background relations of cinema's technologies and their effects on our bodies back into the fore. The "direction," then, of *Frankenstein*'s noetic arrow is both present-oriented and backward-looking; phenomenally vacillating between the embodied fulfillment of classical spectator-diegesis relations and the hermeneutic film-viewer relations of primitive cinema, the film directs our attention once again to the unsettled meaning of cinema's transitional phase, to which I now return.

Dissolve to flashback...

Whale's *Frankenstein* was preceded by at least three prior film versions, the most recent of which was a silent Italian production from 1921, *Il Mostro di Frankenstein*. Before it, two American versions appeared during the turbulent years marked by the primitive paradigm's dissolution and the rise of classical Hollywood: the late-transitional *Life Without Soul* (1915) and the early-transitional *Frankenstein* (1910). Until quite recently, all three pre-Karloff era versions were believed lost forever, and this remains true today for the 1915 and 1921 films.[47] However, the

---

47 According to the entry "Life Without Soul" in the *AFI Catalog of Feature Films*, *Life Without Soul* was a 5-reeler directed by Joseph W. Smiley for Ocean Film Corporation (Ocean's first feature film). It was re-released with new footage in 1916 by Raver Film Corporation. The AFI's plot summary runs thus: "Victor Frawley, an eager young scientist, announces to his fiancée, Elizabeth Lavenza, his discovery of 'the chemistry of life.' Warned by family and friends of the dangers of his invention, Victor falls asleep while reading Mary Shelley's *Frankenstein* and dreams the story of the novel, with himself as the main character. Using his regenerative fluid, Victor fashions a new breed of man, invincible but without soul, whose brutality frightens away even his creator. His life threatened, Victor reluctantly creates a monster mate at the insistence of his 'child.' Fearing the

one-reeler directed by J. Searle Dawley for Thomas Edison's production company in 1910 has surfaced in recent years, offering us a view of the cinema's first take on this story of technical reproduction, the first Frankenstein film proper. Simply being the first, of course, establishes no special claim to originality or lasting significance; and indeed, the stagey "photoplay" produced by former theater actor and stage manager Dawley was neither particularly innovative for its time, nor did it exercise a demonstrable influence on the many Frankenstein films to follow.[48] Yet Edison's *Frankenstein* engages the competition of incompatible techno-phenomenological relations we have uncovered at the root of Whale's film—not in an attempt to subvert the hegemony of Hollywood, which was not yet established, but in response to the uncertain transformation of film-viewer relations that was then underway. Indeed, an antagonism of hermeneutic and embodiment relations characterizes the transitional era in general, and Edison's *Frankenstein* is thus useful in locating historically the structural tensions we will discover recurring again and again in future Frankenstein films. Challenging any single, unified vision, the transitionality at work here plunges us into an experience of overdetermined multiplicity—into a realm that we shall later theorize as that of the postnatural historicity of anthropotechnical interfacing.

---

consequences of the coupling, however, Victor destroys the mate, incurring the wrath of the lonely monster, who kills the doctor's sister and friend in revenge. The monster persists in his bloody destruction, murdering Elizabeth, and finally drives Victor to his own death. The dream over, Victor wakes, thankful for life, and rushes to destroy his evil fluid." As for *Il Mostro di Frankenstein*, even less is known; not even the date is certain, some sources listing it as 1920. The entry in *The Frankenstein Film Sourcebook* (eds. Picart, Smoot, and Blodgett) includes this telling characterization of the plot: "Story: Apparently includes a confrontation in a dark cave between Frankenstein and the Monster."

48 In his self-published *Edison's Frankenstein*, Frederick C. Wiebel, Jr. suggests that Edison's production did in fact have a lasting impact, influencing Peggy Webling's theatrical adaptation upon which Universal's 1931 film was based, and even influencing early designs for the monster's look. However, this is all very conjectural; any influence was most likely far less direct.

3. Monsters in Transit: Edison's *Frankenstein*

> The heterotopia is capable of juxtaposing in a single real place several spaces, several sites that are in themselves incompatible. [...] thus it is that the cinema is a very odd rectangular room, at the end of which, on a two-dimensional screen, one sees the projection of a three-dimensional space [....] Heterotopias are most often linked to slices in time – which is to say that they open onto what might be termed, for the sake of symmetry, heterochronies.
> MICHEL FOUCAULT

Released in the US on March 18, 1910, Edison film no. 6604—with the fitting codename "Vestiglo" for telegraphic orders (Spanish for "fantastic monster")[1]—is a film that sits uneasily between two cinematic worlds. Both historically and structurally, it belongs neither to the realm of early film nor to the classical system. Like any entity not governed by a system of legitimating categories, Edison's *Frankenstein* is a monster of sorts; its monstrosity is that of the cinema's paradigmatic transition, a shift defined less by determinate starting and end points than by indeterminacies that are at once historical, social, material, and formal.[2] Without being

---

1 These codes, listed with each Edison film title, consisted of randomly chosen words, arranged in alphabetical order according to the date of the film's release, that had no apparent connection to the content of the films themselves. An Edison advertisement in *Moving Picture World* (19 March 1910, 436) announces releases from March 15 to March 25, placing the March 18 release of *Frankenstein* after films with the codenames "Vestiging" and "Vestigios," and before "Vestilius," "Violon," "Violoncelo." In all likelihood, therefore, the appropriateness of "Vestiglo" was the result of sheer coincidence.

2 Throughout this chapter, I refer not to Dawley's *Frankenstein* but to Edison's *Frankenstein*, despite the fact that J. Searle Dawley directed the film. This standard practice is in fact quite appropriate because, as Eileen Bowser states, "Before the rise of the star sys-

"representative" of the transitional era, and in a manner not guaranteed by the mere date of its vintage, the film registers many of the central tensions of a cinema in transit—tensions that were all the more pronounced as a result of the transition's uncertain destination. Specifically, Edison's *Frankenstein* stages a contest between the respective appeals of a dramatic story and the film's special effects—a conflict of narrative integration and trick-film spectacle embodied, as we shall see, in a literal play of "smoke and mirrors"—where nothing less is at stake than the identity of the viewer qua spectator in relation to film and its technologies. The film engages, on the one hand, the social processes of monster-making at a time of intense renegotiations of legitimate and illegitimate spectatorial identities; furthermore, it correlates these processes with the cinematic ones of "animation," with the life-giving techniques whose role and significance were being redefined by the social and formal transformations of film.

I undertake this analysis in an effort to partially abstract the structural tensions of the transitional period from their historical roots; this is not done, however, in the spirit of ahistoricism but because the conflicts inscribed in the text and context of Edison's *Frankenstein* are comparable in nature to those repeated in later film versions—and beyond that, they point to a broader phenomenon, to be theorized in Part Two, of anthropotechnical transitionality. That said, we shall never find a simple repetition of clashes "originally" played out in the transitional era. If the contests between alternative techno-phenomenological models of filmic reception and among various socio-cultural conceptions of film and its viewers are particularly prominent and open-ended in the transitional phase, this is due in large part to the general upheaval of cinematic paradigms and institutions that characterizes this period of film history. The very breadth of the changes in filmic production, distribution, exhibition, and reception are arguably unparalleled in any other era, a fact that makes the transitional era a model period of sorts—a paradigm case of interparadigmatic conflict. There is no question, though, of returning to the source; just as it is important to identify structural models that enable comparison across time, it is also necessary to insist that these models only ever function in an unrepeatable historical context that transforms every "application" of a general principle into the productive creation of a new rule. If Edison's *Frankenstein* is to serve as a yardstick of sorts for measuring the techno-phenomenological and social-semiotic tensions registered in later adaptations, it is thus imperative to begin by outlining the narrower context within which the film was produced and consumed.

---

tem, films were perceived and sold by brand name" (103), and "directors' names were not advertised or generally known at this time" (105).

An Interstitial Space

In 1910, the nickelodeon, which had been established a short five years earlier as the first permanent and properly cinematic venue, was already on the decline.[3] With its cheap admission prices, continuous programming, and locations in ethnic and poor neighborhoods, the nickelodeon had turned moviegoing into an accessible form of entertainment for immigrant and working-class audiences with little leisure time or disposable income. Prior to 1905, the settings for cinematic exhibition were highly variable, ranging from county fairs to World Expositions, penny arcades and dime museums to higher-priced vaudeville theaters. And while the advent of the nickelodeon did not altogether eliminate this early variety of screening locations, it certainly re-focused the cinema's major constituency, at least in urban areas, from an earlier predominance of the middle to the lower economic classes. Similarly, while variety in the sense of early film's "variety format" survived the shift—live entertainment such as illustrated songs, small-time vaudeville acts, and educational lectures continued to accompany screen spectacles within the walls of the nickelodeon (Bowser 15-19)—the new venue demonstrated the viability of film to function as the main attraction, liberating it to some degree from its role as one among many in a chorus of entertainments or as technological oddity to be gawked at in a freakshow style revue of novelties. The idea that film could carry the show held out obvious economic promise for the rising cinematic industry; in order to realize this potential to the fullest, however, the class profile of the nickelodeons would have to be upgraded. Alternative venues catering to better-paying audiences began to appear, and enterprising exhibitors solicited better-heeled patrons with more attractive surroundings and higher quality programs.

The film industry's ensuing loss of interest in the nickelodeon coincided with, and was expedited by, an increasing concern on the part of religious and secular reformers over the perceived moral dangers of the cinema.[4] On the one hand, the nickelodeons attracted the less seemly portions of society, thus creating a potentially hazardous environment for women, children, and others who might (supposedly) be easily influenced; and the primitive-film aesthetic of the wares being peddled there seemed to ensure that the experience would be devoid of didactic value.[5]

---

3   A thorough history of the period is provided by Bowser's *The Transformation of Cinema*, which provides the basis of my characterization here.
4   See Bowser, Chapter 3: "The Recruiting Stations of Vice" (37-52) for an overview of the concerns voiced by reformers and officials—and the industry's reactions—with regard to both the nickelodeon itself and the films shown there.
5   Feminist reformer Dr. Anna Shaw pleaded for police presence in the nickelodeons, calling them "the recruiting stations of vice" (*New York Evening World*, qtd. in *Moving*

Thus, "[l]ike prostitution and working-class drinking, the cinema became the site of a struggle over cultural authority" (Miriam Hansen 63). The growing threat of censorship arising from the felt need for reform prompted industry leaders, including the likes of Edison, to jump on the reformers' bandwagon and to advocate the sanitation of movie theaters and film productions alike. Already in 1907, Edison had emphasized the importance for the movie business of producing "films of good moral tone" (*Moving Picture World* 21 Dec 1907; qtd. in Bowser 37). This conviction gained in urgency on Christmas Eve, 1908, when New York's mayor George B. McClellan, Jr. revoked the exhibition licenses for every nickelodeon in the city.[6] In response, the Motion Picture Patents Company (the Edison and Biograph-dominated Trust founded January 1, 1909) supported the establishment in early 1909 of the National Board of Censorship. All of the MPPC member production companies agreed to submit their films to the Board, administered by the civic-reform organization the People's Institute, and to release them only upon official approval. Over the next few years, a new emphasis on film as an artistic medium and a vehicle for moral uplift would increasingly influence the form and content of cinematic productions, steering them away from the appeals of sheer spectacle and towards the development of morally redeeming narratives. And while this redefinition of cinema was necessary in order to deflect mounting social pressures directed towards the motion picture industry, it also quite conveniently contributed to the creation of a more profitable up-scale market.[7] To meet the new demand for high-quality decent entertainment, streamlining measures in production and distribution soon followed the changes in exhibition practices.

In short, by the end of the first decade of the twentieth century, the slow transition from "primitive" to classical cinema had begun, as evidenced by the simultaneous transformations of cinematic outlets, audiences, and products. But while the cinema, conceived abstractly as industry or institution, may have embarked on a transitional phase by 1910, this does not imply that each of the industry's produc-

---

Picture World, 12 March 1910, 370; qtd. in Bowser 38). Magistrate Frederick B. House claimed similarly that "95% of the moving picture places in New York are dens of iniquity"; "more young women and girls are led astray in these places than any other way" (*Moving Picture World*, 11 June 1910, 982, 984; qtd. in Bowser 38).

6 According to Eileen Bowser, "The official reason given for the closing was poor safety conditions, but it was well understood that the real impetus was the supposedly poor moral condition of the darkened rooms and the kinds of films shown in them" (48).

7 According to Eileen Bowser: "With confidence and sincerity, the Motion Picture Patents Company's licensed producers assumed their mission to improve the motion-picture industry and its customers at the same time. To uplift, ennoble, and purify was good business too" (38).

tions, much less every individual act of filmic reception, was "transitional" in any significant sense. In the first place, though the formal techniques elaborated under the classical paradigm can be traced as far back as 1907 (Hansen 23),[8] films with an undeniably early-film aesthetic feel and a primitive mode of soliciting their viewers continued to be produced well into the so-called transitional period. Moreover, with regard to the settings of film reception, nickelodeons still thrived in small towns, and itinerant exhibition outlets typical of the pre-nickelodeon era continued to bring the magic of moving pictures to rural areas. Even within metropolitan city limits, the nickelodeons did not close their doors overnight. Nor was the film industry interested in alienating older audiences. Newly established trade journals at the time emphasized the need to remember these audiences even while pursuing a more economically lucrative base of spectators. And while this mediating approach can also be read in terms of the industry's drive to maximize profits, it received support from reformers' self-proclaimed humanitarian interests. The obvious contempt that many reformers harbored for the socially marginal nickelodeon audiences was counterbalanced by a paternalistic concern for their well-being, a self-righteous sense of duty to the less fortunate. To bring the reformed cinema's newer, more civilized (and therefore civilizing) forms of entertainment to the slums, where it was needed most, could thus itself be construed as a form of social work. The rhetorical posturing of film as a "universal language" with the power to speak to an essential humanity regardless of race, gender, or class standing was instrumental, as we have seen, in establishing the classical paradigm's standardization of viewers under the rubric of the spectator. For the time being, though, older forms of film-viewer relations (along with the spectacles that catered to them and the settings that facilitated them) could exist alongside newer modes—certainly a win-win situation for the emerging industry, for which it made no economic difference whether films imbued with a moral message were also open to non-standard or "subversive" readings.[9]

Characterized by the co-existence of different types of venues serving different audiences, and marked by significant tensions in the motivations for reform, cinema's transition was thus an uneven and discontinuous one. In retrospect, a more or less clear trajectory can be discerned in the developments of the period, but viewed

---

8   As I remarked in a footnote to the last chapter, estimates concerning the dates of the transition vary widely.

9   Bowser writes of the subversion of images through non-standard music (13-15), which, in the case of *Frankenstein*, the Edison company tried to guard against by circulating a suggested score. As Bowser details, other related developments included the use of classical music to upgrade theaters' images and the use of mechanical music-makers to reduce the risk of intentional or unintentional subversion of images.

statically—less, that is, as a "transition" than as an interstitial space of conflicting tendencies—the era is marked by profound structural and historical indeterminacies. If we wish to remain alive to the experiential tensions of transitional era cinema, it would therefore be wrong to reify the period's meaning—either by reducing it teleologically to a developmental stage in the latent classical mode's evolution, for example, or by claiming to identify a set of qualities that demarcate it neatly from both the earlier and the later cinematic paradigms. Not only was it impossible to predict in advance the ultimate resolution of the transition (which already assumes the questionable notion that people at the time consciously believed they were witnessing a transition to something distinctively new[10]), but whatever indications there were that a large-scale metamorphosis of the cinema was underway were matched by the continued appeal of a spectacle-based entertainment and its attendant forms, techniques, gags, and stylistic conventions. As I have hinted with regard to the limitations of a techno-phenomenological reconstruction of the transitional era, we do not find here an alternative model of paradigmatic coherence so much as structural incoherence, an unsettled overlap of clashing—and essentially incompatible—cinematic modes. Accordingly, it would be highly problematic to describe a given film as "representative" of the transitional period, as if "transitionality" were a determinate property ascribable to particular filmic texts. On the contrary, the existence of a cinematic transition is most clearly evident in historical hindsight and at the institutional level, as a competition among different types of films, audiences, and modes of reception.

Nevertheless, many films of the period did in fact register within themselves the central tensions of the cinematic transition and offer to their viewers—who obviously lacked our historical perspective and were also not likely in a position to form a macroscopic view of institutional changes—an experience of the uncertain transformation of film-viewer relations then taking place. Indeed, Edison's *Frankenstein* must certainly count among these films; rooted firmly in early cinematic style but pointing vaguely to the creation of something new, the film offers mixed-mode appeals that fail to coalesce into a stable synthesis. A stylistic hybrid of primitive and proto-classical elements, the 1910 *Frankenstein* discloses the precarious situation of a cinema torn between paradigms. But because this situation is one that is

---

10 In fact they may have believed this, but there was nothing new in that. Early film's appeal was based so heavily on the novelty of moving pictures and the apparatuses behind them, and this novelty had to be constantly renewed, making it inevitable that countless transitions to the next big thing had to be fabricated. In addition, and perhaps more significantly, some of the earliest films posit a form of progress from more to less primitive modes of reception. See, for example, Miriam Hansen's reading of Edwin Porter's *Uncle Josh at the Moving Picture Show* (25-28).

overdetermined by changes in the film industry, its products, and the settings of popular reception alike, any adequate analysis will require mediating between institutional and phenomenological views of the filmic text and its context. In the following, I shall therefore divide my attention between the film's formal, narrative, and aesthetic properties and appeals, on the one hand, and the advertising propaganda and journalistic discourses surrounding the film, on the other.

Primitive Pleasures and the Spectacle of Creation

In a space of under fifteen minutes, the Edison film presents a highly compressed version of Frankenstein's creation of a monster, the threat it poses to his relationship with his unnamed "sweetheart," and the creator's eventual triumph over his *Doppelgänger*. Given the temporal limitations of a single reel of film, it is hardly surprising that the Edison adaptation lacks the sophisticated narrative development, depth of characterization, and psychological motivation that the multi-reel feature-length format would later enable for the classical paradigm. Moreover, the story is told through a series of static theatrical tableaux, each scene (with the significant exception of the creation sequence) consisting of a single, frontal-perspective long shot depicting events that unfold on sets reminiscent of a theater stage, complete with painted backdrops. Since the framing of images remains fixed to the outlines of the studio stage rather than following the actions of the film's characters, the *mise-en-scène* is often imbalanced, drawing the viewer's attention away from the center of the frame—or simultaneously to multiple locations in the image. Typically for the presentational mode of early film, the individual shot therefore functions "as a unit of relative autonomy, as opposed to the classical conception of the shot as a part blending into a continuous narrative space" (Miriam Hansen 34).[11]

---

11 In the terminology of the day, each shot was itself considered a "scene." Though I will speak in the following of the creation sequence—which alternates between third-person views of Frankenstein in his lab and subjective shots of the monster forming in a cauldron—as a single scene, it is important to recall that such a distinction between shot and scene was not made at the time. Instead, though the different views are integrated narratively to form what we would today call a scene, the technique was then called "alternate scenes" (Bowser 58). The written scenario for the film, referred to in the Edison Company records as No. 287, thus planned for twenty scenes, referring to each of the shots in the creation sequence as a "flash scene" (reprinted in Wiebel n.p.). After filming and editing was over, the finished film would in fact include twenty-five "scenes" altogether, though classically trained eyes will most likely count only nine.

In conjunction with the film's narrative ellipses, the "relative autonomy" of the shots prevents the emergence of a clearly structured, self-contained diegetic space. Without the compensation provided by intertitles preceding each scene, "the spatial and temporal connections between successive shots [would] remain confused or unspecified," as Hansen says is typical of early tableaux-based narrative films (34).[12] Not only do *Frankenstein*'s intertitles tell us where and when the respective scenes take place, they also make up for the static camera's inability to focus attention on the relevant action by informing us in advance—often well in advance—of the narrative points to be established.[13] Occasionally, they also provide us with psychological facts about the characters, but they do not include their dialogue.[14]

---

12 Visually, the impression that the individual shots are autonomous units is both heightened and partially contained by the film's use of tinting. Thus, while the shift from a black and white shot to one that is sepia-toned or blue emphasizes the disjunction between the shots, tinting also provides clues regarding location and time of day: interior scenes without natural lighting receive a sepia tint (the film's assembly sheet identifies this as a mixture of orange and yellow), presumably to indicate the presence of candlelight, oil lamps, or the like; a nighttime scene is tinted blue; and daytime scenes with natural lighting are left untinted. As a result, shots are organized into blocks distinguished by their color, an organization that provides information about setting and can even indicate the passage of time. Thus, shots 3 through 20 (from just before the creation scene until just after it) are all sepia-toned, a fact that helps to link them into a larger unit and to emphasize their spatial and temporal closeness to one another. When, in the next scene, Frankenstein returns home, the shot is left black and white, for the sun lights the room through a large window. The following scene has a light purplish tint, though, a twilight color apparently indicating the passage of time, as measured by the sun's decline, between the two shots. As these examples show, tinting helps to bridge some of the gaps between shots, thus going some distance towards the clarification of spatio-temporal relations in the diegetic world. However, the color cues are not sufficient for this purpose and therefore require the aid of intertitles. This is most obvious in the film's first two scenes: both of them are an untinted black and white, but the spatial and temporal gulf between them is the greatest of any two consecutive shots in the film. Thanks only to the titles do we know that the first shot is at Frankenstein's home and the second at a distant college—and that two whole years have passed between them.

13 "Leaders," so called because they "'led' the scene, [...] announc[ing] what the scene was going to be before it started" (Bowser 139), became common after 1907 because of the increasing narrative complexity of story films.

14 See Bowser, 143-45, on the difficulties presented by dialogue: leader-style dialogue made it hard to know who was doing the talking, but there was significant resistance to

These titles carry a great deal of the narrative weight; they alone could almost serve as a summary of the story as depicted in the film: "Frankenstein leaves for college"; "Two years later Frankenstein has discovered the mystery of life"; "Just before the experiment"; "Instead of a perfect human being the evil in Frankenstein's mind creates a monster"; "Frankenstein appalled at the sight of his creation"; "The return home"; "Haunting his creator and jealous of his sweetheart[,] for the first time the monster sees himself"; "On the bridal night Frankenstein's better nature asserting itself"; and, finally, "The creation of an evil mind is overcome by love and disappears."[15]

But even supported by these textual interludes, the film cannot plausibly explain everything one needs to know in order to understand the story's events, their causes, and their motivations. The film thus assumes a general familiarity with the basic plot—a more or less reasonable assumption given the tale's already long established place in popular culture, including its many theatrical dramatizations and its currency as an allusion in contexts ranging from worries over scientific hubris to political satire. An ad in the *Colorado Springs Gazette* dated March 24, 1910 for a showing at The Crystal reads simply: "A Splendid Production of the Story. Don't Miss It." Thus, the mere recognition of the film's title is supposed to suffice to induce viewers to go to the picture show, and a prior knowledge of "the Story" will certainly help them to process what they see. This is to say that *Frankenstein* continues to operate in the mode of what Miriam Hansen terms early narrative cinema's "primitive intertextuality," relying on viewers' knowledge of "plays, novels (or, more often, their theatrical adaptations), folk- and fairy-tales, comic strips, political cartoons, and popular songs" (Hansen 45).[16] The tableau shots of Edison's

---

intercut-type dialogue, which was perceived as breaking into the shot. The latter only became regular practice in 1914.

15 According to Bowser, "In 1908 and 1909, one could 'read' many a film. All the key events and facts were conveyed by the leader, and the image that followed merely illustrated the title" (140). By the time *Frankenstein* was produced, however, changes in narrative construction created pressure to change title practices, because the old means were increasingly seen as conflicting with films' suspense and destroying the illusion of reality "by reminding spectators that they were being told a story instead of actually seeing it happen" (140).

16 By the same token, though, the advertisement in the *Gazette* demonstrates the long distance traveled from the early exhibition context, where "It was the Cinématographe, the Biograph or the Vitascope that were advertised on the variety bills in which they premiered, not *The Baby's Breakfast* or *The Black Diamond Express*" (Gunning, "Cinema of Attraction" 66). Though we typically associate the "feature" film with multi-reel productions, Eileen Bowser reminds us that the term "was an inheritance of the vaude-

Frankenstein do not therefore attempt to construct a self-enclosed narrative world but rather, as Hansen says of a 1903 production of *Uncle Tom's Cabin*, "they function as 'illustrations for a narrative which is elsewhere'" (45, citing Noël Burch)—for a story located in the titles on the screen, in lecturers' spoken words, and in the culture at large.

Furthermore, the film's treatment of the narrative revolves around occurrences that highlight the cinematic means of their presentation and therefore embody a distinctively "primitive" appeal. Most conspicuous in this regard is the creation scene, which trade reviews and Edison's own advertising propaganda alike cast as the film's central attraction. The March 15, 1910 edition of the Edison Company's bulletin of new releases, *The Edison Kinetogram*, which (like the first issue of the London edition, dated April 15) displays *Frankenstein*'s monster (portrayed by Charles Ogle) on its front cover, boasts: "The formation of the hideous monster from the blazing chemicals of a huge caldron in Frankenstein's laboratory is probably the most weird, mystifying and fascinating scene ever shown on a film" (5). The author of *Moving Picture World*'s March 19 "Edison Notes" rubric concurs: "The scene in the laboratory in which the monster seemed to gradually assume human semblance, is probably the most remarkable ever committed to a film" (428). An Edison advertisement in the same issue tells us: "The formation of the monster in a caldron of blazing chemicals is a photographic marvel" (436). And on April 2, a *Moving Picture World* reviewer claims: "The formation of the monster in that cauldron of blazing chemicals is a piece of photographic work which will rank with the best of its kind" (508). When placed alongside other exemplars of "its kind"—that of trick-film effects—these superlative claims about the creation sequence may seem quite ludicrous; certainly, films in the Mélièsian tradition, including those directed by Dawley's mentor Edwin Porter, had produced greater marvels of cinematic magic. What these textual fragments demonstrate, however, is the film's firm rooting in a "cinema-of-attractions" mode of cinematic spectacle, its

---

ville program" that, when originally applied to films, "meant a special film, a film with something that could be featured in advertising as something out of the ordinary run" (191). The "feature film" was thus originally quite imprecise, and prior to 1910, it could be used even to designate single-reel films. Besides the advertisement, there is some evidence that the Edison Company considered *Frankenstein* a special "feature," including the week-long studio shoot devoted to its making (an investment of resources that was unusual for the Edison Company at the time) and the prominent display of the monster on the cover of the *Kinetogram*. (See Wiebel for the film's production schedule.) However, the film may have come a year too late to qualify as a feature film (and to command the higher prices that features were receiving), as the term came, around 1910, to refer to any (and only) multi-reel films.

continued solicitation of (increasingly subordinated but still important) primitive audiences through techniques that aimed to display the fantastic possibilities of moving pictures rather than to develop the film's narrative content.

The scene itself, as I have indicated, is the only one in the film that deviates from the single tableau shot formula.[17] Here there is an alternation between long shots of Frankenstein in his laboratory, where he prepares for and observes the results of his experiment, and medium-length point-of-view shots depicting what he sees in the cauldron. Already before the scene commences, a title card tells us that catastrophe awaits, that "the evil in Frankenstein's mind" (which has nowhere been demonstrated in the film but must be inferred from prior acquaintance with the story) will inevitably result in "a monster" (thus contradicting Frankenstein's stated goal, announced earlier onscreen in a letter to Elizabeth, of creating "the most perfect human being that the world has yet known"). Surrounded by the morbid accoutrements of human skulls and a complete skeleton seated next to his workbench, an obviously excited Frankenstein frantically mixes various ingredients together while his cauldron faintly smokes in the background. He ladles the mixture into the vat, whereupon it emits a puff of smoke, then throws in a handful of powder, resulting in an even greater blast. Frankenstein mimics the rising cloud with gestures of his arms reminiscent of the arcane motions made by a magician, movements that in the context of live entertainment at once enable the wizard's conjuring act and distract the audience from his legerdemain.

The cauldron's encasement (which resembles a large wooden wardrobe) is then closed, its doors barred shut, and Frankenstein peers into it through a peephole-type aperture. The camera cuts to his perspective, and we see the cauldron, which now eerily absorbs the smoke it has emitted while something slowly emerges from its depths. Outside, Frankenstein rubs his hands in anticipation and raises his outstretched arms in delight at his imminent success. Turning back to his experiment, Frankenstein witnesses the unidentifiable thing taking shape more rapidly now, parts flying magically up out of the vat's depths and attaching themselves to what gradually begins to resemble a torso with partially exposed ribcage and skeletal arms. As the scene progresses, this object takes on an increasingly humanoid form as it mysteriously soaks up larger quantities of smoke and then impossibly absorbs into itself the flames that begin to engulf it, seemingly draining them of their power. Interspersed with shots of Frankenstein's reactions—gestures that express a mixture of elation and an inability to believe his own eyes—the camera reveals a head forming, an arm twitching and then waving wildly, bones being covered over with flesh. Finally, when the smoke and fire have been completely osmosed into the body's

---

17 Again, the vocabulary of the day fails to recognize such a distinction between shot and scene. See my previous note in this chapter.

interior, the creature is complete; its wild mane of hair sits atop a hideous visage, and Frankenstein's anticipation gives way to horror. The doors of the wooden enclosure burst open, a long-nailed hand reaches out, and Frankenstein backs away and flees.

Judging by contemporary advertisements and reviews, the Edison Company's self-proclaimed "photographic marvel" was clearly meant to be appreciated as a specifically cinematic spectacle, a display of the wondrousness of motion-picture technology. Importantly, this self-reflexive display is not achieved by means of a diegetic incorporation of machinery—as in later, classical-era versions—but by means of an alchemical operation.[18] Frankenstein's preliminary actions, his pantomimed magic act, make clear that we are about to witness something amazing, fantastic, impossible—not scientifically explainable. Indeed, the miracle not only defies the spatio-temporal laws of physics but also exceeds Frankenstein's own agency, for it is film itself, more so than a character named Frankenstein, that animates the creature. Reverse-motion photography is of course the mechanism behind the illusion, and by its means film, still commonly referred to as "animated photography" in 1910, tropes itself and offers itself up to the viewer as spectacle in the act of animating the creature. The trick effect—achieved by filming a dummy of the monster (consisting of a skeleton overlaid with papier maché or fabric) in the process of burning and then reversing the sequence's order[19]—distinguishes the filmic

---

18   Frederick Wiebel, Jr. argues that it was found necessary to animate the creature in this way in order to avoid implicating science and electricity—and thus Edison himself, the "wizard of Menlo Park"—in an ungodly and blasphemous act of hubris. This must remain speculation, however, as there is no documented evidence of the filmmakers' motivations. Furthermore, the choice is compatible with a simple desire to elicit the spectacle of the live magic show or just to motivate the reverse-motion creation sequence, which for all we know might have been the initial impetus for making the film. Moreover, by the means of alchemy the film could stage an act of creation *ex nihilo* and thereby avoid the novel's charnel-house plundering; this would be practical in terms of both reducing the narrative to fit the limitations of the single reel and also mitigating the risk of censorship on the grounds of blasphemy.

19   As an in-camera effect, the film either had to be cranked backwards through the camera, which is most likely, or the camera had to be turned upside-down so that the filmed sequence could later be spliced into the finished product without rearranging every single frame by hand. This was extremely important in 1910, before optical printers became widespread, for not just the negative but each positive print as well was the handmade product of a quasi-Frankensteinian act of cutting and sewing. Thus, in an uncanny symbiosis of organic and technological reproduction, each print of *Frankenstein* was put together from twenty-five strips of film by a group of women following "Assembly Sheet

spectacle from anything that might be accomplished in a live magic show, thus stripping the mock-magician Frankenstein of the creative agency he initially plays at having; unlike a magician, he has no need to conceal his sleight-of-hand, for he is simply not responsible for the film's conjuration of the creature.[20] In the context of the scene, Frankenstein's primary role is in fact that of a stand-in for the primitive spectator; he channels amazement, disbelief, even fear in the face of cinema's animating powers. Though his actions lend a certain degree of narrative motivation to the spectacle, his main function is similar to early cinema's many Peeping Toms, and the peephole point-of-view shots he affords us are accordingly different from the classical use of subjective perspective. Tom Gunning explains the difference thus: "Rather than providing narratively significant information, or indications of character knowledge or psychology, these glimpses deliver bits of scopic pleasure, spectacle rather than narrative" (qtd. in Miriam Hansen 40). As Miriam Hansen adds, "The scopic pleasure thus delivered [...] may be mediated by the character's look but is still acknowledged and shared with the spectator" (40).

Other Views: Narrative Integration and Multiple Address

The problem, of course, is that the novelty of moving pictures—of film's infusion of life into static photographs—upon which early Peeping Tom films drew for their interest and humor had greatly diminished by 1910. The changes that were by then underway with regard to exhibition practices and the composition and expectations of audiences meant that a purely primitive mode of appealing to audiences was bound to fail—if not in some of the old storefront nickelodeons, then at least among members of the newer, "classier" moviegoing public.[21] It is thus hardly surprising

---

#287" (the document, dated February 14, 1910 is reproduced in Wiebel; also included is a photo of the army of women at work splicing films together for the Edison Company).

20 On the basis of visual evidence, Wiebel suggests that "it looks like [the skeleton] could have been wrapped in nitrate film itself," the flammability of which would have expedited the burning process. This fascinating but unconfirmed idea would give a very literal meaning to my suggestion that the medium of film is in fact responsible for animating Frankenstein's creature.

21 Little is known about the exact circumstances of *Frankenstein*'s exhibition. The film most certainly would have been shown in countless nickelodeons, but since the distribution system of the time granted exhibitors little or no choice with regard to the films they received, and since the line-up of the program changed daily and was not known in advance, advertising in print for a particular film was virtually impossible (and would have been too expensive for many struggling nickelodeon managers anyway), thus making it

to learn that not everyone was as impressed with the creation scene as the *Moving Picture World* reviewers cited above. For example, *The New York Dramatic Mirror*, in a short review from March 26, concedes that "The scene where Frankenstein produces the monster is particularly well done," but, the author adds in the same breath, it is "a bit too long drawn out" (18).[22] Indeed, the creation sequence occupies nearly one-fourth of the film's total running time—arguably a bit too much "photographic marvel" for an emerging class of spectators seeking non-primitive modes of entertainment. Reflecting the new interest in film as a dramatic, narrative medium, the *Dramatic Mirror* emphasizes instead the suitability of "this deeply impressive story" as "a powerful film subject" and praises the film's actors for their "effective expression and skill."[23]

Not only do the theatrical values represented here differ from those of the film industry's trade papers, but the very fact that the *Dramatic Mirror*, a respected theatrical journal devoted to respectable theater, was commenting on films by 1910 signals the changing social perceptions of the cinema and its future.[24] Founded in

---

close to impossible to reconstruct the film's screening history. I know of only three printed sources that advertise or mention showings of the film; these are: the Crystal's ad, cited above, in the March 24, 1910 edition of the *Colorado Springs Gazette*; an ad for a showing at the City Opera House in the March 26 issue of the Frederick, Maryland newspaper *The News*; and a write-up of the Bijou Theater's program in the April 25 *Fitchburg Daily Sentinel* of Fitchburg, Massachusetts. The City Opera House in Frederick featured the film in their "Saturday Matinee and Night" programs, billing it simply as "Edison's latest." Seats for the matinee showing were ten cents for adults, five cents for children; while the evening program cost ten cents for the gallery and balcony, fifteen for first-floor seats, and twenty-five for box seats. The Bijou in Fitchburg, on the other hand, relegated the film, which was by then more than a month old, to "the regular program," which "offer[ed] comedy, drama, and descriptive photography in its most interesting phases, the titles of the several films being 'In the shadow of the cliffs,' 'Method in his madness,' 'The inventor's model,' 'Saraband Dance,' and 'Frankenstein.' This assortment of attractions will be interspersed by the latest popular hits, sung by Florence Brown and James Carroll, and finely illustrated."

22 All subsequent references to this article are likewise found on page 18.
23 A review in the April 1, 1910 edition of *Nickelodeon*, on the other hand, complains that the acting is based on "practically only four gestures, repeating them with very little variation" (177; qtd. in Keil 144).
24 Indeed, the frequently changing names of the periodical, which ran from January 1879 to April 1922, provide an interesting index of the changes in the perception of film and its relation to the theater around the transitional era. The title varies thus: *New York Mirror* (January 4, 1879 - January 19, 1889); *New York Dramatic Mirror* (January 26, 1889 -

1879, the *Mirror* had held out until 1895 before finally adding a section on vaudeville; it continued, however, to defend legitimate theater against the lowbrow phenomena of popular culture. Resistance to film was accordingly great; according to Linda Arvidson Griffith, "Writers on the paper were told that any reference to the movies would be promptly blue-penciled" (62). By the time Frank Woods, writing under the pseudonym "The Spectator," began his regular film column in June 1908, this policy had been irreversibly altered. The *Mirror*, and Woods in particular, became instrumental in developing a critical discourse on film that championed the adaptation of the theater's narrative appeal while articulating the medium-specific differences of theater and film (for example, the potential of the camera to take a closer view, thus allowing for less exaggerated acting styles, and ultimately serving a heightened illusion of reality) that would be central to the cultivation of the classical paradigm—and to the conception of the motion picture as a new and independent art form, its origins in the lowbrow spectacles of the freak show left securely behind.[25] In this vein, the *Mirror*'s review of *Frankenstein* views the film from an angle quite at odds with the primitive appeal of the self-reflexive creation sequence: "When the monster, fashioned in sympathy with the evil in Frankenstein's mind, appears and terrorizes his maker, one finds one's self very nearly accepting it as reality." Praising the film's potential to absorb viewers into the narrative world it depicts, and criticizing its excessive use of techniques that disrupt such involvement, the *Mirror*'s review delineates the battle front that defines the transitional era itself as a competition between early hermeneutic film-viewer relations on the one hand and proto-classical embodiment relations on the other.

If the development of engrossing narratives was to be the main vehicle for the transition to the classical mode, it is important keep in mind that the story film was itself nothing new. The success of the nickelodeon had in fact been founded largely

---

February 10, 1917); *Dramatic Mirror of the Stage & Motion Pictures* (February 17, 1917 - August 17, 1917); *Dramatic Mirror of Motion Pictures and the Stage* (August 18, 1917 - February 1, 1919); *Dramatic Mirror* (February 8, 1919 - February 14, 1920); *Dramatic Mirror: The Screen and Stage Weekly* (February 21, 1920 - October 9, 1920); *Dramatic Mirror and Theatre World* (October 16, 1920 - December 24, 1921); *Dramatic Mirror* (December 31, 1921 - April 1922). Note, in particular, that the inclusion of "motion pictures" occurs in 1917, by when the classical system is commonly said to have been definitively established, and that film then quickly took the upper hand over stage, i.e., received the first position in the title.

25 Woods is sometimes referred to as first serious film critic. Bowser quotes Woods on the topics of acting and "camera consciousness" (89-91) and on the idea that cinema could be art (267).

upon the story-telling potential of film.[26] Now, however, the narrative was also perceived as the way to overcome the tainted image that the nickelodeon had brought to film entertainment generally. Thus, the battle in 1910 was not being waged primarily between narrative and non-narrative films and filmic elements; with the demise of actualities and trick films, this conflict had already been settled.[27] Far more important at this point was to define the right kinds of story, the proper means of their filmic presentation, and the viewers' legitimate relations to them. The rhetoric of uplift demanded that narrative films be given a moral message, and the upward revision of audiences dictated serious, respectable subjects. Literary classics fit the bill in legitimizing the movies for theater audiences and "educating" the lower-class masses at the same time (Bowser 42). The dwindling novelty of moving images required that films involved spectators in the drama rather than causing them to tarry along visible surfaces. If the spectator was to forget the screen as such, actors would accordingly have to suppress their "camera consciousness," which, according to Frank Woods, was still betrayed by exaggerated acting styles even without the direct address of the camera.[28] Greater subtlety was called for, and the camera, itself not restricted to the perspective of a theatergoer in the back rows, was capable of providing it: "facial expression" thus gradually

---

26 As Miriam Hansen reminds us, fictional narratives were dominant by the end of 1904, accounting for the majority of titles submitted for copyright as well as individual prints sold (44).

27 A study conducted by the *Dramatic Mirror* in July 1910, just a few months after the release of *Frankenstein*, provides a clearer picture of the situation. Surveying all of the 242 American releases for the month, the *Mirror* found that 35 percent of the films were "humorous," 34 percent "dramatic," 19 percent "melodramatic," only 3 percent trick and novelty films, and 9 percent "educational" (a category that, according to Bowser, included "scenic and industrial films"). Though the Edison Company advertised *Frankenstein* as a "dramatic" film, it is unclear whether the *Mirror* would have classed it as such or as a "melodrama." According to Bowser, "dramatic films were perceived to be closer to the events of everyday life as experienced by the spectators" (168). Westerns were thus considered by the *Mirror* to be melodramas, and the fantastic events depicted in *Frankenstein* speaks even more strongly for this classification. I return to the changing conception of melodrama, in the later context of Universal's Frankenstein films, in Chapter 7.

28 According to Bowser, "Woods began a campaign on this subject midway through 1909" (89). In a July 10, 1910 article for the *Dramatic Mirror*, Woods makes a strong case for the urgency of shedding "camera consciousness" in order to come "nearer to absolute realism." He asks: "is the mere act of keeping the eyes off of the camera enough? Should there not be absolute unconsciousness that the camera is there—or rather should there not appear to be this unconsciousness?" (15-16; qtd. in Bowser 90).

became the preferred alternative to pantomimic gesture in bringing the story to life.[29]

Of course, the Edison Company was not unaware of the changing tides of critical (and popular) reception, nor did they bank solely on the primitive appeal of trick-film techniques to commend their "liberal adaptation of Mrs. Shelley's famous story," as the film's main title put it. Though the actors' melodramatic gesturing and the camera's near-exclusive reliance on stage-distance tableau shots reveal the film (like most Edison productions of the time) as far less progressive than the films Griffith had begun directing for Biograph, considerable effort was made to pitch the film as a narrative attraction in tune with the new cinematic realities and discourses. The advertisement in the March 19 *Moving Picture World* announced *Frankenstein* as "[t]he most absorbing 'silent drama' ever produced" (436)—no doubt a preposterous claim even in 1910, but one that nonetheless offset the ad's own emphasis on the creation sequence's spectacle-based appeal. Indeed, looking beyond that scene, we cannot ignore the relative development of the film's narrative, which no longer serves merely (as so often with early-film productions) as a motivating excuse for the display of spectacular effects; instead, even if they remain somewhat excessive, *Frankenstein*'s effects are nevertheless integrated into a genuine (if sketchy) plot.[30]

The *Kinetogram* goes to great lengths to explain this plot, offering a long-winded synopsis that attempts to make clear to exhibitors and potential reviewers the story's logic, its moralistic meanings, and the characters' motivations—everything needed for narrative coherence. Moreover, this interpretive summary is introduced with a short account of the story's genesis at Lake Geneva, the author emphasizing that among the tales invented there "Mrs. Shelley's alone remains to be handed down as a work of art" (3). But because this "most harrowing tale that has ever been placed in the field of literature" is said to be unique in "reach[ing] the climax of horror and awful suggestion," the supposedly more refined sensibilities of

---

29 On the rise of "facial expression," changes in acting, and the new camera techniques demanded, see Bowser, Chapter 6 (87-102). As we shall see in Chapter 7, the role of facial expression is a continuing site of Frankenstein films' problematization of film-viewer relations in James Whale's *Frankenstein* and *Bride of Frankenstein*.

30 In Miriam Hansen's words: "In many [early] films the view or plot provides an occasion for demonstrating specifically cinematic techniques and possibilities: the camera's ability to traverse and mobilize space (as in the panoramas and phantom rides); its suspension of spatio-temporal laws (fast, slow, and reverse motion, multiple exposure, split screen) and its geographic ubiquity (film as a substitute for mass tourism); its manipulation of perception through magical transformations (stop-motion photography and substitution splices) and its play with scale and proportions (miniatures and matte shots) [...]" (33).

an audience attracted by a genuine "work of art" demanded that special care be taken in the story's filmic adaptation. Thus, we are told: "In making the film the Edison Company has carefully tried to eliminate all the actually repulsive situations and to concentrate its endeavors upon the mystic and psychological problems that are to be found in this weird tale. Wherever, therefore, the film differs from the original story it is purely with the idea of eliminating what would be repulsive to a moving picture audience" (3). In practice, this meant the elimination of Frankenstein's cutting and sewing of corpses and the re-envisioning of the monster's creation by an act of magic, thus deflecting the threat of censorship and making the film acceptable to decent citizens of the respectable classes.[31]

Beyond the promise of attracting a higher-class clientele to the movies, as I noted above, the other side of the industry's double justification for the turn to cultural masterpieces as film subjects lay in the socially progressive enterprise of reforming the audiences of the still thriving storefront houses. With this educational purpose in mind, the *Moving Picture World* praised *Frankenstein* thus: "The entire film is one that will create a new impression of the possibilities of the motion picture as a means of expressing dramatic scenes. Sometimes the value of the motion picture in reproducing these stories is scarcely realized, yet they will do much for literature in this direction. Very many, for example, will see this picture who have never read the story, and will acquire a lasting impression of its power" (2 Apr 1910, 508). But while the industry was concerned to reform the cinema's image with such ploys, the audiences who were allegedly the intended benefactors often displayed little enthusiasm at the prospect of being educated, reformed, or uplifted by the picture show. As late as 1912, an exhibitor writing in the *Moving Picture World* complained: "Fact of the matter is, folks in this town don't care for the big educationals and classics. They want short snappy stuff, a live Essanay or Edison comedy, a spirited Kalem railroad or adventure film, but let me advertise a religious piece or Shakespeare and it means an off day in the box office" (9 Nov 1912, 643; qtd. in Bowser 133). But besides being a "work of art," *Frankenstein* was also a highly popular subject; it had been adapted to the stage numerous times, not only for the legitimate theater but also as sensational melodrama and burlesque.[32] The story must have seemed, therefore, to present an opportunity to close the gap of disparity between

---

31 It is important to note that, even with the approval of the National Board of Censorship, the danger remained that a film might be suppressed by local censors, thus causing financial losses for producers and distributors. And even more importantly for the *Kinetogram*'s readers, local police in many areas continued to close venues and prosecute exhibitors for showing what they deemed to be inappropriate subjects. See Bowser, 48-52.

32 See Forry and Elizabeth Nitchie for histories of *Frankenstein*'s theatrical dramatizations.

the interests of reformers and those in need of reform and to bring into alignment the appeals of high culture and of cheap entertainment.

The film's multiple address is reflected in the *Kinetogram*: "To those who are familiar with Mrs. Shelley's story it will be evident that we have carefully omitted anything which might by any possibility shock any portion of an audience. To those who are not familiar with the story we can only say that the film tells an intensely dramatic story by the aid of some of the most remarkable photographic effects that have yet been attempted" (5). If the Edison Company could not give traditional nickelodeon audiences the graphic visualizations of gore they might have hoped for, they could at least deliver a fascinating show of cinematic magic. With the necessary pretense of bringing culture to the slums, the film could in fact cater to the tastes of the cultured elite and the illiterate poor alike.[33] That is, it could reinforce the "better" audiences' beliefs in their own superiority and cultural refinement without enforcing among the lower classes a feeling of inferiority—a feat achieved by establishing an interchangeable hierarchy, contingent upon audience and exhibition context, of narrative over non-narrative appeal or vice versa. In other words, though we may detect a condescending view of the unreformed nickelodeon audiences in the Edison propaganda for *Frankenstein*, the film gave to each type of audience (at least the illusion of) that which they presumably sought: on the one hand, by embedding its trick effects in a culturally important narrative, it allowed cultured audiences to indulge in a little primitive excess without feeling bad about it; on the other hand, the prominence with which the effects are presented in the story frame offered other audiences scopophilic pleasure with only minimal (if any) didactic aftertaste. *Frankenstein* thus appears to be an effort on the part of the Edison Company to eat its cake and have it too.

Double Standards

The pleasures of this cake could only be sanctioned, of course, by way of a demonstrable moral message, which the *Kinetogram* purports to make explicit: "the story of the film brings out the fact that the creation of the monster was only possible because Frankenstein had allowed his normal mind to be overcome by evil and unnatural thoughts" (4). Thus, "when Frankenstein's love for his bride shall have

---

33 The dichotomy between "those who are familiar with the story" and "those who are not familiar with the story" or, in the words of the *Moving Picture World* reviewer, "those who have never read the story" and "those who have" (Apr 2, 508) seems to euphemistically code precisely the more expansive difference between the literate and the illiterate, a difference which, in 1910, was drawn largely along lines of class and ethnicity.

attained full strength and freedom from impurity it will have such an effect upon his mind that the monster cannot exist" (4-5). According to the article's author:

This theory is clearly demonstrated in the [...] closing scene, which has probably never been surpassed in anything shown on the moving picture screen. The monster, broken down by his unsuccessful attempts to be with his creator, enters the room, stands before a large mirror and holds out his arms entreatingly. Gradually the real monster fades away, leaving only the image in the mirror. A moment later Frankenstein himself enters. As he stands directly before the mirror we are amazed to see the image of the monster reflected instead of Frankenstein's own. Gradually, however, under the effect of love and his better nature, the monster's image fades and Frankenstein sees himself in his young manhood in the mirror. His bride joins him, and the film ends with their embrace, Frankenstein's mind now being relieved of the awful horror and weight it has been laboring under for so long. (5)

The film's ultimate message, then, is simple enough: provided it is "normal," "natural," and "pure," love conquers all. But beneath the surface, the scene that allegedly demonstrates this point also registers transitional cinema's essential tensions and provides a different, specifically cinematic moral of sorts that is germane to the era's uncertain reorientation of film-viewer relations.

First it is important to note the recurrence here of the same superlative rhetoric used to describe the creation scene. The "never-surpassed" quality of the climactic scene and its ability to "amaze" us compete in the *Kinetogram*'s commentary with the narrative and moral significance of the mirror-play, underlining the alternative possibilities for reception held open to viewers. Trick effects are again responsible for the mirror scene's execution—rather than presenting alternating views of Frankenstein and the monster's reflection in the mirror, in-camera masking techniques allow the viewer to perceive the entire spectacle within the single frame of a long-shot tableau. Here the hierarchical interchangeability I have claimed for the film as a whole—the variable emphasis and subordination of narrative or non-narrative appeals—is apparent as nowhere else, begging the question: Do the effects support the story's resolution, or does the story's conclusion serve merely to frame the effects? On a narrative level, mirroring establishes visually the *Doppelgänger* relation between Frankenstein and the monster, thus making plausible the *Kinetogram*'s reading of the film's central problem: i.e. the root connection between the evil of an isolated mind and the monster of conscience that haunts it. Upon this basis, the trick effect makes way for the film's overt moral and enables narrative closure by establishing an openness to love (and, by extension, marriage and natural means of reproduction) as the cure for the horrors of self-centered seclusion. On the other hand, the scene provides a final dose of cinematographic spectacle to those viewers who may have lost interest since the fantastic displays of the creation scene, thus lending the film an alternative, non-narrative type of closure.

The double appeal of the special effects, functioning either as presentational objects or representational means, marks an uncertainty about what the film is supposed to be—sideshow sensation or serious drama. This indeterminacy is related, moreover, to a more general uncertainty in the transitional period regarding the nature and appeal of film itself. I noted earlier that the creation sequence can be read as a self-troping figuration of film's own life-giving powers, a claim that will seem less far-fetched when we recall that "in the period from 1895 to around 1907, and even later, the term 'animated' often referred generically to *all* films that were shown, and terms such as 'animated photography' were commonplace when referring to films in general" (Ward par. 3). When, today, we employ the term "animation" to refer to cartoons and other forms characterized by their frame-by-frame production processes and by their opposition to live-action film, we invoke a narrowed definition that is itself a product of the transitional period. According to Kristin Thompson,

As late as 1912, Frederick A. Talbot makes cartoons a mere subset of his lengthy section on "trick films" in *Moving Pictures; How They Are Made and Worked*. Animation [in a narrow sense], then, constituted a minor aspect of special effects; quite possibly the majority of audience members at this time had never seen a cartoon. By 1920, however, E. G. Lutz is able to write a whole book on animation and entitle it *Animated Cartoons*. At some point in the intervening eight years, animation had become recognised as a distinct type of filmmaking ("Implications of the Cel Animation Technique" 106-107)

This differentiation thus involved first lumping together (what we now recognize as) narrow-sense animation and the types of trick techniques utilized in *Frankenstein*, and then subordinating both to the dramatic feature; as the term animation became dissociated from film in general, animation took on a supporting role, cartoons—with their formally "disruptive properties" (Thompson 108)—accentuating the more important feature-film attractions on the film bill.[34] The features, in turn, increasingly demanded narrative justification for their special effects.

Even more subtle shifts in terminology bear witness to the transitional demand for narrative coherence and closure at stake in *Frankenstein*'s effects. In 1910, for example, Frank Woods advocated the replacement of the term "moving pictures"

---

34 See Paul Ward, "Defining 'Animation': The Animated Film and the Emergence of the Film Bill," for a discussion of animation's redefinition in relation to changes in production, distribution, and exhibition practices in the transitional era.

(with its kinetic emphasis shared by the notion of film-as-animation) by "motion pictures" (which, though not implying stasis, emphasized the stability of the "picture" as a rounded whole), arguing that the latter term was better suited for higher-quality films and a period of cinematic uplift generally (Bowser 136). Similarly, the term "movies," though popular, was considered by many an obstacle to film entertainment's respectability; writing to their local newspaper in 1913, Hay and Nicholas of the Haynic Theater in Fairmount, Minnesota, inveigh: "It is unpardonable slang, emanating from the gutter, and its use is deplored by everyone who wishes to see the photoplay occupy the dignified position which it deserves" (qtd. in Bowser 136). In each of these cases, the semantic dispute turns on the effort to redefine film as a legitimate form of entertainment, the preferred terms being those that shifted the emphasis from film as a technologically marvelous *process* of animation to a more dignified perception of coherent *products*.

Since, therefore, the creation sequence identifies the monster with primitive film-as-animation, the seductions of which Frankenstein triumphs over in the final scene, the film's narrative development is tied to a larger, non-diegetic story of filmic development: Frankenstein's psychological maturation, as consummated in the mirror scene, allegorizes a historico-normative process of cinematic maturation and spectatorial progress. In the creation sequence, as I have argued, Frankenstein functioned as a Peeping Tom figure, lustfully spying on a perversely monstrous primal scene; he stood outside the spectacle and regarded it with fascination, channeling scopophilic desire and standing in for a primitive viewer likewise expected to regard the scene at a quasi-objective distance. As Miriam Hansen states, "Peeping Toms must be read as figurations of early film-viewer relations" (40)—of hermeneutic relations that placed cinematic technologies and processes on the objective side of the noetic arrow of perception. Such relations operate in the absence of a strong segregation of theater and screen space, under conditions such as those fostered by the variety format of the primitive venue. The fact that Frankenstein's act of viewing not only takes as its object the filmic process of animation but also discovers it to be a monster thus invokes the cinema's illegitimate origins—the "monstrosities" of the freak shows or "fake shows" which, according to one exchange manager, explained the "disfavor" with which the movie business in general was looked upon for years to come.[35] Furthermore, the object thus configured

---

35 Albert J. Gillingham, who testified on behalf of the Motion Picture Patents Company in 1913, stated that when he got into the movie business around 1906 or 1907, "[i]t was looked on with disfavor, as all store shows previously had been shows of an undesirable character. Mostly fake shows. Shows that were showing monstrosities, or had displays outside with a hand organ or a sick monkey. Something of that order" (*US* v. *MPPC* 4:2214 [December 1913]; qtd. in Bowser 37).

reminds us of the risk involved in addressing the screen in a hermeneutic, quasi-objective manner: namely, that the object may turn on the subject and return our gaze—as the direct address of the camera demonstrated playfully in *Kiss* (Edison, 1900), more shockingly in *The Great Train Robbery*, or embarrassingly when voyeurs were discovered spying through keyholes. If the discovery of the Peeping Tom was an occasion for laughter, the humor was often of a rather uncomfortable sort; for the moral reprobation of the perpetrator extended to the primitive viewer who shared his perspective and became an accomplice to his voyeuristic deeds and desires.

Frankenstein's obvious "camera consciousness" (as established in his magic act and carried forth in his gestured reactions to the scene of creation) encourages us to view the spectacle in a hermeneutic mode, but it also, as his reactions change from lascivious pleasure to dread, heightens our perception of the mode's inherent dangers. Devoid of slapstick humor, the discovery of Frankenstein—and of the viewer—by a monster underlines the immorality of visual pleasure unredeemed by a higher purpose. Thus, when Frankenstein later confronts his demon in the mirror, he struggles not only with his own sinful past but with a tradition of viewing that extends from the prurient, pornographic excitement of mutoscope and kinetoscope parlors to the unreformed nickelodeon's amoral appeals of animation for its own sake. Once again Frankenstein doubles for the viewer, but now, as Hansen says of a Peeping Tom picture from 1904, he "points beyond the sheer accumulation of sadistic and voyeuristic pleasures to a later conception of spectatorship as medium of moral truth and social uplift" (41). As a proto-classical spectator, Frankenstein must overcome his hysterical and juvenile fascination with the spectacle of animation, must become "mature and balanced, which means respecting the boundaries between illusion and reality along with the segregation of screen and theater spaces that regulates them" (Hansen 57). The mirror, then, doubles for the projection screen; the monster's image reflects not merely the evil in the creator's mind but also a naïve viewer fixated on the visible surface of the screen. When this image fades and gives way to Frankenstein's own, Frankenstein has successfully "yok[ed] vision and truth," enacted "a moral inscription of the gaze" (Hansen 41) by learning to look through, and not merely at, the reflective surface; like any sane adult wishing to inspect their outward appearance, he learns to embody the mirror as a transparent, truthful medium. In this manner, Frankenstein himself finally gets into the picture, obliterating the distance he maintained earlier between himself and the hermeneutic spectacle and inviting the viewer to do the same. He thus points the way to a respectable mode of spectatorship based on embodiment relations that subordinate the screen and other apparatuses of filmic animation to absorption in the diegetic world.

Frankenstein's rewards for making the transition to spectatorial normativity include his reintegration into the bourgeois world from which he hails and the prize of the girl who has been waiting for him there. Contrasted with the inhuman monster, Frankenstein's humanity is thus defined not only by his openness to intersubjective relations and a mature acceptance of responsibility in the ethical realm, but also as a function of his class identity and masculinity. His triumph over the unnatural creature marks, therefore, not only a refusal of the temptations of early-film viewing practices but also an exorcism of some of the more stubborn obstacles to uplift and reformation: the social and bodily differences of individual viewers. The price of admission to the classical-film pleasures of diegesis, as we have seen, includes a partial suppression of the viewer's concrete body, an act of abstraction from the theater surroundings that allows the spectator to relate to the story as an unseen observer. If Frankenstein has renounced his primitive Peeping-Tom voyeurism, he has opened the door—though again not as wide as some of the Biograph films of the day—for the classical spectator-as-voyeur who, because of the phenomenal split between theater and screen space, is structurally immune to discovery.[36] From this vantage point, the spectator is less vulnerable to the potential threats of filmic images, and the spectatorial subject's assimilation into a generalized humanity heightens the sense of security. However, as the example of Frankenstein reveals, the apparent democratization of cinematic spectatorship masks a bias for certain class and gender identifications (among others) and a concomitant monstrification of deviant forms of otherness. The classical spectator-diegesis relations that Frankenstein seems to anticipate here for the viewer work towards the establishment of an anonymous—sexless, classless, and ultimately body-less—spectating position, but like the equally abstract "human" of liberal humanism, the possibility remains that this ideal subject is structurally white, middle-class, and masculinized.[37]

---

36 See Miriam Hansen's critical discussion of Christian Metz's take on cinematic voyeurism, which she de-ontologizes and relates to classical cinema, distinguishing it from early-film modes of viewing (35-36). Interestingly, in his article "Bits and Pieces," Gary Rhodes compares Frankenstein to the (unseen) voyeur when he writes: "In the sequence, as Frankenstein peers through an opening in the bolted door to see the creature's formation, an almost voyeuristic sensation appears on his face as he watches the creation of life, no different figuratively than witnessing human copulation."

37 See Linda Mulvey's classic text, "Visual Pleasure and Narrative Cinema." I concur with Steven Shaviro, however, who claims that Mulvey's position is unsupported by many popular genre films in the classical mode, and that even where gazes are structured as Mulvey suggests, there are significant "lines of flight" that can be followed out of that pattern. See Shaviro, *The Cinematic Body*, 12-13.

In 1910, however, things had not yet progressed this far. To a large degree, the battle over viewers' bodies was still concentrated at this time on the coarser realities of embodied being: for example, the threats posed to the olfactory senses by smelly, sweaty bodies in close quarters, which theater owners fought by means of ventilation systems and perfumed deodorizing sprays.[38] Besides, the classical narrative system and its methods of spectatorial integration through camera and editing techniques were still far from being perfected. The variable camera distances that would later be so effective in creating continuity and spatial orientation, for example, were still highly controversial, even if the closer views then in question consisted merely in placing the camera at a nine-foot distance from its subject rather than the traditional twelve.[39] Although taking a closer view could mitigate the demand for exaggerated acting, the relatively larger human figures on the screen still seemed, according to one conservative critic, "monstrous to the eye" (*Moving Picture World*, 24 July 1909, 116; qtd. in Bowser 97). Significantly, Edison's *Frankenstein* reserves the so-called "bust shot" (medium length) for the creator-as-primitive-viewer's perspective on the literal monster's creation. In the effort to reform not only Frankenstein's but also the spectator's viewing practices, to integrate and implicate the viewer in the story's moralistic ending, classical-style point-of-view would certainly have drawn a greater contrast with the primitive subjective shots of the Peeping Tom and effected a more radical "moral inscription of the

---

38 "In September 1910 a *World* reporter visiting the Comet at Third Avenue near Twelfth Street in New York's Lower East Side tenement district approved the lighting conditions there. [....] He also approved the ventilating system and reported that an usher wandered the aisles spraying a sweet-smelling liquid. (Advertisements for these deodorizing sprays can be found in the pages of the trade periodicals.)" (Bowser 39).

39 The nine-foot distance that began to emerge around 1909 was referred to as "American foreground" and contrasted with the "French foreground" (corresponding to the older 12 ft. distance), which remained dominant in Europe far longer than in the US (Bowser 94). Moreover, these alternatives were correlated, respectively, with the new "facial-expression" school of filmic and theater acting and the older, exaggerated styles of pantomimic and melodramatic gesture, which, significantly, were known as "the Saxon (restrained/facial) as opposed to the Latin (whole body/exaggerated)" styles (Bowser 88). Even here we find a normative correlation of technical progress, bodily expression, and social hierarchy. As Eileen Bowser writes: "This positioning of Saxon versus Latin gives another clue to the reasons for the changes in style in the course of the Progressive uplift movement. Controlled emotions are approved behavior in Victorian society, the 'excess' of the foreign-born immigrants from Latin countries and the films coming from such countries are to be feared, or at least found ridiculous. Naturalness is equated with restraint" (88).

gaze" (Hansen 41). But, apart from the incompleteness in 1910 of the system in which such methods attained their classical function, this would also have prevented the final display of "smoke and mirrors" magic, the possibility of which depended on the static framing of the tableau shot. Whether a conscious decision on the part of director Dawley or merely the application of early-transitional filmmaking conventions, the result is the same: because the film persists, even at its conclusion, in employing trick effects in a manner that simultaneously presents them as visual spectacle while using them to represent key narrative events, the film's story of spectatorial maturation remains inconclusive, the conflicts between hermeneutic and embodiment relations or primitive and classical forms of voyeurism unsettled.

In sum, as a truly "transitional" film—as determined by its liminality rather than an inclining trajectory towards the classical *telos*—Edison's *Frankenstein* hovers between primitive and proto-classical modes of address and conceptions of film, between alternatives that are at once articulated in terms of viewers' relations to cinematic technologies but that also implicate the class, gender, and ethnic profiles of those viewers. Indeed, whether we focus on the multivocal nature of the film's address, as displayed in its attempt to speak to different audiences with narrative and non-narrative attractions, or more narrowly on the narrative development itself as a story of transit and progress, Edison's *Frankenstein* persistently draws our attention to the intersection and inseparability of techno-phenomenological and social relations, of material-anthropotechnical and socio-semiotic negotiations of monstrosity.

SEEING DOUBLE: MATERIAL AND DISCURSIVE MONSTERS IN THE TRANSITION AND BEYOND

Before moving on, I feel it necessary to clarify the theoretical role and heuristic value I perceive for the transitional era in my project as a whole. In the previous chapter, my initial endeavors to adapt Don Ihde's phenomenological analysis of technology to the medium of film led from the paradigmatic differences between early and classical film to the question of the transition and, specifically, to the historical and structural complications it implies for what might otherwise be an essentially binary model of spectatorial engagements with cinematic technology—an either/or model of hermeneutic versus embodiment relations. Next, in applying the techno-phenomenological perspective more narrowly to Frankenstein films and their self-reflexive potential, I repeated the movement from primitive (*Dog Factory*) to classical (Whale's *Frankenstein*) and again came to rest in the middle with this chapter's analysis of Edison's *Frankenstein*. Having thus circled around and made two passes at transitional cinema, the era has come to occupy a literally central position in my methodology, and I have indicated more generally that the transition's role in a history of Frankenstein films and their reception is one that transcends that period's place in any empirical chronology.

Accordingly, despite its lack of demonstrable influence on later Frankenstein films, my interest in Edison's *Frankenstein* is not just motivated by the completism typical of the collector/fan, nor should the foregoing analysis be understood as an attempt to recuperate an underappreciated "precursor." Instead, what I am suggesting is that in its connection to the larger dynamics of its era (including changes at the institutional level and in the competing discourses on film), the film does more than just offer another demonstration of the self-reflexive analogy between thematic content and media-technological means of presentation at the heart of Frankenstein films—an analogy not insignificantly correlated in this case with transitional cinema's central tension between narrative development and technologically based spectacle; moreover, and this is crucial, Edison's *Frankenstein* expands the scope of the basic analogy, adding to it a dimension of social liminality that connects particular viewers in certain circumstances (and in highly variable ways) to the representations and discourses of marginality, hybridity, and monstrosity projected on the screen. In this way, the film demands that we cultivate a double vision that mirrors the transitional period's own duality of address, its conflicted emphases, trajectories, and simultaneities; it asks us to contextualize filmic texts and acts of reception in two distinct yet intimately correlated registers: according both to aspects of materiality (e.g. the relations of bodies, technologies, and the physical settings of reception) and discourse (including not only the films' own textualities and the critical commentaries that accompany them, but also issues of class, race, and gender as performed both on and off the screen).[40]

Expanding the scope of the discursive register in particular not only reveals further correspondences between thematic contents and the phenomenal "form" of reception (i.e. correspondences between narrative/visual representations of monstrosity and viewers defined by their real or potential deviation from social norms), but also requires us to embed these correspondences in a thick context of mutually determining social and material relations. As we have seen, variations in the implementation of mediating technologies can have important consequences for the

---

40 Mark Hansen invokes a similar methodological "double vision" in his *Embodying Technesis: Technology beyond Writing* (26) to account for the impact of technology on human experience, both in a cultural realm of discourse and in a sub-personal realm of embodied materiality. In the course of the present project I follow Hansen's lead and, in Part Two, generalize "double vision" from a discourse/materiality duality to a much broader focus on phenomenal/aphenomenal and ultimately human/nonhuman negotiations and interactions.

perception of mediated objects; the material means and situation of perception determine, in part, the nature of what we see and the meanings we attach to perceptual phenomena. But because technologies and media are also the objects of discursive signification, the positions they come to occupy in phenomenal relations are not determined solely on the basis of their physical properties but are subject always to prior discursive influences. Moreover, as the example of Edison's *Frankenstein* reveals, the social position of perceivers/viewers can be a determining factor in the form that the embodied reception of images takes—the alternatives of primitive spectacle and proto-classical absorption, which I have theorized as alternative modes of material interaction between bodies and technologies, are aligned in the transitional era with questions of class and other normative determinations of discursive subjectivity. Put abstractly, this is to say that bodies, technologies, and materiality generally are inseparable from the significations, discourses, and ideologies that accompany them. Just as the design, production, and deployment of technologies depend in part on the social meanings, hopes, and fears we associate with them, so too do the social hierarchies and normative overlays inscribed on our bodies influence the material comportment of our bodies in interactions with other humans and with machines.

By holding out to various audiences alternative possibilities for reception—possibilities that are irreconcilable in terms not only of interpreted meanings but also the material relations to technologies required for their respective actualizations—Edison's *Frankenstein* points to the fallaciousness of a reductive technological determinism and challenges views that posit a latent ideology of normative subjectivity inherent in the basic apparatus of cinema. While the paradigmatic difference of the cinema of attractions has often been marshaled against the Lacan/Althusser-inspired apparatus theory made popular in the 1970s—as a refutation, that is, of the sweeping claim that cinematic techniques and technologies invariably tend towards the construction of a masterful spectating position and thus perpetuate Western culture's dominant ideology of the subject[41]—the transitional era's maintenance of multiple, conflicting patterns of subjective relations to the basic apparatus offers the basis for a more radical critique: for here the paradigmatic alternatives are not separated from one another by a historical caesura but coeval with one another and, as in Edison's *Frankenstein*, often present as parallel openings in one and the same film. The determination of which bodies relate to cinematic technologies in a "neo-primitive" and which in a "proto-classical" mode (and,

---

41 The new interest in early cinema came on the heels of apparatus theory and naturally understood itself as, in part, a corrective to the dominant ahistoricism of film studies at the time and a testing ground for then-popular theories and approaches. See Tom Gunning, "Early American Film" (29-32).

furthermore, which ones hover in the indeterminacy of a "transitional" limbo) is thus highly dependent on extra-technological factors: on the social networks of signification that are superimposed upon and internalized in those bodies and technologies.

It does not follow, however, that we must subsume materiality entirely under the system of discourse; bodies and technologies, I maintain, are not wholly constructed but exceed subjective and discursive determinations of their being—which is precisely the basis of their monstrous potential. Because the conflicting meanings inherent in a film like Edison's *Frankenstein* are not served up in ready-made packages and distributed to audience members on the basis of their class or gender as separate, coherent "readings" appropriate to their social standing, but are instead co-present and available in volatile mixtures to individual viewing subjects—especially so, I contend, to subjects defined by their own liminality with regard to dominant social norms—these textual contradictions are capable of exploding the coherence of subjective identity as the locus of experience, expelling viewers from the discursive realm altogether, and thus eliciting an embodied experience of radically material excess. To account for this potential of transitional-era simultaneity and contradiction, the double vision I am calling for must resist the reductive tendencies both of technological determinism and of radical constructivism as well. The multiple phenomenological possibilities of the transitional period urge us to view the relation between materiality and discourse as one of bidirectional interdependence, where experience is conditioned by both "poles" of existence at once. Indeed, the bundle of contests that characterizes the transitional era—technological novelty and spectacle versus narrative integration, hermeneutic versus embodiment relations, freak-show attractions versus institutional respectability, working-class audiences versus middle-class spectators, raucous involvement versus bodily restraint—cuts right across the materiality/discourse divide, making it impossible either to view material configurations in a discursive vacuum or to divorce discursive phenomena from their material substrata. Only by respecting the inseparability *and* distinctness of the two realms, as exposed most poignantly by the uniquely overdetermined dynamics of the transitional era, will we be able to fully appreciate what is at stake in the reception of Frankenstein films generally and, on an even broader level, to theorize the postnatural historicity of the anthropotechnical interface.

Transitional Heterotopias

My argument with regard to the relevance of the transitional phase rests on the premise that it was not *just* a "transition"—that is, a linear passage from one fixed terminus to another—but a historical space resistant to cooptation by the spaces or paradigms surrounding it. The view of the transitional era I have been arguing for in my analysis of Edison's *Frankenstein* is thus apposite with the picture offered by Tom Gunning, who sees in it "less a gradual fade into the classical paradigm than a period of ambivalence and contestation" ("Early American Film" 40)—a period from whose vantage the paradigmatic characteristics of early and (proto)classical film "represent less two different diachronic periods than different synchronic approaches, often present within the same film" ("I film Vitagraph" 231-32; qtd. in Keil 10). As such, the period presents a challenge to utopian and nostalgic historiographies alike, to the complementary linearizations that see either progress towards the classical *telos* or an alienating decline from the arcadian organicism and conviviality of a paradise lost. If the paradigms of early and classical film are (at least as ideal constructs) irreconcilably opposed to one another, the overlapping simultaneity of their elements in the transition (evident in the dual address of distinct audiences, in the active competition between narrative development and trick-film display, and in the unsettled vacillation between hermeneutic and embodiment relations) reveals the cinema of the historically intermediate era as a space of irreducible contradiction: in Foucault's term, a "heterotopia"—an "other space" capable of combining within itself a variety of incompatible "sites" or experiential configurations.[42] For Foucault, heterotopias are both physically real places—he cites cemeteries, prisons, boats, and gardens, among others—and conceptual spaces that, like Borges's famous taxonomy discussed at the opening of *The Order of Things*, exhibit a "quality of monstrosity" (xvi) because they lack the coherence of a "common locus" for their inexplicable juxtapositions (xviii). Combining the materially concrete with the discursively monstrous, the concept of heterotopia thus seems to fit the requirements of the proposed methodological double vision; specifically, it promises to elucidate the multi-layered and contradictory realities specific to transitional cinema and, moreover, to provide a theoretical basis for extrapolating from there to other moments of historical uncertainty and monstrous overdetermination.

Whereas Foucault, in the passage that provides the epigraph for this chapter, applies the term heterotopia to the cinema generally (on the basis of the two-dimensional screen's function as a sort of membrane between the incompatible three-dimensional spaces of the theater and the diegetic world), Miriam Hansen—to whom my approach in this regard owes a great deal—historicizes the concept in order to theorize the transitional period's specific differences from the relative paradigmatic coherence of both early and classical cinema.[43] In effect, Hansen takes

---

42 See Foucault, "Of Other Spaces," from which the epigraph of this chapter is taken (233, 234).
43 See Miriam Hansen, chapter 3.

literally Foucault's idea that heterotopias are tied to specific "slices in time," to ruptures in history and the concomitant reorganizations of individual and collective experiences of temporality. In keeping with her skepticism vis-à-vis the ahistoricism of apparatus theory, Hansen bases her refunctionalized conception of heterotopian cinema not, like Foucault, on the general spatial relations instantiated in the movie theater (relations that, like the basic apparatus of camera, projector, and darkened space, remain largely static over the course of cinematic history[44]) but

---

44 Thus, Hansen writes that the "spatial configuration [described by Foucault] is as old as the magic lantern show and more or less typical of the cinema throughout its history" (107). In fact, however, the phenomenal dimensionalities of screen and theater spaces are not static, as Hansen herself implicitly demonstrates in outlining the paradigmatic otherness of early from classical modes of film-viewer relations. In effect, what Hansen shows is that the emergence of a three-dimensional space on the screen is not a cinematic given but instead tied to the classical paradigm's construction and placement of the spectator, through standardized exhibition practices and continuity techniques, in a spatially elaborated diegetic space. The relatively external position of the viewer in early film, on the other hand, encourages the apprehension of a flatter surface upon which two-dimensional images are projected inside and as a part of the dimensionally richer space of the theater. This is to say that the heterotopian instability of conflicting three-dimensional spaces is, phenomenologically speaking, most pronounced in the transitional era. In contrast to early cinema, which tends to highlight the space of exhibition, and classical film, which sacrifices that realm for the depth of the screen, the true *confrontation* of three-dimensional spaces, upon which Foucault bases his claim that cinema functions as a heterotopia, is most at home in the contests of the transitional period. The surprising fact that Hansen, in her attempts to historicize Foucault's concept, does not argue explicitly along these lines—and it is surprising because the argument, in its entirety, is implicit in what she writes elsewhere in her book—does nothing, however, to damage her general point. If anything, making the argument explicit only reinforces the usefulness of Foucault's term by strengthening its connection to the historical transition. Additionally, it provides a stronger critique of apparatus theory and helps explain the deeper error involved in overlooking the important phenomenological differences between early, transitional, and classical film. For while the single lens of the film camera inherently constructs images in accordance with the principles of Renaissance perspective, the phenomenological actualization of perspectival depth, which is necessary for the ideological inscription of a masterful spectatorial subject in cinematic space, is contingent upon factors that include but are not limited to the physical properties of the apparatus. Fleshed out in terms of the transitional era's phenomenological instabilities, the historically localized concept of heterotopia suggests that apparatus theory is guilty of reducing technological materiality to mere physicality and disregarding not only important social aspects but also the richer

instead focuses on "the fissures, overlaps, and interstices of nonlinear historical processes" (12), concentrating on the "nonsynchronism" and "uneven development" of the cinema between 1907 and 1917 (93). Of particular interest is the continuation of early cinema's presentational exhibition practices and corresponding reception patterns in transitional-era nickelodeons: the persistence of variety-format programming, participatory involvement, and social interaction in neighborhood theaters well after the standardization of filmic products and screenings (along with the emergence of upscale venues and the construction of the classical spectator) had gotten underway. Techno-phenomenological relations thus play a major role in Hansen's argument,[45] but their ultimate significance for her lies in the consequences they have for social-discursive configurations: in the transitional cinema's potential, due to its "margin of participation and unpredictability" (43), to function as an "alternative public sphere" for marginalized groups such as ethnic immigrants and women—for people traditionally excluded from active participation in public life.

On the one hand, the nickelodeons offered these audiences a space apart from the male-dominated bourgeois public sphere and its high-culture entertainments. The cinema thus imperiled traditional configurations of public and private and threatened to upset the power relations that legitimated certain voices and silenced others by refusing them a forum for dialogue; according to Hansen, censorship measures and the rhetoric of uplift bear witness to precisely this threat to the normative status quo.[46] However, the cinema was just one among many manifestations of broader socio-cultural developments that had been straining the public/private demarcation since the nineteenth century. Indeed, an impulse towards indiscriminant (if not universally uncontested) inclusiveness characterized many popular or "lowbrow" entertainments and the rising consumer culture generally, but this alone did not inherently empower their constituencies. For whereas the bourgeois public sphere that had emerged in the eighteenth century systematically excluded women, ethnic minorities, and the lower classes, the "industrial-commercial public sphere" (as Oskar Negt and Alexander Kluge term it) accommodated these outcasts only at the price of their appropriation, assimilation, and exploitation as undifferentiated consumers of commodities.[47] Far from offering a genuine alternative to the exclusionary system, this type of public sphere did not so much respond to the needs and experience of non-normative subjects as it aimed to *structure* them.

---

material dimension in which technologies enter into highly variable relations with human bodies and their environments.

45 And, as I have suggested in the previous footnote, her argument could be strengthened by making the role of these relations more explicit.
46 Similarly, see Annette Kuhn's *Cinema, Censorship and Sexuality, 1909-1925*.
47 On Negt and Kluge's role in Hansen's book, see the introduction to *Babel and Babylon*.

But by eroding the split between the realm of culture and that of the marketplace upon which the bourgeois model staked its claims to legitimacy, the newer—and decidedly modern—sort of public sphere that emerged with phonograph parlors, amusement parks, and department stores brought with it not only a physical infrastructure of meeting places for people from all walks of life and social standing but also a discursive realm that, unlike the opera or the legitimate theater, did not base its right to existence on the ability to address the supposedly "timeless" interests and concerns of a generalized humanity; instead, this realm was both materially closer and conceptually more open to the transitory pleasures and experiences of everyday life, including those of the factory worker, the tenement dweller, and the female shopper. Though the forces of commodity capitalism worked towards the production and reproduction of engineered desires, these same forces also harbored opportunities for alternative or "oppositional" appropriations, spaces for unintended freedoms and unforeseen resistances.[48] If the bourgeois system was marked by its enabling acts of exclusion, at least it implicitly recognized the differences of particular social groups from the generalized humanity it constructed. If, on the other hand, the industrial-commercial sphere damaged that normative construct, it was little better in serving the needs of marginal groups, for it tended to obliterate their differences altogether in fashioning them as consumers. Where, however, the structures of the respective models intersected, where their jostling with one another was enacted in real-world spaces marked by ambiguity and polysemic indeterminacy, here there was room for specific groups both to experience new freedoms of movement and congregation and to recognize their own characteristic differences (as well as commonalities with other marginal groups)—hence fulfilling double conditions for the articulation, on the basis of these groups' own material and social "contexts of living," of a shared experiential framework.[49]

Thus, according to Hansen, the transitional-era nickelodeon, as a site of struggle between bourgeois norms of respectability and the indiscriminant inclusiveness of mass entertainment, was capable of accommodating "autonomous formations" that emerged, more or less accidentally, "in the seams and fissures of institutional development" (93). For ethnic immigrants—themselves situated on the threshold between old-world realities and new—"the cinema seems to have assumed a certain threshold function, oscillating between the tradition of family-centered ethnic entertainment and the more anonymous, more modern forms of commercialized leisure" (104-05). A certain radical potential resulted from this ambiguous position:

---

48 Hansen's argument, upon which I draw here, expands on what Negt and Kluge called a "proletarian" or "oppositional public sphere" that arose in modernity.

49 "Context of living" translates Negt and Kluge's term *Lebenszusammenhang*.

Neither a primeval paradise of viewer participation nor merely a site for the consumption of standardized products, the cinema rehearsed new, specifically modern forms of subjectivity and intersubjectivity at the same time that it addressed older needs and more recent experiences of displacement and deprivation. If it assumed both of these functions, it did so not only because of the liminal situation of its audiences and its own threshold function among commercial entertainments but also because of the particular kind of collectivity actualized in the individual viewing experience. (105)

That is, while the cinema participated in immigrants' broader experience of alienation from real and imagined roots—both as a component in the consumerist erosion of traditional cultural identifications and as a site of the technological shocks and perceptual disorientations experienced in the modern city—it also held out a space for the collective negotiation of those forces and experiences: a place at once within that social and material environment and simultaneously removed from it, a place also for fantasy and temporary escape. Transitional screening practices and the conflicted formal properties of the films themselves contributed to making this a space of heterotopian instability, where social interaction and absorbed detachment were both live possibilities, where traditional identifications and the forces of assimilation co-existed in uneasy dialogue, and where borderline collectives and individuals could re-imagine their pasts and negotiate their present and future positions in American society.

Cutting across class and ethnic boundaries, the forces of modernization and consumerism also had a profound impact on women, setting their identities and status in relation to the public sphere on a trajectory of uncertain transition, and again the cinema of the transitional era had a significant role to play in charting its course. Victorian discourses of femininity, which delineated the proper role of the woman as a domestic, motherly, submissive, and pure creature whose proper terrain was the private space of the family, were being challenged by the image of the New Woman, by the new economic realities introduced by the woman shopper, and by the openness of commercial entertainments to women as paying customers. According to Kathy Peiss, "women comprised 40 percent of the working-class movie audience in 1910" (*Cheap Amusements* 148; qtd. in Hansen 117), a fact that certainly made the industry take notice of women as an economic force of their own; but this novel notion of a *female audience* also exacerbated struggles for the definition and control of women's identities. On the one hand, the ability to attract women was seen as a sign of middle-class respectability that set certain forms of entertainment, like vaudeville, apart from less dignified homosocial ones such as burlesque, etc. (Hansen 115); on the other hand, the presence of large numbers of women in nickelodeons demonstrated the need to police these "dens of iniquity" and "recruiting stations of vice" (Bowser 38). Whether women were instrumentalized to improve the cultural standing of popular entertainments or seen as in need of "protection" from the seductions of the same, such discourses objectified women and failed to acknowledge any real autonomy on their part. But in this crossfire of images, which found a correlate in the conflicting screen images of idealized femininity, self-assured independence, and fallen womanhood, female audiences could negotiate in the transitional cinema alternative spheres of their own. Somewhere between the isolation of domestic duties and the scrutiny of public gazes, the cinema became for temporary collectives of women a heterotopian "site for the imaginative negotiation of the gaps between family, school, and workplace, between traditional standards of sexual behavior and modern dreams of romance and sexual expression, between freedom and anxiety" (Hansen 118). Thus, "the movie theater opened up an arena in which a new discourse of femininity could be articulated and the norms and codes of sexual conduct could be redefined" (118).

The argument can be extended to other marginalized groups who found themselves in the midst of their own transitions at this time. For example, African Americans—whose passage from slavery to meaningful freedom was long and anything but linear, as demonstrated by the history of nominal emancipation, forced segregation, voluntary separatism, and the tough fight for civil rights—began frequenting and organizing black-only movie theaters in this period. While black audiences had heretofore been segregated in balconies or other sections of theaters, if not simply excluded altogether, separate (but hardly equal) venues had become common by 1910,[50] when the black newspaper *The Washington Bee* wrote: "There are better five-cent theaters conducted by colored Americans than any controlled by the Whites, and why do you insist on going where you are not wanted?" (June 4, 1910, 1; qtd. in Strieble 269). The film industry was certainly not producing films with African American audiences in mind, so the images screened in all-black venues were inevitably geared towards the perspectives and ideologies of a white mainstream; even if they harbored dualities of address, the *tertium quid* of a black audience was left out of the loop. But the very fact that an alternative space for the collective reception of these images existed, an unregulated space where blacks could speak freely without fear of being overheard by whites, must have encouraged an atmosphere in which dominant discourses could be actively discussed and challenged.

Add to this the formal instabilities of transitional films, viewed in quasi-live performance conditions marked by local variation (including music chosen and

---

50 Thus, in 1910 *The Washington Bee* is able to report that "there are separate motion picture theaters among the whites and blacks in this country" (July 9, 1910, 4; qtd. in Strieble 269). As Strieble notes, Gregory Waller has provided evidence of a black-run nickelodeon that opened as early as 1907.

performed by blacks for black patrons), which encouraged a strong awareness of the social and material setting of reception: under such conditions, it is hard to imagine African-American audiences as passively absorbed spectators. And yet, the patterns of reception open to black viewers were not necessarily of a merely "oppositional" nature: for opportunities existed here for blacks, as they did for women and immigrants, to appropriate mainstream images according to their own needs, not only to subvert their intended or interpreted significance, but to invest them with other meanings and to experience through them situations and roles from which blacks were excluded in reality. Moreover, because black venues were independent enterprises not affiliated with larger chains,[51] and because these theaters (not only in the transition but for decades into the classical era) would be the last in line for the distribution of films, receiving mainstream houses' worn-out hand-me-downs and rejects, the timeframe of cinema's transition would be quite different—significantly longer—in the context of black exhibition and reception. While the lag between initial release and exhibition in black theaters extended the *duration* of the transitional period for black audiences, the slow pace of African Americans' journey to acceptance and equality preserved the disparity between viewers' experiential realities and the discourses screened by Hollywood, providing this specifically black cinematic transition with a significantly different *quality* from that experienced by white audiences. Together, these factors ensured the lasting relevance of the black movie theater, through the 1960s at least, as an alternative public sphere for negotiating—with the unlikely help of films that continued to speak primarily to someone else or that had exploitation as their goal—a collective identity vis-à-vis a culture of exclusion.

With its historical anchoring in the transitional period, Hansen's revised notion of cinema-as-heterotopia takes on a concrete significance absent from Foucault's general pronouncement that cinema's spatial arrangements alone render it a heterotopia. In particular, this grounding in the transitional era highlights the contingency of heterotopian formations upon specific alignments of social, cultural, economic, and technical configurations all undergoing simultaneous, though by no means synchronous or coterminal, transformations. But while these simultaneities are historically most pronounced—and their overall scale unparalleled—in the transitional era, local instabilities at other times and places in the history of cinema are usefully analyzed with recourse to the concept of heterotopia. The example of African-

---

51 Strieble, whose focus is on a later period (1920-1973), attests to the lasting consequences of such organization. He writes, "ownership of Black movie houses, in contrast to the first-run, White theaters of the day, was not done by regional or national chains, nor by affiliated circuits; because houses operated independently, the dynamics of local conditions affected theaters [...] as much as national structures did" (269).

American reception, with its alternative timeframe of transition, attests to the relevance and legitimacy of an approach that steers a course between historical particularity and conceptual abstraction. Similarly, Miriam Hansen extends the historical scope of heterotopian cinema to account for the possibility of "alternative formations" among female moviegoers in the classical silent era of the 1920s, allowing for a fruitful "slippage between historical and theoretical considerations" (91). Indeed, this type of slippage characterizes the overall thrust of my own project, which through a historicizing view of Frankenstein films aims to theorize the dynamics of human-technological interaction in connection with the material and social impacts that a technology like film has on our agency and self-understanding as humans. The notion of heterotopia, if purged of ahistorical generality yet accorded a certain critical flexibility, becomes an invaluable tool in this pursuit; it exposes, at a variety of historical junctures, alternative (material as well as discursive) openings for viewers that translate into critical openings for analysis—especially for an investigation of the resonances and overlap of threshold situations such as social liminality, technological revolution, institutional reorganization, and aesthetic transformation.

Heterotopian Transitionality:
From Historical Space to Critical Construct

Looked at under the aspect of its potential accommodation of heterotopian alternativity, Edison's transitional *Frankenstein* thus reveals a number of critical points of entry for approaching later Frankenstein films. As we have seen, the film's dual address not only involves a competition between the respective appeals of narrative and spectacle but aligns these with transitional cinema's uneasy position between bourgeois respectability and commercial entertainment. With references to "Mrs. Shelley's work of art" on the one hand and the techno-spectacle of a "photographic marvel" on the other, publicity materials and critical commentaries placed the film squarely in this crossfire between bourgeois and industrial-commercial public spheres, precisely at the intersection that made transitional cinema such fertile ground for the organization of alternatives diagonal to both. In a sense, *Frankenstein* had perhaps always existed at this intersection, oscillating in the nineteenth century between Gothic pulp and high literature or, on the stage, between silly burlesque and serious drama. And these tensions linger on in film throughout the twentieth century, for example in James Whale's 1935 *Bride of Frankenstein*, which by its very nature as a sequel (one of the horror genre's first) depends less on the legitimating categories of author/work than on popular processes of serialization, repetition, and ritualization, but which nevertheless utilizes a frame story that figures

Mary Shelley herself as the author and narrator of the film's events. Or consider 1994's programmatically titled *Mary Shelley's Frankenstein*, a film that wears a claim to authenticity on its sleeve and aims to set itself apart from decades of conventionalized genre films and B-grade productions. Starring and directed by Kenneth Branagh (a Shakespearean actor acclaimed for his "serious" adaptation of Shakespeare to the popular medium of big-budget movies), the lavish period-piece costume film tries to rectify Hollywood's unfaithfulness to Shelley's spirit, yet it cannot altogether suppress awareness of its "vulgar" filmic forebears and thereby escape relation to them.

As the example of transitional cinema makes clear, however, whether or not openings to alternative public spheres exist amidst these gaps or clashes between high culture and popular media will depend on a number of other factors. Particularly relevant with regard to Frankenstein films will be the cinema's various technological transitions—both as they are registered in filmic texts and as they affect the phenomenal relations that constitute spectatorship. As we have seen, for example, the mute monster of Whale's *Frankenstein* self-reflexively problematizes the shift from silent film to talkies. By the time Hammer began its Frankenstein series with *Curse of Frankenstein* in 1957, an equally important technological revolution had transpired in the cinema with the refinement and diffusion of color processes, allowing for a more vivid depiction of bloody extravagance and setting the new wave of horror films apart from Universal's "classics" then entering syndication on American television. The transition itself from black-and-white to color is dramatized by American International's two Frankenstein features, *I Was a Teenage Frankenstein* (1957) and *How to Make a Monster* (1958), each of which shifts to color stock just in time for the explosive finale. Along with color, cinema's TV-era quest for greater dimensional depth and broader sensual engagement led from boxy Academic screen ratios to the predominance of widescreen and involved forays into more experimental, often gimmicky, terrain such as Smell-O-Vision and the literally "shocking" Percepto system. If such techniques were motivated by (in Bazin's term) the "myth of total cinema"—the dream of complete immersion that would make spectators forget they were "just watching a movie"—they were also innovations of an intentionally "spectacular" sort, selling points (for particular films and for the movies generally) that refocused attention on the technological constructedness of cinema and, echoing the tensions of the transitional period, were capable of involving spectators in the to-and-fro of unsettled phenomenal relations. Originally presented in 3D, *Andy Warhol's Frankenstein* (1973) forcefully probes these contradictions, pushing the screen's absorptive potential to its limit only to jolt viewers—by thrusting gall bladders and the like in their faces—into awareness of the paradoxical "flatness" or objecthood of the screen and its images. Finally, the recent emergence of digital special effects and CGI have challenged established relations between camera and reality, not only the line between fact and fiction but also the indexicality at the root of embodiment relations, and therefore also the segregation of spaces central to classical spectatorship; thus, at the dawn of the twenty-first century, in the computer-enhanced monsters of *Van Helsing* (2004) and perhaps more radically in the world of amateur digital animation and video game-based machinima, the monster's relation to technical processes of animation has gained new urgency in probing recent changes in film-viewer relations.

But if phenomenal instabilities of this sort were central to the possibility of heterotopian formations in the transitional era, it is of course by no means clear that they will function similarly in different historical and institutional contexts. When the dichotomy of absorbing narrative versus distracting spectacle loses its clear alignment with class hierarchies, for example, who still benefits from phenomenal instability? If the tension between bourgeois and industrial-commercial public spheres was an enabling condition for the articulation of alternatives in the transitional cinema, what happens when this dichotomy collapses, as it apparently has under late capitalism? In a postmodern world where any and every "alternative" seems susceptible to virtually instantaneous commodification, how much deeper must we dig for resistance to the forces of cooptation? Faced with such odds, many cultural studies-inspired approaches appeal to the competency of recipients to cleverly reinterpret texts that aim to exploit, situate, and contain the radical possibilities of non-normative subjectivities and collectivities. Indeed, in looking for alternative openings among Frankenstein films, it is tempting to follow this fundamentally oppositional strategy: to locate the heterotopian potential of Edison's *Frankenstein* (and transitional cinema generally) in the subversiveness of early-film forms and lower-class appeals vis-à-vis the combined forces of consumerism, classical cinema, and bourgeois values; to seek out subtexts that undermine the ostensible moral messages and conservative ideologies of Universal's and Hammer's Frankenstein cycles; to praise an auteur like James Whale for his assertion of vision and stylistic eccentricity—and his own queerness—in the face of a stultifying studio system; and to focus on marginalized viewers' active resistance to dominant discourses of gender, race, and class through identification with the stigmatized monster rather than with a repentant scientist or his devoted bride.

While such antagonisms, when and where they may apply, are far from irrelevant in appraising *Frankenstein*'s filmic progenies, the oppositional paradigm often does serious violence to the phenomenon of popularity; in demanding avant-garde irony (whether on the part of texts, their authors/directors, or readers/viewers) it denies the value and appeal of "merely" mainstream entertainments and paradoxically marginalizes recipients who are either unable or unwilling to practice the high art of subversion. Furthermore, this critical perspective fails to capture the essence of heterotopia, which is predicated not on the triumph of underdogs against insurmountable odds but on the coexistence of mutually exclusive alternatives in unresolved tension with one another. The transition-as-heterotopia was less a matter of willful circumventions of dominant ideologies than of contextual contingency and "accidental transgression" (Hansen 93). The film industry, in the 1910s as now, was characterized more by profit-driven opportunism than benevolent concern for society's so-called Others, and we may safely assume that many marginalized viewers themselves aspired above all to "normalcy" and acceptance by the mainstream— and that these desires guided their viewing practices and spectatorial identifications. If autonomous formations nevertheless emerged among ethnic, racial, or gendered collectives, this fact cannot be attributed exclusively to conscious decisions and premeditated acts of political organization but must be seen also as the aleatoric result of structural conditions defined by the explosive intersection of incompatible alternatives. Rather than pitting heroic resisters against repressive forces that threaten to close off more liberating possibilities—whether it be the classical paradigm as usurping primitive pleasures, the studio system and genre conventionalization as obstacles to directorial creativity, or censorship as interfering with the integrity of film texts—the notion of heterotopia invites us to view these as productive forces in their own right, as parameters of agency generative of new forms of expression, reception, and experience.[52]

As a model for criticism, heterotopian transitionality emphasizes the chance emergence of discontinuous, interstitial spaces as unintentional by-products of historical developments—indeterminate "plateaus" of experience where chance encounters take place and unforeseen effects unfold against the background of conflicted material and discursive fields of force. Forming at junctures of intense material and social contradiction, these are necessarily unstable constellations, temporary and, in a word, *transitional*. The actualization of such "other spaces" is most likely to occur at times of uncertain cultural, institutional, and media-technological shifts, at points of crisis when the alternatives are still vying for dominance, and especially among liminal social groups whose identities and relations to the dominant public sphere are in the process of (re)negotiation. From this perspective, the question of whether James Whale surreptitiously gives voice to his homosexuality in the muted monster and allegorizes his own liminal predicament will necessarily be subordinate to the question of his films' roles (whether intentional or inadvert-

---

[52] This type of view is supported, for example, by Thomas Schatz's notion of the "genius of the system," as developed in his book of that title; or by Annette Kuhn's view of censorship that, similar to Foucault's refutation of the "repressive hypothesis" (in *The History of Sexuality, Volume 1*), moves beyond what Kuhn calls the "prohibition/institutions model" to see censorship as a productive force in its own right (*Cinema, Censorship and Sexuality* 3).

ent) in negotiating, vis-à-vis the discursive and material spaces of cinema in the 1930s, alternative configurations of (gendered) spectatorial relations towards one another and towards the machinery of the cinema. Similarly, we can ask about the relation of 1950s and 1960s-era Frankenstein films to the social-discursive construction of the "teenager": about the strange ensemble composed of the drive-in theater and its place in the adolescent dating scene, the car (semi-public, semi-private, and parked between mobility and stasis[53]), the monster film's commercial and emotional exploitation of an inherently temporary identity (situated liminally between childhood innocence and the responsibilities of adulthood, marriage, and family), and moviegoers' phenomenal vacillations between the "hereness" of a sexually charged viewing situation and the "thereness" of the screen. Does this configuration facilitate an autonomous formation capable of transcending the spatial isolation of the automobile and the economic and normative interests that sanction the teenager's temporary "freedoms"? On the other hand, the participatory atmosphere at a midnight showing of *Rocky Horror Picture Show*—where spectatorial identification with non-normative, queer, and monstrous subjectivities is the norm, not just as a psychic possibility but as an actuality externalized in costumes and ritually performed in film-accompanying commentaries and enactments of screen events—might be invoked as a paradigm case of heterotopian community, organized autonomously on the fringes of mainstream cinema and in the interstices of public and private life. But is such a self-conscious alternative immune to mainstream cooptation, and, more importantly, what internal and external dynamics are at work in the construction, maintenance, and possible destruction of this "temporary autonomous zone"?[54]

Revised and recalibrated in the manner described here, the notion of heterotopia thus opens a wide field of investigation and brings us a significant step closer to realizing the double vision demanded by Frankenstein films' overdetermined monstrosities. Taking its cue from the productive tensions of the transitional era, this perspective is obviously predicated on a strategic "slippage" between history and theory, and it significantly loosens a number of other oppositions as well: marrying discourse and materiality through a dual emphasis on socio-cultural and material-technical determinants of experience, a heterotopian criticism mediates between the deterministic thrust of apparatus theory and the techno-neutrality implicit in cultural studies' championing of autonomous acts of resistance. It thus partially undoes the dichotomy between pessimistic views of the culture industry and optimistic belief in the power of individuals and collectives to elude the normalizing forces of ideology, maintaining instead that heterotopian alternativity—arising at the temporary

---

53 Compare Foucault's own examples of the train and the boat as heterotopias.
54 The term "autonomous temporary zone" comes from Hakim Bey's book *T.A.Z.*

intersections of competing historical models, spectatorial constructions, technical configurations, and cultural positionings—is as much a result of chance as it is of choice. In fact, the heterotopian perspective goes farther still, suggesting finally the deconstruction of the chance/choice binary itself as contingent both upon negotiations of power in the discursive realm and material expansions and attenuations of human efficacy by technological means.[55] In aligning hopes and fears concerning technology's potential to extend human mastery over nature with socio-political dynamics that determine the differential distribution of choices open to normative and deviant subjects, Frankenstein films are centrally concerned with such jointly discursive and material reconfigurations (and disfigurements) of human autonomy. Because the questions these films raise are ones that cannot be broached by reductively materialist or "discursivist" perspectives, a heterotopian double vision becomes indispensable in approaching Frankenstein's filmic progenies.

But if the generalization from historical transition *qua* heterotopia to a model of heterotopia *qua* overdetermined transitionalities marks an important and necessary step in the right direction, serious difficulties remain for the realization and refinement of this critical perspective. A methodological dilemma of sorts results from the fact that the heterotopia's (critical as well as political) potential derives, on the one hand, from the confluence of material and social factors and, equally, from their irreducible, tension-generating non-identity. It is thus imperative to respect this distinctness, not to collapse bodies or technologies into discursive constructs or, conversely, to reduce social relations to (epiphenomena of) physical ones. However, the task of maintaining this difference while attending to the intersections or coalescences of material and discursive forces is perhaps more difficult than it might at first appear. Miriam Hansen's groundbreaking analysis of transitional-era heterotopias provides a case in point. As I have indicated, Hansen is quite conscious of the significant role that material and techno-phenomenological shifts, lags, and gaps played in constituting alternative public spheres. She thus recognizes the non-neutrality of technology with regard to human subjectivity, but she steers clear of apparatus theory's deterministic exaggeration of it, convincingly demonstrating the possibility of local resistances and non-normative negotiations of subjective and intersubjective relations despite the relative constancy of the basic apparatus. It would seem, then, that she successfully mediates between technological determinism and neutrality and unites the best aspects of apparatus theory and cultural studies.

Yet in her ambitious and commendable effort to locate the possibility of "alternative horizons of experience," Hansen falls back on a common ground shared by

---

55 This is the core of the perspective that I argue for, in a very different context, in my "*Frankenstein*, Bioethics, and Technological Irreversibility."

the opposing perspectives, effectively basing her mediation on their common emphasis on discursive subjectivity as the ultimate receptacle of technology's effects. Against empiricist "notions of perception and cognition based on stable subject-object relations and directed toward instrumental uses in science and technology" (12), Hansen appeals to the "discursive organization of experience" (13) as the enabling basis of heterotopian discontinuity; she thereby challenges the alleged constancy and efficacy of the ideological *dispositif* against which apparatus theory sets the spectator as a passively formed subject, but she leaves the subjectivist framework itself intact. And though she relates the cinema's heterotopian potential to technology's impact—as "shock"—on human perception (109), the discursivist definition of experience effectively blocks the path to countenancing material, bodily impacts beyond the pale of their subjective registration, filtering, and appropriation. Thus, for example, Hansen appeals to Benjamin's notion of the "optical unconscious" and its ability to call forth a type of "memory" that "differs from any form of premeditated, discursive remembering or reminiscing" (110); but rather than pursue this potential opening to a more robustly embodied, non-discursive form of filmic reception, Hansen associates the optical unconscious with a "hidden, *figurative* dimension of film's 'mimetic faculty'" (110, emphasis added) and mobilizes it to redeem the shock-induced destruction of auratic experience in which film participates. She writes:

As a category based on the history of human interaction with nature (*Naturgeschichte*), the optical unconscious would have had a heightened significance for groups like the new immigrants who encountered the impact of industrialization, urbanization and commodification in an accelerated, telescoped form—by *lending expression* to traumatic disjunctions in the social experience of nature. (111, emphasis added)

Thus, as in Hansen's discussion of female reception, the cinematic heterotopia is conceived as "a site for [...] *imaginative negotiation*" and "an arena in which *a new discourse* on femininity could be articulated and the *norms and codes* of sexual conduct could be redefined" (118, emphasis added). Looking beyond the transitional era, Hansen again invokes the optical unconscious—which she then links to "*associational processes in the spectator's head*" (124, emphasis added)—in order to explain the continued possibility of non-standard patterns of reception.

Thus, though her argument ascribes an important causal role to cinema's media-technological infrastructure and the material conditions of reception, Hansen consistently locates the corresponding effects of anthropotechnical interaction in a discursive-normative realm—of figuration, expression, imagination, and association—and, as a result, she confines the scope and significance of these effects to the domain of subjective experience. As I shall demonstrate in Part Two, however, important aspects of technology's impact on human beings radically exceed these limits, and in order to fully appreciate film's receptional dynamics—including their socio-political ramifications—it is essential that we attend more closely to those effects that fall outside of human thought, language, and intentionality. What I am proposing, therefore, is that we supplement rather than simply reject Hansen's perspective, for technologies undoubtedly participate in networks of signification, insert themselves into the semiotic fabric against which social and psychic identities are articulated, and thus have the potential to disrupt and reconfigure our subjective constitutions; beyond this, however, technologies lead a double life in a radically non-discursive realm of materiality, and they impinge upon us directly at the level of human embodiment. To account for the impact of technologies (cinematic and otherwise) at this more fundamental level of human being, it will be essential that we distinguish the socially marked and discursively constituted body (for example, Foucault's "body of the condemned"[56]) from the experientially more basic, phenomenally non-thematized lived body (Merleau-Ponty's *corps vécu*).[57] The latter, as a concretely instantiated and non-iterable basis of embodied experience, provides a nexus connecting materiality and discourse and enables a more robustly double vision of anthropotechnical interaction in the cinema and beyond. However, as we shall see, the phenomenological body is hardly a timeless constant, for it is bound up with technologies and open to transformation; abstracted from the transitional-era experience, anthropotechnical transitionality therefore comes to describe the postnatural historicity of human and nonhuman matter in the betrothal of co-constitution and mutual revision.

In seeking to formulate a theoretical framework that does justice to the dual nature of bodies and technologies addressed—both spoken *about* and spoken *to*—in Frankenstein's filmic progenies, I therefore "slip" farther from history into theory in Part Two, moving into some highly philosophical terrain and ever farther from the cinematic heterotopia's historical basis in the transitional period. In a sense, though, I continue to follow an important lead from the cinema of the 1910s, taking its central tension between narrative integration and technical attraction—a tension that, subject to variation, continues to inform classical-era Frankenstein films—as a structuring principle for my argument. I turn first, in Chapter 4, to the text and

---

56 See Foucault's *Discipline and Punish*.

57 Don Ihde draws this distinction in Chapter 2 of his *Bodies in Technology*. A similar distinction is at work in Mark Hansen's call for a double-vision approach to technology, which I noted in a previous footnote in this chapter, and which guides the argument of Part Two in significant ways. Hansen distinguishes between "*epistemological* (or *artifactual*) *embodiment*" and "*phenomenological* (or *corporeal*) *embodiment*" (*Embodying Technesis* 27).

recent literary critical reception of Mary Shelley's novel—the narrative base upon which all Frankenstein films draw (however tenuously) and from which they deviate (however drastically). In this context, I engage a variety of conceptions of embodiment and materiality and consider how they connect Shelley's text with the technologies of the industrial revolution, ultimately pointing to non-cognitive, affective impacts on embodied experience and agency. Later, in Chapter 5, I locate the revisionary dynamics of anthropotechnical interaction in a broader technoscientific context, from whence I am able to explicate the theory of postnaturalism. Finally, in Chapter 6, I channel my findings into a specifically postnatural media theory that bears on our view of the cinema generally and on the many retellings of Shelley's tale in the technological medium of film, which repeatedly activate radically unsettling experiences of anthropotechnical transitionality.

Part Two

4. To the Heart of (the) Matter: *Frankenstein*, Embodiment, Materiality

> Even in times of narrowly prejudiced thought there was an inkling that life was not limited to organic corporeality. [....] The concept of life is given its due only if everything that has a history of its own, and is not merely the setting for history, is credited with life. In the final analysis, the range of life must be determined by history rather than by nature, least of all by such tenuous factors as sensation and soul.
> WALTER BENJAMIN

In Part Two, I return to Frankenstein films' central dualities (text/technology, narrative content/technological spectacle, embodiment relations/hermeneutic relations) and attempt to situate them within the broader contexts of historically inflected negotiations that humans participate in with regard not only to the cinema but also our larger social environments and increasingly technological lifeworlds. A number of correlations enable and in fact necessitate the intertwinement and opening of the narrower critical focus onto a broader quasi-anthropological level of investigation. If we approach Frankenstein films first of all as "texts," it is in a sense inevitable that we measure their meanings comparatively, by way of the intertextual relations that obtain amongst the films and with Mary Shelley's novel. Disregarding the properly cinematic issues of film-technological mediation for the moment, this "textual" comparison already directs us toward the double vision I have been arguing for. For the novel is centrally about the tangled interrelations between discourse and materiality—between normative codes or ideologies and the material bodies upon which they are technologically inscribed in social, psychic, and cultural spaces. This conjunction of bodily and social factors in the construction and contestation of normative hierarchies has been of central importance in the critical reappraisal of *Frankenstein* that, led by feminist readers, took off in the mid-1970s. A critical interest in rehabilitating marginalized female authors was given special significance and theoretical leverage by this intersection of bodies and discourse that so dramatically impinges on female subjects, whose gender roles and identities are negotiated between biological and social-semiotic determinants of difference. Thus, Shelley's novel became a key text in arbitrating frameworks and identifying strategic possibilities for feminist literary theory, and an initial interest in Shelley's biography was expanded into the larger frames of gendered writing and agency itself. Moreover, the role of technology opens investigations of Shelley's Gothic novel quite naturally onto explorations of the cyborg and other forms of anthropotechnical co-constitution,[1] leading therefore from literary criticism to science studies, feminist philosophy of science, and the cultural study of technology.

In effect, feminist readings of *Frankenstein*, while hardly composing a singular and consonant body of interpretive discourse, have conspired to reveal Shelley's novel as a tale not of one but of two monsters—a tale, that is, of two categorically distinct but inseparably related aspects or *forms* of monstrosity: one discursive and one material. Setting out from feminist engagements with the novel, I aim accordingly to provide a greater depth of field to the methodological double vision demanded by the overdeterminations of transitionality, as explored in the previous chapter. Looked at through the binocular lens of feminist criticism, the novel offers itself as a baseline for approaching Frankenstein films and their reworkings of monstrosity at both irreducible levels of its being—not, certainly, as a standard of authenticity by which to assess the films' merits relative to a literary "original" (e.g. in terms of their degree of "faithfulness" to Shelley's text or intentions), but as a point of reference for coming to terms with the implications of self-reflexive relations between the films' contents or "messages" and the cinematic medium in and through which they are inscribed. Thus, beyond merely orienting a comparative endeavor and offering a yardstick with which to recognize and measure similarities and differences among the films' respective narrative-thematic treatments and ideological codings of monstrosity, revisiting the novel serves to uncover what I take to be a particularly monstrous potential of Frankenstein films—a volatility that results precisely from the tale's retelling in a technological medium whose material efficacy and bodily immediacy resists containment in the trappings of the "text" (including that of Mary Shelley's novel).

In particular, the feminist revision of *Frankenstein* helps to disclose the gaps and overlaps that distinguish and connect the material and discursive monstrosities that, already co-present in Shelley's tale, re-emerge and compete in the changing

---

1   Donna Haraway's mythical figure of the cyborg, as it appears in her famous "Cyborg Manifesto," remains an important point of reference for thinking human-technological interactions. I seek, however, to articulate a somewhat differently inflected view that is more emphatic about the primacy of material relations over semiotic ones.

socio-historical and media-technical circumstances of cinematic production and reception. To make this connection, however, it is imperative that we view the novel not just as offering *representations* of monstrosity that are subsequently reworked, re-represented, or "remediated" in film, but as a text that is itself *materially* imbricated in a historical upheaval of humanity's simultaneously material and discursive "nature"—an upheaval centrally precipitated by the industrial revolution and its lifeworld impacts. That *Frankenstein* problematizes human-technological as well as gender relations is of course no secret. The difficulty, however, lies in conceiving these problematizations not just in the manner of textual commentary or questionings undertaken by the novel but also as contingent upon the book's material interconnection with an extra-discursive reality in the very process of historical transformation. If we can conceive the novel in this double way, then we have a basis for understanding cinema's own double nature and for approaching the potential of Frankenstein films to shed light on—and perhaps even to assist the cinema in *effecting*—reorganizations of human subjectivity that may be less obvious but no less far-reaching than those induced by the industrial revolution.

What is therefore fundamentally at stake in this chapter is our ability to conceive that realm of anthropotechnical interaction that eludes discursive thought and materially resituates embodied agencies, both in the cinema and beyond. But while my undertaking leads me ultimately away from questions of gender and towards human-technological relations, feminist readings of *Frankenstein* remain indispensable to my task. For they suggest that the place of women (and the female author in particular) in patriarchal culture has been defined not only in relation to the codes of male normative discourse, by which females are judged inadequate and in this sense "monstrous," but also through lived, embodied forms of contradiction and alterity that fall outside the purview of those codes and thus escape their containment. It is this latter possibility, though far from being univocally endorsed in feminist theory, that provides the impetus for thinking technology beyond thought, and it is my hope that reflection upon the non-discursive, material monstrosity of anthropotechnical interfaces may be deemed relevant to assessments of gendered embodiment as well.

The feminist rehabilitation of *Frankenstein* provides a foundation, therefore, for this study's perspectival duality and contains the key to articulating its theoretical justification and scope. As we shall see, however, the essential contributions made by feminist criticism and theory towards this end are not provided ready-made but must be wrested from conflicting interpretations and appropriations that are only loosely connected under the rubric of feminism. Indeed, as I shall argue, feminist interpretations, while laying the groundwork for an appreciation of monstrosity's radically double nature, have themselves generally failed to grasp its full implications. On the one hand, many of these readings take the novel's central monster as a symbol or metaphor that foregrounds the social processes of marginalization faced by women and other "marked" subjects (or by Mary Shelley herself) under the structures of patriarchy. In its guise of discursive Other, the monster highlights the injustice of suppressing difference, but it also demonstrates the dialectical constitution of ideological norms that tacitly require such difference, thus contributing to the deconstruction of a supposedly "natural" order of things. Such approaches, by locating monstrosity squarely in the realm of discourse, fail to account for the more elusive form of monstrosity that is so crucial to my project; they are not, for all that, to be discounted out of hand. Indeed, they retain an indispensable power to illuminate the representational structures and political workings of filmic monsters. Moreover, discursive monstrosity is hardly irrelevant to the lived experience of bodily otherness and the role of concrete technologies in the enforcement (and resistance) of dominant social orders; it speaks to the experience of *being* a body that is subject (on the basis, for example, of biological sex or skin color) to a particular "reading" in scientific, legal, medical, or cultural contexts, configured from without—and *through* technologies—as an object of interpretation for a privileged form of subjectivity.[2] This implies, of course, that technologies and bodies are material bearers of discourse, the truth of which cannot be disputed; and yet, as I have intimated in previous chapters, this view only partially accounts for the experiential dualities of anthropotechnical relations. These interpretations therefore winnow out a rich, material realm of experience that should be of central interest to feminism.

In contrast to such thematic readings, and directed to some extent against them, other feminist approaches find *Frankenstein* enacting a more radical sort of deconstruction. Here the novel's monster is denied the stability of being a mere "representation," whether as a metaphor for patriarchal objectification or as an expression of the difference thereby objectified; instead, following Shelley's lead in identifying her book as her own "hideous progeny," it is the text itself which is seen as truly monstrous. Incoherent and contradictory, the novel deconstructs itself and in the process dismantles the privileging of symbolic representation shared by romantic conceptions of the autonomous (and tacitly androcentric) expressive self, by patriarchal culture generally, and, ironically, by feminist readers who fail to appreciate the text's structural resistances to representational coherence. Barbara John-

---

2 In *Bodies in Technology*, Don Ihde tries to account for this type of phenomenon by distinguishing three "senses of body": namely, "body one" (roughly, Merleau-Ponty's *corps vécu*), "body two" (encompassing "locations [that] are not biological but culturally constructed, although they are located upon us as part of our bodily experience"), and "body three" ("the dimension of the technological" as it "[t]ravers[es] both body one and body two") (xi).

son, for example, has argued that—beyond straightforwardly mediating content-level metaphors for the monstrous situation and experience of female otherness—the novel demonstrates the breakdown of such mediation as the necessary result of female autobiography. Enacting what amounts to an allegory in the de Manian sense of the term, linguistic referentiality is thus deflected towards its material, mechanical underside for specifically female purposes. This type of reading is of particular interest in the present context, for it suggests that the novel prefigures the self-reflexive movements I have been tracing in Frankenstein films, short-circuiting semiotic significances and exposing the materiality of their mediation. However, as Mark Hansen has argued, the break with representationalism signaled in Johnson's reading is incomplete; as we shall see, the deconstructionist allegory she uncovers still posits an act of representation as the defining feature of the text: its breakdown *represents* the contradictory experience of a female subjectivity that is essentially *unrepresentable* in the only medium available to Shelley—the patriarchal language of romanticism and the broader masculine bias of Western conceptions of the self. The materiality exposed in the process is, in Hansen's terms, only "relatively exterior" to discourse, still intrinsically tied to it as a support. But, against the background of the industrial revolution, the novel bears witness also to a more radically autonomous level of material reality, to the experiential effects of technologies that stubbornly resist conceptualization, instrumentalization, or any form of subordination to human thought. Literally "in touch" with this monstrously inhuman plane of materiality, the novel deconstructs not just the androcentric bias of representational language but the necessarily anthropocentric frame of human experience itself.

I begin by tracing in more detail the uneasy relations of (bodily) materiality and discourse in feminist readings of *Frankenstein*. Subsequently, I follow Mark Hansen in his attempt to "radicalize" those interventions ("Not thus" 578) by showing that the novel stages a deconstruction of "man" that is effected not by the internal instabilities of (male) language but in virtue of the alterior force of modern technology in its capacity to bypass the symbolic realm altogether. Thus, this displacement of the human perspective is not wholly accountable for in the framework of (feminist) poststructuralism, which despite attempts to conceive a recalcitrant "outside" of representation continues to privilege discourse as the exclusive domain of experience. As we shall see, *Frankenstein*'s exploration of technology points to a historical destabilization of the "lived body" itself, a reconfiguration of the embodied channels and modes of access to the world upon which subjective perception, activity, and experience generally are founded.

Looking ahead to the next chapter, this discovery demands a significant revision of the techno-phenomenological framework as I have theorized it thus far. For it is not just categories of thought or epistemes that are subject to replacement or renewal, but pre-personal forms of embodiment itself. In order to account for this phenomenon, I shall have to supplement the relatively stable Merleau-Pontean conception of embodiment with which I have been operating with a more fluid view; for this purpose I have recourse to a Bergson-inspired notion of material flux as the pre-situated, pre-personal ground of embodiment. In effect, the Bergsonian view turns phenomenology inside out, highlighting the radical contingency of phenomenological descriptions and thereby opening up phenomenology's quasi-synchronic (that is, "situated") perspective to diachronic shifts. If we assume with Merleau-Ponty that human embodiment situates experience, Bergson's metaphysics suggests how this material seat might itself be resituated, thus offering us a means to conceive technologically induced historical change in a way that paradoxically challenges the continuity of human history itself—thus opening onto a properly postnatural history of embodied agency. It is thus in this awkward complementarity of phenomenology and Bergsonism that I seek the philosophical basis of the methodological double vision required by transitionality as a critical paradigm. Mary Shelley's *Frankenstein* leads the way.

FRANKENSTEIN AS A TALE OF TWO MONSTERS: FEMINIST INTERVENTIONS AND BEYOND

Born in the popular mode of the Gothic, giving birth to another popular genre (science fiction), and further popularized on nineteenth-century stages and twentieth-century screens, Mary Shelley's *Frankenstein* was either ignored completely or treated with disdain under the high-cultural biases of the pre-1970s academy. What little praise it received was largely counterbalanced by a patronizing attitude that reduced the work to a mere approximation of the romantic genius displayed by the male authors in whose shadow "little Mary" stood. Biographically marginalized as Godwin's daughter and Percy Shelley's mistress and wife, the woman author thus continued to play "marionette" to a critical tradition that carried forth romanticism's own androcentric biases, a tradition concisely expressed in Harold Bloom's ambiguous appraisal of *Frankenstein*:

what makes *Frankenstein* an important book, though it is only a strong, flawed novel with frequent clumsiness in its narrative and characterization, is that it contains one of the most vivid versions we have of the Romantic mythology of the self, one that resembles Blake's *Book of Urizen*, Shelley's *Prometheus Unbound*, and Byron's *Manfred*, among other works. Because it lacks the sophistication and imaginative complexity of such works, *Frankenstein* affords a unique introduction to the archetypal world of the Romantics. (202)

Like the popular medium of film when it tries to envision a work of great literature, *Frankenstein*'s virtue is to make "vivid" the ethereal visions of genius. By the same token, though, its fatal flaw lies in the mismatch between the heavenly Form to which it is beholden and its own degraded, earthly materialization. Hardly original, in Bloom's view, Shelley's novel is therefore itself only a popularizing medium, an unrefined instrument through which the rarefied truths of romantic poetics are made digestible, stripped of their untranslatable lyrical beauty and condensed as so much prosaic "material." It is therefore only natural, we might add, that *Frankenstein* should be further simplified and reduced to fodder for the media of popular culture. From a feminist point of view, however, what is troubling about Bloom's reading is not simply his valorization of high culture but the way he reserves this realm for men while banishing the female author to the domain of "clumsy" imitators and the "merely" popular. Implicitly, then, his reading propagates the coding of cultural ideals ("imaginative complexity" and intellectual "sophistication") as specifically male; originality, expressive eloquence, and even autonomous selfhood would seem the province of men alone. Intentionally or not, the male critic thus underwrites the deeply entrenched alignments of masculine/feminine, subject/object, and activity/passivity by which standards of submissive propriety and women's treatment as physical property are alike legitimized. In literature as in life, male dominance is sustained by figuring men as masters of the Word and associating women with bare "matter"—both the inert subject-matter of men's discourses and a material body denied the power of expression.

Female Bodies, Women Writers, and the Culture of Compromise

Resisting these fearful symmetries, feminist critics of *Frankenstein* have from the start hovered uneasily between the bodily-material and social-semiotic aspects of women's circumscription and sought in them loci of an alternative significance overlooked or ignored by readers of the patriarchal canon. Ellen Moers's groundbreaking article, "Female Gothic," first published in 1974, links *Frankenstein* precisely to female physiology, relating the tale of monstrous creation to the novelist's own experience with pregnancy, childbearing, and young motherhood. The novel, for Moers, is a "birth myth" that is ultimately rooted in its author's "sex" as determined by her body's reproductive capacities (79). Moreover, Moers locates the general appeal of the Gothic mode, including the specifically "female" form produced by Mary Shelley and other women writers, in its ability "to get to the body itself, its glands, muscles, epidermis, and circulatory system, quickly arousing and quickly allaying the physiological reactions to fear" (77). In this way, Moers's reading establishes the body as the book's productive source and its receptive target alike, as the very channel across which a woman author is able to communicate particularly female truths to other women. But Moers also recognizes the obstacles to such communication, obstacles that arise from patriarchal culture's cooptation and interpretation of women's bodies. She notes male authors' literary mediations of childbearing and the broader social construction of pregnancy and motherhood that situate the female body in the ideological space of medical institutions, literary canons, and legal discourses, distorting the alterior experience of being a woman and becoming a mother.[3] Moers suggests, however, that Shelley rises above these impediments, takes interpretive charge of the materials provided by her biography, and finds an independent voice to express the physical and distinctively female realities obfuscated by male ideals. In this vein, Robert Kiely, whom Moers approvingly cites as providing "one of the rare serious discussions of *Frankenstein* as a woman's work" (86), writes:

> In making her hero the creator of a monster, she does not necessarily mock idealistic ambition, but in making that monster a poor grotesque patchwork, a physical mess of seams and wrinkles, she introduces a consideration of the material universe which challenges and undermines the purity of idealism. [....] The arguments on behalf of idealism and unworldly genius are seriously presented, but the controlling perspective is that of an earthbound woman. (Kiely 161, qtd. in Moers 86)

As such, it is not only demeaning but patently false to view Shelley or her text as "a transparent medium through which passed the ideas of those around her" (Moers 82).[4]

---

[3] Noting the fact that few women writers of the eighteenth and nineteenth centuries were themselves mothers, Moers points to Tolstoy, Zola, and William Carlos Williams as first opening literature to the subject of birth (79). She notes also Thackeray's propagation of an idealized motherly response to the newborn child, despite the fact that his own wife experienced serious post-partum depression (81). In the case of Shelley herself, Moers emphasizes not only the absence of literary precursors but also the lack of material support following the births of her children, the fact that she was not only young but unmarried, and that—unlike Harriet Beecher Stowe and Elizabeth Cleghorn Gaskell, who also experienced the death of a baby—she was not a "respectably settled middle-class wom[a]n" (85). "So," according to Moers, "are monsters born" (79).

[4] It is interesting to note, however, that Kiely himself sees *Frankenstein* as "an instance of genius observed and admired but not shared" (Kiely 161, qtd. in Gilbert and Gubar 221-22)—in other words, precisely as a medium for the ideas of the men around the novel's author.

While inspiring critics to claim *Frankenstein* as an emphatically female (or even feminist) work, Moers's interpretation also set the stage for disagreements over what exactly, apart from its author's biological "sex," made the novel so distinctively a "woman's book," thus spawning debates that touch on feminism's core outlook, strategies, and its very self-conception. Significantly, many of these differences revolve centrally around the body/discourse distinction as implemented in Moers's reading. Retaining Moers's interest in Shelley's biography, for example, Sandra Gilbert and Susan Gubar deflect emphasis away from the author's bodily experience and towards her reading habits and her relation to literature; they highlight the "self-conscious literariness" of *Frankenstein* that they see as crucial to its purported "femaleness" but neglected by critics like Moers (222). From a female perspective, according to Gilbert and Gubar, the novel "rewrites" *Paradise Lost*, interprets Milton—as the spokesman for a misogynistic culture—not in order to protest his message but to "clarify its meaning" for Shelley herself and for women generally (220). Tracing the relations of the novel's characters to the allegorical roles in which Milton typecasts Adam, Satan, Sin, and Eve, Gilbert and Gubar uncover Shelley's pivotal equation of fallenness, femaleness, and monstrosity (234-35); Milton's basic message for women, communicated in his text and enforced in patriarchal society, is thus asserted by the woman author herself. More like Eve than Adam or Satan, Frankenstein's monster is therefore "a female in disguise" (237). His self-narrated tale, "embedded at the heart of the novel like the secret of the fall itself," restores the power of expression to a long line of female and feminized characters silenced by their male authors (235). But whereas the monster's narrative makes plain the injustice of exclusion, it does not fundamentally go beyond this act of exposure; it does not articulate an independent standpoint, free of cultural constraints, from which the female author can express an authentically feminine alternative and combat her characterization as depraved and fallen—most certainly, it does not sidestep social stigmatization and express the raw truth of a woman's body. On the contrary, the monster's predicament, rendered necessary by its outward appearance, underscores the confluence of masculine social norms (including literary conventions) in the shaping of female bodies and demonstrates that even women's relations to their own bodies are necessarily mediated by a male symbolic. It is "Eve's moral deformity"—that is, "[t]he figurative monstrosity of female narcissism" condemned in Milton's representation of Eve (240)—that we find "symbolized by the monster's physical malformation" (241). Further, "the monster's physical ugliness represents his social illegitimacy, his bastardy, his namelessness" (241), perfectly representing the situation of a woman (or of Mary Shelley herself) in patriarchal society. If this announces a truth about the female body, it is the truth of its alienated inauthenticity. Where Moers sees the heroic expression of a woman's body against the odds of male culture, Gilbert and Gubar find instead Shelley's recognition and clarification of the forces that make such heroism impossible for the female author.

In light of this impasse, avoiding the conclusion that Shelley's text was after all just a passive reflection of male ideologies would seem to require viewing *Frankenstein* as an elaborate and subtle compromise. In Mary Poovey's take on what makes the novel both imaginatively original and characteristically feminine, Shelley is shown to have been radically self-divided, "attempt[ing] to conform simultaneously to two conflicting prescriptive models of behavior" (332). Her family instilled in her a desire to "fulfill the Romantic model of the artist," yet that demand was confounded by "prevalent social expectations that a woman conform to the conventional model of propriety" (332). As a result of this contradiction, Shelley's artistic struggle for self-expression was virtually doomed to failure. But neither could she simply resign herself to meek femininity. Internalizing both incompatible ideals, she was forced to modify each and seek an alternative of her own making, to effect a necessarily monstrous compromise that she most dramatically attempts in *Frankenstein*. In the novel, as Poovey would have it:

Shelley explodes the foundations of Romantic optimism by demonstrating that the egotistical energies necessary to self-assertion—energies that appear to her to be at the heart of the Romantic model of the imagination—inevitably imperil the self-denying energies of love. To accommodate this reservation, which implicitly indicts all artistic endeavors as well as more insidious forms of egotism, Shelley essentially feminizes Romantic aesthetics, deriving from her contemporaries' theories strategies that enable her to fulfill her desire for self-expression in an indirect, self-effacing, and therefore acceptable manner. (332-33)

As Nancy Armstrong argues, however, Poovey's notion of compromise presupposes "the belief that the constraints on sexuality existed prior to the act of writing. These constraints arose from the condition of being female, either from within the female self, or from outside that self in a male-dominated 'bourgeois' society, or both" (1253). Ideological forces are thereby naturalized, according to Armstrong, and as the theme of "individual vs. society" dominates interpretation, feminism's interpretive options are radically limited (1254). Armstrong takes particular aim at Poovey's "psychologizing" approach to the monster, the figure of which Poovey reads as Shelley's means of expressing her deep-seated ambivalence regarding the place of the female self. In the monster's autobiographical narration, according to Armstrong,

the nineteenth-century author clearly uses this figure not only to pose the question of origins—whether the self originates in nature or culture—but also to consider what makes that self normal or deviant. Shelley makes the answer to the second question absolutely contingent upon the first, yet it is precisely this question which Poovey's psychological interpretation forecloses [...]. (1255)

For Poovey, that is, the monster functions only to express the woman author's own ambivalent questionings about the deviance or acceptability of female self-expression. Poovey thus avoids the prior question about the productive source of normativity, taking it for granted as something that exists for a female self to accept, reject, or be ambivalent about. Armstrong counters with an alternative reading, asserting that "in a very literal way, [the monster's] origin—like the distinction between truth and fantasy, good and evil, self and society, and even the distinction between nature and culture itself—exists only in and as language" (1256). Only through his reading does the monster develop a sense of (abject) selfhood, thus suggesting that "it is finally 'language' that produces the self, normal or deviant, rather than the other way around" (1256). Judged by the text's own standards, according to Armstrong, Poovey's notion of strategic compromise or negotiation—because it requires a preexistent self, a "true" self capable of doing the negotiation—fails to make sense. Judged in terms of feminism's political efficacy, moreover, Poovey's approach maintains the very "discourse of sexuality" that she aims to dismantle (1257), leaving the "male" standard of autonomy in place and essentializing both the self and gender rather than acknowledging their historical production through discourse.

Minding the Gap: The Body of the Text & the Text of the Body

Charging Moers's and Gilbert and Gubar's critical approaches with the same counterproductive essentialism, Mary Jacobus links this tendency to a particular take on the body. While the Foucauldian paradigm exemplified by Armstrong clearly leaves little room for the physiologically based notions of "sex" and bodily authenticity implied by Moers, Jacobus shows how they may be at work in the more culturalist approach of Gilbert and Gubar as well. Invoking a distinction between American and French forms of feminism, Jacobus diagnoses a general "flight toward empiricism" in America that posits "women's experience" as an authoritative "ground of difference in writing" and assumes "an unbroken continuity between 'life' and 'text'—a mimetic relation whereby women's writing, reading, or culture, instead of being produced, reflect a knowable reality" (138).[5] While she acknowl-

---

5 One may question whether it still made sense in 1982 to draw the distinction along national lines. Certainly, the US publication of *New French Feminisms* (edited by Elaine Marks and Isabelle de Courtivron) in 1980 had eroded the gulf between American and

edges the strategic importance of this approach, Jacobus insists that "to leave the question there, with an easy recourse to the female signature or to female being, is either to beg it or to biologize it" (138).

To insist, for instance, that *Frankenstein* reflects Mary Shelley's experience of the trauma of parturition and postpartum depression may tell us about women's lives, but it reduces the text itself to a monstrous symptom. Equally, to see it as the product of "bibliogenesis"—a feminist rereading of *Paradise Lost* that, in exposing its misogynist politics, makes the monster's fall an image of woman's fall into the hell of sexuality—rewrites the novel in the image not of books but of female experience. (138)

Whether made up front or only covertly and "in the last instance," it is an appeal to a stable bodily difference that unites these seemingly disparate approaches, underwrites their valorization of the distinctively female writer, and brokers generalizations of a female condition that pits "woman" against "patriarchy."

However, with the exorcism of biologism and its underlying empiricist epistemology, the body as a site of strategic contestation does not simply evaporate under an increasingly poststructuralist feminism. The notion of "*écriture féminine*," as Jacobus glosses it, situates "woman as a writing-effect instead of an origin," insists that gender is produced in language rather than the body, and locates its radicalized notion of the "feminine" in the indeterminate space of "the gaps, the absences, the unsayable or unrepresentable of discourse and representation" (138). Yet such an approach also insists that "women must write the body" (138). Not essentialism but a political and cognitive imperative of representation itself therefore dictates feminism's continued concern with the body:

The theoretical abstraction of a "marked" writing that can't be observed at the level of the sentence but only glimpsed as an alternative libidinal economy almost invariably gives rise to gender-specific images of voice, touch, anatomy, to biologistic images of milk or *jouissance*. How else, after all, could the not-yet-written forms of *écriture féminine* represent themselves to our understanding? (139)

French feminist theory to a great extent, and American critics such as Armstrong and Jacobus herself were involved in rendering what remained of the distinction obsolete. Nevertheless, the presence of the bifurcation in Jacobus's text marks a historical moment in American feminism, attesting to the general upheaval and polarization introduced by characteristically "French" theory, and providing a framework within which Moer's, Gilbert and Gubar's, and Poovey's critical approaches can be seen to cohere with one another.

From this constructivist perspective, the valorization of what Kiely calls "the controlling perspective [...] of an earthbound woman," which tacitly unites Moers, Gilbert and Gubar, and Poovey, is unmasked as complicit in a binarization of sex that, by recurring ultimately to physiology, remains rooted in modern medical discourse and reinforces rather than resists an identification of the creative intellect as male and the passive body as female. Laying the groundwork for a performative theory of gender as something one does rather than describing something one naturally is, the idea that a different sort of (non-inert) body erupts in "the gaps" of discourse points, for example, to possibilities for queer identity and a more fluid conception overall of the materiality/textuality dichotomy.

It is in the spirit of uncovering a submerged probing of materiality that I approach those readings, like Barbara Johnson's "My Monster/My Self," that explore Shelley's text in the light of feminism's French connection. While Johnson's claim that *Frankenstein* is an "autobiography" that is "specifically feminist" in enacting a "struggle for feminine authorship" (3) suggests certain alignments with the "American" feminism attacked by Jacobus, her framing of this struggle marks a clear break with that heritage. Rejecting thematic readings that interpret Frankenstein's "demon" metaphorically as a commentary on the monstrosities of either (patriarchal) social injustice, female self-assertion, or subversive compromise, Johnson identifies the text itself as the monstrously productive site of—rather than an instrumental mouthpiece for—an alternative gendered subjectivity. The instrumentality of the text in relation to its author's will is perhaps most famously problematized in the novel's 1831 Introduction, in Shelley's adjuration that her "hideous progeny go forth and prosper" (10). Confusing the boundaries of content and textual container, with this gesture Shelley essentially writes herself into the novel. Nevertheless, it would be wrong to *identify* her with Victor, the monster-maker whom she refers to as the creature's "author," for the relations of inside and outside are more radically unsettled. Averring a reluctance to assert herself in print, Shelley justifies her authorial introduction with the fact that her comments "will only appear as an appendage to a former production" (5). Suggestively, Johnson claims that Mary Shelley herself is here "speaking *as* an appendage to a text" (4). We are confronted, I suggest, with a prototypical case of Derridean supplementarity, an "invagination" of the supposedly self-sufficient text that links its "originary lack" with the burning question of gendered hierarchies (Eve as Adam's invaginated/invaginating supplement) and, by staking out an indeterminate position between externality and interiority, both aligns and refuses to align gender supplementarity with the literal appendages of the narrative monster's body parts.

As an act of self-writing, the text provocatively demands: "In a humanistic tradition in which *man* is the measure of all things, how does an appendage go about telling the story of her life?" (Johnson 4). Rejecting the idea that the novel somehow codes the events of Shelley's life into literary form, and renouncing the associated notion of an authoritative womanhood that would ground female autobiography, Johnson emphasizes that *Frankenstein* seems "more striking for its avoidance of the question of femininity than for its insight into it" (7). It would be "tempting," Johnson concedes, to explain "the story of a man who usurps the female role by physically giving birth to a child" as the means whereby Mary Shelley, in the intimidating company of male genius, "fictively transposed her own female pen envy into a tale of catastrophic male womb envy" (8)—tempting, perhaps, but finally too narrowly psychologizing. As an alternative, Johnson proposes that it is

perhaps the very hiddenness of the question of femininity in *Frankenstein* that somehow proclaims the painful message not of female monstrosity but of female contradictions. For it is the fact of self-contradiction that is so vigorously repressed in women. While the story of a man who is haunted by his own contradictions is representable as an allegory of monstrous doubles, how indeed would it have been possible for Mary to represent feminine contradiction *from the point of view of its repression* otherwise than precisely in the *gap* between angels of domesticity and an uncompleted monsteress, between the murdered Elizabeth and the dismembered Eve? (9)

Again, it is the "gap" that deserves attention in terms of materiality, for it signals a breach of some sort in the fabric of signification, a hole or invagination that points outside of discourse. Because the reality of "self-contradiction" that peeks through is "so vigorously repressed," we cannot infer, with Poovey, that Shelley is engaged in a conscious act of negotiation; to claim that she rises above this repression is merely to vindicate the male romantic imagination as the model for Shelley's own undertaking. Assuming that this would be a mistake, we must therefore have recourse to an agency other than the author's volition, a plane of reality that lies beyond or beneath discourse itself. At least two candidates for this role offer themselves: in the tradition of psychoanalysis, that which speaks through the interstices of repressive regulation is, of course, "the unconscious"; on the other hand, we may entertain the hypothesis that it is matter itself which has been "repressed" in representation and which asserts itself in the gaps of asignification.

With a keen awareness of psychoanalytical theory's patriarchal pitfalls, as well as the dangers inherent in essentializing matter (as exemplified in the recourse to physiology), Margaret Homans brings the two contenders together and links the question of *Frankenstein*'s femininity to the irruption into language of an unconscious realm that is likewise that of (the woman's) material embodiment. In Homans's account of the gendered hole in the text of *Frankenstein*, the "figurative" is punctured by the "literal"; imaginative desire is "literalized," giving way to uncontainable embodiment. Insofar as "women [are] obliged to play the role of the literal in a culture that devalues it" (100), this is an indictment of "androcentric ontology" (110) and an exposure of its deep contradictions. A Lacanian reading of the oedipal conflict provides the connections amongst the psychosocial dynamics of gender, embodiment, and the occurrence in the novel of a rupture in the surface of language. Victor's role mirrors that of the oedipal son:

In flight from the body of the mother forbidden by the father, a maternal body that he sees as dead in his urgency to escape it and to enter a paternal order constituted of its distance from the mother, the son seeks figurations that will at once make restitution for the mother and confirm her death and absence by substituting for her figures that are under his control. (107)

We recall that Frankenstein's pursuit of science is precipitated by his mother's death; that the consummation of his pursuit is followed by a dream the merges Elizabeth and his mother's corpse; that his success does not eradicate death but instead seals the fate of the remaining women in his life; and that his project itself consists, in Homans's phrase, in a very literal "circumvention of the maternal." If the Law of the Father necessitates the son's figurative matricide, his entry into the symbolic order provides compensation by constituting ersatz objects of desire; but "the son cannot wish for these figurative substitutes to be embodied, for any *body* is too reminiscent of the mother and is no longer under the son's control, as the demon's excessive strength demonstrates" (107). As a consequence, women must "at once embody and not embody [...] the object of desire" (100). The monster, with its "female attributes" of "bodiliness" and "identification with matter" (106), is thus a horrifying "literalization of its creator's desire for an object, a desire that never really seeks its own fulfillment" (100-01) but would instead prefer to delay consummation indefinitely, secretly desiring only itself (104, 107). The embodied fulfillment of the male fantasy of obviating the maternal/material is, by virtue of its sheer materiality, an affront to imaginative desire's deferment of itself; indeed, then, the monster articulates a criticism of patriarchal structures generally and of romantic poetics in particular.

But while this critical impulse might be attributed to the strategic deliberation of the author, who ingeniously embodies a daughter's perspective in the monster and sets it against Victor's articulation of the son's predicament, the explosive potential of the text becomes most pronounced in the *clash* of the two views, in the *gap* between creator's and creature's narratives or the *interstice* bounded by "androcentric and gynocentric theories of creation" (113). The "collision" of the two, according to Homans, "results in the denigration of maternal childbearing through its circumvention by a male creator" (113), but this arrogation stands in marked contrast to "a woman's knowledge of the irrefutable independence of the body, both her own and those of the children that she produces, from projective male fantasy" (114). This carnal knowledge is imparted by the experience of real-world, literal childbirth, not by imaginary creation, and it teaches mothers in particular that "children, even pregnancies, do not remain under the control of those who conceive them" (114). As a correction to Moers, then, Homans claims that "[t]he novel criticizes, not childbirth itself, but the male horror of independent embodiment" (115)—a horror poignantly expressed in the social stigma and legal discourse on "illegitimate" birth, which designation marks an insult to the "premium [placed] on the ownership by a man of his wife's body and children" (115), i.e. the relation of the man, as sovereign, to his "dependents." We begin to see how Cartesian dualism—which licenses the distinction between "having" a body and merely "being" one—can be said to constitute the heart of "androcentric ontology." But Shelley's most radical indictment of this ontology begins where her deliberate criticism ends, in the act, that is, of giving free reign to the text's own "independent embodiment" beyond authorial control.[6] Read in this light, Shelley's self-denigration in the 1831 Introduction is less a strategy for making female self-expression acceptable than it is a motherly renunciation of the idea that one can mold a child (or a book) in the image of one's own autonomous desires.

Shelley's insistence that the story is merely a "transcription" of a dream involuntarily suggested by conversations passively overheard between her husband and Lord Byron should not, of course, be trusted blindly[7]; but neither must these claims be read exclusively as the tactics of ironic subversion. Instead, echoing Gilbert and Gubar, Homans suggests that if we take the notion of "transcription" seriously, we find Shelley rewriting rather than protesting male literature, submitting its idealized fantasies to a "literalization" that clarifies their significance (117-18); what sets

---

[6] My reconstruction of Homans's argument in fact ignores certain tendencies in her text to view Shelley in the manner of a Pooveyan volitional negotiator. It is unclear whether Homans intentionally creates the tension between Shelley the scribe, who surrenders herself to the independent agency of the text, and Shelley the potentially heroic or tragic author and critic. Certainly, Homans could claim that the undecidability derives from the imperatives of representation pointed out by Jacobus, or perhaps from the irreducible duality of both being and having a body. In any case, I distill that aspect of Homans's position that posits a non-Pooveyan Shelley because it is here that her argument is both most original and most illuminating in terms of poststructural feminism's relation to bodily materiality.

[7] Mario Praz, prefiguring Harold Bloom's subordination of *Frankenstein* to the canon of male romantic verse, does just this: "All Mrs. Shelley did was to provide a passive reflection of some of the wild fantasies which, as it were, hung in the air about her." (Praz 114; qtd. in Homans 116).

Homans's version of this "bibliogenesis" apart, however, is her scribe's lack of distance from that which she records. Taking Johnson's notion of the "vigorous repression" of female "self-contradiction" to heart, Homans concedes: "as a writer in a culture that defines writing as a male activity and as opposite to motherhood, Shelley too must share the masculine perspective, with its horror of embodiment and its perennial reenacting of Adam's affront at Eve's turning away" (115). As a scrivener, though, Shelley's passivity is a sign not so much of deference to the men around her as of capitulation to the independent agency of inscription itself.[8] Describing her husband as "more apt to embody ideas and sentiments in the radiance of brilliant imagery and in the music of the most melodious verse that adorns our language than to invent the machinery of a story" (Shelley 7), it is precisely this banal machinery that Mary brings to the male ideas she writes down. That these ideas look significantly different in their original and in their literalized forms is not necessarily due to a distorting intrusion on Shelley's part, but can be attributed to the action of transcription itself, which can never simply be a neutral channel (Homans 117). Faithfully mediating the concepts of male literary culture, Homans suggests, Shelley's text becomes yet more than a medium: its own recalcitrant materiality, like that which it portrays, transformatively insinuates itself into the ideas she plugs into her machine, polluting them with its own trajectories; likewise, the "machinery of the story" does not passively conduct Mary Shelley's expressive or critical self (whether a biographical or authorial self) but non-neutrally co-constructs her subjectivity. Moreover, her maternal/material body itself, physically concrete but far from physiologically determined, is opened to transformation by means of its symbiotic interlocking with textual materiality; the sexual body and the textual body rewrite one other. "Bearing men's words"—as Homans describes Shelley's act of literalization, aligning it with the material aspects of childbirth—Shelley allows her text to bear her own body: not an immaculate but a monstrous birth issues forth from the invaginated text.

As we shall see, my approach to the embodied reception of Frankenstein films' characteristic self-reflexivities owes a great deal to the poststructural feminist per-

---

8   As I mentioned in a previous footnote, my presentation of Homans's reading sets aside conflicting tendencies in her approach to highlight that aspect that speaks most directly to the notion of the "gap," as intimated by Jacobus and Johnson. As a "reconstruction" proper, this inherently involves going beyond mere summary. It is worth noting that this is especially true in the following, for though the views I ascribe to Homans are, I maintain, suggestively present in her text, they occur in the midst of a heightened vacillation on her part between a Pooveyan and a Johnsonian view of Shelley's predicament and manner of response. The following thus extrapolates to a greater degree from Homans's written statements to a systematic statement of her underlying viewpoint.

spective of the Johnson-Homans reading of *Frankenstein*. As a first indication of a correlative interplay of discourse/materiality in the medium of film, we note, on the one hand, that "capturing" material bodies on film and "framing" them as images is perhaps one of the most powerful means available for situating these bodies discursively, inscribing them with ideologies and transforming them into signifiers; on the other hand, the photographic medium's own mechanistic materiality, its passive "transcription" of images onto a material surface, has from the beginning lent itself to attempts at uncovering (bodily) realities that elude ordinary perception. From the horse's gallop and Fred Ott's sneeze to what Linda Williams has identified as pornography's "frenzy of the visible,"[9] one of film's great attractions derives from its ability to reveal what happens *between* the frames of our own projective thought, confronting us with material phenomena that normally go unnoticed because they lie *below* certain psychic thresholds. We may surmise, further, that the apparatic "cuts" introduced, for example, by montage as film's predominant "machinery of the story"—its characteristic means of constructing narrative coherence—may function similarly to the "gaps" in the text of *Frankenstein*. Especially at moments of heightened self-reflexivity, this machinery may open up a desemiotized crack in the diegesis, unsettling the "textual" frame of reference that montage itself, among other devices, establishes.

Despite these possible analogies, I nevertheless remain skeptical about whether the materiality uncovered by Homans and Johnson is fully adequate to my purposes—or to those of feminism, for that matter. To begin with, just how material is a concept of embodiment that, like Homans's, is derived from Lacanian psychoanalysis? Even if the equation mother/matter pivots an important inversion of the androcentric perspective of a totalizing symbolic order, can the embodiment that emerges in the asignifying interstice escape the logic of the lack? Can it, in other words, be more than the mere negative of phallic fantasy and truly assert its independence from semiotic overlays? Is the maternal/material body simply another term for the unconscious, which as "the discourse of the Other" is itself, according to Lacan, "structured like a language"? Without attempting to provide definitive answers to these questions, let me intimate briefly one of my own (primarily film-theoretical) reasons for not going down this Lacanian path. The Lacanian psychoanalytic framework that dominated film studies since the 1970s has, regardless of whatever alternative possibilities may or may not reside in Lacanian psychoanalysis itself, proven itself persistently unable to think embodiment or materiality beyond semiotic structures. As Steven Shaviro argues in *The Cinematic Body*, the "founding texts" of this paradigm exhibit "an almost reflex movement of suspicion, disavowal, and phobic rejection" of the pre-theoretical pleasures of film-viewing (11).

---

9   See Williams's *Hard Core*.

Christian Metz, who more than any other theorist was responsible for the Lacanian turn in film studies, characterizes his own undertaking as "an attempt to disengage the cinema-object from the imaginary and to win it for the symbolic, in the hope of extending the latter by a new province" (Metz 3; qtd. in Shaviro 11). Likewise, Laura Mulvey, whose "Visual Pleasure and Narrative Cinema" set the stage for feminist appropriations of Lacanian film theory, renounces viewing pleasure altogether, reducing it to an act of identification with the monolithic forces of patriarchal representation (cf. Shaviro 12-13). While later work within the psychoanalytic frame has challenged the ahistorical, totalizing tendencies exemplified by Metz and Mulvey and acknowledged other possibilities for (among others) women viewers of mainstream cinema, the controlling view of the medium itself, as based on the interplay of signifiers present on the screen and absent signifieds at the source of their production, has largely remained intact. This view, which figures the cinematic image as the embodiment of an ontological lack and therefore theorizes spectatorship as little else than a negotiation with a primordial human condition (gendered or not), essentially blocks the path to recognizing (much less valorizing) the direct material interactions that take place in the cinema—what Shaviro aptly describes as "the visceral embodiment of film viewing, the pleasures and agitations of the flesh, and the literal insistence of the cinematic body" (64).[10]

But even if we can set aside Homans's Lacanian framework, other difficulties of an arguably more fundamental nature persist in the approach articulated by Johnson and Homans. As it functions in their texts, the destabilizing self-reflexive relation between *Frankenstein*'s narrative contents and its material textuality is in an important sense still a means of *reflection on the self*. Identifying Johnson's view of the text "not as a simple allegory of Shelley as writer, but as a textual allegory in the de Manian sense—and one with an irreducibly feminine *difference*" ("Not thus" 577), Mark Hansen points out that her reading unexpectedly validates "the male romantic ideology of self-expression" (578).[11] We recall Johnson's central question: "how indeed would it have been possible for Mary to represent feminine contradiction *from the point of view of its repression* otherwise than precisely in the gap [...]?" (9). Thus, according to Hansen:

---

10 It should be noted that Shaviro considers Carol J. Clover's *Men, Women, and Chainsaws: Gender in the Modern Horror Film*—a text which situates itself within psychoanalytic theory but ultimately "dismantle[s]" it—as "go[ing] a long way toward reclaiming" this neglected, bodily perspective (Shaviro 63, 64).

11 All of the references to Hansen in this and the following section are to his article "Not thus, after all, would life be given."

For all her effort to locate the "question of femininity" in an asignifying "gap" or black hole in the text, Johnson's deft illustration of textual contradiction attains significance only through its status as a "representation" of the female author. While Johnson shifts the focus away from the figure of the monster as a representation of the compromised female self, she cannot escape the larger problematic of representation itself. In her attempt to deflect de Manian allegory toward a specifically feminist end, Johnson is compelled to treat the fragmented and self-contradictory *text* of *Frankenstein* as *an allegory of the equally fragmented and self-contradictory female author*, an allegory in which the text itself assumes the role of *representing* the female self. Far from overcoming the limits of Poovey's thematic reading, Johnson's textual account forms what amounts to its complement: in both cases, the text of *Frankenstein* remains a "mere" figure, whether metaphor or allegory, for the predicament of the female author *within the male textual and social symbolic*. (578)

Clearly, the argument can be extended to Jacobus, who, noting the inevitability of "biologistic images," asks: "How else, after all, could the not-yet-written forms of *écriture féminine* represent themselves to our understanding?" (139). Is, then, the "French" reading still tacitly committed to Moers's physiologically determinate body and "sex" as the foundation of gender? Or does Hansen's argument take aim at an unfortunate, but argumentatively adventitious, choice of words?

Plainly, all parties are in agreement here that authorial intentions are beside the point, so the recourse to representation cannot be excused on the grounds that it is an inadvertent slip of the pen—such lapses are indeed the stuff "gaps" are made of. However, the notion that representability is a pragmatic imperative of feminism as a political undertaking is not so easily dismissed. In order to show, then, that invoking representation genuinely undermines poststructural feminism's marshaling of materiality against the male model of autonomous (and immaterial) selfhood, an independent argument is required that will link the feminists' underlying reasoning to the ideology they attempt to dismantle. Toward this end, I shall follow Mark Hansen in his argument that the appeal to de Manian allegory, which forms the implicit crux of Jacobus's, Johnson's, and Homans's readings, seriously underestimates the workings of matter in Shelley's text, effectively equating it with the mechanical, grammatical underside of language. Partially constitutive and potentially disruptive of meaning, this type of materiality is only "relatively exterior" to discourse and, indeed, to the symbolic imagination. Contending that *Frankenstein* constitutes what he calls a "machinic text" (578), Hansen's reading is apposite with the feminist view—*sans* Lacanian and de Manian theoretical frameworks—that the novel uncovers the romantic imagination's narcissistic blindness to material otherness, that it exposes the poets' practice of "reading" nature as an aggressive imposition of symbolic fantasies that ignore the historicity and alterity of the nonhuman world. Linking Shelley's "machinery of the story" to the literal, non-textual machinery of the industrial revolution, however, Hansen aims to "radicalize" the feminist reading by demonstrating that *Frankenstein*'s explosion of the male model is effected not by the self-deconstructive agency of language but through the radically exterior and historically nuanced influence of modern technology (578-79). It is my hope that this revision will yield a conception of embodiment that is at once ruggedly material and historically flexible, concrete and durable yet permeable to the dynamics of technological change. In short, I seek here the nexus that will illuminate the mutable and heterogeneous set of anthropotechnical interactions that is implicit in cinematic reception and self-reflexively problematized—but not solely by means of representation—in filmic renditions of *Frankenstein*.

From Text to Technology

As should be plain by now, my interest in feminism's critical reception of *Frankenstein* has less to do with specifically hermeneutic questions of the novel's meaning than with the notions of materiality and embodiment that arise when we ask those questions. Indeed, feminism's own concern with Shelley's text has all along been strategic in precisely this sense: reading *Frankenstein* became a key battleground for feminism, a site upon which to define oppositional strategies and negotiate internal coherence, largely *because* feminists recognized that an interpretive encounter with the novel necessarily problematizes (gendered) embodiment and its relations to (patriarchal) culture and discourse. Enlisting the text in a purpose that far exceeds any narrowly literary critical undertaking, feminist readers used the novel to probe those issues most pressing to them—questions, centrally, of the interrelations between political bodies and the body politic.[12] Spanning roughly a decade (from the mid-1970s to the mid-1980s), the readings I have here considered bear witness to a truly transitional phase in both the critical reception of *Frankenstein* and in feminism itself.[13] True to the model of transitionality suggested in the previous chapter, this transition was marked by polarizing conflicts, overlapping alternatives, and moments of liminal indecision. As I have construed them, the central debates revolved around a conundrum of sorts, which might be summarized

---

12 Note that Armstrong takes Poovey to task precisely for being too literary critical, i.e. for adopting a traditional notion of literature and adapting feminism to the traditional role of the literary critic. In effect, Armstrong's criticism of a political complicity between a mainstreamed feminist criticism and the "discourse of sexuality" expresses a requirement that *effective* feminist criticism should not simply be more than but categorically *other than* literary criticism.

13 At stake is nothing less than the transition from second-wave to third-wave feminism.

thus: *how can we (as feminists) theorize the body and (as women) live it too?* As we have seen, physiological conceptions came under attack as stiflingly essentialistic. Constructivist views aimed to reinstate the flexibility required for political efficacy by highlighting the discursive production of gender. But instead of dispensing with corporeality altogether, and resisting the body's total discursification—(hadn't, after all, women's bodies been inmates in the prison-house of language for long enough?)—an alternative notion of materiality arose, one that positioned the female body as an independently generative source of power and thus re-imagined an apparently autarchical patriarchy as a *defensive* strategy, *parasitic* rather than sovereign. In what might be read as a deconstructive revalorization of women's longstanding sociocultural marginalization, embodied materiality was relocated precisely to *the margin* of (male) discourse.

But by placing it just outside the envelope and no further, Hansen's argument suggests, this feminist strategy fails to go far enough. In particular, it closes off a material realm that lies more definitively beyond or below the threshold of language and discursive thought, an experiential realm in which technological materiality and bodily praxis meet *prior to* either conscious reflection or textual inscription. This suggestion will likely seem anathema to theorists of a deconstructionist bent, diagnosable as a recidivism into naïve realism and objectivist essentialism; it will thus be incumbent upon me to demonstrate that no such backsliding is involved. Beyond this negative requirement, two further conditions must be met: it must be shown, on the one hand, that Mary Shelley's own text endorses a view of materiality that is more radically alterior to textuality than poststructural feminist readings are willing or able to countenance and, on the other hand, that there are good, independent reasons to second this endorsement.

Establishing the first lemma involves a reading of the text that sees Shelley's critique of the romantic imagination as connected to, and hinged upon, a critique of instrumentalist conceptions of modern technology—a critique, that is, of the idea that industrial (and post-industrial) technologies can safely be regarded as tools whose employment is neutral with regard to the tool-user's autonomous subjectivity. Both scientific theory's mastery over nature and romanticism's sublimation of it are compromised by the emergence of nonhuman (technological) objects that themselves assert a degree of autonomy, for such technologies resist determination as "applied science" and, by installing themselves recalcitrantly in the nonhuman world, complexify "nature" and undermine poetic strategies of transcendence. Shelley's text therefore "indicts the sublimating gesture for the naive confidence with which it neutralizes the impact of the industrial revolution as such" and reveals a "profound reduction of technology" as an "enabling condition for the advent of romantic ideology" (580). This reduction occurs, according to Hansen, when the romantics figure "industrialization exclusively as a threat to cultural values," as a threat that "can be overcome through the rejuvenating effects of great literature" (580).[14] While not ignorant of the processes of industrialization and urbanization taking place around them, that is, the romantic poets necessarily turn a blind eye to any extra-cultural effects in order that these modern—and centrally technological—phenomena may be susceptible to containment by the cultural means of poetry. Essentially, romanticism enacts a version of what Hansen calls *technesis*—"the putting-into-discourse of technology" (581).[15] As we shall see, de Manian deconstruction enacts another, closely related version. Revealing the inherent shortcomings common to these approaches will thus go a long way towards linking a "hermeneutic" engagement with the text and the larger "philosophical" problem of technology's non-textual being, so that the second lemma of the argument—the reasons, independent of *Frankenstein*, for positing a radically non-discursive stratum of materiality—may be seen to follow from the first. Indeed, Shelley's text lays the groundwork by suggesting that it is what Hansen (drawing on Donna Haraway) calls the "monstrous *ontology* of technical creation" (583), rather than a property of textual inscription, that eludes representation. *Frankenstein* thus grounds its lacunae of reason and of narrative coherence in the altogether inhuman materiality of technology rather than the still marginally human (or discursive) materiality of *écriture*. Moreover, by demonstrating the *transformative* effects of technological materiality, the text of *Frankenstein* itself contributes to mitigating the charge that positing a material domain beyond discourse involves a tacit appeal to an essentialistic, naïve realism or situates matter as an inert *Ding an sich*.

According to Hansen, the monster functions as a "displaced figure for technological exteriority" (582): for technology as a material force beyond the anthropocentric frames of instrumentality or scientific theory. Not simply, as Martin Tropp contends, "a product of technology strictly defined as applied science" (Tropp 30; qtd. in Hansen 581), the monster instead insinuates "a subtle distinction between applied science *and* technology" (Hansen 581), pointing to a type of "technology *beyond* science" (582). That is, "Shelley's text discovers [...] a split between a 'restricted' form of technology as *techne* (or supplement) and a materially robust form of technology as radical exteriority" (584). Indeed, it is only through a "transgression *of* science" that Frankenstein is able to create the monster, by "go[ing]

---

14 In particular, Hansen finds this tendency exemplified in Wordsworth's *Preface to the Lyrical Ballads* and in "critical prose from Coleridge's various musings on literacy to [Percy Bysshe] Shelley's famous *Defence*, where the cultural work performed by poetry is elevated to a prophetic mode—a mode capable of counterbalancing the shortsighted politics of scientific progress, or as we would say today, of instrumental reason" (580).

15 See Hansen's *Embodying Technesis* for a systematic treatment of this tendency as it appears in a wide range of twentieth century theory.

behind the causal laws of Newtonian nature" and returning to the pre-scientific texts of alchemical authors (582). Thus, "the monster is not simply the result of scientific law applied, but rather a *technological product* in a quite specific, post-industrial sense: a product of a process whose 'effects' are neither predetermined nor constrained by theoretical principles of science" (582). Moreover, this type of technology—this type of monster—eludes not only science but any frame of human thought: "Through its resistance to literary or figural 'capture,' the monster embodies a form of invention that emerges as a material force *prior to and independently of* its appearance as the 'new' in the horizon of thought" (587).

To consistently conceive of the creature in this way, it is fundamental that we understand it, as Hansen says, as a necessarily *displaced* figure. This displacement results directly from the limits of textualization, for "insofar as literature's object is and only can be language, there can be no textualization of the technological real that wholly avoids the pitfall of *technesis*. No matter how genuine the desire to respect the robust materiality of technology, any literary presentation of technology *must* use language to speak about the real" (600-01). As an account of something that categorically resists representation, the novel *must* be "fragmented, *constitutively incomplete*" (590, emphasis added); hence, the "clumsy," "compromised," or "self-contradictory" qualities ascribed to Shelley's text result not primarily from the author's sociocultural position or the nature of language itself, but from a historical confrontation of thought with a humanly unthinkable material agency (590). Despite the limitations on communicating such a confrontation, if we conceive Shelley's text as working in and with the material realm it interrogates rather than attempting a *"referential correspondence"* or "non-reductive adequation between materiality and language" (601), it is then possible to see the text as an *enactment* of (rather than metaphor or allegory for) "the fundamental deterritorialization of the human perspective that [...] results from the advent of widespread technological change" (578).

In terms of the narrative, the dynamics of this deterritorialization are most clearly played out in Frankenstein's mountaintop confrontation with his creature and in the progressive transformation of the creator's subjectivity that ensues. Waxing poetic at the sight of Mont Blanc, Victor is jolted from his reveries by the unexpected appearance of the monster; the scene stages a "parody of the sublime" (595), unmasking romantic poetics' ideological suppression of "the priority of the real, in its brute literality, over the imagination" (597) and demonstrating the ultimate ineffectuality of a textualizing sublimation of nature in containing a monstrously unnatural threat. Moreover, the "strange coincidences" leading to Justine's execution for the murder of William and to Victor's own incarceration for the murder of Henry Clerval emphasize the incommensurability of an autonomous technology's alien logic to the human capacities of representation and expression. Nontextualizable, the monster's actions cannot be framed in narrative or apprehended by human institutions; they "constitute instances of pure chance" (604), humanly inexplicable events. Thus, knowing that Justine is innocent, Victor is nevertheless powerless to save her, for his explanation would seem the ravings of a madman. This is not *merely* an indictment of romantic ideology's irresponsibility and moral culpability; it is also an indication of "the radical exteriority of technology's impact with respect to the institution of human law" (604). As "the bearer of an experience which requires for its legitimation—and yet defies—sensory representation" (605), Victor is literally *unable* to construct a coherent tale; his knowledge simply could not be countenanced. Justine's tragic fate and Frankenstein's own brief imprisonment are thus "consequences of the domestication of monstrous chance—its inevitable ascription to some human agent" (606). That Frankenstein escapes execution is in part owing to his class status, an accident of birth that distinguishes him in the eyes of the law from Justine, thus emphasizing the arbitrarity attaching to any such domestication of technology's inhuman materiality under the categories (whether literary, scientific, legal, or moral) of the human(e).

Resigning himself, therefore, to silence, Victor is overtaken by a force beyond his will, so that confessions of his guilt "would burst uncontrollably from [him]," confessions for which he "could offer no explanation" (Shelley 180). If, as is common, we read the novel in terms of Frankenstein's failure to take parental responsibility for his "child," it is tempting to condemn him for recognizing his blame in the deaths of William, Justine, and Henry only now, after it is already too late. However, this reading imposes upon the events of the novel the very humanistic framework that the monster's embodiment of industrial technology calls into question; it therefore misses an important respect in which Victor's responsibility was *not his* to take until now. When he exclaims that "they died by my machinations" (Shelley 180), this must be deemed strictly false, a narcissistic projection of self that typifies romanticism's construction of the autonomous will, carrying it to its logical conclusion and presenting the ultimate domesticating instrumentalization of technology—*unless, that is, Frankenstein has literally become a machine*. The fact that his words "burst uncontrollably" indicates, according to Hansen, that Victor has "been turned into a passive registrar of monstrosity's threat" (608). Forswearing the desire to speak the incommunicable "truth," he submits to "pure machinism"; that is, "he *actually makes* the impossible leap into the real and thus flatly relinquishes the support of the symbolic" (608). At the end of the novel, his subjective volition completely obliterated and replaced by an unswerving automatism, Frankenstein functions literally *as a machine*. In his own words: "I pursued my path towards the destruction of the daemon, more [...] as the mechanical impulse of some power of which I was unconscious, than as the ardent desire of my soul" (Shelley 198).

To the extent that Shelley's text presents a narrative account of technologically induced deterritorialization, it remains, as we have seen, "constitutively incomplete." As an allegory, it may indicate technology's resistance to representation, even to the extent of inscribing insoluble aporiae, but to this extent it still remains focused on representation (or its impossibility) and thus committed (at least negatively) to *technesis* or the domestication of material exteriority. To see, then, how the text goes beyond these limits and, as Hansen claims, also "performs the very techno-logic it explores" (581), we must return to a central preoccupation of deconstructive feminist readings: the question of Shelley's authorship.

Interpreting her much touted "passivity" neither as a calculated response to the exigencies of her social situation nor (exclusively) as ushering in a particularly feminine alternative to the aggressively masculine (romantic) model of writing, Hansen frames Shelley's abdication of authority against the background of industrialization as the consequence of technology's erosion of a centered, human perspective. As we have seen, the novel asserts the radical materiality of *technological* invention—the primacy of "a form of invention that emerges as a material force *prior to and independently of* its appearance as the 'new' in the horizon of thought" (587)—and opposes it crucially to *literary* invention, which, as in the act of poetic sublimation, suppresses materiality and can only set "the new against the background of the old (i.e., within the history of thought)" (587). Considered in these terms, it is clear that Shelley's authorship, if truly open to industrialization and reproductive of (rather than merely representing) its material production processes, cannot be reduced to an active choice to oppose cognition with mechanism, but must instead involve a spontaneous ("uncontrollable") movement that renders Shelley, like the protagonist of her novel, the (necessarily incoherent) voice of machine automation itself.

Because its product, by analogy to an undomesticated novel technology, would be both unprecedented and discursively uncontextualizable, such "automatic writing" would imply an act of creation *ex nihilo*. But, as Hansen notes, Shelley's own theory of literary creation explicitly contradicts this vision. In the 1831 Introduction, Shelley writes:

Every thing must have a beginning, [...] and that beginning must be linked to something that went before. [....] Invention, it must be humbly admitted, does not consist in creating out of the void, but out of chaos; the materials must, in the first place, be afforded: it can give form to dark, shapeless substances, but cannot bring into being the substance itself. (8)

Invention, on this view, is a subject-centered epistemological act of *"recognizing the new"* (Hansen 588), an act that subordinates unpremeditated material emergence to cognitive capture and linguistic expression. And yet Shelley's Introduction also documents the breakdown of this theory, the undermining of her stated will, in connection with Shelley's attribution of her story's creation to a "waking dream" (9). What she sees "with shut eyes" (9) is "[i]tself an impossible invention by the terms of her own humble model, [a] creation from the void [which] manifests the 'working of some powerful engine,' a working that is—crucially—left entirely without explanation" (Hansen 588, citing Shelley 9). Though she credits the vision to her "imagination," this is a force that comes "unbidden, possesse[s] and guide[s]" her (Shelley 8-9); it is itself a "powerful engine" that causes Shelley's tale, like Frankenstein's confessions, to "burst uncontrollably" into view. Not an instrument of the autonomous subject, "imagination" here names something that resists utilization, that employs the author as *its* tool, and that therefore supplants autonomy with automatism. Let us suppose, then, that it names not a psychic entity or faculty at all but rather the unencompassable material reality of technological production that it presents to Shelley in dream-like form. "[M]aking only a transcript" of her dream (Shelley 9), Shelley engages in (or, more appropriately, *is engaged in*) "a form of passive registration" (Hansen 588), equivalent to Frankenstein's eventual machinism; the resulting "text-machine" claims as its victims not only the masculine models she opposes but also her own model of literary invention (587). The self-reflexive relation of "Shelley's paradoxical status as an author and Frankenstein's paradoxical status as an inventor" is inextricably linked to "the paradoxical status of the text itself: as the product of an impossible act of invention (a creation out of the void), the text takes form through an unintended sacrifice of authorial intention and functions *machinically*, outside the scope of intentionality" (Hansen 589). If "passivity" is a strategy, then it cannot be Shelley's own—for ownership is a category of domestication: whether of texts, technologies, nature, bodies, women, or as Donna Haraway might say, of *other* monsters as well.

PARABOLIC MUTATIONS: FROM TEXTUAL ALLEGORY TO MACHINIC PARABLE

At first glance, Hansen's reading might seem to agree in essence with those of Johnson and Homans, the greatest difference being the emphasis placed on industrial technology rather than gendered embodiment as the locus of material agency. However, herein lies an *essential* difference, a fundamental disparity between the ontologies that underlie the respective approaches. Most concisely stated, the deconstructive feminist readings deny the existence of what Hansen characterizes as the "robustly material" stratum in which technological production is said to occur, limiting materiality to the recalcitrance of textual inscription with respect to figural, discursive coherence. As a result, the radical exteriority of technological production is domesticated on the model of literary invention, severely compromising Shelley's "deconstruction" of romantic poetics and obscuring its historical dimension. As Hansen argues, de Man's deconstructive notion of "textual allegory," which forms the crux of the poststructural feminist readings, "contains an essential reference to technology—a reference which harbors an entire theory of technological invention" (591). Establishing a "homology of machine with text" (591), de Man asserts that "[t]he machine is like the grammar of the text when it is isolated from its rhetoric, the merely formal element without which no text can be generated" (*Allegories of Reading* 294; qtd. in Hansen 591). All language is in this sense "mechanical," a fact which opens semantic meaning and reference to a fundamental deconstruction that occurs automatically, "independently of any desire; as such it is not unconscious but mechanical" (de Man 298; qtd. in Hansen 591). Seen thus, the workings of textual allegory are effectively equivalent (i.e. equal in terms of effect) to the effacements of representation and subjective volition hypothesized as the (in)human consequences of industrialization. This convergence, however, is superficial; the underlying causes to which the two approaches ascribe the deconstruction of representation could not be more distinct. Absorbing the machine into language, de Man generalizes this deconstruction as ahistorical, thus cutting off the connection it might have, as in Shelley's case, to concrete technological revolutions.

Derrida, in his reflections on de Manian allegory, goes so far as to turn its disruptive movement into a global theory of "invention," thereby conflating literary and technological forms of production. Specifying the action of invention as "finding," "discovering," or "unveiling" something new, Derrida situates the effects of technology squarely in the realm of thought, as an epistemological event. Coming close to Shelley's "humble" model of literary invention "out of chaos" but not "out of the void" (Shelley 8), Derrida writes that invention "produces what, as *techne*, was not already found there but is still not created, in the strong sense of the word, is only put together, starting with a stock of existing and available elements, in a given configuration" ("Psyche" 43; qtd. in Hansen 593). Moreover, such invention "gives rise to an event, tells a fictional story and produces a machine by introducing a disparity or gap into the customary use of discourse, by upsetting to some extent the mind-set of expectation and reception that it nevertheless needs" (Derrida 43; qtd. in Hansen 593). Technological no less than literary invention is therefore a matter of *recognizing* novelty against the background of established meanings; it perplexes in the realm (or from the margins) of thought and language alone. Genuinely extra-textual, a-subjective materiality has no place in this system.

As a replacement for "allegory," I suggest embracing "parable"—in the sense articulated by Brian Massumi in his extraordinary book *Parables for the Virtual*—as a more appropriate description of Shelley's text. As Massumi employs the term, parable names "[t]he genre of writing most closely allied with the logical form of the example" (21); and the example, in turn, is "an odd beast" (17). Following Giorgio Agamben's suggestion that an example "holds for all cases of the same type" but is paradoxically also "included in these"—that "[i]t is one singularity among others, which, however, stands for each of them and serves for all" (Agamben 9-10; qtd. in Massumi 17)—Massumi adopts what he calls an "exemplary" method to broker an "affirmative or inventive" (rather than merely critical) type of critical writing, one that borrows concepts from unrelated (mostly scientific) disciplines and sets them to work in an alien context, all the while avoiding mere "application" (17). Migrating concepts from their home jurisdictions, stealing them away from their intended purposes, and transplanting them into foreign bodies allows them, according to Massumi, to develop their own productive potential and to effect unexpected, uncontrollable mutations in the host (18-21). It is in this very spirit that I recommend purloining Massumi's terms, for they may hold the key to understanding precisely the relation between the industrial revolution's technical inventions and the machinic production (and productivity) of Shelley's text.

Invention and productiveness play a crucial role in Massumi's critical method, not only as values to strive toward but also as phenomena (of emergence, ontogenesis, qualitative change, and transition) to be uncovered in the realities subjected to critical scrutiny. These are phenomena, according to Massumi, that despite being championed widely have consistently been missed by recent cultural theory. Contending that the poststructuralist notion of "positionality" (as it occurs in the concept of "subject-positions") has been particularly effective in blocking our means of apprehending change—plotting every subject and every "body" on a grid as so many "combinatorial permutations," so that all "cultural emplacements, including the 'subversive' ones, [must finally appear] precoded into the ideological master structure" (3)—Massumi suggests "productivism" and even "inventionism" as felicitous alternatives to constructivism (12). Directed against pan-textualist and omni-discursivist paradigms, the projected theory would break with the domestication of materiality that we find in de Manian deconstruction. The underlying notions of production and invention—pertaining to embodied interactions with a non-inert world that, in addition to its semiotic coding, is also materially concrete and immediate in its impacts—promise therefore a perspective that sidesteps the cognitive-discursive reduction of technological novelty.

The emergent phenomena of production or invention, which Massumi explicitly extends to both natural and cultural processes of change, as well as—and centrally—to liminal cases of crossover from one domain to another (12), are themselves "exemplary" phenomena in the sense described above. In Massumi's words: "An example is neither general (as is a system of concepts) nor particular (as is the material to which a system is applied). It is 'singular'" (17). This singularity implies that invention is simply not assimilable to conceptual thought, that its product is nonetheless not empirically reducible to inert matter. It is both materially real and independently active. From the perspective of systematic thought—whether this be "everyday" discourse and mindsets or a theoretically systematized constructivism—invention/production in this strong sense not only disrupts, deconstructs, or deterritorializes established patterns; it does so from out of the blue, *ex nihilo*.

So Massumi's theory of invention is willing to countenance the ontological exteriority of material, technical production, but what would it mean to say that Mary Shelley's text "exemplifies" industrial technology? According to common usage of the word "example," textual exemplification might suggest "illustration," as employed towards the purpose of explanation or persuasion; as an instrument, the example implies authorial distance from that which is exemplified, and the textual product itself operates in the manner of modeling, representing. On this understanding, metaphor and similitude are the modes in which exemplification functions. This functionality of the example might itself be said to be machine-like: content can be plugged into it in order to derive a rhetorical product (e.g. a model), and the product can in turn be applied to a larger instrumental purpose. But this type of example can only ever be machine-*like*, never really a machine. Indeed, technology is here reduced in the manner of *technesis* to a figure, denied exteriority with respect to discursive thought. To conceive *Frankenstein* as an example in this sense is merely to say that it, or one or more of its thematic parts (e.g. Frankenstein or the monster), is *like* a machine. Modeling technology, the text is not an invention in the strong sense but merely an "application" of technical principles, where the latter—prior to their utilization and, indeed, *as the enabling condition for their employment*—have themselves already been "captured" cognitively and modeled anthropomorphically on the workings of human thought. In this reading, we hear the voice of the policeman, the "exemplary" representative of human social order, as he waves us by: "Move along, please: nothing to see, no monster here."

Can we, then, conceive the text not as an illustration but as an *exemplar*, a true specimen, of technology? It is not, of course, a piece of machinery that can be put to work in a factory, precisely because it is textual. However, this does not mean that it is doomed to be a mere allegory in the de Manian sense, for textuality does not, *per definitionem*, exhaust an exemplar's being; the "singularity" stipulated of the relevant type of example is categorically opposed to unrestricted iterative generality, to pre-scriptive systematicity or "categoricity" itself. It must, therefore, be historically specific and not "of the type" of an ahistorical grammatological machinism. In short, if *Frankenstein* is an exemplar of industrial technology, then it is not a "supplement" to the latter. Paradoxically standing for the class to which it also belongs, the example "is defined by a disjunctive self-inclusion: a belonging to itself that is simultaneously an extendibility to everything else with which it might be connected (one for all, and all in itself). In short, exemplification is the logical category corresponding to self-relation" (Massumi 17-18). It is imperative, however, that self-relation not be confused with self-referentiality, with the linguistic self-enclosure predicated of romantic poetics and theoretically perpetuated by structuralism (including its poststructural and deconstructionist incarnations). Reference, including non-reference, the failure or deconstruction of reference, cannot suffice as a category for grasping the positive singularity of the example—for conceiving Shelley's text as an invention in its own right rather than a merely critical exposure (whether of patriarchy, romantic sublimation, or even *technesis*). Instead, exemplary self-relation is related to *Frankenstein*'s self-reflexivity, which consists not just in a content/form relation but also in the creator/creation parallelisms that, for lack of a better way of speaking, are illustrated *in* the text and enacted *without*, in the text's production or authorship; transversing the boundary between "inside" and "out," the "relation" of self-relation is one of *resonance* rather than containment, the concentric radiation of rippling waves that reflect and form new centers of radiation when they meet with points of resistance.[16] As such, exemplary self-relation is multiplicatively many-centered and therefore, from the perspective of system, a-centric; accordingly, through its extendibility the "self" in self-relation is without determinate or absolute positional moorings.

And yet all of this, by hypothesis, pertains to the level of concrete material reality, is not restricted to the semiotic play of abstract concepts or the movements of psychic phantasy. How so? Let us suppose, apparently uncontroversially, that the steam engine—the real, materially productive industrial machine *par excellence*—embodies an exemplar of technology. Is it possible to specify a relation between it and Mary Shelley's authorship of *Frankenstein*? A relation, that is, beyond one of inspiration and impetus for the author's interpretive-expressive engagement with her own ideas of technology?[17] Certainly, the steam engine fulfills the paradoxical definition of exemplary singularity: it both stands for industrial technology (as its very paradigm) and is simultaneously a real part of the class for which it stands. Paradigmaticity, of course, positions the machine in conceptual space, yet it would be absurd to deny the very material workings of a concrete specimen. Additionally assuming that human bodies (again seemingly uncontroversially, but in fact against

---

16 Compare Massumi, 13-14.
17 That is, I am seeking a relation beyond the political response to machine-breaking that Paul O'Flinn sees the novel articulating and, in the 1831 edition, altering. It is this type of political relation that O'Flinn faults the Universal and Hammer film versions for excising. (See O'Flinn's "Production and Reproduction: The Case of *Frankenstein*.") Ultimately, I am looking for a basis for describing non-ideological and non-conceptual relations between Frankenstein films and (filmic) technologies, but as I aim to show, for example in Chapter 7, this does not mean that such relations are non-political.

the grain of a range of theoretical tendencies) are not only discursively constructed but also materially concrete, is it not obvious that the machine may have a direct, even physical, impact on human beings? At the level of minute vibrations, for example, such physical impacts are even capable of bypassing conscious registration altogether, impinging upon bodies at a pre-personal level immune to figuration or cognitive apprehension. Assuming further that the body's materiality is not restricted to its anatomico-physiological properties but instead encompasses phenomenal propensities (related to corporeal motility, sensation, posture, habit etc.) that in fact extend the body beyond the envelope of the skin, then we need not restrict the scope of technology's material impact to the group of bodies (e.g. those of factory workers) that come into immediate physical contact with machinery. Nor, paradoxically, must we restrict the class of pre- or sub-personal impacts to minute movements that fall below the threshold of personal registration; for the consciously perceived presence and inescapably apparent operations of even the noisiest machine will also imply silent, non-conscious changes in habitualized movement and bodily comportment (for example in the factory worker refunctionalized from a handloom weaver to a power loom operator, incorporated into the machine and determined by its rhythms). While the obviousness of the machine's workings will necessarily imply its being coded and conceptualized, an unthematized but materially *felt* "intensity" will subtend and accompany the subjective perception of the machine as a spatially extended object. As the proximal recipients of technology's impacts leave the factories and carry their reconfigured embodiment with them, these intensities become subject to "communication" in the family, at the marketplace, in the realm of entertainment, and in the social body at large: subject, that is, to an embodied, gestural transmission of affect that takes place below (and possibly quite at odds with) the level of verbal exchanges that explicitly address the subject of technology.[18] Materially radiating from these a-subjective centers (unthematized bodies), resonating in the bodies they come into contact with, which in turn reflect the silently communicated intensities of technological impact and unintentionally propagate an epidemic infection of sorts, radical changes in human embodiment take place without even anyone necessarily taking notice of the fact. Evolutionary invention is not an epistemological event.

Through a series of relatively uncontroversial premises, we have arrived at a material mechanism capable of explaining how Shelley could be infected by industrial technology and induced, without her intentional consent, to embody the rhythms of the steam engine, turning her into a machine productive of another machine: *Frankenstein* as an exemplar of technological invention. (If the steam engine seems improbable as the germinal source of her infection, we might consid-

---

18 Compare Massumi, 23-45.

er that another exemplary industrial technology emerged with and around the factory: the modern city. Indeed, given the historical context and the scope of rapid technological change, the choice of examples is to a certain degree arbitrary. Crucial is that the chosen example exhibits the material singularity discussed here.) Seen thus, the novel is not set off from the material reality it describes but partakes of it, drawing its materials from there, transducing them, and feeding them back into the flux.[19] Neither a metaphor nor an allegory, *Frankenstein* is an exemplary *parable* of historical technological revolution and the concomitant anthropotechnical revision of humanity.

As a parabolic machine, the novel acts not only as a "convertor," translating material impulses into textual form; beyond this, it embodies another material node in the expansive network in which technology's sub-personal impacts are transmitted. Whereas the textualization of romantic sublimation would act as a shock absorber, dampening the felt impact of technological materiality by dissipating it into an ethereally transcendent realm, *Frankenstein* functions as a distributor, reflecting incoming impulses rather than arresting them. Its mode of "reflection" is not that of the mirror (which can only ever show what the observer can see from his or her own perspective), nor of sociolinguistic thematization (where reflection-as-inquiry remains rooted in representation), nor even that of the limit case of philosophical reflection (which, however abstract it may be, can never transcend its centering in the inquiring subject or the "self" of God himself). Instead, the novel's reflection is best understood on the model of the simple physical reflex, whereby the force of an action produces a reaction that alters the trajectory but continues the original movement, conserving the original energy. That *Frankenstein* is also *self*-reflexive means not that it is self-contained, an unmoved mover, for it is conditioned as the recipient of external forces. But this reception is itself productive; through it, the novel is invested with the energy of the machine at the moment of the text's genesis, charged to expel itself in an ongoing chain reaction. On the other hand, as an

---

19 Transduction here is used in a triple sense, corresponding to the three definitions listed in the Oxford English Dictionary: 1. "The action of leading or bringing across." (Marked by the OED as *rare*.) 2. "The action or process of transducing a signal." (I.e. the process of converting, by means of a transducer, one form of energy into another, as in a microphone's transduction of acoustic waves into voltages.) 3. "*Microbiology*. The transfer of genetic material from one cell to another by a virus or virus-like particle." A fourth meaning, which I discuss in Chapter 6, is latent here as well: viz. Gilbert Simondon's notion of a transductive relation as a relation in which the related terms do not precede or exist outside of the relation. (Adrian Mackenzie's *Transductions: Bodies and Machines at Speed* provides a useful introduction to, and an interesting exploration of, Simondon's concept.)

emergent singularity, the text can no more be *traced back* to an original impulse than it can be used up in its reception; it is, ontogenetically speaking, poised *between* the moments of charge and discharge that identify its place—co-ordinate it—in a (mechanical) system. Singularity, that is, marks a liminal position *at the cusp of* systemic positionality, which for its part implies stasis and pre-existence, but which itself emerges in a dynamic movement that, though posited as concretely real, can only be hypothesized in an abstract interval *between* possible positions.[20] Since the novel, on this model, does not pre-exist the charge it (paradoxically) receives from industrial technology but comes into existence simultaneously with the arrival of this charge, it truly embodies the monstrous ontology of the industrial machine: it is characterized by the unexplainable, *ex nihilo* emergence that makes modern technology immune to cognitive capture. And discharging itself onto its readers, *Frankenstein* propagates this ontology more through shocks to the nervous system than by words, turning its recipients into machines like it, recreating them in its own monstrous image.[21]

The point is not that Shelley's (early) readers consciously *feel like* machines, but that in the confluence of forces in which the text partakes (the embodied effects/affects of industrial technology and urbanization) they begin to *function* machinically, receiving and reflecting impacts that gradually permeate the material realm and reorganize the embodied basis of human subjectivity and sociality. The deeper meaning of the industrial revolution, for which *Frankenstein* no less than the steam engine stands as an exemplary technology, consists in a *silent* revolution that undergirds the more noticeable transformations that follow or supervene upon it: a mechanization of the lifeworld that enables, necessitates, and/or undercuts the thematization of technology in ethical, political, socioeconomic, psychic, cultural, or other discursive frames.

Outlook: Re-Embodying the Machine

What I am working towards here is a general model of the anthropotechnical interface as a material pivot in a realm of historical change that both exceeds and grounds our perceptual, conceptual, and linguistic faculties to register change or write history. Accordingly, embodiment—conceived as distinct from and ontologically prior to the discourses and social subjectivities founded upon it—is historically variable, and it varies in response to technological change; the affective body itself is decomposed and reconstituted when inserted into novel technological cir-

---

20 Compare Massumi, especially 6-12.
21 Compare Hansen, "Not thus," 608.

cumstances. Seen thus, embodiment (and, *a fortiori*, subjectivity) is not separable from these circumstances but is born (and re-born) from out of them; technological and human embodiment are co-constitutive, for the former redefines the shape of the latter as it opens new means of contact with the world as environment, while, on the other hand, the technological environment is meaningless or ineffectual without a body thus "environed" and affected. We are approaching here a theory of transitionality as the monstrous (re)birth of the anthropotechnical body in its movement *between* a given material environment and another. Broadly textualized monstrosities—whether they be domesticated as normalcy-enforcing social freakeries or championed as uncontainable destroyers of conceptual order—are, on my model, to be treated as secondary responses to and effects of material passages: transitions that radically elude discourse as they *shift the ground* of embodied experience *upon which we think and speak*. My hierarchizing of material and discursive forms of monstrosity is not meant to deny the reality or power of textual (or even architextual) formations and deformations; rather, this materialist bias is, I contend, fundamental to avoiding ahistorical essentialism—whether of an outright idealist sort (towards which I see certain strands of poststructuralism/deconstruction tending no less than structuralism/constructivism) or of an apparently materialist variety (as when physiology is taken as the basis for stable gender differences or human nature itself). Though it may not be apparent right now, my view of anthropotechnical interaction as a site of revolutionary change takes its cue from a "scientific realist" approach to the biological body as evolutionary product, thereby positing material-environmental interactions that antedate and enable the emergence of human organisms, social formations, language, and thought. Yet the mutations that I propose occur as the result of technology's "unnatural selection" elude scientific description and imply revolutionary changes in the structure of the world—transforming the global context within which *any* description is situated. From a certain (epistemological) perspective, this will be seen as a clearly "anti-realist" theory; yet its thrust is decidedly pre-epistemological: the affective body transformed by the processes of anthropotechnical evolution is not encompassed by the determinations of anatomy and physiology, nor are its affects to be confused with personal feelings, emotions, or psychological quantities.

These claims demand explanation, as do the models of which they are predicated. The next chapter will attempt to bridge some of the expository leaps that I have made here and elucidate some of the consequences for my project's theoretical orientation. There I shall seek to provide a more careful justification of my theory of anthropotechnical transformation both on a general level and with regard to the particular historical context of the industrial revolution, which forms the basis of my generalization. But here we are confronted with perhaps the most glaring of this chapter's loose ends, which concerns precisely the relation and relevance of industrial to cinematic technologies. What do the former have to do with the latter? More specifically, what does the industrial revolution—beyond its being the context in which Mary Shelley wrote *Frankenstein*—have to do with Frankenstein films? What, indeed, does Mary Shelley have to do with the filmic deviations from her text? In each case, my answer is related to the notion of the parable. I have argued that *Frankenstein* (the novel), as a machine, serves as a parable for the industrial revolution as a historical reconfiguration of the affective body. And this revolution can be taken as a parable (or paradigmatic example, if one prefers) for other such transformations, including those effected by the mediating technologies of cinema. Despite differences in their social-historical settings and use-contexts, the steam engine and the apparatus of camera/projector are abstractly similar in reshaping humans' phenomenal relations to the world and the affective capacities of their bodies. And like Mary Shelley's novel, Frankenstein films can serve as parables for the media-technical transitions in which they participate and within which they are enveloped as singular exemplars of broader changes. Mary Shelley's paradoxically passive act of creation, along with its replication in the text she created, stands then as a parable for the embodied impact of such changes—a parable, therefore, for the sorts of non-cognitive transactions that occur between corporeally situated spectators, filmic texts, and the machinery of cinema in historical transition.

A more precise reconnection of this chapter's considerations with the cinema will be the major task of Chapter 6, but some indication of my general trajectory can and must be given now. One of the consequences of pollinating a techno-phenomenological approach to the cinema with the conception of technological production put forward here is that—analogous to Shelley's act of textual production, which produces a machine rather than just a text—cinematic production cannot be limited to the narrow confines of filmmaking, certainly not in the (quasi-romantic) sense in which films are seen to embody the creative vision and expressive will of their directors. Nor, though, should the focus lie exclusively on the technical processes and apparatuses involved, even if these play a central role in bringing about cinematic transitions. Instead, I propose looking closer at how these instances ("style" and machinery, among others) intersect in spectators' acts of reception, which themselves shall be conceived as acts of production. That is, surrendering oneself to the technological milieu of the cinema, like Shelley's act of surrendering herself to industrialization, produces something new: not only a narrative/textual structure (the film "in the spectator's head") but, subtending such structures as the ground of their construction, unprecedented bodily affects—new capacities for engaging with and being engaged by the world.

Consider, for instance, that the world in close-up is not the same as the world seen up close, as if one were to physically inspect the objects of one's daily concerns by placing them just inches from one's face. Indeed, such a fantasy hypothesizes radical changes in bodily comportment, habit, and movement (lots of crouching, climbing, and crawling to achieve the right perspective), but it fails to grasp the *qualitative* change that the empirical world would undergo if one were to put the fantasy into practice. It is easy to imagine that a close-up of a wall clock is in some sense "the same" as the view I achieve by climbing a ladder to inspect the clock or by taking it down and holding it in front of me.[22] But imagine looking at an onrushing car from a position level with and just inches from its front bumper, as opposed to the (still dangerous) distance of ten yards. In the latter case, my heart leaps and my adrenaline-charged body races across the street before I consciously identify and assign a meaning to the sound of screeching brakes; seen up close, on the contrary, I never make it to the other side, never register the electrifying rush and the corporeally relieved slump which, for me, are inseparable from the objective constellation of a near-miss. The close-up, then, shows not the *same* world from the point of view of a quantitative reduction of distance but instead opens up a qualitatively *different* world, one in which I both see the finer details of the bumper and live to breathe a sigh of relief. In this experiential conjunction, however, the conjoined elements—my vision and my autonomic responses—are alike transformed, both in scale (vis-à-vis the proportions established by my body) and in intensity (as registered by my nervous system). Or, as another example, consider the altogether (humanly) impossible perspectives realized in time-lapse and reverse-motion projection: here I do not just witness the familiar world from an unfamiliar angle; rather, my body is subject to a new temporality, to a new causality, and I am reconfigured as a result. Normal patterns of perception and motor response are put out of play, thus in a sense overwhelming subjectivity with a spectacle that defies the objective parameters of its everyday orientation.[23] But this is not (or not just) trau-

---

22 This was considered, in Chapter 2, under the heading of the phenomenal equivalence that Don Ihde describes in relation to optical technologies of magnification. See *Bodies in Technology* 46.

23 For the sake of brevity, I am here omitting an essential reference to historical situation. Such spectacles today may be experienced as perfectly normal, due to our conditioning and familiarity with them. They must surely have been more radical in impact for early film viewers, as I have insinuated in earlier chapters. Just as normal science must follow revolution, so reterritorialization must follow deterritorialization. The thrust of my argument, though, is that normalization is not a return to the status quo but an entry into a transformed reality. My goal is to open precisely these processes of transformation, to which we are typically blind, to historical investigation. The point of these examples is to clear the ground for such investigation by highlighting technology-dependent, *qualitative* differences that militate against the atemporal objectivism at the heart of "normalized" perception—against the very conditions of our historical blindness.

ma, in the sense of a psychic self disrupted; instead, it is a productive reconfiguration of the totality of possible relations between my body and the external world, conceived as an emergent constellation.

As I have argued in relation to exemplary moments in *Dog Factory*, Edison's *Frankenstein*, and Whale's *Frankenstein*, film-viewing carries with it a potential of dissolution: film-textual coherence is subject to interruption by spectacle, and, more radically, seemingly stable subject/object relations can and do break down. Until now, I have approached such moments negatively, from the perspective of empirical and phenomenal formations that are "deconstructed" in diegetic fragmentation or subjective implosion; I am now suggesting a reversal of perspectives, a reorientation that will allow us to grasp what heretofore has announced itself as rupture, gap, or caesura from the angle of positive singularity: as an irruption that hinges transformative *reconstructions* and passages *between* states of being. From this angle, a radically nonhuman matter intervenes through mediating technologies to engage viewers in an unwilled (though perhaps not unwilling) *reinvention* of their bodies, in the process (and in that proportion) producing a new *world* of material relation. Reception *qua* production thus combines passivity and activity, effectively effacing their distinction, in what Massumi calls a "space of *passion*" (61), an "infra-empirical space" of bodily intensities suspended between spatio-temporal states in which a body might act on or be acted upon by empirically identifiable objects (57). Massumi relates his notion of "passion" to Spinoza's definition of the body in terms of "relations of movement and rest," which Massumi paraphrases as the body's "*power* (or potential) to affect or be affected," the simultaneity of which marks the body itself as "transition" (15). As the conjunction of active-passive capacities, the body is viewed here abstractly, not as a conceptual construct but as a material stratum *subtracted* from empirical situations in which it can be actualized as either the recipient or agent of forces in determinate relations.[24] This is what Deleuze and Guattari term the "body without organs"[25]; in relation to the special case of a film actor's embodiment for camera and screen of a radically different form of embodied being—the example is Ronald Reagan's portrayal of an amputee—Massumi terms it "the body without an image" (57); and with a greater em-

---

24 In conversation with Deleuze and Guattari, Massumi develops an elaborate conceptual apparatus, which includes terms such as "virtuality" and "incorporeal materialism" to mark distinctions from the "actual" states and "possibilities" of empirically circumscribed bodies. To avoid unnecessary complication, I dispense with most of Massumi's terminology and retain the terms "corporeality," "embodiment," and even "body" and its derivates. It should be clear, though, that I do not mean objectively determinate *somata*, and if there is any doubt I will be sure to indicate the sense in which I am using the terms.

25 See Chapter 6 of Deleuze and Guattari' *A Thousand Plateaus*.

phasis on spectatorial reception and embodied "abjection" as a pre-subjective interpenetration of flesh and nonobjective image, Steven Shaviro terms it simply "the cinematic body."[26]

Most accessibly, though, as a demonstration that this "passionate" body-in/as-transition is not just an idealized philosophical-theoretical abstraction but a materially efficacious reality, arrived at not through mental but *performative* subtractions of affective intensity from subjective particularizations—what might be called an *abstraction in practice*—Massumi illustrates his theory in terms of biological processes underlying sensory and cognitive delimitations of internal/external realities. Plainly, conscious perception of the outside world is mediated by the body; external stimuli must be relayed via eyes, ears, mouth, nose, and skin to the brain in order that impressions received by outwardly directed senses can be processed as recognizable objects and synthesized into a world in which I, as subject, can act. On the way back out, as well, voluntary action must pass once more through the medium of the body as a motor instrument in order that I can achieve subjective expression or cause objective movement. The phenomenal-empirical world, and my body as part of it, is both agent and patient of actual and potential interaction. However, the really interesting aspect of these transactions is what happens in the middle, in the embodied interval before stimuli become ordered perceptions or before subjective intentions achieve objective expression.

In this passage, *between* subject and object and (temporally as well as ontologically) *prior to* their delineation, discrete senses converge, synaesthetically, in proprioception: "the sensibility proper to the muscles and ligaments" (Massumi 58). Outwardly directed or "exteroceptive" tactility, in particular, is turned inward, "enveloping the skin's contact with the external world in a dimension of medium depth: between epidermis and viscera" (58). Subjective determinations of objective form play no role at this fleshly level, so that we may speak of a bodily filtering or abstraction of pure movement taking place here, the residue of which forms a nonconscious proprioceptive or "muscular memory" informing "skill, habit, posture" (59). Here the passive reception of stimuli comingles, indifferently, with the action of motor response. Our inability to visualize (and subsequently verbalize) the details of the most familiar of our everyday routes, to recall the objective appearance of streets we nevertheless navigate with ease (as if in "auto-pilot"), attests to the praxical primacy of this realm, which is "asubjective and nonobjective" in nature (59).[27]

---

26 Shaviro's repeated appeals to affective states of "abjection" draw on the senses explored in Julia Kristeva's *Powers of Horror: An Essay on Abjection*.

27 On the "auto-pilot" role of proprioception in spatial orientation, see Massumi, Chapter 8, esp. 178-84.

Deeper still than the proprioceptive domain is the "interoceptive" one of "viscerality": the dimension, quite literally, of gut feelings.[28] Here we return to the speeding car discussed above.[29] The important point is that "[v]isceral sensibility immediately registers excitations gathered by the five 'exteroceptive' senses even before they are fully processed by the brain" (Massumi 60). Only in retrospect, after crossing the street safely, do I consciously recognize what has just happened to me, but it was my body, operating autonomously (or autonomically), that got me there. In a very direct manner, then, my body enabled subjective perception, which emerges as a *re*-collection of sense (and sensibility) anticipated by animal viscerality. Situated *between* determinate states susceptible to recognition, viscerality can be defined as "the perception of suspense"; it can be thought of as "a rupture in the stimulus-response paths, a leap in place into a space outside action-reaction circuits" (61). This is the "space of passion," the "body without organs" in an altogether non-mystical guise, derived in practice and shown to be both physiologically and ontologically fundamental to "organized" corporeality.

Together, proprioception and viscerality mark out the realm of pre-personal affect, the cognitive processing and personal recognition of which define emotion or feeling in a world articulated according to distinctions of inside/outside and subject/object (Massumi 61). What we have seen, though, is that the world of empirical and emotional qualification is radically dependent upon a bodily realm that escapes such determination. Thus, "proprioception subtracts qualified form from movement," while "viscerality subtracts quality as such from excitation. It registers *intensity*" (61). Intensity, on this view, is a "nonqualified substance" that despite its lack of qualification is radically non-inert in its interaction with the gut; this substance fills the "maximally abstract spatial matrix" of proprioceptive memory: the embodied record of movement and spatial relation minus their determinate relata (61). From this perspective, the empirical world as we know it is the emergent effect of embodied "indetermination." Beyond outlining a general cosmogony, though, and more importantly for my purposes, this account provides the necessary theoretical infrastructure for countenancing radically non-phenomenal shifts in the structure of the world, via mechanisms not reducible to psychic or textual agencies, and for positioning anthropotechnical interaction as a robustly material factor in such change.

---

28 Massumi, in an endnote, makes explicit that his notion of "viscerality" refers, physiologically, to the enteric nervous system, a "neuronal network in the gut," the workings of which have been shown to be independent of the central nervous system.

29 Indeed, this is one of Massumi's examples, which I have modified, with reference to the close-up, to highlight a difference between cinematic and non-cinematic experience.

My argument is that we interface with mediating technologies directly at this medium depth of corporeality, as a condition of our subjective grasp on and interaction with the world, so that when the "face" of technology is transformed, so too is the "face" of the body; the human-technological "inter-face" itself is revolutionized, and with it the world. Proprioceptively, habits are transformed as we learn new skills and incorporate new technologies; our mesodermic memories are tuned to new movements. Viscerally, the impact of technological novelty, conceived as a clash of familiar modes of apprehending the world with an incommensurable sensorimotor interface, may be even more radical; at this level, shock may be experienced directly on and in the body prior to and autonomously from subjective awareness.

An example seems in order. A staircase, as a simple technology for ascending and descending within architectural spaces, must be seen as more than a physical construction of wood or stone; it is an interface with the world, both human and nonhuman, that opens *for* humans access to material locations that would otherwise remain unreachable. Indeed, building a staircase *creates* such spaces, makes them potentially occupiable, thus constructing in a small but very direct way a portion of the world. Proprioceptively, the staircase evokes a matrix of coordinated movements that we learn as children and apply, mostly unthinkingly, to the various staircases we encounter in the course of our lives. This matrix is abstract, in the sense that it is applicable to a wide range of staircases, more or less independent of their material construction, dimensions, or location; it is nevertheless concrete, encompassing specific patterns and rhythms of muscle contractions and relaxations, precisely timed and balanced against one another. These habitualized movements are only partially accessible to conscious experience, as is adequately demonstrated by the strangeness of posture revealed in Eadweard Muybridge's famous images of staircase locomotion. As with other habitual movements (walking, running, swinging a golf club), self-consciousness in stair-climbing may in fact stand in the way of successful or "natural" execution.

Enter, now, the motor-driven escalator (a technology whose early history coincides in remarkable ways with the early history of cinema[30]). Compared to the staircase, the escalator is a newer technological interface that resembles the stair-

---

30 Similar to film, the escalator has a pre-history or a pre-apparatic phase of design and experimentation that goes back to around 1850. Furthermore, its early exhibition is quite similar to that of film: like cinema, the escalator premiered in 1895, when it was installed as an amusement attraction at Coney Island. It enjoyed similar exhibitions at fairgrounds and Expos over the next few years (coinciding with the primitive era of film). Both film technologies and the escalator were displayed at the Paris Expo in 1900, where, according to the *Encyclopaedia Britannica*, the name "escalator" was first applied.

case both in form (having discrete steps) and function (diagonal ascension-descension as modes of spatial passage). Clearly, though, due to the motorized movement of the stairsteps, the proprioceptive matrix proper to the staircase is of only limited applicability to the escalator. Once on the escalator, one may, of course, choose to actualize the staircase matrix, actively climbing rather than standing and waiting to be delivered by the mechanism. But embarking and disembarking are a completely different matter. Watch a young child getting on an escalator. If inexperienced, the child may place a hand on the handrail, preparing to exert weight on it and pull his or her body up the first step; experience with the staircase has taught the child to do so. But the handrail itself moves, propelling with it the hand. Retracting it, the child looks down at his or her feet, sees the moving steps, but finds no stable point of entry; corporeal indecision, temporary paralysis give rise to visible anxiety. Then a parent takes the child's hand, offering a responsive support that solves the problem of the handrail's unyielding auto-motion, and pulls the child onto the first step, coordinating the child's movement with his or her own. Safely on the escalator, the first steps have been made in the escalator's incorporation by the child, forming the basis of a proprioceptive memory of general applicability to escalators. A new interface with the world is being forged, transforming the child's body and the worldly spaces open to it. Ontogenetically, the child (who literally follows in the parent's footsteps) is repeating the phylogenetic development that led societies with escalators to regard their interface with them as "natural," i.e. similar in kind to the habitual motions of walking, running, and climbing staircases.

But between the introduction (to the child or to society) of the novel technology and its proprioceptive naturalization, a transitional phase of bodily uncertainty intervenes. Nonlinear, this transition falls outside the matrix of old habits, while a new matrix is not yet available to accommodate it. This is a time of viscerally perceived intensity, the shock of the new that disrupts the old but will be forgotten when habit recommences—when, literally, the new has become old. Having developed a proprioceptive schema for the staircase, the child is shocked to find it inapplicable to the escalator. The child's anxiety, I propose, is altogether non-psychic: it is literally visceral in that the absence of a suitable matrix for interfacing with the moving staircase is experienced in the gut rather than the brain; for a brief moment, the child becomes all gut, involuntarily retracting hand, shuffling feet, shifting weight, seeking the safety of orientation that only an unavailable interface-matrix can provide. A proprioceptive interface-matrix, though properly corporeal and non-conscious, is itself the condition for conscious experience. For the child, the parent's outstretched hand is also a proprioceptive interface-matrix, and it draws the child back to subjective awareness, to determinate relationality with the world, from out of the chaos of viscerality.

To grasp the shock of transitional viscerality, and to see that it is indeed both *shocking* and *visceral*, we may approach the situation from a different angle. Consider your own habitual encounters with escalators. Consider that you have not just one but several matrices for interfacing with them: one applies to continuously moving escalators, another to those escalators that are activated and set in motion by stepping on a pressure pad at their point of entry. The differences between your proprioceptive memories of the two are only minimal, but they are quite significant. For example, with the continuous-motion escalator, you can run as fast as you like and, so long as you coordinate your entry carefully, jump onto the first step with a flying leap; with the pressure-pad escalator, you must be careful to step squarely on the activator, not to jump over it, and you would be advised to give the apparatus a moment to start up before embarking. Your body "knows" these things and will usually gauge the appropriate rhythms for you. But habit can also get you into serious trouble. You approach a motionless escalator, step on the pressure pad, and continue on at a pace you have proprioceptively learned to be appropriate for such mechanisms, allowing sufficient time for the escalator's motion to commence. Rather than standing, you unthinkingly choose to climb the steps, tacitly "knowing" that a staircase matrix applies after a certain point (due to the relative immobility of the steps vis-à-vis handrail that results from the synchronicity of their absolute motion). But the escalator has not in fact begun moving, and having had no reason to suspect a malfunction beforehand, you do not consciously recognize this fact until it is too late—you miss a step, stumble, catch yourself or fall. Afterwards, you may feel embarrassment, looking around to see if anyone saw. You may laugh uncomfortably, curse the escalator, or flee the scene as quickly and quietly as possible. But, if you have had this experience yourself, you will agree that it is difficult to describe what exactly happened in the interval, *what it felt like in the process*, between your habitual entry and your recognition of the escalator's malfunction. In the spacetime defined by the mismatch of your proprioceptive matrix to a situation of its inapplicability, you have been thrown out of the space of normal stimulus-response or action-reaction schemata and into a profoundly corporeal realm of burgeoning viscerality. At this level, there is no subject to do the perceiving, acting, or feeling; here there is only pure, unqualified shock, of the same sort that got you across the street earlier. Hence the descriptional impossibility.

With regard to the cinema *qua* anthropotechnical interface, I am proposing that technological transitions challenge viewers' sensorimotor matrices in much the same way, subjecting our bodies to the shock of intensities for which we lack the (corporeal, not just conceptual) means to accommodate and integrate them into the world of subjects and objects. When exposed to them repeatedly, these unqualified intensities, immediate in impact, lay the groundwork for a transformation of bodily-perceptual habits, thus altering the overall shape of our interface with the cinema and with the wider world through the cinema. This is the stuff transitions are made of. But because an interface is itself a condition for conscious experience, we are prone to apprehend change extrinsically and in retrospect, blind to the germinal motor that drives transformation: hence the tendency towards linearization, as with teleological views of the transition from early to classical cinema. Whether cast in terms of dominant style, technical refinement, or social relations, what such views efface is a deeper level of micro-transitions for which no common ground exists to measure the change. Changes in the objective conditions of filmic production and in psychosocial patterns of reception must both be regarded as extraneous, though emphatically not unrelated, to this level of transition, for here we are dealing with the emergence of new global schemata of embodied subject-object relations, and it is in these schemata that particular production-reception models have their basis. Cinematic transitions are matters of "passion." In the mode of the parable, I contend, Frankenstein films offer particularly passionate points of entry into these processes of affective anthropotechnical transition.

That, in a nutshell, is my argument. In Chapter 5, I attempt, by way of a technoscientific interlude on the role of the steam engine in the industrial and thermodynamic revolutions, to secure the theoretical foundations of my view of anthropotechnical interfacing as involving a postnatural history of materially embodied agency. Then, in Chapter 6, I return to the cinema and seek to develop, by way of a postnatural media theory, the view sketched here of filmic transitionality and its far-reaching impacts on the sub-personal infrastructure of human life—on what Deleuze and Guattari call the "molecular" realm of sub-phenomenological intensities that underlie the "molar" formations of human subjectivity.[31] The upshot is this:

---

31 As with virtually all of the concepts at work in Deleuze and Guattari's collaborations, Brian Massumi's *A User's Guide to Capitalism and Schizophrenia* is helpful in understanding the molar/molecular distinction. Massumi writes: "It is crucial for understanding Deleuze and Guattari [...] to remember that *the distinction between molecular and molar has nothing whatsoever to do with scale*. Molecular and molar do not correspond to 'small' and 'large,' 'part' and 'whole,' 'organ' and 'organism,' 'individual' and 'society.' There are molarities of every magnitude (the smallest being the nucleus of the atom). The distinction is not one of scale, but of mode of composition: it is qualitative, not quantitative. In a molecular population (mass) there are only local connections between discrete particles. In the case of molar populations (superindividual or person) locally connected discrete particles have become correlated at a distance. Our granules of muck [in an example that Massumi introduces earlier] were an oozing molecular mass, but as their local connections rigidified into rock, they became stabilized and homogenized, increasing the organizational consistency of different regions in the deposit (correlation). Molarity implies the creation or prior existence of a well-defined boundary enabling the population

passional molecular flows of affect dissolve stable identities, subject-positions, and even the borders between the human and the nonhuman—this is the "sub-organic" realm of transitionality; revising the material basis of subjectivity itself, there can be no conscious, personal experience of such transitions, which occur *between* molar, "organized" arrangements of psychic, social, and phenomenological life.[32] Exceeding the realms of human deliberation or even the impersonal force of ideology, any specific configuration of spectatorial engagement with film reveals itself now as the emergent, temporary product of historical negotiations between human and nonhuman forms of embodiment and agency, locked in a mutually transformative embrace. As I suggest at the end of Chapter 6, rounding out Part Two of this book, Frankenstein films embody non-representational correlates of these transformational processes and thus offer themselves, in the mode of the parable suggested here, as sites for experimentation and for probing the affective realm of anthropotechnical change.

Résumé: Engendered Machines

Before moving on, I must tie up one more loose end. The discussion of the previous section makes it imperative that I return to the feminist readings of *Frankenstein* from which I set out in this chapter and position my theory of the anthropotechnical interface in relation to the conceptions of materiality and embodiment that arose in those readings. Beyond providing the chapter with some much-needed closure, two substantial reasons necessitate this move. First, theoretically, my approach seems to sit uneasily between Moers's empiricism and the deconstructive tactics of Johnson's and Homans's readings, positing physiological-biological processes as the locus of transformation but outlining experiential "gaps" as the effects by which we recognize change and materiality itself. It might seem that I am trying to have it both ways, while it is not clear that synthesis is possible. Following Mark Hansen, I have promised a "radicalization" of feminist readings through the introduction of

---

of particles to be grasped as a whole. We skipped something: the muck as such. A supple individual lies between the molecular and the molar, in time and in mode of composition. Its particles are correlated, but not rigidly so. It has boundaries, but fluctuating ones. It is the threshold leading from one state to another" (*User's Guide* 54-55). Similarly, I seek to discover anthropotechnical transitionality in a "meso-level" of human-nonhuman interactions located between a-centered molecular flux and the situated centeredness of phenomenological subjectivity.

32 With the terms "sub-organic" and "organized," I mean to invoke the Deleuzo-Guattarian concept of the body without organs.

technology as materially exterior to discourse, yet the result looks more like a "compromise" that, like Poovey's view of Shelley as criticized by Armstrong and Jacobus, actually "biologizes" the issue. Far from making an advance, I seem to have returned us to square one, adding merely an apparatic-mechanical account of technology to Moers's anatomico-physiological account of the body. This brings me to the second point, which links theory to politics. Looking back at the course of my argument, it is easy to get the feeling that feminism has been short-changed, that I have appropriated feminist readers of *Frankenstein*, and Mary Shelley herself, as convenient foils (or "fall-dolls," in Mary Jacobus's term) for developing a theory that erases gender and diverts the discussion back to a conversation between male theorists.[33] It can be objected that, like Percy Shelley in his prefatory disclaimer to the first edition of *Frankenstein*, I have made the female author speak my words rather than her own, ignoring her critique of such woman-eliminating practices so dramatically reenacted in Frankenstein's destruction of the uncompleted female monster.[34] Thus, in the patriarchal critical tradition exemplified by Harold Bloom, it can be argued that I have taken Shelley's text as an inadvertent "introduction," not

---

33 Jacobus, in her article "Is There a Woman in This Text?," introduces the notion of the "fall-doll" in her discussion of Stanley Fish's anecdote about the student asking "is there a text in this class?"—an "anec-joke" that is not incidentally a joke between men, for it serves "both to humiliate and to eliminate the woman" (117). As the "fall-doll," the woman "sets Fish's theoretical discourse in motion," but only unintentionally: she is "the idiot questioner disguised as dumb blonde" (117-18). This is part of Jacobus's broader argument against a theoretical strategy of usurping women, taking their words as occasions for elucidating theories that in fact eliminate women: what she calls the "textual harassment" or "specular appropriation of women" (119). It is in the context of this argument, which ranges in focus from Freud to Watson and Crick's discovery of the double-helix structure of DNA to arguments over the meaning of female narcissism, that Jacobus analyzes Frankenstein's misogyny and argues for the turn from an "American" to a "French" form of feminism.

34 Johnson argues that it was perhaps because the novel was successful "in conveying the unresolvable contradictions inherent in being female" that Percy felt the need to add his preface (9). A "gesture of repression of the very specificity of the power of feminine contradiction, a gesture reminiscent of Frankenstein's destruction of his nearly-completed female monster" (9-10). Jacobus also focuses on this act of destruction in her discussion of theoretical gestures designed to "eliminate" women, and Homans takes it as a particularly literal case of the "circumvention of the maternal."

to romanticism but to the anthropotechnical interface, in the process effacing everything that made the novel so important to feminism.[35]

It must be emphasized, first, that I do not see my arguments as in any way invalidating the basic picture offered by Jacobus, Johnson, and Homans of embodied materiality and its relations to discourse. By "basic picture" I mean the image, shared by the critics just named, of a bodily reality that resists textual inscription, opening a gap of asignification in the fabric of discourse. Far from rejecting it, my goal in this chapter has been to find a means of taking up this picture in such a way as to characterize its content—that is, the matter of embodiment itself—more positively than as the recalcitrant stuff that fills textual gaps. Given a textualist starting point, such a negative view is, I suggest, the necessary consequence. But it is by no means obvious that we must approach embodiment from this direction. My appeal to proprioception and viscerality has been an attempt to illuminate the body of the gap from a reverse angle, to effect an inversion of perspective without thereby replacing the focal object. I am not *rejecting* the deconstructive approach so much as supplementing it with another point of view. Deconstruction is particularly suited to locating textual gaps, so to speak from the "outside," while it is less well suited to the task of occupying those gaps and exposing what they are like on the "inside." An examination of proprioception and viscerality helps in this regard.

And while my metaphors (inside/outside/other-side) may be subject to easy deconstruction, the shift of perspective on embodiment that they signal is not incompatible with the deconstructive indictment of biologism. Taking a "positive" view of the gap is not tantamount to endorsing positiv*ism*, for the proprioceptive-visceral body, while grasped initially in physiological terms, is not itself a term in the system of physiological discourse. Most crucially, my reversal of perspectives does not involve a return to empiricism and approach the body as the cogito's passive other but goes "behind" the subject/object dichotomy to the ground of its (material)

---

35 I shall address these objections in the order I have introduced them; strictly speaking, though, my responses are inseparable from one another, due to the inextricability of feminist theory from politics. In the present context, a simple reformulation reveals the connections. Having argued that the deconstructive feminists' appeal to de Manian textual allegory underestimates the exteriority of materiality to discourse, does my subsequent attempt at reinstating this alterity not implicate my project precisely in the biologism that poststructural feminism identified as the essentialistic stumbling-block preventing an empirically oriented feminism from realizing its full political potential? And is the return to physiology not precisely a means of obviating feminism as a political force? In order to answer these questions, I must show both that I avoid essentialistic notions of the body and that my model of human-technological interaction is politically relevant in a way that should interest feminism.

construction. Importantly, though, this ground is not held to be foundational in any ultimate sense; rather, it marks a particular (pre-personal) level of organization (and disorganization), itself decomposable in a groundless regress of material strata (cellular, atomic, subatomic) while also imbricated in the progressive emergence of higher-level systems (organs, systems of organs, bodies, ecospheres, social collectives, and linguistic-symbolic matrices). On this view, the relations between strata are not genetically determined by the body any more than they are transcendentally fixed by the Word of God. The same goes for the relations between the sexes.

Thus, though I have framed my account in naturalistic language, I have not thereby naturalized ideological discourses, contingent social formations, or gender roles. The proprioceptive-visceral body is neither a genetic origin nor a transcendental signifier. It is still very much a gap. As a space of pre-personal transition, it is, in Massumi's words, "less a space in the empirical sense than a gap in space that is also a suspension of the normal unfolding of time" (*Parables* 57). The affective changes that take place here find "expression," so to speak, back in the empirical world, which is always already articulated as a differential play of significance-relations. "Affect contaminates empirical space through language" (62), so that deconstructive strategies remain central to the task of uncovering the material dynamics and unqualified intensities—which are anything but determinate "sense-data"—that pivot sub-phenomenal transitions. What I am saying, in effect, is that it is exceedingly difficult to think the positive (the proprioceptional-visceral interface) without reference to the negative (textual and phenomenal gaps); this is the flipside of deconstruction's problem of thinking negatively without falling back into a positive metaphysics. As I see it, my approach and that of deconstruction are strategically reversible perspectives.

Still, it might be felt that I am strategically pulling a fast one on the deconstructive feminist critics. I had better be up front, then, about the critical implications that my model does have for their views of embodied materiality. These consequences concern the perceived "details," so to speak, of the "basic picture" described above. The first consequence of my positive characterization of the gap's negativity with relation to discourse is that we can link such gaps more confidently to materiality and corporeality, thus strengthening the very tentative connection drawn by Jacobus, for whom embodiment (in the form of "biologistic images") answers a pragmatic imperative of representational thought and political intervention. Indeed, without abandoning politics, we can, I think, eschew the entire problematic of representation by marshaling a conception of embodiment that is radically opposed to being captured as an "image." My notion of a pre-personal embodied interface thus militates directly against the residual representationalism that unsettles the otherwise anti-representational paradigm of deconstructive feminism, as in

Johnson's last-minute appeal to the concept in her claim that *Frankenstein*'s textual aporiae represent the inherent contradictions of female selfhood.

Such claims are, I think, rightly read as feminists' own attempts to strengthen the bond—implicitly recognized as having been weakened by deconstruction's methodical skepticism—between discursive gaps and the materiality of female embodiment, to establish the bond's "positivity" without reverting to physiological (or metaphysical) positivism. And none of the critics considered undertakes this task more vigorously than Homans, who links female embodiment to a Lacanian unconscious. I have already noted my skepticism with regard to Lacanian psychoanalysis and its usefulness for my project, but I can now state these doubts more positively: Homans's approach unduly narrows embodiment by framing it, negatively, in terms of consciousness (as that which is categorically not-conscious), thereby blocking from view certain corporeal dynamics that have, in themselves, no intrinsic connection to subjectivity whatsoever.[36] Under the headings of proprioception and viscerality, I have been considering processes that humans share with the animal world from which we hail, ascribable to organisms with limited, different, or no subjectivities at all, and whose "worlds" are not structured by oedipal conflicts or ontological lacks. A Lacanian view, while it may illuminate a range of human phenomena, obfuscates such sub- and non-human physical processes and

---

36 As Ruth Mayer has pointed out to me, there is a rich pre-Freudian history of conceptions of the unconscious that might be better suited to thinking embodiment in positive, i.e. non-privative, terms and therefore capable of serving as a basis for mediation between the approaches of poststructural feminism and my own postnaturalism. Mayer explores some of these conceptions in connection with her new-historical investigation of the American Renaissance in *Selbsterkenntnis – Körperfühlen: Medizin, Philosophie und die amerikanische Renaissance*. Compare also Brian Massumi's reading of the unconscious in the light of Deleuze and Guattari's work: rejecting Freudian and Lacanian models, "the unconscious is everything that is left behind in a contraction of selection or sensation that moves from one level of organization to another: It is the structurations and selections of nature as contracted into human DNA. It is the multitude of excitations of rods and cones and nerve cells as contracted into a perception of the human body. It is the perceptions of the human body as contracted into larval selves. It is the larval selves as contracted into fledgling selves. It is the fledgling selves as contracted into the overself of the person. It is an interlocking of syntheses, natural and cultural, passive and active: productions of production, productions of recording, productions of consumption. Production. Becoming. It is continually changing as all of those levels are superposed and actualized to different degrees as the body jumps from one more or less indeterminate threshold state to the next. The only things the unconscious is not are present perception and reflection (personalized redundancy)" (*User's Guide* 82-83).

retains (at least negatively) a subject-centric and anthropocentric approach to the body.[37] (The resistance to bodily pleasure in Metz's and Mulvey's film theories appears, then, to be integral rather than accidental with regard to their Lacanian orientation.) As with explicit appeals to representation, invoking a Lacanian unconscious surreptitiously reintroduces that which the deconstructive approach shuns most: positivism.

Finally, and this is the criticism I have made most explicitly, the de Manian focus of the deconstructive feminists' readings is reductive of technology, underestimating its material exteriority to discourse. The account of corporeal-technological interface developed in this chapter corrects that limitation by severing technology from the mechanical aspects of language, thereby opening our reading of Shelley's text, as well as a multitude of other phenomena (including the cinema), to a more historical—and ultimately more material—account of their deconstructive or deterritorializing mechanisms.

To be honest, though, it is somewhat euphemistic to claim that this theorization of the anthropotechnical interface merely corrects the details of a "basic picture" I share with Jacobus, Johnson, and Homans. Again, I must place my cards on the table to put to rest a lingering suspicion that there's something up my sleeve. For though it may be possible, as I have argued, consistently to read feminist gaps in terms of biological openings of pre-personal embodiment onto its material environment, subject to change through contact with non-textual technologies, certainly this reading effects a fundamental displacement of (at least one variety of) feminist projects. Let me be clear about this. The manner in which I have sought to (re)materialize textual gaps not only opens the feminist critics' inquiries to domains in which their interests are only questionably addressed or served; more fundamentally, my attempt at backlighting the gap reaches back to a stratum of embodied being that is prior to gender differentiations, perhaps even more basic than biological sex, thus implying that gender is not as central to questions of subjectivity as feminists have generally asserted.[38] This is a displacement of feminism as a politi-

---

37 See also Mark Hansen's argument, in Chapter 7 of his *Embodying Technesis*, that Lacan's real is, so to speak, "not real enough" for the project he undertakes of according to technology an autonomous, non-phenomenologically reduced agency, which would effectively break with the tradition of *technesis* and allow us to think technology's corporeal impact independently of psychic structures.

38 Compare Massumi's discussion of Deleuze and Guattari's uneasy relations to gender politics, which, based in a contrast between the "BwO" (body without organs) and the "OwB" (organs without a body) as a critique of (Lacanian) psychoanalysis's supposition of prelinguistic indifferentiation between the infant's and the mother's body, comes to a head in their call to "become-woman." See Massumi, *A User's Guide*, 84-89.

cal undertaking, for it resituates feminist criticism, via feminist conceptions of embodiment, as taking aim at a secondary or tertiary level of embodied becoming. To this extent, the anthropotechnical interface would seem to supplant gender politics, apparently claiming for itself a more basic level of ontological and practical urgency.

For all that, I maintain, this reorientation does not in any way undermine or circumvent feminism—at least not post-second-wave feminism. On the contrary, the broader basis upon which feminism is placed grounds the possibility of specifically gender-oriented inflections on the theme of environmental interaction, allowing for a robustly material (and technological) reappraisal of "female experience" that avoids the pitfalls of empiricism, biologism, and positivism. With her myth of the cyborg, Donna Haraway may be read as a feminist theorist who long ago began practicing the "displacement" of feminism I am here advocating. And I suggest that more focused analysis of the proprioceptive schemata typical to women in particular sociohistorical situations may provide a fruitful means of locating embodied gender differences,[39] while a parallel concentration on the disruptive gaps of visceral shock may outline a history of important micro- and macro-level reorientations that should be of central concern for feminist theory and politics. Finally, because the indeterminate molecularity of the pre-personal body is taken not as a foundation but as one among many levels of organization, my approach maintains a certain pragmatic relativism; feminism need not eschew more traditional concerns with ideological, cultural, and socioeconomic forces of domination in favor of biotechnical materiality, for these modes of inquiry may complement each other much as pre-discursive corporeality and discursive sociality coexist, each as real as the other. On the whole, then, the non-destructive "displacement" of feminism must be counted as a positive consequence of my theory, for rather than defusing or limiting feminist inquiry it broadens its scope more definitively beyond the prison-house of language and multiplies relevant perspectives.

Consider the consequences for the interpretation of *Frankenstein*. Rather than leaving us with one ultimate reading, consideration of the anthropotechnical interface suggests certain relations between a number of approaches, arraying perspectives according to which of the different levels of the text's contextually delimited connections with reality they address. One of these, the reading expounded in this chapter, may seem to be of limited use to feminist concerns. For at the level of Shelley's proprioceptive-visceral interface with the steam-engine and industrial urbanization, conceived as a matter of pre-conscious propensities and undifferentiated intensities rather than empirical relations, the author's femaleness may seem to

---

39 Feminist phenomenology provides an important starting point. See, in particular, Iris Marion Young, *On Female Body Experience*.

be quite inessential. At this level, it is difficult to establish the supposed femaleness of the text, as required (or at least desired) by feminist critics in order to marshal *Frankenstein* as a challenge to the male canon. In fact, though, the relevance of the anthropotechnical interface for specifically feminist engagements is not difficult to establish. Given the inexhaustible stratification of reality I have posited, it cannot be the case that everything emerges of its own accord from the pre-personal body as the ultimate source of production. Given the interdependence of strata, there must be both upward and downward movement between levels of complexity. Specifically, there must be empirical entry points into the non-empirical spacetime of the proprioceptive-visceral body-in-transition.[40] (The escalator for the child was one such point, the malfunctioning escalator another.) Just as human subjectivities plan and construct the machines that may ultimately displace those very subjectivities, so do social situation and gender play a role in a given subject's preparation for and openness to embodied revision. If Shelley's text is the product of such an anthropotechnical revision that, due to the direct bodily transmission of industrialism's novel affective intensities, swept silently across her society and effected a general deterritorialization of the human perspective, it surely cannot be considered irrelevant that a young woman author submitted herself so radically to transformation while the men around her, whose poetic "genius" defined itself in terms of a special relation to nature, sought to insulate themselves and their culture to the change.

Thus, emphasizing the radically non-discursive nature of industrialism's embodied impacts situates *Frankenstein* and its author between a range of coexistent planes, with respect to which different interpretive foci will be appropriate and various conclusions can be drawn. From one perspective, Mary Shelley is hardly unique, and the empirical fact of her womanhood seems accidental, for "she" is merely a body that was subject like all other bodies at the time to the forces of industrialization. From another perspective, in relation to the degree of her particular openness to technology's sub-personal impacts, and as compared to the defensive closure of those around her, the question of gender gains importance; Shelley appears exceptional, her embodied difference making her such an able critic of her male peers. Between these levels of passive relation and active criticism, in the in-

---

40 This is the requirement that enables Deleuze and Guattari to speak of "making yourself" a body without organs. On this requirement hinges nothing less than the political relevance and allegedly liberating potential of "becoming-other." Without it, there would be only the chaos of involuted chance which, from the perspective of any individual, would amount to determinism.

between space of "passion," Shelley and her novel appear neither absolutely unique nor wholly typical, but as exemplary: singular.[41]

Similar conclusions can be drawn when we turn to the side of reception. The notion that the text functions as a machinic vehicle for the further transmission of deterritorializing intensities does not render irrelevant the special attraction it may have held early on for women readers, nor does it nullify feminism's more recent interest in that receptional history. If anything, the anthropotechnical reorientation adds here a promising new dimension to feminist investigations. Did women, at the proprioceptive and/or visceral level of their embodiment, maintain a special relationship to industrial technology? Clearly, the industrial revolution introduced large numbers of women (as well as children) to the world of work, employing them in factories as cheap, unskilled labor. While the social dimensions of this transition have not been lost on feminism, more attention to the embodied rhythms of factory life is needed, specifically to the reorientations of proprioceptive matrices that women, in particular, underwent when they left home and family and began operating powerlooms and the like. The visceral shocks of factory work and urban life, I have suggested, disrupted old habits and recalibrated bodies to the new rhythms of industrial technology. But because pre-industrial gender roles defined different empirical points of entry into industrialization's revolutionizing of the body, there is no reason to expect that the outcome was the same for men and women; because transitionality can be defined externally by the situations between which change occurs, there is every reason to believe that qualitative differences obtained.

Perhaps we can even find in these differences a non-positivist (and technology-inflected) basis for Moers's notion that the appeal of "female Gothic" to women lay in its ability "to get to the body itself, its glands, muscles, epidermis, and circulatory system" (77). When tuned to the transformations of (gender-differentiated) glands, muscles, and so forth leveraged by the human-technology transactions of the industrial era, Moers's idea that *Frankenstein* was a perfect medium for the communication, between a female author and female readers, of truths specific to the female body is then open to a non-essentialistic reading, one that still captures something "essential" about the (historically variable) embodied conditions of women's receptivity. Purged of its strictly physiological and ahistorical conception of materiality, Moers's approach to *Frankenstein*'s bodily "communication" in fact provides a useful model for thinking about Frankenstein films, pointing the way to

---

41 Other such singular cases might be sought in Poe, Baudelaire, and Turner, for example. On the first two, see Benjamin's "Some Motifs in Baudelaire." On Turner, see Serres's "Turner Translates Carnot" (also discussed by Mark Hansen in his reading of *Frankenstein*). In this company of men, however, Shelley's gender might be seen as making her paradoxically "more singular than the other singularities."

a non-cognitive, non-"expressive" notion of film reception that, by way of something like "mimesis" in Benjamin's corporeal-materialistic sense (to which I return in Chapter 5), links the transformational indeterminacy of anthropotechnical revision to the determinate situations of gendered, classed, and ethnic social bodies.

One final comment about the foregoing apologetics: in my attempt to demonstrate the compatibility of an anthropotechnically oriented line of investigation with the political goals of feminism, I have appealed to strategic reversals of perspective and made allowances for pragmatic selections of contextual relevance. But clearly, by positing definite relations between contextual orders or strata—above all, the ontological primacy of corporeality vis-à-vis discourse—the reorientation I have suggested integrates alternative viewpoints *in a particular manner*, transforming them by means of their non-arbitrary ordering. Positively, as we have seen, this integration of perspectives recommends new directions for traditional inquiry, e.g. correlating industrial production and literary reception on the basis of gender-inflected proprioceptive matrices. Negatively, the anthropotechnical reorientation imposes serious constraints on theory—not only underwriting the ban on positivistic notions of the body, for example, but also decentering the textual means whereby deconstructive feminists originally decentered physiology. I remain adamant about my claim that the anthropotechnical interface is not conceived as providing the last word on *Frankenstein*—or any other cultural phenomenon for that matter—but it does set limits to the perspectival choices that can be made. A pragmatic sort of relativism is maintained, but it is circumscribed within definite—*material*—bounds. I emphasize these dialectical consequences because they are central to understanding the methodological double vision I aim to put into practice in the cinematic realm. Like the novel itself, *Frankenstein*'s filmic progenies are multilayered, not reducible to the molecular intensities that, in the pre-personal interface of bodies and machines, may be said to produce their most radical moments; such productions always explode into personal and suprapersonal contexts and structures, which they may disrupt *or* reinforce as they assume objective shape, narrative form, and ideological significance. At this representational-discursive level, material positivities may *become* asignifying gaps, and gaps may *become* metaphors, symbols, and mere "things." If I have downplayed these stabilizing processes in this chapter, it is not because I regard them as illusory or unimportant. Rather, it is because I am convinced that the materiality of embodiment, in its technologically variable openness to the environment, forms a non-foundational ground from which representation cannot be divorced.

In her study of postmodern filmic "body horror," Judith Halberstam takes Shelley's *Frankenstein* as a preeminent "textual technology" for normatively "disciplining" subjects; the novel provides for Halberstam a historical point of reference against which to measure transitions between variously inflected constructions of "normal" humanity. Halberstam writes, "Monsters are meaning machines," and she is right: "They can represent gender, race, nationality, class, and sexuality in one body" (21-22). Frankenstein's monster is subject to an "infinite interpretability" (31), which means, according to Halberstam's allegorical reading, that in addition to policing boundaries it also holds open an unassimilable margin that enables "posthuman" and specifically "queer" mutations. This type of approach, I reiterate, is terribly important, and if focusing on the anthropotechnical interface prevented us from taking it seriously, this would surely have to count as grounds for rejecting my theory. On the other hand, if we fail to relate "textual technologies" to radically non-textual ones, we end up with a one-sided view of the body as it figures in cinematic "body horror"; for the object of disciplinary action—and this goes for cinemas as much as for factories, prisons, or psychiatric wards—is not just the subject but material embodiment as the "sensible" (i.e. sensing *and* sensed, sensitive *and* more narrowly sensible) locus of being: the "passionate" flesh of the world itself.[42] Monsters may *become* meaning machines, but they start out life in this aoristic realm of the flesh.[43]

Accordingly, beyond the dualities of content and form, text and technology, diegetic construction and embodied reception—where each pair articulates a particular methodological delimitation of double vision—mine is a plea for an expansively *ontological* double vision: let us affirm that conditions of "infinite interpretability" are correlated with an inherent instability of signification, but let us assert as

---

42 My point is not to indict Halberstam of these shortcomings. Certainly, her analysis stops short of the anthropotechnical interface, but it is unclear whether she thereby *reduces* the body in the sense I am warning against—whether, in other words, she takes the discursive realm as *exhausting* technologies and bodies (however indeterminately), or whether hers is a purely methodological choice. In either case, consideration of the anthropotechnical interface is, as I have argued, compatible with the thrust of her analysis, and each approach stands to learn a great deal from the other.

43 By "aoristic" (from the Greek *aoristos*, meaning "indefinite," as in the indefinite grammatical tense common to ancient Greek and Sanskrit), I mean to indicate that the prepersonal affective body is both prior to the distinctions of subject and object fundamental to the space of the empirical world, and that it maintains a paradoxical relation to time as well: in a sense outside of empirical time but not properly "ahistorical." The Greek term is a negation of *horistos* (limited or defined), from the verb *horizein* (to limit or define), from *horos* (boundary or border). Accordingly, flesh is monstrous because it refuses to respect boundaries, and it explodes horizons—including those invoked by phenomenology. This monstrous body, which all of us are but which none of us *has*, is thus not only subjectively unthematized but also decidedly pre-phenomenological.

the material ground of this instability the inexhaustible stratification of reality.[44] Subject to this double exposure, *Frankenstein* and its cinematic offspring unfold their illimitable parabolisms; at once narratives with a (repeatedly undermined) moral—parables in the narrow sense—and also material sites or transducers of broader anthropotechnical revolution, they exhibit that quality that defines for Massumi the truly "exemplary" event: "a belonging to itself that is simultaneously an extendibility to everything else with which it might be connected" (*Parables* 18). Spiraling outward from an ever-shifting center of indeterminacy and folding back in infinitely aleatory rhythms, we find in these machinic texts a parable for the inexhaustible multiplicity of the cosmos itself.

---

44 Compare Massumi, *A User's Guide*, where a similar point is made, drawing on Deleuze and Guattari, first with respect to the split subject of Lacanian psychoanalysis (83-84), and then vis-à-vis Saussurian linguistics and its post-Saussurian afterlife (90-92).

5. Of Steam Engines, Revolutions, and the (Un)natural History of Matter: A Techno-Scientific Interlude

> But we had better get back to shore, lest we enter into a boundless ocean and not get out of it all day. So put forward the arguments and demonstrations, Simplicio—either yours or Aristotle's—but not just texts and bare authorities, because our discourses must relate to the sensible world and not to one on paper.
>
> GALILEO[1]

In the previous chapter, I have used *Frankenstein* to make some rather large claims, and the cosmic note on which I ended may make the reader skeptical as to whether the text can in fact support these claims. I have tried to illustrate some of the more contentious notions, such as anthropotechnical evolution, but my small-scale example of the escalator may have left the reader wondering whether one can really extrapolate to the large-scale revolution I have associated with industrialization. Moreover, at the heart of these claims is implied a radical reorganization of the techno-phenomenological approach which demands a more careful examination. That is, the postulation of a "silent revolution" in the material realm has effected a quiet revolution on the theoretical-methodological front. This is, to borrow Massumi's term, a "Bergsonian revolution" (*Parables* 7), and it displaces the phenomenological framework with which I have approached the cinema in previous chapters just as surely as it dislocates the textualism characteristic of poststructural feminist readings of *Frankenstein*. Allowing for radical revisions of the embodiment that, according to Merleau-Pontean phenomenology, materially situates human intentionality, my extrapolation from the "deterritorialization of the human perspective"

---

1   *Dialogue Concerning the Two Chief World Systems*, 113.

that Hansen sees indexed in *Frankenstein* implies a technologically induced eclipse of phenomenality itself. Methodologically, this revolution is highly problematic indeed. Most obviously, since I have been supposing a domain of force that is anterior to phenomenality, immune to representability, I have been forced to speak in the very mode I ascribe to *Frankenstein*: that of the parable. Imagining a mechanism for the transfer of intensities that fall outside the scope of imagination, the story I have told is necessarily couched in terms that strain not only the expressive capacity of prose but also the conventions of logical coherence itself. One may with justification wonder, therefore, whether the paradoxes introduced in this parabolic account are not simply a cover for poetic nonsense and a hyperbolically immaterial take on matter.

Dispelling this suspicion is no easy task. To address the issue at all, I must specify more precisely the nature of the tension between phenomenology and the account of (technological) matter as emergent singularity; further, I must explain what exactly I hope to gain by pitting the two against each other. First the latter: the confrontation pivots a theory of transitionality that is simply not possible without acknowledging the claims of both—irreducibly opposed—perspectives. Without assuming the situatedness that phenomenology grounds in human embodiment, there can be no point (or field) of reference for gauging qualitative change; but for such change to occur, we must assume that embodiment itself is somehow displaced and reorganized by the emergence of radically novel, unprecedented productive forces. Without the latter, the parameters of human being remain static; without the former, there is flux but no history. Historical transition, that is, requires the oppositional co-operation of situation and displacement. Theoretically speaking, situated embodiment is the ground upon which emergent production arises as figure. But "theoretically speaking" indicates here an abstract, quasi-transcendent perspective that is not to be confused with the interplay of ground and figure in the phenomenal realm; the "figure" of radical change eludes disclosure in the phenomenal field altogether, for it implies the movement of the "ground" itself (material embodiment) upon which figures appear to us as such. Thus, addressing the nature of the two perspectives' opposition, Massumi writes:

The Bergsonian revolution turns the world on its head. Position no longer comes first, with movement a problematic second. It is secondary to movement and derived from it. It is retro movement, movement residue. The problem is no longer to explain how there can be change given positioning. The problem is to explain the wonder that there can be stasis given the primacy of process. (*Parables* 7-8)

From this perspective, "positionality is an emergent quality of movement" (8). To be sure, movement or motility is central to the lived body, and to this extent phenomenology can also claim to show that "positionality"—by which Massumi means the discursive determination of subjects as the primary focus of poststructuralism—is emergent, contingent upon the dynamic primacy of material embodiment. Moreover, motility implies the possibility of change, which in turn requires temporality, so that historicity is an essential property of the phenomenal subject, a direct consequence of embodied situation. But the Bergsonian perspective posits a more radical domain of historicity, a realm in which matter itself has a history that is incommensurable with human temporality and the history of thought, imperceptible to the historical subject because it pertains to the evolutionary history of (human) embodiment itself. Hence the essential tension.

As articulated in the previous chapter, my parable of *Frankenstein*'s parabolic machinism is meant to stand as an "example" for the revolutionary processes of anthropotechnical evolution that the industrial revolution exemplifies. It will be objected, however, that I have not truly demonstrated anything yet, that I have merely cobbled together a conceptual framework within which a process becomes (arguably, perhaps) thinkable. But the process itself remains hypothetical, and the coherence (or, as the case may be, productive incoherence) of my reading is predicated upon an extremely controversial premise: viz. that the industrial revolution really involved such a far-ranging reconfiguration of humanity as to merit calling it an evolutionary development. Skeptics will demand positive proof of this claim, but my appeal to a realm of material efficacy beyond or below phenomenal disclosure precludes exactly the possibility of providing this proof. It is thus easy to dismiss all talk of sub-personal affective intensities and the mechanisms of their transmission as so much superstitious (read: unfalsifiable) mumbo-jumbo. What metatheoretical justification I have offered for my approach amounts to a sort of transcendental argument. Such an argument attempts to explain a phenomenon by way of showing what the conditions of its possibility are, but the phenomenon in question must itself be assumed to obtain—and that is precisely what is at issue here. What reasons do we have to believe, against all observable appearances, that the industrial revolution actually marks a quantum leap of sorts in the makeup of matter and, contingent thereupon, in the constitution of human beings? Everything hinges upon this question, but have I not backed myself into a position from which any answer I provide will presuppose a materially ineffectual and theoretically dispensable *Ding an sich*?

I do not take the charge lightly; it marks a very real circularity in my argumentation. To show that this is an inevitable *formal* circularity rather than the vicious, logical sort known better as question-begging, I shall have to revert from the Massumian "affirmative" mode of parabolic story-telling to a more traditional, "negative" mode in order to defend the plausibility of my theory. What this negative route amounts to is piling another transcendental argument on top of the last, showing that an identifiable change takes place with the industrial revolution that cannot be explained with recourse to the empirically oriented epistemological framework from whence issues the problem of "proof" or "evidence." (In this connection, we may note that the call for "demonstration" contains a demand for "demonstrification," a demand that the hypothetically monstrous material alterity of industrial technology be tamed and empirically "justified"—brought to justice before the tribunal of thought.) My argument, in short, is that higher-level changes are registered in discursive thought, marked by conceptual upheaval (paradigm shift, epistemic revolution), but that on pain of reducing materiality to a discursive construct and positing something like *écriture* or textual allegory as the agent of change—an option that I presume to be unacceptable to my scientifically-minded, materialist interlocutors—we shall have to posit a level of material transformation generative of epistemic paradox but itself immune to cognitive capture. From there we can make our way back to the conclusion that the industrial revolution involves a radical revision of humanity on the order of an *ontological*—or, with Massumi, *ontogenetic*—revolution.

SCIENTIFIC REVOLUTION: A MATTER OF DISCOURSE OR THE DISCOURSE OF MATTER?

The first place to look for the outward signs of change is in the relation of science to technology. Against the common view that technology represents the practical application of scientific theory, it has been well documented in the case of the industrial revolution that *science followed technology's lead*, not the other way around. In particular, the development of thermodynamics was essentially guided by preoccupation with already developed automated machines. Summing up the position of many recent historians of science, Rachel Laudan writes: "science owes more to the steam engine than the steam engine owes to science" (10). That thermodynamics represents one of the great scientific revolutions of the modern age cannot be doubted, but theory's dependence on technology indicates that it would be wrong to reduce it to a revolution of science alone. If we assume that a "paradigm shift" occurs here, we must posit either a theory-structural or a material catalyst of change. Quite naturally supposing that the physical structure of the universe is constant, unchanged in its essence by the rise of industrial technology, it is intuitively appealing to explain theory-change in terms of the new paradigm's better theoretical "fit" with reality: correspondence is the key. Pressed, however, to explain how we *know* that a theory (more approximately) corresponds to reality, recourse must be had to instrumental effects: the theory "works" better. This can mean at least two things: 1) it more adequately *explains* observable phenomena, and/or 2) it *translates more easily into practice*, for example allowing for the construction of new machines that were unthinkable under the old science. But, to take up the first possibility, it is in the nature of paradigm shifts that a more or less internally coherent view of the (physical) universe is replaced by another more or less coherent model; both models explain "more or less" everything, and if the old paradigm is suddenly found to explain "less," it can in principle be augmented in an *ad hoc* manner to make up the difference.[2] In terms of explanatory adequacy, the preferability of the new paradigm must therefore be grounded in its theoretical elegance, simplicity, or ontological parsimony. Because there is no independent guarantee that the universe is itself parsimonious, however, the notion of correspondence begins to give way to a coherence theory of truth[3]; thermodynamics more "economically" explains heat/work relations than caloric theory, but economy is (exclusively, for all we know) a quality or value of human thought.

Might we not say, though—now taking up the second interpretation of theoretical "work"—that success in praxis is a *sign* of a paradigm's correspondence to reality? That the productive potential of the new science, as materialized in the invention of new technologies, is evidence that it captures something essential about the underlying mechanisms of the universe? Or is it that the requirement of objective veracity is itself subordinated to pragmatic instrumentality? In the case of the industrial revolution, we are confronted with an apparently insoluble paradox. For although the science of thermodynamics certainly enabled the construction of more efficient machines, its laws emerged as an afterthought to technological innovations that developed without its help. Of course, the steam engine might be retroactively reclaimed by science: demonstrating pre-existent but hitherto unobserved physical principles, the steam engine offered itself as a new tool, the factory as a new laboratory, for scientists to study the laws of nature. The fact that the technological infrastructure was, historically speaking, anterior to the science that instrumentalized it may seem paradoxical, but this anachronism is not a clear indication that things did not in fact work this way. However, to the extent that this recuperation subordinates technology to the role of theory's handmaiden, it also undercuts any possibility for situating the catalyst of scientific revolution in "the real world," in the law-like structures of the universe. For if technology is merely the tool of science, and scientific thought is autonomous with regard to its material supports, then the mounting pressure that causes one paradigm to give way to another can

---

2   This is the so-called Duhem-Quine thesis. See the volume *Can Theories Be Refuted? Essays on the Duhem-Quine Thesis*, edited by Sandra Harding, for original statements from Pierre Duhem and Willard Quine, as well as more contemporary discussions.

3   Classic texts on truth theory are collected in *Theories of Truth*, edited by Frederick F. Schmitt.

only come from science itself. As a material *extension* of scientific discourse and thought, the successful "translation" of theory into praxis demonstrates only thought's correspondence to itself, its self-enclosed coherence rather than its adequation to the world. The fact that a paradigm shift occurs can therefore only indicate the self-deconstructive workings of scientific discourse itself. The thermodynamic revolution would amount, accordingly, to nothing more or less than the result of a specifically scientific sort of "textual allegory."

This conclusion may be fine for out-and-out constructivists, but it must certainly be unacceptable to anyone committed to the existence of an external (mind-independent) physical reality not reducible to an impotent, formless *Ding an sich*.[4] Perhaps we can circumvent the deconstructivist argument—if not the failure of correspondence in a strong sense—by positing institutional rather than discursive pressures as the mechanism of change. Recognizing that scientific theories do not drop pre-formed from heaven but are developed by flesh-and-blood humans working under social conditions of competition, vying for fame or wages, we might wish to re-frame the question of scientific revolution as a sociological problem. Indeed, this is the consequence that, in one way or another, most readers (proponents and detractors alike) have drawn from Thomas Kuhn's once revolutionary philosophy of science.[5] But this move is of no help to the cause of materialism, as becomes clear if we ask from whence institutional pressures arise. On the one hand, institutions may be contextualized in progressively larger social frames (academic departments, universities, inter-university research programs, professional associations, industry affiliations, programs of national interest, international communities, etc.); but the attribution of theory-change to political strife and negotiation at any

---

4 The condition that physical reality not be reducible to "an impotent, formless *Ding an sich*" might seem redundant, already contained in the notion of mind-independent externality. But in fact a thoroughgoing constructivism should have no problem with such externality if it *were* merely a formless, passive recipient of conceptual qualifications (however these may be defined). Indeed, as a primarily epistemological position, constructiv-constructivism should be agnostic regarding the existence of inert matter; so conceived, it entails no commitment on the debate between idealism and materialism as metaphysical positions. But while not strictly bound to idealism, it seems that constructivism is open only to a materialism so-called.

5 It should be noted, however, that Ian Hacking has identified the attribution to Kuhn of the thesis "that philosophy of science should become part of the sociology of knowledge" as one of the "widespread misapprehensions" of his work (Hacking, Introduction 4). Indeed, Kuhn himself is critical of the sociological re-framing and appropriation of his work outside the philosophy of science. See, for example, Kuhn's "The Trouble with the Historical Philosophy of Science."

level will be open to the interpretation that scientific crisis and revolution instantiates merely the structurally inevitable contradictions between various positions on an overarching grid of discourse. On the other hand, the individuals engaged in science-as-politics are themselves decomposable, for example, to the play of psychic forces and libidinal energies; though such mechanisms might promise to explain the emergence of new ideas not prescribed by an aging scientific paradigm or matrix of discursive positionality (episteme), both the agents and the products of change are rendered more ideal than real; accordingly, the workings of paradigm-shifts become ultimately indistinguishable from textual allegory. Either way, whether we move up or down the scale, materiality as a historical force is shown to be dispensable or—and this seems equivalent to me—internal to discourse itself.

Weighing the Options: Ontological-Epistemological Commitments

We are faced, therefore, with the following options: we may a) *abandon the notion of material reality altogether*, i.e. adopt some form of idealism. Strictly speaking, though, not even a thoroughgoing constructivism, as an epistemological (as opposed to ontological) stance, requires this much of us.[6] Somewhat less radically, then, we may b) *cling to our belief in mind-independent reality, but at the price of rendering it irrelevant*; ontological materialism (or dualism), that is, can be bought as part of a package deal that, in terms of epistemology, requires us to adopt coherence theories or even "no-theory theories" of truth and knowledge. On this view, the physical world may be "out there," but science, we must admit, is all about us. To avoid this self-enclosure of human thought and the bloodless materialism it entails, we might c) *pressure the notion of scientific revolution, denying either its actual occurrence or its very possibility*. Here we would not be in poor company; prompted by quandaries related to those outlined here, many philosophers—drawing on the later Wittgenstein and American pragmatism, for example—have argued that we can and should dispense with the notion of "paradigms," at least in the sense that they are held to be radically incommensurable. Perhaps the most famous, and most fundamental, of these attacks has been advanced by Donald Davidson, who argues on the basis of the pragmatic demands of translation that we simply have no means of recognizing something as a language if we are not willing to grant that a speaker's beliefs (e.g. concerning the objects in our immediate physical surroundings) are in important respects similar to our own; thus, we cannot make sense of the very idea of an untranslatable language, and we cannot imagine

---

6   See my previous footnote in this chapter.

the meaning (or, more accurately, the meaningfulness) of an incommensurable conceptual scheme, *Weltanschauung*, or paradigm.[7]

The argument has the perhaps appealing consequence of dismantling poststructural matrices of discourse, but does it not also rule out the possibility of human change altogether—thus paradoxically converging with an all-too-static structuralism—and ignore an important sense in which scientific (among other) revolutions have demonstrably changed our world? Instead of rejecting scientific revolutions out of hand, then, we might d) *attempt to tone down their radicality*. Kuhn's basic approach, because historicist and attendant to the actual practice of science, parts dramatically with an older philosophy of science (and epistemology generally) that saw its task as the "rational reconstruction" of science (or any knowledge), a normative and ahistorical task that consisted in piecing together the rationality of true (scientific) beliefs.[8] As a descriptive undertaking, philosophy of science following Kuhn was instead put on a par with science itself; thus, it has been suggested, Kuhn's was basically an "epistemology naturalized" in the sense famously articulated by W.V.O. Quine.[9] It is the hallmark of such an approach, according to proponents, that it is able to sidestep the challenges of skepticism that have haunted modern epistemology by simply abandoning the (hopeless) search for a firm foundation for empirical knowledge. Giving up the desire to transcendentally ground knowledge, naturalism assumes that all belief is fallible but that the large majority of our beliefs must be true, the reason being that humans (and our beliefs) are *a part of* the natural world about which we form beliefs. Denying the distance between a world "out there" and a mental realm "in here," the naturalistic framework need not commit itself to strong metaphysical theses about the ultimate nature of reality. Content with the world as we empirically know it, debates between realism and idealism become moot.[10] Davidson's argument—which itself operates natural-

---

7   See Davidson's classic essay, "On the Very Idea of a Conceptual Scheme."
8   For example, the logical empiricism of Rudolf Carnap and Carl Hempel sought firm foundations for scientific knowledge in the inherently rational realm of formal logic and mathematics. Classic texts are Carnap's *Logische Aufbau der Welt* and Hempel's *Aspects of Scientific Explanation*.
9   Ronald N. Giere, for example, claims that "[a]lthough he did not use exactly these words, Kuhn was advocating a *naturalized* philosophy of science" (380). Quine's classic text, entitled "Epistemology Naturalized," is contained in his *Ontological Relativity and Other Essays* and has been widely anthologized.
10 Of course, "realism" is a notoriously ambiguous term that means many things to many people. Naturalists themselves often lay claim to the epithet "realist," but in a sense different from that opposed by metaphysical idealists. See, for example, Hilary Putnam's collection of essays, *Realism with a Human Face*, in which he argues for an "internal"

istically in this sense, relying on the actual practice of science (field linguistics) rather than setting itself apart—purports to show that Kuhn's program, due to its assertion of a strong incommensurability thesis, still retains an allegiance with the outmoded metaphysical problematic and therefore falls into the trap of idealism, along with its attendant consequences; i.e. if paradigms *structure* our experience, revolution implies radical relativism or else skepticism. The question, then, is this: Can we disabuse the Kuhnian approach of its ontological excesses, retaining its basic naturalism, without giving up either a commitment to "robust" materiality or the possibility of revolutionary change?

The crux of the problem seems to be Kuhn's notion that "after a revolution scientists work in a different world" (*Structure* 135). To demystify them, we can look at paradigms simply as scientific traditions or research programs competing to explain a single world shared by embodied humans as social beings; it is thus tempting to reinterpret revolutions as primarily sociological or political, not ontological, events. As we have seen, however, this approach tends to support option b), leading to a dubiously materialist (or ontologically agnostic) social constructivism. While sociocultural dynamics must surely have their place in a naturalistic framework, science (including revolutionary science) cannot be *reduced* to the social if it is to retain its claim to being *about* the physical world. Indeed, naturalized epistemology is committed to the idea that the social world and the physical world are not separate but rather form a continuum; but to avoid the cluster of idealism, constructivism, and discursivism, the connection between the two realms must be such that it is not arbitrary whether we prioritize the human or nonhuman aspects of nature. Taking empirical science as its model, and taking it seriously as an engagement with a mind-independent reality, an "evolutionary epistemology" therefore posits a strong, causal link between the material world and our beliefs about it, seeing knowledge as the product of our biological evolution. Effectively marrying realism and pragmatism, knowledge (and, at the limit, science) is both instrumental or praxis-oriented and firmly anchored in "the real world." As a means of survival, it is inherently instrumental, but in order for this instrumentality to be effective— and/or as the simplest explanation of such effectivity—the majority of our beliefs

---

realism. Similarly, Arthur Fine argues for what he calls "The Natural Ontological Attitude" (or NOA) in his article of that title. The basic idea in both cases is that a "commonsense" realism is acceptable, but capital-R "Realism," which involves access to a mind-independent world, is metaphysical overkill. More recently, a movement called "speculative realism" has emerged which aims to reclaim the metaphysically robust notion of realism called into question by the likes of Putnam and Fine. In Chapter 6, I announce my allegiance to the general project of speculative realism, and explore several aspects of that project as guiding the formulation of a postnatural media theory.

must actually *correspond to* the reality of which they form part.[11] Clearly, this view maintains a strong commitment to materiality, but does it still leave room for revolution?

A Naturalistic Theory of Theory-Change

Convinced that an evolutionary perspective offers the most promising account of human knowledge compatible with a non-negligible materialism, I would like to pursue this question in some detail. As a case study, I turn to Ronald N. Giere's article "Philosophy of Science Naturalized," a concise but important attempt to coordinate evolutionary naturalism (à la Darwin) with revolutionary science (à la Kuhn). Asserting that "[h]uman perceptual and other cognitive capacities have evolved along with human bodies" (384), Giere's is a starkly biology-based naturalism. Evolutionary theory posits mind-independent matter as the source of a matter-dependent mind, and unless epistemologists follow suit, according to Giere, they remain open to global arguments from theory underdetermination and phenomenal equivalence: since the world would appear the same to us whether it were *really* made of matter or of mind-stuff, how do we know that idealism is not correct? And because idealism contradicts the materialist bias of physical science, how do we *know* that scientific knowledge is sound? According to Giere, we can confidently ignore these questions once the philosophy of science has itself opted for a scientific worldview. Of course, the skeptic will counter that naturalism's methodologically self-reflexive relation to empirical science renders its argumentation circular at root, but Giere turns the tables on skeptical challenges, arguing that they are "equally question-begging" (385). Given the compelling explanatory power and track record of modern science and evolutionary biology in particular, it is merely a feigned doubt that would question the thesis that "our capacities for operating in the world are highly adapted to that world" (385); knowledge of the world is *necessary* for the survival of biological organisms such as we are. Because this is essentially a transcendental argument, it does not *break* the circle in which the skeptic sees the

---

11 Of course, not everyone who follows this line of reasoning retains the talk of correspondence, and not everyone means the same thing by it. A "deflationary theory of truth," as put forward in Tarski's formalistic correspondence theory does not in itself imply a metaphysical thesis. This kind of correspondence is therefore perfectly compatible with positions such as Putnam's internal realism or Fine's NOA. It is only when it is coupled with metaphysical realism—which Putnam defines simply as the view that "there is exactly one true and complete description of 'the way the world is'" (*Reason, Truth, and History* 49)—that it becomes unacceptable to naturalists.

naturalist moving; instead, it asserts that circularity is an inescapable consequence of our place in nature. I shall return to the circle argument in some slightly different guises shortly, but I would first like to point out an important consequence of entering this circle. Accepting evolution as the basis of human knowledge implies an endorsement of the view that "we possess built-in mechanisms for quite direct interaction with aspects of our environment. The operations of these mechanisms largely bypass our conscious experience and linguistic or conceptual abilities" (385). More on the significance of this thesis later.

Another consequence is that norms (whether ethical, epistemic, or otherwise) must be explained in purely naturalistic terms, or else abandoned as chimeras. Whereas science is (arguably) free to cordon off the limits of its explanatory jurisdiction on this side of normative questions, a naturalistic theory of science is not.[12] It must be able to demonstrate that there are good reasons to believe x or y if science is not to turn out as mere knowledge so-called. Such reasons must be sought, however, in a descriptive account of true belief's value for survival, for example, rather than in the irreducibly prescriptive terms of rationality's inherent value or the *a priori* self-justification of epistemic justification. Certainly, naturalism opens itself to charges of relativism, but it swiftly contains the threat; as Giere says with regard to cultural relativism: "It is not physically possible that there should exist on earth a culture totally alien to us" (386). Differences exist, but they are bounded by the limits of our corporeal natures. This argument, reminiscent of Davidson's argument against incommensurable conceptual schemes, may give us pause, especially if we approach the problem from a feminist or otherwise politically interested perspective; does it not commit us to an essentialistic view of "human nature"? On the contrary, insists Giere, the implications are just the opposite: "one of the main points of an evolutionary perspective is that there is no sharp boundary between animals and humans, and thus between irrational and rational" (387). Further: "We have given up essentialism in biology. It is about time we gave it up in epistemology, and for similar reasons" (387).

Normativity, on this view, is no more illusory than cognition; like mind, however, norms are dependent on the physical. Disciplines such as sociology, anthro-

---

12 Of course, a range of disciplines that have laid claim to the honorific title of science—from eugenics to sociobiology, for example—have chosen not to draw the lines thus. From a different perspective, feminist epistemologies and philosophies of science suggest that more reputable sciences' hands-off approach to normative questions masks a deeper complicity between scientific "objectivity" and the suppression of necessarily "situated" subjectivities, thus making science—*especially* when it claims to be disinterested or apolitical—an inherently political affair. Accordingly, the failure to confront normativity is not only irresponsible but itself embodies a pernicious normativity.

pology, psychology, and cognitive science describe to us their workings, so a naturalistic account of scientific theory choice will draw upon their resources—so long as the mental or the social are seen not as providing the last word but as describing a certain level or aspect of an emphatically physical reality. Like any beliefs, scientific theories are therefore amenable to empirical descriptions that respect the primacy of the physical. But this does not mean that they are *determined* by biology or, more positively expressed, that their truth is *guaranteed* by the mechanisms of evolution. Since science is a highly abstract (cognitive and social) undertaking, it must be significantly more open to the whims of social and political influence than the everyday knowledge upon which our survival in the world depends. Nonetheless, the processes governing high-level theory formation are continuous with, not categorically distinct from, those evolutionary processes that have shaped the low-level knowledge fundamental to our survival. A naturalistic approach therefore looks at how practicing scientists, as intelligent but fallible social organisms rather than idealized rational agents, actually choose between competing theories in various historical circumstances (390-91).

We note, in relation to naturalism's circular form, that the possibility of choice is central to the possibility of revolutionary variation, and the occurrence of the latter attests to the reality of the former. If science were a continuous, cumulative affair, the naturalistic approach might be seen to face a science-theoretical version of the old nature vs. nurture conundrum: unbroken continuity could be seen as a sign that, firmly grounded in reality by our evolutionary biology, science itself evolves relentlessly toward a more perfect understanding of reality; on the other hand, this so-called progress might simply indicate the effectiveness of social control processes, indoctrination, and disciplinary power in shaping theoretical belief. There could be no deciding between the alternatives, each apparently reducible to the other. But the actual discontinuity of science suggests that neither biology nor society can be ultimately determinative of scientific theory. Historical discontinuity may thus be taken as empirical evidence for the naturalistic hypothesis that scientists form, test, accept, and reject theories under the dual pressures of sociality and biological materiality. (As an aside, one might even seek in this insight a *scientific* justification for a *politically* motivated opposition to the complementary positions of biological essentialism and totalizing constructivism, both of which would explain away political choice as illusory.[13]) Because the historical movement of sci-

---

13 Though I am not aware of anyone explicitly making this argument, an implicit appreciation of its logic must surely form part of the reason for feminists' interest in Kuhnian style philosophy of science. Of course, the argument remains strictly circular, which might account for why the argument has not been explicitly made, but if epistemological naturalism is correct, this circularity may not need worry us.

ence is *not* linear, choices must really be made—not by isolated geniuses but against the background of scientific traditions and "peer pressure," but nevertheless in an attempt to understand the material reality to which scientists are bound by the physicality of their own bodies. Given that the paradigms of "normal" (i.e. non-revolutionary) science are conservatively resistant to change, where does the impetus for revolution come from? Why do scientists at a given point in time choose to reject the old and embrace the new?

It would be more than surprising if a general answer could be given to this question (and it is the generality of constructivist/textualist mechanisms that make them suspect); lest we impose upon history the uniformity of a static or even eschatological framework (whether evolutionary or otherwise), each individual case must be investigated on its own grounds. To illustrate the applicability of his naturalistic perspective in such cases, Giere turns to the geophysical revolution of the 1960s: the rapid overturn of a model of the earth as a once much warmer body that had cooled and contracted, leaving the oceans and continents more or less fixed in their present positions, by the continental drift model which set the stage for the now prevalent plate tectonics theory (391-94). As Giere points out, the matching coastlines of Africa and South America had long suggested the possibility of movement, and drift models had been developed in the early twentieth century but were left, by and large, unpursued; it was not just academic protectionism that preserved the contractionist model but a lack of hard evidence capable of challenging accepted wisdom—accepted because it "worked" well enough to explain a large range of phenomena. The discovery in the 1950s of north-south ocean ridges suggested, however, a plausible mechanism for continental drift: if the ridges were formed, as Harry Hess suggested, by volcanism, then "sea floor spreading" should be the result, and the continents would be gradually pushed apart by its action. Paleomagnetists' discovery, also in the 1950s, of large-scale magnetic field reversals provided the model with empirically testable consequences (the Vine-Matthews-Morley hypothesis): if the field reversals were indeed global and if the sea floor was spreading, then irregularly patterned stripes running parallel to the ridges should match the patterns observed in geological formations on land. Until this prediction was corroborated, there was still little impetus to overthrow the dominant theory, but magnetic soundings of the Pacific-Antarctic Ridge in 1966, along with sea-floor core samples, revealed the expected polarity patterns and led, within the space of a year, to a near complete acceptance of drift hypotheses among earth scientists.

Without recourse to apparently idealistic talk of researchers living "in different worlds," naturalism can explain the radical and sudden revolution in geology, according to Giere, by appealing only to a few very plausible assumptions about human psychology and social interaction—assumptions that are fully compatible with physicalism. These concern what he calls the "payoff matrix" for accepting one of the competing theories (393). Abandoning a pet theory is seldom satisfying to an individual, and the rejection of a widely held model is likely to upset many researchers, revealing their previous work as no longer relevant. Resistance to change is all too easily explained; only those so-called visionaries who, out of rebellion or simple idiosyncrasy, had invested their energy into demonstrating the plausibility of an alternative would have a strong interest in establishing a new paradigm. However, humans also take satisfaction in being right, and scientists hope to be objectively right about those aspects of the world they investigate. This interest, as Giere points out, does not have to be considered "an *intrinsic* positive value" among scientists, for it is tempered by psychosocial considerations (393): both the fear of being ostracized by a differently-minded establishment and the promise of rewards (the gratification of fame or professional advancement) should the winds start blowing differently. The geo-theoretical options became clear— indeed, first came into existence as *vital* rather than merely logical alternatives— with the articulation of a drift model with clearly testable consequences. We may surmise that researchers began weighing their options at this time, though it is not necessary to consider this a transparently conscious act of deliberation. What *was* essential was the wide agreement among researchers that the predictions regarding magnetic profiles, if verified, would be extremely difficult to square with a static earth model and compellingly simple to explain if drift really occurred. Sharing this basic assumption, the choice was easy when the relevant data came in (394).

Accordingly, a shift of paradigms need not be a mystical event, and it can be explained in purely naturalistic terms, without appeal to irreducibly normative notions of epistemic justification. The really interesting thing about this case, though, is the central role that technology played in structuring theoretical options and forcing a decision, which Giere notes but only in passing. The developing model first became truly relevant through the availability of technologies capable of confirming its predictions: technologies for conducting magnetic soundings of the ocean floor and for retrieving core samples from the deep. Indeed, the Vine-Matthews-Morley hypothesis depended on technology not only for its verification, but for its initial formulation as well: ocean ridges could not have been discovered without instruments capable of sounding the ocean floor, and the discovery of magnetic field reversals depended on a similarly advanced technological infrastructure.[14] A reliance on mediating technologies is central to the practice of science, and Giere suggests that an appreciation of this fact helps distinguish naturalism from "methodological foundationism" or the notion that justified beliefs must recur

---

14 As is so often the case, science benefitted from military technologies, including both sonar equipment and magnetic anomaly detectors developed for locating enemy submarines.

ultimately to a firm basis in immediate experience (394). His account of the geological paradigm shift therefore

assumes agreement that the technology for measuring magnetic profiles is reliable. The Duhem-Quine problem [i.e. the problem that it is logically possible to salvage empirically disconfirmed theories by *ad hoc* augmentation] is set aside by the fact that one can build, or often purchase commercially, the relevant measuring technology. The background knowledge (or auxiliary hypotheses) are embodied in proven technology. (394)

In other words, the actual practice of science (or technoscience) does not require ultimate justificational grounding, and the agreement on technological reliability ensures, according to Giere and *contra* Kuhn, that disagreeing parties still operate in the *same* world.

Natural Science and Technological Multistability

While I agree that Giere's description of the way technology is implemented by scientists is a plausible account of actual practice and its underlying assumptions, I question his extrapolation from the practical to the theoretical plane. With regard to technology, I contend, the circle problem resurfaces with a vengeance. As posed by the skeptic, Giere is right, in my opinion, to reject the circle argument as invalidating naturalism's methodologically self-reflexive application of scientific theories to the theory of science. Our evolutionary history, I agree, genuinely militates against the skeptic's requirement that we be able to provide grounds for all our beliefs; our survival depends upon an embodied knowledge that is presupposed by, and therefore not wholly explicatable to, our conscious selves. But as extensions of embodiment, the workings of our technologies are equally opaque to subjective experience, even—or *especially*—when they seem perfectly transparent channels of contact with the world. Indeed, Giere seems to recognize this when he says that "background knowledge (or auxiliary hypotheses) are *embodied* by proven technology" (394, emphasis added). In other words, scientists *invest* technology with a range of assumptions concerning "reliability" or, more generally, about the relations of a technological infrastructure to the natural world; their agreement on these assumptions is the enabling condition for technology to yield clear-cut decision-making consequences. Appearing *neutral* to all parties involved, the technology is in fact loaded, subordinated to human aims as a tool.[15] Some such subordinating process

---

15 This, of course, is a technology-based formulation of the popular claim that all observation is always already "theory-laden." One advantage of formulating it in terms of mate-

seems, from a naturalistic perspective, unavoidable for embodied humans. However, *agreement* on technological utility—on both whether and how a technology is useful—is not guaranteed in every case. Moreover, it is not just a set of cognitive, theoretical assumptions ("auxiliary hypotheses") with which scientists entrust technologies, but also aspects of their pre-theoretically embodied, sensorimotor competencies. Especially at this level, mediating technologies are open to what Don Ihde has called an experiential "multistability"—capable, that is, of instantiating to differently situated subjectivities radically divergent ways of relating to the world.[16] But it is precisely the consensual stability of technologies that is the key to Giere's contextualist rebuttal of "foundationism." And while I have no doubt that Giere's analysis is true to the facts of the specific case of the geological revolution, I question whether these facts can (or should) be generalized to an overarching naturalistic theory of scientific theory choice.

Downplaying multistability is the condition for a general avoidance of the circle argument, for a pragmatic avoidance of idealism and/or skepticism. This, I believe, is most certainly the way things work in actual practice, at least in cases like the one Giere describes; (psycho)social-institutional pressures work to ensure consensus on technological utility. But does naturalism, self-reflexively endorsing science as the basis of its own theorization, then necessarily reproduce these pressures? Feminists in particular may protest on these grounds that the "nature" in naturalism in fact encodes the white male perspective historically privileged by science because embodied by the majority of practicing scientists. What I am suggesting is that the tacit, largely unquestioned processes by which technological multistability is tamed in practice form a locus for the inscription of social norms directly into the physical world; for in making technologies the material bearers of consensual values (whether political, epistemic, psychological, or even the animalistically basic preferability of pleasure over pain) scientific practice encourages certain modes of embodied relations to the world—not just psychic but *material* relations themselves

---

rial technologies, however, is that it offers a concrete mechanism for non-conscious theoretical investment and, in the process, suggests that "theory" is perhaps the wrong word: for at issue are precisely pre-theoretical relations that, materially embodied by active corporeal organisms vis-à-vis their physical environments, lay the practical groundwork for any properly theoretical articulation.

16 Multistability is a recurrent theme in Ihde's work. Consider the following statement: "I argue that the very structure of technologies is multistable, with respect to uses, to cultural embeddedness, and to politics as well. Multistability is not the same as neutrality. Within multistability there lie *trajectories*, not just any trajectory, but partially determined trajectories" (*Bodies in Technology* 106). At stake are therefore "multiple intrinsic possibilities of the technologies" (107).

embodied in technologies. It goes without saying that this can only occur at the expense of other modes of being-embodied.

More generally stated, the real problem with naturalism's self-reflexivity is not that it fails to take skeptical challenges seriously or that it provides a false picture of actual scientific practice, but that in extrapolating from practice it locks certain assumptions about technological reliability into theory, embracing them as its own. While it is contextually—indeed physically—necessary that assumptions be made, and that they be embodied or exteriorized in technologies, the particular assumptions are contingent and non-neutral. This may be seen as a political problem, which it is, but it also more than that. It is, moreover, an ontological problem of the instability of nature itself—not just of nature as a construct but of the material constitution of real, flesh-and-blood human organisms and their environments. Once we enter the naturalist circle—and I believe we have good reason to do so— we accept that evolution dislodges the primacy of place traditionally accorded human beings. At the same time, we accept that the technologies with which science has demonstrated the non-essentiality of human/animal boundaries are reliable, that they show us what reality is really, objectively like. This step depends, however, on a bracketing of technological multistability. If we question this bracketing, as I do, we seem to lose our footing in material objectivity. Nevertheless convinced that it would be wrong to concede defeat to the skeptic, we point out that adaptive knowledge's circularity or contextualist holism is a necessary requirement of human survival, that it follows directly from embodiment and the fact that the underlying biological mechanisms "largely bypass our conscious experience and linguistic or conceptual abilities" (Giere 385). But if we admit that technological multistability really obtains as a fact of our phenomenal relations to the world, this holism seems to lead us back precisely to Kuhn's idealist suggestion that researchers (or humans generally) may occupy incommensurably "different worlds." If we do not wish to abandon materialism, then we must find an interpretation of this idea that is compatible with physicalism.

Indeed, it is the great merit of naturalism that it provides us with the means for doing so; however, it is the great failure of the theory that it neglects these resources. The failure, which consists in reproducing science's subordination of technology to thought—in fact compounding the reduction, as contextually practiced, by subordinating it to an overarching (i.e. supra-contextual) theory of science—is truly necessary for naturalism, for to rectify its oversight of multistability is to admit the breakdown of a continuous nature itself. To consistently acknowledge the indeterminacy of human-technology-world relations and simultaneously maintain materialism requires, to begin with, that we extend Giere's insight about biological mechanisms to specifically technological mechanisms of embodied relation to the world: they too "bypass our conscious experience and linguistic or conceptual abilities." If we take the implications seriously, this means that technologies resist full conceptualization and are therefore potentially non-compliant with human (or scientific) aims; reliance on technology is not categorically different in kind from reliance on our bodies: both ground our practice and knowledge in the material world, but neither is fully recuperable to thought. Extending naturalism in this way means recognizing that not only human/animal but also human/technology distinctions are porous and non-absolute. But whereas naturalism tacitly assumes that the investment of technology with cognitive aims is only "natural" and therefore beyond question, the multistability of non-cognitive investments of corporeal capacities implies that there is more to the idea of "different worlds" than naturalism is willing or able to admit: on a materialistic reading, it is nature itself, and not just human thought or science, that is historically and contextually multiple, non-coherently splintered, and subject to revolutionary change. Serious consideration of technology leads us, that is, to embrace a *denatured* naturalism, a *techno-evolutionary* epistemology, and a *material* rather than social constructivism.

Before elaborating on this conclusion, I should point out that my reasoning is not guilty of any crude sort of question-begging. Clearly, my argument rests on an appeal to phenomenology, and it may be questioned whether this is compatible with naturalism. As a method, phenomenology is descriptive rather than prescriptive, so it need not introduce any irreducibly normative notions. And, at least following Merleau-Ponty, phenomenology's objects of description are also ontologically compatible with naturalism; the phenomenological subject is not a free-floating rational entity but inextricably attached to a body whose physiology has been shaped, in communication with the material environment, by the mechanisms of evolution. (In philosophical jargon, the subject "supervenes upon" the biological body.) The methodological focus on subjectivity and noetic processes implies, with respect to science's objectivist descriptions of reality, an *operational dualism*, not a metaphysical one; in this respect, it is little different, structurally speaking, from the distinction between social-institutional and physico-biological forces in Giere's analysis. Moreover, the argument from the experiential multistability of mediating technologies appeals not to merely logical possibilities but to real, historically vital alternatives of embodied experience of the world, so the argument is not involved in the skeptic's tacit appeal to "foundationism" and the tired game of "but how do you know you're not a brain in a vat?" That is, the argument respects naturalism's basic insight that idealism is the complement of metaphysical (i.e. "foundationist") realism, that it issues from the same problematic that leads epistemologists to posit an Archimedean point upon which knowledge rests and that allows skeptics to question knowledge *in toto* on the grounds that no such point exists. The attraction of naturalism is that it sidesteps this problematic and suggests a materialistic interpretation of revolutionary change that avoids the objectionable ascription of world-changes to the causal power of human thought or scientific theory. The goal itself is commendable; nor do I question the basic approach of metamethodological self-reflexion. What I do object to is the *uncritical* endorsement of empirical science's instrumental methodology, which leads to a neutralization of technology and a tacit reinstatement of a stable human nature. In effect, naturalism goes too far in its denial of relativism. Its pursuit of a scientifically grounded knowledge of material reality suggests that, because theory supervenes on materiality, conceptual revolution cannot be *the cause* of radical changes in the structure of the world, and I emphatically second this conclusion. But by bracketing out the phenomenal relativity implicit in technological multistability, naturalism establishes this conclusion at the price of obfuscating very real, very material changes in the structure of the lifeworld from which conceptual revolution may follow as an *effect*.

Postnaturalism

Several pages ago, I laid out a number of options, labeled a) through d), for thinking about the relations between materialism, knowledge, and scientific revolutions. These alternatives implied, respectively: outright idealism, a so-called materialism of little consequence, the denial of historical revolution, or the latter's naturalistic neutralization. Assuming, now, that each of these consequences is deemed unacceptable, a more radical alternative is called for. I propose, therefore, that: e) *revolutionary changes in matter itself are historically indexed—but not caused—by conceptual upheavals, including but not limited to scientific paradigm shifts*. Whereas naturalism tones down the radicality of revolutionary relativism, this approach (which I dub postnaturalism to indicate its intimate but critical relation to naturalized epistemology) aims at a further radicalization by remitting the causal mechanisms from the cognitive-theoretical to the material-technological realm.

Like the "instrumental realism" discussed by Don Ihde in his book of that title, the postnaturalist position asserts that more often than not the "interface" between science and technology is such that technology drives science rather than the other way around.[17] But whereas most instrumental realists, in Ihde's sense, recognize the central role played by technological instrumentation (as science's necessary embodiment and the material context in which it is embedded) both in the fulfillment and indeed the prior *definition* of epistemic tasks, their focus remains very much on the construction and confirmation of theory. Occasionally such approaches even note technology's *production* of contemporary technoscience's objects of study, thus

---

17 See Ihde's *Instrumental Realism: The Interface between Philosophy of Science and Philosophy of Technology*.

positing a sort of instrumentation-driven feedback loop between observation and the entities observed (think, for example, of atom-smashers or laboratory-engineered, non-naturally occurring chemical elements), but still here the "realism" of instrumental realism is largely cast in terms of a representational match between an admittedly "carpentered" world (to use Ihde's term) and an observing-theorizing subject[18]; such approaches continue to form a strict complement to the anti-realism of social constructivist readings of similar phenomena (for example in Latour's early work[19]).

Postnaturalism, on the other hand, goes farther in asserting what Mark Hansen calls the "radical exteriority" of (natural and technological) matter to representational thought and socially negotiated significance, thus displacing the centered subject by insisting on the inextricable interconnection of intentionality and historically variable technospheres. To this extent, postnaturalism is apposite with actor-network theory and variant science-studies approaches in the work of Latour or Haraway, for example; highlighting the distribution of agency among human and nonhuman "actants" within technologically mediated networks, they too assert that material reality is dynamic rather than static, active rather than passive, even historically produced yet not amenable to the human aims of its apparent or would-be producers. The latter seems a useful approach to what I above called *material* constructivism. However, postnaturalism breaks with such approaches when, as sometimes occurs, their "material-semiotic" concentration becomes more semiotic than material—to the extent, that is, that cyborgs and "quasi-objects" focus materiality in the realm of its intersection with representational discourse (in processes of "inscription," in Latour's term) and ignore a larger sphere of technological impact that outstrips a semiotically established "generalized symmetry" between human subjects and technical devices.[20]

---

18 See, for example, Ian Hacking's *Representing and Intervening* and Robert Ackermann's *Data, Instruments, and Theory*, as well as Ihde's discussion of them in *Instrumental Realism*.

19 See, for example, Latour and Woolgar's *Laboratory Life*. As will become apparent later, I do not think the same can be said of Latour's later work, to which I have recourse in Chapter 6.

20 As I noted in the previous footnote on Latour, and which applies to Haraway as well, this is not meant to be a blanket indictment of these approaches, for they do not always succumb to textualization in this manner. Sometimes, however, they do, such as when Haraway locates the destabilizing power of her "odd boundary creatures—simians, cyborgs, and women"—in the fact that "Monsters signify" (*Simians* 2). Arguments that Latour sometimes gives the upper hand to semiotics rather than materiality can be found in Mark

Following Hansen's call for a *"new realism"* (*Embodying Technesis* 30) that, in addition to the social and cultural (including scientific-theoretical) construction and contextualization of technologies, also acknowledges their place in what N. Katherine Hayles calls the "unmediated flux,"[21] postnaturalism embraces Hansen's "methodological double vision" and accords an asymmetrical primacy to an extra-discursive materiality of technology by virtue of which it "can actually alter the very material conditions for perceptual and cognitive social life" (Hansen 36). Rehabilitating a dualism between phenomenal appearance and an underlying noumenal reality, this realism nevertheless avoids configuring materiality as (in Wittgenstein's words) a "wheel that can be turned though nothing else moves with it"; for though categorically immune to complete cognitive-representational capture, the unmediated flux, by virtue of our embodied grounding in and direct experiential contact with it, is not inert and humanly irrelevant but (to conclude Wittgenstein's aphorism) indeed very much a "part of the mechanism."[22] "Embodiment, in short, constitutes our practical means of interaction with the material flux and with the material reality of technology beyond the theater of representation" (Hansen 41). Impinging directly upon our bodies, technologies can thus transform us in ways that simply escape the purview of narrowly epistemological frameworks. This is not to say, of course, that technologies do not *also* enter conscious experience and discursive signification, nor is it to claim that non-representable transformations leave no mark in the cognitive-discursive realm; but to the extent that the latter effects *are* registered there, it is in a purely negative manner, as a disruption of conceptual-linguistic frameworks.

Here we approach one of the decisive advantages of postnaturalism over exclusively semiotic or textualist approaches to technology, which are unable and often quite simply unwilling to countenance anything "outside the text." Insofar as they avoid straightforwardly *reducing* "tech" to "text," such approaches are still unable to *account for* its material impacts; at the limit, as in de Manian textual allegory, they simply *mystify* technology's workings by attributing them to the causal agency of textuality itself—gesturing, as I see it, to what amounts to an elegantly reified *je-ne-sais-quoi*. As a semiotically immanent critique of constructivistic anti-realism, Hayles's discussion of "constrained constructivism" provides an interesting case in point. Starting from strictly constructivist premises, Hayles questions the role of constraints that limit—for surely not just *anything* goes—our alleged construction of reality. Plotting the relations between representation and constraint as affirmative

---

Hansen's *Embodying Technesis* (30-47) and in Andrew Pickering's *The Mangle of Practice* (9-20).
21 See Hayles's essay "Constrained Constructivism."
22 Wittgenstein's aphorism is from *Philosophical Investigations*, Part I, §271.

and negative positions on a semiotic square, Hayles aims to demonstrate, from *within* the space of language, how representations can never match unmediated reality but, through the function of negation, must nevertheless have indirect recourse to an *unrepresented* form of external reference; thus, the negating action of constraint "opens an escape hatch from the prison house of language" ("Constrained Constructivism" 81). Tellingly, though, this connection to the unmediated flux, because it is approached *through the medium* of language, can only be described as an "elusive negativity" (83). In later writings, Hayles herself supplements this account with a more "positive" view of embodied experience as the pre-representational medium linking discourse and radically non-discursive materiality, including that of technology.[23]

Seen in this light, the virtue of postnaturalism lies in its naturalist point of departure. Taking the material evolution of organic bodies for granted, methodologically speaking, means that we *begin* by assuming that our linguistically elusive interface with the unrepresentable material real is already, literally, *fleshed out*. Since postnaturalism is not so much a reversal as a radical continuation of naturalism's course, it preserves a strong commitment to materiality as its ontological base, as the historically and metaphysically necessary foundation of thought and theory, and is therefore neither tempted to reify textuality nor forced to box its way out of semiotic squares. Nevertheless, postnaturalism—as the prefix already indicates—is not self-sufficient, and Hayles's discussion of "elusive negativity" therefore remains instructive in another way.

The point might be expressed thus: naturalism is sensible epistemology; in terms of its basic trajectory, I believe, it is probably the most sensible theory of knowledge we can hope for. Postnaturalism, on the other hand, is *not* sensible epistemology, not because it is unreasonable but because it points to something that is subjectively *insensible* and therefore *beyond the jurisdiction of epistemology altogether*—viz. a noumenal (i.e. non-phenomenal) realm of material flux. Naturalism may bequeath to us our materialism, but as an empirically based approach it certainly cannot describe what lies beyond the realm of empirical accessibility. And yet, in a negative manner like that described by Hayles, this alterior realm announces itself from *within* the epistemological framework of naturalism itself. This begins with a paradox: natural science aims for an objective description of reality, yet its discovery of organic evolution contradicts the possibility of a single, static standpoint from which to deliver this description. So long as we are doing epistemology, we are right to bracket out this paradox. Contrary to the skeptic, knowledge is not fundamentally invalidated, as naturalism rightly claims: we have to make knowledge claims to live, but we should know, as pragmatists (like John Dewey)

---

23 See, for example, "The Materiality of Informatics" and *How We Became Posthuman*.

and feminists (such as Sandra Harding and Donna Haraway) remind us, that all knowledges (in the plural) are situated knowledges.[24] Or, in phenomenological terms, since intentionality is inherently relational, objectivity is always relative to a situated subject. Parallel to Hayles's concept of "constrained constructivism," we can call this a "constrained objectivism." Naturalism therefore quite sensibly assumes that the evolutionary interaction of material organisms and their environments is a fundamental, though non-invalidating, constraint on our knowledge. Postnaturalism does not question this assumption but instead points out, chiasmatically, that our *knowledge of* this constraint is itself based on a further *constraint on* our knowledge, that it depends on the (bracketed) material embodiment of corporeal intentionality in technologies that themselves form part of the environment in which our bodies act, react, and evolve. Again, we draw no skeptical conclusions; instead, postnaturalism emerges from naturalism by simply *setting aside* epistemology, by following the paradox beyond the knowledge-enabling bracket and calling to the fore as figure that which forms the ground of scientific inquiry. What we find behind the bracketed anthropotechnical interface is still a *je-ne-sais-quoi*, so that the negating "post-" of postnaturalism points to what (from the perspective of phenomenality, which is to say from *any* situated perspective) remains the "elusive negativity" of the material flux.

Stated differently, the unmediated flux cannot be reduced to science's physical laws, anatomical structures, and physiological capacities any more than it can to psychosocial pressures, for these are all descriptions relative to a contextually seated subjectivity, mediated through the mechanisms of (among others) conscious perception, technologies, and inscription practices. Scientific descriptions may in fact be very *good* ones, but they cannot claim to be completely commensurable with the noumenal realm. This, then, is the kernel of truth in constructivism: that knowledge simply cannot aspire to an absolute status. But constructivism no less than objectivism is constrained—so that, regardless of their varying ontological commitments, the forms of knowledge they theorize tend (ideally) towards convergence, as both are the products of (non-arbitrary) processes of negation: products of what in a Bergsonian idiom we could call "subtractions" from the flux. Because it is constrained—or to the extent that it is responsive to representational *and* material constraint—knowledge *pertains to* but cannot *encompass* the real. At the intersection of unqualified matter and a qualifying mind, the objects of knowledge are situated in what Latour calls the "Middle Kingdom," the realm of "quasi-objects" that span the nature/culture divide and are "simultaneously real, discursive, and

---

24 See, for example, Dewey's "Propositions, Warranted Assertibility, and Truth"; Harding's *The Science Question in Feminism*; and Haraway's discussion of Harding in "Situated Knowledges."

social" (*We Have Never Been Modern* 64). The hybrid both/and of the epistemic-phenomenal realm, because it issues from restrictions on the unlimited constructability of *and* from limitations on our unhindered cognitive access to the alterior real, in fact indicates that knowledge is a doubly negative affair: the world as we know it is a world of not-subject/not-object. Starting from the notion that knowledge is contextually grounded in our non-conscious organic transactions with the physical environment, and followed to its paradoxical post-epistemological conclusion, naturalism gives way to a view of a very Bergsonian body that is no longer encompassed by anatomy and physiology (its relative determinations) but acts, in relation to flux, as a "center of indetermination."[25]

It will be noticed, then, that my postnaturalism is not a novel theory *per se* but rather a particular derivation of a group of pre-existing positions (metaphysical, epistemological, phenomenological) set in definite relations to one another. Significantly, the derivation operates much in the manner of deconstruction, revealing empirical science as contingent upon contrary acts of investment, or "in-scription," *as well as* withdrawal, subtraction, "de-scription": *un-writings* of nature. Rather than ascribing the "gaps" to the workings of *différance* or *écriture*, however, I follow naturalism in tracing them to a material reality that necessarily pre-exists discourse and cognition as the condition of their possibility. Thus, what I have described is a non-textual, *material* aporia that arises from the juxtaposition of a situated perspective and the ground upon which experience is situated. In effect, then, postnaturalism grants that epistemic contextualism is an accurate description of knowledge, that knowledge is real and pertains to what is objectively "out there"; at the same time, though, this realism is relativized to a quasi-synchronic perspective upon a material domain that cannot be exhausted by any single perspective, and that enables situational and historical (or diachronic) variation. The world that presents itself to a situated subjectivity is describable in phenomenological terms, but the material flux is not. Faced with this division of spheres, with phenomenal relativity on the one hand and noumenal inaccessibility on the other, it may seem that realist epistemology is just thrown in for good measure, that it really has no claim in this system. However, the reality of knowledge—as knowledge *of* reality—follows from the material embodiment which places us at, or *as*, the interstice between the noumenal and the phenomenal, between flux and stasis. To deny the objectivity of knowledge, on the grounds that it is not absolute, is to deny the materiality which defines our situational subjectivity. It is thus to deny the reality of positions between which systemic change can occur. By admitting knowledge, we are able to recognize (theoretically if not phenomenally) the radicality of revolution

---

25 See Bergson's *Matter and Memory* or, for an accessible introduction to Bergson's thought, the collection of essays *The Creative Mind*.

as a literal world-change, as a shift *between* contextual knowledge systems that is not *caused by* knowledge but instead owes its occurrence to a prior mechanism of "articulation"—or the division of flux into subjects and objects—and a concomitant movement of "reticulation"—or the web-like "mapping" of actual and possible relations amongst them.

Spontaneous, for all intents and purposes *ex nihilo*, division and mapping *precede* "all intents and purposes" as they might issue from a projecting ego or constructing communitas; articulation/reticulation occur through—or *as*—embodiment, which as a material center of indetermination links situational determinacy with its a-centric substratum. Technologies, though, transform our modes of access to (or subtraction from) the material real, change the very shape of our embodiment when introjected into the pre-personal ground of experience; expanding and attenuating sensory capacities and intentional modalities, they give rise to a newly configured reality. Just as embodiment cannot be reduced to its anatomico-physiological description, so do technologies exceed mechanical-technical determinations; as *lived*, technologies are symbiotically, non-dualistically, attached to the embodied lifeworld as an integral part. Viewed (metaphorically) "from below," from the perspective of its emergence through articulation and reticulation, the phenomenal lifeworld that includes a new technology is incommensurable with a lifeworld in which it is lacking, for the technology is not just articulated as an object, not *only* a machine towards which one might relate, but is itself a condition for the mappings of possible relations between subjects and objects.[26] From this perspective, a lifeworld is itself a historical event, part of a chronology that "precedes" the history (and range of possible futures) contained in every lifeworld. This transcendent history is not, however, a Hegelian history of Spirit but the very history of embodiment's material immanence, from which perspective phenomenology's "natural attitude" as ground is displaced to appear as a variable figure in the history of nature's transformation. Seen thus, anthropotechnical interfacing effects a radical revolution of matter itself, and embodiment is its site. Because such shifts occur *between* situated perspectives, where there can be no subjective measure, they remain phenomenally elusive. If not totally invisible, material revolutions certainly lack the opacity required for objecthood, so that their "appearance" to us is in a diffuse manner, as bodily affect: indeterminate feelings of wonder, awe, confusion, a feeling that we can't quite place or an inchoate sense that we're somehow not at home anymore (*das Unheimliche*).[27] In such a way, the deeper (nonhuman) history of embodiment

---

26 In *Embodying Technesis*, Mark Hansen identifies and criticizes a "machine reduction" of technology at work in Freud, Heidegger, Derrida, and others.

27 At the end of his essay on *Frankenstein*, Mark Hansen also invokes the uncanny and highlights its pre-Freudian formulation, by Ernst Jentsch, as an experience of undecida-

comes to non-representational expression, inarticulately communicating a material evolution that is incompletely described by biology or natural history.

We may surmise that the romantic strategy of sublime transcendence, which by harnessing the indifferent mutability of nature exempts itself from human history, was an attempt to tame precisely these bodily intimations of change, to silence the murmurings of a body transformed by industrial technology. Indeed, though Mary Shelley may not have consciously shared the ontology put forward here, the conflux of technology and history around pre-personal embodiment allows us to see the profound appropriateness of basing her critique of romantic poetics in a monstrous body: for although the latter, like sublime nature, also signals a realm of passage that transcends human temporality, its reorganization of nature effaces the foundation upon which the poet seeks to embody nature's eternal perspective, to view the world and its history *sub specie aeternitatis*. That perspective is itself resituated, thrown back into history, by the emergence of a machinic body. The anthropotechnical interface punctuates the supreme history of nature, denatures it, and places it in a larger history of embodiment. Instantiating a rupture, break, or gap in perspectival situatedness, the monster participates, as a "constraint," in a metahistorical transformation. It marks the ungraspable *transitionality* that, as the affective, non-cognitive bond between noumenal flux and phenomenal-systemic stasis or between transcendent and situated histories, anthropotechnical embodiment ontologically *is*.

POSTNATURALISM AND THE THERMODYNAMIC REVOLUTION

In order to make these abstract claims more concrete, it remains to demonstrate how the postnaturalistic derivation of embodied transitionality applies to the case of the industrial revolution. Let us return to the steam engine as an alleged site, as Hansen has it, of a historical "deterritorialization of the human perspective." From an empirical point of view, it must seem fantastic to claim such power for the primitive piston-driven heat engines that now rest idle as museum displays. The workings of such machines, far from anomalous exceptions to nature, are readily explained in the scientific terms of thermodynamic heat/work conversion processes. It would seem, then, that the only thing mysterious about the steam engine is the quasi-romantic nostalgia with which it is sometimes perceived, its function as a symbol of human ingenuity in the days before big-business technoscience took over. We note, however, the marked contrast between this view and that of the

---

bility with regard to the animate or inanimate nature of technological objects ("Not thus" 609). The uncanny, in this sense, will be relevant to my assessment, in Chapter 7, of James Whale's Frankenstein films and in particular the image of the monster.

nineteenth-century romantics, for whom the steam engine and the factories it powered represented a fundamental threat to human freedom. Is this not evidence that we inhabit a very different world?

The answer, of course, depends on the interpretation of the question. Most would be willing to concede that the sociocultural context of our life and labor has undergone radical change, even that the material structure of our world would be fundamentally different had the industrial revolution not occurred. Indeed, without our knowledge of thermodynamics, the present state of the world would be unthinkable: for the new science found ready application in the construction of internal combustion engines, upon which our cars are based, and in the improvement of heat engines that led directly to the modern power plant and the electrification of our homes (not to mention the condensing clothes dryers, refrigerators, air conditioners, and other appliances plugged into the power grid). To the extent that thermodynamics depended for its explication upon the industrial steam engine, Isaac Asimov's claim—that the absence of the automobile would make more of a difference to our lives than had Einstein not formulated the theory of relativity—must be extended to James Watt's low-pressure engine or Newcomen's atmospheric engine upon which it improved.[28] Seen thus, the impact of these machines is rightly called revolutionary, but does it amount, as I have suggested, to an *ontological* revolution in the very structure of physical nature? I will argue for this counterintuitive thesis in three steps: 1) beginning from an empirical-naturalistic perspective, a historical reconstruction of the steam engine's role in thermodynamics reveals theoretical underdetermination and logical uncertainties, which demand 2) a techno-phenomenological reduction of underlying anthropotechnical (scientist-instrument) relations, set in the broader context of industrialization's multistable lifeworld impacts; 3) the results of this analysis are then approached from a postnatural, postphenomenological perspective, rehistoricized vis-à-vis the history of embodiment or the embodied history of flux.

1) Science and the Steam-Engine: A Naturalistic Approach

As numerous historical accounts have shown, the relations between thermodynamic science and steam-engine technology were complex and bilateral: an existing technology fueled scientific knowledge that in turn enabled innovations with far-reaching effects for human life right up to the present day. The fact that "science owes more to the steam engine" than the other way around does not prevent us

---

28 Asimov's suggestion is reported in Mark Hansen's *Embodying Technesis* 1, 2.

from fitting these developments into a naturalistic explanation of scientific theory change. Accordingly, in addition to industrial applications, the steam engine functioned as an instrument with which to study heat phenomena, and it defined for scientists the theoretical options between the old view of heat as a material substance (caloric), which is neither created nor destroyed but always conserved, and the "dynamical" theory of heat, according to which only energy is conserved in heat-dissipating conversions to mechanical work. That the steam engine's scientific instrumentality was historically and practically secondary to its industrial utility and arose in close connection with engineers' ultimately economic efforts to improve efficiency does not damage this account; what is important, from a naturalistic perspective, is that scientists eventually *agreed* on the scientific relevance of the machine. Given the lively interchange between natural scientists and engineers, a basic sort of agreement seems to have been reached quite early in the history of the steam engine. But it was not until around 1850 that scientists began to agree on the steam engine's *reliability as a decision-enabler* with regard to the choice between caloric and mechanical theories of heat. The question had simply not been posed as such by investigators; caloric theory guided their interactions with the steam engine, and the technology taught them more about the properties of caloric. The theory had developed a paradigm-like resiliency with regard to explicit challenges (like Count Rumford's cannon-boring demonstrations[29]), whereas the steam engine posed no apparent difficulties at all. In fact, there was a very simple reason for this: existing steam engines were extremely inefficient, converting only one or two percent of the heat supplied (through coal, for example) into mechanical work. As such, it was easy to believe that the same amount of caloric came out as went in.[30] Had the caloric/kinetic alternative in fact been posed to the steam engine, a decision would have been underdetermined by available evidence.

While improvements in materials and design had been made by mid-century, they were not so great that the steam engine could directly enable a decision between the two theories. Unlike the magnetometer in the geological revolution considered earlier, the steam engine's role in the theoretical confirmation of thermodynamics was in fact never so immediately focal. Nevertheless, it maintained a diffuse but dominant presence in the deliberations and experiments leading to the new science's ratification, such that its significance can truly be claimed as central to the theoretical decisions coded as the first and second laws of thermodynamics. These laws were formulated very much in the steam engine's shadow; the industrial ma-

---

29 See Sanborn C. Brown, "Count Rumford and the Caloric Theory of Heat"; also Masao Watanabe, "Count Rumford's First Exposition of the Dynamic Aspect of Heat."

30 See, for example, Lynwood Bryant, "The Role of Thermodynamics in the Evolution of Heat Engines," 154.

chine was therefore quite as decisive in theory-change as the aforementioned magnetometer, though in a much more *mediate* manner. Its role was mediate first in the sense that the steam engine *qua* scientific instrument was embedded in a larger context of (literally) experimental instruments: thermometers, barometers, magnets, dynamos, and batteries, among others, the precision and indeed significance of which were not always clear to researchers. Often these other technologies were more directly responsible for providing the results that would lead to the acceptance of thermodynamics. But mediation defined the steam engine's instrumentality in a second, more crucial sense—that of a high degree of abstraction with which the apparatus was approached by scientists—and in its idealized form, as I shall argue presently, the steam engine articulated the very framework within which the conservation of energy and the law of entropy could emerge as theoretical options.

The steam engine's route from the motive force of industry to a scientific decision-machine was long and contorted. I offer here only a highly abbreviated version of this history, starting with the publication, in 1824, of the French military engineer Sadi Carnot's *Réflexions sur la puissance motrice du feu*.[31] Motivated by the practical goal of producing more efficient steam engines (and with a view to the political and economic implications for an industrially disadvantaged post-revolutionary France), Carnot set to work on a very theoretical problem: he aimed to rectify the lack of a mechanical analysis of the steam engine and thus to set it on an equal scientific footing with water-, air-, or animal-driven engines, the principles of which had been studied in detail.[32] The most important contribution of Carnot's *Réflexions* was the abstraction of an idealized heat engine (frictionless, cyclical, with no conduction between parts of different temperatures, and therefore thermodynamically reversible) that defined efficiency in relation solely to the difference in temperature between two reservoirs (a furnace or boiler and a condenser or cold sink), regardless of the medium or "working substance" employed (e.g. steam, alcohol vapor, or air). Given these two reservoirs, Carnot's ideal machine represents the maximally efficient use of heat in the production of work (realized, for example, in the movement of a piston) that can possibly be achieved. Assuming a cycle that consists of adding heat (H) to a substance, doing work (W) through expansion, dumping heat (h) to a cold sink, and returning the medium to its initial state, Carnot reasoned that any such cycle could (theoretically) be improved upon except for a perfectly reversible one—i.e. one in which the same amount of heat would be transferred back from the cold sink to the furnace by doing the same

---

31 A translation, by Robert Fox, is available under the title *Reflexions on the Motive Power of Fire*.

32 See D.S.L. Cardwell, "Power Technologies and the Advance of Science, 1700-1825," 189.

amount of work upon the machine as the machine had done on its environment (thus turning the heat engine into a heat pump or refrigerator). For, holding the temperatures of the reservoirs constant, if an enhanced engine could produce more work (W*, where W* > W) given the same addition of heat (H) at the furnace, then the surplus work (W* − W) could be expended usefully, leaving the original amount of work (W) produced by the unenhanced machine; that amount, in turn, could be applied in reverse to fully restore the heat (H) to the furnace. And since less work would be required than could be obtained, the machine could operate perpetually without need for renewed heat input! Alternatively, if we imagine an engine that could produce the original amount of work (W) by means of a smaller addition of heat (H*, where H* < H), then a reversal of the process could yield the higher amount (H) through the application of the same work (W). Repeating the cycle, heat could therefore be transferred continuously from a cooler body (the cold sink) to a hotter one (the furnace) with a net work expenditure of zero. Assuming that perpetual motion machines and zero-cost refrigerators are impossible, Carnot established reversibility as the ideal limit of efficiency.

If Watt's steam engine drove the industrial revolution, Carnot's idealization of it was the motive force of the scientific revolution that culminated in the laws of thermodynamics. All of the basic problems or anomalies addressed by thermodynamics—and quite possibly the solutions as well—may be seen as implicit in Carnot's treatment. Assuming the truth of caloric theory, Carnot viewed heat as a fluid that cascades like water over a waterwheel or moves through a hydraulic pump, yielding work as it flows without itself being expended in the process.[33] On this assumption rests the very ideal of reversibility, Carnot's model of which makes conceivable a combination heat engine/heat pump system that redistributes, without diminution, a fixed amount of heat; this conception only makes sense if the (as yet unformulated) first law is false, i.e. on the condition that heat is not *converted* into mechanical work and thereby *lost* as heat. Yet Carnot's denial of perpetual motion, as a part of his argument that there can be no better engine than a reversible one, is predicated on what will later be codified as the second law, which in one formulation says that it is impossible, "without any expenditure of force or any other change, to transfer as much heat as we please from a *cold* to a *hot* body"—for heat "always shows a tendency to equalize temperature differences and therefore to pass from *hotter* to *colder* bodies" (Clausius, "On the Motive Power of Heat" 90[34]). Still

---

33 Cardwell argues that a variety of machines must have inspired Carnot's thinking, with hydraulic water engines exerting a greater influence than waterwheels (see, especially, 200-205).

34 Compare also the original English translation, "On the Moving Force of Heat, and the Laws regarding the Nature of Heat itself which are deducible therefrom" (103).

later, this principle will receive an alternate formulation, according to which the entropy of a closed system cannot decrease (remaining constant only in a perfectly reversible system) and, in fact, tends toward a maximum (so that perfect reversibility is revealed as a purely fictional limit).[35] If, therefore, the ideal of perfect reversibility is a fiction, then so is the conservation of heat.[36] Carnot's machine generates the first two laws of thermodynamics, but in fact it was slow to do this work, and actual theory development was much less deductive than this discussion might suggest.

Without going into too much detail, then, we must consider the historical course of engagement with Carnot's work, which was initially ignored but taken up a decade later by Émile Clapeyron.[37] In his *Mémoire sur la puissance de la chaleur*, Clapeyron expands on Carnot's principles, providing graphical depictions and mathematical extrapolations of his ideal cycle in terms of heat/work relations. Most importantly, perhaps, Clapeyron derives an approximate value for what would become known as the "mechanical equivalent of heat"—a coefficient of central importance to the first law's full quantitative articulation, the experimental confirmation of which was crucial for that law's acceptance. Significantly, though, Clapeyron's results were derived without abandoning the substantial theory of caloric and the principle of heat conservation; again, the inefficiency of real steam engines and the uncertain precision of instrumentation helped preserve caloric theory from the danger of empirical disconfirmation. But even as, in the 1840s, the conservation of energy began to articulate a clear threat to the conservation of heat, theory-underdetermination remained a real problem. In 1842, the German physician Julius Robert von Mayer also found a value for the heat/work conversion coefficient, and he recognized the implication that heat is not indestructible, stating that "the steam-engine serves to *decompose* heat [...] into motion or the raising of weights" (76, emphasis added); nevertheless, Mayer did not see himself forced to adopt the kinetic theory and say that heat just *is* (molecular) motion. But without this component, energy conservation, notions of which had been around since the time of Newton, could not become the principle (or law) of thermodynamics *as we*

---

35 In Clausius's "Ueber verschiedene für die Anwendung bequeme Formen der Hauptgleichungen der mechanischen Waermetheorie."
36 Indeed, Carnot himself became doubtful of caloric theory, and in manuscript notes written after the publication of his book he elucidates the principle of energy conservation and even derives a value for the heat/work conversion coefficient. It is therefore occasionally conjectured that, had Carnot not died early, he might have put forward both laws and established thermodynamics decades earlier than was the case. See Robert Fox's introduction to the English translation of the *Refléxions*, 31-32.
37 See Stephen Brush, 16.

know it—not, that is, part of an integrated system that, by displacing a prior system, was once revolutionary *per se*.[38]

James Prescott Joule, who in the following years presented his own results on the mechanical equivalent of heat, based on a variety of experimental methods, was more inclined to draw the connection with the kinetic theory as *the* alternative to caloric. Strictly speaking, though, the experimental demonstration that energy may be converted from one form to another did not establish the primacy of any particular form, as is required for the kinetic theory (Brush 21). Lacking conclusive empirical evidence for the existence of atoms, writers such as Joule (in his "On Matter, Living Force, and Heat" from 1847) and the physician Hermann von Helmholtz (in "The Conservation of Force," also from 1847) resorted to general (*a priori*) philosophical principles concerning the definition of matter and the necessity of causation to buttress their views. Both of these writers took specific aim at Carnot, as mediated through Clapeyron, whose theories they saw not as precursors of the new science but as the purest embodiments of the old. Part of the reason for this focus, however, must have been the sheer convenience of Carnot's ideal engine rather than any particular allegiance on his part, much less representative status, with regard to caloric theory; for Joule, whose own experiments dealt with magnets and water canisters (among other things) rather than steam engines, Carnot's abstract model provided an easy means of illustrating a departure from the earlier view of heat, not a means of proving kineticism.[39] Joule's and Helmholtz's remained minority voices at first; and the acceptance of the kinetic theory, as being of a piece with an incipient thermodynamics, would have to wait until the company of others (such as Krönig and Clausius) shifted scientists' "payoff matrices" (in Giere's term) in its favor. Though not without considerable opposition (for example, from Ernst Mach), the path was being paved, first with rhetoric and later peer pressure rather than empirical results, for the shift from so-called phenomenological to statistical thermodynamics and the integration of atomic theory.

In the meantime, Joule's attacks on Carnot and Clapeyron had caught the attention of William Thomson (later Lord Kelvin), in whose writings a tone of crisis and

---

38 Thus, Stephen Brush lists nine others, besides Mayer and Joule, who have been credited with statements of the conservation of energy. He notes: "Some of these statements give one the impression that the author does not believe himself to be proposing a new physical principle, but is merely making explicit the current scientific view that perpetual motion is impossible, and force cannot be created or destroyed unless some kind of conversion takes place. The list could probably be increased indefinitely by adding the names of writers who made this type of statement" (Brush 20).

39 See, for example, Joule's "On the Changes of Temperature produced by the Rarefaction and Condensation of Air," especially 382-83.

a view of the new science as truly revolutionary became most pronounced. Initially, Thomson held to the non-convertibility of caloric and presumed against Joule, noting (in a footnote) the latter's "remarkable discoveries" and confessing the "mystery" still surrounding "these fundamental questions of natural philosophy" ("On an Absolute Thermometric Scale" 102); but instead of pursuing these questions, Thomson ingeniously put Carnot's engine to work in deriving an absolute temperature scale. Carnot's model (mediated again by Clapeyron) had the advantage of being medium-independent, so the mechanical work occasioned by the transfer of heat from a warmer reservoir to a compressor only one degree cooler would serve as a basis upon which to calibrate thermometers employing various fluids—thus solving a very practical problem of scientific instrumentation, upon which hinged the reproducibility of experimental results. Interestingly, this work was done without reading Carnot directly, whose text was then (in 1848) unavailable. So when Thomson procured a copy, he took it upon himself (in 1849) to provide to the English-speaking community an "Account of Carnot's Theory of the Motive Power of Heat." Still relying on caloric theory, Thomson's confidence had nevertheless been rocked, and the crisis tone in his writing reached a fever pitch; now science was seen to be faced with a disjunctive choice between two absolute alternatives: *either* Joule *or* Carnot. Asking, again in a footnote, "the very perplexing question" of what happens to the potential work that is lost through the outward conduction of heat in a less than ideally insulated system (as in any real steam engine), Thomson finds science unable to answer but confesses that Joule may have found "the foundation of a solution." But, he continues, to follow Joule and dispense with "Carnot's fundamental axiom" (i.e. the indestructibility of caloric) would create "innumerable other difficulties—insuperable without farther experimental investigations, and *an entire reconstruction of the theory of heat from its foundation*" ("Account" 118-119, emphasis added). Thus did Carnot's engine serve to articulate the choices defining a revolution.

Soon Thomson himself would defect and begin collaborating with Joule. And Rudolf Clausius would show that the contradiction between Carnot and Joule was real, but that a synthesis was possible by retaining the former's ideal engine while abandoning caloric in favor of the latter's dynamical (and ultimately kinetic) theory of heat.[40] In the process of recalibrating the heat engine for energy conservation, Clausius would give explicit formulations of the first two laws and thus set the theory of heat on its new, thermodynamic foundation. Soon would come entropy, Maxwell's hungry demon, and the heat death of the universe.

As regards the molecular or atomic basis upon which this revolution proceeded, however, we have seen that decisive evidence was lacking, so that *a priori* princi-

---

40 See Clausius's "On the Motive Power of Heat."

ples filled the gap; skeptics, though increasingly in the minority, thus continued to question the necessity of positing unobservable entities whose motions produce heat. More radically, perhaps, we find a scientist, H.L. Callendar, writing as late as 1910 on "The Caloric Theory of Heat and Carnot's Principle," defending caloric as compatible with energy conservation:

> The only defect of the caloric theory lay in the tacit assumption, so easily rectified, that the ordinary calorimetric units were units of caloric. The quantity measured in an ordinary calorimetric experiment is the motive power or energy of the caloric, and not the caloric itself. If this had been realised in 1850, it would have been quite unnecessary to recast and revolutionise the theory of heat. (Callendar 188)[41]

According to Callendar, a modified conception of caloric, still conceived as a material substance, names precisely that which Clausius called entropy, with the advantage that the second law becomes less abstract and difficult to fathom (178-79). Indeed, from a purely logical point of view, why not a caloric theory of motion instead of a kinetic theory of heat? Why prioritize any particular form of energy as fundamental to all others? The natural, which is to say naturalistic, answer is that, in connection with the social negotiation of "payoff matrices," scientists overwhelmingly agreed on what would count as evidence and embodied their agreement in technological instruments, first and foremost the steam engine. The Duhem-Quine problem, the problem of holistic relativism, was itself answered holistically—i.e. pragmatically, *technologically*—rather than foundationally.

Yet, as Thomas Kuhn points out in a pre-*Structure of Scientific Revolutions* article, the pioneers of thermodynamics overwhelmingly drew their evidence for the destructibility of heat directly from experiments conducted by caloric theorists, reinterpreting the same results that had once provided strong reason to posit caloric now as the grounds for rejecting it. Though later findings would vindicate this choice, it is far from clear how it initially came to be made, for it depended not on new data or even new instruments but on a reinterpretation of instrumental "reliability": *that* the experimental infrastructure was reliable was assumed by caloricists and kineticists alike, but the *meaning* of that reliability underwent a change. As Kuhn explains:

> In this area of research, [...] theoretical and experimental techniques developed together into a region where neither was entirely secure. [....] No caloricist was ever forced to maintain his theory in the face of clear-cut experimental counter-evidence. On the contrary, the caloricists

---

41 The quote is from the abstract appended at the end of Callendar's paper, though near verbatim statements can be found in the paper itself.

occasionally produced experimental evidence for relationships that we are quite unable to confirm today. An examination of Laplace's first theoretical value for the speed of sound or of the consistent results gained by those who first investigated the variation of heat capacity with pressure may well tempt the puzzled historian to proclaim with Oscar Wilde that, where theory and experiment are both insecure, "nature imitates art." ("The Caloric Theory of Adiabatic Compression" 140)

In the light of Kuhn's classic book, which appeared shortly after this statement, and especially in light of the book's later reception, we may read Kuhn's remarks as indicating either the role of social pressures on scientific theory or the idealistic disjunction of "worlds" corresponding to paradigms. However, I would like to take the phrase "nature imitates art" more literally, reading "art" in the specific and older sense of technology, as Kuhn surely intended.[42] What this interpretation points to, then, is the multistability of human-technological transactions involved in the thermodynamic revolution, which must therefore be submitted to a techno-phenomenological analysis. As we shall see, phenomenal multistability is analogous in some ways to the undecidability of theories that results from empirical underdetermination, but the former must be regarded as more fundamental and materially concrete than the latter. We arrive at the second stage of the postnatural derivation.

2) The Machine in the Industrial Lifeworld: Techno-Phenomenological Variations

To understand the variable relations between scientists and their instruments, we must rewind to the industrial revolution again and locate the steam engine in a broader range of phenomenal relations to variously situated subjectivities. We may start with the industrialist, for whom the steam engine represents an unprecedentedly efficient means with which to realize his desire for profit. In Ihde's terms, his is an *embodiment relation* to the machine—a highly abstract one, to be sure, quite unlike the hands-on incorporation of a hammer, a cane, or a telescope. Nonetheless, there is a sense in which the steam engine forms a lens through which the industrialist views the world, in which the machine gathers together and structures for him a range of phenomenally objective entities and processes (related, for example, to logistical flows of resources, information, labor, products, and money), and in

---

42 Andrew Pickering suggests that Kuhn progressively moves from a view of incommensurability that "embrace[s] experimental techniques as well as worldviews and gestalts" to the narrower, more problematic view that has "made the linguistic and conceptual aspects of incommensurability central" (*Mangle*, footnote 190).

which it reflects back on and defines the perceptual, decisional, and actional parameters of the industrialist's subjectivity. Because, in these regards, the machine is not detachable from, but instead integrally conjoined to, the industrialist's subjectivity and definitory of (to borrow a Wittgensteinian term) a particular "form of life," we are concerned here with properly phenomenological, and not merely psychological, relations.

At another extreme, the displaced artisan or cottage worker with a tendency towards Luddism relates to the steam engine in a radically different manner. Perceived as a threatening other—a competitor in the job market or a steely, smoking replacement for organic muscle and sweat—the machine occupies what Ihde calls an *alterity relation*.[43] If the steam engine ideally approximates transparency in the embodiment relation enacted by the industrialist, here it assumes near total opacity as the telic object of intentional concern. This objecthood of the machine, its appearance as noetic *telos* or end, stems from its functioning as an obstacle rather than a means: the machine is seen to *block* rather than facilitate the achievement of goals (livelihood, social harmony, unmediated contact, the satisfaction of skillfully producing wares from start to finish). Again, this is not merely a psychological attitude or a social-semiotic determination of the technology, though it is (or becomes) those things as well; it is, moreover, a material relation between embodied humans and their physical environment, expressed most directly not in political slogans but in forms of bodily comportment and interaction—of which machine-breaking is perhaps only the most obvious one. Interestingly, the paradigm case in which a technology becomes objectively opaque (a precondition for phenomenal alterity) is precisely the case in which it is *broken*[44]; the broken hammer (or the malfunction-

---

43 See Ihde, *Technology and the Lifeworld*, 97-108. One might think of alterity relations as approximating those relations that normally (or perhaps ideally) structure humans' interpersonal relations, as the basis for dialogue between equals rather than instrumentalization. The Luddite's relation to the steam engine would thus instantiate a particularly negative counterpart to Buber's Ich-Du relations or the alterity that Lévinas takes as the basis for his ethics of the Other. See Martin Buber, *Ich und Du*, and Emmanuel Lévinas, *Totality and Infinity*.

44 The example that follows, taken from Heidegger's analysis of the hammer, makes apparent that objective opacity is not *equivalent* to phenomenal alterity: the broken hammer becomes a terminus of intentional concern, but it is not thereby invested with agency. Machine-breaking is thus a means of disrupting "normal" relations to the steam engine, making the machine obtrude as an object from out of the otherwise semi-transparent network of material, socioeconomic, and ideological realities that it in part organizes. But the Luddite's relation to the machine as to a menacing agency precedes the actual event of destruction, providing its justification. Machine-breaking is thus the practical culmina-

ing machine) is no longer, in Heidegger's terminology, "ready-to-hand" in our embodied engagement with the world, no longer absorbed in goal-directed concerns, but becomes conspicuously "present-at-hand" as unusable *Zeug* (a term which combines both "equipment" and mere "stuff").[45] Significantly, the Luddite actively strives to realize this situation, and the felt necessity of intervention indicates that the steam engine is not perceived as a passive receptacle of intention or meaning but as a material assemblage with a menacing agency of its own, one that must be counteracted (broken) to preserve human autonomy.

Between the extremes of the industrial capitalist and the Luddite activist lies a range of phenomenal possibilities, not all of which are precisely determinate. The interactive relation of a factory worker, e.g. a power-loom operator, to the steam engine is more practical ("hands on") than that of the factory boss but less adversarial than that of the machine-breaker; within these bounds, multiple and shifting relations occur. On the one hand, the steam engine can be an unrelenting dictator, determining for the worker the pace of action and the rhythm of life itself, without regard for organic limitations. When its demands exceed the worker's capacities, alterity again defines the machine. The power-loom operator, who is less a weaver than a helping hand for the machine, interacts with the steam engine mediately, through the loom(s) he or she oversees; as an attendant, the operator's primary tasks include monitoring the automated weaving process, replacing emptied bobbins of yarn, and repairing broken threads. Breakage is thus central to the worker's activity, yet it is absorbed into normal functioning, i.e. it defines the normal course of operation as laid out in the loom operator's job description. Because it is expected, this sort of breakage does not of necessity lead to an alterity relation, and the latter can arise with or without the machine's actually being broken; breakage itself is therefore subject to a contextual redefinition. But an unexpected series of otherwise expected "breakages" (for example, weft yarn is lacking and warp yarns snap simultaneously or in rapid succession on multiple looms under one's supervision) constitutes a real malfunction, which it is beyond the worker's abilities to manage and which causes the machinery to obtrude as object: as a machinic other that makes impossible demands on the human body. Yet such a pileup of mishaps is not necessary for otherness; the worker's own fatigue may suffice. In that case the

---

tion of the Luddite's prior investment of agency in the steam engine, which shows that physical breakage is not *necessary* for alterity. But neither does breakage *entail* alterity, as the case of the broken hammer demonstrates. At most, machine-breaking can *expedite* others' perception of the machine as a non-innocent agency by revealing, as object, its role in a network that treats humans as resources or dehumanized "things."

45 Heidegger's tool analysis is found in *Being and Time*, Division One, Chapter III: "The Worldhood of the World."

apparatus may keep humming along, while the operator falls out of step with its tune. Here the appearance of breakage is shifted to the organic body, which is revealed as inadequate as a source of labor (unable to match the machine's production of mechanical work), insufficient as fuel (expended faster than the coal in the furnace or the yarn on the bobbins), or deficient as an extension of the machine (analogous to an ill-designed or inefficient motor-driven power tool).

That an alterity relation may result from or imply not the machine's but *the body's own "breakage"* (which, given the health hazards and the risk of injury in the industrial factory, could become a very literal reality) points to significant reversals that more generally structure the worker's relations to the steam engine. When the power-loom operator successfully copes with his or her tasks, in contrast to the overwhelming experiences just described, the loom itself may be incorporated in an embodiment relation, and the steam engine driving it may recede into the background; a sort of "dance" ensues—a finely choreographed performance in which human worker and technological apparatus seem mutually to respond to one another's gestures. The flow of the dance depends on a whole troupe of performers, each playing his or her part: the stoker tends the furnace, a man oils the looms, a child sweeps the floors, a woman prepares the bobbins. All participants must execute their parts in time. Like the members of a symphony orchestra, each must incorporate his or her instrument as an extension of self, so that specialization and coordination can give rise to a tune that is more than the sum of its parts—the factory as philharmonic. However, when looked at from a reverse angle, we see that smooth operation is less a function of human mastery, of technology's incorporation by the workers, than of the workers' *being-incorporated* by the factory (giving literal meaning to their "employment"). From this angle, the steam engine acts as the symphony's automated conductor, the workers arrayed around it like the orchestra with its various sections; the dance or tune performed follows *the engine's* rhythms, in relation to which even the floor supervisor or factory boss are at best first violins. At the level of the well-functioning factory, there is an *inverse embodiment relation* between the factory "hands" and the steam engine.

It is this level which defines the engineer's relations to the machine, for the primary desideratum of his interactions is the improvement of efficiency, as measured against the gold standard of the highly productive factory. Again, we can discern multilayered and reversible relations at work. As the machine's maker, it would seem that the engineer, if anyone, should be in control of the machine: if the factory forms a sort of inhuman body, it is the task of the engineer to provide it with a mechanical heart—the steam engine. It is the engineer's responsibility to keep this organ beating, and he can be said to determine its pace. On his shoulders devolves not just an obvious economic responsibility but the very weight of human control and mastery, shifted from the pre-industrial tool-user to the industrial engineer as fabricator of autonomous tools. The engineer's acts of design and construction stand, then, as a bulwark against humanity's incorporation by the machine. However, his mastery is never complete. Rather than a unilateral assertion of human power and ingenuity, we find in fact a complex *negotiation* of agencies taking place in the engineer's tasks of analysis, design, production, and maintenance.

First, we note the dialectical nature of the engineer's efficiency-based project; the positive goal of progress (i.e. building better engines) is predicated centrally on a recognition of lack or deficiency: an existing state of inefficiency must be eliminated. Occasionally this is a straightforward matter, as when the engineer is called upon to repair a broken machine and restore order to the factory. But, at some level at least, even the functioning steam engine is by definition broken in the engineer's eyes; it is not as efficient as it could be. To overcome this problem, and as a preliminary step towards constructing a better engine, the engineer may analyze existing machines, physically or conceptually dissecting them or studying them in action in order to understand the principles of their functioning and the reasons for their failure. A *hermeneutic relation* is then instantiated; the machine's author becomes its devoted reader, interpreting the material "text" to discover the hidden physical processes inscribed in its mechanism. With this knowledge in hand, the engineer starts to tinker with the machine—making adjustments, testing, replacing old parts with newly constructed ones, and re-testing. Clearly, interpretation does not end where revision (or "tinkering") begins. But, as the engineer begins manufacturing new parts, his hermeneutic relation to the steam engine is interspersed with instances of embodiment relations. He *utilizes* a steam engine and the power tools it runs—as extensions of himself, his plans and designs, but also of his sensorimotor capacities—in order to machine new parts, new power tools, and ultimately new engines. But rather than subordinating the machine to his will, the engineer enters into a process of negotiation with the engine, going back and forth between a subjective incorporation and an objective manner of regarding it.

Indeed, this to and fro in the process of tinkering—a process encompassing acts of analysis, testing, modification, and production—points to a more fundamental alterity relation that underlies and enables the alternation between hermeneutic and embodiment relations. For the tinkerer, the machine's otherness is clearly not that which is apprehended by the Luddite, whose aggressive acts of machine-breaking respond to a vision of the machine as an independently aggressive perpetrator of spirit- and body-breaking acts. The engineer's mission, on the contrary, is to repair, to restore, and to overcome a pre-existing state of breakage *qua* inefficiency. With regard to the engineer, machinic alterity is also different from the steam engine's otherness relative to the factory worker, though both may be seen as engaged in a race against the fatiguing demands the machine places on body and brain. Tinkering is indeed a competition, a contest of wills between human ingenuity and the cunning of the machine, which always conceals the key to its optimization; but for the contest to be won, for it to take place at all, the engineer must strive to establish a level playing field, must negotiate some ground rules, and must therefore *cooperate* with his machinic other. Cooperative alterity is instantiated in a dialogical relation; the engineer poses a question, not merely to himself, but to the engine: How can I get you to do what I want (i.e. be more efficient)? The adjustments and alterations made in the process of tinkering are modes of addressing the other, attempts at eliciting a response and at *coaxing* the machine into cooperating. Only if the machine responds to the engineer's embodied queries can new knowledge arise through analytical testing, and this know-how (both cognitive and somatic in nature) forms the basis for the engineer's instrumentalization of the machine (as in the production of new parts).

Cooperative alterity is again dance-like, involving a *mutual tuning* of the engineer's intentions to the machine and of the machine to human intentions.[46] The engineer's goal of increased efficiency is constantly revised; if an ideal of total productivity abstractly informs his undertakings, in practice he must lower his sights to a relative and shifting notion of what is realistically feasible for the machine vis-à-vis its present state of development. On the other hand, the machine must constantly improve to meet the engineer's goals, and each improvement sets new parameters for the next. In the bilateral process of tinkering, breakage *qua* inefficiency is *distributed amongst the machine and the engineer*; not only is the presently existing machine judged inadequate in its material construction, but human thought is also shown as deficient or compromised in its ability to think the ideal. These are the conditions which make tuning, as a bidirectional process, necessary. The aim of the cooperative enterprise is then a mutual optimization, the reciprocal unfolding of human and technological potentials, neither of which is knowable in advance but rather emergent in the course of interactive practice. The horizons of the engineer's intentionality are constrained by the machine's materiality, by its formal properties and its sheer physicality, and these are not transparently malleable to thought or ideal designs (as the persistent failure of perpetual motion machines sufficiently demonstrates). Moreover, these constraints actively shift the horizons of thought (redefining what is thinkable or realistic at a given moment), and they reshape the contours of subjectivity itself: not only the engineer's conscious self-conceptions or the social definitions of his profession as an engineer are revised, but also the possible material relations he may engage in practically with respect to the machine and the world beyond.

---

46 Both the notion of the dance ("the dance of agency") and "tuning" are central to Andrew Pickering's approach to the role of machinery in experimental science, as put forward in his *Mangle of Practice*. I return to Pickering's analytical model later in this chapter.

The engineer Carnot's abstraction of an ideal heat engine may be read as a response to the to and fro of engineer-engine alterity, as an attempt, that is, to establish absolute parameters for the interaction of human and machinic agencies. Carnot, who can be said to have taken "tinkering" to its hermeneutic extreme, approaches the steam engine and reads off the ideal limit of its efficiency, defining in this stroke the limits of what is both mechanically and humanly feasible: Carnot's model does not so much arrest the practical process of "tuning," which continues to take place in the engineer's workshop, as it extracts from it an invariant structure that owes its legitimacy to the heretofore undefined constraints of both rational thought and physical nature. Carnot's thought experiment, in other words, is responsive to material constraints, codified as the impossibility of a perpetual motion machine, and these in turn determine the rational limit of the engineer's intentional goals, concretely defining for the first time the unknown quantity of total productivity. In this way, Carnot provides a means of measuring practical success on an absolute scale and inaugurates a specifically scientific relation to the steam engine.

As we have seen, Carnot's model machine stands at the center of thermodynamic science, and since this ideal engine derives from the engineer's practical interactions with real machines, we must ask in how far scientific practice repeats or alters the relational patterns established by engineering practice.[47] Again, the question is how the steam engine came to function as a decision-enabler for physical science, or how it was able to pivot a scientific revolution, and this question is inseparable from the phenomenal relations obtaining between scientists and the industrial machine. We may note, as a first approach, that Carnot's model licenses unprecedented claims of objectivity, transforming the steam engine for the first time into a respectable object or instrument of scientific inquiry; for, unlike real engines, Carnot's ideal is not in need of modification, so that further tinkering is unnecessary. Thus stabilized, the steam engine is made available to scientists, who can now take it up as a component of serious inquiry. But what type of relation then obtains?

---

47 On a broad, structural level, one may identify a certain isomorphism between the process of tinkering and that of scientific experimentation. For the scientist alternately embodies instruments, consults them in a hermeneutic manner, makes variations, tests effects, and mathematizes the results. As in engineering practice, this involves, as Pickering demonstrates in *The Mangle of Practice*, a process of mutual tuning, an effort at making non-human reality communicate with human thought by means of reciprocal adjustment. However, this general isomorphism does not attest to any particular effect of engineering practice (or industrial-era mechanical engineering) on thermodynamic science. Rather, the similarities, in themselves significant enough, can be shown to hold for modern scientific practice in general, and they lay the groundwork for the current convergence of science and industry in "Big Science" or technoscience.

Does the engine of industry, as appropriated by the theoretical scientist, function as a means or an end, as an experimental instrument or as an observational object? In effect, I submit, both modes are present in the period leading up to the formulation of the two laws. On the one hand, the ideal engine remains semi-opaque as a gauge or indicator of relevant aspects of the physical universe beyond it, thus continuing the hermeneutic aspect of the engineer's engagement; schematically, the relation can be diagrammed thus:

$$\text{scientist} \rightarrow (\text{engine} - \text{world})$$

This type of relation can be seen in the derivation, going back to Clapeyron, of determinate values for the coefficient relating heat to mechanical work; these values are taken as descriptions of the objective world, but they are obtained by interpreting the machine as a *gauge* of independent processes. On the other hand, the ideal engine was also appropriated as a gaze-channeling, theory-focusing *lens* or knowledge-producing *tool*, thus mirroring the engineer's embodiment relations; schematically, the engine is incorporated in such cases into the left-hand side of the noetic arrow:

$$(\text{scientist} - \text{engine}) \rightarrow \text{world}$$

This mode is instantiated, for example, in Kelvin's instrumentalization of the Carnot machine to produce an absolute temperature scale. In contrast to Clapeyron's analytical approach, which attends to the machine in the manner of a thermometer—that is, by "reading" it as a passive indicator of independent events and relations—Kelvin's approach employs the machine in an active, productive effort to *create* a better thermometer, thus putting the engine to work in and *on* the outside world. But despite their differences, the relations exemplified in Clapeyron's and Kelvin's interactions with the machine have one important thing in common. In each case, whether a hermeneutic or an embodiment relation is realized by the scientist, these relations have been severed, through Carnot's abstraction, from the underlying alterity relation to which they responded in engineering practice. For whether or not actual steam engines play a role in their research, thermodynamic scientists ultimately relate to a pristinely mathematized machine, one unsullied by the physical realities of friction, convection, and the like. A machine, therefore, which has been freed from its bonds to the engineer's body and made amenable to an image of the scientist as occupying a disinterested, corporeally disengaged, and ideally rational perspective.

Here we approach the conditions for what was earlier discussed as the "reliability" of the steam engine, defined in terms of an unstated consensual agreement that allows a technology to generate clear-cut theoretical implications. What we find is that this reliability (upon which scientific objectivity rests) depends upon a bracketing of alterity, a closure of the open-ended negotiations between engineer and engine; but crucially, this closure also preserves—*in a particular manner*, as one might say of any such transformative *Aufhebung*—the former moments of hermeneutic and embodiment relations to the machine. Specifically, and in accordance with the abstractly defined heat engine to which scientists relate, these relations are to a certain extent dematerialized; more importantly, though, in terms of establishing the engine's role in revolutionary theory-choices is the fact that the engineer's *oscillations* between hermeneutic and embodiment relations are arrested and stabilized in scientific theory. The former movement between these modes, as distinct moments in the engineer's material dialogue with a machinic agency, gives way to a specific *alignment* or *coordination* of them, such that they are arrayed to form a sort of *self-referential system*: on the one hand, the steam engine is *incorporated* into physicists' subjective standpoints, as an abstract lens through which phenomena are perceived and cognized; but, on the other hand, this lens is directed at the world through *a second mediating instance*, viz. the engine as hermeneutic device. Synchronized with one another, a correspondence is established between observer-side incorporations of the technology and the machine's objective filtering of physical phenomena, creating a noetic situation which can be symbolized thus:

$$(\text{scientist} - \text{engine}) \rightarrow (\text{engine} - \text{world})$$

This correspondence, I contend, is the secret achievement of Clausius's reconciliation of Carnot and Joule, who, especially in William Thomson's writings, had been figured as incommensurable alternatives. On the one hand, Clausius shows that Joule's findings are compatible with a *hermeneutic* interpretation of the steam engine (as demonstrated already by Clapeyron's discovery of a heat/work coefficient on the sole basis of a mathematical analysis of Carnot's machine). On the other hand, the assumption of caloric as an indestructible substance is shown to be unnecessary to Carnot's theory, which is otherwise "conspicuously verified by experience" ("Motive Power" 68)—by which Clausius means, significantly, that the model engine's basic principles are confirmed in industrial practice. At stake here is the legitimacy of a science-oriented *embodiment* relation to the industrial machine; compare, for example, the opening sentence of Clausius's classic text, "On the Motive Power of Heat":

Since heat was first used as a motive power in the steam-engine, thereby suggesting from practice that a certain quantity of work may be treated as equivalent to the heat needed to produce it, it was natural to assume also in theory a definite relation between a quantity of heat and the work which in any possible way can be produced by it, and to use this relation in drawing conclusions about the nature and the laws of heat itself. (65)

Here, not only is the practical employment of the steam engine explicitly recognized as the historical basis of theory, but the machine's specifically scientific "use" is endorsed as legitimate and, in a word (Clausius's own): "natural." Thus naturalized, the steam engine is incorporated as a theoretical lens and absorbed into a closed hermeneutic system, the product of which is the integrated theoretical system of the first two laws, along with their molecular (kinetic) interpretation.

By aligning hermeneutic and embodiment relations to the industrial machine in such a way as to allow for their *simultaneous instantiation* by scientists, Clausius completes the steam engine's stabilization, neutralizes alterity-based oscillations, and makes the thermodynamic revolution, which had recently appeared so shocking to Thomson, seem quite inevitable. The role of the industrial machine in thermodynamic science can now retreat from view, for a *new correspondence* between scientific subjectivities and the objects of empirical science has been constituted by the distribution of industrial technology across the subject/object divide. What was above symbolized thus:

$$(\text{scientist} - \text{engine}) \rightarrow (\text{engine} - \text{world})$$

is subject to an equivalent schematization that will make the point plainer. By overlaying, one on top of the other, these two relations:

$$\text{scientist} \rightarrow (\text{engine} - \text{world})$$
$$(\text{scientist} - \text{engine}) \rightarrow \text{world}$$

and by dropping the outermost set of parentheses, we derive the following:

$$\text{scientist} \rightarrow (\text{engine}) \rightarrow \text{world}$$

This symbolization is meant to indicate not that two separate noetic acts are executed, but that the bracketed engine stands now, invisibly and integrally, at the heart of the scientist's intentional relation to the world. The engine and its role in scientific theory are subject to a "vanishing act,"[48] which conjures the appearance of a direct, unmediated relation:

$$\text{scientist} \rightarrow \text{world}$$

---

48 The phrase is taken from Pickering (*Mangle*, footnote 188).

It is the engine's disappearance which grounds thermodynamic science's claim to objectivity, understood in terms of theory's correspondence to the physical structure of the universe, the organizing laws of which are taken to be older than and independent of the industrial revolution. In fact, though, this objectivity is itself historically situated, for Carnot's engine has installed itself as a refractive prism at the very heart of scientists' intentional acts. The noetic arrow itself has been reconstituted, the very conditions of experience revised by the steam engine—which in theory as in practice supplants hydraulic machines and undermines classical mechanics, placing scientific thought and perception on a novel footing.

The physical scientist's relation to nature, we may claim, is now centrally, though invisibly, mediated by the steam engine. In fact, though, this description is only approximately correct, because the engine's distribution across the objective and subjective poles of intentionality problematizes the notion of mediation itself. That is, it would be inaccurate to conceive thermodynamic scientists as autonomous individuals looking at an independent nature *through* the engine as a mediating instance; rather, the engine is thoroughly imbricated into every aspect of the world in which such acts of looking take place. As the initial diagram of the scientist's relations—viz., (scientist – engine) → (engine – world)—makes clear, it is less a matter of the machine standing *between* subjects and objects as it is the case that the engine is absorbed into the basic constitution of both: henceforth, a scientist-engine faces an engine-world. Both the intentional agent and his or her (or its?) intended objects are now machinic in nature; nature itself has become machinic.

3) Beyond Nature

We are coming to the third and final stage of the postnatural derivation, to the postnatural stage proper. But because the implications of my findings thus far are not unambiguous, I shall have to go slow and specify precisely how (and how not) the step "beyond" naturalism is to be made. According to my analysis so far, it is due to the role of the steam engine as a hidden factor in the basic subject-object relations open to them that post-industrial scientists come to occupy, in Kuhn's phrase, a radically "different world" than pre-industrial researchers. However, at the risk of repeating myself, the point I wish to make is not that the world is merely a theoretical construct or that the laws of thermodynamics fail to correspond to the world "out there," but that, in accordance with the foregoing discussion, *the material conditions of objective correspondence are themselves subject to radical transformation.* As a component in physical science's theorization of the world, the revolution-hinging "reliability" of the steam engine involves the *correlation* of, on the one hand, an anthropotechnical revision of embodied subjectivity and, on the other, a techno-natural revision of the nonhuman environment. As I have been suggesting, these were not just conceptual but robustly material transformations, effected on the bodies and surroundings of laborers and Luddites, industrialists and engineers, as they interacted with the non-inert technologies of their industrial lifeworld; against that background, the specifically scientific achievement of correlating subject-side and object-side changes under the umbrella of a revolutionary scientific paradigm is thus inseparable from the embodied practices of production, design, tinkering, and tuning that precede and condition the emergence of thermodynamics.

In other words, what we find in the thermodynamic revolution is a case of theory *catching up* with experience, scientific theory-change *responding to* a much broader lifeworld-change. I emphasize this point because it marks a decisive reversal of the notion, still pervasive in much of post-Kuhnian philosophy of science, that world-change happens in a top-down manner, as the result of observation's determination through theory: our beliefs, expectations, and theoretical commitments color perception in such a way as to cause us to see the world differently, to perceive *different* objects than would otherwise be the case. There is, of course, plenty of psychological and social-psychological evidence for this sort of phenomenon, but the change of perspective I am trying to accomplish here requires putting aside such evidence and taking leave from the realm of psychological or cognitive explanation altogether. This also applies, by the way, to the Kuhnian explanation of incommensurability in terms of the semantic mismatches that ensue when, for example, a theoretical concept (such as caloric) drops out of scientific discourse, thereby altering not only a local taxonomic structure but shifting the web of significance *in toto*; accordingly, the terms "energy," "heat," and "work" would refer to something different—incommensurably different—before and after the formulation of thermodynamics' laws. My contention is not that this is untrue, but only that the causal efficacy of the conceptual should not be overestimated, and that—at least in terms of ontology—semantic-theoretical shifts should not be prioritized over material transformations such as those connected with the impact of the steam engine.

That the metaphysical horse of material reality should be put back before the epistemic cart of theoretical discourse is, naturally, a central tenet of naturalism. And indeed, it may not be immediately apparent exactly where, in the course of my analysis, naturalism gives way to postnaturalism. Take, for instance, the problem of thermodynamic theory's empirical underdetermination, the conditions of which have now been described from a techno-phenomenological perspective. As we saw earlier, in the first (naturalistic) phase of my argument, the thermodynamic revolution could not be effected by empirical data alone; underdetermination required that observation be supplemented by arguments from *a priori* principles and by the sheer exertion of social pressures. Moreover, decisive data leading to the ratification of the first two laws and their kinetic interpretation was supplied by researchers whose experimental results had once been subject to a radically different interpretation, quite at odds with the new science. I have suggested, in the second (phenomenological) phase of my argument, that this divergence is best analyzed in terms of the self-referential system of scientist-engine-world relations, wherein the engine comes to insinuate itself into both the subjective and objective poles of the basic noetic relation, reconfiguring the means and objects of perception alike. In accordance with a non-skeptical, naturalistic theory of science, this techno-phenomenological analysis of the deeper meaning of technological-instrumental "reliability" can be seen as a re-description of the holistic structure of epistemic justification that follows from an evolutionary perspective on human biology and cognition. That structure has been shown to revolve around the relational patterns of humans' practical engagements with the world, specifically as they are mediated by technologies; knowledge itself is a sort of survival technics that responds quite directly to material reality and enables, as a sort of by-product, the production of science's abstract systematizations of higher-order knowledge claims as they are arrayed between the subjects and objects constituted in the holistic field obtaining at a given moment of evolutionary history.[49] Accordingly, the objectivity of thermodynamics rests on its distillation, from out of the plurality of real or potential interactive practices characterizing the industrial lifeworld, of the abstract parameters that circumscribe the space of such practices. In the course of the thermodynamic revolution, the steam engine is lifted out of its polyvalent relations to industrialists, Luddites, factory workers, and engineers and turned into what, in another context, Ihde has called an "epistemology engine"—a material device that, as Ihde argues for the camera obscura in early modernity, comes to function also as a metaphorical model for knowledge, thereby inventing an episteme and producing new knowledge claims.[50] We can imagine this taking place by means of an implicit reduction (in a quasi-phenomenological sense) to something like an eidetic structure: to an apparently invariant "essence" common to all of the human-engine relations that the industrial lifeworld holds open. The stabilized steam engine with which thermodynamics operates may therefore be seen as the ideational embodiment of an invariant structure of industrial experience itself, of experience as situated in and mediated by industrial technology. The knowledge generated through the ideal machine is thus objective in the sense that it corresponds to the general conditions of such

---

49 The view of knowledge as a technology is supported also by John Dewey, in connection with his pragmatic notion of knowledge as praxical correspondence. See Larry Hickman's *John Dewey's Pragmatic Technology*.
50 See Chapter 5, "You Can't Have It Both Ways: Situated or Symmetrical," in *Bodies in Technology*.

experience. But then this objectivity is situational and historical, for it is tied inextricably to the multistable relations and embodied practices from which the ideal engine is abstracted.

Clearly, this relativistic analysis challenges the constancy and foundational position of "nature," but in a manner still familiar from the phenomenological tradition. Following from a general methodological focus on noetic *relations* as opposed to subjects and/or objects in isolation, the later Husserl's conception of the "objective-scientific world" as derivative of the pre-reflective lifeworld (as developed in *Crisis of European Sciences*) points in this direction, as does the early Heidegger's claim that "Nature is itself an entity which is encountered within the world and which can be discovered in various ways and at various stages" (*Being and Time* 92): either as "ready-to-hand" in the context of human concern and practice—whereby "[t]he wood is a forest of timber, the mountain a quarry of rock; the river is water-power, the wind is wind 'in the sails'" (100)—or as the merely "present-at-hand" that subsides independently of and without regard for humanity. For Heidegger, the latter mode is parasitic upon the former; the perception of nature as disinterested and disengaged is only a "limiting case" (94) of our own interested engagement with the world, the norm for which is supplied by the active use of tools and other technological equipment. Accordingly, the ahistorical "nature" described by natural science is discovered through an act of negation, constituted by assuming a perspective that "depriv[es] the world of its worldhood" (94)—which means not so much that science is inherently "artificial" or that it involves a "perversion" of nature through technological intervention but, quite to the contrary, that a specifically scientific viewpoint presupposes an *interruption* of what Heidegger describes as the "non-thematic circumspective absorption in references or assignments constitutive for the readiness-to-hand of a totality of equipment" (107). In other words, nature itself is a by-product of technology, and science, the study of nature, is made possible by the type of disconnect between human intentionality and the environment that ensues when an instrument breaks or goes missing. Empirically—or "ontically," in Heidegger's terminology—a technology may be destructive of nature; but ontologically, nature is seen to be the product of technology's privation.

Phenomenology, as we see here, tends to *uproot* naturalism in a way apposite with the last section's argumentation. But insofar as phenomenological investigation situates itself at a "deeper" level of analysis than that of science (as in Heidegger's ontological as opposed to ontic inquiry), and in fact more generally as a result of its methodological injunction against making metaphysical judgments (*epoché*), phenomenology cannot really be said to *undermine* naturalism; on the contrary, there is no *direct* engagement with the epistemic claims of science, no commitment as to the veracity of its theories. Because of this, phenomenology alone cannot *establish* postnaturalism, which, as I have defined it, involves commitments both to central claims of natural science (biological evolution) and to a strong metaphysical thesis (materialism). At best, phenomenology serves as a go-between or bridge from naturalism to postnaturalism, much as it does in the structure of my three-part derivation; in fact, though, I contend that phenomenology is a *necessary* bridge, so that postnaturalism—which involves not a rejection of naturalism but a materially deconstructive *departure from* it—will also necessarily be *post-phenomenological* in a specific sense. That is, postnaturalism uses phenomenology to unearth relational ambiguities that, within the context of empirical science, must remain invisible in the production of knowledge; in its interpretation of these ambiguities, however, postnaturalism steps outside the frame of phenomenology proper and fundamentally exceeds its resources.

Consider the present case, where I have employed phenomenology to reveal multistability as the hidden ground of thermodynamic science's stabilizing neutralization of the steam engine's technological alterity; my goal, of course, was to expose the historical situatedness of thermodynamics' knowledge claims as a function of the material-technical context in which they are embedded. Implicitly, the analysis suggests that the system of human-technology-world relations naturalized in thermodynamics' specific appropriation of the industrial engine replaces, to the point of effacing, an earlier, very different system embedded in a qualitatively different lifeworld—for which, presumably, a techno-phenomenological analysis could also be provided. Between the two analyses, phenomenology would thus point to the *occurrence* of a "world change," but a positive characterization of the transition, much less an explanation, is clearly beyond the scope of its resources.[51] The problem is not just that the *epoché* precludes phenomenology from identifying a causal mechanism, though this too is certainly a problem; moreover, with its (altogether reasonable) insistence on situatedness as a basic condition of all existence, phenomenology rules out any sort of mediation between radically differently situated epochs, indeed rules out any genuine mutual recognition of situational difference, except as that difference is filtered to appear within the horizon of one's own situation. Unless phenomenology can somehow transcend the conditions of its own existential involvements, it cannot therefore occupy a standpoint that would encompass both sides of the divide; limited to a single perspective at a time, it can do no more than point to an inexplicable gap in phenomenality itself—or, in the spirit of Donald Davidson, deny the very possibility of radical change.

And phenomenology has traditionally, if not explicitly, done just that: the later Husserl, for example, would seem to have recognized Galileo as a true revolution-

---

51 We have encountered this problem before, in Part One, in the context of the transitional era of 1910s cinema.

ary whose "surreptitious substitution of idealized nature for prescientifically intuited nature" (*Crisis* 49-50) was every bit as radical as any Kuhnian paradigm shift, but in fact it is only on the basis of Husserl's continued belief in the prescientific lifeworld as the constant and foundational realm of experience that he is able to countenance the change entailed by modern physics. It is this contrast between the transhistorical foothold of the primary lifeworld and the derivative world of science (found not only in Husserl but also in the existential phenomenology of Merleau-Ponty, for whom science is a "second-order expression" of a more "basic experience of the world" (ix)) that gives the phenomenologist the means to compare and to recognize historical difference. But to maintain such a transhistorical realm of experience is effectively to deny the possibility of global-scale change. This more radical sort of transformation, which does not respect the categories of primary and secondary experience, is so deeply problematic for phenomenology because it implies the replacement of one complete frame or horizon of phenomenal experience by another; and clearly, such a frame, which encompasses all possible relations between subjects and objects, all possible manners of appearing and experiencing within a given lifeworld situation, cannot itself appear as a phenomenal object. The world-change thesis therefore requires the assertion of a non-phenomenal "outside," a space radically alterior to any frame of situated human experience, where the suprahistorical progression of frames can take its course. Strictly speaking, then, the idea of such global ontological shifts must appear, from a phenomenological perspective, if not wholly nonsensical then at least inexplicable.

Significantly, a number of phenomenologists have themselves been led to transgress the bounds of phenomenology's traditional jurisdiction precisely when they have turned their attention to the historicity of science and technology. Most famously, in this regard, is the later Heidegger's anti-phenomenological conception of philosophy as the "history of Being" (*Seinsgeschichte*), which purports to trace the progression of fundamentally incommensurable epochs of Being, and according to which a mathematizing technologization of the world as "standing-stock" (*Bestand*) is the mode of Being's disclosure in the modern period.[52] Less well known, but perhaps more pertinent in the present context, is the Dutch phenomenological psychiatrist J.H. van den Berg's "metabletic" treatment of the thermodynamic revolution, metabletics being his term for "the study of radical changes in the course of history" (49). The interesting thing about van den Berg's study, *The Two Principal Laws of Thermodynamics*, apart from its thematic focus, is that unlike Heidegger's concentration on quasi-transcendent "names of Being," van den Berg attempts to locate mechanisms of change in the material world itself, claiming that

---

52 See, for example, Heidegger's *On Time and Being* and "The Question Concerning Technology."

a "profane transubstantiation" of material substances (e.g. metal, wood) precedes and enables the revolutionary shift in scientific theory (105-114). The industrial furnace, according to van den Berg, effects an explicitly "metaphysical" change in the "nature" of wood, which it takes as fuel for the steam engine: "A change that cannot be observed in the wood's chemical structure, yet one that has all-pervasive consequences" (78). The laws of thermodynamics are said to follow from and to remain dependent upon such transformations, which pertain to the total frame of human experience rather than some discrete, secondary realm only. Thus, the industrial machine not only upsets social structures, cultural formations, and scientific discourses, but also revolutionizes matter itself, which constitutes the alterior realm in which world-changes are possible. Thermodynamics, accordingly, does not provide a better representation of the physical universe than did earlier science; rather, the new physics pertains to a new *physis*, to a new matter created by and contingent upon industrial technology and concomitant developments. This, rather than social constructivism, is behind van den Berg's claim that a return to agrarianism would cause thermodynamics' laws to become "obsolete" (100). Not conceptual but *material incommensurability* distinguishes post-industrial from pre-industrial reality—for van den Berg, not just the universe of thought but the physical universe itself is subject to radical revision.

While this extreme relativism may seem unnecessarily extravagant, van den Berg's metabletics brings us a step closer to understanding the connection between postnaturalism and post-phenomenology. As van den Berg's translator Bernd Jager points out, the transformational events that concern metabletics are not those of "metaphor," which today as in the ancient Greek *metapherein* refers to reversible passages that connect two realms and preserve similitude; rather, metabletics pertains to changes of the type "metabolism," which shares with metabletics the root *metaballein* and refers to abrupt and radical changes which efface, digest, or absorb all traces of an earlier state (4-9). Metabolic changes do not occur on a human scale, are not commensurate with human perception or discourse, and are therefore not subject to social or cultural construction (or deconstruction, for that matter); in contrast to metaphorical changes, which leave intact a humanly accessible context within which such changes may be cognized and recognized, metabletic shifts are properly sub-conceptual, sub-phenomenal, and literally material. The method by which van den Berg seeks to discover such transformations is of particular interest here. He maintains that metabletics does not reject naturalistic descriptions but only asserts their limitations, which he seeks to uncover with phenomenology (van den Berg 68-69). Applied to the history of science, this allows for a series of phenomenal variations or Gestalt shifts on the theme of the human and nonhuman forces driving discovery. Compare van den Berg's concluding remarks:

every significant innovation can be approached from the side of the artist or scientist who proposed and elaborated it. An important discovery brings about a change in the outlook and understanding of the one who makes the discovery. It can also be approached from the side of the newly elaborated or discovered matter as announcing a change in the established order of the natural world. It is possible for us to imagine the process of natural scientific discovery as a progressive revelation of the nature of material relations. It is also possible to assume that the natural world, like the cultural world, undergoes periodic changes that are noticed and recorded by observant scientists. In this way we come to think of every important scientific discovery as confronting us with matter metamorphosed or transubstantiated in either a profane or a sacred sense. (114)

In effect, van den Berg uses phenomenology to point up the multistability of appearances, but he then goes on to posit transformations that are strictly incompatible with phenomenology: noumenal or "fundamental changes that take place within the very substance of things" (78), the assertion of which implies a non-phenomenal historicity of matter itself.

It remains, however, a great leap from the hypothetical *possibility* of "periodic changes" in matter to the notion that the physical universe does *in fact* undergo such revolutions, to which scientific revolutions in turn respond. Assuming that a *demonstration* of that thesis is impossible, that positive verification through empirical evidence cannot be produced for categorically non-phenomenal events, it should at least be possible to establish the plausibility of the hypothesis. This, indeed, is the weak point of van den Berg's argument, while its strong point is the delineation of something like a general method: the *confrontation* of naturalism and phenomenal multistability, as I have been arguing in this chapter, points to a mutual deconstruction and a path beyond. Naturalism places human experience squarely on the basis of nonhuman reality, while phenomenology notes the necessary recourse of naturalism to the phenomenal realm as it is governed by the structures of human thought and perception. Each perspective, prioritizing either the subjective/human or the objective/nonhuman, undercuts the other in an exchange of ground and figure—each alternative supplants and absorbs the other like the well-known vase/faces-in-profile Gestalts (also known as Rubin's vase, after Danish psychologist Edgar Rubin). The impasse, it would seem, is insoluble, but it can in fact be taken as the basis for a higher-level phenomenological reduction: What, such an investigation asks, do the two Gestalts have in common? What, in other words, unites them in their disparity and enables alternation between them? In the case of the vase/faces pair, it is a boundary that reversibly demarcates the inside and outside borders of the forms. Analogously in the case of naturalism and phenomenology, there is a reversible border between the subjective and objective, between the human and the nonhuman; this border is precisely technology as an extension of material embodiment, which is itself both something I am and something I have, both an instrument of the human will and an excessive alterity. Occupying an irreducible middle ground between a reversible inside and outside, bodies-with-technologies are the highly variable "invariants" at the intersection of the naturalism/phenomenology variation. And while I am using a phenomenological vocabulary to express this, it should be clear that phenomenology, when self-reflexively applied in this way, catapults itself beyond its own limits, for the liminal body-with-technology uncovered here no longer pertains to the situated experience of phenomenology but describes instead the sub-phenomenological space of situation itself—a noumenal substrate of phenomenality as such. I made a similar point earlier with greater emphasis on the methodological self-reflexivity of naturalism as a means of avoiding skeptical challenges: assuming the evolutionary exigency of knowledge as its own non-infallible justification, body-environment interactions are taken as simultaneously enabling and constraining knowledge. Recognition of this "ecological" constraint contextualizes knowledge, allowing the skeptic's decontexted charge of circularity to be acknowledged but then set aside as being of little consequence. As I argued, though, the circle problem resurfaces in the science-technology interface, in researchers' reliance on "reliable" technologies, wherein materially embodied constraints on knowledge are presupposed by and presuppose a bracketed knowledge of constraint—art imitates nature imitates art and so on, *ad infinitum*. In the manner of a feedback loop, naturalism therefore anticipates what I have here identified as the impasse between prioritizations of the human and the nonhuman, with the implication that the hybrid materiality of the anthropotechnical interface conditions all access to objective reality and, in a postnatural sense, *actually undergirds nature itself*.

Thus, from whichever direction we approach the impasse, that of phenomenology or of naturalism, we arrive through this confrontation of perspectives at a non-empirical stratum of materiality that, in the evolutionary conjunction of organic and inorganic variation, constitutes the postnatural space of anthropotechnical embodiment. This material realm must be pre-empirical, as it concerns the very means of our access to the world: embodiment and technology, conceived not as organic or technical objects but as the bidirectional pathways through which experience and agency must pass. It is here, I contend, that global shifts are made possible— holistic revolutions that reconfigure human subjects and nonhuman objects alike through the irruption of a more fundamental, non-dualistic matter with a history of its own. Clearly, though, such a strong metaphysical claim will meet with suspicion and, perhaps, evoke charges of mysticism. I have referred to van den Berg in staging my argument, largely because his materialism contrasts so well with Heidegger's lofty history of Being *qua* procession of master concepts. Yet, in the end van den Berg invokes a religious image, that of "transubstantiation," to describe the material revolution effected by industrial technology. And indeed, the advent of a new materiality, subject to new laws, must appear miraculous if apprehended from the side of naturalism. In this regard, van den Berg's concept alludes to what Hayles calls the "elusive negativity" of the material flux, which, as I discussed earlier, constitutes a privative description of an amorphous positivity from the angle of our inability to represent it conceptually. Such a mismatch, of course, also characterizes theological conceptions of God. But if this casts doubt on his argument, it is interesting to note that besides transubstantiation van den Berg has at his disposal another concept with which to describe material transformation, one drawn from natural science and free of transcendental connotations: *metabolism*.

Characterizing the breaks and shifts at the center of van den Berg's non-teleological history of metabletics, Bernd Jager invokes the "abrupt and complete change undergone by plants and animals as they are eaten and digested and as they are made to form part of the body of an alien organism" (5). As a "unidirectional change that leaves no memory of its passing" (5), metabolism "does not honor the thresholds that protect the identity of neighboring domains. Instead, it destroys all distance and difference between them as it turns the one into the other" (6). The industrial revolution, as a metabolic transformation, "eroded distinctions between animals and human beings and between living beings and inanimate things" (9), thus outstripping the discursive or "metaphorical" categories by which humans position themselves in the world. Seen thus, metabolism offers a much better description of the postnatural hybrid material intermixture of the human and nonhuman in the undifferentiated plenum of anthropotechnical interface. But whereas van den Berg's diagnosis of the industrial era's material revolution accords more or less with my own, he adds to it the therapeutic aim of reinstating metaphor and rescuing the human perspective's phenomenal integrity from monstrous disorientation. The significance of transubstantiation, in this context, lies in its recoding of chaotic material flux as a source of wonder and awe, by which van den Berg attempts to restore or renew the discursive thresholds that order the lifeworld and situate humans between the merely organic and the majestically divine—distinctions flattened by modern science and technology. In the end, his turn from metabolism to transubstantiation marks van den Berg's failure or refusal to follow through with the postnatural, post-phenomenological promise of his program. For him, the advent of the industrial factory becomes the occasion for a miracle, an *Ereignis* not unlike the appearance of the god in Heidegger's Greek temple, so that van den Berg's transgression of phenomenology, no less than Heidegger's with his quasi-theological "destiny" of Being, leads not to postnaturalism but to a dubious sort of super-naturalism.

If we guard duly against this tendency, metabletics can still remain instructive in its staging of the confrontation between naturalism and phenomenology, and the image of metabolism, with its undifferentiated indifference to metaphorization, offers an important cue to the impasse's possible *dis*solution into a non-dualistic space of flux and indetermination (as opposed, that is, to its "solution" in favor of a divinely sanctioned human nature). As a non-subjective material process, metabolism points to a space that is "infra-empirical" rather than transcendental, and which pertains, in Deleuze's terminology, to a "molecular" stratum of reality. What distinguishes metabolic processes in this sense from the "molar" perspectives of naturalism and phenomenology, with their opposed but equally asymmetrical weightings of one side or the other of an inseparable but nevertheless dualistic pair (subject/object, active mind/inert matter, human/nonhuman), is a material fullness and lack of qualitative differentiation between the "parts" involved, a non-directed symmetry in the absence of cardinal points or non-relative coordinates. Just as an animal devours dead or living organic matter and, through processes outside its control, integrates it into a body that grows, maintains itself, reproduces, and dies within shifting ecological parameters, so too does the anthropotechnical body mutate non-deterministically by absorbing into itself environmental materials of the most diverse sorts, synthesizing them into new structures and functional pathways that, viewed from above, constitute nodes in an evolving network of relations between apparatic innovations, cellular and organic changes, and other internal and external exigencies. As a metabolic process, anthropotechnical evolution is an a-centric and non-hierarchical process of transformation that is not only indifferent to consciousness but cannot be said to favor the organic or the natural either. It is spatially liminal and temporally transitional, always outside and in-between the molar "situations" of human experience and empirical nature.

To relate this image back to my discussion of the steam engine's role in thermodynamics, I turn to Andrew Pickering's notion of the "mangle," an exemplary postnaturalistic concept. Starting from a (basically naturalistic) view of life as a matter of "coping with material agency, agency that comes at us from outside the human realm and that cannot be reduced to anything within that realm," Pickering asks us to see science as an extension of this enterprise, and to view machines as central to its execution (*Mangle* 6-7).

Scientists, as human agents, maneuver in a field of material agency, constructing machines that, as I shall say, variously capture, seduce, download, recruit, enroll, or materialize that agency, taming and domesticating it, putting it at our service, often in the accomplishment of tasks that are simply beyond the capacities of naked human minds and bodies, individually or collectively. (7)

"The machine," in this performative view, "is the balance point, liminal between the human and the nonhuman worlds (and liminal, too, between the worlds of science, technology, and society)" (7). This picture obviously accords with my analysis of the steam engine's transition from industrial to scientific technology, as does the notion that the actual practice of science involves "a kind of delicate material positioning or tuning" (14), a matter of adjustment which *"works both ways*, on human as well as nonhuman agency" (16), both of which are conceived as *emergent*—not pre-given but mutually articulated in a *"dance of agency"* (21) that is centered in technologies as the material mediators of a dialogical encounter. Compare the following statement with what I have said about engineering practice as the basis for thermodynamics' specifically scientific relation to the steam engine:

The dance of agency, seen asymmetrically from the human end, thus takes the form of a *dialectic of resistance and accommodation*, where resistance denotes the failure to achieve an intended capture of agency in practice, and accommodation an active human strategy of response to resistance, which can include revisions to goals and intentions as well as to the material form of the machine in question and to the human frame of gestures and social relations that surround it. (22)

These are precisely the dynamics described in the last section's analysis of tinkering, which, as a phenomenological analysis, was of course asymmetrically human-oriented. Taking a broader view, however, Pickering's "mangle of practice" pushes beyond this human orientation and imagines a more symmetrical relation between human and nonhuman agency as "constitutively intertwined" (17). When—subsequent to bidirectional revisions of goals, intentions, and material responses through technologies—machinic "captures" of material agency at some point coalesce with theoretical models and explanations, then human and nonhuman agencies are *"interactively stabilized"* in machinic assemblages (17). This corresponds to my analysis of thermodynamics as involving a realignment of noetic relationality, consummating the marriage of hermeneutic and embodiment relations in the steam engine's "vanishing act" as it is dispersed across the subject-object divide to create a new scientist-nature correspondence.

Significantly, Pickering's mangle theory emerges as a response to a confrontation not unlike that between phenomenology and naturalism, an impasse between human/nonhuman prioritizations that arises in the field of science studies in the course of debates between representatives of the sociology of scientific knowledge (SSK) and actor-network theory (ANT).[53] Canonical SSK, as Pickering argues,

---

53 The specific context is the so-called "chicken debate" initiated by Harry Collins and Steven Yearley's essay, "Epistemological Chicken," to which Michel Callon and Bruno Latour reply in their "Don't Throw the Baby Out with the Bath School!" In what follows,

insists that there are only two possible approaches to the study of scientists' interactions with the material world: either to bracket out the truth claims of scientists' accounts, "which should be analyzed sociologically as the products of human agents"; or "to take material agency seriously, on its own terms," in which case "we yield up our analytic authority to the scientists themselves" and indulge, allegedly, in "a simple rehearsal of scientific/engineering accounts of how the world is, from which the human and the social simply disappear" (Pickering, *Mangle* 12). Opting for the former alternative, SSK is clearly analogical, in terms of asymmetrically favoring the human perspective, to phenomenology, while the latter alternative, which SSK identifies with ANT, has clear affinities to naturalism's prioritization of nonhuman matter. ANT, for its part, denies the identification, responding to what it sees as a false dilemma with a third alternative, one which insists on a basic symmetry of agencies that is unavailable to the perspective either of science or of its sociological study. As far as symmetry goes, Pickering praises ANT for helping to break "the spell of representation" and for indicating "a way to a thoroughgoing shift into the performative idiom" (13), sidestepping the impasses of opposed asymmetries, whether those of SSK/science or of phenomenology/naturalism. But, on the other hand, he faults ANT for establishing this symmetry by way of an appeal to semiotics, which "looks like a kind of retreat, a return to the world of texts and representations that one does not wish to make" (13). The semiotic turn would make human and machinic actants interchangeable, perhaps, but at the price of weakening our notion of their materiality. And, to return to the problematic that has structured this chapter, it would seem to imply that revolutionary change is a matter of linguistic-conceptual self-deconstruction and the workings of "textual allegory" à la de Man.

The image of the mangle, then, can be seen as a material inversion of ANT's semiotic side,[54] one which establishes human/nonhuman symmetry in terms not of signs and their substitutions but of embodied interactions and the material emergence of agencies in the give-and-take of practice. Pickering's mangle theory suggests a non-mystical view of change as involving a material progression of interactive stabilizations characterized by their "*machinic incommensurability*" with one another (32). As Pickering writes of the revolution in particle physics in the 1970s, but which applies equally well to the thermodynamic revolution:

SSK and ANT refer to positions staked off in this context. Clearly, each side is more complex and nuanced, but the picture that emerges retains a generic accuracy.

54 As I remarked before, this semiotic side is not all there is to ANT, and so I do not wish to be taken as expressing a wholesale condemnation of the approach. On the contrary, I find much of use in ANT, and I will put a small bit of it to work in the next chapter.

The theories of the old physics were tied to the world via performances of one set of machines; the theories of the new physics engaged with a largely disjoint set. Representations of the world certainly changed in going from the old to the new physics, and they changed in an incommensurable fashion, since there was no neutral domain of machines, phenomena, and facts to which both could be held accountable. But no clever and debatable arguments about how representations infect the world are needed to make sense of this. The incommensurability resided in the shift of machinic grip made by the [scientific community]. (189)

The steam engine, as we have seen, did not simply outperform pre-industrial technologies; it radically recast questions of efficiency, which had to be reformulated from the ground up, and in the process challenged physicists to develop new instrumental techniques that in turn opened onto a new set of theoretical questions. In this way, the advent of an incommensurable paradigm can be traced to an empirically describable performative process, which, in general terms, looks something like this:

As active, intentional beings, scientists tentatively construct some new machine [or, as in the case of thermodynamics, they take it over from the realm of industry]. They then adopt a passive role, monitoring the performance of the machine to see whatever capture of material agency it might effect. Symmetrically, this period of human passivity is the period in which material agency actively manifests itself. Does the machine perform as intended? Has an intended capture of agency been effected? Typically the answer is no, in which case the response is another reversal of roles: human agency is once more active in a revision of modeling vectors, followed by another bout of human passivity and material performance, and so on. (21-22)

From a phenomenological perspective, I have described these reversals in terms of an alternation between hermeneutic and embodiment relations as they are instantiated by human agents vis-à-vis the steam engine. However, if we loosen our focus on the human side of things, and attempt, post-phenomenologically, to take into view the larger performative ensemble, which also means adding a temporal or processual dimension to the punctual vantage of phenomenal-empirical situatedness, a different sort of picture arises.

Methodologically, Pickering's description of alternating rounds of passive/active complementarities may be understood as enacting a perspectival alternation or Gestalt shift between human and nonhuman prioritizations, meant to draw attention to the shared conditions of each, from whence symmetry emerges in the realm in-between—in the reversible border or region that connects the two and enables their transposition. Because this region, what Pickering calls the mangle, lies between moments or periods of stabilization, it is less susceptible to empirical or phenomenological description than the reversible situations from whose alternation we negatively derive its existence. But the external parameters of its discovery indicate something of this realm's nature: not only is the middle realm between humans and their environments occupied by technologies, but it is precisely they that reversibly bear transpositions of activity and passivity as their empirically undifferentiated material embodiments, i.e. as the very substratum of agency. Passive reception and active production, to return to terms I have used before, alternate and merge in something like Massumi's "space of passion," which I discussed in Chapter 4 in terms of pre-subjective proprioceptive and visceral sensibilities, and which we find here again in the non-biological matter of pre-objective technologies as they are implicated in the non-phenomenal procession of experiential horizons. This finding, I contend, confirms my view of the hybrid materiality of the anthropotechnical interface as an evolutionary force, as the site of sub-phenomenal material transitions that ground the very possibility of conceptual-discursive revolutions.

As for the steam engine, Pickering's model of the mangle helps us to see it as more than an empirical entity produced by engineers, studied by scientists, and employed as an instrument; more than this, the engine-as-mangle exceeds even phenomenological determinations that place it variously between subjects and objects as a variable or mobile medium; instead, the steam engine may now be conceived as the productive material interval between unprecedented situations, novel agencies, and bodies that did not exist in the same form prior to the engine's emergence. In other words, the industrial-cum-scientific engine was a locus for the production of a new world, populated by agencies, both human and otherwise, that were not pre-existent but that emerged in and through their being-mangled in the performative ensemble of steam engine practices. As such, it is a non-subjective, non-objective region of "constitutive intertwinement" governed by indeterminate interchanges, unexpected reversals, unknown variables, and indefinite parameters—the engine is the very process in and through which all these unknowns become knowable and, more fundamentally, in which potential subjects and objects of knowledge are constituted in the first place. During the processes of tuning, tinkering, or mangling, now considered from a postnatural perspective, the terminal poles or agencies are not yet or no longer determinate but in a state of metabolic flux—a state of becoming that can be explained, again, by reference to the pre-personal biological processes of proprioception and viscerality, but which is qualitatively different from all pre-industrial becomings by virtue of the steam engine's annexation into the "space of passion." By this addition, a qualitative change is effected in anthropotechnical embodiment, which, as I have suggested before, is best conceived in a Bergsonian vein as a "center of indetermination," subtracting out of the undifferentiated flux of material positivity a particular set of actualities, selecting out the situations, articulating the objects, and reticulating the relational networks that correspond to the particular sensorimotor modalities, openings, or pathways of a given somatic-technological aggregation.

Slowly, a positive image of anthropotechnical transitionality emerges from the intersection of negative determinations, discovered in the liminal materiality that spatially and temporally fills the gap between subject-centered and object-oriented perspectives. Clearly, the image is irreducibly at odds with asymmetrical perspectives that take either the subject-world or the object-world as already constituted, and it is precisely in its decentering of both that a mangle-type approach is simultaneously post-phenomenological and postnatural.[55] Indeed, this act of decentering may be seen as the definitive gesture of postnaturalism, and its implications are far-reaching and hardly uncontroversial. On the one hand, the view explicated here may be seen to provide a more robustly material, micro-level counterpart or complement to poststructural processes of "subjectification" (Foucault), mapping out subject-positions quite independently of discourse, and with the added advantage that matrices of "positionality" (as Massumi calls it) now appear far less totalizing, as they are themselves repositioned to be co-emergent with their elements. This newfound "primacy of process" (Massumi, *Parables* 8), however, introduces new riddles and difficulties, for if a mangle-ish focus avoids reifying *écriture* and steers clear of ANT's (occasional) semiotic reduction, it also makes the appearance of stability, the arrest of flux in discursive or material formations, all the more difficult

---

[55] Pickering prefers to speak of the mangle's "posthumanism": "The performative idiom that I seek to develop thus subverts the black-and-white distinctions of humanism/antihumanism and moves into a *posthumanist* space, a space in which the human actors are still there but now inextricably entangled with the nonhuman, no longer at the center of the action and calling the shots. The world makes us in one and the same process as we make the world" (26). While I agree wholly with this view, I am nevertheless uncomfortable with calling it posthumanism, for the latter term gathers much of its fashionable appeal (similarly to postmodernism) from an equivocation with regard to its object of (at least partial) negation: humanism or humanity. The reciprocities described in Pickering's quote apply to human beings, so the "post-" here is certainly aimed at humanism of one sort or another. And whether it is the "liberal humanism" of modernity or a broader form of anthropocentrism, implying some sort of fixed human nature or perspective, Pickering again has all my sympathies: that is, I agree wholeheartedly that we must break these illusory and politically pernicious tendencies. And yet, it seems to me, to call this break posthuman paradoxically reifies the human, anthropocentrically places the human right back at the middle of debate, whereas the real issue has only tangentially to do with the human. I, on the other hand, would prefer to contextualize the issue by attacking the larger question of scientific naturalism, while affirming, to adapt Bruno's Latour's stance on modernity, that "we have never been human."

to fathom. The symmetry of metabolic materiality implies, as Pickering acknowledges, that "[c]aptures and their properties [...] *just happen*," that the emergence of agencies, relations, representational systems, and the rest in the dance of agency is quite simply a matter of "brute chance" (*Mangle* 24). Hence, "[t]he world of the mangle lacks the comforting causality of traditional physics or engineering, or of sociology for that matter, with its traditional repertoire of enduring causes (interests) and constraints" (24). This severing of links is the ontological price one must pay in order to explain the occurrence of incommensurability—where, as I made explicit at the opening of this chapter, "explanation" is conceived in the sense of a rather perverse transcendental argument. And, if we shift back to the perspective of human cognition, this ontology clearly has epistemological consequences: the whole field of knowledge, on this view, is an emergent system, characterized by an obvious historical relativity.[56] And yet, viewed from a pragmatic, non-representationalist or performative perspective that eschews debates over realism and antirealism centered around "correspondence" to reality, we may see with Pickering that "the manglings that constitute relativistic linkages through time are the selfsame manglings that confer upon science [its] objectivity" (208).

The products of scientific practice, then, including scientific knowledge (as well as machines, instruments, disciplines, social relations, and so on) are significantly detached by the mangle from the subjectivity of human agents (who are, nevertheless, integral to their production). This detachment from the intentional structure of human agency through encounters with material and disciplinary agency (themselves proper to no individual subject) is the basic sense of the objectivity of science that the mangle makes available to us. (195)

It is important to note, however, that Don Ihde—who sees his own form of "post-phenomenology" coming close to the technoscience studies of Pickering, Latour, and Haraway, even affirming with them that "If I 'make' technologies, they, in turn, make me" (*Postphenomenology – Again?* 20)—sees Pickering's strategy here as an attempt at "having it both ways" (*Bodies in Technology* 80), as an impossible attempt at marrying the situatedness of experience emphasized by phenomenology with the symmetry of agency achieved by semiotic reduction. Noting that symmetrically flattened transformations "simply occur" (77), Ihde recognizes "a new, non-Cartesian equivalent of 'the view from nowhere,'" thus provoking the question: "Who describes the symmetries?" (78). Ihde proposes that symmetrical views may in fact be the product of video games, email, multimedia, and virtual reality technologies, which serve as a sort of postmodern "epistemology engine," replacing the camera obscura and its image of correspondence with a view of cognitive construc-

---

56 Compare Chapter 6: "Living in the Material World," in Pickering's *Mangle*.

tability, perspectival arbitrarity, multiplicity, and masking (80-85). Such technologies, when abstracted from their material contexts and made into "paradigmatic metaphors for knowledges themselves" (69), lead precisely back to the disembodiment and illegitimate transcendence of existential situatedness that anti-Cartesian paradigms aim to overcome. They lead, according to Ihde, to three major errors in symmetrical theories: "(a) the perspective from which the symmetry is drawn is unknown, (b) the absence or transcendence of the narrator again creates a god-trick of nonsituatedness, and (c) the question of for whom the system operates also hides the politics of semiotic systems" (80).

Pickering, for his part, responds to Ihde's challenge by "transposing his notion of an epistemology engine into that of an *ontology engine*," maintaining that "certain machines can help us think about ontology, rather than deceiving us about epistemology" ("Ontology Engines" 213). In fact, though, this methodological-epistemic claim (technologies *help us think* about ontology) is tightly coupled with a much more radical, properly ontological claim (technologies *produce* new ontologies, new worlds). The tacit relation between the two may be stated thus: while Ihde is right that the latter claim, taken on its own, involves something like a "god-trick" (which term he borrows from Haraway), the former claim offers a bridge by means of which embodied humans could arrive at the latter conclusion, without the need for transcendence, and precisely *through* their practical interactions with technologies. The human perspective is decentered *in practice*, by its confrontation with technologies that actively assert themselves as recalcitrant and that model systems of evolutionary adaptation that have no need for recourse to representational consciousness. Pickering illustrates with cybernetic mechanisms, but we have seen much the same in engineers' and scientists' interactions with the steam engine, which I claim now as an ontology engine in both senses of the term. First, prior to its scientific stabilization, it exhibited unruly properties that challenged human actors to address it as an agent and to repeatedly revise their own embodied and cognitive comportments towards it and the world; in this role, the steam engine served as an epistemic or existential clue to agential symmetry, and it is this fact that makes phenomenological analysis indispensible as a bridge between naturalism and postnaturalism. Second, though, and more radically: what the steam engine in that role points to is its own ontological indeterminacy, its transformative role in the abyss of metabolic materiality that is not conceptualizable directly but is suggestively modeled in the cosmic implications of thermodynamics—for example, the entropic heat-death of the universe. The productive, generative role of the steam engine *qua* ontology engine is neutralized in the vanishing act executed in scientific stabilization, but its generated products of thermodynamic ontology remain, indicating that a non-representational correspondence is emergently achieved: a temporary alignment of subjects and objects on the model of the steam engine, subject to its characteristic laws. With respect to the engine's distribution and absorption into both poles of noetic relationality, I have spoken of the anthropotechnical body's annexation of the steam engine. The flipside of this, to more properly characterize the pre-subjective, pre-objective ontological effects, could be described as follows: the engine absorbs or metabolizes the world itself, the industrial world *becomes* an engine.

What Pickering's move from epistemology engines to ontology engines implies, then, and what I am trying to suggest with the notion of non-representational correspondence, is that symmetry is not only a matter of human/nonhuman relations, even though our only cues to it are to be found in that domain. Beyond this, however, is the symmetry between historically emergent situations and the ontological ground of situation itself: technologies pivot qualitative changes in the material structure of the world that mark, simultaneously, events in human as well as cosmic history. This non-representational type of correspondence brings us full circle, back to the cosmic-scale level of theory with which I closed the last chapter and which is to provide, in alternation with phenomenologically situated analyses, one of the lenses for a double vision of anthropotechnical transitionality or evolution. It is therefore not a question of shifting from epistemology to ontology (though, following naturalism's basic impulse, which insists on knowledge's essential dependence on the material world, ontology should certainly "come first"); rather, at stake is an alternation between molar states, systems, or systematizable situations (phenomenal-epistemic strata) on the one hand and, on the other, the molecular, aleatory, metabolic ground of becoming from which these "states" emerge. Non-representational correspondence identifies correlations between molar and molecular aspects of technologies (and other forms of embodiment), upon which basis subphenomenal becomings are linked to larger realms of being—to organic, ecological, phenomenal, epistemic, discursive, and social configurations and reconfigurations.

Against traditional epistemological notions of correspondence, Pickering writes, "the representational chains of science terminate not in 'the world itself' but in specific captures and framings of material agency" (*Mangle* 187). For Pickering, this leads to a "noncorrespondence realism," to a view of knowledge which is "agnostic about correspondence" (183). What I am proposing as a complement to this is a form of ontological, radically non-epistemological correspondence, whereby *"the world itself" just is the changeable collection of captures and framings of material agency*—not limited to those captures contingently actualized in theory or in practice but encompassing the virtual totality of captures and framings of material agency potentially available for actualization in a given moment or duration of cosmic history. Pickering implies as much with his suggestion that "the mangle is, as the physicists put it, *scale invariant*" (234); Pickering extrapolates progressively from the scientific laboratory and suggestively expands the mangle's scope to include, first, the realm of industrial technologies and shop-floor labor, which then opens onto society at large, and out across large-scale historical developments. Finally, Pickering speculatively transforms the mangle into "an evolutionary theory of indefinite scope" (247)—into nothing less than "a potential [...] theory of everything" (248). By removing references to human practice and agency and loosening the focus on specifically machinic forms of nonhuman agency, the mangle comes to model a truly cosmic form of evolution, in which "the selection environment is not given in advance [...], but itself emerges within the evolutionary process—in uncertain captures of material or disciplinary agency and achievements of interactive stabilization" (247). The model is "irreductive" (247) in the sense that it recognizes no final determinants or "nonemergent mechanisms of selection" (248), such as genes, quarks, or fixed natures of any sort; it can be applied equally to the evolution of scientific theories, of organisms, or "of the cosmos as a whole—of inorganic as well as organic matter—as evolving within fields of agency in dialectics of resistance and accommodation" (248). Such "agencies," then, would be raw material forces impinging on one another, and "captures" or "framings" would be the bare fact of impingement, the fact that certain forces (e.g. heat, light, gravity, etc.) meet with resistance from other material forces, that they do not simply pass through certain material configurations or bodies but act upon the "sensorimotor pathways" or "perceptual capacities" to which they correspond (where sensation and perception are understood in a broad, Bergsonian sense which does not require but does not rule out subjective consciousness). At this level, the steam engine, which harnesses previously untapped forces and sets energies free in novel ways incommensurable with the reversible mechanics of wind-, water-, or animal-powered technologies, can be said to have effected a non-epistemic cosmological revolution, far more fundamental than that experienced by science, by altering the most basic relations of correspondence—those between pre-subjective receptors and the material forces to which they are tuned. Resonating across nature, society, in bodies, thoughts, words, and cultural products—no stratum of reality was immune to revisionary tuning through the disruptive force of this ontology engine.

CODA: FICTION MEETS FRICTION

While I hope that the reader has found this techno-scientific interlude to be engaging on its own terms, I realize that its relevance for my overall project may still not be completely apparent. In Chapter 6, I will put my findings most directly to use in articulating a postnatural media theory and fleshing out what I have called a cinematic double vision. Before doing so, however, I would like to return briefly to *Frankenstein* and the "parabolic" reading I put forward (against the more common "allegorical" ones) in the last chapter, according to which Shelley's text instantiates a machinic "exemplar" of industrial technology—which in the terms I have used here means that the novel is characterized by a non-representational correspondence to the steam engine. It is now possible, I believe, to determine more concretely the nature of this relation. In this context, I would like also to elucidate the alternation between human-centered and thoroughly postnatural perspectives in an extra-scientific, properly cultural context, thus paving the way for the next chapter and a re-entry into the world of film.

At stake in the characterization of *Frankenstein* as a parable of machinic agency is the notion, recently discussed, of symmetry between historically emergent situations and the material ground of situation—between, in this case, a work of literature and the "center of indetermination" defined by the impact of the steam engine *qua* ontology engine. What we need, then, is a means of connecting pre-objective materiality (conceived as radically exterior to discourse) with the cultural realm of literary products and the discursive agencies of their producers and consumers. Generally speaking, my answer to the conundrum should be clear by now: it is the affective body-plus-technology that bridges the gap. But, we may ask further, by what method can we locate the specific resonances involved in a given case? In pursuit of an answer, let us consider Michel Serres's essay "Turner Translates Carnot," which is also a point of reference for Mark Hansen's treatment of *Frankenstein*.

Serres's essay begins with a description of a painting by George Garrard, commissioned in 1784 by brewer Samuel Whitbread, which Serres reads as a "tableau" or pictorial "tabulation" (55) of pre-industrial "equipment," a chart or "balance sheet" of mechanical forces as they are harnessed in the tools of the day (54). Accordingly, the painting depicts four, "and only four" (54), productive sources of mechanical force—"men, horses, wind, and water"—which, along with the instruments for applying and transmitting force, for bearing, lifting, transporting, or (in Pickering's terminology) "capturing" force, constitute an "exhaustive" image of anthropotechnical relations just prior to the industrial revolution (54-55). "All this," writes Serres in a manner reminiscent of the early Heidegger, "makes a world" (55); for both theorists, the equipmental trappings of human practice define a global context of significance, from which science (in this case classical mechanics) abstracts its general principles but which is also susceptible to artistic expression (among other forms of manifestation).

With the introduction of the steam engine, however, the unity of this world is shattered by a force that Serres clearly conceives along the sub-phenomenological, postnatural lines I have drawn above, and which is correlated at a higher level with a reconfiguration of the human lifeworld. Note the interplay of molecular forces and molar (de)formations in the following passage:

What is the Industrial Revolution? A revolution operating on *matter*. It takes place at the very sources of dynamics, at the origins of force. One takes force as it is or one produces it. Descartes and Newton, crowned by Lagrange, chose the first alternative: force is there, given by the biotope, the wind, the sea, and gravity. It is beyond our control except insofar as men and horses are subject to it, but it is not under our dominion when it is a question of heavy bodies, of air, and of water. With it one produces motion, work, by using tools—those mentioned earlier. The mediating function of the tools is inscribed in their form, their lines, their geometry: Garrard's form, Lagrange's formal demonstrations. Then a sudden change is imposed on the raw elements: fire replaces air and water in order to transform the earth. Fire will consume *Analytical Mechanics* and burn down Samuel Whitbread's warehouse. It will destroy the wooden shed, the wooden ships. Fire finishes off the horses, strikes them down. The source, the origin, of force is in this flash of lightning, this ignition. Its energy exceeds form; it transforms. Geometry disintegrates, lines are erased; matter, ablaze, explodes; the former color—soft, light, golden—is now dashed with bright hues. The horses, now dead, pass over the ship's bridge in a cloud of horsepower. The brig-schooner is in dry dock, disarmed: the new ship, which wins the big prize, is called the *Durande*. Here comes Turner. (56)

What this beautifully embellished passage expresses is a view of revolution which, like Pickering's, emanates from the void of chaotic materiality to destabilize the achievements of a prior interactive stabilization—the well-tuned ensemble of humans, objective nature, and the pre-industrial tools, machines, and other means of capturing or taming material agency now overturned by an as yet untamed or incompletely harnessed fire. "Theorem: beneath the forms of matter, stochastic disorder reigns supreme. To smelt is to rediscover chance as fundamental. The furnace is the engine for going back towards chaos. The foundry is where creation starts over at zero. History is recast beginning with primitive matter" (61). Yet if Serres's view converges here with Pickering's notion of mangling, it is important to note that he is not concerned primarily to prove this essentially postnaturalistic thesis; true to the designation "theorem," Serres treats it as a quasi-deductive product of previously assumed axioms, while the true concern of his essay lies in William Turner's paintings as a non-representational expression of the revolution—not yet a determinate capture but an early, diffuse, and pre-subjective perception (again, in a broad, Bergsonian sense) of the new world, still in the process of becoming. "There is no longer any representation in Turner's foundry. The painting is a furnace, the very furnace itself. [....] We pass from geometry to matter or from representation to work. By going back to the sources of matter, the painter has broken the stranglehold of copying in the arts" (62).

The path beyond copying is paved, however, by a different sort of mimicry, a material identification or correlation that collapses the distance between the subject and the object of perception, the painting and the painted, or the painter and the viewer. Turner, according to Serres, "passes from the rationalized real, from the abstract or mathematical real, to the burgeoning real that radiates from the furnace where edges collapse" (58). Having given himself over to dissolution, Turner's paintings disperse material objects into indefinite "cloudy masses" (59), and "the entire world becomes a steam engine between Carnot's two sources: the cold and the hot" (57). As Serres demonstrates for a variety of Turner's paintings, this correlation organizes the visible scene, or the cosmos itself, as "a thing-nature" (60) circulating between two reservoirs. But the correlation is not a representation, for the irruption of chance or the untamed force of fire means that "there is no relation to man" (60): no stable ground upon which to stand and constitute oneself as a subject that apprehends, from a distance, a metaphorical similarity (which always implies an underlying difference) between the world and the steam engine. Instead, there is the unity of metabolism as the engine engulfs the world and eradicates perceptual distance by unsettling the ground of anthropotechnical embodiment.

In *Techniques of the Observer*, Jonathan Crary fleshes this out in terms of a "breakdown of the perceptual model of the camera obscura" enacted in Turner's paintings (138), especially in his images of the sun. If the camera obscura had been employed by scientists "to avoid looking directly into the sun while seeking to gain knowledge of it," and thus as "a defense against the madness and unreason of dazzlement" (139), Turner discards the protective medium and regards the cosmic furnace directly, "dissolv[ing] the very possibility of representation that the camera obscura was meant to ensure" (139). According to Crary:

His solar preoccupations were "visionary" in that he made central in his work the retinal processes of vision; and it was the carnal embodiment of sight that the camera obscura denied or repressed. In one of Turner's great later paintings, the 1843 *Light and Colour (Goethe's Theory)—The Morning After the Deluge*, the collapse of the older model of representation is complete: the view of the sun that had dominated so many of Turner's previous images now becomes a fusion of eye and sun. On the one hand it stands as an impossible image of a luminescence that can only be blinding and that has never been seen, but it also resembles an afterimage of that engulfing illumination. If the circular structure of this painting and others of the same period mimic the shape of the sun, they also correspond with the pupil of the eye and the retinal field on which the temporal experience of an afterimage unfolds. Through the afterimage the sun is made to belong to the body, and the body in fact takes over as the source of its effects. It is perhaps in this sense that Turner's suns may be said to be self-portraits. (139-41)

But *not*, I would add, portraits of a self.

What Serres and Crary both see in Turner's paintings are materializations of a new form of vision, highly volatile products of a dawning new perception not yet assimilated to conscious experience, of receptive faculties still being tuned to novel material forces. Not yet readable in terms of thermodynamic science, the principles of which were yet to be formulated, nor assimilable to the stylistic forms of Impressionism, which had not yet emerged as a distinct artistic movement, Turner's paintings propagate this new vision directly, bodily, through the abysmal identification described by Crary, whereby the viewing subject coincides with the painting subject not by virtue of their shared perspective vis-à-vis the depicted objects but rather by means of a material collapse, an enfolding of the world into the painting, of the painting into the body, and of bodies into one another, pointing towards their convergence on a plane of material fullness in flux.

I dwell on this image not merely for its intrinsic beauty, but because it, along with the analysis by which it is revealed, holds an important key for re-thinking *Frankenstein* as a machinic parable and, concomitantly, for conceiving the relations between cultural criticism and postnaturalism. The first thing to note is that the foregoing analysis does not and cannot directly demonstrate that an emergent change of human and nonhuman agencies takes place with the industrial revolution. Instead, Serres proceeds negatively, by juxtaposing the "tabulations" of human-technology-world relations put forward by Garrard and, in germinal form, by Turner. On its own, this juxtaposition reveals only a gap; it cannot define the matter that fills it. That, in turn, can only be deduced on the basis of a prior assumption of the postnaturalist thesis. Only then do the formal correspondences between Turner's paintings and the steam engine with its dual reservoirs become significant as indicators of an a-centric embodied process of mangling. But if such cultural analyses are dependent in this sense upon the foundation of a prior ontological investigation, they are not for that matter irrelevant to the theory of postnatural flux, which would truly be an empty metaphysics if it did not concern itself with the concrete emergence of historical agencies. Cultural phenomena not only represent higher-order emergent products of molecular manglings, thus providing content for postnatural analysis, but they also point to a threshold of central importance to the relations between symmetrical manglings and asymmetrical situations. The formal correspondences revealed in the analysis of Turner's paintings point, I submit, to mid-level or meso-manglings, emergent exchanges taking place somewhere between micro- and macrocosmic strata, between laborers' embodied interactions with industrial machines and scientists' abstract theorizations, between curvatures of spacetime and turns in social organization, and between the void of chaos and the reterritorialization of situated subjectivity. The resemblance involved in the paintings' non-representational correspondence to the steam engine is of the sort described by Walter Benjamin with his materialistic notion of mimesis—a sensuous, non-conscious relation to flux which obtains at the very cusp of articulated embodiment, at the precipice where organized states of being begin and end against the backdrop of a formless abyss.[57] This is the minute space in which the corporeal interface-matrices discussed in the last chapter are formed, dissolved, and reformed. And precisely this space, activated by non-representational correspondences between the molar and the molecular, is the realm of primary concern for a postnatural cultural criticism.[58]

What I am suggesting, to put it somewhat differently, is that Massumi's "space of passion" becomes palpable for cultural criticism at a certain intersection of analytical and practical strata, that the specific resonances, as I called them above, between cultural products and metabolic indeterminacies can be located in the loopings of form, content, production, and reception that are simultaneously in and not in the realm of articulated experience, spanning the embodied membrane between being and becoming. The key here is to take the right perspective on the self-reflexive correspondences between culture and chaos, and to position analysis precisely at the threshold. Pickering points the way: "It is [...] reasonable to see cultural studies and the mangle as delineating two perpendicular axes [...], the mangle staking out the time dimension of scientific practice while cultural studies engage in transverse cultural mappings" (*Mangle* 224). Like Serres's tabulations or "tableaux," cultural studies provides "snapshots: transverse cuts through cultural webs" (*Mangle* 222)—"synchronous mappings" of culture, which for Pickering refers broadly to the realm of "made things," both material and discursive (3, 218). Cultural studies in this sense is therefore concerned with the reticulated interrelations amongst articulated agencies obtaining at a given time and place; seen thus, it is concerned with the totality, even if only taken in slices, of a given "situation"— both with the human and the nonhuman, the subjective and the objective conditions and perspectives that define a world. Plotted onto the diachronic axis of the mangle, these quasi-spatial mappings gain the depth of a temporal dimension. The intersec-

---

57 Mark Hansen sees Benjamin's concept of mimesis, as developed in his later essay "On Some Motifs in Baudelaire," as fundamental to his own attempt at rethinking technology's impact as aesthetically embodied and yet molecularly pre-subjective. My thinking about Benjamin's notion has been shaped crucially by Hansen's discussion. See Chapter 9 of Hansen's *Embodying Technesis*, "On Some Motifs in Benjamin: (Re)Embodying Technology as *Erlebnis*, or the Postlinguistic Afterlife of Mimesis," 231-63.

58 As I remarked in a footnote to Chapter 4, in the context of introducing Deleuze and Guattari's molecular/molar distinction, my view of meso-level processes accords with Massumi's explication of Deleuze and Guattari's concepts and the middle realm between them: "A supple individual lies between the molecular and the molar, in time and in mode of composition. Its particles are correlated, but not rigidly so. It has boundaries, but fluctuating ones. It is the threshold leading from one state to another" (Massumi, *User's Guide* 55).

tion of the two axes defines a plane of history[59]—the realm of alternations between situation and displacement, between the two poles required for true development or meaningful change. For, as I claimed at the opening of this chapter, lest the parameters of human being turn out to be statically ahistorical, there must be an indeterminate material flux beyond the pale of phenomenal situation; but for sub-phenomenal flux to become historical, it must impinge upon embodiment in such a way as to revise it and effect the passage from one phenomenal orientation to another. We are considering here a middle realm between symmetry and situation, anthropotechnical embodiment as the very spacetime of history.

Medium depth manglings therefore constitute the coordinates plotted on this historical plane; these are the "resonances" that connect materiality *qua* radically emergent singularity on the one hand to the mappable multiplicities of culture on the other, revealing very definite contours and concrete determinants of anthropotechnical transitionality. For example, when looped through a historically emergent, sub-personal embodiment, what would otherwise be the merely formal correspondences between Turner's paintings and Carnot's engine indicate in fact a significant reorganization of the principles of emergence or of perception. Beyond representation, the corporeally mimetic union of machinic and artistic forms in the indistinct, "passionate" bodies of passive producers and active recipients defines the fulcrum on which turns anthropotechnical history. This is the case, as we have seen, with Turner's solar afterimages, which double for the furnace and undermine distinctions of objective being, subjective construction, artistic vision, and spectatorial reception.

Similarly, one might wish to revisit Benjamin's discussions of Edgar Allan Poe and Charles Baudelaire with a theory of the mangle in hand and reconsider the correspondences he finds between their literary output and the experience of being "jostled by the crowd" ("On Some Motifs" 172), the "series of shocks and collisions" encountered in big-city traffic (175), the automatic execution of unskilled machine work (175-76), and the rise of photography (186-88). We have seen already the usefulness of the mangle in consideration of industrial labor, but the navigation of urban spaces is equally well thought of in terms of a decentered "dialectics of resistance and accommodation": think, for example, of the experience of being pulled along by the flow of the crowd, to which one submits or one resists, but whose agency cannot be ignored; the push and pull of elbows and the attempt to avoid them; the shock of collisions or near-collisions, especially when the very

---

59 It should be borne in mind that the figure of the plane is merely a representational convenience. Polysemic overdetermination in the cultural realm and multistability in the techno-phenomenological realm ensure that the spacetime marked out by the intersection of molecular flux and phenomenal situation is many-dimensional.

effort to steer clear of an approaching pedestrian is reciprocated in reverse, each movement to the left or right exasperatingly matched by the would-be passer-by; and of course the conveniences and dangers, the pleasures and precautions, and the unconscious adaptations of comportment connected with modern means of transportation. The "complex kind of training" to which Benjamin suggests "technology has subjected the human sensorium" (175) in the modern city is, as these examples demonstrate, a matter of negotiating and renegotiating one's place in a realm dominated by unpredictable and inhuman agencies.

Much like the example of the escalator in the last chapter, these are processes that involve the acquisition of habit or, as Benjamin puts it, the "drilling" (176) of "reflex action" (178), where even a smile can "function as a mimetic shock absorber" (176). As such, stimulus and response are swallowed by a radically presubjective realm of embodiment. But the empirical situation remains as an objective correlate, inaccessible to the subject dissolved in "passion," but determinable from without by a sort of differential calculus as the interval between concrete entry points and exits. It is the simultaneity of these two realms, the empirical and the infra-empirical, that we take into view when we take as our grid of analysis the dual axes of cartographable formations and mangle-ish emergence. And it is by means of this duality that non-thematic correspondences such as those described by Serres and Benjamin become recoverable to analysis, and by which they become meaningful as the meso-manglings of a transitional embodiment, poised between phenomenal situations and sub-phenomenological symmetries. The painting as engine, the poem as confrontation with the modern city—these are not simply discursive formations, metaphors or allegories, but parabolic traces of a robustly material history of anthropotechnical embodiment.

Thus do the processual metaphysics of the mangle and the structural mappings of cultural studies work together, "reinforc[ing] and interactively stabiliz[ing] one another" (Pickering, *Mangle* 224) in a specifically postnatural cultural criticism, the task of which is to reveal the specific resonances at work in a particular intersection of axes and to plot vectors of change at a particular historical juncture. With regard to the exemplary case of *Frankenstein*, we begin by noting a number of formal correspondences that point to the steam engine as the source of the novel's specific or operative resonances—as the decisive force behind the dissolution and reorganization of interface-matrices. As expressed in *Frankenstein*, these correspondences are of course colored somewhat differently than in Turner due to the author's gender, the novel's closer temporal proximity to the French revolution, its greater distance from the ratification of thermodynamics' first two laws, and, of course, the different medium in which Shelley works—to name but a few of the material/cultural variables that any analysis, postnatural or otherwise, must in some way account for. As for the correspondences, the steam engine's hot and cold reservoirs find correlates in contrasts such as: the heat of electric sparks (lightning destroys an oak and a "spark of being" animates the dead) set against the arctic cold of the novel's frame story; the sunny summer days at Lake Geneva in the shadow of the eternally cold peaks of the Alps, where Frankenstein will encounter his creature and hear his tale next to a fire, surrounded by ice; or, more abstractly, the young Frankenstein's humanistic optimism and his eventual realization that his transgressions have created an inhuman monster. Each set of reservoirs defines a sort of engine, and there are more engines to be found: that "powerful engine" that Shelley will later, in her Introduction, identify as the animator of the creature in her waking dream (9); but also the monster itself, that unnatural assemblage powered by differentials of life and death, reason and instinct, human and machine; and thus Frankenstein too, whose pursuit of the monster into the ice is driven not by subjective desire but by a "mechanical impulse" (198), machinic automatism rather than human autonomy. Indeed, the relation between creator and creature is one of symmetry, precisely in the sense of the mangle as applied to the engineer/engine pair: Frankenstein's agency is decentered in practice, through his give and take with a nonhuman agency that eludes capture. And Shelley's relation to her text, her own "monster," mirrors this exactly: recall her passivity vis-à-vis the text, which comes to her "unbidden" of its own accord (9), so that Shelley, like her creature Frankenstein, is subject to words "burst[ing] uncontrollably" from her (180). Her agency too is uprooted, rendered symmetrical to that of her text, which is itself an engine or collection of engines, its circulating fluid the narrative flowing between its various reservoirs. Note the engine's cyclical structure, like that of the Carnot engine: beginning and ending in the arctic waste, the "origin" buried within is less a starting point than a station in a cycle that repeats regularly between each expansion and condensation of the medium. But this is not a perpetuum mobile, as there is no coming back from the ice: here we find a structural correlate of entropy, the irreversibility of thermodynamic time. Fiction meets friction.

Looked at from a postnatural perspective, the text's formal resemblances to the steam engine are tied mediately to the formless materiality of non-discursive flux, whereby the link of relation is to be found in the liminal embodiment of anthropotechnical interface through which correlations loop as a condition of their significance. Only in this material medium can the text escape the representationalism of merely metaphorizing the machine and thus enact what Hansen calls its "*a-signifying performance* of a technological machine" ("Not thus" 603). In this regard, Shelley's predicament as author is crucial, as we saw in the last chapter: the eclipse of asymmetrical grounding she experiences as a passive scribe—when seen as the impact of untamed matter on her unthematized body, rather than the expression of social deference or the effect of linguistic self-deconstruction—links her text to a process of mimesis, to the pre-conceptual "tuning" of embodiment to an intuited world in upheaval. The symmetry and interchange of passive and active agencies in her authorship produce the text as an objective or, in Latour's term, quasi-objective correlate of Shelley's no-longer-subjective negotiations; like Turner's suns, *Frankenstein* may be seen as a sort of self-portrait, but again *not* a portrait of self. Mechanically reproducing what might be called Shelley's a-centric perception from the border regions between symmetry and situation, the text remains an unclosed quasi-object by preserving an openness to agencies that are not tamed by its narrative: for example, the aporetic series of "strange coincidences," as Frankenstein calls them, which lead to Justine's execution for little William's murder and Victor's temporary imprisonment for Clerval's murder, resist textualization and demonstrate the workings of an autonomous technology as unrepresentable chance, as Mark Hansen has shown.[60] By holding open this gap and refusing the closure of objecthood, the text offers the reader a vantage in precisely that a-subjective space at the cusp of symmetry occupied by its author; thus, like Turner's afterimages, which reproduce in the act of reception the very image of authorial dispersal, *Frankenstein* propagates Shelley's liminal or quasi-experience of technology's deterritorialization and reterritorialization of embodiment by means of mimesis—the reader is provided the opportunity to undergo, as an embodied rapport, the non-representational correspondence to the steam engine that the text *qua* cultural product approximates as formal equivalences.

Critics have long been fascinated by *Frankenstein*'s concentric structure of nested narratives. Seen now from the angle of a postnatural cultural criticism, the novel's expansive, radial form mirrors—as another non-representational correspondence—that liminal resonation of industrial-technological becoming which was intuited by Shelley in an a-centric perception (not quite her own) of the embodied border between molar situation and molecular symmetry, a perception which reverberates in the novel's inner circle, the monster's tale of emergence, extending outward to implicate Frankenstein and Walton as tale-tellers as well, resounding again in the reader, and drawing ever expanding cultural and ultimately cosmic circles. At their center, as we have seen, is the steam engine as it a-centrically transforms—from a space between form and formlessness, culture and chaos—the embodied shape of the historical world. If, then, the novel serves to transmit intensities generated by the industrial era's exemplary ontology engine, it is simultaneously a highly efficient "storytelling engine," as Michael Chabon has said of the Sherlock Holmes stories with a view to their proliferating stories within stories, their narrative gaps that beg to be filled by clever readers-cum-writers, and their

---

60 In Hansen's words, "The chaotic impact of sheer chance on narrative structure should be understood *as the novel's manner of embodying the experiential impact of the industrial revolution*" ("Not Thus" 603).

innovative techniques for integrating an awareness of fiction's construction into the fiction itself, thereby problematizing the distinction between narrative and medium and lending to both of them a self-propelling momentum of their own ("Fan Fictions" 46-49). Similarly, *Frankenstein*'s cultural/cosmological duplicities—tensions which go all the way down and include the self-reflexive doublings and confusions of author/text, creator/creature, narrative content/medial form, depicted technologies/techniques of depiction, and phenomenal centeredness/sub-phenomenal circulation—may be said to constitute the reservoirs of this storytelling engine, apparently inexhaustible in its ability to generate ever new self-replicating centers of indetermination, further tales in different media, with historicities that beg to be plotted along cultural as well as cosmic axes.

6. Re-Focusing Cinematic Double Vision: Seriality, Mediality, and Mediation in Postnatural Perspective

> As soon as we start from the middle, as soon as we invert the arrows of the explanation, as soon as we take the essence accumulated at the two extremes and redistribute it to the whole set of intermediaries, as soon as we elevate the latter to the status of full-fledged mediators, then history in fact becomes possible.
>
> BRUNO LATOUR[1]

Now that we have discovered *Frankenstein* as a storytelling engine, as a non-representational cultural correlate of the industrial steam engine *qua* ontology engine, all that is left, or so it might appear, is to establish the medium of film and/or the apparatic appurtenances of cinema as ontology engines in their own right—*et voilà*: we end up right back where we started, with the Frankenstein/film analogy from which I set out in Chapter 2, and which in its simplest form claims that a) cinema is itself a Frankensteinian technology of (re)animation, and b) Frankenstein films are (representationally) *about* precisely this life-giving operation of the medium. The problem with this analogy, as I argued in Chapter 2, is that it suggests that both the cinema and the Frankenstein story possess some sort of essential and unchanging (though variously specifiable) traits as the condition of their correspondence. But these traits will either be too specific to be applicable beyond a limited time-frame (e.g. the identification of montage as the animating principle limits the analogy's purchase in comparative endeavors by restricting its purview to classical or, at most, post-primitive film), or, at the other extreme, they will be too general to be of real historical interest (e.g. by widening the scope of

---

1 *We Have Never Been Modern*, 81-82.

filmic animation—by reducing it, say, to the bare facts of photographic inscription, storage, and reproduction via projection—a monolithic ontology of film is established that obscures any substantial change in its material operations).

The analogy, in other words, tends to rob both the medium and the basic narrative content of Frankenstein's filmic progenies of their histories. As I have demonstrated with reference to *Dog Factory* and the Edison and Whale versions of *Frankenstein*, however, the particular conjunctions of narrative-discursive contents and contexts and media-technological materialities that come together in Frankenstein films are of interest precisely for their illuminations of historically specific media transformations or, at the cosmic scale, the anthropotechnical transitions with which they are correlated. At certain moments, at certain interstitial and potently indeterminate junctures, that is, the Frankenstein/film analogy seems briefly to ring true, there exists then a resonance between the tale as told and the technologies of its telling, an impermanent and emergent correspondence that is neither abstractly ahistorical nor entirely concrete and empirically determinate. Seen in this way, the essential truth of the analogy is only an occasional truth; *on occasion*, the self-reflexive stagings of a Frankenstein film can be seen not to suggest an essential correspondence between cinematic technologies and Frankensteinian creation but *to perform a certain act of mediation*—in the sense of being a mediator, go-between, or middle-man between conflicting parties—*that corresponds to the changing, that is, transitional medial forms by which it is framed*. The task, then, for a postnatural cultural criticism of Frankenstein films will be to locate those occasions and to identify the specific modalities and resonances between the as yet to be defined notions of mediation and mediality. Before this task can be undertaken, it will therefore be necessary to make a foray through media theory and to connect the concept of medium to the postnatural perspective introduced in the last chapter. In effect, media (and the medium of film) will indeed be revealed as ontology engines, which means that I shall accord them a role that is not reducible to the empirical-technical objectifications (e.g. concrete apparatuses, devices, circuits, and carriers of data) that exhaust a naturalistic perspective, but that instead approximates a transcendental function in determining the parameters of life as such. However—and the following qualification is crucial to a postnatural conception of media—the more-than-empirical function of media only ever *approximates* transcendence, is always also less-than-transcendental, because it is inextricably *grounded in the concretely embodied apparatic entities and structures of historically evolving media technologies*. In arguing for these claims, I will follow Mark Hansen in his engagement with Bernard Stiegler and Gilbert Simondon, among others, and steer a course *between* the empirical and the transcendental—a middle or "medial" course that is congenial to the meso-level analysis I recommended at the end of Chapter 5.

If, as I have argued, the occurrence of technological change marks an upheaval of the parameters of embodied experience, then the transitions between media-technological configurations challenge phenomenological coherence and re-situate human subjectivities, human life itself, on a new ground. In my arguments regarding the nature of anthropotechnical transitionality, I have been concerned to show how it involves a movement *between* grounds, situations, and interface-matrices that quasi-transcendentally structure perception and action in an empirical-phenomenal environment. The postnatural (which is to say more-than-empirical but less-than-Hegelian) history I have described is defined by this alternation between relatively stable stations and transitional irruptions that—because they mark the appearance of a material change that is not encompassed within the parameters of contiguous stations but which is also never without concrete embodiment (and its attendant trajectories of impingement and resistance)—defy the distinction between the transcendental and the empirical. Recognizing the inherent difficulty of characterizing something of this sort as more than a purely negative gap without thereby positivizing it into an empirically objectified phenomenon, I have proposed that we may approach transitionality by means of an oscillating double vision that alternates between molar and molecular, phenomenological and sub-phenomenal strata in order to capture the liminal materiality that occupies the meso-level realm in which anthropotechnical changes are negotiated—the embodied interstice, in other words, between human culture and cosmic becoming. Pickering has referred to these acts of negotiation under the headings of the "dance of agency" and the "tuning" of human and nonhuman agencies, but they may also be described with Latour's term "mediation," understood as a productive process in which agents meet, are transformed, and re-defined by way of a non-neutral "mediator" that is capable of registering and conveying the perturbative forces of each, not as a passive "intermediary" but as a constitutively necessary pathway in the networks within which intersecting entities and agencies are individuated and given identity.[2] Hansen's concept of medium as "environment for life" opens the operation of technical media to such a view, though with an emphasis on the cosmic aspect of anthropotechnical mediations.[3] Later, I shall supplement Hansen's rethinking of mediality with a view of the concrete mediations (again in the Latourian sense) that are performed by Frankenstein films; as mediators, I shall argue, the films transformatively link the cosmic realm in which media *qua* anthropotechnical milieux

---

2   Compare the epigraph above. Latour's *We Have Never Been Modern* is a wonderful, exhilarating exploration of this process of mediation.

3   The concept is explored in Hansen's "Media Theory," to which I return later in this chapter.

undergo transition, on the one hand, to the phenomenal domain of human culture on the other.

My historicizing rehabilitation of the Frankenstein/film analogy therefore refocuses cinematic double vision—which is intent on discovering the ligaments articulating together narrative-discursive structures and functions with the material-technical or medial parameters of life—as a specifically postnatural cultural criticism. In line with the picture I have offered of an analysis that alternates between views of, in Pickering's terminology, the diachronic axis of symmetrical manglings and the synchronic "snapshots" of cultural situation, I aim to initiate a method for tracing the Frankensteinian storytelling engine's cinematic afterlife through its various instantiations in such a way as to link the isolated filmic productions into a *series* that reveals meaningful, though non-representational, correspondences to the infra-empirical history of anthropotechnical destabilizations that have been effected through filmic technologies *qua* ontology engines. As the binding links constitutive of the films' seriality, the serially staged figures of Frankenstein and the monster become the central focal objects of a monstrous double vision, occupying a spatio-temporal milieu on the mediating cusp between diegetic contents and media technologies, between human and nonhuman agencies, between phenomenal states and sub-phenomenal transitions, and thus between positive and transcendental media histories.

Prelude: Maurice and Henri at the Cosmic Picture Show

Before I turn to the concept of medium as such and thence to Frankenstein films' serial mediations, allow me to bring back to the fore the metaphysical landscape that undergirds the postnatural perspective generally and, in particular, its methodological correlate of (cinematic) double vision. As I intimated at the opening of Chapter 5, the basic picture may be summarized by way of a confrontation between the carnal phenomenology of Merleau-Ponty and the evolutionary vitalism of Bergson. In the course of this confrontation, staged as the postnatural derivation, the techno-phenomenology from which I initially set out to approach Frankenstein films—and the cinema generally—has undergone a marked shift towards the "techno" side of things and away from the human orientation of orthodox phenomenology. What Massumi calls the "Bergsonian revolution" enacted here involves a radical displacement of the experiential situatedness that Merleau-Ponty's phenomenology locates in human embodiment. More specifically, material embodiment remains central in the Bergsonian paradigm as a pre-subjective ground (as a sort of selective filter) of experience, but embodiment itself is endowed with a deep history that renders the "natural" perspective of phenomenology (or the invariants discovered through eidetic reduction) radically contingent. Moreover, the subordination of phenomenological situation to Bergsonian evolution expands the scope of inquiry beyond the capacities of the specifically human, opening the realm of sensorimotor activity to the experiential-agential correlates of nonhuman forms of embodiment—including those of nonhuman organisms and, potentially, those of technological entities as well. Techno-phenomenology, in other words, assumes that there is a plethora of embodied perspectives or standpoints that are no less real for the fact that phenomenology cannot countenance or occupy them, and between which standpoints occur inter-agential transactions and evolutionary transformations, defining a sub-phenomenological space of liminal matter and a sub-phenomenological time of transitionality. However, supplanting phenomenology in this way is not equivalent to "disproving" it or rendering it useless, and thus techno-phenomenology remains phenomenological in that it investigates the contours of a given object in a given situation with the tools provided by phenomenology, but with the important difference that techno-phenomenology relativizes its findings (along with the objects of investigation and, indeed, the phenomenological investigation itself as an elaboration of subject-object relations and their conditions) as contingent and temporary products of what Pickering refers to as an "interactive stabilization." Thus, though they are not foundational in any absolute sense, these analytical slices or "captures" of situated being are the key to tracing a movement or history—not only of human culture but of the forms of situatedness and embodiment that compose its substratal basis. In this way, to put it schematically, Bergson and Merleau-Ponty provide the two lenses of the double vision being developed in the guise of postnatural cultural criticism.

As such, I am committed to the idea that there can be a productive relation of complementarity between the two perspectives, a relation tentatively specifiable as that between the "inside" of a given human situation (the domain of phenomenology) and the a-centric "outside" of flux (the province of a Bergsonian metaphysics). Anthropotechnical evolution, accordingly, is that which relates or mediates between the two realms, i.e. *the relation of inside and outside itself*—the very boundary where "radical exteriority" (Hansen) presses up against the horizon of human phenomenality, warping and bending that horizon without entering into it as such, while the interior expands and contracts like a flexible bubble in accordance with the environmental transformations of materially embodied affective-actional "input-output" capacities and relations. Hence, the double vision I am proposing is not just a matter of methodology; rather, it is grounded squarely in a genuinely metaphysical complementarity that is anything but obvious, but which is indispensable to my view of the impact that technological novelty can have. On this view, a new technology, far from being just a prosthetic extension of thought or pre-defined subjectivity, constitutes in fact an unprecedented sensorial or receptive opening onto the world (or, in a Deleuzo-Bergsonian idiom, a new obstruction that can reflect the light of the material flux and make new facets of it, or "images," apparent for the living being[4]). New "subtractions" from the whole (or perceptions) therefore become possible, and a new horizon of active experience forms as the material universe perceived in this reflection "incurves" around the new center of indetermination that we become in conjunction with the technology. The technology acts *upon* the lifeworld at the same time that it acts *within* the lifeworld.

This simultaneous existence and action of technologies both within and without the phenomenal realm, i.e. as at once empirical objects and quasi-transcendental conditions of experience, is another formulation of what it means for something to be an ontology engine. On the basis of this view of technical duplicity, which ultimately founds double vision not only as an analytical practice or a way of looking but as an honest-to-goodness ontology, we may say that my postnaturalism makes common cause with the recent endeavors of the so-called speculative realists, a group of contemporary philosophers dedicated to breaking the spell of what Quentin Meillassoux, in what may be seen as the founding gesture of the young movement, has identified as "correlationism." According to Meillassoux:

the central notion of modern philosophy since Kant seems to be that of *correlation*. By 'correlation' we mean the idea according to which we only ever have access to the correlation between thinking and being, and never to either term considered apart from the other. We will henceforth call *correlationism* any current of thought which maintains the unsurpassable character of the correlation so defined. (*After Finitude* 5)

Defined by a common opposition to this doctrine rather than any unified alternative to it, "speculative realism" denotes a loose alliance of divergent and at times incompatible positions.[5] Among these are extreme scientific reductivist positions,

---

4   The notion that Bergson's primordial flux consists of "light" which is "obstructed" stems primarily from Deleuze (see *Cinema 1*, 60-61). While this reading is largely consistent with Bergson, it is in fact correlated with a transformation of Bergson that we shall return to shortly.

5   The "movement" was founded at a 2007 conference on "Speculative Realism" held at Goldsmiths College, University of London. One of the "founders," Ray Brassier, has recently said: "There is no 'speculative realist' doctrine common to the four of us: the only thing that unites us is antipathy to what Quentin Meillassoux calls 'correlationism'—the doctrine, especially prevalent among 'Continental' philosophers, that humans and world cannot be conceived in isolation from one other—a 'correlationist' is any philosopher who insists that the human-world correlate is philosophy's sole legitimate concern. Anti-

such as Ray Brassier's, sometimes referred to as "eliminative materialism" or "transcendental nihilism."[6] But there are also positions that might better accommodate the technological duality at the heart of double vision. In particular, postnaturalism harbors significant (though limited) metaphysical sympathies with the "object-oriented philosophy" or "object-oriented ontology" advanced by philosophers Graham Harman[7] and Levi Bryant[8], along with video game critic, theorist, and designer Ian Bogost, who ventures the following "elevator pitch" of his philosophy:

Ontology is the philosophical study of existence. Object-oriented ontology ("OOO" for short) puts *things* at the center of this study. Its proponents contend that nothing has special status, but that everything exists equally—plumbers, cotton, bonobos, DVD players, and sandstone, for example. In contemporary thought, things are usually taken either as the aggregation of ever smaller bits (scientific naturalism) or as constructions of human behavior and society (social relativism). OOO steers a path between the two, drawing attention to things at all scales (from atoms to alpacas, bits to blinis), and pondering their nature and relations with one another as much as with ourselves. (Bogost, "What is Object-Oriented Ontology?" n.p.)

Divorcing objects from any necessary relation to subjects (whether empirical, transcendental, or collective) and granting them an agency and relationality all their own, this manner of pursuing the anti-correlationist program has an obvious affinity with Latour's ANT, and the object-oriented approach defines a place for objects such that they are neither fully encompassed by natural science nor absconded into the lofty heights of transcendental principles—i.e. OOO's objects exemplify precisely the type of liminal existence led by the postnatural ontology engine. However, proponents of object-oriented approaches—especially Harman—have expressed serious misgivings about processual, vitalist ontologies such as Deleuze's and Bergson's, so that my postnaturalism, while compatible with OOO in many ways, is probably closer in spirit to another brand of speculative realism, viz. the latter-day *Naturphilosophie* developed by Iain Hamilton Grant. Based primarily on his

---

correlationism is by no means a negligible unifying factor—but our alternatives to correlationism are fundamentally divergent and even incompatible in several regards" ("Against an Aesthetics of Noise" n.p.). The other three founding members to whom Brassier alludes are Meillassoux, Iain Hamilton Grant, and Graham Harman.

6   See Brassier's *Nihil Unbound*.
7   See, for example, Harman's *Prince of Networks*, as well as his earlier *Tool-Being* and *Guerilla Metaphysics*.
8   Bryant's engagement with object-oriented ontology or, as he calls his own brand, "onticology" has taken place largely on his blog "Larval Subjects" (http://larvalsubjects.word press.com/) and, more systematically, in his book *The Democracy of Objects*.

reading of Schelling, combined with a clear Deleuzean influence, Grant argues for a dynamic, non-inert notion of matter, and against the sharp distinction of the organic from the inorganic, in order to envision nature as possessing a history that outstrips any anthropocentric determination of it. Nature, on this view, not only exceeds scientific descriptions of it but is also, and more importantly, dissociated from the transcendental conditions of experience that Kant locates in the subject. But Grant sees "somatism," the philosophy and physics of formed bodies, as a metaphysical error; thus, he effectively negates the view that objects *per se* can have a quasi-autonomous being.[9]

In the end, due to its dual tutelage of Merleau-Pontean and Bergsonian philosophies, postnaturalism would seem to converge with some combination of object-oriented and neo-vitalist approaches (and Steven Shaviro has recently considered whether such a combination might not be feasible[10]) that may or may not be compatible with existing strands of speculative realism. Whatever the case may be, the critique of correlationism and the attempt to go beyond the metaphysical and methodological anthropocentrisms that dominate modern thought from German Idealism to pragmatism, phenomenology, deconstruction, and cultural studies; the attempt to disconnect thought and being and to open a robustly realist path towards what Meillassoux calls the "Great Outdoors," a realm radically indifferent to human or even animal life; in short, speculative realism's attempt to open philosophy to "radical exteriority"—this core project is not only apposite with the basic impulse of postnaturalism, but it articulates a criterion that may be brought to bear on a double-vision approach to technical media. Specifically, what would it mean to think media beyond correlationism? Is a medium not precisely a conjunction of human thought or experience and nonhuman being, a means of passage between the two or a connecting pathway that defines our modes of access to the world? Is it possible, in other words, to think media non-anthropocentrically, that is, without an essential reference to the human? Obviously, the answer must be negative for any view that reduces media to instrumental artifacts and systems crafted "by the people, for the people." Less obviously, the answer will also be negative for a theorist like Friedrich Kittler, who sees in the digital convergence of media not only the end of media as such—for the notion of a medium, for Kittler, only makes sense when it can be opposed to other media—but also the impending end of humanity, the

---

9   See Grant's *Philosophies of Nature after Schelling*.
10 See Shaviro's blog post "More about objects." Shaviro's envisioned marriage of object-oriented and process-oriented takes, for the latter conjunct, not Bergson but Whitehead as its point of orientation. This follows on Shaviro's recent engagement with Whitehead in *Without Criteria* and is due to be developed further in his forthcoming book, *The Universe of Things*.

dawning of a properly posthuman era, due to an essential link between media and the human summed up in the famous opening line of Kittler's *Gramophone, Film, Typewriter*: "Media determine our situation" (xxxix). In other words, though Kittler's interest is devoted to the unintentional, non-instrumental, inhuman logics which technical media can display, his view of media history implies what we might dub a strong *media correlationism* by virtue of which the end of media spells the obsoletion of the phenomenological—the end of the "situation" determined (still, but not much longer) by media—and therefore the end of "so-called man." Kittler's theory of media *a priori* is no more capable of escaping the logic of correlationism—or, consequently, of defining media as ontology engines—than is the *a posteriori* empiricism of a media theory that perceives only artifactual products created by autonomous inventors and engineers, and passively employed by human agents and societies. The question of how to avoid media correlationism, therefore, is not one that is decided as a choice between media neutrality and media determinism.

I shall address media theory *per se* in a more methodical manner shortly, but I would like to note here that the question of media correlationism brings us to the heart of the matter with regard to the necessity of a specifically *double* vision; this necessity, I contend, can be demonstrated in terms of cinema—where Merleau-Pontean and Bergsonian lenses have been applied, respectively and in isolation, by Vivian Sobchack and by Gilles Deleuze. Let us begin with Sobchack, whose important book *The Address of the Eye* offered a sophisticated application of Merleau-Ponty's embodied phenomenology to the theorization of film experience. Now such a phenomenology is clearly correlationist: intentionality is precisely the correlation of subject and object, and orthodox phenomenology is unable or unwilling to think anything apart from this correlation and its enabling conditions. Limiting the scope of investigation in this way is exactly the function of *epoché*. But, we may ask, so what? Do we really need a non-correlationist media theory? To answer this question, let us consider what happens when we restrict ourselves, with Sobchack, to a "monocular" phenomenological view—unaccompanied, that is, by a second perspective that would ground phenomenology's centering of being in a broader realm of a-centered becoming and in this way complete the binocularism under consideration.

In opposition to what she takes to be the limited perspectives of classical and poststructural film theories, which for Sobchack tend either to subjectively "psychologize" film or to empiricize and objectify it, or else to conflate and confuse the perceptive and expressive acts involved (*Address* 15-18), Sobchack insists that we must consider the "*whole correlational structure* of the film experience" (18), i.e. re-think the experience in terms of the intentional relations that unify its parts. The real genius of Sobchack's approach is displayed in the manner in which she uses this basic phenomenological apparatus to situate the subject-pole and object-pole orientations of non-phenomenological film theories in an overarching theoretical perspective of her own, where both the legitimacy of their interests but also the partiality of their vision are plain to see. Thus, in Sobchack's view film has both an objective materiality and a quasi-subjective capacity to see, mirroring our own dual existence as subjects and objects alike of perception and expression—and based like our own in the reversibility of *embodiment* in an emphatically Merleau-Pontean sense. The communicational capacity of the filmic medium to speak to and move its spectators is therefore grounded in film's "privileged equivalence with its human counterparts in the film experience" (22), which for Sobchack "is certainly *not* to say that the film is a *human* subject," but instead "to consider the film a *viewing* subject—one that manifests a competence of perceptive and expressive performance *equivalent* in structure and function to that same competence performed by filmmaker and spectator" (22). And this intentional equivalence stems from the functional isomorphism that Sobchack posits between human and filmic *lived bodies*, which correspond in exceeding their physiologies and apparatic mechanisms and in centering experience in and as a reversibly subjective and objective materiality (205-219). Sobchack's argument is organized around an elaborate and original application of Ihde's concepts of embodiment relations and hermeneutic relations to film experience (171-203), which is revealed as an experience both *of* film and *by* film—a dialectical exchange between human and filmic agencies or "a co-operative visual exploration of the visible world" (141).

But as important and groundbreaking as Sobchack's argument is, it is flawed in a fundamental respect, viz. in its overly ideal vision of "the film experience as such" (191), which leaves little room for deviation and which effectively establishes the norm of classical cinema as the hidden *telos* of the medium. (It is for this reason that I have re-adapted Ihde's concepts for my own purposes in Chapter 2, effectively simplifying their application to film in my attempt at historicization rather than relying on Sobchack's more complex, but also more abstract and formalistically ahistorical, use of them.) Thus, on the basis of her phenomenological analysis of a well-functioning cinematic communication *qua* dialogue of human and filmic embodied agencies, Sobchack attacks valorizations of filmic self-reflexivity (219-248) on the grounds that self-reflexive films involve an objectification of film's own body, which for her is a sign of "inauthenticity" or perceptual "untruthfulness" (247) that bears comparison to the "disabling and dysfunctional relation" to one's body characteristic of "hypochondria," "illness," or "old age" (218)—unhealthy situations of bodily self-objectification and diminished functionality. Clearly, my engagement with Frankenstein films is devoted to the idea that there can be more to "dysfunctional" or monstrous self-reflexivity than that, including—most centrally—a non-representational expression of anthropotechnical transitionality. And indeed, beyond the merely stylistic aberration of a too-self-conscious cinema, it is a cinema of transitionality that Sobchack's theory marginalizes, as is evidenced most directly in her (as she puts it) "brief intentional history" of film's body (248-259). Reviving the notion that cinema underwent a process of maturation from early to classical film, but recast as a story of film progressively actualizing *the entelechy of its lived body* by "realiz[ing] its perceptive and expressive intentions" (251) through technological refinement and a growing sense of stylistic appropriateness, Sobchack reinstates the view of early film as a clumsy, infant-like caricature of mature cinema (252). More importantly, in terms of my own interests, she thereby cancels out the specificity of the transitional era as a heterotopian possibility rather than just an intermediary between helpless immaturity and confident, healthy adulthood—where the ideal form of non-deviant film embodiment happens to coincide with a pre-electronic cinema governed by classical continuity principles. In other words, "the film experience as such" is the experience of classical Hollywood, the norm from which the primitivity of early film and the decadence of digital old age deviate.[11]

Thus, Sobchack's phenomenological media correlationism makes transitionality unthinkable, a fact which attests to the need to displace or render more radically contingent the lived bodies that connect human and medial agencies in her account. As I have argued, it is precisely this decentering that defines the task of Bergsonian becoming in the context of postnatural double vision. Because Sobchack lacks a Bergsonian lens to counterbalance her Merleau-Pontean one, her teleological history of cinema turns out to be the humanistic flipside of Kittler's antihumanistic prehistory of digital de-phenomenalization. What the two approaches share is not just a correlationist view of media but, tied to it, a lack of flexibility with regard to anthropotechnical change. For both of them, it's an all or nothing affair: if it's not normatively classical cinema, then it's hardly cinema; if it's not analog experience, then it's hardly experience. Again, my contention is that the needed flexibility can be obtained by placing centered experience in the broader spacetime of a-centered flux—by re-situating Merleau-Pontean situation as a mobile island in a Bergsonist sea—which will dissolve the link of correlationism by extending to experiential situatedness itself the embedding gesture whereby existential phenomenology once inserted transcendental intentionality into the contingency of concrete, embodied

---

11 Sochack comments on the alleged hostility of electronic media to human and filmic embodiment in the concluding section of her book (300-302), as well as in "The Scene of the Screen: Envisioning Photographic, Cinematic, and Electronic 'Presence'." Originally published in 1994, a revised edition of the latter essay is included in Sobchack's 2004 collection of essays, *Carnal Thoughts: Embodiment and Moving Image Culture* (135-161).

matter. I turn, therefore, to a consideration of Deleuze's adaptation of Bergson for his philosophy of cinema, which, I hope to show, offers us a context in which to reconsider the concrete relations between Merleau-Pontean and Bergsonian perspectives in a cinematic double vision (as a check, that is, on my still quite abstract postulation of metaphysical complementarity above). Specifically, assuming that I have now established the need for a non-correlationist media theory for the purpose of thinking anthropotechnical change, do we really need to retain the phenomenological perspective at all? Or can we dispense with it and focus only on flux in thinking media beyond their anthropocentric determinations and uses? Put another way: are the two lenses of the postnatural spectacles a) compatible and b) equally necessary?

For her part, Sobchack sees Deleuze's project in his cinema books as in some sense "parallel" to her own (*Address* 30). She claims, on the one hand, that Deleuze misunderstands the complexity of Merleau-Ponty's phenomenology and "neglects the *embodied situation* of the spectator and of the film," but, on the other hand, that he nevertheless "moves on to assert (phenomenologically) the *direct* and *preverbal* significance of cinematic movement and images" (31). To be sure, Sobchack recognizes a fundamental difference of a film theory that takes off from Bergson as opposed to Merleau-Ponty; citing Bergson's claim that "Questions relating to subject and object, to their distinction and their union, should be put in terms of time rather than of space" (*Matter and Memory* 77), Sobchack responds drily: "It is not time, but space—[...] the historical space of situation—that grounds [her own] response to those questions [...]" (*Address* 31). But with her suggestion that the endeavor of Deleuze's *Cinema 1* is nevertheless "similar" to her own undertaking (31), it is clear that Sobchack underestimates just how fundamental the difference is between the two approaches, which amounts not to a choice between time and space as elements of a single system—that of situated experience—but as marking out completely different orders of being: the situated space of empirical reality as opposed to the a-centered flow of evolutionary time. Deleuze, for his part, is happy to emphasize the great distance between the two approaches, which he finds summed up in the difference between the phenomenological thesis that "all consciousness is consciousness *of* something" and what he takes to be the stronger Bergsonian thesis: "all consciousness *is* something" (*Cinema 1* 56). Deleuze explicates this difference against the background of Bergson's rejection of cinema on the grounds of its production of a "false movement" (i.e. its impossible synthesis of movement from a succession of instantaneous, static images: the "cinematographic illusion"), contrasted with Merleau-Ponty's view of the cinema as an "ambiguous ally" capable of reduplicating or simulating the action of "situated intentional consciousness," thus "suppress[ing] both the anchoring of the subject and the horizon of the world" and "substitut[ing] [...] a second intentionality for the conditions of natural perception" (57).[12] Now the brilliance of Deleuze's appropriation of Bergson for the cinema lies in his argument that the latter's metaphysics is—despite what Bergson himself thought—essentially a cinematic metaphysics, i.e. one that unwittingly champions the cinema as a means for thinking the relation between "a flowing-matter in which no point of anchorage nor centre of reference would be assignable" (57) and the formation of "centres [...] which would impose fixed instantaneous views" (57-58). The deduction of conscious experience from material flux was the great task of Bergson's thought; according to Deleuze, cinema is an invaluable aid in this task because of the following "advantage" it has over consciousness: "just because it lacks a centre of anchorage and of horizon, the sections which it makes would not prevent it from going back up the path that natural perception comes down. Instead of going from the acentred state of things to centred perception, it could go back up towards the acentred state of things, and get closer to it" (58).

The crucial step in Deleuze's confrontation of Bergsonian metaphysics with cinema is made in his recapitulation of Bergson's deduction, as laid out in *Matter and Memory*, of consciousness from matter (*Cinema 1* 58-66), beginning from an originally chaotic "gaseous state" of pure, uninterrupted movement (58). In order to avoid the symmetrical impasses of idealism and reductivist materialism, unable both to maintain the existence of an external world *and* to explain how subjective mental states correspond to that world, with which they are continuous but not identical, Bergson postulates from the start that matter, movement, and "image" all name the same thing. These images are therefore impersonal, not essentially connected to a subject—which, *ex hypothesis*, does not yet exist—but not categorically incapable of being attached to one. In this "state of matter too hot for one to be able to distinguish solid bodies in it," as Deleuze puts it, which "constitutes a kind of plane of immanence," "*movement-image* and *flowing-matter* are strictly the same thing" (58-59). In this flux, there is constant motion, but not of a mechanical sort, for "mechanism involves closed systems, actions of contact, immobile instantaneous sections," whereas the plane of immanence is the "bloc of space-time" from which "closed systems, finite sets, are cut" (59). And here Deleuze connects film and flux:

The plane of immanence is the movement (the facet of movement) which is established between the parts of each system and between one system and another, which crosses them all, stirs them all up together and subjects them all to the condition which prevents them from

---

12 Deleuze is referring here, as the basis of his readings, to Chapter 4 of Bergson's *Creative Evolution* and to references to cinema made by Merleau-Ponty in *Phenomenology of Perception*, for example 78.

being absolutely closed. It is therefore a section; but [...] it is not an immobile and instantaneous section, it is a mobile section, a temporal section or perspective. It is a bloc of space-time, since the time of the movement which is at work within it is part of it every time. There is even an infinite series of such blocs or mobile sections which will be, as it were, so many presentations of the plane, corresponding to the succession of movements in the universe. And the plane is not distinct from this presentation of planes. This is not mechanism, it is machinism. The material universe, the plane of immanence, is the *machine assemblage of movement-images*. Here Bergson is startlingly ahead of his time: it is the universe as cinema in itself, a metacinema. (59)

Everything depends, of course, on the identity of images as they exist either in the a-centered flux or as elements in framed sets or slices thereof. It is this identity, as I mentioned before, that will eliminate the gulf between subjective representation or conscious thought and reality as its content, and ultimately hinge a theory of material subjects that the universe could do without, i.e. a non-correlationist metaphysics. But we have yet to see how these contingent centers of being, these "cinematic" framers of images that we are, come to be. At this point, we still have not moved beyond the flux of impersonal images.

Before we do so, however, Deleuze introduces a perspective that emphasizes the radical difference between phenomenology and Bergsonism, at least as he understands them. To explain the notion of impersonal images—"images in themselves which are not for anyone and are not addressed to anyone" (59)—Deleuze offers that "the plane of immanence is entirely made up of Light. The set of movements, of actions and reactions is light which diffuses, which is propagated 'without resistance and without loss'. The identity of the image and movement stems from the identity of matter and light" (60). According to Deleuze, "This breaks with the whole philosophical tradition which placed light on the side of the spirit and made consciousness a beam of light which drew things out of their native darkness" (60)—and phenomenology is in this tradition by virtue of treating perception "as if the intentionality of consciousness was the ray of an electric lamp ('all consciousness is consciousness *of* something...')" (60). Here, for Deleuze, is the crucial difference:

For Bergson, it is completely the opposite. Things are luminous by themselves without anything illuminating them: all consciousness *is* something, it is indistinguishable from the thing, that is from the image of light. But here it is a consciousness by right [*en droit*], which is diffused everywhere and yet does not reveal its source [*ne se révèle pas*]: it is indeed a photo which has already been taken and shot in all things and for all points, but which is 'translucent'. If, subsequently, a *de facto* consciousness is constituted in the universe, at a particular place on the plane of immanence, it is because very special images will have stopped or reflected the light, and will have provided the 'black screen' which the plate lacked. In short, it is not consciousness which is light, it is the set of images, or the light, which is consciousness, immanent to matter. As for *our* consciousness of fact, it will merely be the opacity without which light 'is always propagated without its source ever having been revealed'. The opposition between Bergson and phenomenology is, in this respect, a radical one. (60-61)

As we shall see, with his understanding of Bergson's notion of the photographic basis of flux, projected onto embodied subjects as onto cinema screens, Deleuze is laying the groundwork for a subtle but fundamental transformation of Bergson, one that is of central relevance for the notions of non-correlationist media theory and cinematic double vision.

It is with the equation of matter = movement = image = *light* in mind that we must approach Deleuze's further discussion of Bergson's deduction of consciousness, which begins with the introduction of "an *interval*" on the plane of immanence, or "a gap between the action and reaction" (*Cinema 1* 61). This interval distinguishes "living images" from the rest, which are subject to a push and pull on all sides; the living image, by contrast, possesses a "specialised facet, which will later be called receptive or sensorial," which functions to isolate certain images but not others (61). Living images, in Bergson's words, "allow to pass through them, so to speak, those external influences which are indifferent to them; the others isolated, become 'perceptions' by their very isolation" (*Matter and Memory* 28-29; qtd. in Deleuze 62). Continuing his ontologization of cinema, Deleuze glosses this non-conscious act of perception as an act of "framing" (62)—thereby sealing the analogy of the cinema screen and the living being (as bodily organism with or without an articulated consciousness) *qua* center of indetermination (62). From here, it is an easy series of steps to the derivation of an essentially cinematic subjectivity, the "first material moment" of which is the subtractive action of perception (63), accompanied by the "curvature" of the universe as a "horizon" for action—"the second material aspect of subjectivity" (64-65). In between, in the interval or gap between incoming action (or perception) and outgoing action (i.e. action proper), there is affection—"a coincidence of subject and object, or the way in which the subject perceives itself, or rather experiences itself or feels itself 'from the inside' (third material aspect of subjectivity)" (65). Affection "re-establishes the relation" between the inward and outward motions interrupted by the living being as a center of indetermination (66). In conclusion, Deleuze claims:

All things considered, *movement-images divide into three sorts of images when they are related to a centre of indetermination as to a special image*: perception-images, action-images and affection-images. And each one of us, the special image or the contingent centre, is nothing but an assemblage [*agencement*] of three images, a consolidate [*consolidé*] of perception-images, action-images and affection-images. (66)

We are, therefore, perfectly analogous to film, which also consists of these image types. And though this conclusion bears some comparison to Sobchack's imputation to film of a quasi-human lived body, Deleuze's analogy in fact represents a radical inversion of her phenomenological thesis. For here it is the human agent that approximates the nonhuman, cinematic one, and not the other way around. As a result, film is not bound normatively to copy the example set for it by the situated subjectivity of intentional consciousness; instead, film itself sets the standard, offering to us a means, an image, with which to "extinguish" ourselves (66-70) and reach back to the a-centered flux of transitionality itself. As Deleuze goes on to argue in *Cinema 2*, film can even offer images of pure temporality—time itself, freed from situation and movement altogether.

If this were in fact the whole story, we might have a basis here to argue, siding with Deleuze against Sobchack, that a non-correlationist media theory can dispense with phenomenology altogether—that, in effect, *double* vision is quite unnecessary for understanding the cinema or anything else for that matter. A Bergsonian lens focused on flux alone would provide the means for grasping the dynamics of anthropotechnical transitionality. But, as I mentioned above, Deleuze has transformed Bergson's thought with the line of reasoning that takes off from an identification of image, matter, and movement with *light*. Mark Hansen, whose *New Philosophy for New Media* is in a significant sense centered around an effort to reclaim Bergson from Deleuze's appropriation, has identified the change as a deformation of Bergson's affective faculty and a bracketing of its richly embodied nature (Hansen, *New Philosophy* 6). Rather than the active affections described by Bergson, which "always interpose themselves between the excitations that I receive from without and the movements which I am about to execute, as though they had some undefined influence on the final issue" (*Matter and Memory* 1-2), Deleuze assimilates affection, in the guise of the affection-image, to perception, which for Deleuze is a passive framing. This, according to Hansen, is fundamentally at odds with Bergson, for whom the "central concepts of affection and memory [...] render perception constitutively *impure*"—and this impurity "correlates perception with the concrete life of the body" (*New Philosophy* 4). Bergson is explicit about the fact that his discussion of perception as analogous to photography (*Matter and Memory* 31-32) is designed to illustrate only the notion of "*pure* perception" (39), whereas the latter is in fact a theoretical construct abstracted (for purposes of argumentation) from the factual reality that affection is always "alloyed" to perception (59-60). Thus, as Hansen argues, Deleuze's "homology" between framing and the body as a center of indetermination is based on a "progressive disembodying of the center of indetermination," which is effected by the replacement of embodied affection with "affection as a concrete type of image—the affection-image—defined exclusively by the protracted interruption of the sensorimotor circuit, the interruption, that is, of the *form* of the movement-image" (*New Philosophy* 6). This sets the trajectory, then, for the course that peaks in Deleuze's notion of the time-image, which overcomes the subordination of time to movement through space and therefore, according to Hansen, "can be understood as a realization of the cinema's capacity to instance the universal flux of images, or more exactly, to divorce perception entirely from (human) embodiment" (6). Further, "[b]y rendering cinema homologous with the universal flux of images as such, Deleuze effectively imposes a purely formal understanding of cinematic framing and thus suspends the crucial function accorded the living body on Bergson's account" (7).

What this means, in the most basic terms, is that the body, in Deleuze's appropriation of Bergson, is reduced to "the passive correlate of linkages between images" (Hansen, *New Philosophy* 7)—or, in the term Deleuze borrows from Bergson, the "black screen." What Deleuze ignores is Bergson's insistence on the theoretical nature of this screen, which, from the perspective of his later correction of the theory of pure perception, must be seen as a caricature of the rich dimensionality of embodied perception, a caricature which fails to "take into account the fact that our body is not a mathematical point in space" (Bergson, *Matter and Memory* 60). As Tim Lenoir puts it in his foreword to Hansen's *New Philosophy*, "In this account the body becomes relatively passive, a site of technical inscription of movement-images instead of the active source framing otherwise formless information. On the one side is the world of preformed images, technically framed as movement-images; on the other is the sensorimotor apparatus of the individual that passively correlates them" (xxi). For Bergson, things are not so cut-and-dry; for affection—and Massumi's notion of "passion" is true to this insight—inherently mixes the inside and the outside. But, ignoring Bergson's argument against pure perception, Deleuze subordinates affection to it as one mode among others, thereby neutralizing the impurity affection introduces and eliminating bodily "passion" in favor of a passive body. As I have indicated above, all of this is included in Deleuze's meditation on light and obstruction: "As for *our* consciousness of fact, it will merely be the opacity without which light 'is always propagated without its source ever having been revealed'" (*Cinema 1* 61). Once we have identified Deleuze's mistake (or appropriational strategy) here, we see that his opposition to phenomenology—based on his reversal of the roles of light (transferred from consciousness to matter) and of darkness (from external reality to subjectivity as a mere material obstruction)—is unnecessarily and unrealistically exaggerated. When we restore, as Hansen has undertaken to do, the creative aspect of affection by which perception is always infected with the concrete embodiment attaching to any center of indetermination, we "discover [...] that the frame in any form—the photograph, the cinematic image, the video signal, and so on—cannot be accorded the autonomy Deleuze would give it since its very form (in any concrete deployment) reflects the demands of embodied perception, or more exactly, a historically contingent negotiation between technical capacities and the ongoing 'evolution' of embodied (human) perception. Beneath any concrete 'technical' image lies [...] *the framing function* of the human body *qua* center of indetermination" (Hansen, *New Philosophy* 8).

To bring this back to the discussion of media correlationism and double vision, we can say that a Bergsonian lens certainly yields a non-correlationist metaphysical foundation for thinking about the cinema, but that it in no way dissolves embodied situation into pure flux. Instead, as we have seen, the centers of indetermination that arise within the a-centered flux—whether human, animal, cinematic, or other—cannot be divorced from their concrete embodiment. Film may help us to imagine or intuit alternative modes of being, but it cannot dissolve our somatic being any more than it can transcend its own in a pure image of chaos. The justification for a phenomenological perspective emerges *from within* the Bergsonist meditation on flux. And an object-oriented perspective asserts itself *from within* a process-oriented or evolutionary vitalism. Moreover, as Hansen suggests, it is precisely embodiment—conceived as essentially endowed with a non-conscious, affective material "underside"—that insures us against ahistorical formalisms and enables us to account for the transitionalities marking an anthropotechnical evolution. Clearly, then, my plea for a double vision does not mean that an unmodified Deleuzo-Bergsonian perspective should be installed parallel to a Merleau-Pontean one on the model of Sobchack's film theory. The arguments I have presented here have aimed to reveal the shortcomings of both, but my aim has not been entirely critical. It is my continued belief that the two perspectives can each profit from being played against the other: Deleuze's Bergson relativizes and renders contingent Sobchack's Merleau-Ponty, while the latter brings the former back down to earth or back into dialogue with the situated beings we happen to be.

So much, in theory, for double vision. In practice, it will have to prove itself as a productive means of approaching cinema and, in particular, Frankenstein films. But there might be a lingering doubt about whether the result of the confrontation between Sobchack and Deleuze has really ended up yielding a *non-correlationist* approach to media. Hasn't the argument against Deleuze's abstraction of framing from embodiment in fact brought media and mediality right back to the fold of anthropocentrism, saving it at the last moment from the gaping abyss of universal flux? And what is that flux if not precisely the Great Outdoors? Perhaps, one might say, the enterprise has been doomed from the start, quite simply because the anthropotechnical evolution sought in the postnatural perspective is theorized as *between* a phenomenal "inside" and an aphenomenal "outside." However, this would imply a narrow conception of correlationism—or a narrow view of why, for that matter, we should be interested in avoiding it. If the point of critiquing correlationism were to escape the phenomenal realm altogether, we would probably be better off in Zen monasteries than in movie theaters. I take it, though, that the critique of correlationism is designed to decenter our *de facto* centered perspectives— not to destroy the phenomenal realm (as in Deleuze's time-image or in Kittler's post-media future) but to imbue it with a historical depth that exceeds that of an empirical history, to rend open its infrastructure for comparison with the infrastructure of other human and nonhuman modes of being. Any such comparative endeavor will certainly require keeping (at least) one foot in the situation that material embodiment assigns us. Not that we could do otherwise. But this doesn't mean that we are doomed in our endeavor to see with other eyes—this, of course, is one of the central functions of cinema. As for media in this postnatural perspective, they are no longer thought here from *within* the horizon of correlationism but, we might say, *as* that horizon—as *the very correlators* of the phenomenal, the concrete, and the empirical on the one hand and the noumenal, the abstract, and the transcendental on the other. This means that media are themselves not merely artifactual and instrumental—a correlational view of media *for us*—but are precisely media, that is, milieux *for anthropotechnical historicity* itself. This view of medium as originary correlator, which I will argue for in the next section, might in fact be said to represent the only possible form for a non-correlationist media theory: as we have seen in relation to Deleuze's cinematic philosophy, a simple rejection of the phenomenological component of postnatural stereoscopy in favor of a one-eyed view of flux will yield something that's non-correlationist, to be sure, but (as even Kittler agrees) it sure as heck won't be media theory—that is, a theory *of media*— anymore. For whatever else they are, media are always also concretely embodied in objects, but in objects with a special relation to our own embodiment. They exceed their correlation as intentional objects by materially informing the shape of intentionality as such. Thus, media are thought non-correlationally as *connecting* the inside of empirical-phenomenal situation with the outside of non-situated becoming, as *grounding* the very possibility of correlationist metaphysical perspectives from the liminal, non-correlational, material cusp that defines anthropotechnical historicity.

Let me close with one final suggestion for conceiving the interplay of perspectives constituting a productive cinematic double vision. In the course of developing an object-oriented approach to video games, Ian Bogost has provocatively proposed doing an "alien phenomenology" for inanimate objects and technical systems.[13] We

---

13 See Bogost's "The Phenomenology of Video Games." Bogost has also given a presentation on this topic, entitled "Alien Phenomenology: A Pragmatic Speculative Realism," at

might say that Sobchack, with her notion that film has a lived body, and Deleuze, with his notion that human subjectivity is merely an iteration of cosmic cinema, each in their own way contribute something to an alien phenomenology of film. Each, however, fails to carry it out: Sobchack assimilates the filmic body normatively to the human body, and Deleuze reduces the framing function of affective embodiment to the technical framing of the cinematic apparatus. The failure, as I see it, lies in the isolation of the two perspectives. What we require, I suggest, is an oscillating vision that will understand the correspondences between a particular form of cinema and a particular human situation, as revealed in Sobchack's study, but that will also learn to relativize this correspondence on the basis of the nonanthropocentric contingency introduced by Deleuze—and from there begin to feel out the differences between various historically dominant modes of cinematic embodiment and, on that basis, to intuit more radically idiosyncratic manifestations of affective and embodied deviation (rather than merely normative deviance). Would it be possible, on the basis of a cinematic double vision, to imaginatively feel our way into profoundly different, non-anthropomorphic filmic bodies and to describe their difference from our own being, that is, their specific positions between objective framings and subjective framers of material experience? If something like this is possible—and this of course remains to be seen—then the task of cinematic double vision could be understood as a sort of anthropotechnical ethnography, one that would offer, by means of its break with correlationism, a hope not unlike that promised (though certainly not always fulfilled) by traditional ethnography: that we may become more tolerant, open, and just with respect to difference and variation—in both the human *and the nonhuman* realm of agency.

MEDIA IN THE MIDDLE

In this chapter so far, I have been shuttling back and forth between two extremes, between a general metaphysics and the specific case of cinema; however, it is imperative that we turn our attention now to the link that enables movement between these extremes, and that we carefully consider the middle term between them: *media*. Only in this way will it be possible to firmly establish by what rights cinematic double vision can stake its claims in the newfound wilds of postnatural cultural criticism. As we have seen, cinematic double vision is grounded in a view of media in general as, so to speak, doubly articulated: media are both concretely embodied empirical objects *and* pre-objective conditions of perception, intention-

---

the 2009 conference of the Society for Literature, Science, and the Arts. Since then, he has developed his perspective in a book-length study titled *Alien Phenomenology*.

ality, or object articulation itself. This conception of media links up, in turn, with the double-lensed metaphysics I have outlined and in fact defines the liminal spacetime of postnatural historicity or anthropotechnical transitionality. As such, media can be seen not only as the middle term (of an argument) that links my ontology and the correlated practice of cinematic double vision, but also as the (metaphysical) middle term between cosmic becoming and human culture: we return, that is, to the notion of media as ontology engines. Media *history* is then of particular interest, as it reflexively connects two distinct realms of development—referring, on the one hand, to an empirical or positive history of apparatuses and systems for the conveyance of cultural communications, and, on the other hand, to a deeper history of subphenomenal transitions that defines the historicity of anthropotechnical assemblages.

Accordingly, the theoretical coherence of my entire project turns on a specific concept of medium, and it is thus necessary that we develop and contextualize this concept before moving on. In the following subsections, I shall: 1) explore the relation of media and history and, in connection with this exploration, rule out several types of media-theoretical approaches as incompatible with postnaturalism; 2) consider Niklas Luhmann's systems-theoretical concept of media as possibly outlining the general shape of a postnatural media theory; 3) investigate and expand Mark Hansen's notion of medium as an "environment for life," which he develops in dialogue with Bernard Stiegler and Gilbert Simondon. In the end, I hope to arrive at a non-correlationist, postnatural media theory that will connect the extremes of metaphysics and the movies and thus provide a framework in which to reassess the monstrous mediations performed by Frankenstein films.

Media/Historicity

For purposes of orientation, I turn first to an article on "the genetic function of the historical in the history of visual media" by the German media philosopher Lorenz Engell.[14] Though operating in the context of a very different theoretical vocabulary (namely, that of systems theory), Engell links media and historicity in a manner that is not unlike the double vision I have here outlined. According to Engell, "The specific focus of media historiography is grounded in the function that media and history assume for one another" (33-34).[15] It is a question, then, of specifying these functions *as* mutual or co-determining. Contending that history is not simply given

---

14 The title, in German, is "Die genetische Funktion des Historischen in der Geschichte der Bildmedien."

15 All citations from Engell's text are my translation.

but is instead "a product of historical observation and description [*Geschichtsbeobachtung und Geschichtsschreibung*]," Engell infers:

> Media are thus indispensible for the historical constitution of the world, and if the historical world did not already have media at its disposal in the first place, it would have to invent them. Every history of media is therefore simultaneously – potentially, virtually – a contribution to the history of history and to the medialization of the medial; and, conversely, every medium in its historical dimension can be queried as to what function it is capable of fulfilling with regard to the (self-)historicization of the world. Media history can therefore also offer an overview of the genesis and transformation of the conditions of the possibility of history, for there is history only insofar as there are media capable of constituting it. (34)

Now "the genesis and transformation of the conditions of the possibility of history" sounds like precisely the area of concern that I have marked with the terms postnatural historicity and anthropotechnical transitionality, so let us pursue Engell's linking of media and history further. He continues: "Media history is rooted in the self-relation of the historical, in the fundamental reflexivity of a historically constituted world, just as history is to be found in the self-relation of the medial" (34). This does not mean, according to Engell, that media are nothing more than their "history-generating function," or that history is nothing more than its "medial conditionality," as if all history were reducible to media history (34). Instead, two nonequivalent views are said to be compossible: on the one hand, "media history can indeed be treated as an ordinary sub-district of the historical so that it settles into the role of a variously interesting component of a cultural or social history (or a history of technology or art)," but then "the special nature of media history [...] does not come to light. In media history, rather, the historical world itself can reveal itself as a reflexive one" (34). Here, then, we have Engell's media-historical double vision, which would seem to relate the empirical and cosmological in the manner I have identified as a desideratum of postnatural media theory.

In explicating his dual view of media(l) histor(icit)y, Engell identifies three distinct (descriptive) layers coordinated in a historiography of media. At the most basic level, there is qualitative change (*Wandel*), defined in opposition to cyclical variation—that is, novel and irreversible change set against the background of repetition and predictable reoccurrence (34-35). A step up from change is evolution, constituted as a "sequence" that concatenates individual changes (*Wandlungsschritte*) and relates them to each other causally in such a way that "one developmental step can be viewed as the precondition for the next and the result of the previous one" (36). In other words, the relation between change and evolution could be characterized thus: first there is an event, then a line of development consisting of a series of events. In addition to (and situated atop) these first two layers, a third stratum is formed by history—the object of historiography. Whereas evolution, according to Engell's treatment, is something that a system (e.g. organism, society, or medium) *undergoes*, history is something it *has* as a matter of self-relation to its own past (45). Only after evolving to a certain level of complexity can (and must) such self-relation occur (46). As with the evolution of natural species from inanimate matter, developments of the evolutionary sort can be described without recourse to the self-referentiality that, at least partially, defines consciousness as a self-distancing reflectivity in the present of now-past events; but while our own consciousness is the case with which each of us is most familiar, it seems certain that the necessity of such self-relation—and with it, of history—imposes itself at a lower level of organizational complexity. According to Luhmann, "Contrary to fundamental assumptions of the philosophical tradition, self-reference (or 'reflection') is in no way a special property of thought or consciousness, but rather a very general principle of system formation with particular consequences regarding evolution and the construction of complexity" (*Theories of Distinction* 156). Similarly, Bergson correlates indetermination (i.e. the self-relation of affection which contaminates pure perception and thereby allows for free, that is, mechanically non-determined action) not with an autonomous consciousness but with the degree of complexity of an organism's nervous system. History, accordingly, is materially emergent and does not presuppose discursive subjectivity.

History does, on the other hand, presuppose media, as Engell argues. The reason is that a historical system, always operating in its own present, must relate to itself in such a way as to locate events of which it carries traces in the present as events in its own past, must therefore constitute for itself a past, *as* past, apart from the present. This history-generating temporalization implies an externalization of the past, as closed, from the continuing present in which the system individuates or "subjectivizes" itself (Engell 46). Observing itself, the system describes, as object, those events and evolutionary developments that it places in the past. And this description, which need not be taken as a conscious act, requires for its execution a medium of sorts—an orienting relationality as the precondition of self/other (or system/environment) differentiation. From self-relation emerges a relation to an external other (*Fremdverhältnis*) (47), a primitive form of intentionality, perhaps, which can be said to constitute the medium of historicity. Phenomenological intentionality, which includes temporality as a function of self-relation,[16] can be seen as a medium of this type, but this does not mean that mediality or historicity is necessarily a phenomenal relation. Relationality or mediality here refers, in a very formal way, to the means by which a system structures (its relation to) that which it is not;

---

16 See Edmund Husserl's *Vorlesungen zur Phänomenologie des inneren Zeitbewusstseins*; also his *Texte zur Phänomenologie des inneren Zeitbewusstseins*.

hence the articulation of a distinction between system and environment or between inside and outside.[17] Putting aside a number of difficult questions regarding the compatibility (or not) between systems theory's generally constructivist epistemology and postnaturalism's pursuit of a non-correlationist media theory, the question that presents itself is thus: can the notion of mediality at work in this conception of systemic historicity be extended from its function of articulating system/environment boundaries and be made to account also for the metaphysical distinction of phenomenal versus noumenal? If so, it might be able, at least abstractly, to accommodate the postnatural notion of media as ontology engines—by which I mean, in particular, the idea that changes in concrete media within the phenomenal realm are responsible for reshaping the entirety of the phenomenal realm, both in its internal functioning and in its relation to the non-phenomenal realm.

Before we can evaluate this possibility, we must note a further peculiarity of the systemic approach outlined by Engell, an aspect which we have encountered already but left uncommented until now. If all history requires media, then media history is inherently reflexive: in order for a medium to have a history, it must have evolved to a level of complexity that allows it to observe itself and, *by way of media*, to orient itself with respect to its environment, including other media. In other words, media self-differentiate and thereby establish both their external relations (medial system/environment) and internal ones (defining, above all, the medial system's own history). According to Engell:

The respective medium therefore begins at a certain point in its evolution to produce self-observations and self-descriptions; thus, it also realizes self-symbolization and self-distancing; it gains access to its own, past developmental states and thereby acquires likewise the ability to assume an extrinsic relation [*Fremdverhältnis*]. This can be seen, for example, when existing, functioning media are forced through media change to historicize themselves [*durch den Medienwandel zur Selbsthistorisierung gezwungen*], when, that is, other media constitute themselves as "new" (and thus, in terms of evolution as well as history, as relatively presuppositionless) in opposition to the "old," established media, which are thereby compelled to historicize themselves. (47)

Media become historical by means of their relations to other media, and history is medial by virtue of media's self-historicization:

---

17 See, for example, Niklas Luhmann, "Das Risiko der Kausalität." Here Luhmann claims that media "repräsentieren nicht die Welt, wie sie ist, sondern sind Eigenleistungen beobachtender Systeme, mit denen sie eigene Unterscheidungen ausarbeiten, erinnern, modifizieren, um sich selbst zu orientieren" (109).

the medium constitutes, along with its history, itself as well; precisely herein lies the fundamental significance [*Sinn*] of any historiographical project. Thus, in turn, the history of media – or of a medium – becomes describable as the development of the self-relation and self-production [*des Selbstbezugs und der Selbstverfertigung*] of this medium; and, conversely, a medium's development can be described as a process of its (self-)historicization [*(Eigen-)Historisierung*]. (47-48)

This recursive aspect of mediality, this historicizing reflexivity of medial activity, would seem to exacerbate the problem of compatibility between systems-theoretical and postnatural approaches to media. There is a feeling of circularity, of endless regress, in this notion of self-historicization, and we may well wonder if the self-reflexive processing described here is not merely a formalization of the correlationist circle that anthropocentrically links thought and being as a hermetically sealed universe. All the more so when we note the extent of the constructivism involved, which sets in not at the meta-level of historiographical reflection, but already at the micro-level of analysis: Engell, in accordance with Luhmann, claims that "evolution is not a 'property' of the observed but rather a descriptive form that arises from the interests and possibilities of observation, a product of observation or a construct that emerges in the constitution of meaning [*Sinnkonstitution*] but which is always – and necessarily – attributed to the observed" (47). Indeed, the question of what separates merely cyclical repetitions of patterned variations from genuinely qualitative changes (*Wandel*)—the basic elements whose sequencing constitutes evolution—is itself said to be "a question of perspective and of description" (35). It is far from obvious how this constructivism could be compatible with the metaphysics of postnaturalism and the role it attributes to the non-phenomenal realm. Again, I defer the question for the moment, but allow me, for now, merely to intimate that the difficulties outlined here are not as insurmountable as they may appear, and that a systems-theoretical approach may contribute fundamentally, though perhaps more formally than substance-wise, to a postnatural understanding of media as the "originary correlators" of the phenomenal and noumenal, as I put it in the last section. As for the self-reflexivity at the heart of Engell's perspective on media historicity, I hope to show that it is less an obstacle to an anti-correlationist view of media than a central ingredient that will facilitate a re-linking of the cosmic and the cultural in the concrete practices of Frankenstein films, conceived as serialized (and serializing) mediators of medial change.

First, however, I would like to concentrate on the typological autopsy of media-theoretical approaches and their media-historical implications that Engell conducts in the context of his stratified view of the mediality of history. At the elementary level of qualitative change, Engell, following Luhmann, identifies three descriptive possibilities: such change can be characterized as a) externally induced, i.e. a "reaction" to changes or pressures in the environment; as b) internally determined, i.e. an act of self-correction or self-optimization in accordance with a system's internal trajectory or, in Ihde's term, "telic inclination"; or, finally, as c) radically "experimental," "risky," "unnecessary," and "morphogenetic" (35-36). At the cosmic level of postnatural historicity, I am of course interested primarily in cases of morphogenetic change, which Engell fittingly associates with "industrial revolutions, from the Neolithic revolution to computing" (36). This does not mean, however, that externally or internally driven changes are of no interest to a theory of anthropotechnical transitionality. Indeed, my argument concerning the steam engine as an ontology engine, where the industrial revolution was shown in Chapter 5 to have unfolded as a process of mangling, can be read as an analysis of the way an emergent morphogenetic change resulted from a to and fro between the internal programs and external pressures of human and nonhuman agencies in dialogue. As such, mine is an account not of change *per se* but of evolution, i.e. a higher-level causal sequencing and structural relating of lower-level change events. As for evolution, there are two basic types that this ordering can take: on the one hand, teleological evolution, which sees a "direction" in every line of development, "quite often accompanies the diagnosis of change as a process of external and self-adaptation" (37); on the other hand, "*eigendynamische*" evolution—an evolution according to a novel, original, or emergent dynamic of its own—corresponds to a focus on change as morphogenetic and, because it lacks the directedness provided by internal or external determinants, allows for the logic of its lines of development to be reconstructed only after the fact (37). Clearly, this description of *eigendynamische* evolution accords with my characterization of industrialization's material impact as a "silent revolution," discoverable only in retrospect, whose global impact on embodied experience went largely unregistered in the symbolic domain of discourse.

With Engell's developmental categories in hand, we are thus already able to say quite a bit about what a postnatural media theory can or cannot be. As a minimal requirement, in accordance with the postnatural analysis of the steam engine, the requisite theory must hold open a place for morphogenetic change and *eigendynamische* evolution, and so we can rule out any purely "externalist" or purely "internalist" theories of media. In the first case, media cannot be conceived as determined from without, reduced to instruments that are neutral with regard to the being of their users and creators, and thus subject to a straightforward social history of their development, i.e. "as epiphenomena, as *Überbau*, as reflexes" (Engell 39) vis-à-vis human actors, economic determinants, social functions, and the like. In the second case, media cannot be seen as autonomous, developing exclusively according to their own internal programs. Both externalist and internalist accounts of media will be, in terms of the media histories they imply, teleological and therefore incompatible with postnaturalism. Of course, Ihde's phenomenological analysis of mediating technologies already implied that any pure externalism or internalism must be wrong; and, besides, there are hardly any serious contenders for such a "pure" media theory. But, apart from caricatures such as the "vulgar" Marxist, real live theories also display problematic tendencies, leanings, and dominant foci that become visible—and objectionable—only in the light of evolutionary categories. To name just one example, Sobchack's phenomenological film theory can hardly be critiqued from the standpoint of Ihde's account of technological mediation, as the former is a sophisticated application of the latter, one that respects the non-neutrality and bi-directional causality of human-technological interactions. Nevertheless, as we have seen, Sobchack's "intentional history" of film is clearly internalist in the sense being considered here, the causes of filmic development being ascribed to the teleological unfolding of the medium's hidden destiny as determined by its authentic embodiment.

Engell conjectures that teleological models may be especially appealing at moments of uncertain, violent development, when media are in transition; then there is a heightened "need for exposure or elaboration of some sort of patterns and schemata of the developmental process [...], knowledge of which could reduce the moment of surprise, increase predictability, and restore to the whole of the transformation process a – negative, if necessary – orientation of meaning [*Sinnorientierung*]" (43). This diagnosis corresponds, as we have seen, to Sobchack's normative embrace of classical film and her rejection of the electronic media that have fundamentally transformed film experience. More importantly, though, we see here what is at stake for a postnatural media theory: it is the fact of transitionality itself that is blotted out by the teleological models implicit in externalist and internalist theories of media change. This, then, is the central reason why a postnatural conception of media must be capable of countenancing morphogenetic change, for only thus can it account for transitions (such as the transitional era of film of the 1910s or the more recent electronic and digital transitions) as anything but teleological developments of progress or decline.

However, as the case of the steam engine demonstrates, internal and external pressures and determinants remain relevant, especially if they are conceived as acting in concert with one another, and thus a media theory that puts this interchange and mutual influence of internal and external causes at the center of focus is significantly more interesting than a theory that favors one over the other. This foregrounding of bi-directional causal interactions is precisely the function of the poststructuralist concept of the *dispositif*, which takes aim, as Engell puts it, at "medial phenomena in which material conditions and properties of apparatic, technical objects are made imbricable [*verschränkbar*] with physiological, psychological, epistemological, and sociological structures" (41). In actual practice, the apparatus theory of the 1970s tended to elide transitionality as much as a strictly internalist or externalist teleology: the specific imbrication of inherent and extrinsic causal forces tended towards a reversible determinism—of the cinematic apparatus itself by an ideology that extends back at least to the Renaissance, and of the spectator as dominated and positioned by the apparatus.[18] Nevertheless, the underlying theory of the *dispositif* contains other potentials and resources that might be mined for the task of thinking a medial "dance of agency." Asked in a 1977 interview about his own understanding of the term *dispositif,* Foucault responded:

What I'm trying to pick out with this term is, firstly, a thoroughly heterogeneous ensemble consisting of discourses, institutions, architectural forms, regulatory decisions, laws, administrative measures, scientific statements, philosophical, moral and philanthropic propositions – in short, the said as much as the unsaid. Such are the elements of the apparatus. The apparatus itself is the system of relations that can be established between these elements. ("The Confessions of the Flesh" 194)

Paul Rabinow has argued that Foucault was in the process here of distancing himself from "structuralist" modes of thought, particularly from the Lacanian and Althusserian obsession with deep structures of the unconscious, ideology, and signification, which Foucault rejected in favor of surface relations; concomitantly, he was also distancing himself from his own earlier archaeological focus on discourse (Rabinow 49-52). Foucault's conception of the *dispositif,* in contrast to the more common usage of the term in film theory, thus resembles the networks of humans and nonhumans described in actor-network theory: networks which involve "translations" and "mediations" that bring forth through relation something more than the sum of their individual parts. In other words, the *dispositif* as network can be thought of as bringing together agencies or forces and pitting their internal structures and external determinations against one another *in such a way as to bring forth an unanticipated, emergent morphogenetic change.* Seen thus, we can ratify Engell's claim that "[t]he model of the *dispositif* thus effects the mediation [*Vermittlung*] not only of material and functional descriptions of media, but also especially those of an *eigendynamische* and an externalist perspective on development" (41). Media, on this view, become "mediators" rather than mere "intermediaries," to put it in terms that Latour explains thus:

An intermediary – although recognized as necessary – simply transports, transfers, transmits energy from one of the poles of the Constitution [i.e. the system by which modernity sepa-

---

18 See, for example, the essays in Part 3 of *Narrative, Apparatus, Ideology,* edited by Philip Rosen.

rates all entities into either cultural or natural, subject or object, obscuring the role of hybrid quasi-objects]. It is void in itself and can only be less faithful or more or less opaque. A mediator, however, is an original event and creates what it translates as well as the entities between which it plays the mediating role. (*We Have Never Been Modern* 78)

As I noted earlier, this connection of media (or mediality) and mediation (in Latour's sense) will be crucial to my historicizing rehabilitation—or better: refunctionalization—of the Frankenstein/film analogy.

At present, however, we are still concerned to understand what media are. Basically, we have only gotten as far as saying that, whatever media may be, a theory of their mediality must not close off the potential for morphogenetic change and *eigendynamische* evolution; this, then, is a necessary condition of a postnatural media theory. And while we have considered one way in which morphogenetic developments—i.e. transitions in the emphatic, postnatural sense associated with a radically exterior matter in flux—may be related to internal and external causal forces—i.e. forces that can be located within the realm of a given phenomenal and empirical situation—there are certainly other ways of relating them. Assuming that variations here are differences that would make a difference, then the mere inclusion of morphogenetic emergence may only be necessary, not sufficient, for the theory of media sought here. And indeed, this suspicion is borne out when we consider the media-historical practice of Friedrich Kittler, who also emphasizes morphogenetic change and chance events but nevertheless produces a deterministic picture of media development. This is due, as Engell astutely observes, to the "interplay of pure emergence on the one hand, that is, the sudden, autonomous, and in any case not causally reducible [*nicht auf Ursachen reduzierbaren*] appearance of surprising incidents, which then crystallize into inventions, epiphanies, etc.; and a grand overarching program [*Programmatik*], a governing cumulative progression, which is operative in media evolution on the other hand" (41). That is, morphogenesis is restricted in Kittler's treatment to episodic events that are subordinated to a tale of "the self-adaptation, the self-refinement of the medial sphere" (41) as the evolution of hardware. Here is Engell's insightful diagnosis:

Media's constitutional [*grundgesetzliche*] self-realization and dissemination tendency is thus combined with individual events, usually even attributable to individual persons, and with singular fluctuations. Accordingly, it is occurrences, often select incidents from the works and lives of the great inventors, that ultimately entail self-revisions of the whole medial system, that is, of the structure of the medial world itself. Here the motif of external adaptation and external control is reversed in the most significant way. In the first place, the pressure to adapt now works in reverse; the – if, at all, there is one – non-medial world or at least its extra-medial zones themselves become subject to a pressure to adapt. Thus, as it were, a medial *a priori* is formulated for all (cultural) evolution [...]. In the second place, in this perspective media evolution adapts, if it at all operates with respect to an outside, to external conditions that it itself has produced. Accordingly, every extrinsically oriented adaption of the medial system is just a form of indirect, reflexive self-adaptation. (41-42)

In Kittler's treatment of media history, that is, the internal *telos* of media, the entelechy of technical hardware, trumps both externalism and morphogenesis. Media's reactions to the circumstances of the outside world are seen as adaptations to media's own exteriorizations of itself; Kittler's strategy is therefore an implicit internalization of externalist perspectives. Moreover, the internal law of medial unfolding is set above, and made to *absorb*, the chance events of morphogenetic change. The sudden reversals and emergent whims of nature and technology, which in a postnatural perspective mark the impingement of a radically exterior materiality on a system unable to process it, are for Kittler after all just working towards the telic goal of media.

What this amounts to is a neutralization of emergence, a denial of *eigendynamische* evolution by means of reducing the morphogenetically novel to the merely *coincidental*, by locating it, that is, in the realm of the *incidental* or *situational*. Indeterminacy, in other words, is rendered a phenomenal illusion; or, with Bergson, "indetermination"—the disengagement of causes and effects by means of bodily affection—is eliminated by the transcendental program of media that engulfs all of life and all of reality in its technical embrace. At the latest, this elimination is consummated with the apocalypse of digital convergence. Clearly, then, it is not enough for a postnatural media theory merely to hold open a space for the morphogenetic; it must also place such change in the right relation to the immanent causalities identified by internalist and externalist perspectives on evolution. And the right relation, I contend, is that which I have considered in terms of a revised apparatus framework: an interplay between the causal forces of internal structure (the "telic inclination" of a given medium) and environmental pressures (including the medium's use by humans, but also its physical situation, wear and tear, political decisions, aesthetic choices, wars, earthquakes, late breakfasts, solar eclipses, insomnia, and workers' strikes, to name a few) together give rise to emergent, unprecedented changes that, from within the immanent framework of empirical-phenomenal situation, can only but appear as pure chance. In the evolution of media, that is, the a-centered material flux brushes up against and transforms the domain of centered being.

To review, briefly, why this arrangement of causal forces is the correct one, let us consider each of the alternatives. First, even before we have made the postnatural turn, Ihde's phenomenology of technology-in-use demonstrates that we cannot realistically eliminate either internal or external causal forces; this is the implication of technology's non-neutrality, its resistance to determination through human volition, in combination with its converse lack of totalizing sway, i.e. the fact that technology does not completely determine its own use. Second, the postnatural derivation teaches us that morphogenetic change must also play a role; else we are unable to countenance transitionality as anything but an interim phase that leads linearly from one fixed state to another. So we must specify relations among all three causal types. Internal and external pressures would seem, *prima facie*, to be of the same basic sort, i.e. ontologically similar in terms of their immanence within the empirical realm; Ihde's analysis suggests as much as well, but, of course, the proof is in the pudding. So consider what happens when one of them is elevated to the ontologically higher status of transcendent condition. On the one hand, a transcendental internalism such as Kittler's ends in determinism, cancelling out transitionality. On the other hand, to raise externalism to the superior position is simply to follow vulgar Marxism in reducing media (and culture, etc.) to epiphenomena. A more sophisticated version incorporates a social history of technology into media history in such a way as "to attribute the material development of media to social development," as Engell puts it. According to Engell, "Brian Winston's model of media genesis can be seen as such an attempt to divest the technical emergence of media of its *Eigendynamik* and thus of its originlessness [*Ursprungslosigkeit*] and to tie it back – if indeed 'technology' is granted an independent core of its own – to movements external to it, namely to those of society and economy" (41).[19] As these two examples demonstrate, the transcendentalization of one causal factor, be it internal or external, leads necessarily to an absorption by it of the other: in the case of Kittler, externalism is reversed and absorbed by media's internal program, and in the case of Winston, internal structure or force is merely an expression of external determinants. More importantly, in both cases *eigendynamische* transitionality is rendered impossible. Thus, we can conclude that internal and external determinants must be located immanently with regard to the phenomenal realm. The only other permutations left as possibilities, then, are the revised apparatus configuration that I favor and, on the other hand, a "flat" or leveling arrangement that would place internal, external, *and* morphogenetic transformations in the phenomenal-empirical realm. However, this opposition misses the point of the postnatural solution, for I am not claiming that morphogenesis or chance constitutes a transcendental condition or law—what, indeed, would a law of absolute lawlessness be like?—but rather, and this distinction is crucial, that the emergence of morphogenetic change must be seen as transcendental *with respect to the immanent causalities of a given situation*. The latter, by definition, cannot causally determine the radically novel

---

19 The reference is to Brian Winston's *Misunderstanding Media* and the revised edition, *Media Technology and Society, A History: From the Telegraph to the Internet*.

forces which they nevertheless occasion; the morphogenetic marks a *disengagement* of reigning causal forces (as in Bergson's affection) as the precondition of non-determined transitionality. In other words, and as I have intimated before, the indeterminacy I am after is a matter of *quasi-transcendence*, not opposed to immanence by means of an absolute gulf between the phenomenal and the noumenal, but instead conceived as the impact of a sub-phenomenal or infra-empirical flux of matter—the *same* matter of which the empirical world is composed. Media, I am suggesting, are the membranes upon which these perturbations are materially recorded. They are, by virtue of their openness to situationally defined forces of intrinsic and extrinsic causes *and* to pre- or sub-situational materiality alike, the "originary correlators" of the phenomenal and the noumenal.

Media Systems and Metaphysical Form

Let us now back up for a moment and take stock of the respective roles and positions of media in postnatural and systems-theoretical perspectives. As we have seen, a systems-theoretical approach to media is very different from traditional media theories; it is more abstract, less concrete or positive, than theories that deal with the specific media and technical apparatuses of film, television, writing, and so on. In the writings of Niklas Luhmann, such diverse things as money, acoustics, meaning, art, time, and space are at times considered media. A typical complaint, then, is that the systems-theoretical conception of media is just too abstract, that it's not really about media as we know them. On the other hand, though, the abstractness of the concept can be put to positive use, as Lorenz Engell's application amply demonstrates; for it is in virtue of its abstract formalism that the systems-theoretical notion of media can be made to serve as a schematic framework for comparing other, comparatively more positivist media theories. My own argument has benefitted from this formalism, and by virtue of piggybacking on Engell's analysis, the developing postnatural media theory may be seen to have inherited its abstraction as well. Both approaches are concerned less with particular media than with mediality as such, and specifically with the historicity of mediality. And in both cases, the historicity of mediality is seen to be reversibly related to the mediality of history itself.

We return, though, to an issue left dangling in the last section, namely the apparent tension between the epistemological constructivism of systems theory and the insistent metaphysics of postnaturalism, which is committed to a robust, nonconstructivist realism of matter beyond the horizon of the human-world correlation. As I indicated earlier, I do not believe these differences are insurmountable; in fact, systems theory may be able to define the general shape of postnatural media theory—but Luhmann's concept of media might have to be subjected to a sort of perversion for this to be the case. In particular, systems theory's methodological self-restriction to the immanent realm of systemic relations, which results in the theorization of media as always related to the operative distinctions that structure a given system—and thus ultimately *immanent to* that system—would seem to stand in the way of the postnatural notion that media are operative at the metaphysical limit, at the boundary *between* systemic situations and an absolute outside of systemless matter in flux. Thus, in contrast to the usual worries that systems theory's treatment of media is too abstract, my concern is that it paradoxically *may not be abstract enough* to capture the dynamic processes concretely embodied by media. In effect, I shall be concerned here to stretch the system-theoretical concept, as put forward by Luhmann, beyond its original scope—or, more precisely, to deterritorialize it, to dislodge or detach it from its home turf, *by abstracting it even further*—not for the sheer sake of formalist abstraction but in order to make the concept fit to describe *the concrete historical work* of media in a postnatural perspective.

Schematically, my approach can be seen as staging a confrontation between Luhmann and Bergson, much as I have done with Merleau-Ponty and Bergson before. This is not, however, a repeat of the previous encounter, because there are two main components of the present juxtaposition, only one of which can be seen as having an analogue in the earlier one. The first (analogous) component consists in the fact that systems theory's constructivist epistemology is to be relativized, vis-à-vis Bergsonian metaphysics, as the result of a methodological decision that is structurally not dissimilar to that of the phenomenological *epoché*. In short, because systems are conceived as self-referentially closed situations or relational structures, systems theory restricts itself to the description of its own observations of the workings of self-observing systems; though very different in scope and aim, systems theory and phenomenology therefore resemble one another in their demarcation of a relational and reflexive field of concern (self-observing observation, intentionality as primitive relationality) and in their renunciation of an attempt to transcend their own involvement in the objects of their study. Recognizing this basic similarity allows us to situate systems theory and phenomenology together on one side, Bergsonian metaphysics on the other. However, the second, more important aspect of the confrontation between Luhmann and Bergson works in precisely the opposite direction; effectively, it consists in demonstrating the *formal congruence*, as opposed to substantive agreement, of Luhmann's media theory and Bergsonian metaphysics. Only on the basis of this similarity of form can I claim to stretch (or mobilize) Luhmann's concept, as opposed to simply replacing it with a different one. Generally speaking, the comparability is based on the fact that systems theory is not just concerned to theorize the structure of a single system but instead investigates the relations and intersections of multiple systems and is therefore necessarily concerned with the zones of demarcation between systems and their environments, with the membranes where systems begin and end; and media are crucial to the definition and delimitation of systems—thought as quasi-spatial structures and as temporal processes alike—by setting historically evolving parameters for the possible forms that may emerge in a system from out of its overly complex environment. Media therefore function in a manner similar to the subtractive action of Bergsonian perception vis-à-vis the universal flux of images. If, therefore, we relax the stipulated restrictions on the scope of media in the systems-theoretical paradigm, so that they are allowed to operate at this level of metaphysical abstraction, they may then formally describe nothing less than the flexible membrane where the phenomenal aspect of the world ends and flux begins. The projected payoff of this abstraction is that we learn something about the *form* of postnatural media, i.e. the formal parameters of the site where affective, anthropotechnical transitionality occurs.

Let us begin with Luhmann's relation to metaphysics, which he discusses in *Social Systems*. Metaphysics, according to Luhmann, can be thought of as "teachings about the self-reference of being" (99). Classically, this "thinking of being" (99) paired thought and logic in such a way as to "*order the relationship between thinking and being*" (100; emphasis in original). By marking contradiction as a divergence of thought and being, their correlation was adaptively ensured by favoring logically non-contradictory patterns of thought. Knowledge's supposed correspondence to the world, on this model, is then in fact a matter of constructivist coherentism, but (illusory or not) this means of correlating thought and being through logic, according to Luhmann, makes sense "for a society confronting a 'nature' it cannot control or itself create" (100). This changes, however, with "the transition to modern society," for increasingly "society engages in continual discussion with a self-created reality: with persons who are what they are through socialization and education, and with a physico-chemico-organic nature that is directed by technical processes" (100). Thought and being become so intermixed that the old method of revealing divergence through logical contradiction (and enforcing correlation through its avoidance) is rendered unreliable; metaphysics breaks down. And yet Luhmann's own theory of "meaningfully self-referential systems," as he himself recognizes, bears a certain resemblance to metaphysics. On the one hand, the theory "lies outside the domain of metaphysics in the classical sense and likewise outside the domain of modern subject-metaphysics" in a number of respects: it does not claim to get at objective being itself, nor does it anchor meaning (or reality) in the subject. "But in its domain it formulates a concept of self-referential closure that includes formulating this concept within what is formulated. Its relevance for metaphysics resides in this isomorphy of the problem's formulation" (101). Ultimately, it is this "isomorphy" that I wish to exploit in my effort to hijack systems theory for postnatural media theory.

The obstacle, though, is made clear in Luhmann's explication of the "consequences for the possibility and the situation of scientific analysis":

> The old interpretation was that science depends on a corresponding rationality in its object. The version of this interpretation as an available ontology was abandoned by transcendental philosophy. It was replaced, in correlation with the inclusion of self-reference in the "subject," by the hypothesis that reality is unknowable "in itself." The re-objectivation of self-referential systems carried out here does not falsify this thesis, but rather generalizes it: every self-referential system has only the environmental contact it itself makes possible, and no environment "in itself." (101)

Luhmann's basic orientation is therefore an extension of what, with Meillassoux, we have come to call correlationism. It is a more general form of correlationism than is involved in phenomenology, for it is not concerned with the intentional relation between a subject and an object, but instead with the correlative internal and (relatively) external relations of systems in general. Another statement, part of which I quoted earlier, shows that the epistemological limitations announced here are perceived to derive from ontological conditions:

> Contrary to fundamental assumptions of the philosophical tradition, self-reference (or "reflection") is in no way a special property of thought or consciousness, but rather a very general principle of system formation with particular consequences regarding evolution and the construction of complexity. The consequence that there are many ways of observing the world, according to which system-reference each is based on, should then be inevitable. Or, to rephrase it, evolution has led to a world that has very many different possibilities of observing itself without marking one of these possibilities as the best or only correct one. Every theory that measures up to this state of affairs must therefore be located on the level of the observation of observations, on the level of second-order cybernetics in the sense of Heinz von Foerster. (*Theories of Distinction* 156)

In adapting systems theory for my own purposes, I shall of course be concerned to reverse its progressive distancing of itself from the unthematized materiality to whose evolution, paradoxically, it sees itself methodologically indebted. I shall argue, in effect, that systems theory restricts itself unnecessarily when it claims categorically that there is "no environment 'in itself.'" To mount this argument, however, I must first examine the role of media in the construction of systems, for it is here that systemic self-enclosure and the exclusion of the noumenal is codified, with the result that a truly productive media theory is prevented from unfolding its potential as a fully generalized theory of mediality, i.e. as a theory of media as originary correlators.

Inspired by psychologist Fritz Heider's distinction of medium and thing, defined as the difference between a "loose coupling" and a "tight coupling" of elements of a given sort,[20] Luhmann approaches mediality as a *relation* between a given medial substrate and the forms that may be constituted in it.[21] Substrate and form are always composed of the same basic "stuff," the same elements, whatever they may be in a given case; the difference, then, between substrate and form lies in their respective organization of these elements: a substrate is a loose coupling, i.e. a relatively unordered mass of particles, while forms are tight or strict couplings, that is, relatively ordered combinations of elements. Thus, for example, the loosely coupled molecules of the air can be temporarily ordered into forms, wave patterns, by the tone-emitting action of a radio's loudspeaker; the tones that become perceivable by such means are themselves a medium out of which specific couplings or combinations can be formed to produce music. Similarly, the letters of the alphabet constitute a medium in which specific orderings, words as forms, can be composed; and words, in turn, constitute a medium for the construction of sentence forms, sentences a medium for textual forms, and so on. As these examples show, the distinction substrate/form is strictly relative, i.e. a medial substrate exists only in relation to the forms it enables and vice versa. Accordingly, a medium does not lead an independent, objective existence but is related to an observer or system as "the operative deployment of the *difference* of medial substrate and form" (*Die Gesellschaft der Gesellschaft* 195; my translation). Luhmann's differential media concept thus bears a special relation to Gregory Bateson's famous definition of information as "a difference that makes a difference." Mediality is not just any difference but, we might say, the difference that makes the differences that make a difference—an information-generating and, more fundamentally, a system-structuring difference that orients by means of defining the objects and structures that can count for a system, as well as specifying the elements of their composure. Moreover, medial substrates and forms are not only structurally tied to one another, but temporally as well: mediality is conceived as the *process* of the coupling and decoupling of forms. A medial substrate is both the "whence" and the "whither" of forms: the source from which articulate forms emerge and the pool of disarticulation into which they return.[22] The emergence and perishing of forms, or its obverse: the departure from and return to the substrate—these are rhythms that define the very

---

20 See Heider's *Ding und Medium*.
21 For a detailed treatment, see Chapter 3 (165-214) of Luhmann, *Die Kunst der Gesellschaft* (translated as *Art as a Social System*). See also Chapter 2 (190-412) of Luhmann, *Die Gesellschaft der Gesellschaft*.
22 Thomas Khurana characterizes the medial substrate as the *Woraus* and the *Worein* of forms (101).

temporality of a system. Time and space alike are therefore constituted by or in media, i.e. through the interplay of forms and substrate, which relate to each other as the actualization and passing of positive patterns enabled by an invisible horizon of virtual or potential organization.[23]

Already we see here a number of clear points of comparison with the metaphysics of postnaturalism. Process orientation is perhaps the most obvious commonality, and the virtuality or potentiality of forms in the medial substrate strongly suggests the relation of Bergsonian flux (or Deleuze's plane of immanence) to specific framings of it. Luhmann's medial substrates are not empty or neutral spaces, not *un*-structured matter but a weakly structured (loosely coupled) set of elements that non-passively constrains the selective action of formation. Likewise, Bergson's flux consists of matter that is formless only in the sense of not yet framed or filtered in the subtractive act of perception; it is not, however, without force and (in Deleuze's term) "molecular" structure. In both cases, this is related to the common makeup of the respective realms: just as substrate and form share a common elemental structure, i.e. are composed of the same basic units arranged in lesser or greater degrees of organizational order, Bergson's flux and the empirical-phenomenal situations founded upon it are also made of the same basic stuff: matter *qua* images. The latter are essentially the same whether perceived or unperceived, the only difference being their relation to a center of indetermination that organizes them (and we can here think of the sense of "organization" implied in Deleuze and Guattari's concept of the body without organs). The molecular and the molar, like substrate and form, are materially identical. And if meaning or meaningfulness (*Sinn*), for Luhmann, is the criterion of a system's selections of forms, so are the needs and interests of an organism, for Bergson, the decisive factors in determining which images it will or will not "subtract" from the universal flux and perceive. Affective embodiment, in short, can be conceived as a proto- or arche-medium: the difference (of substrate/form or material flux/perceived image) that makes the differences that make a difference, i.e. that generates a phenomenal situation (the molar) through its contact with the environmental flux (the molecular).

To better understand what kind of transformation of systems theory is involved in this move, let us consider Thomas Khurana's succinct formulation of "four peculiarities [*Besonderheiten*] of the conceptual apparatus" of Luhmann's media theory.[24] These include: 1) the "complex temporality" involved, 2) the "intrinsic

---

23 The medium itself becomes visible through the forms that the substrate invisibly supports (see, for example, *Die Kunst der Gesellschaft* 168). And a substrate can be made visible by shifting media: for example, words as the substrate of sentence forms become visible as such by means of a medial praxis that takes letters as the substrate.
24 All citations are from Khurana, "Niklas Luhmann – Die Form des Mediums."

transformability of the medium," 3) a "changed understanding of constitution," and 4) the "specific 'materiality' of the medium" (106-111). First, Khurana points out the paradoxical relation between what I have called the structural and temporal linkages between substrate and form: they are considered both inseparable, and therefore "simultaneous," and nevertheless temporalized as a process in which the substrate is "always *before* or *after* the form" (106). Defining the difference between forms as "actualization[s] of the present" and the substrate as a reservoir of pastness and futurity, media are *constitutive* of time, and this fact distinguishes Luhmann's theory from any view of media as merely modulating the temporal perception of its users (106-107). In a Bergsonian view, we might say that media, such as film or recorded music, do not just telescope or retard temporal passage with respect to an objectively "real" or neutral clock time, but they instead constitute genuine experiential "durations" of their own. Moreover, the notion that temporality is constituted in the process of substrate/form alternations is isomorphic with my argument—at the heart of my plea for double vision—that historicity, as opposed to pure flux, is constituted only in the alternation of situation and displacement.

Second, Khurana points out that media, on the basis of Luhmann's processual treatment, are always subject to transformation. This is because of the dynamic linking of substrate and forms, whereby the substrate constrains possibility by defining parameters that are nevertheless only relatively stable, i.e. non-absolute, because they are *constitutively* inseparable from the "practical process" of coupling and uncoupling of forms (107-108). Because of this bi-directional influence, transformation is an inherent possibility, for "composition and decomposition levels" are subject to displacements and substitutions in which substrates are taken as forms or forms themselves are made into a higher-level substrate, e.g. "through repetition with minimal variation" (108). As we shall see later, such mechanisms are central to Frankenstein films' negotiations or mediations of medial transitions. For the moment, though, we can restate Khurana's point thus: Luhmann guarantees the possibility of medial transitionality by establishing what Gilbert Simondon defines as a "transductive" relation between substrate and media—i.e. an irreducible relation in which the related terms do not precede or exist outside the relation—as opposed to a more traditional distinction of apparatuses and (separable) content, where change is primarily a matter of content-level variation, or else requires intrinsic (teleological) or extrinsic (e.g. human) causal agencies to affect apparatuses. The advantage, then, of Luhmann's conception is that *eigendynamische* transitions are enabled by the transductive inseparability of substrate and form that, as a dynamic process, subjects both to transformation through emergent connections—much in the manner of the equally transductive relations of Latour's "mediations."

This brings us to Khurana's third point, viz. that Luhmann's media theory is not reducible to talk of transcendental conditions of possibility (109). This is the direct consequence of the transductive relation between the substrate and the concrete process of the coupling and decoupling of forms: the substrate is inseparable from "the immanent changes" in the realm of forms, so it can at best be described as having a "quasi-transcendental character" (109). As is already indicated by their identical elemental structures, the substrate is "not essentially heterogeneous [with respect to form] in the same sense as, in classical versions, the transcendental with respect to the empirical" (109). This, of course, is an aspect that is of central interest to a postnatural theory of media as ontology engines. However, as Khurana points out, what it means for systems theory is that the difference between "the constitutive" and "the constituted" or between "the enabling" and "the enabled" becomes a distinction that is "operatively made in the 'empirical' system itself" (110). This stands, then, in an uneasy relation to the double vision I am trying to establish. On the one hand, following Bergson's view of images in flux, I am also committed to the idea that the "inside" and "outside" of experience are not qualitatively different but share a common materiality that is at odds with classical distinctions of the transcendental and the empirical. My conclusion, though, is not that there is nothing outside the system—that the notion of the outside is merely an effect of internal distinctions, as Luhmann suggests—but that an alternative solution is available by conceiving media as operative between the noumenal and the phenomenal. With Bergson, this is the position occupied by the affective body, a pre-systemic position that is inconceivable as a medium in the systems-theoretical paradigm (because it is not bounded by a system) but which formally fulfills the definition of mediality as the unity of the difference between a medial substrate (material flux) and the forms it enables (the subtracted images that constitute the perceived world). Bodies, like media, are subject to "re-entry" in George Spencer-Brown's sense: on the one hand, they are pre-conditions for the articulation of concrete forms but, on the other hand, they become forms themselves. In this sense, the quasi-transcendental becomes immanent, but this does not mean that bodies, or media, are only effects of systemic distinctions, that they are identical to differences drawn within the empirical. The empirical is founded not on transcendental categories but on an infra-empirical materiality.

Materiality, finally, is the topic of the fourth "peculiarity" (as identified by Khurana) of Luhmann's theory. The positive side of things is that media, for Luhmann, are not completely reducible to objectified "apparatuses, technical infrastructures, merely physical substrates, or the like" (Khurana 110). Nor, as Khurana points out, is a medial substrate passive or neutral, despite the fact that it "has the character of a 'material'" with respect to the forms it enables (110). This would seem to be in agreement with the basic trajectory of the techno-phenomenology I have developed in dialogue with Ihde and Pickering, which emphasizes technology's non-neutrality and relational excess over and above physical objecthood. But the agreement is merely superficial. For, as Khurana notes, the substrate's *"material character* [...] is geared toward something different than what is classically treated as the *materialities of communication*. It aims, rather, at a 'non-meaning' [*Nicht-Sinn*], which is in no way extrinsic to the order of meaning and cannot be seen as externally given, but only as the condensate of a meaning practice [*Sinnpraxis*] itself" (110-111). While meaning, in Luhmann's perspective, is hardly a subjective or even primarily linguistic matter, the relation of it to materiality cannot be squared with a postnatural perspective. In Luhmann's treatment, the material *character* of media replaces a robust materiality, substituting a determination that is, in Mark Hansen's term, merely "relatively exterior" to discourse. Indeed, this weakening of materiality, which is essentially a correlationist view of matter, is the conclusion that is logically entailed by the notion, discussed above, that the quasi-transcendental unity of mediality as difference of substrate and form is *identical* or reducible to an operative difference within an empirical system.

But the restriction of media to a strictly intra-systemic role is in fact quite unnecessary: it results from a confusion of epistemological and ontological problems. As we saw earlier, Luhmann explicitly "generalizes" the Kantian position that "reality is unknowable 'in itself'"—an epistemological problem of access—to the conclusion that "every self-referential system has only the environmental contact it itself makes possible, and no environment 'in itself'" (*Social Systems* 101)—an ontological statement regarding the constitution, as opposed to knowledge, of reality. Luhmann's media theory offers an "alternative formulation" of the system/environment theory ("Interview" 121), and it harbors the same ontological generalization of systemic self-enclosure and of a constructivist, correlationist reduction of matter. Thus, according to Luhmann, the "distinction between medium and form [...] is meant to replace the distinction substance/accidence, or object/properties—a guiding distinction, crucial for any object-oriented ontology, that has long been criticized" (*Art as a Social System* 102). "The distinction between medium and form suggests another primary distinction designed to replace and render obsolete the object-oriented ontological concept of matter. In traditional notions of matter, one thinks of the wax mass that suffers the engraving and erasure of inscriptions. From a systems-theoretical standpoint, by contrast, both media and forms are constructed by the system and therefore always presuppose a specific system reference. They are not given 'as such'" (103). To be sure, the passive notion of materiality attacked here is certainly deserving of criticism; however, Luhmann's critique goes too far in eradicating matter as such, allowing ontology to be dictated by epistemology. When we realize this and (as I have argued we can and should) put aside epistemological worries in favor of a renewed metaphysical confidence, the path is then cleared for an extra-systemic, system-*genetic* view of mediality that is not transcendentally and ahistorically "given 'as such'" (as Luhmann puts it) but transductively related to the systemic situations and concrete forms it enables, and thus subject to the historical evolution I have described as anthropotechnical transitionality.

In sum, by dispensing with Luhmann's restrictions on the scope of media, by opening them to an absolute outside through attachment with the original medium of the historically evolving affective body, we regain contact with the radical exteriority of pre-systemic materiality. Luhmann's media theory, thus generalized, describes the *form* of this contact, i.e. the form of media *qua* originary correlators, which define time and space as essentially medial processes that, situated between the phenomenal and the noumenal or the systemic and the a-systemic, are inherently open to an *eigendynamische* transitionality that outstrips any immanent determination of its causality but is never divorced from the concrete.

Life at the Limit

The consequences of this expansion of media are most clearly spelled out by Mark Hansen, specifically in terms of his concept of "the medium as an *environment for life*" ("Media Theory" 299). Identifying the need to interrogate "an ineliminable oscillation between the materiality and the phenomenality of media" (297) as the crucial task of contemporary media theory, Hansen undertakes "an effort to address both the theoretical and the historical dimensions of media" in a manner that sees these dimensions as ultimately "inseparable, if not in fact indistinguishable, from one another" (298). The reason he gives for this is one that integrates, effectively, Lorenz Engell's thesis of the co-constitutive nature of media and history with my metaphysical retooling of Niklas Luhmann's media theory and, in consummation, grounds postnatural double vision in a conception of media as the basic relays between the human, the technical, and the environment. The reason, according to Hansen, for the inseparability of media theory and media history is that the aforementioned "ineliminable oscillation" between medial materiality and phenomenality "marks an 'originary' correlation of technics and thought, one that comes 'before' history and that is, for this very reason, necessarily expressed by history, by the history of technics as much as that of thinking" (298).

A specific implication of this view is that, contrary to McLuhan's "well-nigh pop-Hegelian project for understanding media [...] that would find its first principle in the incessant and ongoing shift from message to medium" (298), there is in fact a transductive relation between message and medium that resists reduction in terms either of technical determinism or social constructivism (298-299). The deeper reason, though, lies in "the co-originarity of technics and the human, in the sense that the break giving rise to the human as a distinct species simply is the invention of technics" (299)—a thesis put forward by philosopher Bernard Stiegler on the basis of work done by paleontologist André Leroi-Gourhan.[25] According to Stiegler, humans are intrinsically, and not just incidentally, technical beings; instrumental views of technology, which assume the separability of human agents from their tools, are fundamentally flawed in their ignorance of the role technology plays in the historical and cultural formation of the human, or what Stiegler refers to as the process of "epiphylogenesis": the co-evolution of the human and the technical, according to which the human is able to evolve "through means other than life."[26] The human as such commences with an "originary prostheticity," a dependence upon "organized inorganic matter" (technics as a third domain between the living and the inanimate) that forms the horizon of our historical experience of time, memory, and consciousness. Human life is unthinkable without technical objects, which for Stiegler are always "memory aids" and which can therefore take the explicit form of "mnemotechnics" (such as writing or, centrally, cinema), i.e. externalized materializations of memory through which humans inherit the (cultural) past and which therefore condition further development or non-genetic evolution.[27]

Drawing on Stiegler's idea of epiphylogenesis, Hansen elaborates his conception of "the medium as an environment for life" as follows:

Such a conceptualization draws explicitly on the implications of recent work in biological autopoiesis (which, among other salient claims, demonstrates that embodied life necessarily involves a 'structural coupling' of an organism and an environment), but it does so, importantly, in a way that opens the door to technics, that in effect contaminates the logic of the living with the distinct and always concrete operation of technics. From this perspective, the medium is, from the very onset, a concept that is irrevocably implicated in life, in the epiphylogenesis of the human, and in the history to which it gives rise *qua* history of concrete effects. Thus, long before the appearance of the term 'medium' in the English language, and also long before the appearance of its root, the Latin term *medium* (meaning middle, center,

---

25 Stiegler's views are developed in the series *La technique et le temps*, the three volumes of which have been translated into English as *Technics and Time, 1: The Fault of Epimetheus*, *Technics and Time, 2: Disorientation*, and *Technics and Time 3: Cinematic Time and the Question of Malaise*.
26 See Stiegler's *Technics and Time, 1*, especially 169-179.
27 On the notion that all technics is a "memory aid," and on the distinction between technics generally and mnemotechnics in particular, see for example Stiegler's "Our Ailing Educational Institutions," a translation of chapter 4 of *La technique et le temps*, vol. 3, *le temps du cinema*.

midst, intermediate course, thus something implying mediation or an intermediary), the medium existed as an operation fundamentally bound up with the living, but also with the technical. The medium, we might say, is implicated in the living as essentially technical, in what I elsewhere call 'technical life'; it is the operation of mediation – and perhaps also the support for the always concrete mediation – between a living being and the environment. In this sense, the medium perhaps names the very transduction between the organism and the environment that constitutes life as essentially technical; thus it is nothing less than a medium for the exteriorization of the living, and correlatively, for the selective actualization of the environment, for the creation of what Francisco Varela calls a 'surplus of significance', a demarcation of a world, of an existential domain, from the unmarked environment as such. (299-300)

Thus, as Hansen goes on to explain, "medium" in this sense does not refer to "a specifically and narrowly technical entity" but instead "names an ontological condition of humanization," one that *"necessarily involves the operation of the living, the operation of human embodiment"* (300; emphasis in original).

This emphasis on embodiment is fundamentally at odds with the autonomy with which Kittler would endow technical media, and it exposes Kittler's theory of media convergence and demise as based on a restrictive view of media artifactuality that is blind to the medial co-constitution of the human and technics (301). In opposition, then, to deterministic notions of technical autonomy, but also against instrumentalist or otherwise passive conceptions of technology (and media), Hansen appeals to Gilbert Simondon's quasi-autonomous view of technical development, whereby technics is seen as having an evolutionary lineage that is not subordinated to, but is essentially correlated with, the quasi-autonomous evolution of the human. The relational influence exercised between the two is thought as a "reciprocal (though asymmetrical) *indirection*" (302). That is, according to Hansen:

rather than operating through causal interference, technics impacts the human being and the human impacts the technical as respective perturbations to the organization-maintaining (and hence system-preserving) operation of the other. Technics and the living impact one another by triggering crises in the organizational closure of the other, such that each must change, and change not through submission to external forces, but through self-(re-)structuring that follows operational rules and preserves constitutive organizational principles. What results then is a mutual, bidirectional, asymmetrical dialectic of indirection: a punctuated, nonlinear, and extremely complex recursive catalysis of the living by technics and of the machinic by embodiment. (302)

Medium, naming the link between the alterior systems and developmental dynamics of the human and the technical, has thus been opened to the a-systemic outside, expanded beyond systemic determinations to encompass inter- and therefore extra-systemic relations—including, centrally, "the demarcation of a world [...] from the unmarked environment as such" (300). The "reciprocal indetermination" of the link (i.e. the medium) is reminiscent of the inter-agential dynamics described by Pickering's mangle theory, marking the emergence of an *eigendynamische* causality that is occasioned, but not caused in a strict or deterministic sense, by the interaction of human and nonhuman (technical) agencies. Accordingly, Hansen's medium as environment for life names precisely the anthropotechnical interface as the evolving site of postnatural transitionality and deep historicity.

As to the alleged *asymmetry* of indirection, Hansen claims that "the principles of human embodiment [...] retain a certain privilege in the transductive dialectic of the living and the machinic, namely the privilege of furnishing the very rules according to which each can change, and thus, the privilege of providing a model for the capacity of both to impact the other" (302). In effect, this privileging of embodiment is related to Hansen's rethinking of Stiegler's philosophy of technology, which according to Hansen "forges a much needed position *between* positivism and abstraction" ("Realtime Synthesis" n.p.) by situating the quasi-transcendental horizon of technics squarely within the empirical, in the form of concrete technical objects which contingently but ineluctably *instantiate* the temporalizing function of *différance*. I will not enter into the details of the debate that is involved here between Stiegler and Derrida.[28] Instead, I want to concentrate on Hansen's appeal to embodiment as his means of achieving the same transformative problematization of the transcendental and empirical that he ascribes to Stiegler while, at the same time, marking a real divergence from Stiegler's conception of anthropotechnical relations. At stake in this debate, I contend, is a matter that is of crucial concern for postnatural media theory with respect not only to Stiegler (and, clearly, to explicitly symmetrical positions such as ANT), but also in terms of the relations between Bergsonian metaphysics and Merleau-Pontean phenomenology, and particularly with regard to the possibility of cinematic double vision as negotiating between the positions exemplified by Deleuze and Sobchack.

Where Hansen parts ways with Stiegler is in connection with the latter's view of cinema's potential to colonize human experience and subordinate it to a technical logic capable of dictating not only memorial constructions of the past but also the very production of the future. Cinema, for Stiegler (and in keeping with his localization of Derridean arche-writing in concrete, historical regimes of inscription technologies), designates not only a specific apparatus but also the entire epoch institut-

---

28 One locus of the debate is the filmed interview which forms the bulk of *Echographies of Television*. Hansen's "Realtime Synthesis" includes a detailed discussion of what is at stake in the debate between Derrida and Stiegler.

ed in the nineteenth century by recording technologies such as photography and phonography and continuing through television and digital technologies. Cinema, we might say, is conceived as something between a positive apparatic "capture" (as Pickering might put it) and the overall or macro-level framework of mangling in our era. It is an ontology engine in a strong sense: for Stiegler, as Hansen puts it, cinema "is the paradigm for the experience of the self, for self-consciousness, for what philosophers call 'self-affection' (Kant) or 'internal time-consciousness' (Husserl), as it takes shape in our world today" ("Realtime Synthesis" n.p.). The reason is that the images of cinema (in both the narrow and broad senses) constitute "tertiary memories," as Stiegler calls them, building on Husserl's distinction of primary retention and secondary memory: cinema, in other words, stores experience in an externalized, material form that allows for its reproduction, and this has radical implications for the structuring of personal and collective experience.

Husserl had distinguished primary and secondary retention by way of an analysis of a temporal object, i.e. an object that is not only (like all objects) encountered in time but that is itself constituted temporally: in Husserl's case, a melody. Primary retention designates the relatively immediate experiential process by which a melody is constituted as a coherent object while listening to it, a process which requires that successive notes be experienced in relation to those just past and retained in the present. Secondary retention, on the other hand, refers to the memory that is activated when the melody is recalled after the conclusion of a primary audition; secondary retention, or recollection, is therefore parasitic with regard to the lived experience constituted by primary retention. Now, to simplify Stiegler's complex argument (which draws on and expands Derrida's prior deconstructive engagements with Husserl[29]), the distinction between primary and secondary retention is hardly absolute, as is demonstrated by listening twice to an identical recording of a melody.[30] Here we find that a second audition is different from the first: it may afford details unnoticed before, might be more accessible or more engaging, or it might fail to captivate and prove boring due to familiarity. My immediate experience of the melody the second time around is informed by my past experience of it, by my secondary retention of the first go-round, which subsequently focuses perception *qua* primary retention as selective. Moreover, this influence of secondary retention on a subsequent primary retention only becomes apparent through the availability of a tertiary memory (a sound recording or a film, for example) that furnishes consciousness with a repeated experience of an identical

---

29 See Derrida's *Speech and Phenomena* and *Edmund Husserl's Origin of Geometry: An Introduction*.

30 See Chapter 4, "Temporal Object and Retentional Finitude," of *Technics and Time, 2: Disorientation*.

recording of experience, i.e. the *same* temporal object. Not only are the distinctions between primary, secondary, and tertiary forms of memory not absolute, then, but their ordering is precisely reversed: tertiary memory injects secondary memory into primary retention. The effect is that tertiary memories, i.e. technical recordings of experience not lived first-hand, are capable of shaping human subjects' lived experience, monopolizing primary retention: that is, dominating the very locus of temporal consciousness in the present, out of which flows the future as well. The threat, according to Stiegler's argument, is exacerbated in "the televisual epoch of cinema" with the advent of live media, which potentially collapse the temporal difference between consciousness and temporal object altogether:

> the two coincidences proper to the televisual epoch of cinema (direct transmission and live production of images) engenders a temporal object of a new kind, such that what occurs is immediately formatted photographically and registered as a 'just past' 'it has been', that is, as a primary retention collectively and massively retained via this tertiary retention which the telediffused program indubitably and immediately already is. In these temporal objects which news programs are, it becomes impossible to distinguish between the primary memory 'just past' and image consciousness [i.e. tertiary memory], since what occurs occurs immediately by the image consciousness. ("The Time of Cinema" 106).

Hansen's response, in a nutshell, is that Stiegler overestimates the power of the technical and impoverishes the robustness of the human, specifically by bracketing crucial aspects of embodied agency. Following an objection raised by Jean-Michel Salanskis,[31] Hansen argues that Stiegler has reduced primary retention to a discrete, referential form of intentionality rather than, as in Husserl, a continuous operation in which the "adherent past" is glued together: i.e. retention as, in Salanskis's words, "a sort of infinitesimal operator capable of giving us, by the path of a dynamic production, the linear continuum" (qtd. in Hansen, "Realtime Synthesis" n.p.). For Salanskis, this implies a paradox in the concept, or a split between a discrete, referential aspect of primary retention and the continuous, nonreferential aspect that Hansen takes to be the primary (if not sole) component of primary retention as such. On the basis of the latter, Hansen reads Husserl's primary retention as "fundamentally nondiscrete and almost certainly nonconscious (beneath the threshold of what can be experienced phenomenologically)" ("Realtime Synthesis" n.p.). This, for Hansen, is a corporeal operation, the bodily production of time or temporal experience, or "the differential of the body," as he terms it. And the consequence of the body's meting out of time and making it available to consciousness, which positions the body at the cusp of the unmarked environment and the world of

---

31 The text in question is Salanskis, "Ecce Faber."

experience, is that primary retention is not subject to the cooptation by tertiary memory that Stiegler envisions. The "mnemotechnical constitution of time" prioritized by Stiegler is thus secondary to the "corporo-technical constitution of time" that Hansen identifies as an infra-empirical condition of experience. Hence the asymmetrical privileging of human embodiment in the medial transduction of human and technical agencies.

Although I agree with Hansen's argument concerning the embodied basis of temporal experience and the consequence it has for Stiegler's view of cinema, I would like to propose a slight modification, or perhaps addition, to the overall picture that it suggests of anthropotechnical relations. But first let us briefly take stock of the convergences and divergences amongst Luhmann's, Stiegler's, and Hansen's theories of mediality. The four "peculiarities" of Luhmann's theory identified by Khurana can serve as points of reference for the comparison and, thus, as a framework in which I will be able to articulate my own emendations.

Khurana's four points can be summed up in the terms temporality, transitionality, quasi-transcendentality, and materiality. *Temporality*, for Luhmann, was given concretely (i.e. intra-systemically) through the paradox of media: the simultaneity of substrate and form on the one hand, and the temporal spacing of before and after, on the other, which is defined processually by the relative position of the substrate in its function as a reservoir from which forms emerge (hence prior to forms) and into which they dissolve (hence after them). Formally, this corresponds to Stiegler's quasi-positivization of *différance*, his relocation of the transcendental horizon of time to the empirical realm, where time is constituted through the concrete technical objects that condition human life. It therefore also corresponds to Hansen's endorsement of human-technical transduction as the basis of his concept of the medium as environment for life, with the important difference that the primary source of time is transferred to human embodiment as the differential of the body. In all three cases, temporality is constituted within media. As to the second point, *transitionality*, this was guaranteed in Luhmann's theory through the emergent *Eigendynamik* resulting from the transductive relationality of substrate and form, and this conforms with the emergent evolution of epiphylogenesis in both Stiegler and Hansen, who see the transduction of human life and technics as initiating feedback loops that create changes irreducible to immanent causes (relative, that is, to the quasi-autonomous lineages of either the human or technics). Third, *quasi-transcendentality*, as opposed to absolute transcendence, characterized the relation of Luhmann's substrates to the forms they enable; for Luhmann, this involved a radical restriction of the scope of media, making them immanent to particular systems (or, more precisely, defining them as functions of operative distinctions made within a system). Earlier, I argued that the systems-theoretical model of media could be extended to the noumenal/phenomenal split itself, abstracted to cover the formation of the empirical as a whole from out of the flux of the non-empirical material environment, without thereby slipping back into a properly transcendental role. This extension is carried out, implicitly, in Stiegler's view of the cinema and, more explicitly, in Hansen's generalized concept of the medium as environment for life.

Fourth and finally, as regards *materiality*, Luhmann reduced materiality to a position of "relative exteriority" vis-à-vis meaning, effectively making out of it one more intra-systemic construction; as I argued earlier, and in connection with the expansion of Luhmann's media concept, the ontological generalization of systems theory's methodological constructivism is unnecessary and unwarranted. The first step, then, towards a more robust notion of materiality is to dispense with the view that systemic closure is total, that there is no contact with an absolute outside, an "environment 'as such'" (in Luhmann's words), but only with a system's self-constructed one. But there is more to materiality than this, as we have seen in Hansen's criticism of Stiegler. The latter diminishes the materiality of embodiment by failing to account for its concrete grounding of time (and space) in the continuous, non-conscious, and non-referential underside of anthropotechnical mediality, thus ignoring a material functioning that is immune to colonization through the images of tertiary retention. It is here, in the infra-empirical depths of the body, itself an evolutionary product of genetic and epiphylogenetic heredity, along with "natural" and anthropogenic environmental pressures, that the empirical and the non-empirical materially meet. Stiegler's underestimation of embodiment is correlated with his specific view of technology, which overemphasizes the memorial or mnemotechnical aspect of technics at the expense of its own materiality. Indeed, this priority of mnemotechnics renders Stiegler's a properly correlationist view of technology, one that aligns technical objects with consciousness, and specifically with a discrete and referential functioning of conscious thought. Only by restoring the unthematized bodily operations put forward by Hansen can we understand the full material implications of humans' transductive relations to the technical: as Hansen puts it, "the impact of technics on embodied life can only take place within primary retention understood as an infinitesimal operation, whereas its impact on memory involves a 'referential form' of retention that introduces a 'discrete polarity' between a retaining and a retained" ("Realtime Synthesis" n.p.). This distinction, unavailable in Stiegler's philosophy of technology, explains how it is possible for anthropotechnical evolution to take place, as I have claimed, by way of "silent revolutions": namely, because there can be *no referential memory* of the primary material impact.

Now it is in this connection that I would like to propose a final augmentation to round out the picture of media as anthropotechnical transducers. If we accept Salanskis's notion that primary retention is inherently paradoxical, that it is effectively *split* between a referential and a non-referential aspect, then it remains possible to recognize the advent of tertiary memory (including the cinema) as an evolutionary event with far-reaching consequences for the structure and operation of human consciousness. (Hansen seems unsure as to whether he is willing to grant the existence of such a split, but Stiegler's thought experiment, in which a second audition of a recording differs significantly—and non-retrospectively, i.e. at the time of listening—from the first, would seem to warrant it.) What would happen, though, if we instituted a complementary split in tertiary memory, if we granted to technical recording a non-referential, continuous aspect of its own? In other words, what if we granted the technical object a form of embodiment that, parallel to our own, marked its own material boundary between discrete objecthood and environmental flux? To be clear about it, the suggestion is not that tertiary memory is split between cognitive and noncognitive aspects, as one might say about our own primary retention, but rather that it has both a discrete and a continuous side, where the significant difference is that between a referential and a nonreferential facet. This would seem to make perfect sense when we consider that film, for example, is both a representational and a presentational medium, both image and matter.[32] On this basis, we are able to reconstitute a certain human-technical symmetry that allows us to conceive of films (and not just film or cinema as a general condition) as quasi-agential entities, actors in Latour's sense, without thereby conflating them with human agents or confusing their materiality with the type of embodiment that characterizes humans. Films *qua* tertiary retentions are then not reduced to being mnemotechnologies (or their referential memory-contents) but, similar to the continuous, embodied facet of primary retention, also embody a technical materiality that impacts on phenomenological reality (and culture) in a non-deterministic, transductive manner that situates cognitive life squarely in a realm staked out between robustly material agencies—between the subpersonal operation of the body, on the one hand, and the subphenomenal, infra-empirical material agency of technics on the other. Tertiary retention's non-referential counterpart to the dynamic embodiment underpinning primary retention can be thought in terms of "metabolism," which we have discussed earlier as a "unidirectional change that leaves no memory of its passing" (Jager 5), i.e. an infinitesimal material operation underpinning but outside the properly mnemotechnical function of technical objects.

With memory flanked *on both sides* (that is, on the side of primary *and* of tertiary memory) by a non-discrete, smooth space of matter, the human-technical

---

32 To put it somewhat differently—and parallel to Deleuze's characterizations of phenomenology and Bergsonism as claiming, respectively, "all consciousness is consciousness *of* something" and "all consciousness *is* something"—we might characterize this duplicity by saying both that "film is constituted by images *of* something" and "film is constituted by images *as* something."

transduction—or, following Hansen, the medium as environment for life—is itself more deeply anchored in a realm of *distributed materiality* or *distributed embodiment* (to coin a counterpart term to "distributed cognition"). The *dual evolutionary lineages* of the human and the technical, as suggested by Simondon, are accordingly each grounded in a continuous and non-inert matter from which they emerge temporally, i.e. in history, in the space of *mutual* territorializations,[33] or mediations, that bring forth the discrete formations of subjective being, memory, culture, and technical artifactuality where they meet; the quasi-autonomous development of each lineage then recognizes no prerogative of human or animal embodiment, so that the asymmetry of Hansen's transductive medium between them is significantly weakened or leveled. The payoff, though, besides further counteracting Stiegler's all-too-cognitive view of technics, is that we reach a more robustly anti-correlationist account of media *as the originary correlators*. By taking a wholly ahuman realm of non-organic metabolic materiality into account, we counteract the impression of anthropocentrism that adheres to the asymmetrical privileging of the human bodily synthesis of time and space as the primary determinant of empirical reality. We then conceive the production of the empirical, the constitution and maintenance of its spatio-temporal foundations, as a matter of distributed embodiment—of the transduction of materially intersecting entities, each with their own form of embodiment, their own manner of marking the boundary, embodying the membrane, between material flux and the emergent realm of discrete objects. In effect, we read Latour (taking ANT's symmetry, the primacy of objects, the focus on acts of mediation as productive of networks) together with Bergson (the vitalist impulse, the primacy of process, material construction by way of subtraction from a universal flux). We therefore combine, as a further aspect or implication of anthropotechnical transduction, process-oriented and object-oriented ontologies, conceiving them as indissolubly integrated, as defining the joint material conditions of temporality or historicity, of evolutionary transitionality, and of the material immanence of transcendence *qua* infra-empirical mediality. Process and object, according to this speculative realism, mark the originary interplay of substrate and form, defining together the medium as originary correlator.

The most immediately palpable implications of this admittedly abstract metaphysical suggestion are likely to seem banal, hardly worthy of the theoretical effort. For what this postnatural theory of media allows us to think, on the one hand, is a collection of facts that science and common sense very much take for granted. For example, a plastic bag is not just a repository of memory but an object with an objective structure that is independent of subjective intentionality or even the exist-

---

33 Simondon speaks of the formation of a "techno-geographic milieu" (56; qtd in Hansen, "Realtime Synthesis" n.p.)

ence of a human body. Not that it could have come into being without human effort, but it certainly can, and very probably will, outlast the human species. A world without humans, but not without time and space, a pre-anthropological history of process and object, a post-anthropological future in which plastic bags rustle in empty streets, articulating spaces and durations in which discrete objects struggle against a metabolic flux—in short, a secular scientific view of matter and entropy, combined with a more or less commonsense (non-reductive) view of "things," conceived without any baggage of the ecstatic being of *Dasein* and the like[34]—this is what postnatural media theory makes thinkable. (As if it weren't thinkable already, protests the skeptic, and without the need for an elaborate metaphysics...) On the other hand, however, this theoretical endeavor has not been altogether in vain. For not only does the transductive notion of distributed embodiment imply some surprising ideas about the non-linear course of evolution, about the inextricable interrelations of living, inanimate, and technical materials, and about the emergent cosmological structures of reality; moreover, it has some significant implications for media theory, which is, after all, what it was designed to illuminate.

These implications can be elaborated in terms of the standoff between Deleuze and Sobchack, the impasse of their approaches marked and—tentatively, speculatively—*aufgehoben* in cinematic double vision at end of this chapter's prelude. There, I suggested that Ian Bogost's notion of "alien phenomenology" might hold the key to resolving the deadlock between, on the one hand, Sobchack's ascription to film of a lived body that, unfortunately, she assimilates normatively to (a particular vision of) human embodiment and, on the other hand, Deleuze's establishment of a homology between the nonhuman technical framing of cinematic images and Bergson's theory of (pure) perception, by which Deleuze unfortunately effects a "progressive disembodying of the center of indetermination" (Hansen, *New Philosophy* 6). Recognizing that each approach was incomplete in itself, my proposal was that we institute an oscillating vision that would appreciate, with Sobchack, film's embodiment and its attendant phenomenological capacity to initiate or engage in dialogue with the embodied subjectivity of the human; but that would be capable also, following Deleuze, of offsetting and historicizing that perspective by means of a radically non-anthropocentric contingency rooted in non-phenomenal flux. Alien phenomenology would then be a matter of imaginatively feeling out the interstice

---

34 At stake in this view of "things," which is opposed to Heideggerian determinations as much as scientific reductions, can perhaps be approached in terms of the distinction, introduced by Latour in "Can We Get Our Materialism Back, Please?," between an essentially idealist conception of matter that underpins "thin descriptions" of physical objects and a more robustly material materialism that sees things, in its "thick descriptions," as assemblages of forces that exceed the geometrical space of the isolated object.

of embodied difference between specific instantiations or forms of the human and the technical (for example, the filmic). I asked earlier if such a phenomenology of the nonhuman, or of the transductive relation between changing manifestations of the human and the nonhuman, might be possible. In effect, my entire meditation on media here, my engagement with Engell, Luhmann, Stiegler, and Hansen towards the construction of a postnatural media theory—all of this can be read as an effort to establish that possibility, to ground cinematic double vision in a metaphysics that makes conceivable the intuition of material difference and evolution.

The result, on the one hand, can be summed up as a partial rehabilitation of Deleuze's homology: by granting technical objects (or tertiary memories) a radically nonhuman form of embodiment and agency, Deleuze's "progressive disembodying of the center of indetermination" is counterbalanced with what might be described as my "progressive re-embodying of the technical frame." This implies thinking technical "things," such as films, as engaging in their own forms of relationality and material indetermination, quite apart from the organic agencies around which our own perspectives take shape. Concomitantly, this opens Sobchack's notion of human-film dialogue to the possibility of interchanges between radically non-homologous forms of embodied agency. By establishing the human-technical transduction as a medium not of memory (as in Stiegler), nor biased towards the human (as in Hansen), but rather as a dynamic field of distributed embodiment, more intense negotiations between human and nonhuman agencies become thinkable—and certainly more interesting dialogues than the teleologically scripted interchanges marked out by Sobchack's "brief intentional history" of the filmic body (a history that is both all-too-intentional, i.e. teleologically modeled on human embodiment, and all-too-brief, i.e. determined to run out of steam with the alleged perfection of the classical Hollywood system and prior to the decadent embodiment of electronic mediality). It becomes possible, in short, to consider these interchanges as taking place in a materially embodied history, which means first and foremost in the indeterminate spacetime of non-telic *transitionality*.

That, schematically, is the payoff of a postnatural media theory for cinematic double vision. In the next section, I shall attempt to illustrate more concretely what this might mean by returning to Frankenstein films and considering them in the light of their (non-obvious) serial natures, by means of which the films are able to reflect on medial transitions, changes in the specific medial form of cinema, and to mediate (in Latour's sense) between the human and nonhuman agencies in transit. Thus, in the guise of the mediation/mediality pair, we return to the Frankenstein/film analogy, which we are now able to read as a non-representational and non-allegorical correspondence between cultural situation and cosmological becoming, established concretely as a function of filmic self-reflexivity. Such correspondence, we can now say, is rooted in the inherently linked and inherently *medial* transductions of culture and cosmos, situation and flux, form and substrate, message and medium. These transductions become variously thematic and/or problematic at times of transitional upheaval, when transformations of the anthropotechnical relations constitutive of media force media to focus on their own mediality (itself transductively related to media's historicity). As a series that spans many such transitions, Frankenstein films are therefore able to explore the logic of their own forms of tertiary memory and nonhuman embodiment, e.g. the logic of their revisionary effects on experience via the comparisons, virtual or real, that they enable: the technical storage and reproduction of experience (i.e. tertiary memory itself), in the form of the monster as a product of quasi-cinematic technologies of animation, constitutes one of the central self-reflexive foci of Frankenstein films' visions. The films' self-conscious employment of iconic images and figures (e.g. approximations, imitations, and parodies of the monster's image as established by Boris Karloff) offers, then, an interesting study in the selective variation of primary retention through the influence of tertiary memory-enabled repetition—i.e. the effects of seeing the same film twice—as this medial phenomenon is self-reflexively transformed into the ground for a different sort of play with repetition and variation, viz. the production of qualitative difference through the redundant repetition of more or less the same story, told through more or less the same images. Of course, this "more or less" is where the variation's at, but the sameness of the same is a central reality of Frankenstein films, which rely heavily on predictable plots and flat characters (not just flat-headed ones). In this interplay of sameness and difference, the logic of seriality is at stake, and the logic of mediality as well: Luhmann notes that one way to elaborate his distinction of medial substrate/form is "by means of the distinction between redundancy and variety" (*Art as a Social System* 105). As he explains:

The elements that form the medium through their loose coupling—such as letters in a certain kind of writing or words in a text—must be easily recognizable. They carry little information themselves, since the informational content of an artwork must be generated in the course of its formation. The formation of the work creates surprise and assures variety, because there are many ways in which the work can take shape and because, when observed slowly, the work invites the viewer to contemplate alternate possibilities and to experiment with formal variations. (105)

As we have seen, transitionality is an inherent possibility of the reversible and mobile transduction of substrate and form. A series like the one constituted by Frankenstein films, a series which operates with a continual repetition of "easily recognizable" elements, is able to illuminate the change involved in medial transitionality by staging its (e.g. narrative or visual) variations in a minimal (and if not unobtrusive then at least limited) way, thus opening the series' medial substrate to a kind of "slow observation" that highlights operational and material shifts over time—shifts of elemental arrangements that, considered punctually and apart from their historicity, "carry little information themselves." In this way, as I shall argue presently, the serially staged figures of Frankenstein and the monster themselves become media (i.e. substratal elements) composable into forms that selectively construct their own media history, and thereby serve as mediators of medial (i.e. both artifactual and anthropotechnical) change. It is for this reason that I take these figures as the central focus of cinematic double vision.

SEGUE: SERIALITY AND THE MEDIATION OF MEDIAL CHANGE

In theorizing a relation of seriality among the diverse adaptations, aberrations, versions, visions, remakes, renditions, sequels, spin-offs, parodies, and portrayals that go under the heading of Frankenstein films, my purpose is to create a framework in which to consolidate and reinterpret the findings of Parts One and Two, in order to finalize the setting for the concluding Part Three of this study. To establish the films' seriality, which (by definition) inheres not in individual episodes but between them as a matter of their relatedness, I approach them here from a distance and take a general, synoptic, and quasi-structural view of the films and their interrelations. In this way, we will be able to perceive the films as the cinematic unfoldings of a powerful, *eigendynamische* "storytelling engine" (in Michael Chabon's term) set in motion by Mary Shelley's novel but quickly autonomized as a self-propelling force of its own. Tracing the serial logic of this developmental lineage reveals acts of self-historicization, moments of medial self-reference such as those described by Lorenz Engell. These are occasioned by the films' negotiations of their relational positions, *qua* parts, with respect to the cumulative whole of an overarching series, which remains dynamically open-ended and subject to revision. Serial non-closure establishes a momentum that keeps part/whole relations in motion, ever shifting in a monstrous mereology that is played out in both narrative and medial terms, as we shall see, hence linking the workings of the storytelling engine inextricably to the development of the filmic medium *qua* ontology engine—which, like all media, leads a dual existence as concrete apparatic object and co-articulator of an anthropotechnical milieu. Frankenstein films' content-level treatment of transformative human-technological interrelations, in turn, virtually predestines the serial installments to be mediators of medial transitionality. As is clear, then, by reworking the Frankenstein/film analogy as a matter of a serially actualized mediation/mediality transduction, we take into view a wide range of topics, phenomena, oppositions, theoretical aspects, and analytical levels, which together encompass a veritable catalog of this study's concerns so far:

Table 1: Postnatural Terms and Topics

Human	Nonhuman	Anthropotechnical
Situation	Flux	Transitionality
Message	Medium	Mediality
System	Environment	Membrane
Phenomena	Noumena	Selective Actualization
Action	Passivity	Passion
Culture	Cosmos	Deep Historicity
Steam Engine	Epistemology Engine	Ontology Engine
Metaphor	Allegory	Parable
Molar	Molecular	Meso-Level
Form	Substrate	De/Formation
Object	Process	Boundary De/Formation
Author	Text	Storytelling Engine
Creator	Creature	Co-Constitution
Subject	Object	Quasi-Object
Classical	Primitive	Transitional
Centeredness	Circulation	Indetermination
Inside	Outside	Liminality
Film	Technology	Self-Reflexivity
Media	History	Medial Self-Historicization
Empirical	Transcendental	Infra-empirical
Naturalism	Supernaturalism	Postnaturalism
Nature	Technology	Epiphylogenesis
Cause	Effect	Affect
Merleau-Ponty	Bergson	Double Vision
Internalism	Externalism	Morphogenesis
Production	Reception	Interface
Medium	Intermediary	Mediator
Autonomy	Determinism	*Eigendynamik*
Body	Environment	Distributed Embodiment
Parts	Whole	Monstrous Mereologies

Table 1 offers only a partial listing of terms that have played key roles in the development of a postnatural perspective on *Frankenstein*, film, and the anthropotechnical interface. The mediation/mediality pair can be seen as an abridged or synoptic crystallization of the heterogeneous relations laid out here, a condensed view or conspectus that can be variously actualized to connect, review, and rethink the thematic and methodological vacillations elaborated under the headings of technophenomenology, postnaturalism, cinematic double vision, and the like.

Effectively, this rethinking of terms takes us back to the very beginning, to the question of definition posed in Chapter 1: What is a Frankenstein film? Having argued that the category cannot reasonably be limited to adaptations in any strict sense, but that a thematic focus on technical creation or human-technological hybridity was an insufficient condition for inclusion, I tentatively considered Frankenstein films under the rubric of genre. This treatment was abetted by the fact that the various films often seem to have more in common with one another than with Shelley's novel. However, as I noted then already, although there is heuristic value in thinking of the films this way, they do not in fact constitute a coherent genre. Instead, they run the gamut of golden age horror, science fiction, gory trash cinema, melodrama, comedy, film musical, and even pornographic exemplars; indeed, it is at least thinkable that the thematic content of the *Frankenstein* story invites such a crossing and confusion of generic boundaries. To grasp the resulting network of heterogeneous elements, then, we might expand our concepts even further and speak instead of an overarching Frankenstein "franchise," spanning various media, discourses, and forms of deployment, of which Frankenstein films are but a subset. There is indeed something to be said for the franchise concept, which is often invoked in connection with Henry Jenkins's notion of "transmedia storytelling," but *Frankenstein*-inspired film and other media productions do not work together to construct the same sort of expansive world that is usually implied by this concept, and which Jenkins defines at one point as "the art of world making" (*Convergence Culture* 21). Instead, each film tends to contradict the others and to erect its own diegetic world atop their ruins. Even the films of the two best-known Frankenstein film cycles, the Universal Studios and Hammer Film series, fail to create amongst themselves coherent narrative worlds.

Seriality is my alternative proposal for rethinking Frankenstein films' constitutive categorial interrelations. On the surface, the series might seem the least hopeful category, as I have already highlighted the palimpsest-like succession of narrative worlds and the lack of linear continuity between the films. So I will have to specify an alternative kind of seriality, and this brings us directly to the mediality of the films. For, as I shall argue, Frankenstein films constitute a series not on the basis of narrative connections between productions but on the basis of medial linkages (which includes transmedial, intermedial, or plurimedial connections as well). And in the space of these connections, the establishment of which opens a non-diegetic interstice between historically and technically disparate filmic instantiations of the *Frankenstein* story, a range of mediations takes place. Modeled on Latour's use of the term, which operates in the context of a general blurring of human/technology borders, mediation here links the function or activity of media with the social domain of conciliation, intercession, refereeing, and dispute resolution. That is, it playfully and strategically associates the mediality of technological media with the social activity of human mediators, who serve as middle-men or go-betweens to facilitate negotiations between conflicting parties in commercial, legal, or paralegal contexts. And, as we have seen, Latour's concept of mediation involves an emergent creative aspect that is distributed amongst human and nonhuman agents alike, and that transductively *generates* (rather than passively conveying information between) the terms of its networked relations. It is on this basis that we shall be able to conceive the medial linkages between Frankenstein films as transformative relations that modify the individual elements by associating them as parts of an emergent and ongoing series.

There is of course an appeal being made here, as in the Frankenstein/film analogy considered in Chapter 2, to a correspondence between media-technical operations and narrative treatments of human/technological hybridization processes. But, by way of Latour's mediators, this correspondence is open to an interpretation that is not allegorical but, in the Massumian sense elaborated in Chapter 4, parabolic: i.e. non-representationally expressive of materially emergent, ontogenetic changes (that is, transformations of the sort theorized in detail in Chapter 5 and, in terms of mediality, in the present chapter). In the role of quasi-objects, mediators connect human subjects and societies with the thingly world and articulate networks that transform and (re)define agencies of both sorts. These mediators elude the dichotomy between active subject and passive object, as well as that between the natural-organic and the technical. In connection with Frankenstein films, the value of this mediation concept unfolds beneath superficial thematic connections, viz. in terms of the light it casts on the medial construction of Frankenstein films' serial forms of narration. The proliferating interrelations among Frankenstein films subject these films to constant revision and rehistoricization, thus instituting structural or quasi-narratological principles of multistability and transitionality that correspond to the techno-phenomenological and social-semiotic principles of transition *qua* heterotopia discussed in Chapter 3. The association is not purely coincidental, for these structural principles of serial narration arise historically in the context of the technological and social upheavals of the nineteenth century—in connection with dynamic modern processes originating in the industrial revolution and exemplified as well in transitional-era cinema and other periods of significant media-technological change and attendant sociocultural-aesthetic debate. What I have in mind here is a particularly modern modality of plurimedial storytelling, namely: a figure-centered proliferation of narratives that are staged repeatedly and with variation in various media, and which establish themselves firmly in the landscape of popular culture, where they thrive independently of the controlling instance of an author. Figures such as Frankenstein and his monster develop an *Eigendynamik*, a quasi-autonomous momentum, that allows these figures to cross medial and generic borders and therefore to make medial shifts and transitions visible. Consequently, they are able to serve as mediators or middle-men between various medial forms—in order to negotiate, redefine, reconcile, or even sharpen their differences. Media-technological transitions, as I have argued throughout this study, involve revisions of the parameters of experience and agency itself, and a figure like Frankenstein's monster constitutes one of the sites where popular culture seeks to cope with such change.

The figure's ability to serve as an interlocutor or mediator in this sense stems from two interrelated properties—or rather: activities—that it shares in common with other serially staged figures (like Dracula, Tarzan, Batman, Superman, Sherlock Holmes, Fu Manchu, or James Bond). First, these figures move lightly between various media and medial forms—between newspapers, novels, theatrical stages, comics, radio, film, television, and video games. Second, in the process they establish self-reflexive relations to their changing medial frameworks, especially when making the leap from one medium to another or at times of intensified media transformations. Such serial figures, and in this sense Frankenstein's monster is typical or even prototypical, tend to be liminal or hybrid entities that, in terms of their narrative construction, span boundaries such as those between human and animal, natural and artificial, normal and monstrous; significantly, though, the problematizations of conceptual borders effected by these figures is mirrored by their liminal medial situations: a figure like Frankenstein's monster, as we have seen, straddles ontological and social determinations of the human while straddling numerous media divides (novel, stage, film, etc.) as well. Such figures therefore lend themselves to reflection—and themselves engage in self-reflection—on the course and meaning of media changes.

Thus, to review briefly these self-reflexive relations with which we are now quite familiar, the monster portrayed in Mary Shelley's novel already casts its ontological questionings as, in part, questions of media: the conceptual pair humanity/monstrosity is treated in the book in such a way that it is inseparable from the tale of the monster's language acquisition through a small canon of literary works. In stark contrast to this, the creature of the classic Frankenstein films of the 1930s is transformed from a highly articulate to a mute being, a change that informs the iconic image of the monster even today. In this new form, the monster still poses questions regarding the limits of the normal and the natural; in its historical context, however, this excessively visual—that is, photographic—monster also embodies a media-ontological question that is intimately tied to the transition from silent to sound film and which foregrounds the still problematic image/sound relations of the early sound cinema.[35] Thus, the monster of the movies, like the monster of the printed page, oscillates between diegetic and non-diegetic roles and functions and articulates variable interrelations between narrative and medial liminalities which, due to the serial nature of the figure's repeated staging, are subject to historical— and indeed media-historical—comparison. One might ask whether the monster's medial self-reflexivity is a product or reflection of its narrative construction as a transgressor of boundaries, or whether the situation is not precisely the other way around. However, following Hansen's revelation of the transduction of medium and message, we can safely put aside such questions as largely beside the point and, in any case, hopelessly insoluble. At stake here instead is the *relative autonomy* of the monster as a serial figure, which we discover by reconceptualizing its role in articulating the relations of narrative content and medial form (or, with Luhmann, narrative form and medial substrate): as an irreducibly hybrid mediator between competing media, medial forms, and the changing networks articulated by media, the monster and other serial figures play an important role in giving a concrete form to the media shifts and transitions that they document. Serial figures such as the monster are themselves, in other words, the transductive correlators of media and messages; they are media in Luhmann's sense, i.e. the unity of the difference between substrate and form, defining the parameters of formation (here, storytelling) and, through the process of formation and deformation, themselves undergoing transformation over time. They are the faces of medial change, the very embodiment of borders that are transformed, renegotiated, mediated in the transitions between media and medial forms. As a result, serial figures such as the monster are medial storytellers par excellence: the stories told by these figures are not merely told *in* media. They are, moreover, stories *about* media—if not in fact key episodes in the narrative of media history itself.

Let me be clearer about what it means to characterize the monster as a serial figure.[36] In general terms, seriality stands opposed to the type of closure that ideally

---

35 See Robert Spadoni's *Uncanny Bodies*, to which I return in Chapter 7, for a detailed treatment of this aspect.

36 My thoughts on this subject have been developed in dialogue with Ruth Mayer, with whom I collaborated on a research project titled "Serielle Figuren im Medienwechsel," and with the larger interdisciplinary research group on "Ästhetik und Praxis populärer Serialität/Popular Seriality: Aesthetics and Practice" in which we still participate. See the contributions to Kelleter, *Populäre Serialität*, which collects statements from many of the group's participants, including Denson and Mayer, "Grenzgänger." Also relevant to the

characterizes literary or artistic "works." A serial aesthetics corresponds to continuation and repetition as aspects of series—in contrast to an aesthetics of the self-sufficient artwork, an aesthetics which values uniqueness and coherence. Series tend not to make sense if their constituent parts, installments, or episodes are viewed as works in this sense. The characters, actions, and developments of narrative series must instead be understood in the framework of a continuing, unfinished narrative in order for them to appear significant. Seriality therefore presupposes a recipient who is in a position to reconstruct relevant continuities, for which purpose a memory of past events and an openness to future developments is crucial. We can dub this situation of the recipient a *medial* one. In other words, with regard to the narrative, the recipient is situated temporally and structurally in the pluripotent middle of things, *in medias res*. Series build their suspense upon this medial situation, which is why they exert a great deal of effort to position their readers, viewers, or other recipients precisely in this situation. But for this situation to remain suspenseful and attractive, the structural repetitions and continuities must be varied and occasionally interrupted. An aesthetics of seriality is therefore based on a to and fro between repetition and innovation, between those moments, on the one hand, that reinforce recipients' memory by connecting the series' present to the series' past and, on the other hand, those unexpected turns of event that prevent recipients from imagining that they know what's coming next. To recognize these moments of continuity-creating repetition and uncertainty-fostering innovation, which together articulate the suspenseful situation of enraptured serial reception, a viewer or reader must develop an awareness of the developmental history of the series. Because of this, serial structures tend to develop a dynamics of self-referentiality: series demand an aesthetics that reflects upon this developmental history and thereby continually enables variation—e.g. through narrative or technical innovation or complexification.[37]

There are, of course, many types and forms of serial narration, corresponding to different genres, media, and historical and cultural settings. For our purposes here, a relevant distinction can be made in terms of the characters that populate two basic types of serial narratives. On the one hand, there are the *serial figures* I have been considering here: stock characters who appear again and again in significantly different adaptation forms, contexts, and in various media over relatively long

---

concept of serial figures articulated here are Denson and Mayer, "Bildstörung"; Denson, "Marvel Comics' Frankenstein"; and Mayer, *Serial Fu Manchu*.

37 These dynamics are explored by Frank Kelleter and Andreas Jahn-Sudmann, whose partner project in the seriality research group dealt with processes of "one-upmanship" in so-called Quality TV in contemporary American television. See Jahn-Sudmann and Kelleter, "Die Dynamik serieller Überbietung."

periods of time. These are to be distinguished, on the other hand, from *series figures*: i.e. figures that are developed in a continuing narrative (e.g. in a soap opera, a novel series, or a saga).[38] Series figures tend to take on an increased psychological depth over the course of their narrative development, their biographical histories and uncertain futures being a primary concern for readers or viewers and a motor force for plot development. Serial figures, by contrast, are generally presented as "flat" and, as Umberto Eco once wrote of Superman, repeatedly experience a "virtual beginning" with each new production (117). Seen in this way, the seriality of the serial figure has something in common with the seriality that defines the serial killer: both commit ritualized, repetitive acts that may allow for formal or situational variation but which fail to constitute a line of development at the content level, so to speak. That is, there is no developmental logic that would connect one deed with the next; the serial figure learns no more from his or her deeds than the serial killer, who seems psychologically to be caught in an endless loop of repetition compulsion. The series of stagings that constitutes the career of a serial figure therefore has more in common with a series of murders than with the continuing seriality of a conventional television drama. We can say, then, that series figures lead their existences *in* series, where they grow and develop, while serial figures exist *serially*, as repeatedly instantiated, flat beings.

Looked at in general terms and without regard for any particular instantiation, the monster of the Frankenstein films is unsurpassed in its flatness: without any psychological interiority to speak of, the creature is often reduced, either by design or by default, to a killing machine—pure surface, devoid of depth. Most of the films tell more or less the same story of graveyard robbery and the assembly of parts, artificial birth and unnatural death, of the threatened villagers reunited through their communal hunt for the monster by the light of their torches. Settings, names, and other circumstances are subject to change, but the core of the story generally persists, which is why the seriality of the Frankenstein films is fundamentally different from that of a continuing series. Even when there are (usually only minimal) narrative continuities between two films (e.g. among installments of the Universal or Hammer series), the monster experiences a paradigmatic "virtual beginning": without having learned the slightest bit from its past, the monster repeats behavioral patterns and actions in a—literally—mechanical fashion. The viewer of a Frankenstein film therefore does not absolutely need the memory required by the typical television drama (not to mention the extreme demands made by recent

---

38 The serial figure/series figure distinction was coined by Ruth Mayer and developed by the two of us in a series of publications. Most programmatically, we articulate the distinction in our jointly authored "Grenzgänger: Serielle Figuren im Medienwechsel."

"Quality TV" programs[39]). Nor is openness to future revelations a major requirement, for the viewer generally knows more or less right from the start how things will eventually end up anyway. Nevertheless, the formal-structural characteristics that I have identified for series in general are not put completely out of play. The self-referentiality with which a series marks its moments of repetition and innovation is still present, but it tends to be deferred from the level of narrative content to the level of medial articulation. A Frankenstein film is generally quite aware of its seriality, stages itself as an heir to its precursors, and thus situates itself amongst their ranks. It acknowledges its belongingness to the series by taking up prominent and iconic elements of earlier Frankenstein films, quoting them visually or otherwise commenting on them. Against this background of commonality, the film is then able to assert its innovative difference from the tradition and stake a claim for a specific—rather than an arbitrary—position within the series. These positioning attempts are usually made not by way of narrative variation but, first and foremost, by way of technical-medial innovation. Frankenstein films try to outdo each other technologically by employing increasingly spectacular special effects, or they distinguish themselves from their predecessors with an emphatic use of new film technologies (such as sound, color, 3D, or CGI). The serial self-referentiality of the series "Frankenstein films" thus gives way to a full-blown medial self-reflexivity. The developmental history traced out by the individual installments of the series is not primarily the narrative line of development that is so essential to a linear, continuing series but rather the technical line of development of specific mediality forms to which the films have been witness. The most important innovations are usually concentrated around the monster, whose creation is the central thematic and technical event of the individual films and simultaneously the organizational principle for the series as a whole. The material bearers of serial belonging and differentiation—or repetition and innovation—are therefore concentrated in the obligatory creation sequence and in the visual appearance of the monster. And because of the monster's technical constructedness within the diegesis as well, it is an especially self-reflexive being: it doubles in exemplary fashion the medial processes and circumstances that enable its very existence. This means, then, that the creature's recurring "virtual beginning" is only half of the story. On the one hand, because of the tireless re-creations and resurrections of the monster at the content level of the films, this new beginning is a very literal rebirth. On the other hand, however, the medial history of the figure—representative as well for the medial history of the films—resonates materially and cumulatively in each new incarnation of the mon-

---

39 For a discussion, not restricted to so-called Quality TV, of the narratological characteristics of recent television series, see Jason Mittell's "Narrative Complexity in Contemporary American Television."

ster, which can never be perceived in complete isolation from its earlier manifestations.[40] A specifically medial line of development is therefore inscribed in the monster's body, where it is displayed in a non-linear fashion.

We are approaching a more precise determination of the serial figure's activity as one of "mediation." What is decisive here is the fact that a serially staged figure like Frankenstein's monster is situated simultaneously *in* a narrative and also without, that is, *between* narratives. Only by means of this liminal position can the figure constitute its seriality: namely, by providing a basis of comparison for the narratively isolated stagings that therefore connects them with one another. The thematic doubling of this liminality in the ontological constitution of a figure that challenges the distinction between human and machine further reinforces the figure's series-producing intertextuality—i.e. the in-between-ness of the monster with regard to the texts that narrate its story. For this doubling promotes a self-reflexive acknowledgement of the creature's medial constructedness, which allows it to escape the bounds of the single episode. In this way, the figure is able to transcend the diegesis and mediate between the competing texts to produce the overarching unit of the series. However, this type of serializing mediation is far from being a primarily intertextual activity, because, as I have argued, the serial figure is not primarily a basis of comparison for narrative differences but for the various medial conditions that both enable and are displayed by the specific stagings of the character. In order to function as such a basis of comparison, the serial figure executes a Gestalt-shift: it becomes a background upon which the medial ground of a specific production can appear in turn as figure. An abstract figure therefore serves as the background against which the medial development of the whole series of concrete instantiations can be reconstructed. Strung together as a series, the chain of individual stagings narrates nothing less than a selective history of medial forms—a partial media history for which the constituted series functions as a second order medium.

Between these two levels of narration—between the diegesis of a particular production on the one hand and the aggregate series of productions as a media-historical unit on the other—the monster articulates another, literally "medial" narrative as well: a story told from a middle altitude, where the figure's oscillation between narrative content and medial form is most dynamic. At this level, the situation of the figure is structurally similar to the situation of the viewer (or reader), whose attention, thanks to the serial dynamics of self-referentiality and/or self-reflexivity, also swings back and forth between narrative contents and mediating technologies. Earlier, I referred to this position of the spectator as a "medial" situation, a designation that is all the more fitting in light of its correspondence to the

---

40 Jane Gaines makes a similar point with regard to Superman in her "Superman and the Protective Strength of the Trademark."

self-reflexive position of the serial figure. Due to this correspondence, the serial figure is able to serve as a mediator proper: as a go-between for humans and media in historical and reciprocal transformation. With the popular serial figure, I contend, a forum is created (symbolized in Figure 1) wherein the significance of popular mediality forms for the social fabric of the technicized lifeworld can be probed experimentally and renegotiated. Under the "social fabric of the technicized lifeworld" I understand, as should be clear by now, not merely a human system or structure of interrelation under the influence of modern technology but rather a dynamic assemblage of networks composed of human and nonhuman agencies alike, the interactions of which effect transformations on both sides. By self-reflexively problematizing the variability and contingency of medial forms, serial figures enable for us a sort of dialogue with our technological interlocutors—thus consummating the marriage of Sobchack and Deleuze. The monster of the Frankenstein films mirrors or models the material interfaces of bodies and apparatuses which, in normalized and non-self-reflexive interactions, allow human users to act in concert with technical media in such a way that the events of a narrative come to the fore rather than the mediating technologies. But the figure of the monster self-reflexively inverts these normalized relations—especially when it moves from one medium to another or at times of heightened media transformation. And those are precisely the times when uncertainty prevails with regard to the manner in which humans can or should relate to their media. What announces itself as a purely human conflict over the aesthetic, social, and moral implications of new media or medial forms can often in fact be seen as an anthropotechnical conflict that is carried out between humans and the technical media that co-define the parameters of human activity.[41] And yet we usually (and understandably) lack the imaginative or empathetic capacities required to place ourselves in the position of nonhuman apparatuses and to conduct a dialogue with them directly. For this we need a mediator who can "represent" (in the sense of *vertreten*, to stand proxy, rather than *darstellen*) each side to the other to work towards a mutual understanding of the significance of media-technological changes. This is precisely what a serial figure like Frankenstein's monster provides—and its ability to act in this mediating role is the result of its double transgression of boundaries on narrative-thematic and medial levels alike.

---

41   I argue for this thesis, in the context of transitional-era cinema and film aesthetics, in my "Between Technology and Art: Functions of Film in Transitional-Era Cinema."

Figure 1: The mediating activity of the serial figure

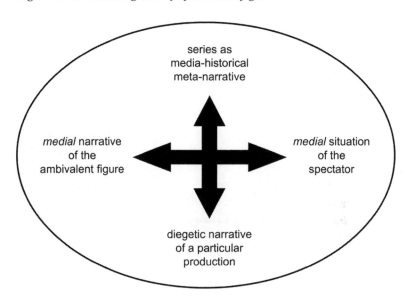

I would like, finally, to illustrate this perspective by recalling my analyses, undertaken in Chapters 2 and 3, of the Edison and Whale versions of *Frankenstein*. This brief review should serve to demonstrate the manner in which the findings of Part Two, culminating in this chapter's articulation of a postnatural media theory, theoretically inform and revise the perspective taken in Part One, thereby setting the stage for Part Three's return to a more direct form of analytical engagement with Frankenstein films. As we saw in Chapter 3, Edison's film of 1910 was situated between the early, image-technology oriented "cinema of attractions" on the one hand and the coming narrative-oriented classical Hollywood style on the other. This transitional position made the film witness to a cinema torn between conflicting conceptions of cultural values, formal and media-technological dispositions, and economic imperatives. Edison's *Frankenstein* tried, or so it would seem, to circumvent these structural contradictions and to satisfy the conflicting claims of all the parties involved. Advertising propaganda for the film emphasized, on the one hand, the "photographic marvel" of the creation sequence (advertisement in *Motion Picture World*, 19 March 1910, 436) and, on the other hand, the origin of the narrative in "Mrs. Shelley's [...] work of art" (*The Edison Kinetogram*, 15 March 1910, 3). Accordingly, the film aimed to be a technological spectacle and narrative high culture both at the same time. Of course, *Frankenstein* was already a staple of popular culture and the subject of countless stage adaptations—including melodramatic and burlesque versions that hardly respected the artistic integrity of "Mrs.

Shelley's [...] work of art." And so one finds a multiple address—if not also moral double standards—in the film, which defines the scope of the monster's mediating activities in the film's historical context.

The so-called "marvel" of the creation sequence, we recall, consisted in the presentation of a physically impossible spectacle: a *creatio ex nihilo* by means of reverse-motion footage of a burning mannequin. Clearly speaking to media-aesthetic expectations deriving from the illusionistic tradition of cinematic magic that, in the context of early film, exhibited the novel technology and invited viewers to attend more to filmic images than their referential content or the objects they depict, Frankenstein's reactions emphasize the wondrous nature of the trick effect and channel the scopophilic pleasure of a "primitive" viewer, for whom he stands in as an onscreen proxy. In the creation sequence, as I argued earlier, the object of wonder was filmic "animation" itself, hence a self-reflexive topos which links cinematic and monstrous acts of creation. From a phenomenological point of view, this self-reflexivity was hardly conducive to an immersive suture of the spectator into a visually and narratively constructed diegesis. On the contrary, the perceived images, the perceiving viewer, and the perception-enabling apparatus of camera, projector, screen, and venue were all situated in more or less the same—nondiegetic—space. In order to change this phenomenological situation, which was precisely the task of classical continuity principles, trick effects would have to be consistently subordinated under a greater narrative purpose. And, indeed, Edison's *Frankenstein* exhibits some degree of effort—though still a bit indecisive—towards this type of integration, especially in the final showdown between Frankenstein and the monster.

This standoff, carried out in the medium of a mirror, constitutes the film's narrative climax and (according to the *Edison Kinetogram*) communicates the moral of the story—namely: love conquers all, even a monster. But considering the identification of the monster with the technology of film in the creation sequence, Frankenstein's battle is not merely with a monster but with the medium of film as an animating technology, especially since trick effects are essential to the staging of the conflict. The film's narrative closure is therefore mixed with a self-reflexive countercurrent which also provides a final occasion for narratively unredeemed, technology-oriented pleasures. But the situation is still more complicated, because Frankenstein's victory—if we understand it as a self-reflexive event—is simultaneously the triumph of the phenomenology of narrative integration, which is directed against precisely the sort of self-reflexivity that is employed in staging the battle. The mirror functions here like the projection surface of the cinema screen that frames the image of the mirror. The similarity is not merely abstract but in fact visually perceptible due to the scene's technical means of production: the images in the mirror are not reflections of its depicted environment; rather, they are themselves flickering filmic images. The result is a film within the film, and Frankenstein is again a film viewer. His battle with the monster is a battle with filmic images and especially with his manner of relating to them, i.e. with the primitive type of reception that he exemplified in the creation sequence. But this time he is reformed, as he wins the ability to identify himself with the depicted content of the images. Instead of staring at the surface of the medium, he is now able to look through rather than at the mirror—i.e. to perceive himself and not the mirror as an object. With this achievement, Frankenstein is therefore finally in a position to devote his attentions to the reality of his environment—which means, for us, to the world of the diegesis.

In the context of transitional-era cinema, to reiterate a thesis advanced in Chapter 3, the film's narrative development is linked to a larger, non-diegetic narrative of filmic development: Frankenstein's psychological maturation, which is consummated in the mirror scene, allegorizes a historical-normative process of cinematic maturation and of media-psychological progress of the spectator towards a proto-classical relation to film. But because the staging of this normalizing meta-narrative can only be effected via a monstrous self-reflection, the allegory remains incomplete. The monster may have been conquered on the level of the diegesis, and indeed this defeat is structurally reproduced at the higher, abstract level of the media-historical meta-narrative—but the monster nevertheless survives at the middle, "medial" level, at the level of mediation. For the supposedly integral diegesis of the film, whose closure Frankenstein achieves in overcoming his technology-oriented fascination, and therefore also the higher-order story (or history) of medial development that champions such closure and integrity—both of these narratives are in equal measure dependent upon the radical non-closure of the recursive self-reflexivity which the monster as mediator embodies: they depend, that is, on the monstrous in-between-ness that allows the figure of the monster to literally "incorporate" into the film much larger border conflicts between humans and their media. As a mediator, the monster confronts viewers with the still germinal, not yet sharply defined alternatives between "primitive" and "classical" modes of spectatorship, which are staged not as a merely human choice but as modes of techno-phenomenological interaction that mark out medial human-technological hybridization options in the process of transformation. The figure of the monster is itself an embodiment of medial transitionality.

This claim can be partially unpacked in terms of Don Ihde's hermeneutic relations and embodiment relations, which I associated in Chapter 2 with early film and classical Hollywood cinema. As we saw there, early film functioned along the lines of hermeneutic relations, demonstrating the technologies of camera and projector to audiences whose attentions were directed both at moving pictures and the machines producing them, where no clear split between the real-world space of the cinema and the virtual space of the screen was yet articulated. Here viewers were encouraged to look *at* rather than *through* cinema's medial technologies. By contrast, embodiment relations came to define the dominant model of ideal transparency in classical Hollywood, which sought to integrate its spectator into a diegetic world by means of editing techniques that create the illusion of spatio-temporal continuities and that de-emphasize the constructedness of filmic narratives and the role of the machinery involved in their production, storage, and reproduction. On this model, spectator and filmic apparatus are ideally fused as a unit jointly directed at the constitution, perception, and emotional investment in the story world. In Figure 1, the movements along the vertical axis between diegesis and meta-narrative are essentially effected through oscillations between these two modes: between the medial transparency of embodiment relations and the opacity of hermeneutic relations to film and filmic technologies. The figure of the monster enables such oscillations on the basis of its duplicity as a figure in a narrative that also self-reflexively mirrors and interrogates its own conditions of mediality. The figure thus constitutes a mobile mediality, ambivalent and on the move between the subjective and objective poles of spectatorial perception. To maintain this position is to tarry on the brink, in a situation such as that described in Chapter 5, according to which the steam engine instituted an unstable, double form of relationality just before it executed the "vanishing act" (as Pickering puts it) that stabilized it as a new basis of perception and action. It is in this sense of tarrying on the brink that the monster embodies the transitional phase, conceived as a dynamic flux rather than a determinate state or a telic passage. And this indeterminate, intermediately oscillating position can be said to constitute the very content or focus of the dialogue between the figure and the spectator, symbolized in Figure 1 as the horizontal axis of interaction. At stake, then, in this dialogue is the uncertain affective transformation of perceptual and actional parameters, of subjects in relation to objects, that ensues when the mediating technologies that constitute such relations are put in motion. At least on a small scale, it is the technologically induced upheaval and redefinition of agencies that the monster serves to negotiate, define, and mediate.

It is in the nature of things, however, that the radical ambivalences I am describing, and which are indexed to a particular historical situation, are subject to stabilization over time and in relation to the degree to which medial technologies become familiar, routine, and habitual. The dialogical potential of the film fades. But here is where the serial nature of a figure like the monster, which implies a cumulative concrescence of incarnations over time, enters into the picture. The vertical axis in Figure 1 can also be read in terms of a reversible form/substrate relation according to Luhmann's conception of media. A particular instantiation of the *Frankenstein* story can be viewed as a form in relation to a serially existing narrative substrate, thus defining a space of temporal progression via the reservoir out of which the presently existing form emerged (past) and into which it will be decomposed (futurity). On the other hand, the various versions collectively constitute the series, which they variously alter and reconstruct as a form when they self-reflexively abstract a media-historical meta-narrative from out of the resources of their own diegetic worlds. In both cases, the serial figure, the monster, is the element of de/formation, i.e. the common element that, through loose or tight coupling, is constitutive both of forms and substrates. By maintaining a reversible relation between specific instantiations and the serial pool, each of which can interchangeably serve as form or substrate, the de/formable monster holds open an indeterminate space in which to inscribe the transitions between its incarnations and, under circumstances of renewed change, to reactivate its memory of change for another bout of negotiations. The particular ambivalences witnessed by a concrete film may fade historically from view, but the monster *qua* mediality itself embodies a temporality and an ongoing transitionality that is continuously regenerated and reactivated as nothing less than a medium of (medial) historicity: not only a historical record but a site for the manifestation of material change, which it embodies, much like Shelley's novel as read in Chapter 4, as a postnatural parable of the transductive relation it exemplifies, i.e. that of mediality/mediation. In structure, though perhaps not in scope, the monster therefore resembles the steam engine *qua* ontology engine: both a concrete form and an articulator of the parameters of formation, the de/formable serial figure powers the storytelling engine of *Frankenstein* as its circulating medium.

Thus, the 1931 version of *Frankenstein*, produced more than a decade after the rise of classical Hollywood, sees the engine set to work again in the midst of another media-historical transition: the shift from silent film to the talkies. Clearly, a monster at this juncture has other concerns than his counterpart from 1910. Structurally, though, something very similar takes place. As we saw in Chapter 2, the monster is again the locus of a self-reflexive problematization of filmic mediality, but updated in relation to the then current state of the cinema. On the one hand, the scars on the body of the monster might be seen as objective correlates of the splicing techniques by which film narratives are now constituted and by which spectators are integrated into the worlds opened up to them. In addition, the creation sequence is itself staged like an act of filmic production, effecting what Marc Redfield calls a "teasing alignment of monster-making and movie-making" (par. 6). By means of such alignments, the film makes the quasi-transparent embodiment relations that dominate classical cinema partially opaque; the movie renders the principles of its own construction into objects that can be inspected and interrogated in the manner of a hermeneutic relation. Again, the monster is at the center of these shifts, articulating the alternatives.

And again the monster is keyed to the historically transitional moment, becoming a hyperphotographic being whose muteness serves to highlight the film's use of sound, which itself seemed eerie and artificial to many early audiences and, contrary to arguments that it expanded the sensory basis of immersion in the diegetic world, actually served to undermine the illusion of realism while the transition from silents to talkies was still underway.[42] In this context, the mute monster opens a dialogue with the spectator on the subject of the changing conditions of medial realism, self-reflexively linked to a narrative of the artificial production of a hybrid human-technological being. Later, when the sound transition has been completed, it will be largely forgotten that that narrative's specific meaning and relevance was once defined by the long period of experimentation with sound recording and storage technologies, by synchronization problems, and by the obtrusive presence of loudspeakers to unaccustomed audiences either marveling at a technical achievement or terrified at the prospect of the silent-era's aesthetic standards being irrevocably compromised. This forgetfulness seems to be one of the conditions for the iconization of Karloff's portrayal of the monster, which in 1931 constituted a radically ambivalent figure capable of mediating a significant change in the parameters of viewers' interactions with their media-technological lifeworlds. As an icon, the post-transitional afterlife of the Karloff figure undergoes phenomenal stabilization and is flattened out into a sort of visual cliché. However, due to its role in the process of serial accumulation, it comes to serve as a standard against which to measure future stagings and therefore to gauge material processes of change. At least potentially, it remains poised to articulate new transitions and to mediate further reconfigurations of human and technological agencies when the opportunity arises.

What I have been arguing, then, is that the monster, as a serialized mediator, is not just a representation but itself an *instantiation* of the inherently transitional anthropotechnical interface, a facet of the medium as environment for life, co-articulating the historical milieu of human-technical relations. The various filmic incarnations can be seen, then, as snapshots of various states of the liminal membrane between the phenomenal and the noumenal (i.e. between an emergent situation and the non-actualized environment), as this border is continually renegotiated between the transductively related material agencies of the human and the nonhuman. In Part Three, I aim to consolidate this perspective by applying cinematic double vision, now refocused, to a closer view of the confrontations between human and nonhuman agencies and embodiment forms as they come to a head in Frankenstein films to mediate affective transitionalities. In Chapter 7, I concentrate my energies once more on James Whale's *Frankenstein*, now considered alongside its sequel *Bride of Frankenstein*; collectively, by establishing the iconic image of the monster and solidifying a serial procession, these films laid the groundwork, or

---

42 This is the basis of Spadoni's argument that *Frankenstein* channels an "uncanny body" mode of sound-transitional film experience into the horror genre. I return to this argument in the next chapter.

the medial substrate, for the various forms of Frankenstein films that would follow. Moreover, they captured a unique moment in the postnatural history of medial life, harnessing transitional energies and using them to elicit a fearful symmetry of human and technical perspectives that, as we shall see in the concluding Chapter 8, continues to reverberate in later productions' engagements of their own broadly medial settings. Establishing this symmetry of the human and the alien, and relentlessly renewing the assertion of its own autonomy and transformative power over its human spectators, the monster of the movies instructs us, ultimately—as Donna Haraway has recently put it in her twist on a phrase from Latour—that we have never been human.[43]

---

43 "We Have Never Been Human" is the title Haraway gives to Part I of her remarkable "dog book," *When Species Meet*.

Part Three

7. Universal Monsters and Monstrous Particulars

> Let the monster look from every billboard—His face is your good fortune!!
> *FRANKENSTEIN* (1931) PRESSBOOK[1]

> A horror story, the face is a horror story.
> GILLES DELEUZE AND FÉLIX GUATTARI[2]

In the serial procession of Frankenstein films as a whole, a special place is held by Universal Studios' productions of the 1930s and 1940s. Among these it is particularly the two films directed by James Whale, Universal's "original" *Frankenstein* from 1931 and its sequel *Bride of Frankenstein* from 1935, that play a definitive role, not only kicking off Universal's series but setting standards against which Frankenstein films are inevitably still compared, even up to the present day. With regard to the nature of these standards, it is not just that Whale's films are somehow superior in conception and execution to the rest of the Universal series, which following 1939's *Son of Frankenstein* steadily declined in terms of narrative complexity, characterization, and attention to technical detail (no doubt lending the later films, including such multi-monster mash-ups as 1943's *Frankenstein Meets the Wolf Man* and 1944's *House of Frankenstein*, a charm all of their own); no, the continued influence of Whale's renditions owes less to the "quality standards" they established than to their institution of *standard patterns* of action, narration, and visualization that serve as baselines for later productions—patterns that subsequent films can either follow (via emulation, extrapolation, modification) or break with (in a privative relation that is still a relation *to* Whale's films), but which they are hardly able to ignore. In other words, Whale's films serve as the basis for a *standardization* of Frankenstein films, a process which admits possibilities for both

---

1 Reprinted in Philip J. Riley, ed. *Frankenstein*, n.p.
2 *A Thousand Plateaus*, 168.

repetition and difference, and thus marks the genesis of a specifically filmic serialization—a medial differentiation of the Frankensteinian storytelling engine that establishes Frankenstein's filmic progenies as a quasi-independent lineage next to literary and especially theatrical lines of development. (Edison's *Frankenstein* was in this regard not yet independent of the theater, nor could it have been given the role and social standing of the cinema at the time; it should therefore come as no surprise that the 1910 film failed to exert an influence of the magnitude that Whale's films have had on a specifically cinematic serial lineage, a lineage which could only be constituted in a medium capable of historicizing itself as post-transitional, i.e. sufficiently stabilized as an independent medium governed by non-arbitrary, even if non-absolute, norms.)

Among the aspects of Whale's films to which any later version is necessarily beholden, none surpasses in significance and power the now iconic image of the monster as portrayed by Boris Karloff. All subsequent incarnations (and, retrospectively, prior ones as well) are inevitably judged against Karloff's embodiment of the monster, which defined the creature's look for the entirety of the Universal series and beyond. Indeed, one could say with reference to this iconic image, Universal's monster became the "universal" monster, both onscreen and off. The familiar image of the flat-headed, bolt-necked creature has become a general-purpose stereotype that is more or less synonymous with *Frankenstein*, thus eclipsing Shelley's novel as the original "source" of most popular associations with the story. It is the Karloffian image, or a variation on it, that stands alone (e.g. in print or televisual media) as a warning against technologies perceived as harboring the unpredictable potential to escape our control (as in the context of biotechnologies ranging from so-called Frankenfood to human cloning, where quite often the image serves less as an illustration than, on the contrary, ethical and theological arguments serve as mere captions to the image). But it is not just the universal familiarity of the image that is of interest here; there is another sense of universality evoked by the Universal monster: in Whale's films, this monster can be seen alternatively flirting with, questioning, enacting, disseminating, and/or criticizing "universalism" in the sense of essentialism—i.e. speculatively engaging notions of human nature as defined vis-à-vis a form or image of monstrosity that may itself harbor pretensions to a universal condition or essence of some sort (thus, for example, the monster might be seen as embodying the transcendental Other, as allegorically proclaiming the inalienable rights of oppressed or marginal groups, or even as representing an inherently conflicted humanity via a properly monstrous humanism).

Thus, two sets of questions come together around the iconic image of the monster: questions about the role of Whale's films in the larger medial process of serialization, and about the (diegetic as well as nondiegetic) role of the monster in that process. These topics are, so to speak, connected materially in the Karloffian image. And, in addition to this material connection, we might identify a thematic one as well; consider, that is, that the two sets of issues are linked by a common concern with (and/or problematization of) relations of the universal and the particular (and oscillations between them): relations, on the one hand, of an emerging serial totality to specific (in this case privileged) filmic instantiations, and relations, on the other hand, of a totalizing normativity to the monstrous particularity of the serial figure (here in its iconic form). In this context, the universal/particular thematic possesses both a "media-technical" and a "discursive-ideological" aspect, and yet both of these, according to the argument of Chapter 6, are to be conceived as properly *medial* aspects, each transductively conditioning the other. Seen thus, the so-called technical and ideological questions converge as two ways of addressing human-technical relations—which does not mean that they ask identical questions or questions that are reducible to a single perspective, but that they are inseparably concerned with historical negotiations of the anthropotechnical interface. According to a postnatural perspective, such negotiations are never centered solely in human discourse and action but involve genuine interactions amongst human and nonhuman agencies, interactions which I aim to illuminate from both sides of that divide. In this chapter, I start from the human side of things, taking up what is arguably the most obvious point of human interest in Whale's films—viz. that of the narrative contents mediated by the films taken as storytelling devices—from whence I work my way towards the nonhuman materiality of the technical medium. In line with the perspective outlined at the end of Part Two, the stories told by Whale's films harbor an excess that refuses narrative closure, pointing to a material encounter between historically situated agencies, human and nonhuman alike, and simultaneously opening a margin for serial continuation on a medial (rather than primarily narrative) basis. Thus, though I begin here with narrative aspects of the films, it is with a view to demonstrating the irreducible transduction of medium and message, which I have re-framed as the transduction of mediality and mediation—thus bringing us full circle to a human-technical dialogue on the historicity and contingency of the anthropotechnical interface or medium as it is configured at any given time (and which can be made visible only in historical series). By proceeding from the human to the nonhuman—from the human contexts of authorial production and spectatorial reception to the nonhuman materialities of image technologies and technical images—I aim to show (again drawing on Bogost's provocative suggestion) how a sort of "alien phenomenology," understood here as a non-correlationist exploration of the nonhuman agency of film, asserts itself from within a human-centered interpretive approach to Whale's films.

The image of the monster, I contend, functions as the central relay between the human and the nonhuman, between narrative and the non-discursive materiality of the medium, or more generally between the molar and the molecular; accordingly, the trajectory of my analysis is one that takes off from narrative content in what might be its most molar aspect—viz. that of the genre affiliations articulated in the type of story told and in the conventional manner of its telling—but leads us to a molecular level of affectively powerful images that, though present within the narrative explication of a story world in its function as a conventionalized or generically stabilized unit, nevertheless resist signification and instead exist on a plane of radically non-anthropic matter. As a mediator connecting these realms, the monster in the middle is always more than any particular reading, and it therefore holds open a space for dialogue of the type described in Chapter 6. However, the process of iconization tends to close off dialogical possibilities, to reduce the image from an ambivalent multiplicity to a signifying singularity, obscuring the alternative potentials for human-nonhuman interaction marked out in a temporary and transitionally unstable historical moment. Recovering the pre-stabilized openness of the now iconic image bears upon the meaning of the series of Frankenstein films as a whole, due to the series' constant references (both positive and negative) back to that image. And it bears specifically, as we shall see, on the political dimensions of anthropotechnical interfacing.

My argument, to be mounted here in two phases, can be summarized as follows. Whale's films stage a melodramatic tale of the monster's progressive humanization, and this process sheds light on the politics of embodiment (or embodiment of politics) at stake in cinematic spectatorship, ambivalently raising questions that focus our attention on the historical configuration of normative patterns for interfacing with film technologies.[3] In exploring this political dimension, we are led to consider a genetic or molecular level of pre-personal affective interface, a material domain which undergirds the "molarization" processes of both the monster's becoming-human and the viewer's becoming-classical-spectator; in the second phase of my argument, I locate this elemental level at work in images of the monster's face. It is this face which hinges the possibility of melodramatic identification, which frames the monster's nascent subjectivity as a bearer of human significance, and which, in the process of iconization, comes to serve as the medium of a visual cliché. And yet, as I shall argue, the monster's "faciality" (as the term is used by Deleuze and Guattari to denote a precondition of signifying subjectivity[4]) disintegrates in the series of shots by which the monstrous visage is initially introduced onscreen in 1931. These images, which dramatically cut in to ever closer views of the creature's face, hold within them an alternative form and politics of interfacing than that of

---

3   This argument, which occupies the first half of this chapter, was originally put forward in my "Incorporations: Melodrama and Monstrosity in James Whale's *Frankenstein* and *Bride of Frankenstein*."

4   See Chapter 7 of Deleuze and Guattari's *A Thousand Plateaus*.

the mutual humanization of monster and spectator—a possibility of becoming-animal, becoming-technical, becoming-monstrous. In the monster's face, or so I argue, an alien-phenomenological viewpoint asserts itself against the noetic correlationism of traditional (i.e. human) phenomenology, and a momentary opening onto a radically alterior materiality is made available to a non-subjective, affective experience: a monstrous singularity at the very heart of the Universal (and/or universal) monster.

INCORPORATIONS: MELODRAMA AND MONSTROSITY

When critics discuss them today, James Whale's Frankenstein films are usually treated either as horror films or as science fiction—or as a hybrid mix of the two genres.[5] Certainly, it is difficult to think of these films in terms other than horror and/or sci-fi: their formal, narrative, and visual qualities virtually define for us the "classic" image of a bygone era (a "golden age") in the history of filmic horror, whereas the thematic conflicts depicted are paradigmatic for a certain strand of what we call science fiction. Significantly, however, these genre categories were not automatically applied to the films at the time of their appearance in the 1930s. It is well known that "science fiction," a term first widely used in the 1920s to designate written (usually pulp) fiction, did not come to name a film genre until after World War II; but also the concept of the horror film was still under construction, so to speak, not unheard of but not yet firmly established in the pre-Code years. To be sure, a recognizable genre took form around increasingly frequent uses of the term "horror" over the course of what is now known as the classic horror cycle, which began with *Dracula* in February of 1931 and ended in 1936 with *Dracula's Daughter*; and yet the concept itself of the horror film remained not only somewhat indeterminate but also, significantly, contested in struggles over the moral legitimacy of the films so described. In this regard, the written correspondence between Universal Studios and industry censors on the topic of Whale's films, which are so central to the image of golden-age horror, provide an interesting index of the genre's emergence. In these letters, the term "gruesomeness" (one of the Motion Picture Production Code's so-called "Repellent Subjects") is repeatedly used to characterize (and to justify censorship of) those elements that make *Frankenstein* a horror film for us, but that made it, for the correspondents, part of a nascent and

---

5   Indeed, this hybridity sometimes occasions uneasiness for critics whose interests lie in one of the conventionally defined genres. Thus, for example, Michael Sevastakis, in his discussion of early American horror films (xvi), and J.P. Telotte, in the context of science fiction (72), both feel compelled to defend their interest in these hybrid specimens.

troubling class of films still lacking a convenient label. Provoked by his involvement with the case of *Frankenstein*, and detecting a larger trend coming on, industry censor Jason Joy penned the following letter to Will H. Hays (of Hays Code fame) on December 5, 1931, the day after the film's New York opening:

Dear General:

Perhaps it would be wise to obtain an early estimate of the audience reaction and critical opinion concerning *Dracula* and *Frankenstein* by Universal; *Dr Jekyll and Mr Hyde* by Paramount; and *Almost Married* by Fox, all of which are in distribution or are about to be distributed. Paramount has another "gruesome" picture about to be put into production and Metro-Goldwyn-Mayer has *"Freaks"* which is about one-half shot.

Is this the beginning of a cycle which ought to be retarded or killed? I am anxious to receive your advice.[6]

One month later, on January 11, 1932, Joy wrote again to Hays on the topic of this "cycle," now identified somewhat apprehensively as constituted of "so-called horror pictures," which were gaining industry attention due to the fact that *"Frankenstein* is staying for four weeks and taking in big money at theatres which were about on the rocks." Disturbed by the development, Joy assured himself: "The fact that the supply of such stories is necessarily limited will lead eventually to straining for more and more horror until the wave topples over and breaks."

As the wave continued to swell over the next few years, the terms and the tone of this discourse remained relatively stable. Talk of "gruesomeness" continued, in 1933 and 1934, to dominate pre-production censorship discussions concerning the screenplay for the planned sequel *The Return of Frankenstein*; and when the film, now titled *Bride of Frankenstein*, was reviewed in March 1935 by the head of the new Production Code Administration, Joseph I. Breen, it was rejected on the grounds of "its excessive brutality and gruesomeness" (letter to Harry H. Zehner, dated March 23, 1935). When an edited version was reviewed the following month, Breen found it (in his letter of April 15) "acceptable under the *letter* of our Production Code, but very dangerous from the standpoint of political censorship"—a prophecy that proved accurate shortly thereafter, as Ohio censors demanded major cuts to the film. Breen wrote on this occasion (in a letter dated May 8) to Hays, asking how far his office should go to defend the integrity of films passed under the

---

6   All of the letters referenced in the following pages are held at the Margaret Herrick Library of the Academy of Motion Picture Arts and Sciences in Los Angeles, where I had the opportunity to view them.

Production Code and, more philosophically, whether the Code itself should correspond to the sensibilities of non-industry censor boards. Breen notes a generally high level of agreement, "but in the case of so-called horror pictures, crime films, etc., it is not always so."

In these instances, the qualifying epithet "so-called," as applied to "horror pictures," speaks of course to the relative novelty of the young genre, to the uncertainty that attends attempts to name the new; but beyond this, it signals also a cautionary reaction to extravagant, horror-crazed marketing campaigns and, not lastly, reflects the fact that the Code, through which lens the censors in their official functions viewed all films, provided no terms for recognizing the genre *qua* genre— except, that is, as a motley collection of "gruesome" pictures which, by definition as it were, had to be handled with care and, ultimately, resisted. The lack of recognition denoted by "so-called horror picture" is therefore double: the expression indicates both an inability and an unwillingness to recognize the existence of a bona fide horror genre. As if to say, with the stereotypical monster-movie policeman: "No monster here, move along now." Even after the classic horror cycle had come to an end, we find Breen repeating the protective gesture in exchanges with Katherine K. Vandervoort, a concerned Director of Attendance at White Plains Public Schools worried about the harmful effects on children of such films, occasioned specifically by the 1937 re-release, as a double horror bill, of *Dracula* and (with cuts dictated by the Breen Office) *Frankenstein*. Responding in a letter dated November 26, 1938, Breen confesses his distaste for "these, so-called, 'horror' pictures" (with scare quotes added, presumably, for double protection against the disreputable category) but notes the "very substantial market" for them, adding as a consolation that no new films of the type have come out of Hollywood for "about three years." The danger, it would seem, was over; if not just a bad dream, then at least one could say "so-called horror" had been merely a fad rather than a lasting genre. In hindsight, of course, we know better, and the term "so-called horror picture" seems incredibly quaint at this late date; the tactics of misrecognition encoded by the phrase proved ineffective, and Breen's sigh of relief premature, for the *Dracula/Frankenstein* double feature inspired a second horror cycle, spearheaded again by Universal Studios with their 1939 *Son of Frankenstein* (thus also reviving the Universal Frankenstein series, which in its post-Whale incarnation refused to die until the farcical *Abbott and Costello Meet Frankenstein* appeared in 1948). If not at the start of the 1930s then certainly at the end of the decade, the existence of the horror genre could no longer plausibly be disavowed.

In the meantime, not only censors had problems recognizing and identifying the new genre on its own terms. Critics like Mordaunt Hall, writing in the *New York Times* on December 5, 1931—the same day Joy wrote to Hays about the unsettling "cycle" on the horizon—struggled to locate *Frankenstein* generically, assimilating it to other, more familiar categories: Hall describes the film as a "stirring Grand Guignol type of picture" that "is naturally a morbid, gruesome affair" (echoing the language of the just-ratified but not-yet-enforced Code). In terms of filmic relatives, Hall draws the likely comparison with *Dracula*, which he judges to be "tame" next to *Frankenstein*, and anticipates affinities with Universal's then forthcoming adaptation of Poe's *Murders in the Rue Morgue* (which, starring Bela Lugosi, appeared in 1932). Thus, like Joy, Hall senses the imminent birth of a cycle, but the word "horror" is missing from his characterization of the film and the emerging genre in which it participates. Instead, Hall describes *Frankenstein* as the elaboration of "melodramatic ideas," much as *Dracula* had been described by another reviewer as a "grotesque, fantastic, slightly unhealthy melodrama" upon its release earlier in the year.[7] If this characterization is surprising to us, it is important to recall, as Steve Neale reminds us in his treatment of melodrama in *Genre and Hollywood*, that the now common identification of melodrama with the woman's film, with "weepies," and with family melodramas is largely an academic conceit, and one of quite recent vintage at that (179-204). The film industry and film critics, by contrast, long employed the term "melodrama" (and cognates such as "meller") to characterize films of all sorts, including gangster films, thrillers, and horror—not only in 1931, before the genre was articulated as such, but throughout the first classic horror cycle and into the next. Thus, in 1939 we find the *Motion Picture Herald* referring, without irony, to *Son of Frankenstein* as "Melodrama" (January 21, 1939: 40; qtd. in Neale 185)—a designation that was in no way at odds with that of "horror."

Melodrama, the Grand Guignol, and the gruesome—these terms all applied quite naturally to "so-called horror" in the 1930s, in a sense in which it is awkward to combine them today. Appreciating this fact is, as Neale has argued, essential to a historically informed understanding of Hollywood genres, including but not limited to that of horror. In the context of my own project, which recognizes Frankenstein films as genre films without collapsing them into a film genre, I take it that this historical awareness is also essential to understanding Frankenstein films as a series. As I have pointed out, this series, despite precursors such as Edison's *Frankenstein*, is not constituted as a specifically filmic series until the 1930s; it is born with Whale's films and with Karloff's appearance as the monster. Looking at these films in terms of horror and/or sci-fi tends to obscure the historical specificity of the filmic objects with which spectators were confronted at that moment; in particular, the materiality of an uncertain spectator-film interface is potentially assimilated to our own generically organized sensibilities when we view the films this way. By highlighting reactions to Whale's Frankenstein films in which the term "horror" is

---

7   Richard Watts Jr. "On the Screen." Review of *Dracula*. *New York Herald-Tribune*. 13 Feb 1931. 20. (Cited in Spadoni 7).

either absent or contested, I have been trying to loosen the grip of our generic preconceptions, but this has only been a ground-clearing exercise for a closer engagement with the films' incorporations of, as Hall put it, "melodramatic ideas." As I aim to show here, investigating the films in these terms is not only truer to the historical perception of these films, but it promises also to shed light on the corporeal stakes of spectatorship, understood as a variable interface between human and nonhuman agencies or forms of embodiment.

Clearly, then, when I speak of the "incorporations of melodrama" in Whale's Frankenstein films, I do not mean just to suggest that these films incidentally *add* melodramatic forms to their melange of horror and sci-fi; rather, three senses of "incorporation" are at issue here. My use of "incorporations of melodrama" is self-reflexive in the sense that the films' formal structuring and realization, which accords in many respects with patterns of classical stage melodrama (as I shall demonstrate in the first subsection, "Incorporations I"), corresponds thematically to the stories told: *Frankenstein* and *Bride of Frankenstein* are *melodramatic tales of the quest for a fitting body* (the theme of the following subsection, "Incorporations II"). By embarking on this quest, Frankenstein enters a love triangle with science, and his bride-to-be must compete with its disembodied seductions. The creature, on the other hand, is in search of a bride for himself; struggling against the odds imposed by society, the monster also becomes something of a melodramatic hero—in a process that calls into question the limits of embodied difference within the normative framework of human subjectivity. This brings me to the third respect, equally self-reflexive, in which Whale's Frankenstein films engage the relations of incorporation and melodrama: namely, they highlight and problematize the intimate connection of discursive subjectification and bodily practice in the spectatorial hermeneutics of melodrama (explored in "Incorporations III"). Linda Williams has famously identified melodrama, along with horror and pornography, as one of the cinema's "body genres,"[8] and it is my conviction that this characterization can be fundamentally enriched with the view of embodiment developed in Part Two; to recapitulate that view, materially distributed agencies in flux are "captured" in dialogical interactions, crystallized in the form of technical devices or praxis-oriented corporeal interface-matrices that underlie and structure subject-object relations. Such captures can, through habituation, become thoroughly naturalized, but they can also—and occasionally must—dissolve again into a-subjective, "passional" flows and make way for new means of interfacing. Melodrama, as I see it, is alternately concerned with such passional flows and with their containment; as Christof Decker puts it, melodrama typically involves "a fundamental ambivalence of feeling," alternating to and fro between "a stimulation and a control of affect" (Decker

---

8 See Williams's "Film Bodies: Gender, Genre, and Excess."

14; qtd. in Kelleter and Mayer 13).[9] My suggestion is that we think these dynamics—melodrama itself—as a mode of experimental interrogation of interface-matrices as they are constituted at a given historical moment.[10] Viewing Whale's

---

9   As I see it, this ambivalence militates against any wholesale condemnation of melodrama as a vehicle of ideology, as much as it obviates celebratory views—especially widespread in cultural studies—that would identify in melodrama an inherently liberating potential. Both views, in my opinion, neutralize melodrama's indeterminate ability to move us, to affect us, by reducing the scope of affective impact to a subjective level at which one is manipulated and made to internalize norms of social relation and psychic hygiene or at which, alternatively, clever readers or viewers ironically subvert these forces and experience empowerment by determining for themselves the use and meaning melodramatic texts have for them. Both scenarios, I believe, are contextually possible modes of engagement, but they are never the whole story; moreover, while the former exaggerates the power of narrative media in the direction of determinism, the latter reduces melodramatic productions to passive raw material, a gesture that is of a piece with neutralizations of media and of technology. In both cases, what is effaced is the margin of dialogical openness at the pre-subjective level of anthropotechnical mediality/mediation. By widening the scope of affective impact beyond the narrow realm of subjectivity, I therefore follow Mark Hansen's call for a transformation of cultural studies into "technocultural studies" (as put forward in his "Realtime Synthesis").

10 I thus wish to expand on a view expressed by Frank Kelleter and Ruth Mayer, who write: "the specific achievement of literary and filmic melodrama might well be to symbolically enact conflicts and problems that seem irresolvable at the time of enactment, thus not so much mapping a way out of a cultural predicament than rather staging it in the manner of a tableau. This might be one reason for the prominence of melodramatic performances in times of cultural transition and paradigm shifts" (13). My expansion of this view consists, effectively, in opening it to include *sub-symbolic enactments* of conflicts, taking the tableau as a "snapshot" (in Pickering's term) of the embodied membrane of anthropotechnical transduction (or a particular view of its possibilities) at a moment of *pre- or proto-cultural, material transition*. In other words, melodrama is taken as a means or mode of engagement with problematizations of embodied forms initiated by movements in the medial substrate of anthropotechnical relationality. Classical stage melodrama, around the turn of the nineteenth century, responded to tumultuous times and tried to locate the proper place of the human in the world, which task it approached in emotional and likewise moral categories; also at issue here, I suggest, was an attempt to forge a stable interface-matrix—that is, an effort to obtain, secure, define, or render coherent a set of meso-level (i.e. medial in the sense theorized in Chapter 6) parameters of embodied agency that could regulate contact with human and nonhuman environments. Accordingly, the bodily responses evoked by tear-jerking or hair-raising melodrama are not merely incidental to

Frankenstein films in terms of melodrama and incorporation therefore means looking at the dialogical possibilities that they held open, the reconfigurations of agencies and anthropotechnical relations that they encoded, and the medial shifts in the embodied membrane between the empirical-phenomenal and the non-actualized environment that they captured and deposited at the *locus classicus* of the Frankenstein film series.

Incorporations I: Monstrous Manichaeism

In order to situate this analysis, let me begin by establishing the melodramatic nature of Whale's films. First, we should note the close historical relationship between the Gothic novel and theatrical melodrama. According to the argument of Peter Brooks's classic study, *The Melodramatic Imagination*, both genres represented reactions to the perceived loss of the "Sacred," to the ethical and epistemological "void" left by modernity's progressive demythologization of the universe (16-20). Their common cause was to demonstrate the existence of a realm of moral and spiritual truth beyond mundane reality in an age of doubt. Towards this end, they had to resort to excessive means, breaking with conventions of verisimilitude: psychological motivation in melodrama, like physicalistic realism in the Gothic novel, were sacrificed for a higher, moral purpose. These generic affinities help explain the common borrowings from Gothic literature by melodramatic theater, as in the case of *Frankenstein*'s nineteenth-century stage career; and given the debts owed by silent-era cinema to that theater tradition, these historical affinities set the stage for the conjunction of "Grand Guignol" and "melodramatic ideas" in Mordaunt Hall's previously mentioned review of Whale's *Frankenstein*.

As the goal of classical melodrama was "to locate and to articulate the moral occult," which Brooks defines as "the repository of the fragmentary and desacralized remnants of sacred myth" (5), constant recourse was had to "an underlying manichaeism" (4) of good and evil as the polarized forces driving the world (and its dramatic representation).[11] The metaphorical "conflict between light and darkness"

---

an aesthetics of overwrought emotion and emotional display, but central to a politics of pre-subjective embodiment. In the cinema, similarly, melodrama probes the medial membrane of anthropotechnical (spectator-film) relations, and it is capable, especially at transitional moments of heightened media-technical transformation, of putting us corporeally in touch with molecular affective processes that underlie the more obvious molar configurations of subjective emotion, identity, and identification at stake in melodrama.

11 Brooks's conception of melodrama, developed to explain classical stage melodrama and with a view towards the modern novel, may seem, in this respect, too "essentialist" to

(5) is likewise the motor of Whale's narratives, and it is made literal in the *mise-en-scène*: an alternation between the dark settings of diabolic undertakings and the well-lit locales of innocence and virtue underscores the cosmic stakes of the plot. *Frankenstein* opens with a nighttime grave robbery; assistant Fritz steals a brain from the university by cover of night; and the famous creation scene takes place, of course, on a stormy night. Daytime scenes are interspersed to provide relief from the suspense and horror of these events: the Gothic setting of Frankenstein's tower lab is juxtaposed with bright scenes in his father's house and garden, where fiancée Elizabeth (played by Mae Clarke) lives, fearing her betrothed has gone astray. Elizabeth herself is clad in white, and backlighting produces a veritable halo around her, emphasizing her innocence and natural goodness. Contrasts of light and dark thus contribute to characterization, which, in keeping with melodrama, is established by means of visual signs. As Brooks claims for melodrama in general, "the characters have no interior depth, there is no psychological conflict" (35); instead, "melodrama exteriorizes conflict and psychic structure" (35), so that characters are swept along the surface of the manichaean forces indicated by light and dark, black and white.

As I have been suggesting, the alternation of light and shadow is more than just an element in Whale's visual aesthetic. For here the visual is intimately connected to the narrative dynamics of the films. The visibility of Elizabeth's purity, for example, is central to the establishment of conflict in the plot of *Frankenstein*. Her natural innocence is the polar opposite of Frankenstein's artificial experiments; she is clearly the legitimate recipient of his affections, but he has been seduced by technology. The sanctioned union of their marriage is threatened, and Mae Clarke's exaggerated acting style reinforces Elizabeth's sincere concern for Frankenstein's well-being. Her visually conveyed virtue, juxtaposed with Frankenstein's dark pursuit of science, establishes a central conflict between natural and artificial forces as the driving motor of the plot. Frankenstein (portrayed by Colin Clive) is thus figured, as Brooks claims of "man" in melodrama, as "playing on a theatre that is the point of juncture, and of clash, of imperatives beyond himself that are non-mediated and irreducible" (13). He is intersected by natural and unnatural desires, but in time

---

deal with later, filmic manifestations such as the "family melodrama." Ben Singer offers a useful corrective in defining melodrama as a "cluster concept" (*Melodrama and Modernity* 44). He includes "moral polarization"—along with pathos, overwrought emotion, nonclassical narrative structure, and sensationalism—in his list of melodrama's "primary features" (58), but adds that not all of these need be present in every case or type. My primary reliance on Brooks, and particularly my emphasis on manichaean structures, is justified in the present context by the theatrical and filmic traditions of "sensational melodrama" informing Whale's films.

he repents and returns to Elizabeth. Significantly, this takes place in an idyllic outdoors scene, where he expresses regret and agrees with Elizabeth that the wedding should take place "soon." His repentance is thus marked by a return to Nature—literally, in the setting of beautiful foliage, and metaphorically, in turning away from the unnatural seduction of technology and back to a "natural" (i.e. heterosexual) relationship.

The conflict of desires to which Frankenstein is subject—by which he is driven as a character—does not, however, indicate the presence of a psychologically deep realm in which he is "torn" in any serious sense. Whereas classical melodrama generally externalized the forces of good and evil in clearly identifiable heroes and villains, later adaptations of the mode often located the confrontation within a single character. Brooks cites Victor Hugo's theater in this regard, claiming that "any illusion of interiority, depth, or psychological complexity that this struggle gives is dispelled upon close examination. The forces themselves remain integral, and the character who is the arena of their struggle never gains psychological coherence or consistency. He is himself a kind of theatre of the sign" (93).

If this is the case in *Frankenstein*, its sequel comes a good deal closer to the structures of classical melodrama. Frankenstein having returned to the fold, the main narrative begins with a scene of virtue and (marital) bliss. But, typically for melodrama, "there swiftly intervenes a threat to virtue" (29) in the person of one Dr. Pretorius, who violates the sanctity of the couple's bedroom to solicit Frankenstein's help in a diabolical undertaking: the creation of a female counterpart to the monster. Pretorius (Ernest Thesiger) is clearly a villain: robed in black, his face is consistently lit from below, casting deep shadows across it. The motivation for his monstrous project is unclear, apparently lacking altogether. Brooks offers that "evil in the world of melodrama does not need justification: it exists, simply" (33). The epithet "mad" underlines Pretorius's unmotivated, arbitrarily volitional, and completely irrational evil. Within seconds of his appearance onscreen, his complete characterization has been established with certainty. His arrival gives credence to Elizabeth's suggestion, expressed in exaggerated melodramatic rhetoric, that "the devil" is behind all human pursuits of forbidden knowledge. If Pretorius is this devil, Elizabeth's angelic appearance (now embodied by actress Valerie Hobson) has been heightened to emphasize the cosmic scale of conflict, and religious imagery abounds in the film. This time there is no question, though, about Frankenstein's moral position. Taking strength from Elizabeth, he is able, at least initially, to resist the temptations of "the dark side." Later, the kidnapping of Elizabeth gives Pretorius the necessary leverage to blackmail Frankenstein. Not hubris, but iron necessity as a result of virtue's imperilment dictates Frankenstein's pact with the devil. His complicity in Pretorius's plan is the necessary price of melodramatic heroism, for only so can virtue be saved from certain doom. In *Bride of Frankenstein*, therefore, the relative sophistication of the earlier film's manichaean conflict is simplified—externalized and personalized—and the moral roles of the characters are as clearly visible as the clothes that they wear.

According to Brooks, melodrama's manichaean structure is a means to its moral goal: the "recognition of virtue" in a post-sacred era (27). "The polarization of good and evil works toward revealing their presence in the world. Their conflict suggests the need to recognize and confront evil, to combat and expel it, to purge the social order" (13). As a "drama of recognition" (27), melodrama requires the recognition of evil as a prerequisite to the public recognition of virtue and the reestablishment of value generally—both within the dramatization and in its relation to the spectator (49). In Whale's films, the purging of the social order is enacted in the villagers' pursuit of the monster. Though Frankenstein himself is responsible for the creature's existence, the monster embodies the unnatural force to which, in 1931, Frankenstein is attracted but which he eventually resists. Moreover, the creature is responsible for the death of an innocent child; in the melodramatic repertory, "children, as living representations of innocence and purity, serve as catalysts for virtuous or vicious actions" (34). In 1935, the monster holds Elizabeth captive; the creature is thus a threat to virtue in both cases, one that must be eliminated for the common good of society.

Finally, the decisive turn from Shelley's Gothicism towards a melodramatic *Frankenstein* comes in the films' "happy endings." As Brooks points out, melodrama "tends to diverge from the Gothic novel in its optimism, its claim that the moral imagination can open up the angelic spheres as well as the demonic depths and can allay the threat of moral chaos" (20). Whereas Shelley's novel ends with the mutual destruction of unnatural creature and hubristic creator, Whale's films condemn the monster while reuniting Frankenstein with Elizabeth in a purged social order. Significant here is not merely the difference between optimism and pessimism, but that a specifically moral aim is expressed in the melodramatic restoration of order. "Melodrama is less directly interested [than the Gothic novel] in the reassertion of the numinous for its own sake than in its ethical corollaries" (20). That is, in subjecting virtue to peril, but in staging its eventual victory over evil, melodrama insists on the "existence of a moral universe which [...] can be made to assert its presence and its categorical force among men" (20). In 1931, the monster must die (apparently) for its threat to the "natural" social order, while the repentant Frankenstein is able to escape the burning windmill where the final standoff is staged. A toast is then made to his health, his marriage, and the birth of a child. In *Bride of Frankenstein*, the now wholly virtuous Frankenstein complies with Pretorius's evil plans to create a mate for the original monster (who, alas, is not dead); but, rejected by his intended "bride," the monster recognizes his own lack of virtue and destroys himself, Pretorius, and the would-be mate, allowing Frankenstein and

Elizabeth to escape back to normality. In both cases, order is restored, nature saved, and "normal" familial relations reestablished.

Incorporations II: The Search for a Fitting Body

Having focused up to now on the incorporation of melodrama *into* Whale's films, I am concerned here with the way in which these films embody "melodramas *of* incorporation." The most obvious reference of this expression is to the plot level, for both *Frankenstein* and its sequel concern the search for a fitting body: Frankenstein's attempt to create a living being from corpses in 1931, and the resulting monster's search for a female companion in 1935. However, the full significance of these corporeal quests goes well beyond the narrative level. Whale's melodramas of incorporation engage larger questions concerning the formal and political characteristics of melodrama generally. This becomes most apparent at the intersection of monstrosity, muteness, and corporality figured in the composite bodies of the monster and his bride.

In the first film's opening credits, Frankenstein's creation is referred to as "The Monster," and the actor's name (Boris Karloff) replaced by a question mark: "?" This may seem to be of merely marginal interest in terms of the film proper, but we can read it as a first announcement of some basic dilemmas with regards to the creature: for the creature, there is a dilemma of *identity*, and for us one of *classification*. Stitched together from various bodies, how can we say *who* this is? More fundamentally, though, *what* is it in the first place? The word "monster" and the "?" are in a sense equivalent; for a "monster" is an aberration from the natural order, thus unclassifiable because lacking a corresponding concept. Conceptually undefined, "monster" is a variable, an "x" in the place of that which cannot be identified. For what it is, if truly monstrous, is *unspeakable*. Interestingly, in Whale's film this unspeakable quality of monstrosity is turned back on "The Monster" itself: the creature is denied speech, and thus the means of defending itself against designations thrust upon it from without.

I have already noted the irony and self-reflexive significance of the fact that, right at the beginning of the sound era of motion pictures, a mute creature should gain the iconic status that Karloff as the monster achieved. The mute role is, however, pervasive in classical melodrama, a fact that Brooks links to the expressive impulse of the genre: accordingly, melodrama is essentially a struggle to articulate the moral forces in the world. Muteness thus provides a dramatic obstacle to "the expressionism of the moral imagination" (55)—as when a mute character is falsely accused of some crime—but its significance goes beyond plot motivation. Brooks devotes an entire chapter of *The Melodramatic Imagination* to what he calls "the text of muteness" (56-80). Under this heading, he concerns himself with the many non-verbal means of expression appealed to by melodrama, from mute tableau, music (from which melodrama derives its name), to the expression of emotion through the exaggerated gestures characteristic of melodramatic acting. The literally mute character thus has a place in the larger context of the melodramatic aesthetic, and it is relevant here to consider briefly the historical and ideological roots of this constellation.

Historically, the mute character derives from pantomime. The pre-Revolutionary patent system in France, which censored verbal expression in non-sanctioned theatrical productions, led to great innovation in the visually expressive repertoire of popular theater (Brooks 63). Without the spoken word to convey meaning, scenery had to be expressive (46), banners and flags with printed text supplemented the action (63), and music underscored emotional states (48). After the official end of censorship, the visual devices retained an importance in popular theater, and, most importantly, the central use of gesture as an expressive means in pantomime was translated into what we now know as "melodramatic" acting. Brooks claims that "the whole expressive enterprise of [melodrama] represents a victory over repression [...] conceive[d] [...] as simultaneously social, psychological, historical, and conventional: what could not be said on an earlier stage, nor still on a 'nobler' stage, nor within the codes of society" (41). Here we approach the link between the historical and ideological reasons for the continuing appeal of muteness in a melodramatic theater allowed to speak. For related to the lowly roots of popular theater no less than to lofty philosophical reflections on the origins of language, "a deep suspicion of the existing sociolinguistic code, as of its image in the classical theatrical code" (66) was in the process of according a deeper significance to embodied, non-verbal gesture. Here, it was believed, a truer, more immediate expression could be achieved than through linguistic means. The quest for the origins of language led back to mute gesture as a universal, natural language capable of communicating "ineffable" meanings.

The appeal of muteness for theatrical melodrama, as a "democratic" genre concerned to reassert the presence of moral forces in a post-sacred era, consisted in its supposed ability to make this higher drama immediately legible to all spectators. The decline of the sacred had eroded the consensual basis for the communication of ultimate values by conventional means. Thus, in Brooks's words:

The use of mute gesture in melodrama reintroduces a figuration of the primal language onto the stage, where it carries immediate, primal spiritual meanings which the language code, in its demonetization, has obscured, alienated, lost. Mute gesture is an expressionistic means— precisely the means of melodrama—to render meanings which are ineffable, but nonetheless operative within the sphere of human ethical relationships. (72)

As the "democratic" theater was gradually eclipsed in popularity by film, elements of the former naturally found their place in the latter. I do not wish to suggest, however, that this was an even process of linear "development." For one thing, between the appearance of melodrama around 1800 and the rise of film, approximately a century later, the very modernity to which melodrama responded had changed. A more pronounced capitalism, the "hyperstimulus" of urban modernity, and new technologies all transformed the stage melodrama, which became more sensational and technology-dependent (both in its formal realization and in the diegetic employment of machines onstage).[12] For a time, film coexisted with 10-20-30s melodramatic theater (so called for the price of admission: ten, twenty, or thirty cents); the exhibition of early film—a "cinema of attractions"—was in fact, as we have seen, incorporated into an encompassing "variety format" (Miriam Hansen 29) which brought theatrical performance, film, and other entertainments under a single roof. It was the advent of the nickelodeon that, due to economic savings for audiences and exhibitors alike, ultimately enabled film's takeover of melodrama (Singer 167-68). But rather than undergoing a radical transformation, sensational stage melodrama was essentially *continued* by filmic melodrama of the early and transitional eras: not only the narratives, but also the *mise-en-scène* and theatrical style of these films (not to mention the actors, writers, and others involved) were simply imported from the theater.[13]

Moreover, with a new restriction on the spoken word, this time by way of the technological limitations of silent cinema, the excesses of melodramatic acting styles were reinvested with necessity. Muteness was no longer a choice, and gesture was once again required as a central expressive means. Significantly, cinema made a virtue out of its necessity, repeating the strategy of classical melodrama. Indeed, cinema was in quite a similar situation as the theater of a hundred years before. For essentially, the problem of the post-sacred "void" was one of the disintegration of "a unified audience committed to identical social and moral values" (Brooks 82), to which melodrama reacted with its "universal language" of mute gesture. By the twentieth century, an intensified modernity had only exacerbated the problem of the fragmented audience, and the emerging institution of cinema formulated for itself a remarkably similar solution: the medium of film itself, due to its non-verbal means, was figured widely in the transitional period, as we saw in Chapter 2, as a "univer-

---

12 See Singer, especially Chapters 5 and 6. Singer adopts the term "hyperstimulus" from New York social reformer Michael Davis, who coined it in 1911 (65).
13 This is not to say that filmic melodrama exactly reproduced sensational stage melodrama, but the initial continuity—which flowed into transitional-era perceptions of cinema as "canned theater"—greatly overshadows the disparities. See, in this regard, Singer, especially Chapter 7.

sal language" legible to literate and illiterate, rich and poor, recent immigrant and long-established citizen alike.[14] (Significantly, Universal Studios, the company that would later give us Whale's Frankenstein films, exploited the universal-language argument for the "democratic" nature of cinema, emphasizing in the transitional era that the company's name was also its program.)[15]

In this context, we might say that Karloff's mute monster was something of a carryover from silent film into the sound era,[16] much as the mute character in melodrama was retained after the necessity imposed by censorship was abolished. We can thus postulate a genealogical line of descent leading from pre-Revolutionary pantomime and its connection to philosophical speculations about the origins of language, by way of melodrama and silent cinema, to the creature of Whale's 1931 production. But if, as I have said, there is an irony in the monster's muteness at the beginning of the sound era, we are now in a position to see how deep that irony goes. For the "ineffability" of meanings allegedly expressed by mute gesture is a function of their inarticulability by linguistic means. So conceived, "the ineffable" comes quite close to "the monstrous" as that which is unspeakable because it eludes conceptual classification. But where mute gesture (and film itself) allegedly reaches the plane of *natural* language at its origin—a universally legible form of expression—the muteness/monstrosity of the creature is a result of *unnatural* forces that account for its incomprehensibility.

We are back to the manichaean forces—nature and anti-nature—which led Frankenstein on his quest for the fitting body. But we see that the monster is even more centrally, because corporeally, located at the point of their intersection. The monster is thus poised to become a melodramatic hero himself, to assert his virtue in the face of great social—and, as we see, ontological—odds. In *Bride of Frankenstein*, the monster embarks on an odyssey towards expression, morality, and humanity—the central terms of melodrama[17]—and his search for recognition leads him in the footsteps of his creator: onto a quest for a fitting (i.e. complementary, female) body.

---

14 See Miriam Hansen, especially 76-81.
15 See Miriam Hansen 78.
16 Robert Spadoni offers a compelling argument for this thesis, to which I return later in this chapter.
17 Note that Ed. Thomas and Forrest J. Ackerman, in a postscript to their May 1935 review of an advance screening for *Fantasy Magazine*, write that: "The story, instead of inspiring horror, as the former did, awakens the deepest compassion for the Monster. Karloff makes him lovable and engaging, his helpless exploits as a murderer entirely excusable." Interestingly, the film is referred to as a "scientifilm." Reprinted in Riley, *The Bride of Frankenstein* 17.

The pivotal scene, and indeed one of the most overtly melodramatic of the film, occurs when, persecuted and pursued into the forest, the creature is drawn towards a hut, visibly moved, by the sound of music: a hermit plays Schubert's "Ave Maria" on his violin. The lonely blind man bids the creature inside, welcoming him as a "friend." Showing empathy for a fellow "afflicted" creature, he shares his food and drink and offers the monster his bed. Melodramatic music underscores the hermit's prayer of thanks to God, who "hath brought two of thy lonely children together, and sent me a friend." A close-up reveals a tear rolling down the creature's cheek, and a cross on the wall glows eerily as the shot fades to black. We then see the two sitting together, the old man offering an English lesson. The creature repeats the words "bread" and "drink," commenting "good, good," and the two seal their fellowship with an impromptu eucharist of bread and wine and a vow of friendship. The creature's movement into the realm of language and human interaction culminates in an internalization of morality, as he pronounces, "Good. Bad." He appears more human now than ever before, "enlightened"—and indeed the lighting on his face is soft, the shadows on it almost absent. Eyes wide open, he seems to understand the great truth of a fundamental moral distinction, recognition of which is so central to the melodramatic mode.

But the fellowship cannot last, for hunters discover the "monster" and "rescue" the old man. Again driven from human society, the creature takes refuge in a crypt. Here he finds a female corpse, strokes its face, and mutters, "Friend." He spies from the shadows as Pretorius enters and prepares a meal on the casket of the dead woman who is to provide the bones for the "bride." The creature, ever in search of a friend, approaches the doctor, and a conversation ensues. Tempted by the necrophiliac "devil," the creature confesses, "I love dead. Hate living." Inspecting his future bride's skull, he marvels at the prospects offered by Pretorius: "Woman. Friend. Wife." The contrast between the pious hermit and the evil Pretorius thus personalizes the manichaean forces driving the creature.

Now under the control of Pretorius, the creature abducts Elizabeth to blackmail Frankenstein into the "supreme collaboration" of constructing a female creature. Forced now against his will to work with the diabolical doctor, Frankenstein leads Pretorius and two assistants to his tower laboratory for the climactic creation scene. More elaborate and extravagant than its 1931 counterpart, this creation sequence is a powerful, frenzied montage of high and low-angle shots, canted, complementary Dutch angles, and percussive editing. At the end of it all, a mummy-like creature moves its hand and Frankenstein repeats the now obligatory words: "It's alive!"

Shortly thereafter we see the two scientists on either side of the now fully dressed female as they drop their ends of the flowing white "wedding gown," Pretorius ambiguously announcing, "The bride of Frankenstein." The musical score mimics wedding bells, and the "bride" (played by Elsa Lanchester) steps forward.

A series of shots, cutting in to ever closer views of her face, reveals a glamorous contrast to the first creature, but marked, nonetheless, by telling scars under her chin. Her movements are jerky, robot-like, and she screeches as the original "monster" approaches and says, "Friend?" Looking confused, sad, and pleading, he takes her hand; a low-angle close-up of her face depicts the "bride" screaming, rejecting her would-be mate.

Devastated, the creature threatens to destroy the tower by pulling a conveniently placed self-destruct lever. Even Elizabeth has appeared in time for the final catastrophe, trying to persuade Frankenstein to come with her. But he replies, "I can't leave them! I can't!" The creature insists: "Yes, go! You live!" And to Pretorius: "You stay. We belong dead." The camera reveals the creature's hand approaching the lever, followed by a hideous headshot of the bride hissing. The creature sheds a tear, pulls the lever, and the destruction commences. An external shot depicts the tower exploding, and we see Frankenstein and Elizabeth escaping just in the nick of time. Ascending a hill, the couple embraces to watch the fireworks and the tower crumbling. The camera narrows in on them as Frankenstein utters, "Darling, darling." Fade to black and end of story.

The monster thus demonstrates his internalization of the hermit's lesson in morality; goodness and nature triumph over the forces of evil, and order is restored. If melodrama is a "drama of recognition," the creature's self-sacrifice implies the highest form of virtue's recognition. As Brooks emphasizes, the reward of virtue is secondary to its recognition in melodrama, virtuousness itself more important than the consequences of being good (27). The monster thus accepts death as the necessary price of virtue, and in Frankenstein and Elizabeth's closing embrace, in their final gaze at the decimation of the tower, we can imagine something like a feeling that justice has been served—"justice," indeed, on a number of levels. First, the justice sought by the villagers has certainly been done: the monsters are dead. And simultaneously the monster himself has done justice to humanity, to normality: he has seen the error of his ways and spared the protagonist and his wife as a result. With the couple's gaze doubling that of the audience, this double sense of justice adds up to a happy ending and the sense that "all's well that ends well." It also allows the spectator to engage in a reciprocal doing of justice to the monster. Recalling the creature's transformation into humanity in the course of the film, the almost sentimental gaze of our heroes invites us to give the creature his due by accepting him as one of us for his honorable and morally upright act. We can see him now for what he has been all along: very much like us, with a sense of honor, dignity, justice, and respect for the natural order of things.

If the monster is crisscrossed by the forces of nature and anti-nature, only the destruction of his hybrid body can restore nature's reign. For this hybridity is at odds with the integrity of moral forces demanded by melodrama, and the monster's recognition of this, though it dictates death, is a triumph for that natural element of his being. He sees that there can be no relief from his torments in the companionship of an equally hybrid body. Only those born wholly natural, like Frankenstein and Elizabeth, can share the rewards of virtue. The quest for a fitting body is over. "The only fitting body is a natural body," the film seems to tell us.

Incorporations III: Spectators, Melodrama, and the Politics of Embodiment

But this is only half the story, and here we arrive at the question of melodrama's politics of the body. Moving in concentrically larger circles from text to context (but setting the stage for the next section's reverse movement from large to small, or from molar to molecular), I hope to demonstrate here how Whale's Frankenstein films open up crucial questions concerning the spectatorial politics of melodrama—questions that bear on the political stakes of Frankenstein films generally as they interrogate, enact, and enforce processes of humanization both on the screen and off.

First, we should note that the "humanness" implicitly accorded the Karloff creature is in fact predicated on a misogynistic essentialization of gender roles. Having acquired language and internalized a basic morality, what the monster still lacks to be on a par with his human creator is the ability to reproduce sexually—indeed, he lacks "sexuality" *per se*, his "maleness" vis-à-vis a woman. The bride is therefore necessary for the monster's humanity. But she refuses to complete him and must therefore be destroyed—thus, paradoxically, completing him in negative fashion, by becoming Other to his Otherness, and giving him the opportunity to confirm the dominant patriarchal notion of humanity. Refusing to serve the creature's interest and submit to him in a pseudo-natural (heterosexual, procreative) relationship, the bride represents a recalcitrant, deviant form of feminine sexuality. She is monstrous in her failure to submit to male dominance. The death of this unnatural couple thus makes way for the "happily ever after" of the normal, natural, heterosexual couple. Thus, there seems to be a certain ironic *injustice* in doing the monster the justice of accepting him as human. For his internalization of a humanistic morality (with the notions of justice, honor, etc.) has led not only to self-destruction (itself questionable enough), but also to his injustice towards—indeed the destruction of—the deviant female Other. He has forgotten, in effect, his own Otherness in appropriating the dominant (male, heterosexual) image of humanity. The temptation to feel sympathy for the creature and to accept him as human, then, reinforces the exclusionary sort of humanity that he has indeed achieved.

Originally, the film was to end quite differently: The final script, as well as the preview version of April 6, 1935—not quite two weeks before the premiere of the film as we know it—had both Frankenstein and Elizabeth dying in the tower along with the bride, the monster, and Pretorius.[18] Whale changed his mind and reshot the ending just days before the April 19 opening, allowing the couple to live. Though his motives are unclear, the fact that Whale's last-minute decision followed the preview screening seems to suggest that it was a response to the audience's reception.[19] Of course, the original ending codes a radically different message, one hard to square with the moral logic of melodrama; the change is thus of great significance, especially for someone like Whale, who, as a homosexual, was himself something of an outsider in Hollywood. That is, Whale had a personal stake in the ending of the film, for the triumph of normality at the expense of monstrosity includes an indictment of "deviant" sexualities. Scott MacQueen reports an anecdote according to which Whale, while viewing the film years later, laughed out loud at the ending and was hushed by a woman who did not suspect his identity.[20] It is speculated on this basis that Whale had given Hollywood audiences what they wanted, but in full consciousness of the political implications of the changed ending. Accordingly, he was laughing at the simplistic expectations encoded in Holly-

---

18 The script is contained in Philip J. Riley, ed. *The Bride of Frankenstein. Universal Filmscripts Series, Classic Horror Films – Volume 2*. Absecon, NJ: MagicImage Filmbooks, 1989. In his foreword to this edition, Forrest J. Ackerman writes: "the betrothal and destruction of the Monster and his mate went through several drastic changes. An early concept was to have Fritz cut out Elizabeth's heart for use in the female monster. This idea was discarded as too macabre. It was changed in the film to another ghoul releasing Elizabeth, who arrives at the laboratory only minutes before the Monster pulls the lever that blows up the structure, bringing down rocks and rubble upon the Monster, his mate, Pretorius, Henry and Elizabeth, who is struggling to enter the locked lab door. After filming, Universal opted for a happy ending and reshot, having the Monster allow Henry to escape with Elizabeth. However, the destruction of the laboratory was too expensive to redo and if you look closely you can still see Henry and the Monster's mate by the laboratory door as the explosion occurs" (17).

19 Already the first film experienced a similar last-minute change. As Mordaunt Hall wrote in his review of *Frankenstein* in 1931: "As a concession to the motion picture audience, Frankenstein is not killed, but he is badly injured. Two endings were made for this production, and at the eleventh hour it was decided to put in the one in which Frankenstein lives, because it was explained that sympathy is elicited for the young scientist and that the spectators would leave disappointed if the author's last chapter was adhered to."

20 MacQueen recounts the story in his audio commentary to the DVD released in 2002.

wood conventions,[21] but he was also ironically staging his own predicament: for he was forced through such conventions to deny his own outsider status and play to the expectations of the mainstream—expectations in which melodrama plays a major role.[22]

This is not to say that Whale passively sacrificed himself and his alleged Otherness in the face of a patriarchal studio system—not, at least, without raising serious questions. The creature's hybrid ontology problematizes the role accorded the body in melodrama: to the naturalization of morality implicit in melodrama's appeal to mute gesture, the monster opposes the possibility that behind culture's conventions lies not natural goodness but indeterminate monstrosity. In its hybridity, the monster is an ontologically "queer" creature, and it is precisely queerness that is so threatening to the moral values of the villagers—to the integrity of all inhabitants, good or evil, of the melodramatic universe. In recoding mute embodiment as queer, Whale destabilizes the very premises that make possible the melodramatic ending he gives the audience.[23] But as the reaction of the woman in the anecdote reveals,

---

21 By way of contrast, Hall wrote in his 1931 review of *Frankenstein* that the film "aroused so much excitement at the Mayfair yesterday that many in the audience laughed to cover their true feelings."

22 For a reading of *Bride of Frankenstein* as a queer text along these lines, see Gary Morris, "Sexual Subversion: The Bride of Frankenstein." *Bright Lights Film Journal* 19 (July 1997). <http://www.brightlightsfilm.com/19/19_bride1.php>. See also Vito Russo's classic study of homosexuality in Hollywood, *The Celluloid Closet*, where Russo writes: "In both films the homosexuality of director James Whale may have been a force in the vision. Director Robert Aldrich recalls that 'Jimmy Whale was the first guy who was blackballed because he refused to stay in the closet. Mitchell Leisen and all those other guys played it straight, and they were onboard, but Whale said, 'fuck it, I'm a great director and I don't have to put up with this bullshit'—and he *was* a great director, not just a company director. And he was unemployed after that—never worked again'" (50). Russo goes on to position the monster and Dr. Pretorius as precursors of the many openly gay characters who, beginning in the 1960s, were violently killed or committed suicide in connection with their homosexuality (51-52).

23 The term "queer" did not, of course, have the same connotations then as it does now, but it is interesting to see it used in characterizations of early horror films and their monsters. Mordaunt Hall, writing in the February 13, 1931 edition of the *New York Times*, said of *Dracula* the following: "As the scenes flash by there are all sorts of queer noises, such as the cries of wolves and the hooting of owls, not to say anything of the screams of Dracula's feminine victims, who are found with twin red marks on their white throats." And later that year, in his December 5 *New York Times* review of *Frankenstein*, Hall writes: "As for the monster, he is burned when the villagers set fire to the windmill. From the

that ending continues to function as a "happy" one for (at least some) spectators. Not just an act of private irony, though, Whale's deconstruction of pre-linguistic nature sheds light on the moral "logic" of melodrama and begins to illuminate the role of the spectator in the "justification" of this system.

In a passage of central significance to Brooks's study of the melodramatic mode in the modern novel, Henry James remarks on Balzac that, though his characters don't act realistically, their actions accord with the moral drama in which they are seen to participate—"they owe their being to our so seeing them" (qtd. in Brooks 9). Generalizing on James's insight, we can say that the whole moral system of melodrama owes its existence to our noetic investment, our willingness or ability to believe and to "see" in a certain way. Indeed, this "seeing as" is the central goal of melodrama, which aims at the inscription of moral values in the bodies it depicts and, reflexively, at the incorporation of these values into the bodies of its spectators. It naturalizes a normative version of "the body" through its vague gesturing at ineffable meanings and demands of the spectator that the gap of incommensurability between individually lived embodiment and discursive constructions be neutralized. The model of nature at the heart of melodrama's recourse to mute gesture is the ground upon which commensurability is sought, and this commensurability is to be the basis for a new moral consensus in the face of the post-sacred void.

The monster embodies the process: its queer incommensurability is transformed by the expressive means of linguistic articulation and the internalization of a sanctioned morality. Discourse and incorporation come together to complete the process whereby the melodramatic happy ending is enabled. But the zero degree of queerness and monstrosity—as opposed to the natural universalism of romantic goodness—points to our own starting position in the becoming-spectator of melodrama: we are first of all embodied beings, and on this level of mute (i.e. non-discursive) embodiment, no body is a fitting body. Melodrama, at least in one of its capacities, is thus a normalizing technology aimed at taming the explosive potential of bodily difference; in this sense, melodrama is itself an invitation for the spectator to under-

---

screen comes the sound of the crackling of the blazing woodwork, the hue and cry of the frightened populace and the queer sounds of the dying monster." The significance of these statements lies in the fact that, as Robert Spadoni argues (and to whose argument we turn shortly), early horror films channeled sound-transitional experiences of early talkies as "uncanny," causing viewers to ascribe these experiences to the diegetic contents of the films. We see this in Hall's talk of "queer sounds," which attributes the queerness to narrative events, but which responds to a transitional perception of the embodied reception situation. It is precisely this vacillation between diegetic and extra-diegetic phenomena that ultimately powers Whale's queering of the mute monster and the bare embodiment for which he stands.

take the quest for a fitting body—his or her own. Whale's adaptation of the melodramatic mode allows, though, for a critical questioning of the ways in which non-discursive embodiment and discursive constructs of "the body," incorporation and inscription, come together in the creation of a spectator willing and able to enact the noetic "seeing as" required by melodrama.

As we have seen, melodrama, as the "expressionism of the moral imagination," sets stock in mute gesture as a primordial language. As Brooks points out, though, it constantly comes up against the limits of expression resulting from gesture's "desemanticized" nature (68-75). This leads to problems in script-writing: how are the gestures to be described in terms other than the grandiose meanings to be conveyed? Concomitantly, spectators face the problem of how to interpret the gestures enacted on stage. Recourse is thus had to "translators," characters who explain the meanings to other characters and to the audience. Perceiving the "close relationship between gesture and writing" (Brooks 78), the modern novel in its melodramatic mode picks up on and transforms the problematics of the "mute text"; according to Brooks, "gesture in the novel becomes, through its translation, fully resemanticized." The novel thus imagines "the identity of gesture and writing, *écriture*, [as] the inscription of meaning" (78).

Mute expression thus involves melodrama in a struggle over the relation between "incorporating acts" and "inscription"—terms N. Katherine Hayles invokes to explain the complex interplay between individual embodiment and "the body" as a discursive construct (*How We Became Posthuman* 192-207). Embodiment is the monstrous, intractable condition of our non-discursive, individually and contextually instantiated state of physical being—a pre-semantic or desemanticized *Leib*. "The body" is a discursively defined normative ideal or average, the "normal" or "fitting" body—a (re-)semanticized *Körper*. Inscription practices record—and thereby transform by making commensurable to discourse—embodied being in the construct of the body. Incorporating practices, individually enacted gestures, are not, however, pure *Leib*—not the "pure" language of primordial nature; nor are they identical with "writing." Gestures are possible only upon the basis of our embodiment (physicality is one precondition of their enactment), but they are always enacted in the social space of discourse. Gesture thus offers no escape from a degenerate linguistic code, but neither does language swallow our bodies whole. Incorporation involves a *negotiation* between an ineffable or monstrous embodiment and a normative body.

This negotiation helps to explain the process of the monster's becoming-human: here monstrosity—embodiment—clearly loses out to normativity. What I am suggesting, though, is that the interaction of incorporation and inscription is crucial to melodrama generally. On the narrative level, muteness poses an obstacle to expression, the eventual triumph over which indicates the resemanticization of gesture—

the victory of discourse over the indeterminacy of embodiment. The ultimate significance of melodramatic incorporation lies, however, in its "higher" goal of moral reconstruction. Melodrama attempts to make "humans" of us all, to make us *feel* the force of its moral imperatives, and for this purpose incorporation is indispensable. A "successful" spectator, in the terms defined by melodrama, is one who truly incorporates melodramatic morality, whose enabling noetic investment in the melodramatic universe is grounded and expressed in normalized bodily practices and affects. Ideally, we enact the becoming-human of the monster in our becoming-spectator with regard to melodrama, transferring semanticized body images into our own bodily praxis; an "appropriate" and "humane" reaction to the monster's sacrificial consummation of humanity might be to shed a tear. Whale, in laughing, was himself a poor spectator of melodrama, a fact plausibly explained by his queerness—his refusal to become "human" in the essentialized terms of a patriarchal mainstream. In connection with his queering of pre-linguistic nature, we can therefore read his films as an ironic critique of bourgeois, patriarchal ideology. But a straightforward reading remains a live possibility, as the reaction of the anecdotal woman reveals. Significantly, her irritation is expressed in a reproving bodily gesture aimed at silencing Whale's irreverent outburst. Ultimately, Whale's films are open to both sentimental and ironic readings. In their multi-leveled incorporations of melodrama, they thus gesture toward the fact that the hermeneutic strategies of spectators are differentially grounded in—and bounded by—their incorporations of highly political discursive contents by means of embodied affective responses. In this way, *Frankenstein* and *Bride of Frankenstein* highlight the stakes of melodramatic incorporation and tell us not so much that "ideology is in the eye of the beholder," but rather that politics is rooted squarely *in the body*.

Furthermore, there are crucial implications for cinematic spectatorship generally. As Miriam Hansen has documented, the figuration of "film as a new universal language [...] coincided in substance and ideology with the shift from primitive to classical modes of narration and address that occurred, roughly, between 1909 and 1916" (79). At stake here, as we saw in Chapter 2, was a normative conception of "the spectator" as opposed to the diverse masses of empirical audiences.[24] The rise of the feature film (notably melodrama) and the development of narrative and formal devices designed to position the spectator with regard to diegesis, to absorb viewers into the illusion of the screen and thereby divorce them from "the physical and social space" (83) of the venue—these point to the construction of a "viewer as a temporarily incorporeal individual" (84): a member of an essentialized human

---

24 See Miriam Hansen, Chapter 2. See also Annette Kuhn's "Women's Genres: Melodrama, Soap Opera and Theory" for the distinction between audiences and spectators in the context of melodrama.

community without ethnicity, race, gender, or social class (80-81). The absorptive identification aimed at in the emerging classical style dictated, among other things, a shift from "primitive" pantomimic acting to "naturalistic approaches that emphasized facial expression instead of broad physical gesture" and from characters "as moral or comic types" to "psychologically motivated individuals with whose predicaments, aspirations, and emotions the viewer could identify" (80). Karloff's monster, restricted as he was (initially) to the old pantomimic means, and whose scarred face complicated identification considerably, was in a sense a return of "the primitive"; his hybridity points towards the deeper meaning of the "transitional" period of film—the transformation of corporeal audiences into incorporeal spectators. Open as they are to multiple readings, his monstrous corporality and ambiguous humanity highlight the practices of inscription and incorporation at play in the negotiation of spectatorship and offer a potential, if only partial, undoing of the by then long-established classical spectator. Ultimately, the monster points us toward a rediscovery of what Miriam Hansen calls the "significant margin [that remained even in the classical era] between textually constructed molds of subjectivity and their actualization on the part of historical viewers" (90). It is this margin, I would suggest, which lends Whale's Frankenstein-film melodramas—with their excesses and hindrances to "absorptive realism"[25]—the potential to unmask their own normalizing methods of incorporation and even to disrupt anthropocentric modes of engagement in favor of an affective experience of anthropotechnical transitionality.

ABOUT-FACE:
ANTHRO-, TECHNO-, XENO-PHENOMENOLOGY

As I announced at the outset of this chapter, my argument here has been following a trajectory that leads from the human to the nonhuman, which means, in this case, from the diegetic and narrative-thematic constructions engaged by a human spectator to a sub-personal and distributed material encounter with cinema as an alien agency. Hence, I have been concerned to show that a non-psychological affective excess inheres in, and *emerges from*, contact with the films *qua* discursive event (i.e. from the films approached as storytelling devices addressed to socially situated subjectivities defined by their discursive interactions and politico-semiotic relations). This is important to my claim that an alien-phenomenological perspective, and an experience of the non-correlationist excess that is the radically nonhuman body of these films, asserts itself from within rather than from without—in other words, that this experience of an alien encounter is a reality of engagement with

---

25 The term is Singer's (177).

these particular filmic objects rather than a mere projection of my own spectatorial fantasies (or techno-theoretical predilections) onto them. To be sure, my argument is designed with a view towards more general theoretical consequences for thinking the cinema in terms of anthropotechnical interfaces, but that hardly means that it is a matter of indifference to my argument *which* films we view and under *what* specific material and historical circumstances. And if the technology-philosophical and media-theoretical orientation of my approach, as articulated in Part Two, suggests that cosmic-scale transitions are at play in inducing experiences of alterior material agencies, there is also a more local, aesthetic aspect involved here: some films, like Whale's Frankenstein films, are simply better at inducing the experiences that interest me than others, and this has something to do with the way that particular filmmakers harness the energies and agencies of transitionality in their films. (These filmmakers are like the scientists and engineers discussed in Chapter 5 in this respect: not wholly autonomous but not passive either—they engage in transformative experimental negotiations with the material forces of novelty.) In such instances, historical setting, media-technological transition, narrative convention, and aesthetic innovation come together in such a way as to broker an experience of subterranean, seemingly occult powers, forging subjectively unrecuperable and fleeting moments of contact in which one might briefly glimpse the molecular, metabolic flux of anthropotechnical change. In the remainder of this chapter, I turn to the achievement in Whale's films of this monstrous contact, which runs counter to the "molarizing" processes of humanization outlined above, and which lies sedimented beneath a number of retroactive conventionalizations: viz. the ensuing consolidation of the horror genre, the serialization of Frankenstein films, and the iconization of the Karloffian image. I turn, then, to the films' successful capture of alien, monstrous particulars made available for experience at the heart of the universal monster.

Locating the "Uncanny Bodies" of Whale's Frankenstein Films

Part of the reason for Whale's success in this regard has been identified by Robert Spadoni in his important book *Uncanny Bodies: The Coming of Sound Film and the Origins of the Horror Genre*. The thesis of Spadoni's study is that the horror genre was produced by means of channeling an "uncanny" experience of film reception that briefly dominated the sound transition, by preserving and transforming this experience into the foundation for viewers' perceptions of sound-era monsters. As Spadoni puts it, "[t]he sound transition acted as a kind of filter through which strained all the other materials and forces that coalesced into the first sound horror films Hollywood produced" (4). Tod Browning's *Dracula* appeared at the tail end of the transition—which, according to the chronology proposed by Donald Crafton, concluded in May 1931[26]—and set this filtering process in motion. *Frankenstein*, appearing half a year after the close of the transition, picked up on *Dracula*'s precedent and secured the place of horror among the genres of the new era. What fueled these films was an experience, already fading from memory then and all but unrecoverable now, of the first talking figures to appear on screen, a perception of human figures rendered "ghostly" by the novelty of sound, which foregrounded the artificiality of cinema in a manner not unlike early film's emphatic demonstrations of moving picture technology (6, 8-30). Such figures, as Spadoni documents, appeared to audiences strangely transformed, out of kilter, "uncanny" in the senses Freud borrowed from Ernst Jentsch: alive but somehow inanimate, or inanimate but somehow alive (Spadoni 6).[27] As transitional phenomena, these sensations were quickly "stabilized," as Spadoni aptly puts it, "neutralized" in such a way that sound could be seen as contributing to, rather than detracting from, filmic realism; but "*Dracula* and *Frankenstein* [...] 'trapped' within their forms the uncanny reception energies" and "converted [them] into the solid basis for an enduring genre practice" (7).[28]

I have highlighted Spadoni's uses of the terms *stabilization, neutralization*, and *trapping* because they are reminiscent of Pickering's descriptions of the machinic "captures" that take place in science conceived as a "dance of agency." It will be useful, I believe, to keep these resemblances in mind as we explore Spadoni's notion of the "uncanny body" of classical horror, for what emerges is a picture of filmmakers and moviegoers *negotiating* with material forces that are crafted—not through unilateral domination but by means of the bidirectional process that Pickering calls "interactive stabilization"—into filmic texts and images that, over time, will progressively lose their initially powerful ability to activate experiences of transitionality. Accordingly, what we find in Whale's Frankenstein films is a cinematic counterpart to the varied negotiations with the steam engine, which, as outlined in Chapter 5, progressed from an early mode of registration as corporeal shock to the eventual intellectual taming and scientific "vanishing act" effected in thermodynamic theory. Similarly, Whale's Frankenstein films bear witness to the passing, by way of naturalization, of the unsettling transitional force of a shift in the

---

26 See Crafton's *The Talkies*.
27 See Freud's "The Uncanny." Jentsch's 1906 treatment of the subject has been translated as "On the Psychology of the Uncanny."
28 In my article "Tarzan und der Tonfilm: Verhandlungen zwischen 'science' und 'fiction'," I expand upon Spadoni's argument that a very similar process applies to the filmic representation of Tarzan; the iconic portrayal by Johnny Weissmuller, I argue, was also tuned to and animated by the dynamics of the sound transition.

medial fabric of anthropotechnical co-constitution. The monster, as we have seen, allegorizes this normalization process in the course of his melodramatic career, but he also carries traces that can be excavated to reveal an encounter with the not-yet-conventionalized, or not-yet-molarized, agency that is the radically alien embodiment form of early sound film, prior to its correlation to human subjectivity.

Figure 2: The Uncanny Body

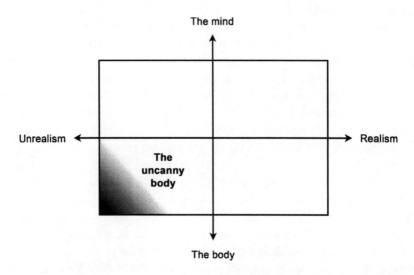

What Spadoni refers to as the "uncanny body" of early sound film is defined, in terms that require a bit of explanation, as a "zone of sensation in which the *unreal* and the *bodied* nature of sound film come across the most forcefully" (11). This zone is located on a plane of coordinates defined by a horizontal "unrealism/realism" axis and a vertical "body/mind" axis, as seen in Figure 2.[29] It is important to note that Spadoni's use of "realism" is defined in terms of medial "transparency" (10), so that the term "unreal" as it occurs in the definition of the uncanny body does *not* primarily mean a number of things that are commonly implied by the term "unrealistic" (e.g. logically or physically improbable, narratively fantastic, etc.); instead, it refers to an opacity of the filmic medium that corresponds to an awareness of its artificiality and technical constructedness—an awareness that Spadoni, following Yuri Tsivian, calls the viewer's "medium sensitivity" (13-19). The horizontal axis of Spadoni's grid can therefore be redescribed, according to the vocabulary I adopted from Don Ihde in Chapter 2, by placing embodiment relations on the right and hermeneutic relations on the left. This interpretation is borne out by

---

29 The diagram appears in Spadoni 11.

the opposition established in the following statement: "Within the chorus of praise for the realism of [transitional-era sound] films were indications that sound simultaneously was *getting in the way* of viewers' sensations of the figures speaking and singing on the screen" (11, emphasis in original). Crucial to the operative notion of "unrealism," then, is the medium's standing out as an object in its own right, protruding in front of the content it mediates.

As for the mind/body distinction, Spadoni associates "mind" with "the disembodied, 'intellectual' appeal" of the use of sound in the 1932 film adaptation of Eugene O'Neill's play *Strange Interlude*, which used voice-overs to present characters' thoughts directly, without the need for lip movement or corporeal gesture (9-10). Spadoni's initial cue here is therefore one that refers to the attachment, or disconnection, of onscreen characters' voices and bodies, but the true potential behind the notion of "the *bodied* nature of sound film" lies, I submit, in its ability to foreground the materiality of filmic sound itself and its registration through a form of resonating contact with the viewer's body. Seen thus, "mind" refers not only to the disembodiment of filmic figures' voices, but more generally to the construction (and reconstruction following the sound transition) of the "viewer as a temporarily incorporeal individual" that defines the idealized classical spectator according to Miriam Hansen (84). "Body" then refers to the situation characteristic of early film, before a spectatorial subjectivity had been abstracted from the space of the theater by means of the classical cinema's segregation of it, through continuity principles, from the diegetic space of the screen; and it likewise characterizes the sound transition, during which period these distinctions were temporarily suspended.

Seen thus, the uncanny body corresponds to a corporeally situated viewership according to the techno-phenomenological pattern of hermeneutic relations, as opposed to the model of disembodied spectatorship under embodiment relations privileged by classical Hollywood. But Spadoni's grid, with its three remaining quadrants besides that of the uncanny body, draws a somewhat more nuanced picture of normative and non-normative spectatorial possibilities than I was able to draw, with the help of Ihde and Miriam Hansen, in Chapter 2. For although "disembodiment" and medial transparency did in fact come, in the 1910s, to fit together as a pair in the course of the transition to the classical film paradigm, and though this combination (which would be located in the upper right hand corner of Spadoni's diagram) retained a certain privilege in classical film theory's aesthetic ideal of filmic productions worthy of the title "art," the other two quadrants mark out real, non-empty possibilities that have been actualized in filmic practice. Thus, I propose, a range of non-deviant, popular forms of viewer-film relation, characteristic of conventional modes of what Linda Williams dubs "body genres"—with their regulated excesses, their conventional means of activating bodily responses—are at home in the lower right-hand quadrant of Spadoni's grid; let us call this the normal, as opposed to uncanny, body.[30] By contrast, the upper left-hand region is occupied, for example, by modernist and avant-garde modes of high-cultural deviance—by "intellectual," and often *conceptually* self-reflexive, modes of violating classical principles, as opposed to the "materialist" manner of the uncanny body; let us call this the uncanny mind. (To be clear: the idea is not that abstract, avant-garde, or "art film" modes are *incapable* of invoking the uncanny body, in a way that popular modes uniquely can. But the question, which explains why the distinction usually works out this way, is this: does a given film promote an intellectual acknowledgement, recognition, or appreciation of filmic materiality, or does it induce a distributed, somatic, and pre-personal experience of it?) By filling in the blanks on Spadoni's diagram thus, we are able to see the entire right-hand side as mapping out a spectrum of tendencies within mainstream cinema, where the "normal mind" mode retains a theoretical privilege in the classical history of film aesthetics while the "normal body" defines a popular, but generically stabilized, form of body-centric production and reception. The left-hand side describes, accordingly, a correspondent range of non-normative options. The upper half of the diagram, spanning the spectrum from normative to non-normative extremes, is united by a relative disembodiment of spectatorial subjectivity and dematerialization of spectatorial engagement, which can imply either the segregation of spaces identified by Miriam Hansen or the heady appeal and interpretive demands of film with high-art aspirations.[31] It is, of course, the lower half that interests me more, and especially the nature of the distinction between normal and uncanny body modes, which I would like to coordinate with the distinction of molar versus molecular—"the body" (or *Körper*)

---

30 In "Film Bodies: Gender, Genre, and Excess," Williams situates her discussion of body genres (drawing on arguments put forward by Rick Altman) in terms of the way that the account of the classical Hollywood style presented in Bordwell, Thompson, and Staiger's seminal study is unable to accommodate melodrama and other genres that rely on "spectacle, episodic presentation, or dependence on coincidence except as limited exceptions or 'play' within the dominant linear causality of the classical" (3). By mapping the bodily sorts of excesses emphasized by Williams onto Spadoni's grid, we are able to see mainstream, popular cinema as split between (or hierarchized according to) a disembodied idealization of classical norms on the one hand, championed by classical film theory and maintained as well by more contemporary models, and an embodied mode on the other hand that is excluded by those norms, relegated to a lower cultural status, but no less established and widespread.

31 Indeed, the union of these projects in transitional-era film aesthetics and in actual film practice might be seen as responsible for the privileged status of the viewing subject over the viewing body, despite the widespread appeal and success of body genres. See, on this topic, my "Between Art and Technology: Functions of Film in Transitional-Era Cinema."

versus a distributed embodiment (anthropotechnical *Leib* or body without organs)—as these might correspond to generic and/or media-technical stabilization versus transitional negotiation or mangling within the cinema.

Before I pursue this last suggestion, which is crucial to my view of Whale's Frankenstein films, allow me to spell out the critical scope and type of analysis enabled by Spadoni's grid as I have expanded upon it here. I claimed above that the molecular affective experience of alien encounter that I am after arises through conjunctions of historical situation, media-technical transition, genre convention, and aesthetic innovation. The matrix that I have extrapolated from Spadoni's mapping of the uncanny body is useful in the pursuit of such experience because its operative distinctions of mind/body and normal/uncanny can be used to locate a range of experiential differences across all of these categories, which can then be mobilized to identify the specific material agency of a film in its historical, technological, and social contexts. Thus, to illustrate the general mechanics of the approach, we can start with the insight that the uncanny body and the normal mind typify the dominant historical paradigms of early and classical cinema, respectively. Relevant changes in media technology (such as sound, color, digitization, etc.) and media technique (such as continuity principles, practices of aural orientation and coordination with visually constructed spatiality, etc.) can be mapped on top of these periodizations to yield a more subtle phenomenological view of dominant paradigms and transitional disruptions. Genre conventions, as we have seen, correspond to various modes that can be located on the grid (body genres dominating the lower right, perhaps certain types of detective films or "puzzle films" in the mode of *The Sixth Sense* and *Memento* landing in the uppermost reaches of "mental" appeal among popular genres,[32] while others like science fiction are characterized by periodic shifts between "intellectual" speculation and body-based spectacle); and these generic differences can be re-mapped onto the initial historical and media-technical mappings, thus complicating the picture once more. Finally, within this grid of determinants, we are able to map stylistic choices and aesthetic innovations onto the coordinate plane, where they find their place as the means of channeling the many forces and agencies at play. The result of such a multi-layered mapping is a nuanced picture or "snapshot" (in Pickering's term) of films in context, of the agential assertions of specific filmic bodies as they negotiate positions amongst producers, consumers, technologies, and discourses. The type of nonhuman body revealed in this snapshot is defined by both external and internal relations: by the normative patterns and expectations that it contextually fulfills or fails to fulfill, and by the rhythmic material alternations between modes (i.e. quadrants

---

32 On "puzzle films," see the anthology of that title: Warren Buckland, ed. *Puzzle Films: Narrative Complexity in Contemporary Cinema*. West Sussex: Wiley-Blackwell, 2009.

on the grid) that accompany the internal movements of narrative development, *mise-en-scène*, and the unique temporal course marked out by a film's overall sequence of sounds and images. Accordingly, a film might shift between normal mind and body modes, interrupted perhaps by a "utopic moment" (in Landon's term) of the uncanny body type, and then return to its origin; the specific pattern of these movements, which is always relative to historical, media-technical, and generic constraints, defines *this* filmic body: the particular cinematic capture of agency that this film is. And our map, or a set or series of such context-sensitive snapshots, can be used to trace the historical development of this body's metamorphosis over time.

In the first half of this chapter, I demonstrated how Whale's Frankenstein films articulated a melodramatic tale of humanization—both the monster's and the spectator's—that progressed by means of taming the anomalous or monstrous potentials of the body. With respect to Spadoni's grid, these melodramas of incorporation place themselves clearly on the lower right-hand side; they are body-genre masterpieces of the "normal body" variety, and this is true whether we treat them as melodrama or as horror. However, as I pointed out earlier, the very notion of a horror genre is one that took form alongside—and with direct reference to—Whale's Frankenstein films, so that our view of them today as golden-age horror is the product of a major transformation both of the films and of the region marked out as the space of the "normal body." For if, as Spadoni argues, early horror called forth experiences that derived from the uncertain transition to sound, then an "uncanny body" haunts the films, and this must be recovered if we are to approach the films on their own terms. Besides, as I pointed out at the beginning of the chapter, melodrama may exercise normalizing powers on the body by channeling unruly affects into more manageable, subjectively correlated emotions, but in order for it to do so this "mode of excess"—by which phrase Brooks defines melodrama as more than a determinate genre—must be in contact with those pre-personal affects in the first place. Perhaps we can follow the dominant molar, humanizing development of Whale's films in reverse, taking it as an index of broader concomitant processes of generic stabilization, in order to discover a molecular undercurrent of passional flows at the root of both. Recall now that Whale's self-reflexive problematization of normative (spectatorial) embodiment recoded the natural ground of the normal body as uncanny and queer; this may be read as an affront to the hypothesized normalization process by which the horror genre, Whale's own Frankenstein films, and their monster experienced a shift to the right along the uncanny/normal axis. In other words, Whale parried that line of development by making a contrary, perpendicular move: a sublimation of the uncanny body along the vertical axis, by means of which a subtext of the uncanny mind mode emerges—a "critique" or "commentary" on the films' ostensible political messages, a subtle (and, accordingly, hermeneutically demanding) means of undermining their apparent endorsement of a conservative politics of proper (sexual and spectatorial) embodiment, which it is tempting to read in the conceptual terms of irony. If we are to take Whale's critique seriously, however, we will have to retrace its path back downward, back to the uncanny transitional agencies from which it draws its energy.

This very cursory mapping of tendencies therefore reveals that the two basic trajectories in Whale's Frankenstein films, the horizontal movement of normalization and the vertical movement of "mentalization," are intimately related one to the other. The former movement designates a historical course of changing perceptions of the films, which is correlated with a range of processes, including the media-technical normalization of post-transitional sound, the generic stabilization of horror as a normal-body-type body genre, and the narrative and extra-diegetic demonstrification of the monster both *qua* character and *qua* iconic image. The second, vertical movement subjects these processes to a reflexive, conceptual problematization that ironically points to a pre-conceptual layer of embodied agency. Taken together, the two trajectories suggest that Whale's Frankenstein films are themselves animated by *an agency that radiates outward from the uncanny body* as the point of their origin. Sedimented beneath the weight of the twin subjective appropriation forms of sentimentally normalized and ironic readings alike, this agency, as Spadoni's analysis helps us to substantiate, is the diffuse molecular power of a fleeting transitional moment.

Face to Face with the Monster: Towards Affective Ground Zero

Let us return, then, to Spadoni's argument that *Frankenstein* "traps" the weird energies of the sound transition and diverts them for its own purposes, thus clearing the way for the formation of horror as we know it—and horror as we know it is definitely a sound-era creation, full of sonic as much as visual terrors, such as shrieks and "things that go bump in the night." But, as Spadoni convincingly argues, these latter phenomena—the "[u]nseen bumps and audible screams" of horror (2)—are in an important sense only carryovers, conventionalized remnants of the uncanny body of early sound film, the experiential force of which dissipated steadily from the moment of the sound transition's inception, as viewers increasingly got used to the sight and sound of talking pictures. As long as the transition was underway, the novelty of cinematic sound could still be appealed to, and sensations of the strangeness of the affair still attended the experience of viewers heeding such appeals. Though a stroke of genius in its own right, the deflection of these sensations into a vampire story's arsenal of fear-inducing techniques was, due to *Dracula*'s late-transitional vintage, therefore all but natural. But if Browning's film evoked the uncanny body of early sound film more or less by default, the post-transitional *Frankenstein* could do so only with a greater degree of design. And if Whale's self-reflexive plays indicate a highly self-conscious mode of creative agency, Whale's successful "capture" of the uncanny body—conceived as the result of an interactive "dance of agency," a distributed process of mangling—manifests itself elsewhere: above all, in the face of the monster, which, beneath the iconized veneer familiar to us all, undermines self-reflexivity of the conceptual sort with a non-reflective surface that refuses subjective correlation; the facial image, I wish to say, harbors a Teflon-like substrate to which phenomenological intentions just won't stick. It is this substrate, this non-iconizable material excess of the monstrous facial image, that, in 1931, mediated the molecular force of transitionality.

To recover an experience of that visage, which would bring us face to face with the alien agency of *Frankenstein*'s filmic body, requires that we peel back the layers of popular-cultural associations that have accrued upon it over the years, that we rewind all the subsequent Frankenstein films and return to a situation prior even to *Bride of Frankenstein*'s melodramatic/ironic humanization of the face as the source of articulate words and expressive tears. We must try to imagine how terrifying the monster's face was to its first audiences, who did not even have the comfort of a fixed genre label "horror" at their disposal with which to categorize, process, and thereby mitigate the disturbing nature of their experience. Indeed, this pre-stabilized horror film's particular power to frighten was linked directly to the pre-iconic perception of the monster; as Spadoni points out: "How scary the film was on its first release is suggested by the fact that at that time, and unlike any time since then, the view of Boris Karloff's monster as a sympathetic figure was not unanimously taken for granted" (93). Then, the still unfamiliar monster caused fear by virtue of its unpredictability—the 1931 incarnation may have been less violent and bloodthirsty than the inhuman killing machine to which it (sometimes) devolved in the 1940s (and even more so in post-Universal productions), but the latter creature (or better: creature "type") is so predictable and conventionalized in its mechanical action that the horror it inspires remains largely in the diegetic realm, affecting its onscreen victims more than its real-world viewing audiences. In 1931, however, the monster's greater unpredictability was not only a matter of viewers' prior lack of exposure, or even of the pre-stabilized state of horror, but, attendant to those factors, also a function of the monster's reactivation of the "unpredictable, context-contingent responses" typical of the sound transition, which were then "converted into responses [...] provoked not by technological novelty and other temporary, reception-based dynamics but by text-embedded triggers that are, comparatively speaking, context independent" (97). In other words, the monster is animated by a transitional materiality, but the textualization of this force begins right away. The outward radiation, of which I spoke above, from a molecular agency of the uncanny body sort towards normalized and dematerialized avatars ensures, or so it would seem, that the monster's true face is doomed to misrecognition from the start.

Recognition, though, is the category of melodrama, which Brooks declares the "drama of recognition" (27). It is therefore the wrong category with which to approach the *pre*-humanized face of the monster and the experience it could engender. Thus, despite the monstrous facial image's almost immediate degradation to a ubiquitous marketing gimmick, and despite the seemingly total transfer of its uncanny monstrosity to the diegesis (upon which basis *Frankenstein* served as a shining example for the subsequent generic stabilization of horror), it is possible, I maintain, to locate a gap in the net of textuality cast upon the image. In this gap, which is also a sort of hole in the narrative, the monster assaulted his first viewers with a physical shock, subject only to a visceral sort of processing, but which was just as quickly forgotten. Ground zero, where the impact of this experience is the greatest, and which marks a point of contact with an alien agency, is reached in the scene when the newly animated monster makes his first appearance onscreen.

We see Frankenstein and his former teacher Waldman seated at a table. As the two discuss the creature, eerie footsteps become at first faintly audible and then gradually louder. Frankenstein extinguishes the light above the table, and the two men prepare for the imminent entry of the monster, peering, full of contagious anticipation, offscreen to the viewer's left. We see, by way of a low-angle shot that more or less matches their perspective, a closed door that—the footsteps having reached their maximum volume—slowly opens to reveal the monster, who is facing *away* from us and who now backs into the room. There is a cut to a medium-shot view of the monster, still backing in, now turning around slowly toward the camera. At the very instant that his face is in profile, it is thrust—due to the monster's tottering gait, his weight shifting from one leg to another—out of the shadow and into the light, where the monster hesitates for a split second before shifting back to the other side and continuing his robotic pirouette. Another forty-five degrees, but only a half second later at most, and the next shift of weight coincides with a semi-profile, a three-quarter view with deep shadows cutting into the facial features, emphasizing especially a darkened and dead-looking eye socket, the monster's eyes now turned uncannily towards the camera/the viewer. The creature's final step brings the face into a frontal, full face position, and there is a sudden cut to a medium close-up, held for approximately a second, the monster still staring blankly into the camera—and now another jarring cut to a tightly framed close-up of the grey face, again held for a second that seems like an eternity, a timeless moment in which nothing stirs, no sound is heard, no connection is made to the outside world. This is a caesura that suspends—only briefly if we are to believe the clock—not only the film's narrative development but also the basis of spectatorial engagement according to classical norms. Moreover, the scene does so not by way of allegorical or otherwise conceptual self-reflexivity but by means of a very material assertion of a filmic agency that is uncannily indifferent to the interests humans have in narrative coherence, discursive significance, or experiential meaningfulness.

"This sequence more than any other," Spadoni asserts, "crystallizes the film's formal affinity with the uncanniness of early sound films" (109). As Spadoni details, a number of factors have already come together to induce a certain degree of "medium sensitivity" on the part of the viewer; these range from the obviously artificial nature of outdoor sets to shaky camerawork and apparently crude editing techniques (104-105). Non-diegetic music, which could have "cushioned" the impact of the film's artificiality, is lacking throughout the film, thus "foreground[ing] the photographic qualities of the image" and "forc[ing] viewers into a more direct contact with the film's overtly synthetic nature" (104). The mounting medium sensitivity is mobilized to full effect just before the monster appears. Especially the absence of music makes the offscreen footsteps stand out as phenomenal objects in their own right, rather than *merely* indicating the monster's approach; this they do as well, but with a sonic excess attached that simply *sounds* and does not *mean*— thereby recalling the difficulty viewers had coordinating sounds and images in their first encounters with the talkies. After the door opens, the mechanical, clockwork fashion of the monster's turn toward us—which through an interplay of movement and lighting rhythmically marks the milestones of ninety degrees, forty-five, and zero—continues to foreground the technical nature of the spectacle, which seems the product more of disinterested calculation than a naturally occurring event; the camera, accordingly, offers not a transparent window onto reality but asserts itself as a quasi-scientific or mathematical instrument, complicit in some strange experimental perversion of time and space. And, as Spadoni emphasizes, the monster's direct address of the camera, breaking a now long-established taboo of classical filmmaking, causes the viewer's medium sensitivity, his or her awareness of the scene's mediality, to coalesce with the perception of the constructed monster. According to Spadoni, "[t]he monster's glassy-eyed stare represents a moment of self-conscious filmmaking. This self-consciousness intensifies with the cuts that push viewers into the close-up of the monster's face" (111). But while this statement is no doubt true with respect to the intentions of the film's director, the *effect* of the scene is one that works against self-consciousness by flattening the distance— which is requisite for reflection—between the viewer, the screen and/or camera, and the monster as object.

Spadoni rightly points out that the effect of the axial cuts by which the frontal image of the monster's face is twice enlarged, violating the thirty-degree rule and constituting jump cuts, is "to punch [Whale's] monster out of the screen and into the space of the theater" (111), and to establish on film an experience of the "physically emergent figure" depicted by promotional posters of the monster breaking through walls (99). But while the progression of cuts from medium shot, to medium close-up, to close-up, all made along a single line of approach, does indeed have this effect, it seems that there is more involved here than just transgressing the segregation of spaces instituted by the classical paradigm. Thus, while I am in agreement with Spadoni's assessment of the scene's central function in conjuring and channeling an uncanny body that derives from the sound transition, and though I grant that part of the effect is to break through the screen and enter the theater space, I believe that we must go one step further and ask: what does this uncanny body do when it finally gets to the space occupied by the viewer, when it encounters the viewer's body? In developing my answer to this question, I will effectively be attempting to extend Spadoni's concept of the uncanny body by a molecular level of diffuse material interaction between human and alien filmic agencies—thus fleshing out my alignment, which I hinted at earlier, of the film-theoretical distinction of normal body versus uncanny body with the broader distinction of molar versus molecular embodied agencies, as they are constituted in "classical" and "stabilized" versus "transitional" configurations.

First, however, it may not be clear what the close-up of the monster's face has to do with transitionality. Spadoni makes the relation clear by "compar[ing] the distorted quality of the monster's head with the sometimes troubling appearances of heads in earlier sound films, especially when they were shown vocalizing in close-ups" (103). Having noted instances of "commentators during the sound transition finding faces in close-ups appearing grotesque, and others finding synchronization especially unconvincing in shots so framed," Spadoni argues that, "for these reasons, perceptions of the uncanny body probably intensified with cuts to a close-up view." The effect was this: "Close-ups spurred viewers to transfer, without regard for a filmmaker's intentions or a film's narrative, the discursive attributes of a shot [i.e. the formal or technical aspects of its execution] onto its diegetic contents." And this provided a unique opportunity for the post-transitional filmmaker at the formative stage of the horror genre's development:

With *Frankenstein*, Whale accomplishes something similar on the viewer's behalf, only he makes the transfer stick, and he jettisons the requirement that the head be framed in any particular way. In his film, the distorting and enervating effects of the early sound film close-up become the concrete attributes of one diegetic subject, regardless both of the distance between it and the camera and of the level of a viewer's medium awareness. (103)

Now, Spadoni's argument here explains quite a bit about the way Whale's film "trapped" or tamed the energies of the transition in the material icon of the Karloff image, but it tells us very little about how those energies erupted into the film in the first place. And this omission is in a sense necessary to the perspective Spadoni outlines in this passage, which is synoptic in nature and directed more at the lasting impact that Whale's film had in the consolidation of filmic horror rather than the immediate impact it had on its first viewers.[33] In particular, it is remarkable that, despite their obvious relevance, Spadoni does not relate his observations on the unsettling nature of sound-transitional close-ups directly to the close-up of the monster's face. If it is true that Whale "jettisons the requirement that the head be framed in any particular way" and thus detaches the monstrous face, imbued with transitional uncanniness, from the transitional context, this is only made possible through the scene in which the face is first revealed, where it is *of the essence that the head be framed in a very particular way*. For this scene establishes the very possibility of detachment by first exposing the head from all sides, thus turning it into an object *per se* rather than a flat image, and the cut-in to the close-up seals the deal by making the head emerge from the screen, separated from the monster's diegetic body. This non-diegetic decapitation stubbornly resists integration as pertaining to "one diegetic subject," but the experience also lays the necessary groundwork for its retroactive textualization. This, then, is the very genesis of the monstrous face's iconicity, the initiation of a process that will turn that face, seen from whatever angle and from whatever distance, into a sort of eternal close-up. But the brief gap in the narrative by which we are introduced to the face does not, or does not yet, belong to that process; for if it enables the transfer and accrual of meaning onto the facial image by constituting the object to be iconized, it does so by means of radically disrupting spectatorial subjectivity, entering the screening venue, and affectively imprinting the close-up not on the viewer's psyche but on his or her body. At stake now are the mechanisms for doing so. Again: what does the film's uncanny body do when it finally encounters the viewer's body?

Da Capo, or Losing Face:
Faciality and the Politics of Image Correlation

In fact, there are two questions involved here, both a question of "what" and a question of "how." First the what: The close-up of the monster's face does materially what Whale's self-reflexive queering of mute embodiment tries to do conceptually: it dismantles the molar norm of normal-body embodiment and derails the humanization process that, on the surface of Whale's Frankenstein films, works towards

---

33 To be clear, Spadoni's analysis is elsewhere very good at illuminating the momentary experiences, but in this particular argument they are subordinated to the long-term view that emphasizes the process of stabilization and normalization.

taming both the monster and the spectator. The close-up therefore provides a proactive, *advance* destabilization of, or inoculation against, the retroactive forces of normalization that will befall the monster in the course of his diegetic humanization and extra-diegetic iconization; and in contrast to the conceptual, allegorical sort of self-reflexivity which is attributable to James Whale the auteur, this must be seen as an unpremeditated (because incalculable) artifact of a transitional dance of agency, a *parable* of anthropotechnical evolution that, similar to Mary Shelley's novel, undermines both authorial and spectatorial subjectivities by opening them to a molecular realm of "passion."

The real question, though, is *how* the close-up manages this feat. My answer, in brief, is that it dissolves the link by which human subjects correlate images to their own "sensory ratios," attacking in particular the integrity of *the face* (both the monster's and the viewer's), thereby dismantling the channel through which subjects communicate, empathize, and order their environments. As a result of this operation, human and nonhuman agencies are able to confront each other in a more direct yet diffuse manner, without discursive-subjective mediation—which means that they come to commingle in the open of the medium itself, in the milieu of originary correlation that underlies all the more perniciously reductive forms of correlationism (such as *technesis* and all manners of yoking materially alterior agencies to human thought—which undertaking is shared also by Frankenstein's attempts to tame the monster, by interpretive reductions of the literary or filmic creature to a mere *Doppelgänger*, as well as by the sentimental acceptance of it as "one of us"). The close-up thus opens onto an affective experience of distributed embodiment that demands we acknowledge the alien agency of film—which is always the alterior agency of *this* filmic body, just as human agency is always the agency of *this* human being—as transformatively bound up with us in the anthropotechnical network of medial materiality, which is only ever contingently and tentatively stabilized, always potentially subject to global-scale transitionalities.

Before I elaborate this take on the close-up further, let me emphasize that my view of it as a "parable" (in Massumi's sense) of the autonomous media-technical agency of film in transition does not contradict, but rather supplements, Spadoni's emphasis on Whale's aesthetic channeling of that agency. What I am saying is that even if we attribute to Whale a conscious decision to employ the close-up of his monster to recall the uncanny experience of sound-transitional close-ups (or, for that matter, the earlier experience of the closer views that accompanied the transition, around 1910, to "facial-expression" acting styles, deemed by one critic "monstrous to the eye"[34])—even if, that is, we accept Spadoni's judgment that the scene

---

34 The expression is from *Moving Picture World*, 24 July 1909, 116 (qtd. in Bowser 97). As I noted in Chapter 3, the closer views in question corresponded to a seemingly harmless

in question "represents a moment of self-conscious filmmaking," it remains the case that the ultimate force of the close-up is one that radically outstrips directorial control. It is perfectly consistent, in other words, to maintain both that Whale knew what he was getting us into (i.e. that he consciously cultivated an experience of transitional instability) and that he had no idea where it would take us (precisely because of the incalculable nature of transitional instability). Thus, even if it was Whale's intention to undermine normalizing tendencies with the close-up, these intentions are still only incidental to the experiential product that marks his success, which itself remains, as I said above, an unpremeditated artifact of a transitional dance of agency.

Bearing this in mind, let us recall that the melodramatic normalization of the monster, especially as it is played out in the sequel *Bride of Frankenstein*, is coordinated with a series of scenes in which the monster's face is visually transformed from a terrifying sight to the pitiful countenance of a misunderstood creature. A key moment in this process takes place in the hermit's hut, when the monster is moved to tears by the generosity of the blind man; the close-up of the crying monster, whose face is dramatically softened and enlightened, marks the crossing of a central threshold: in this face is displayed a newly constituted subject, who can now, with the hermit's guidance, learn to speak and gain a sense of moral value—and with whom spectators can therefore come to identify. Later, when the monster is rejected by his would-be bride, an important contrast is drawn between his expressive—initially hopeful but gradually disillusioned—face and her hideous head. Lacking human expressiveness, the bride's scarred head hisses animally in a series of low-angle close-ups, to which are juxtaposed a close-up of the saddened male creature, again with tears rolling down his cheeks, just before he pulls the lever that will destroy the tower lab, exterminating himself, the bride, and the evil (and queer) Dr. Pretorius. What these scenes exemplify is the central role played by the face in melodrama as a politics of body containment and normalization; especially the image of the crying face occupies a privileged position in the repertoire of this body genre, due to its ability to resonate with spectators in the form of the "tear-jerker."

The process that coordinates the monster's face with his increasingly normalized subjectivity accords with the theory of the face formulated by Deleuze and Guattari in *A Thousand Plateaus*. Here, in the chapter entitled "Year Zero: Faciali-

---

change from a 12 foot camera distance to a 9 foot distance, but they set the stage for the transitional shift from "primitive" pantomimic acting to (in Miriam Hansen's words) "naturalistic approaches that emphasized facial expression instead of broad physical gesture," whereby characters were transformed from "moral or comic types" to "psychologically motivated individuals with whose predicaments, aspirations, and emotions the viewer could identify" (80). For more on the topic, see Bowser, Chapter 6.

ty," the face is seen as the locus of capitalism's mixed semiotics, which produces signifying subjectivities at the expense of embodiment. In the face, according to Deleuze and Guattari, "[b]odies are disciplined, corporeality dismantled, becomings-animal hounded out, deterritorialization pushed to a new threshold—a jump is made from the organic strata to the strata of signifiance and subjectification" (181). Consisting of a "white wall/black hole system," which corresponds to the reflective and inscribable surface of the skin in its interaction with the eyes as the passageways of subjectivity into and out of a hidden, interior realm, the face engulfs the body and tames it: normalizes it and eradicates its monstrosity.

This machine is called the faciality machine because it is the social production of face, because it performs the facialization of the entire body and all its surroundings and objects, and the landscapification of all worlds and milieus. The deterritorialization of the body implies a reterritorialization on the face; the decoding of the body implies an overcoding by the face; the collapse of corporeal coordinates or milieus implies the constitution of a landscape. The semiotic of the signifier and the subjective never operates through bodies. It is absurd to claim to relate the signifier to the body. At any rate it can be related only to a body that has already been entirely facialized. (181)

Facialization creates the "normal body" and institutes the molar human, to whom is attached an entire world of meaningful things: one's own body now has determinate meaning (expressive gesture, symptom, etc.) and the landscape is full of objects that signify, that exist only insofar as they are objects *for* the facialized subject. The face/head distinction, exemplified in the juxtaposed close-ups of monster and bride, marks a threshold corresponding to human versus animal, being-in-the-world versus merely existing in an environment[35]; facialization is therefore not, as Deleuze and Guattari emphasize, a psychic or phenomenological process—for example, an act of projection or the result of a Gestalt-shift—but the very precondition for the emergence of the phenomenological realm, i.e. for the emergence of a totalizing intentionality (171-172). The system of faciality "grid[s] all of space" (179), leaving no remainder or outside, and thus excludes as impossible (and renders imperceptible) the molecular becomings of a passional body without organs. The only hope, therefore, is to *dismantle* the face, which means not returning to a primitive state but transforming the face into something new:

---

35 Compare also Chapter 4, "Body, Meat and Spirit, Becoming-Animal," in Deleuze's *Francis Bacon: The Logic of Sensation*. Furthermore, consider that the (animal) sound/(human) speech threshold is intimately related to the body-head/subject-face threshold constitutive of the female monster's difference from the male monster's humanness *qua* signifying subjectivity.

Only on your face and at the bottom of your black hole and upon your white wall will you be able to set faciality traits free like birds, not in order to return to a primitive head, but to invent the combinations by which those traits connect with landscapicity traits that have themselves been freed from the landscape and with traits of picturality and musicality that have also been freed from their respective codes. (189)

Clearly, the monster fails to do anything of the sort. But what, indeed, would it mean for him to succeed?

In effect, the project of dismantling the face is an anti-correlationist project, in the sense of "correlationism" recently articulated by the speculative realists: Deleuze and Guattari are trying here to imagine what it would be like to unyoke being from human thought, to experience the interplay of agencies that subtend and exist independently from the subject, the psyche, the person. Interestingly, this project, which is for them an explicitly political project (188), includes an attempt, with its pursuit of liberated "traits of picturality," to conceive pictorial images in a non-correlationist way. What is the being, the agency of the image, if not its ability or even predestination to be seen by me or someone like me, by someone of the generically human "type"? The monster's failure to dismantle the face is correlated with my own failure to honor the autonomy of the image. "The close-up in film treats the face primarily as a landscape," which means that it treats *me* as a face correlated with it; "that is the definition of film, black hole and white wall, screen and camera. But the same goes for the earlier arts, architecture, painting, even the novel: close-ups animate and invent all of their correlations" (172). This is to say again, only now from a different, more properly postnatural angle, exactly what we saw in the first half of this chapter: that the taming of the monster, the rendering normal of its body, is correlated with a taming of the spectator and his or her body. The close-ups of the crying monster are simply the most effective means by which Whale's Frankenstein films do what classical Hollywood does as a matter of course: namely, to produce the spectator as a generalized "incorporeal individual" (Miriam Hansen 84) capable of emotionally identifying, above all on the basis of facial expression, with the character types depicted on the screen.

As I have suggested, though, the close-up by which we first encounter the monster in the 1931 film holds a radically different potential: that of a de-facialized image, a non-correlated image of filmic mediality itself, apart from instrumentalist and humanistic reductions of it. Deleuze's treatment of the "affection-image" in *Cinema 1* helps us to see it this way. I should note, however, that Mark Hansen sees Deleuze's engagement with the close-up there as a radical reversal of the course charted with Guattari in *A Thousand Plateaus*. According to Hansen, Deleuze's solo analysis of "the close-up fundamentally revalorizes facialization as a liberation of affect from its ties to the body," thus offering a "positive conception of facialization" in which "the face is now endowed with the function of expressing the intensity of the body abstracted or purified, as it were, from its spatiotemporal functions" (132). Against Deleuze's affection-image, Hansen explores the use of digitally-generated close-ups in interactive new-media artworks, theorizing a "digital facial image" (DFI) that highlights the role of the human body in the affective synthesis of images: "whereas Deleuze celebrates the close-up as a liberation of affect *from the body*, the DFI aims to catalyze the production of affect *as an interface between the domain of information (the digital) and embodied human experience*" (134). But whereas Hansen sees a radical reversal of Deleuze and Guattari's theory of facialization, I see Deleuze's treatment of the affect-image as continuous with it. The three roles ascribed to the face in *Cinema 1*—namely individuation, socialization, and communication (99)—are consistent with the view of the face as a locus of "signifying subjectivity," and Deleuze tells us that "the face, which effectively presents these aspects in the cinema as elsewhere, loses all three in the case of close-up" (99). As Deleuze explains: "There is no close-up of the face. The close-up is the face, but the face precisely in so far as it has destroyed its triple function—a nudity of the face much greater than that of the body, an inhumanity much greater than that of animals" (99). In other words, the affection-image is a face dismantled, deterritorialized in the manner described in *A Thousand Plataeus*—an anti-correlationist image in which "faciality traits [are set] free like birds" (189).

More important, however, than the question of consistency between Deleuze and Guattari's facialization and Deleuze's affection-image, is the charge of disembodiment that Hansen levels against the latter. As we saw in Chapter 6, Hansen demonstrates that Deleuze's appropriation of Bergson subordinated affection to perception, rendering it a mere conduit between the stimulation and (re)action of a body, and thereby making it available to cinema as an effect of technical framing. In this manner, Deleuze instituted a "homology" between film and the body that underestimated the role of human embodiment in an effort to render affect autonomous from human subjectivity. Effectively, for Hansen, Deleuze overshoots the mark by making affect autonomous from embodiment itself, an implication which Hansen finds exemplified in Deleuze's insistence that "the close-up, the close-up of the face, has nothing to do with a partial object" (95). Deleuze continues: "As Balázs has already accurately demonstrated, the close-up does *not* tear away its object from a set of which it would form part, of which it would be a part, but on the contrary it *abstracts it from all spatio-temporal co-ordinates*, that is to say it raises it to the state of Entity" (95-96, emphasis in original). But whereas Hansen reads this as rendering human embodiment irrelevant, Mary Ann Doane reads Deleuze's autonomization of the close-up as "an attempt to salvage spectatorial space, to reaffirm its existence and its relevance in the face of the closed, seamless space of the film," which is "also an attempt to reassert the corporeality of the classically disembodied spectator" (108). Now Doane is hardly convinced by Deleuze's attempts, seeing them as part of a broader "hystericization of film theory when confronted with the close-up" (96), a tendency to exaggerate the close-up's "separability" from narrative connections, which expresses "a desire to stop the film" (97). The close-up, on this reading, allows theorists such as Deleuze to apprehend not the object depicted in close-up but the close-up itself as object, thereby focusing on the screen as a giant protruding entity in the space occupied by my body. The abstraction "from all spatio-temporal co-ordinates," which for Hansen refers to the coordinates of embodied being, a sense of which is suspended in the spectator, refers for Doane merely to an *Aufhebung* of the coordinates of diegetic spacetime, thereby *enhancing* the viewer's sense of embodiment.

My purpose in raising this issue is not to engage in a dispute over the correct interpretation of Deleuze's text, which seems to support a variety of readings. Instead, it is my conviction that both Hansen and Doane miss an important opportunity, which may or may not correspond to Deleuze's intended meaning, but which plausibly colludes with his view of the close-up as "Entity" in a manner that neither disembodies affect nor correlates the image exclusively with *my* body, but that sees it as a function of an alterior, nonhuman agency with its own form of embodiment. The Entity in question can be read, that is, along the lines of object-oriented ontology's insistence on the independence of objects from the noetic yokes that subjects place around their necks, which therefore situates them in a non-phenomenological space that eludes not just discursively constructed spectatorial subjectivities but also the phenomenological body to which Doane sees Deleuze returning. This suggestion continues my partial rehabilitation of Deleuze's homology between cinema and human embodiment, which I embarked upon near the end of Chapter 6. There I proposed that we conceive film as a (non-teleologically evolving) center of indetermination in its own right; accordingly, it is capable of affection in a way that does not disembody affect, as Hansen fears, but rather *distributes embodiment*, making affect not a mere conduit between passive stimulation and active response (between human perception and action, photographic exposure and projection) but a mediator in a strong, Latourian sense: the material realm of "passion" that *engenders* inside and out, perception and action, prior to the correlationism of the facialized world. This realm is shared by, or distributed across, human and nonhuman agencies alike; film, and the affection-image in particular, therefore constitutes an opening onto the Great Outdoors of anthropotechnical transduction, the medium as environment for agential interaction and molecular change.

However, it is hardly the case that we always, or even very often, recognize this opening for what it is. Again, recognition is the wrong category: as a function of the face, it is precisely what gets in the way of a non-correlationist view that stops seeing the image with the eyes of a subject and starts letting the image act in the element of molecular materiality, where it can only be glimpsed as an "uncanny body." When, in 1931, the Karloff monster was first revealed, it was an unrecognizable "head without a face,"[36] full of the destabilizing power of media-technical transitionality; when it emerged from the screen and entered the space of the theater, thereby disturbing the anyway tentative traction that the classical spectator had in early sound cinema, it not only abstracted itself from the coordinates of the diegesis but disrupted the phenomenological coordination of the viewer's body as well. Refusing to be recognized, the face failed to take form: the facial traits of the monster failed to cohere in a pattern of recognizable, human expressiveness as a cue to the signifying subjectivity of another like myself. Failing to facialize, the image could not be captured as a landscape, could not be made to correlate with a face, and the viewer's own face was thereby disorganized. Unhinged from the frame of the screen and from the frame of *noesis* alike, the image of the monster asserted itself as an autonomous force, the autonomous expression of a nonhumanly embodied agency that, outside the channels of empirical recognition (faciality as the locus of identity and identifiability; phenomenologically situated corporeality; concretely individuated technical media), initiated an affective wrestling match that refused closure in the sense of emotional subjectification. A specifically alien-phenomenological perspective was opened, allowing viewers to see themselves *as seen by the image*, which is to say molecularly, without recognition. With the disintegration of faciality came a temporary undoing of the strictures of molar humanity, and the molecular agencies underpinning human and nonhuman, organic and technical forms of embodiment momentarily entwined themselves in an exploratory dance, probing the mutually articulated milieu of the medium.

The dance, of course, was brief. The head so introduced became recognizable—*instantly* and *ineluctably* recognizable as a face, an icon. On the other hand, the brief encounter left an indelible mark on the subsequent serialization of Frankenstein films, one sedimented beneath the monster's universalization. For in this encounter was enacted a synthesis, from out of the interaction of mutually impinging molecular agencies, of an affective deformation and reshaping of the anthropotechnical interface that laid the groundwork for the future of filmic horror, for subsequent viewings of this and other Frankenstein films, and for a revision of human relations to technical media generally. Before I close out this chapter, allow me to turn briefly to this phenomenon.

Earlier, I noted that Mark Hansen formulates his theory of the digital facial image, or DFI, in direct opposition to Deleuze's affection-image. In rehabilitating Deleuze's analysis for the purposes of a so-called alien phenomenology, I have called into question the basis upon which this opposition between the DFI and the

---

36 The phrase is taken from Deleuze's *Francis Bacon: The Logic of Sensation*, 15-16.

affection-image is drawn. Now I would like to suggest that, once reconfigured in accordance with my suggestions, Deleuze's cinematic concept converges with the functions of Hansen's new-media analysis in such a way as to complete a composite picture of anthropotechnical transition, illuminating it from both sides of the human/nonhuman divide. Again, Hansen sees his own theory of the processes of interactive engagement with digitally generated faces as "diverg[ing] fundamentally from Deleuze's analysis of the close-up: in [the DFI], the face does not so much *express* the body, as *catalyze* the production of a *supplementary* sensorimotor connection between the body and a domain (informatics) that is fundamentally heterogeneous to it" (133). Or again: "whereas Deleuze celebrates the close-up as a liberation of affect *from the body*, the DFI aims to catalyze the production of affect *as an interface between the domain of information (the digital) and embodied human experience*" (134). In these statements, "the body" always refers to the human body, so that the affection-image's transcendent expression of the body by the face is taken to mean the detachment of affect from its source in the human body; simultaneously, affect is taken to be the prerogative of human (or at least organic) embodiment. My response to these stipulations has been to expand the affective domain by granting to technical media such as film their own robust forms of embodiment, i.e. imputing to them a nonhuman center of indetermination that complicates the picture of technical media as passive input/output throughfares, making them unpredictable mediators that are, in a word, *uncanny*—though inanimate, they seem to be strangely alive. As a result, the "expression" of the body manifested in Deleuze's facial close-up should be read not as a detachment of affect from the actor's or the viewer's body, and thus as a liberating detachment of it from the spatiotemporal coordinates of the (implicitly human) body, but as a manifestation *qua* image of the *technical* body that opens onto a "passional" realm that is neither wholly mine nor wholly its. The fundamental heterogeneity that Hansen ascribes to the digital is already present in film; whereas Hansen sees the alterity of digital information as requiring an unprecedented framing by means of an expansion of the affective capacities of the human body, which organizes non-indexically anchored pixels, for example, into recognizable images commensurable to human sensory ratios, I see this as the status quo for all forms of emergent image interfaces. That is, this radically volatile act of framing, which is so uncanny in our present transition to digital imaging forms, is an aspect of all such transitions between familiar and novel modes of anthropotechnical interfacing, and is subject to naturalization processes that eradicate the uncanniness over time.

This is not to discount Hansen's model or its ability to illuminate what takes place in our interactions with new-media art and digital media, but to generalize it to cover transitionality itself as regards shifts between specific modalities and medialities of image correlation.[37] This generalization does not collapse the difference between Deleuze's and Hansen's model, but sees them as tracing out opposing, but complementary, analytical trajectories that converge on the milieu of images' distributed embodiment. That is, Hansen sees Deleuze's concept as abstracting and autonomizing affective power *from* the body *to* the image, while "the DFI results in a transfer of affective power *from* the image *to* the body" (130); but once we amend (our reading of) Deleuze's model as suggested above, we no longer have these two opposed movements of body → image *versus* image → body, but instead a trajectory (Deleuze's) running thus: *technical* body → image, which is *followed* or *continued by* the trajectory (Hansen's) which runs thus: image → *human* body. Together, these models mark the continuous movement of affect from an alien technical agency, by means of an image manifesting the product of a nonhuman center of indetermination, across the divide to a human center of indetermination as it affectively appropriates and processes that image. Moreover, this process, as the meeting of two affective agencies in the medium of the image, is subject to reversals in which the flow of affect runs from human to nonhuman loci. Schematically, the result of combining the DFI (generalized to cover pre-digital media in transition) with the affection-image (as a non-correlationist model of imaging technologies' materially autonomous functioning) looks like this: technical body ↔ image ↔ human body. The image is a *mediator* in the milieu of the anthropotechnical interface, the material site where transitions are affectively negotiated.

Seen in this way, the historicity of an image is defined in terms that exceed its discursive and intertextual relations, extending materially to the dialogical co-constitution of anthro-phenomenological and xeno-phenomenological capacities. The neutralization of the monstrous close-up's originally destabilizing power of "defacement," which gives way to a humanized creature and an iconized face, is therefore predicated on the realignment of agential powers, and the redistribution of embodiment amongst them, that takes place by way of the transitional image. The image itself, in other words, reshapes the milieu in which its body becomes normal rather than uncanny; uncanniness is attendant to the process of reshaping, normality its inevitable effect. Hansen explains the DFI's ability—and I would extend this ability to any patently transitional image—to "*catalyze* the production of a *supple-*

---

37 Certainly, my suggestion *relativizes* Hansen's theory of the DFI by relating it to the transitional context in which we live; that is, I do not deny the radical alterity of digitality to human embodiment, but I question whether this alterity is categorically different from that of previously transitional and subsequently naturalized image technologies. On the other hand, I do not wish to deny the specific medial differences of digital images from all sorts of analog ones, and it is precisely in its ability to foreground these *specific* differences that the DFI might serve as a *general* model of image-correlation transitionality.

mentary sensorimotor connection between the [human] body and a domain [...] that is fundamentally heterogeneous to it" in terms of the process of "affective attunement," as explored by psychoanalyst Daniel Stern[38]; according to Hansen:

> like the affective modality of preverbal parent-infant interaction, this supplementary sensorimotor connection capitalizes on the contagious dynamics of affectivity in order to attune the body to a stimulus that is novel—and, in this case, that is so precisely because of its radical heterogeneity to already developed human perceptual capacities. It is as if affectivity steps in precisely where no perceptual contact can be made. (133)

This accords with my analysis, in Chapter 4, of the child's development of an interface-matrix appropriate to the unfamiliar escalator, as well as with my argument, in Chapter 5, concerning the occurrence of a "silent revolution" vis-à-vis the steam engine's reconstitution of anthropotechnical relations. The sequence in which the monster was introduced to viewers in 1931 put a similar process in motion: a close encounter with an alien agency, followed by a "dance of agency" and "interactive stabilization" (as Pickering puts it) by means of affective attunement, resulting eventually in the normalization of the transitionally novel image. As I have attempted to show here, this image deposited the monstrous particular of a transitional, pre-stabilized image-correlation matrix at the heart of the universal monster; the icon itself—apprehended as the emergent product of a process by which an initial uncanniness can be observed decaying, attuned, and normalized over time—constitutes therefore a non-static, composite image of mediality in process, an image of human and nonhuman agencies embraced in the openness of their originary correlation.

---

38 See Stern's *The Interpersonal World of the Infant*, Chapter 4.

8. Lines of Flight: Transitional Thoughts by Way of Conclusion

I take of the continuity of a particular becoming a series of views, which I connect together by "becoming in general." But of course I cannot stop there. What is not determinable is not representable: of "becoming in general" I have only a verbal knowledge. As the letter x designates a certain unknown quantity, whatever it may be, so my "becoming in general," always the same, symbolizes here a certain transition of which I have taken some snapshots; of the transition itself it teaches me nothing. Let me then concentrate myself wholly on the transition, and, between any two snapshots, endeavor to realize what is going on. As I apply the same method, I obtain the same result; a third view merely slips in between the two others. I may begin again as often as I will, I may set views alongside of views for ever, I shall obtain nothing else. The application of the cinematographical method therefore leads to a perpetual recommencement, during which the mind, never able to satisfy itself and never finding where to rest, persuades itself, no doubt, that it imitates by its instability the very movement of the real. But though, by straining itself to the point of giddiness, it may end by giving itself the illusion of mobility, its operation has not advanced it a step, since it remains as far as ever from its goal. In order to advance with the moving reality, you must replace yourself within it. Install yourself within change, and you will grasp at once both change itself and the successive states in which it might at any instant be immobilized.

HENRI BERGSON[1]

---

1   *Creative Evolution*, 307-08.

Throughout this book, I have tried to find a means for going beyond the merely "verbal knowledge" of transition that Bergson here warns against; I have sought to formulate a framework that would answer the call of Frankenstein films and allow us to "install ourselves within change." The theory of postnatural historicity I have developed attempts to "grasp at once both change itself and the successive states in which *it might* at any instant be immobilized," positing an alternation between phenomenal-empirical situations and the underlying processes of "passional," molecular displacements at work in the evolution of anthropotechnical interfaces—and defining in this way a medial or meso-level milieu of transitionality itself. The cinematic double vision that I have based upon this view responds to the dualities of address by which Frankenstein films non-representationally correspond to the dynamics of transition—by which, that is, their interplays of representation and presentation, of narrative and spectacle, of embodiment relations and hermeneutic relations, and of taming humanizations and xenomorphic destabilizations double the progressions that continually transform human/nonhuman relations. As we have seen, there are both cultural and cosmic vectors of such transformation, and Frankenstein films, both individually and collectively, bring these vectors together and challenge their spectators to grapple with the monstrous alterity of cinema's technical agencies, to confront material otherness in the open of the Great Outdoors, in the originary medium of distributed embodiment. At the same time, though, the images by which these films issue their challenges are historically indexed and subject to capture and neutralization, so that they become mere "snapshots"; then, divested of their transitional force, these images come to indicate not the postnatural historicity of agency but instead lines of development that have been retrospectively tamed and made to represent processes of maturation and normalization.

James Whale's Frankenstein films are paradigmatic for both aspects or movements. With respect to the call or challenge issued by Frankenstein films, the scene in which the monster is first introduced onscreen is "exemplary" in the sense of the parable. And with respect to the retroactive process of normalization, there can be no better example than the face of Karloff introduced at that fateful moment, melodramatically humanized in 1935, and fixed forever after as an unmistakable icon. Taken together, these two aspects constitute a composite image of transitionality itself, exemplifying "at once both change itself and the successive states in which *it might* at any instant be immobilized." It is this double nature of the films' images, their ability both to evoke an experience of transitional singularity *and* to outline the opportunities for arrest and generalization, that makes Whale's films paradigmatic for the characteristic potential of Frankenstein films generally. Indeed, Whale's films establish the framework for the ongoing filmic serialization of Frankenstein films by turning these two trajectories into the very *medium* of the series: an experience of anthropotechnical transitionality forms the medial substrate, while generalized images concretize into specific forms or "snapshots." By means of their interplay—temporally expressed as a play of repetition and variation, and visually embodied in the monster who mediates between the universal and the particular or the molar and the molecular—a series emerges, and Frankenstein films' application of their own sort of "cinematographical method therefore leads to a perpetual recommencement." As a series, Frankenstein films therefore enact a continual rebirth of self-differentiation into the twin forces of transitional instability and situational stabilization.

Focused on these dual reservoirs that drive the storytelling engine and make it a constant interrogator of the ontology engine of film, our double vision reveals the series as encompassing a distinctly double history: on the one hand, there are developments of a broadly narrative nature, including the changes that subsequent Frankenstein films carry out on established patterns of plot, characterization, or the themes they are used to address; on the other hand, the series also contains an implicit history of mediality or anthropotechnical interfacing. Each of these histories, in turn, displays its own lines of normalization (conventionalization of generic and quasi-generic traits, iconization and humanization or reductive mechanization of the monster, as well as the habituation or naturalization of media technologies such as sound, color, CGI, etc.); but, in addition to these, both the narrative and the medial histories of the series also hold within them *lines of flight* that signal breaks and lead beyond regularizing progressions: these are affective openings onto experiences of the molecular, postnatural historicity of the anthropotechnical interface, and they arise through the films' work of mediation, in the Latour-inspired sense detailed in Chapter 6.

I would like, by way of conclusion, to address the issue of how we might locate these lines of flight in the further course of Frankenstein films' serial development. My treatment, though, will be brief and episodic, and the reason for this is twofold. On the one hand, I cannot possibly hope to deal with all the twists and turns that the Frankenstein series has taken since James Whale's films appeared in the 1930s; the series is far too rich and diverse, and the sheer number of incarnations is too great for me to provide a comprehensive view. On the other hand, such a treatment is quite unnecessary anyway: my arguments have already been made, and by now they will have been deemed successful or unsuccessful; if convinced, the reader will, I believe, readily see that the perspective I have developed applies to the dynamics of the films' further serial course, whereas conversely no amount of further elaboration will persuade the skeptical reader of my thesis. I have argued that it is a quasi-generic feature of Frankenstein films (realized differentially through serial progression and according to historical circumstances) that they pose an experiential challenge to us as viewers, and it is the job of postnaturalism, as a metaphysics of anthropotechnical change, to help us comprehend and meet that challenge. But if

I have failed to convey the force of the films' challenge, so that the reader is unable to feel it for him- or herself, or if the reader denies that my model is able to account for it, then all further exemplification would just be adding snapshots on top of snapshots. Under such circumstances, "I may begin again as often as I will, I may set views alongside of views for ever, I shall obtain nothing else." If, however, I have succeeded in making heard the "call of the postnatural wild" that I take these films to be, then we may see these snapshots as endowed with both a static surface and a dynamic underside that is an affective record of our postnatural historicity itself. In the hopes that this vision is not only possible but that it has been made actual through my endeavors, I venture finally a selective look at the further proliferation of Frankenstein's filmic progenies.

THE CONTINUING ADVENTURES OF THE UNCANNY BODY

So how do we recognize the lines of flight submerged beneath the normalized histories of de-monstrification and image correlationism? What is it, exactly, that we are looking for? Consider again the close-up of the monster's face, which paradoxically disintegrated faciality and laid the groundwork for iconicity as well. In this image, as I have pointed out, is contained in germinal form both prongs of the conflict that connects Frankenstein films to the dynamics of transitionality—both a destabilizing molecularity and the molar means of containing it. Establishing the paradigmatic duality of Frankenstein films, this close-up is in fact the genetic element of the series as a whole: the series, in effect, is an elaboration of the juxtaposition that the close-up presents, an endless play of repetition and variation of its twin trajectories. The close-up therefore "exemplifies" the series in that it both *belongs to the series* and in a sense *contains it as its generative source*. As Agamben says of the example, "[i]t is one singularity among others, which, however, stands for each of them and serves for all" (10). It is thus a parable in Massumi's sense, exhibiting the *inventive self-relation* he associates with that concept by both conforming to a pattern and wringing that pattern out of an unpatterned flux in the first place. The close-up of the monster's face is thus a *parabolic mutation* of the material medium in which patterned agencies are co-articulated. Invention, self-relation, mutation: these are the characteristics of the hidden history we are after, attributes of a line of flight.

We are looking, then, for moments that are exemplary in this sense, which clearly cannot mean that they *repeat* the example set by the close-up, but that they follow it in *exemplifying their own transitional moment*. In other words, these instances will involve an unprecedented mutation of the relations between molecular and molar forces, between alien and human agencies, and between the medial substrate of the series and the forms of which it is capable; such parabolic moments effect these redefinitions by virtue of their contact with the anthropotechnical interface, the changes in which they transformatively mediate into dual-pronged images that will generate the series' basic conflict anew, hence resetting the parameters of experiential engagement within which repetition and variation take place. Exemplary as they are, they will both absorb past examples (so that they function in the non-epistemic manner characteristic of silent revolutions), and they will configure themselves as perfectly normal as well—the example conforms to the pattern it forges. If it is these dual-pronged or pluripotent moments that hold within them the lines of flight we are after, we clearly cannot expect them to announce themselves for what they are. We shall have to resort to the aid of extrinsic indicators, such as the "medium sensitivity" that led us to the "uncanny bodies" explored by Spadoni.

Medium sensitivity, as in the case of the sound transition, is heightened during periods of media change—when an old and a new form stand side by side, when perceptions of the new still stand out against memories of the old, or when various media compete and provoke innovation in one another. The virtual explosion of television into American homes in the early 1950s created a situation of the latter type. Cinema was forced to compete with the new medium, and it used color and widescreen processes, among other things, in its efforts to differentiate itself and assert itself against television.[2] In this context, the Frankenstein film experienced its renaissance. Most famously, Hammer released *The Curse of Frankenstein* in May 1957, landing an unexpected hit that revitalized not only the Frankenstein film but also the horror genre itself. The Hammer Frankenstein films that would follow, constituting a series of seven films in total that endured until 1974, offer the only systematic alternative to Universal's vision to date, one that famously focuses on the creator rather than any single creature. The true innovation, though, was color, which was used in *The Curse of Frankenstein* to great effect. Eastmancolor, introduced in 1950, made this possible by providing a more affordable alternative to Technicolor's three-strip process, which had involved higher costs for film stock and required special cameras; the new "tri-pack" film stock placed the three primary color-sensitive layers on one strip of film, thus making it compatible with existing camera equipment. Nevertheless, *The Curse of Frankenstein* was a huge gamble, financially and otherwise, for the small Hammer Studios. As David Pirie explains in his history of the British horror film, the entire British film industry was in an unprecedented crisis, and no one was hit harder by the combined impact of

---

2   See Chapter 5, "Technology and Spectacle," in Peter Lev's *The Fifties: Transforming the Screen* for an overview of the new technologies. See also Janet Wasko's "Hollywood and Television in the 1950s," Chapter 6 in the same volume, for an account of the varied relations that Hollywood maintained with television in that decade.

television and Hollywood's spectacular widescreen and color reaction to it than those companies, like Hammer, who specialized in small features (22). Moreover, the existence of a market for a new Frankenstein film was highly questionable: "The general feeling was that the science-fiction boom had come to an end. No-one, apart from Hammer, was even considering the possibility that the public might be interested in classical horror, a field which had died many years before, and the trade papers of the period are comparatively snide in their remarks about the Baron's imminent British revival" (Pirie 32). Not to mention the fact that Universal was threatening legal action if it deemed that Hammer's production violated any of their copyrights, most centrally the copyright on the monster's makeup. Shifting focus to the Baron, who in the course of his career would animate numerous creatures of various types and by various means, was one way of avoiding this threat.[3] There was also considerable resistance from British censors, who wanted to kill the project before filming had even started, on the basis of what one reviewer called its "monstrous script" alone (qtd. in Pirie 38). Hammer persisted, however, and commenced filming in 1956, knowing full well that their product would be slashed by the censors. "But," as Pirie explains, "they did have a trick up their sleeves":

[Producer Anthony] Hinds was well aware the BBFC would rarely have seen a colour horror movie and certainly never a British horror movie in colour. He therefore ensured that the BBFC's crucial decisions on cuts were made on a black and white print, carefully neglecting to remind the BBFC the film was in colour. This was a master-stroke, for when matters came to a head in January 1957 [...], Hammer could always point out that the BBFC had already been informed in writing they were dealing with a colour film. (39)

Realizing their oversight, the censor board demanded to see the entire film again in color, but by then it was too late in the day for them not to pass the film, and it thus received a certificate with only minor cuts made in April 1957.[4]

Certainly, then, the British censor board was suddenly sensitized to the medium of color film stock, but did *The Curse of Frankenstein* induce medium sensitivity in cinemagoers as well? Quite apart from the problem of generalizing over diverse viewing audiences, it is difficult to answer this question in a straightforward manner. The reason is that viewers, at this historical juncture, were sensitive to differ-

---

3 Compare Pirie 82. Various critics have accordingly pointed out that Frankenstein becomes the real monster of the Hammer cycle. See, for example, McCarty 19, and O'Flinn 41.

4 See Pirie 37-45 for a fuller account of Hammer's dealings with the censor board. See also Chapter 4 of Wayne Kinsey's *Hammer Films: The Bray Studios Years* for pre-production and production history.

ences in visual media as a matter of course: television, which by then had even seen the birth of its own experimental color processes, jostled with Technicolor and Eastmancolor, with 3D, Cinerama, and CinemaScope, along with a variety of other widescreen systems. These differences were actively highlighted, put forward in the sense of advertisements for media in general rather than just the particular productions to which they pertained.[5] It is hard, in this context, to know whether the presence of color in *The Curse of Frankenstein* contributed anything of its own in this atmosphere of a general medium sensitivity with regard to the growing number of screens and screen types in existence. What we can say, however, is that the film *harnessed* that sensitivity and focused it for its purposes of horror. This commences in the film's first images, which present a textual preface to the film, set in white "Gothic" letters (perhaps reminiscent for audiences of Nazi propaganda posters) upon a blood red background—introducing a color motif which is to be repeated throughout the film, most centrally, of course, in the depiction of blood. The preface, which acknowledges the existence of the series in which the film partakes, reads: "More than a hundred years ago, in a mountain village in Switzerland, lived a man whose strange experiments with the dead have since become legend. The legend is still told with horror the world over.... It is the legend of..." And here comes the title screen: "The Curse of Frankenstein" in giant letters and underscored with a musical crescendo. The lush red background is held throughout the credits, for nearly two minutes, before the film's narrative begins; and it is this background, I suggest, which marks one of those turning points in the Frankenstein film series that readjust the poles of repetition and variation, narrative and spectacle, molar and molecular. For all of the vivid images of blood and guts that follow refer constantly back to this obstinate red background. The camera's insistent concentration on eyeballs, brains, detached hands, and bodily fluids, by which the film paved the way for the body horror of splatter, is tied inextricably to this blood red background, thus infusing images *of* blood with a medial excess over and above their diegetic capture of the color red. In Godard's words: "Ce n'est pas du sang, c'est du rouge." Or it is both blood *and* red, but not both at once in harmony. The visceral impact of the film's images of viscera, then, is predicated on the irresolvable tension that marks a bifurcation between diegesis and medial materiality, confronting the viewer with the uncanny body of mediality in transition: the distributed embodiment of a pluripotent, not yet stabilized, anthropotechnical interface. Here, then, lies a line of flight that, like the iconic image of Karloff's face, will inevitably be sedimented and absorbed into a regularized line of development. It subsists, though, and bears witness to the untamed power of images freed from the subjugation of anthropocentric correlation.

---

5   Again, see Chapter 5 of Peter Lev's *The Fifties*.

Following the success of *The Curse of Frankenstein*, Frankenstein exploded again onto screens—this time both cinema and television screens. As a result of a contract between Screen Gems and Universal-International, fifty-two of Universal's pre-1948 classic horror films were released for television syndication under the package name "Shock!" beginning in October 1957.[6] Among the films were *Frankenstein, Son of Frankenstein,* and *Frankenstein Meets the Wolf Man*.[7] The package was such a huge success that a second set of twenty films, this time called "Son of Shock," was released in May 1958. Included in this follow-up were the rest of the Universal Frankensteins (apart from *Abbott and Costello Meet Frankenstein*): *Bride of Frankenstein, Ghost of Frankenstein, House of Frankenstein,* and *House of Dracula*.[8] Hammer got to work right away on a sequel to *Curse*, already submitting a script for *The Revenge of Frankenstein* (originally referred to as *Blood of Frankenstein*) to the censors in 1957 and conducting filming in early 1958.[9] But they also sought their own inroads into television, making a deal with Columbia to produce a pilot episode for a Frankenstein TV series that would consist of tales, narrated by the great-great-grandson of Frankenstein himself, of the doctor's early experiments and other incidents in the course of his career. Three full seasons of thirteen episodes each had been planned out in considerable detail as part of Hammer's pitch, but all of this was thrown overboard when Michael Carreras, son of Hammer chairman James Carreras, flew to Hollywood in November 1957 to oversee production of the pilot. There he discovered that the original pilot script had been rejected, and it looked as though Hammer was being gradually cast out of the deal altogether.[10] A pilot was made, but nothing like what had been planned. As David Pirie puts it:

In the end a plodding Universal-style script called *Face in the Tombstone Mirror* was shot with a story by its director Curt Siodmak (who had worked on some of the less distinguished Universal efforts) and a pilot script from Catherine and Henry Kuttner. Unlike [Jimmy] Sangster's original approach, *Face in the Tombstone Mirror* retreated into sub-Universal

---

6   See Kevin Heffernan, *Ghouls, Gimmicks, and Gold*, 140.
7   Kevin Heffernan includes an appendix with a complete list of titles included (254).
8   A complete list of titles appears in Kevin Heffernan, 255.
9   Wayne Kinsey cites a letter from James Carreras, dated 7 July 1957, in which Carreras reports that "Tony Hinds and Michael [Carreras] are busy at work on the *Blood of Frankenstein* and I feel sure that we have another terrific winner on our hands" (*Hammer Films: The Bray Studios Years* 85). David Pirie discusses the negotiations with censors on the topic of the sequel (42).
10 See Pirie, 86-88.

territory with almost indecent haste and the lumbering monster is reborn in entirely traditional fashion within five minutes. Predictably the series never happened. (88)[11]

In the meantime, other companies responded to the success of Hammer's *The Curse of Frankenstein*. Notably, the recently formed American International Pictures, which specialized in films catering to a teenage audience, produced *I Was a Teenage Frankenstein*, released in November 1957 as a follow-up to their own successful *I Was a Teenage Werewolf* from July of the same year.

Teenage Frankenstein actively sought to evoke medium sensitivity by dramatically switching from black and white stock, which is used throughout the majority of the film, to color stock for the final minutes of the film. The monster, whom Professor Frankenstein has put together from the corpse of a teenager collected from a car accident, along with various spare parts, has a hideously disfigured face until a suitable donor can be found—and killed. Now a handsome teen with a freshly transplanted face, the monster is to be dismantled and shipped back to England, but he resists and throws Professor Frankenstein into the alligator pit located beneath his house. When the police arrive, the monster backs into a panel of electrical equipment of some sort, and it is at this point that the film switches to color for the electrocution. A certain Dr. Karlton, present at the scene, checks the collapsed monster's pulse and determines his death, remarking: "I'll never forget his face after the accident," and, wincing, repeats the word "never" as the image dissolves to a close-up of that face, tracking ever closer to it, revealing in color all its hideous details. But while there can be no question that *Teenage Frankenstein*'s abrupt change to color induced a sort of medium awareness, I doubt that it evoked an experience of the uncanny body. If anything, the use of color in the final close-up would seem to make plain the presence of the mask pulled over the actor's face. Certainly, this stands in conflict with narrative integration, but the effect is somewhat humorous rather than horrifying. It does not succeed in challenging the viewer in the same way the Karloff close-up did in 1931.[12]

AIP's sequel, *How to Make a Monster*, appearing in July 1958, tried a somewhat different tack. To be more precise, it in fact repeats the former film's strategy of switching from black and white to color stock for the final ten minutes or so (thus justifying the challenge of promotional posters: "See the ghastly ghouls in flaming color!"), but it adds another twist in its efforts to achieve medium sensitivi-

---

11 Curt Siodmak had worked, in particular, as a writer on Universal's *Frankenstein Meets the Wolf Man* and *House of Frankenstein*.

12 This is not to say that humor cannot pose such a challenge. We saw in Part One that *Dog Factory*'s humor involved a complex interplay of phenomenal relations, and we may be able to detect similar moments in *Rocky Horror Picture Show* or *Young Frankenstein*.

ty: specifically, the film is autothematic, i.e. a film about filmmaking.[13] That is, it is a sequel that frames and reveals its immediate predecessors, *I Was a Teenage Werewolf* and *I Was a Teenage Frankenstein*, as the filmic productions that they were by focusing on the makeup specialist who created the figures for American International, portrayed in the diegesis as Pete Dumont. Dumont, who has built his reputation on monsters like Teenage Werewolf and Teenage Frankenstein, learns that the studio is planning to stop producing horror, and he swears revenge against the men responsible. In order to get even, Dumont hypnotizes the actors starring in the film *Werewolf Meets Frankenstein* that is currently in production and causes the "monsters," in full makeup, to kill the new studio bosses. Certainly, the film is interesting for its intertextual references to previous Frankenstein films, which the autothematic framing itself promotes, and hence for its acknowledgement of Frankenstein films' ongoing serialization. It presents, therefore, a media-historicizing take of sorts on the series, as I have argued in Chapter 6 that Frankenstein films characteristically do. But it remains too deliberate, too aware of itself to evoke an experience of the uncanny body sort and open up a molecular line of flight.

How to Make a Monster might be compared to another autothematic, or quasi-autothematic, film of the same year: *Frankenstein 1970*, released just weeks after AIP's film. Starring Boris Karloff not as the monster but as Baron Victor von Frankenstein, the aging and childless heir to the original Baron Frankenstein, *Frankenstein 1970* is of course also very aware of its relation to the overall series of Frankenstein films. A trailer for the film repeatedly displays Karloff's name in bold letters, mentioning it just as often in a voiceover, and the narrator announces: "The one, the only king of monsters brings you the demon of the atomic age!" The film, shot entirely in black and white but presented in anamorphic CinemaScope, is quasi-autothematic in that it portrays a modern-day Castle Frankenstein as the setting for an American television crew's shooting of a horror show to commemorate the occasion of the 230th anniversary of the original Frankenstein's creation of a monster. The Karloff character has signed the deal with the TV crew in order to acquire funds for a much-needed nuclear reactor so that he can continue where his ancestor left off. Perhaps the most interesting part of the film is the television director's idea to incorporate the Baron himself into the TV show, where in a live segment designed to introduce the filmed footage shot on location at the castle he is to deliver a mood-setting monologue about his forefather and his experiments, appropriately delivered from the castle crypt where both the creator and his creature lie

---

13 I am indebted to Jörg Schweinitz's discussion, in "'Wie im Kino!' Die autothematische Welle im frühen Tonfilm," of autothematic films of the early sound era, where the technique served much more effectively to evoke medium awareness in the sense that attracts Spadoni's attention to horror films of the same era.

entombed. Trying to make the idea palatable to Frankenstein, the director paints a bright picture of television stardom. The lead actress remarks, "Well do you think a series right here from the castle is such a bad idea?" The impressively eerie and completely improvised monologue that Frankenstein delivers as a rehearsal proves, indeed, that it wouldn't be such a bad idea. (And interestingly, the series imagined here sounds remarkably like the TV series that Hammer wanted to make.)

The interesting thing about this quasi-autothematic twist (which is much more interesting than the film's monster) is that it highlights an awareness of the film's own construction and conventionality (and participation in Frankenstein films' seriality as well) in a manner that is similar, in some respects, to the way film musicals function: focusing on a closely related medium that is not quite its own (here TV; in the case of the musical, live stage acts) allows for an oscillation between medial transparency and medium sensitivity (where the latter is a mixed-mode sensitivity based on the contrast between the represented and the framing medium). The "utopic" nature of the musical's song-and-dance numbers has something in common with the function of science fiction's special effects, and, as Robert Spadoni argues, the musical is in fact closely related to the horror film in that they both "seized on the abrupt tonal shifts that early sound filmmakers sometimes effected in their films unintentionally" (27). This gave rise, in the musical, to the familiar pattern Spadoni describes: "A film shifts gears when a number starts, then shifts back again after it is over" (27). And while the impact of the sound transition can hardly be marshaled as a determining factor in 1958, the pattern by which musicals aligned the dream-like nature of the number with the representation of another medium might still be instructive. For Frankenstein's rehearsal of his monologue is indeed something like a musical number, sufficiently compartmentalized from the film's narrative, which itself is framed as a television equivalent of the musical's backstage setting; the monologue, then, is a performance that can be compared to the musical's stage performances, and it similarly disrupts the narrative flow by presenting itself *as* a performance that is both meant for the other medium (TV, stage) but also in this way highlights its own filmic nature—especially as the number abruptly ends, in this case with a scream that jars us back into the framing narrative.

Do we find another uncanny body here, another line of flight? It is hard to say, and it is not an empirical question anyway. The monologue/number might, however, be capable of recalling the experience of live television that it thematizes. And the "liveness" of the bodies appearing on early television, which was all live, was problematically uncanny: live in the sense of happening in "real time," those bodies could nevertheless seem strangely mechanical in the context of early television's highly medium-sensitive viewership, thereby problematizing the viewer's own embodiment, which shared its temporality with the spatially distant onscreen bodies. We can imagine this experience of the uncanny as motivating the science fiction explorations of the television series *Tales of Tomorrow*, a *Twilight Zone*-like series launched by ABC at an early hour of television broadcasting, in 1951. And in its second season, on January 18, 1952, *Tales of Tomorrow* even staged its own adaptation of *Frankenstein*, starring Lon Chaney, Jr. as the monster (which role he had played before, in 1942, as Karloff's successor in *Ghost of Frankenstein*). The episode is notorious for Chaney's allegedly drunken performance. On live television, without the possibility of a retake, Chaney's monster is strangely careful with the furniture that he goes through the motions of smashing. In one case, he raises a chair high over his head, then gently sets it down before raising his empty arms to mimic the motion of bringing the chair crashing down. Clearly, Chaney believed his performance was a rehearsal, not the real thing being broadcast live. He at one point says something about saving a chair for later, when he apparently thought the real performance would take place. Drunk or not, the tension between rehearsal and live performance that Chaney demonstrates here might be found lurking in the background of Karloff's rehearsal of his monologue in *Frankenstein 1970* as well, as an invocation of the televisual uncanny body.

As for Chaney's performance in *Tales of Tomorrow*, the uncanny body it confronts us with is instructive in another way: while a television viewer in 1952 would have had only one chance to see the show, today it is available online to be viewed as often as one likes. Nor, of course, must the linear progression of the narrative be respected. In the text accompanying a full copy at archive.org, the uploader notes the exact time of one of Chaney's goofs, so that the viewer so inclined can skip directly to it; and on YouTube one can find short clips that excerpt only the episode's best or, of course, its unintentionally funniest moments. Our own medium sensitivity when watching once-live television in the endlessly replayable, spliceable, and mashable medium of digital video indeed involves an uncanny sense of the mismatch between a unique historical moment and its total digital deterritorialization. This mismatch, we might say, opens a line of flight in the context of our own transitional moment. The embodied situation of the computer user seated before the monitor, mouse in hand, is subject to destabilization through the molecular flow of bits that have transformed the live event into a decontexted string.

And as we turn to our own precarious moment, we find that Edison's *Frankenstein* has experienced a similar transformation. In Part One of this project, the 1910 film came to stand as a paradigm of Frankenstein films' transitional challenges— i.e. a parable of these films' abilities to induce phenomenally unstable experiences of transitionality itself—but the Edison film preceded and was therefore not itself a part of the specifically filmic serialization process initiated by Whale's films. This has changed, however, as the series has opened onto the digital realm, in which various media and media productions commingle in a strangely revisable temporality. I am not suggesting, as some critics do, that the digital spells the end of history or of media, but it certainly does transform both of those. And here Edison's *Frankenstein* is instructive again, after a full century in existence, for the majority of which the film was forgotten and then believed lost forever. As I pointed out much earlier, any "influence" attributed to the film with respect to the series that kicks off with Whale and Karloff is highly questionable—if, that is, we are looking for direct and demonstrable influences on the historically situated acts of conception that bore the fruits of Universal's, Hammer's, Warhol's, Mel Brooks's, Rocky Horror's, Kenneth Branagh's, or other filmic Frankensteins. On the other hand, though, from the distance of a hundred years, Edison's film is now exercising a retrospective influence on the perceptions of viewers who discover this "first" Frankenstein film. Widely available now on DVD and online, the once lost film rewrites our histories of Frankenstein films and transforms our visions of their media-historical significance. Moreover, the material accumulation of visual "noise" over the years, including the watermarks added by the surviving print's late owner, but also the transformation of the images as they migrated from disintegrating nitrate stock to video to DVD to YouTube—these medial phenomena record a rich revisionary history of anthropotechnical interactions, a give and take between the material agencies of humans and nonhumans, rendering the film into a multifaceted image that could itself be interrogated as an image of postnatural historicity.

As one example, consider the soundtrack put together for the DVD on the basis of the musical scores passed down (or, more accurately, filed away and forgotten) by the Edison Company. Synthesized electronically and stored digitally, this sonic image contrasts with and to a certain degree constructs an image of the physical real as comprised of unrepeatable sounds and noises produced in the various screenings of 1910. But we are hardly trapped today by the intentions of the Edison Company, and the YouTube proliferation of the film is perhaps truer to the transitional spirit of 1910 film exhibition when it replaces this reconstructed "authentic" score with alternative musical accompaniments. The user AbendKomponist has composed an original score full of (digital) wind instruments, strings, chimes, and piano; the Video Cellar Collection copy at archive.org substitutes a recording of Paul Dukas's *The Sorcerer's Apprentice* (of Mickey Mouse/*Fantasia* fame); Carlos Devizia superimposes the film on top of images from *Gray's Anatomy* (1918) and underscores it with techno music and a spoken Esperanto text; and Life Toward Twilight, self-described as the "dark ambient, post-industrial project" of Detroit artist Daniel Tuttle, offers one of the most interesting musical renditions, a mesmerizing score that casts the film's visual images in a very different light, in no small part as a result of the occasional sounds that accompany those images in a diegetic or expressionistically quasi-diegetic function—thus exploding the notion that silent film accompaniment must respect an absolute wall that separates non-diegetic sound from diegetic image. In no sense are these soundtracks "authentic," but the proliferation of anachronous musical scores challenges our preconceptions about the medial historicity of silent film by bringing them into connection with our own medial transition currently underway.

Recoding our perceptions of the Frankenstein film, including even our view of Karloff's iconic monster as the "original" of its type, Edison's *Frankenstein* joins the ranks of the Frankenstein film series, now situating itself at our end rather than at the beginning of that series' history. Now, prospering among the short clips of YouTube, where it is far more at home than any of the feature films ever could be, the Edison monster becomes capable again of articulating a "medial" narrative—a tale told from a middle altitude, from a position half-way between the diegetic story, on the one hand, of the monster's defeat by a Frankenstein who grows up and "comes to his senses" and, on the other hand, a non-diegetic, media-historical metanarrative that, in contrast to the story of medial maturation it encoded in 1910, now articulates a tale of visual media's currently conflicted state, caught between historical specificity and an eternal recurrence of the same. The monster's medial narrative communicates with our own medial position, mediates possible transactions in a realm of experimentation, in which human and nonhuman agencies negotiate the terms of their changing relations. With its digitally scarred body, pocked by pixels and compression "artifacts," the century-old monster opens a line of flight that, if we follow it, might bring us face to face with the molecular becoming of our own postnatural future.

Works Cited

Ackermann, Robert J. *Data, Instruments, and Theory*. Princeton: Princeton UP, 1985.
Agamben, Giorgio. *The Coming Community*. Trans. Michael Hardt. Minneapolis: U of Minnesota P, 1993.
Armstrong, Nancy. Review of *The Proper Lady and the Woman Writer: Ideology as Style in the Works of Mary Wollstonecraft, Mary Shelley, and Jane Austen*, by Mary Poovey. *MLN* 99.5 (December 1984): 1251-1257.
Baldick, Chris. *In Frankenstein's Shadow: Myth, Monstrosity, and Nineteenth-Century Writing*. Oxford: Oxford UP, 1987.
Bazin, André. "The Myth of Total Cinema." *What is Cinema? Volume 1*. Trans. Hugh Gray. Berkeley: U of California P, 2005. 17-22.
—. "The Ontology of the Photographic Image." *What is Cinema? Volume 1*. Trans. Hugh Gray. Berkeley: U of California P, 2005. 9-16.
Benjamin, Walter. "On Some Motifs in Baudelaire." Trans. Harry Zohn. *Illuminations*. Ed. Hannah Arendt. New York: Schocken, 1968. 155-200.
—. "The Work of Art in the Age of Mechanical Reproduction." Trans. Harry Zohn. *Illuminations*. Ed. Hannah Arendt. New York: Schocken, 1968. 217-251.
Bergson, Henri. *Creative Evolution*. Trans. Arthur Mitchell. Mineola: Dover, 1998.
—. *The Creative Mind: An Introduction to Metaphysics*. Trans. Mabelle L. Andison. Mineola, NY: Dover, 2007.
—. *Matter and Memory*. Trans. N.M. Paul and W.S. Palmer. New York: Cosimo, 2007.
Bey, Hakim. *T.A.Z.: The Temporary Autonomous Zone, Ontological Anarchy, Poetic Terrorism*. 2nd ed. Brooklyn: Autonomedia, 2003.
Bloom, Harold. Afterword. *Frankenstein*. By Mary Shelley. New York: Signet, 2000. 199-210.
Bogost, Ian. "Alien Phenomenology: A Pragmatic Speculative Realism." Plenary lecture. Society for Literature, Science, and the Arts, 2009 Annual Conference. Georgia Tech Global Learning Center. 6 November 2009.
—. *Alien Phenomenology: Or, What It's Like to Be a Thing*. Minneapolis: U of Minnesota P, 2012.

—. "The Phenomenology of Video Games." *Conference Proceedings of the Philosophy of Computer Games 2008*. Eds. Stephan Günzel, Michael Liebe, and Dieter Mersch. Potsdam: Potsdam UP, 2008. 22-43.

—. "What is Object-Oriented Ontology? A Definition for Ordinary Folk." Blog post. 8 December 2009: <http://www.bogost.com/blog/what_is_objectoriented_ontolog.shtml>.

Bordwell, David, Janet Staiger, and Kristin Thompson. *The Classical Hollywood Cinema: Film Style and Mode of Production to 1960*. New York: Columbia UP, 1985.

Bortolotti, Gary R., and Linda Hutcheon. "On the Origin of Adaptations: Rethinking Fidelity Discourse and 'Success'—Biologically." *New Literary History* 38.3 (Summer 2007): 443-458.

Bowser, Eileen. *The Transformation of Cinema, 1907-1915*. Berkeley: U of California P, 1990.

Brassier, Ray. "Against an Aesthetics of Noise." Interview with Bram Ieven. *nY* 2 (July 2009). <http://www.ny-web.be/transitzone/against-aesthetics-noise.html>.

—. *Nihil Unbound: Enlightenment and Extinction*. London: Palgrave Macmillan, 2007.

Brooks, Peter. *The Melodramatic Imagination: Balzac, Henry James, Melodrama, and the Mode of Excess*. New Haven: Yale UP, 1976.

Brown, Kelley R. *Florence Lawrence, the Biograph Girl: America's First Movie Star*. Jefferson, NC: McFarland, 1999.

Brown, Sanborn C. "Count Rumford and the Caloric Theory of Heat." *Proceedings of the American Philosophical Society* 93.4 (September 1949): 316-325.

Brush, Stephen G. *The Kinetic Theory of Gases: An Anthology of Classic Papers with Historical Commentary*. Ed. Nancy S. Hall. London: Imperial College Press, 2003.

Bryant, Levi R. *The Democracy of Objects*. Ann Arbor: Open Humanities Press, 2011.

Bryant, Lynwood. "The Role of Thermodynamics in the Evolution of Heat Engines." *Technology and Culture* 14.2 (April 1973): 152-165.

Buber, Martin. *Ich und Du*. 1923. Stuttgart: Reclam, 1995.

Callendar, H.L. "The Caloric Theory of Heat and Carnot's Principle." *Proceedings of the Physical Society of London* 23 (1910): 153-189.

Callon, Michel, and Bruno Latour. "Don't Throw the Baby Out with the Bath School! A Reply to Collins and Yearley." *Science as Practice and Culture*. Ed. Andrew Pickering. Chicago and London: U of Chicago P, 1992. 343-368.

Cardwell, D.S.L. "Power Technologies and the Advance of Science, 1700-1825." *Technology and Culture* 6.2 (Spring 1965): 188-207.

Carnap, Rudolf. *Der Logische Aufbau der Welt*. Hamburg: Felix Meiner Verlag, 1998.

Carnot, Sadi. *Reflexions on the Motive Power of Fire.* Trans. Robert Fox. Manchester: Manchester UP, 1986.
Chabon, Michael. "Fan Fictions: On Sherlock Holmes." *Maps and Legends: Reading and Writing along the Borderlands.* San Francisco: McSweeney's, 2008. 35-57.
Clausius, Rudolf. "On the Motive Power of Heat, and on the Laws that can be Deduced from it for the Theory of Heat." *The Second Law of Thermodynamics: Memoirs by Carnot, Clausius, and Thomson.* Ed. W.F. Magie. New York: Harper and Brothers, 1899. 65-107.
—. "On the Moving Force of Heat, and the Laws regarding the Nature of Heat itself which are deducible therefrom." *Philosophical Magazine* 2 (Series 4, July-December 1851): 1-21, 102-119.
—. "Ueber verschiedene für die Anwendung bequeme Formen der Hauptgleichungen der mechanischen Waermetheorie." *Annalen der Physik und Chemie* 125 (1865): 353-400.
Clover, Carol J. *Men, Women, and Chainsaws: Gender in the Modern Horror Film.* Princeton, NJ: Princeton UP, 1992.
Collins, Harry M., and Steven Yearley. "Epistemological Chicken." *Science as Practice and Culture.* Ed. Andrew Pickering. Chicago and London: U of Chicago P, 1992. 301-326.
Crafton, Donald. *The Talkies: American Cinema's Transition to Sound, 1926-1931.* Berkeley: U of California P, 1997.
Crary, Jonathan. *Techniques of the Observer: On Vision and Modernity in the Nineteenth Century.* Cambridge, MA: MIT, 1990.
Davidson, Donald. "On the Very Idea of a Conceptual Scheme." *Inquiries into Truth and Interpretation.* New York: Oxford UP, 1984. 183-198.
De Man, Paul. *Allegories of Reading: Figural Language in Rousseau, Nietzsche, Rilke, and Proust.* New Haven: Yale UP, 1979.
Decker, Christof. *Hollywoods kritischer Blick. Das soziale Melodrama in der amerikanischen Kultur, 1840-1950.* Frankfurt: Campus, 2003.
Deleuze, Gilles. *Cinema 1: The Movement-Image.* Trans. Hugh Tomlinson and Barbara Habberjam. Minneapolis: U of Minnesota P, 1986.
—. *Cinema 2: The Time-Image.* Trans. Hugh Tomlinson and Robert Galeta. Minneapolis: U of Minnesota P, 1989.
—. *Francis Bacon: The Logic of Sensation.* Trans. Daniel W. Smith. London: Continuum, 2003.
Deleuze, Gilles, and Félix Guattari. *A Thousand Plateaus: Capitalism and Schizophrenia.* Trans. Brian Massumi. Minneapolis: U of Minnesota P, 1987.
Denson, Shane. "Between Technology and Art: Functions of Film in Transitional-Era Cinema." *Funktionen von Kunst.* Eds. Daniel Martin Feige, Tilmann Köppe, Gesa zur Nieden. Frankfurt: Peter Lang, 2009. 127-142.

—. "Frankenstein, Bioethics, and Technological Irreversibility." *Studies in Irreversibility: Texts and Contexts.* Ed. Benjamin Schreier. Newcastle: Cambridge Scholars Publishing, 2007. 134-166.

—. "Incorporations: Melodrama and Monstrosity in James Whale's *Frankenstein* and *Bride of Frankenstein.*" *Melodrama! The Mode of Excess from Early America to Hollywood.* Eds. Frank Kelleter, Barbara Krah, and Ruth Mayer. Heidelberg: Universitätsverlag Winter, 2007.

—. "Marvel Comics' Frankenstein: A Case Study in the Media of Serial Figures." *Amerikastudien/American Studies* 56.4 (2011): 531-53.

—. "Tarzan und der Tonfilm: Verhandlungen zwischen 'science' und 'fiction'." *"Ich Tarzan." Affenmenschen und Menschenaffen zwischen Science und Fiction.* Eds. Gesine Krüger, Ruth Mayer, and Marianne Sommer. Bielefeld: Transcript, 2008.

Denson, Shane, and Ruth Mayer. "Bildstörung: Serielle Figuren und der Fernseher." *Zeitschrift für Medienwissenschaft* 7 (2012): 90-102.

—. "Grenzgänger: Serielle Figuren im Medienwechsel." *Populäre Serialität: Narration-Evolution-Distinktion. Zum seriellen Erzählen seit dem 19. Jahrhundert.* Ed. Frank Kelleter. Bielefeld: Transcript, 2012. 185-203.

Derrida, Jacques. *Edmund Husserl's Origin of Geometry: An Introduction.* Trans. John P. Leavey. Lincoln: U of Nebraska P, 1989.

—. "Psyche: Inventions of the Other." Trans. Catherine Porter. *Reading de Man Reading.* Eds. Lindsay Waters and Wlad Godzich. Minneapolis: U of Minnesota P, 1987. 25-65.

—. *Speech and Phenomena, and Other Essays on Husserl's Theory of Signs.* Trans. David B. Allison. Evanston: Northwestern UP, 1973.

Derrida, Jacques, and Stiegler, Bernard. *Echographies of Television.* Trans. Jennifer Bajorek. Cambridge: Polity Press, 2002.

Dewey, John. "Propositions, Warranted Assertibility, and Truth." *Contemporary Readings in Epistemology.* Eds. Michael F. Goodman and Robert A. Snyder. Englewood Cliffs, NJ: Prentice Hall, 1993. 199-205.

Doane, Mary Ann. "The Close-Up: Scale and Detail in the Cinema." *Differences: A Journal of Feminist Cultural Studies* 14.3 (Fall 2003): 89-111.

Dumont, Frank. *The Witmark Amateur Minstrel Guide and Burnt Cork Encyclopedia.* New York: M. Witmark and Sons, 1899.

Eco, Umberto. "The Myth of Superman." *The Role of the Reader: Explorations in the Semiotics of Texts.* Bloomington: Indiana UP, 1984. 107-124.

Engell, Lorenz. "Die genetische Funktion des Historischen in der Geschichte der Bildmedien." *Archiv für Mediengeschichte* 1 (2001): 33-56.

Fine, Arthur. "The Natural Ontological Attitude." *The Philosophy of Science.* Ed. David Papineau. New York: Oxford UP, 1996. 21-44.

Forry, Steven Earl. *Hideous Progenies: Dramatizations of* Frankenstein *from the Nineteenth Century to the Present.* Philadelphia: U of Pennsylvania P, 1990.

Foucault, Michel. "The Confessions of the Flesh." *Power/Knowledge: Selected Interviews and Other Writings 1972-1977*. Trans. Colin Gordon. New York: Pantheon, 1980. 194-228.

—. *Discipline and Punish*. Trans. A.M. Sheridan Smith. New York: Pantheon, 1977.

—. *The History of Sexuality, Volume 1: An Introduction*. Trans. Robert Hurley. New York: Vintage, 1990.

—. "Of Other Spaces." *The Visual Culture Reader*. 2nd ed. Ed. Nicholas Mirzoeff. London: Routledge, 2002. 229-236.

—. *The Order of Things: An Archaeology of the Human Sciences*. New York: Vintage, 1973.

Freud, Sigmund. "The Uncanny." Trans. David McLintock. *The Uncanny*. London: Penguin, 2003. 121-162.

Gaines, Jane. "Superman and the Protective Strength of the Trademark." *Logics of Television: Essays in Cultural Criticism*. Ed. Patricia Mellencamp. Bloomington: Indiana UP, 1990. 173-192.

Galilei, Galileo. *Dialogue Concerning the Two Chief World Systems*. Ed. and trans. Stillman Drake, with an introduction by Albert Einstein. Berkeley and Los Angeles: U of California P, 1967.

García, Pedro Javier Pardo. "Beyond Adaptation: Frankenstein's Postmodern Progeny." *Books in Motion: Adaptation, Intertextuality, Authorship*. Ed. Mireia Aragay. Amsterdam: Rodopi, 2005. 223-242.

Giere, Ronald N. "Philosophy of Science Naturalized." *Readings in the Philosophy of Science*. 2nd ed. Eds. Baruch A. Brody and Richard E. Grandy. Englewood Cliffs, NJ: Prentice Hall, 1989. 379-398.

Gilbert, Sandra M., and Susan Gubar. *The Madwoman in the Attic: The Woman Writer and the Nineteenth-Century Literary Imagination*. New Haven: Yale UP, 1979.

Glut, Donald. *The Frankenstein Catalog*. Jefferson, NC: McFarland, 1984.

Gomery, Douglas. "Technological Film History." *Film History: Theory and Practice*. Robert C. Allen and Douglas Gomery. New York: Alfred A. Knopf, 1985. 109-130.

Grant, Iain Hamilton. *Philosophies of Nature after Schelling*. London: Continuum, 2006.

Griffith, Linda Arvidson. *When the Movies Were Young*. 1925. New York: Ayer Company, 1972.

Gunning, Tom. "The Cinema of Attraction: Early Film, Its Spectator and the Avant-Garde." *Wide Angle* 8.3-4 (1986): 63-70.

—. "Crazy Machines in the Garden of Forking Paths: Mischief Gags and the Origins of American Film Comedy." *Classical Hollywood Comedy*. Eds. Kristine Brunovska Karnick and Henry Jenkins. London: Routledge, 1995. 87-105.

—. "Early American Film." *American Cinema and Hollywood: Critical Approaches.* Eds. John Hill and Pamela Church Gibson. New York: Oxford UP, 2000. 29-45.

Hacking, Ian. Introduction. *Scientific Revolutions.* Ed. Ian Hacking. New York: Oxford UP, 1981. 1-5.

—. *Representing and Intervening.* Cambridge: Cambridge UP, 1983.

Halberstam, Judith. *Skin Shows: Gothic Horror and the Technology of Monsters.* Durham and London: Duke UP, 1995.

Hansen, Mark B. N. *Embodying Technesis: Technology Beyond Writing.* Ann Arbor: U of Michigan P, 2000.

—. "Media Theory." *Theory, Culture & Society* 23.2-3 (2006): 297-306.

—. *New Philosophy for New Media.* Cambridge, MA: MIT Press, 2004.

—. "'Not thus, after all, would life be given': *Technesis*, Technology, and the Parody of Romantic Poetics in *Frankenstein.*" *Studies in Romanticism* 36.4 (Winter 1997): 575-609.

—. "'Realtime Synthesis' and the Différance of the Body: Technocultural Studies in the Wake of Deconstruction." *Culture Machine* 6 (2004). <http://www.culturemachine.net/index.php/cm/article/view/9/8>.

Hansen, Miriam. *Babel and Babylon: Spectatorship in American Silent Film.* Cambridge: Harvard UP, 1991.

Haraway, Donna J. "A Cyborg Manifesto: Science, Technology, and Socialist-Feminism in the Late Twentieth Century." *Simians, Cyborgs, and Women: The Reinvention of Nature.* New York: Routledge, 1991. 149-181.

—. *Simians, Cyborgs, and Women: The Reinvention of Nature.* New York: Routledge, 1991.

—. "Situated Knowledges: The Science Question in Feminism and the Privilege of Partial Perspective." *Simians, Cyborgs, and Women: The Reinvention of Nature.* New York: Routledge, 1991. 183-201.

—. *When Species Meet.* Minneapolis: U of Minnesota P, 2008.

Harding, Sandra, ed. *Can Theories Be Refuted? Essays on the Duhem-Quine Thesis.* Dordrecht: D. Reidel, 1976.

—. *The Science Question in Feminism.* Ithaca: Cornell UP, 1986.

Harman, Graham. *Guerrilla Metaphysics: Phenomenology and the Carpentry of Things.* Chicago: Open Court, 2005.

—. *Prince of Networks: Bruno Latour and Metaphysics.* Melbourne: re.press, 2009.

—. *Tool-Being: Heidegger and the Metaphysics of Objects.* Chicago: Open Court, 2002.

Hayles, N. Katherine. "Constrained Constructivism: Locating Scientific Inquiry in the Theater of Representation." *New Orleans Review* 18.1 (1991): 76-85.

—. *How We Became Posthuman: Virtual Bodies in Cybernetics, Literature, and Informatics.* Chicago: U of Chicago P, 1999.

—. "The Materiality of Informatics." *Configurations* 1 (1992): 147-170.

Hearn, Marcus, and Alan Barnes. *The Hammer Story: The Authorised History of Hammer Films*. 2nd ed. London: Titan Books, 2007.

Heffernan, James A.W. "Looking at the Monster: *Frankenstein* and Film." *Critical Inquiry* 24.1 (Autumn 1997): 133-158.

Heffernan, Kevin. *Ghouls, Gimmicks, and Gold: Horror Films and the American Movie Business, 1953-1968*. Durham and London: Duke UP, 2004.

Heidegger, Martin. *Being and Time*. Trans. John Macquarrie and Edward Robinson. New York: Harper & Row, 1962.

—. *On Time and Being*. Trans. Joan Stambaugh. Chicago: U of Chicago P, 2002.

—. "The Question Concerning Technology." *The Question Concerning Technology and Other Essays*. Trans. William Lovitt. New York: Harper & Row, 1977. 3-35.

Heider, Fritz. *Ding und Medium*. 1926. Berlin: Kulturverlag Kadmos, 2005.

Helmholtz, Hermann. "The Conservation of Force." *The Kinetic Theory of Gases: An Anthology of Classic Papers with Historical Commentary*. By Stephen G. Brush. Ed. Nancy S. Hall. London: Imperial College Press, 2003. 89-110.

Hempel, Carl. *Aspects of Scientific Explanation and Other Essays in the Philosophy of Science*. New York: Free Press, 1965.

Hickman, Larry A. *John Dewey's Pragmatic Technology*. Bloomington and Indianapolis: Indiana UP, 1990.

Hitchcock, Susan Tyler. *Frankenstein: A Cultural History*. New York: Norton, 2007.

Homans, Margaret. *Bearing the Word: Language and the Female Experience in Nineteenth-Century Women's Writing*. Chicago: U of Chicago P, 1986.

Husserl, Edmund. *The Crisis of European Sciences and Transcendental Phenomenology: An Introduction to Phenomenological Philosophy*. Trans. David Carr. Evanston, IL: Northwestern UP, 1970.

—. *Texte zur Phänomenologie des inneren Zeitbewusstseins*. Ed. Rudolf Bernet. Hamburg: Meiner, 1985.

—. *Vorlesungen zur Phänomenologie des inneren Zeitbewusstseins*. Ed. Martin Heidegger. Halle: Max Niemeyer Verlag, 1928.

Hutcheon, Linda. *A Theory of Adaptation*. New York: Routledge, 2006.

Ihde, Don. *Bodies in Technology*. Minneapolis: U of Minnesota P, 2002.

—. *Instrumental Realism: The Interface between Philosophy of Science and Philosophy of Technology*. Bloomington and Indianapolis: Indiana UP, 1991.

—. *Ironic Technics*. Copenhagen: Automatic Press, 2008.

—. *Postphenomenology – Again?* Working Papers from the Centre for STS Studies. Aarhus: U of Aarhus, 2003.

—. *Technics and Praxis*. Boston: D. Reidel, 1979.

—. *Technology and the Lifeworld: From Garden to Earth*. Bloomington and Indianapolis: Indiana UP, 1990.

Jacobus, Mary. "Is There a Woman in This Text?" *New Literary History* 14.1 (Autumn 1982): 117-141.

Jager, Bernd. "The Historical Background of van den Berg's *Two Laws*." *The Two Principal Laws of Thermodynamics: A Cultural and Historical Exploration*. By J.H. van den Berg. Trans. Bernd Jager, David Jager, and Dreyer Kruger. Pittsburgh: Duquesne UP, 2004. 1-31.

Jahn-Sudmann, Andreas, and Frank Kelleter. "Die Dynamik serieller Überbietung: Amerikanische Fernsehserien und das Konzept des Quality TV." *Populäre Serialität: Narration-Evolution-Distinktion. Zum seriellen Erzählen seit dem 19. Jahrhundert*. Ed. Frank Kelleter. Bielefeld: Transcript, 2012. 205-224.

Jenkins, Henry. *Convergence Culture: Where Old and New Media Collide*. New York and London: New York UP, 2006.

Jentsch, Ernst. "On the Psychology of the Uncanny." Trans. Roy Sellars. *Angelaki* 2.1 (1995): 7-16.

Johnson, Barbara. "My Monster/My Self." Review of *Frankenstein*, by Mary Shelley, *My Mother/My Self*, by Nancy Friday, and *The Mermaid and the Minotaur*, by Dorothy Dinnerstein. *Diacritics* 12.2 (Summer 1982): 2-10.

Joule, James Prescott. "On the Changes of Temperature produced by the Rarefaction and Condensation of Air." *Philosophical Magazine* 26, (Third Series, 1845): 369-383.

—. "On Matter, Living Force, and Heat." *The Kinetic Theory of Gases: An Anthology of Classic Papers with Historical Commentary*. By Stephen G. Brush. Ed. Nancy S. Hall. London: Imperial College Press, 2003. 78-88.

Keil, Charlie. *Early American Cinema in Transition: Story, Style, and Filmmaking, 1907-1913*. Madison, WI: U of Wisconsin P, 2001.

Kelleter, Frank, ed. *Populäre Serialität: Narration-Evolution-Distinktion. Zum seriellen Erzählen seit dem 19. Jahrhundert*. Bielefeld: Transcript, 2012.

Kelleter, Frank, and Ruth Mayer. "The Melodramatic Mode Revisited: An Introduction." *Melodrama! The Mode of Excess from Early America to Hollywood*. Eds. Frank Kelleter, Barbara Krah, and Ruth Mayer. Heidelberg: Universitätsverlag Winter, 2007. 7-17.

Khurana, Thomas. "Niklas Luhmann – Die Form des Mediums." *Medientheorien: Eine philosophische Einführung*. Eds. Alice Lagaay and David Lauer. Frankfurt: Campus, 2004. 97-125.

Kiely, Robert. *The Romantic Novel in England*. Cambridge, MA: Harvard UP, 1972.

Kinsey, Wayne. *Hammer Films: The Bray Studios Years*. London: Reynolds & Hearn, 2002.

—. *Hammer Films: The Elstree Studios Years*. Sheffield: Tomahawk Press, 2007.

Kittler, Friedrich. *Gramophone, Film, Typewriter*. Trans. Geoffrey Winthrop-Young and Michael Wutz. Stanford: Stanford UP, 1999.

Kristeva, Julia. *Powers of Horror: An Essay on Abjection*. Trans. Leon S. Roudiez. New York: Columbia UP, 1982.

Kuhn, Annette. *Cinema, Censorship and Sexuality, 1909-1925.* London: Routledge, 1988.

—. "Women's Genres: Melodrama, Soap Opera and Theory." *Home Is Where the Heart Is: Studies in Melodrama and the Woman's Film*. Ed. Christine Gledhill. London: BFI, 1987. 339-349.

Kuhn, Thomas S. "The Caloric Theory of Adiabatic Compression." *Isis* 49.2 (June 1958): 132-140.

—. *The Structure of Scientific Revolutions*. 2nd ed. Chicago: U of Chicago P, 1970.

—. "The Trouble with the Historical Philosophy of Science." Robert and Maurine Rothschild Distinguished Lecture, 19 November 1991. An Occasional Publication of the Department of the History of Science. Cambridge, MA: Harvard UP, 1992.

Landau, Diana, ed. *Mary Shelley's Frankenstein: The Classic Tale of Terror Reborn on Film*. New York: Newmarket Press, 1994.

Landon, Brooks. "Diegetic or Digital? The Convergence of Science-Fiction Literature and Science-Fiction Film in Hypermedia." *Alien Zone II*. London: Verso, 1999. 31-49.

Latour, Bruno. "Can We Get Our Materialism Back, Please?" *Isis* 98.1 (2007): 138-142.

—. *We Have Never Been Modern*. Trans. Catherine Porter. Cambridge, MA: Harvard UP, 1993.

Latour, Bruno, and Steve Woolgar. *Laboratory Life: the Social Construction of Scientific Facts*. Los Angeles: Sage, 1979.

Laudan, Rachel. Introduction. *The Nature of Technological Knowledge: Are Models of Scientific Change Relevant?* Ed. Rachel Laudan. Dordrecht: D. Reidel, 1984. 1-26.

Lavalley, Albert J. "The Stage and Film Children of *Frankenstein*: A Survey." *The Endurance of* Frankenstein: *Essays on Mary Shelley's Novel*. Eds. George Levine and U.C. Knoepflmacher. Berkeley: U of California P, 1979. 243-289.

Leitch, Thomas. *Film Adaptation and its Discontents: From* Gone with the Wind *to* The Passion of the Christ. Baltimore: Johns Hopkins UP, 2007.

Lenoir, Tim. Foreword. *New Philosophy for New Media*. Mark Hansen. Cambridge, MA: MIT Press, 2004. xiii-xxviii.

Lev, Peter. *The Fifties: Transforming the Screen, 1950-1959*. Berkeley: U of California P, 2003.

Lévinas, Emmanuel. *Totality and Infinity*. Dordrecht: Kluwer, 1991.

"Life Without Soul." *American Film Institute Catalog of Feature Films*. Online edition.
<http://www.afi.com/members/catalog/AbbrView.aspx?s=&Movie=16531>.

Lindsay, Vachel. *The Art of the Moving Picture*. 2nd ed. New York: Macmillan, 1922.
Luhmann, Niklas. *Art as a Social System*. Trans. Eva M. Knodt. Stanford: Stanford UP, 2000.
—. *Die Gesellschaft der Gesellschaft*. Frankfurt: Suhrkamp, 1997.
—. Interview with Hans Dieter Huber. *Texte zur Kunst* 4 (September 1991): 121-133.
—. *Die Kunst der Gesellschaft*. Frankfurt: Suhrkamp, 1995.
—. "Das Risiko der Kausalität." *Zeitschrift für Wissenschaftsforschung* 9/10 (1995): 107-119.
—. *Social Systems*. Trans. John Bednarz, Jr., with Dirk Baecker. Stanford: Stanford UP, 1995.
—. *Theories of Distinction: Redescribing the Descriptions of Modernity*. Ed. William Rasch. Stanford: Stanford UP, 2002.
Mackenzie, Adrian. *Transductions: Bodies and Machines at Speed*. London: Continuum, 2002.
MacNamara, Brooks. "Scavengers of the Amusement World: Popular Entertainment and the Birth of the Movies." *American Pastimes*. Brockton, Mass.: Brockton Art Center, 1976.
MacQueen, Scott. Audio Commentary to *Bride of Frankenstein*. DVD. Universal, 2002.
Mank, Gregory William. *It's Alive! The Classic Cinema Saga of Frankenstein*. San Diego: A.S. Barnes, 1981.
Marks, Elaine, and Isabelle de Courtivron, eds. *New French Feminisms: An Anthology*. Amherst: U of Massachusetts P, 1980.
Massumi, Brian. *Parables for the Virtual: Movement, Affect, Sensation*. Durham and London: Duke UP, 2002.
—. *A User's Guide to Capitalism and Schizophrenia: Deviations from Deleuze and Guattari*. Cambridge, MA: MIT Press, 1992.
Mayer, Julius Robert. "The Forces of Inorganic Nature." *The Kinetic Theory of Gases: An Anthology of Classic Papers with Historical Commentary*. By Stephen G. Brush. Ed. Nancy S. Hall. London: Imperial College Press, 2003. 71-77.
Mayer, Ruth. *Selbsterkenntnis – Körperfühlen: Medizin, Philosophie und die amerikanische Renaissance*. München: Wilhelm Fink Verlag, 1997.
—. *Serial Fu Manchu: The Chinese Supervillain and the Spread of Yellow Peril Ideology*. Philadelphia: Temple UP, 2013.
McCarty, John. *The Modern Horror Film: 50 Contemporary Classics from "The Curse of Frankenstein" to "The Lair of the White Worm"*. New York: Citadel, 1990.
McFarlane, Brian. *Novel to Film: An Introduction to the Theory of Adaptation*. Oxford: Oxford UP, 1996.

Meillassoux, Quentin. *After Finitude: An Essay on the Necessity of Contingency.* Trans. Ray Brassier. London: Continuum, 2008.
Merleau-Ponty, Maurice. *Phenomenology of Perception.* Trans. Colin Smith. London: Routledge, 2002.
Metz, Christian. *Film Language: A Semiotics of the Cinema.* Trans. Michael Taylor. New York: Oxford UP, 1974.
—. *The Imaginary Signifier: Psychoanalysis and the Cinema.* Trans. Celia Britton, Annwyl Williams, Ben Brewster, and Alfred Guzzetti. Bloomington: Indiana UP, 1982.
Mittell, Jason. "Narrative Complexity in Contemporary American Television." *The Velvet Light Trap* 58 (2006): 29-40.
Moers, Ellen. "Female Gothic." *The Endurance of* Frankestein: *Essays on Mary Shelley's Novel.* Eds. George Levine and U.C. Knoepflmacher. Berkeley: U of California P, 1979. 77-87.
Morris, Gary. "Sexual Subversion: The Bride of Frankenstein." *Bright Lights Film Journal* 19 (July 1997). <http://www.brightlightsfilm.com/19/19_bride1.php>.
Mulvey, Linda. "Visual Pleasure and Narrative Cinema." *Screen* 16.3 (Autumn 1975): 6-18.
Münsterberg, Hugo. *The Photoplay: A Psychological Study.* New York: D. Appleton, 1916.
Musser, Charles. *The Emergence of Cinema: The American Screen to 1907.* Berkeley: U of California P, 1990.
Neale, Steve. *Genre and Hollywood.* London: Routledge, 2000.
—. "Questions of Genre." *Screen* 31.1 (1990): 45-66.
Nestrick, William. "Coming to Life: *Frankenstein* and the Nature of Film Narrative." *The Endurance of* Frankenstein: *Essays on Mary Shelley's Novel.* Eds. George Levine and U.C. Knoepflmacher. Berkeley: U of California P, 1979. 290-315.
Nitchie, Elizabeth. "The Stage History of *Frankenstein.*" *The South Atlantic Quarterly* 41 (1942): 384-398.
O'Flinn, Paul. "Production and Reproduction: The Case of *Frankenstein.*" *New Casebooks: Frankenstein.* Ed. Fred Botting. London: Macmillan, 1995. 21-47.
Peake, Richard Brinsley. *Presumption; or, the Fate of Frankenstein.* Ed. Stephen C. Behrendt. *Romantic Circles.* <http://www.rc.umd.edu/editions/peake/>.
Peiss, Kathy. *Cheap Amusements: Working Women and Leisure in Turn-of-the-Century New York.* Philadelphia: Temple UP, 1986.
Picart, Caroline Joan ("Kay") S. *The Cinematic Rebirths of Frankenstein: Universal, Hammer, and Beyond.* Westport, CT: Praeger, 2002.
—. *Remaking the Frankenstein Myth on Film: Between Laughter and Horror.* Albany: State U of New York P, 2003.
Picart, Caroline Joan ("Kay") S., Frank Smoot, and Jayne Blodgett. *The Frankenstein Film Sourcebook.* Westport, CT: Greenwood Press, 2001.

Pickering, Andrew. *The Mangle of Practice: Time, Agency, and Science.* Chicago and London: U of Chicago P, 1995.

—. "Ontology Engines." *Postphenomenology: A Critical Companion to Ihde.* Ed. Evan Selinger. Albany, NY: State U of New York P, 2006. 211-218.

Pirie, David. *A New Heritage of Horror: The English Gothic Cinema.* London: I.B. Taurus, 2008.

Poovey, Mary. "My Hideous Progeny: Mary Shelley and the Feminization of Romanticism." *PMLA* 95.3 (May 1980): 332-347.

Praz, Mario. *The Romantic Agony.* Trans. Angus Davidson. London: Oxford UP, 1933.

Pudovkin, V.I. *Film Technique and Film Acting.* Trans. Ivor Montagu. New York: Bonanza, 2007.

Putnam, Hilary. *Realism with a Human Face.* Ed. James Conant. Cambridge, MA: Harvard UP, 1990.

—. *Reason, Truth, and History.* Cambridge: Cambridge UP, 1981.

Quine, Willard Van Orman. "Epistemology Naturalized." *Contemporary Readings in Epistemology.* Eds. Michael F. Goodman and Robert A. Snyder. Englewood Cliffs, NJ: Prentice Hall, 1993. 313-323.

Rabinow, Paul. *Anthropos Today: Reflections on Modern Equipment.* Princeton: Princeton UP, 2003.

Redfield, Marc. "*Frankenstein*'s Cinematic Dream." *Romantic Circles Praxis Series.* Ed. Jerrold E. Hogle. (June 2003). <http://www.rc.umd.edu/praxis/frankenstein/redfield/redfield.html>.

Rhodes, Gary D. "Bits and Pieces: American Cinema and Radio Representations of Shelley's Monster Before and During the Creation of Karloff." *Monsters from the Vault* 9 (1999).

Riley, Philip J., ed. *Abbott and Costello Meet Frankenstein: Universal Filmscripts Series, Classic Comedies – Volume 1.* Absecon, NJ: MagicImage Filmbooks, 1990.

—, ed. *The Bride of Frankenstein: Universal Filmscripts Series, Classic Horror Films – Volume 2.* Absecon, NJ: MagicImage Filmbooks, 1989.

—, ed. *Frankenstein: Universal Filmscripts Series, Classic Horror Films – Volume 1.* Absecon, NJ: MagicImage Filmbooks, 1989.

—, ed. *Frankenstein Meets the Wolf Man: Universal Filmscripts Series, Classic Horror Films – Volume 5.* Absecon, NJ: MagicImage Filmbooks, 1990.

—, ed. *The Ghost of Frankenstein: Universal Filmscripts Series, Classic Horror Films – Volume 4.* Absecon, NJ: MagicImage Filmbooks, 1990.

—, ed. *House of Dracula: Universal Filmscripts Series, Classic Horror Films – Volume 16.* Absecon, NJ: MagicImage Filmbooks, 1993.

—, ed. *House of Frankenstein: Universal Filmscripts Series, Classic Horror Films – Volume 6.* Absecon, NJ: MagicImage Filmbooks, 1991.

—, ed. *Son of Frankenstein: Universal Filmscripts Series, Classic Horror Films – Volume 3*. Absecon, NJ: MagicImage Filmbooks, 1990.
Rosen, Philip, ed. *Narrative, Apparatus, Ideology: A Film Theory Reader*. New York: Columbia UP, 1986.
Ross, Steven J. "How Hollywood Became Hollywood: Money, Politics, and Movies." *Metropolis in the Making: Los Angeles in the 1920s*. Eds. Tom Sitton and William Deverell. Berkeley: U of California P, 2001. 255-276.
Russo, Vito. *The Celluloid Closet: Homosexuality in the Movies*. New York: Harper & Row, 1981.
Salanskis, Jean-Michel. "Ecce Faber." *Les Temps modernes* 608 (2000): 235-278.
Sanders, Julie. *Adaptation and Appropriation*. New York: Routledge, 2006.
Schatz, Thomas. *The Genius of the System: Hollywood Filmmaking in the Studio Era*. New York: Pantheon, 1989.
—. *Hollywood Genres: Formulas, Filmmaking, and the Studio System*. Boston: McGraw-Hill, 1981.
Schmitt, Frederick F. *Theories of Truth*. Malden, MA: Blackwell, 2004.
Schor, Esther. "Frankenstein and Film." *The Cambridge Companion to Mary Shelley*. Ed. Esther Schor. Cambridge: Cambridge UP, 2003. 63-83.
Schweinitz, Jörg. "'Wie im Kino!' Die autothematische Welle im frühen Tonfilm. Figurationen des Selbstreflexiven." *Diesseits der "Dämonsichen Leinwand": Neue Perspektiven auf das späte Weimarer Kino*. Eds. Thomas Koebner, Norbert Grob, and Bernd Kiefer. Frankfurt: edition text + kritik, 2003. 373-392.
Scruton, Roger. "Photography and Representation." *Critical Inquiry* 7 (1981): 577-603.
Serres, Michel. "Turner Translates Carnot." Trans. Marilyn Sides. *Hermes: Literature, Science, Philosophy*. Eds. Josué V. Harari and David F. Bell. Baltimore and London: Johns Hopkins UP, 1982. 54-62.
Sevastakis, Michael. *Songs of Love and Death: The Classical American Horror Film of the 1930s*. Westport, CT: Greenwood, 1993.
Shaviro, Steven. *The Cinematic Body*. Minneapolis: U of Minnesota P, 1993.
—. "More about objects." Blog post. 25 January 2010: <http://www.shaviro.com/Blog/?p=857>.
—. *The Universe of Things: On Speculative Realism*. Minneapolis: U of Minnesota P, forthcoming.
—. *Without Criteria: Kant, Whitehead, Deleuze, and Aesthetics*. Cambridge, MA: MIT, 2009.
Shelley, Mary. *Frankenstein: Or, the Modern Prometheus*. New York: Penguin, 1994.
Silverman, Kaja. *The Subject of Semiotics*. New York: Oxford UP, 1983.
Simondon, Gilbert. *Du Mode d'existence des objets techniques*. Paris: Aubier, 1958.
Singer, Ben. *Melodrama and Modernity: Early Sensational Cinema and Its Contexts*. New York: Columbia UP, 2001.

Small, Christopher. *Mary Shelley's Frankenstein: Tracing the Myth*. Pittsburgh: U of Pittsburgh P, 1973.

Sobchack, Vivian. *The Address of the Eye: A Phenomenology of Film Experience*. Princeton: Princeton UP, 1992.

—. *Carnal Thoughts: Embodiment and Moving Image Culture*. Berkeley: U of California P, 2004.

—. *Screening Space: The American Science Fiction Film*. 2nd ed. New Brunswick, NJ: Rutgers UP, 1997.

Spadoni, Robert. *Uncanny Bodies: The Coming of Sound and the Origins of the Horror Genre*. Berkeley: U of California P, 2007.

Stam, Robert. "Beyond Fidelity: The Dialogics of Adaptation." *Film Adaptation*. Ed. James Naremore. New Brunswick, NJ: Rutgers UP, 2000. 54-78.

Stern, Daniel. *The Interpersonal World of the Infant*. New York: Basic Books, 1985.

Stiegler, Bernard. "Our Ailing Educational Institutions." Trans. Stefan Herbrechter. *Culture Machine* 5 (2003). <http://www.culturemachine.net/index.php/cm/article/view/258/243>.

—. *Technics and Time 1: The Fault of Epimetheus*. Trans. Richard Beardsworth and George Collins. Stanford: Stanford UP, 1998.

—. *Technics and Time 2: Disorientation*. Trans. Stephen Barker. Stanford: Stanford UP, 2009.

—. *Technics and Time 3: Cinematic Time and the Question of Malaise*. Trans. Stephen Barker. Stanford: Stanford UP, 2011.

—. "The Time of Cinema: On the 'New World' and 'Cultural Exception'." Trans. George Collins. *Tekhnema: Journal of Philosophy and Technology* 4 (1998): 62-113.

Strieble, Dan. "The Harlem Theater: Black Film Exhibition in Austin, Texas: 1920-1973." *Moviegoing in America: A Sourcebook in the History of Film Exhibition*. Ed. Gregory A. Waller. Oxford: Blackwell, 2002. 268-78.

Svehla, Gary J., and Susan Svehla. *We Belong Dead: Frankenstein on Film*. 2nd ed. Baltimore: Luminary Press, 2005.

Telotte, J.P. *Replications: A Robotic History of the Science Fiction Film*. Urbana: U of Chicago P, 1995.

Thompson, Kristin. "Implications of the Cel Animation Technique." *The Cinematic Apparatus*. Eds. Stephen Heath and Teresa de Lauretis. London: MacMillan, 1980. 106-119.

Thomson, William. "An Account of Carnot's Theory of the Motive Power of Heat; with Numerical Results Deduced from Regnault's Experiments on Steam." *Mathematical and Physical Papers, Volume 1*. Cambridge: Cambridge UP, 1882. 113-155.

—. "On an Absolute Thermometric Scale Founded on Carnot's Theory of the Motive Power of Heat, and Calculated from Regnault's Observations." *Mathematical and Physical Papers, Volume 1.* Cambridge: Cambridge UP, 1882. 100-106.
Tropp, Martin. *Images of Fear: How Horror Stories Helped Shape Modern Culture (1818-1918).* Jefferson, NC: McFarland, 1990.
Utterson, Andrew, ed. *Technology and Culture: The Film Reader.* London: Routledge, 2005.
Van den Berg, J.H. *The Two Principal Laws of Thermodynamics: A Cultural and Historical Exploration.* Trans. Bernd Jager, David Jager, and Dreyer Kruger. Pittsburgh: Duquesne UP, 2004.
Vertov, Dziga. "Kinoks: A Revolution." Trans. K. O'Brien. *Technology and Culture: The Film Reader.* Ed. Andrew Utterson. London: Routledge, 2005. 99-104.
Waller, Gregory. "Black Moviegoing and Film Exhibition in Lexington, Kentucky, 1906-1927." Paper presented at Society for Cinema Studies Conference, Washington, DC, May 27, 1990.
Walton, Kendall L. "Transparent Pictures: On the Nature of Photographic Realism." *Critical Inquiry* 11 (1984): 246-277.
Ward, Paul. "Defining 'Animation': The Animated Film and the Emergence of the Film Bill." *Scope* (December 2000). <http://www.scope.nottingham.ac.uk/article.php?issue=dec2000&id=289&section=article>.
Wasko, Janet. "Hollywood and Television in the 1950s: The Roots of Diversification." *The Fifties: Transforming the Screen, 1950-1959.* By Peter Lev. Berkeley: U of California P, 2003. 127-146.
Watanabe, Masao. "Count Rumford's First Exposition of the Dynamic Aspect of Heat." *Isis* 50.2 (1959): 141-144.
Wiebel, Jr., Frederick C. *Edison's Frankenstein.* N.p.: The Frederick C. Wiebel, Jr. Fine Arts Studio, 2003.
Williams, Linda. "Film Bodies: Gender, Genre, and Excess." *Film Quarterly* 44.4 (Summer 1991): 2-13.
—. *Hard Core: Power, Pleasure, and the "Frenzy of the Visible".* 2nd ed. Berkeley: U of California P, 1999.
Winston, Brian. *Media Technology and Society, A History: From the Telegraph to the Internet.* London: Routledge, 1998.
—. *Misunderstanding Media.* Cambridge: Harvard UP, 1986.
Wittgenstein, Ludwig. *Philosophical Investigations.* The German Text, with a Revised English Translation. Trans. G.E.M. Anscombe. Malden, MA: Blackwell, 2001.
Young, Iris Marion. *On Female Body Experience: "Throwing Like a Girl" and Other Essays.* New York: Oxford UP, 2005.

Zakharieva, Bouriana. "Frankenstein of the Nineties: The Composite Body." *Frankenstein: Complete, Authoritative Text with Biographical, Historical, and Cultural Contexts, Critical History, and Essays from Contemporary Critical Perspectives*. By Mary Shelley. Ed. Johanna M. Smith. Boston: Bedford/St. Martin's, 2000. 416-431.